A Professional Approach

Microsoft® Office
PowerPoint®

Comprehensive

Pat R. Graves

McGraw Hill **Technology Education**

Boston Burr Ridge, IL Dubuque, IA Emeryville, CA Madison, WI New York San Francisco St. Louis
Bangkok Bogotá Caracas Kuala Lumpur Lisbon London Madrid Mexico City
Milan Montreal New Delhi Santiago Seoul Singapore Sydney Taipei Toronto

The McGraw·Hill Companies

Technology Education

1333 Burr Ridge Parkway
Burr Ridge, Illinois 60527
U.S.A.

Microsoft® Office PowerPoint® 2003: A Professional Approach, Comprehensive
Student Edition

For information on translations or book distributors outside the U.S.A., please see the International Contact Information page immediately following the index of this book. Some ancillaries, including electronic and print components, may not be available to customers outside the United States.

1234567890 QPD QPD 01987654

Book p/n 0-07-225444-0 and CD p/n 0-07-225443-2
parts of
ISBN 0-07-225442-4

This book was composed with Corel VENTURA™ Publisher.

www.mhteched.com

Sponsoring Editor
Gareth Hancock

Developmental Editor
Lisa Chin-Johnson

Project Editor
Jenny Malnick

Technical Editors
Eileen Mullin, Darren Choong,
EK Choong, Craig Leonard

Copy Editors
Robert Campbell, Marcia Baker

Proofreaders
Stefany Otis, Linda Medoff

Indexer
Valerie Robbins

Composition
Elizabeth Jang, John Patrus,
Dick Schwartz

Illustrators
Melinda Lytle, Kathleen Edwards

Interior Design
Leggitt Associates, Creative Ink, Inc.,
Peter F. Hancik

Contents

UNIT 1   BASIC SKILLS

UNIT 3   CUSTOMIZING A PRESENTATION

UNIT 4 ADVANCED TECHNIQUES

UNIT 5   CHARTS, TABLES, AND DIAGRAMS

UNIT 6   MAKING PRESENTATIONS AVAILABLE TO OTHERS

What does this logo mean?

It means this courseware has been approved by the Microsoft® Office Specialist Program to be among the finest available for learning *Microsoft® PowerPoint 2003*. It also means that upon completion of this courseware, you may be prepared to take an exam for Microsoft Office Specialist qualification.

What is a Microsoft Office Specialist?

A Microsoft Office Specialist is an individual who has passed exams for certifying his or her skills in one or more of the Microsoft Office desktop applications such as Microsoft Word, Microsoft Excel, Microsoft PowerPoint, Microsoft Outlook, Microsoft Access, or Microsoft Project. The Microsoft Office Specialist Program typically offers certification exams at the "Specialist" and "Expert" skill levels.* The Microsoft Office Specialist Program is the only program in the world approved by Microsoft for testing proficiency in Microsoft Office desktop applications and Microsoft Project. This testing program can be a valuable asset in any job search or career advancement.

More Information:

To learn more about becoming a Microsoft Office Specialist, visit www.microsoft.com/officespecialist. To learn about other Microsoft Office Specialist-approved courseware from McGraw-Hill/ Technology Education, visit http://www.mhteched.com.

*The availability of Microsoft Office Specialist certification exams varies by application, application version, and language. Visit www.microsoft.com/officespecialist for exam availability.

Microsoft, the Microsoft Office Logo, PowerPoint, and Outlook are trademarks or registered trademarks of Microsoft Corporation in the United States and/or other countries, and the Microsoft Office Specialist Logo is used under license from owner.

Preface

Microsoft® Office PowerPoint® 2003: A Professional Approach, Comprehensive Student Edition is written to help you master Microsoft Office PowerPoint for Windows. The text takes you step-by-step through the features that you're likely to use in both your personal and business life.

Case Study

Learning the features of PowerPoint is one component of the text, and applying what you learn is another. That is why a Case Study was created and appears throughout the text. The Case Study offers the opportunity to learn Word in a realistic business context. Take the time to read the Case Study near the front of this book. The Case Study is about Good 4 U restaurant, a fictional business located in New York City, New York. All the documents for this course involve the Good 4 U restaurant.

Organization of the Text

The text includes six units. Each unit is divided into lessons, and there are 15 lessons, each building on previously learned procedures. This building block approach, together with the Case Study and the following features, enables you to maximize the learning process.

Features of the Text

- ☑ *Objectives* are listed for each lesson.
- ☑ Required skills for the *Microsoft Office Specialist* are listed for each lesson.
- ☑ The *estimated time* required to complete each lesson (up to the "Using Online Help") is stated.
- ☑ Within a lesson, each *heading* corresponds to an objective.
- ☑ Easy-to-follow *exercises* emphasize "learning by doing."
- ☑ *Key terms* are italicized and defined as they are encountered.
- ☑ Extensive *graphics* display screen contents.
- ☑ *Toolbar buttons* and *keyboard keys* are shown in the text when used.
- ☑ *Large toolbar buttons in the margins* provide easy-to-see references.
- ☑ Lessons contain important *Notes*, useful *Tips*, and helpful *Reviews*.
- ☑ *Using Online Help* introduces you to a Help topic related to lesson content.
- ☑ A *Lesson Summary* reviews the important concepts taught in the lesson.
- ☑ A *Command Summary* lists the commands taught in the lesson.

- ☑ *Concepts Review* includes true/false, short answer, and critical thinking questions that focus on lesson content.
- ☑ *Skills Review* provides skill reinforcement for each lesson.
- ☑ *Lesson Applications* ask you to apply your skills in a more challenging way.
- ☑ *On Your Own* exercises let you apply your skills creatively.
- ☑ *Unit Applications* give you the opportunity to use the skills you learn in a unit.
- ☑ Includes an Appendix of Microsoft Office Specialist Certification standards, a Glossary, and an Index.

Microsoft Office Specialist Certification Program

The Microsoft Office Specialist certification program offers PowerPoint certification at the "Specialist" level. This certification can be a valuable asset in any job search. For more information about this Microsoft program, go to www.microsoft.com/officespecialist. For a complete listing of the skills for the PowerPoint 2003 "Specialist" certification exam (and a correlation to the lessons in the text), see the appendix, "Microsoft Office Specialist Certification."

Professional Approach Web Site

Visit the Professional Approach Web site at www.mhteched.com/pas to access additional materials including tutorials, additional projects, online quizzes, and more!

Conventions Used in the Text

This text uses a number of conventions to help you learn the program and save your work.

- ☑ Text to be keyed appears either in **boldface** or as a separate figure.
- ☑ Filenames appear in **boldface**.
- ☑ Options that you choose from menus and dialog boxes appear in a font that is similar to the on-screen font; for example, "Choose Print from the File menu." (The underline means you can press Alt and key the letter to choose the option.)
- ☑ You are asked to save each document with your initials followed by the exercise name. For example, an exercise might end with this instruction: "Save the document as *[your initials]*5-12." Documents are saved in folders for each lesson.

If You Are Unfamiliar with Windows

If you are unfamiliar with Windows, review the "Windows Tutorial" available on the Professional Approach Web site at www.mhteched.com/pas before beginning Lesson 1. This tutorial provides a basic overview of the operating system and shows you how to use the mouse. You might also want to review "File Management" (also on the Professional Approach Web site) to get more comfortable with files and folders.

Screen Differences

As you practice each concept, illustrations of the screens help you follow the instructions. Don't worry if your screen is slightly different from the illustration. These differences are due to variations in system and computer configurations.

Acknowledgments

We thank the technical editors and reviewers of this text for their valuable assistance: Eileen Mullin, EK Choong, Darren Choong, Craig Leonard, Susan Olson, Northwest Technical College, East Grand Forks, MN; John Walker, Doña Ana Community College, Las Cruces, NM; Mary Davey, Computer Learning Network, Camp Hill, PA.

Thanks to all members of the Professional Approach Series team at McGraw-Hill for their commitment and dedication to this project. Special thanks to Jenny Malnick, Project Editor, for coordinating all the pieces of this puzzle and to Elizabeth, John, Carie, Tabi, Kelly, Lucie, Tara, Jean, Peter, Dick, Jim, Melinda, and Kathleen on the production and illustration teams for creating such an attractive and effective textbook. We hope that everyone learning from this textbook will find it easy to use and understand.

Installation Requirements

You will need Microsoft Office PowerPoint 2003 to work through this textbook; it needs to be installed on the computer's hard drive or on a network. Use the following checklist to evaluate installation requirements.

Hardware

- ☑ Computer with 233 MHz or higher processor and at least 128MB of RAM
- ☑ CD-ROM drive and other external media (3.5-inch high-density floppy, ZIP, etc.)
- ☑ 400MB or more of hard disk space for a "Typical" Office installation
- ☑ Super VGA (800 × 600) or higher-resolution video monitor
- ☑ Printer (laser or ink-jet recommended)
- ☑ Mouse
- ☑ Optional: Modem or other Internet connection (required for Using Online Help exercises)

Software

- ☑ PowerPoint 2003 (from Microsoft Office System 2003)
- ☑ Windows 2000 with Service Pack 3 or later, or Windows XP or later operating system
- ☑ Optional: Browser (and Internet access)

Internet Access

Access to the Internet is required for most of the Using Online Help exercises. Many of the help features are only available online. Microsoft Office Online is also a valuable resource for additional clip art, photographs, templates, and other resources.

CASE STUDY

There is more to learning a presentation graphics program like Microsoft Office PowerPoint 2003 than simply keying text on colored backgrounds and calling the result a "presentation." You need to know how to use PowerPoint in a real-world situation. That's why all the lessons in this text relate to everyday business tasks. You will learn how to create well-organized presentations that are designed effectively, too.

As you work through lessons, imagine yourself working as an intern for Good 4 *U*, a fictional New York restaurant.

Good4U

Good 4 U Restaurant

The Good 4 *U* restaurant has been in business for only a little over three years—but it's been a success from the time it served its first veggie burger. The restaurant—which features healthy food and has a theme based on the "everyday active life"—seems to have found an award-winning recipe for success. (Figure 1 shows the interior of the largest dining room in the restaurant. It features plants and a wide expanse of windows looking out over Central Park South, a tree-lined avenue on the south side of New York's Central Park.)

The food at Good 4 *U* is all low-fat. The menu features lots of vegetables (all organic, of course!), as well as fish and chicken. The restaurant doesn't serve alcohol, instead offering fruit juices and sparkling water. Good 4 *U*'s theme of the "everyday active life" is reflected on the restaurant's walls with running, tennis, and bicycling memorabilia. This theme really reflects the interests of the two co-owners: Julie Wolfe who led the New York Flash to two Women's Professional Basketball Association championships in her ten years with the team; and Gus Irvinelli who is an avid tennis player and was selected for the U.S. Amateur team. Even the chef, Michele Jenkins, leads an active everyday life—she rides her bicycle ten miles a day in and around Central Park.

Two years ago, Roy Olafsen was a marketing manager for a large hotel chain. He was over-weight and out-of-shape. In the same week that

FIGURE 1 Interior of Good 4 *U* restaurant and a sampling of the fresh food prepared daily.

his doctor told him to eat better and exercise regularly, Roy received a job offer from Good 4 *U*. "It was too good to pass up," he said. "It was my chance to combine work and a healthy life style." As you work through the text, you'll discover that Good 4 *U* is often involved in health-oriented products, as well as events that focus on athletics.

In your work as an intern at Good 4 *U* restaurant, you will have a chance to meet many of the people who work at Good 4 *U*. You will certainly interact with the four key people shown in Figure 2. In fact, you will find that you will be doing most of your work for Roy Olafsen.

All the presentations you will use and create in this course relate to Good 4 *U* restaurant. As you work with the presentations in the text, take the time to notice the following things:

- The types of presentations needed in a small business to carry on day-to-day business.

- The design of presentations. Real businesses must often focus on designing eye-catching, informative presentations for customers. The business's success often depends on developing attractive and compelling presentations that sell its services to customers.

- The "Tips for Designing Presentations" on the next page. Good presentations generally follow these basic guidelines.

As you use this text and become more experienced with Microsoft Office PowerPoint 2003, you will also gain experience in creating, editing, and designing the sort of presentations generated in a real-life business environment.

FIGURE 2 Key employees

JULIE WOLFE
Co-Owner

GUS IRVINELLI
Co-Owner

MICHELE JENKINS
Head Chef

ROY OLAFSEN
Marketing Manager

In your first meeting with Roy Olafsen, he gave you the following tips for designing presentations. These tips can be applied to any presentation.

Tips for Designing Presentations

- Prepare a distinctive title slide. Make sure the title identifies the presentation content.

- Maintain a consistent color scheme throughout the presentation for a sense of unity.

- Keep the background simple, and modify it to help create a unique theme for your presentation.

- Choose colors carefully so all text can be seen clearly. You must have a high contrast between background colors and text colors for easy reading.

- Write lists with parallel wording and be concise. Limit bulleted text to no more than seven words on a line and no more than seven lines on a slide.

- Avoid small text. Body text on slides, such as for bulleted lists, should be no smaller than 24 points. Text for annotations may be slightly smaller, but not less than 20 points. Establish a hierarchy for text sizes based on text importance and then use those sizes consistently.

- Think and design visually to express your message. Use graphics such as boxes, lines, circles, and other shapes to highlight text or to draw diagrams that show processes and relationships. Illustrate with pictures and clip art images.

- Select all images carefully to make your presentation content more understandable. They should not detract from the message. Avoid the temptation to "jazz up" a slide show with too much clip art.

- Keep charts simple. The most effective charts are pie charts with three or four slices and column charts with three or four columns. Label charts carefully for easy interpretation.

- Provide some form of handout so your audience can keep track of the presentation or make notes while you are talking.

- Include multimedia elements of animation, transitions, sound, and movies if these elements strengthen your message, engage your audience, aid understanding, or make your presentation more compelling.

- Your final slide should provide a recommendation or summary to help you conclude your presentation effectively.

Basic Skills

LESSON 1

What Is PowerPoint?

OBJECTIVES

MICROSOFT OFFICE
SPECIALIST
ACTIVITIES
In this lesson:
PPO3S-1-2
PPO3S-4-1
PPO3S-4-4
PPO3S-4-6
PPO3S-4-7

See Appendix.

After completing this lesson, you will be able to:

1. **Start PowerPoint.**
2. **Explore PowerPoint.**
3. **Use text placeholders.**
4. **Use tabs and views.**
5. **Name and save a presentation.**
6. **Run a slide show.**
7. **Print slides and handouts.**
8. **Close a presentation and exit PowerPoint.**

 Estimated Time: 2 hours

Microsoft PowerPoint is a powerful but easy-to-use presentation graphics program you can use to create professional-quality presentations. PowerPoint can be used in a variety of settings by people in many different career fields. For example, a day care worker may develop a presentation showing parents pictures of their children in all of the year's activities, or a minister may utilize PowerPoint to display notes on the sermon or display song lyrics for the congregation. An instructor may use it for notes for a lecture to help keep the students focused and their notes organized, or a hotelier may develop a presentation to help market their hotel at conferences and meetings. PowerPoint is also an effective tool for creating flyers and other printed products because of its versatile drawing and layout tools.

This lesson begins with an overview of many PowerPoint features and will help you become accustomed to the application window.

Starting PowerPoint

There are several ways to start PowerPoint, depending on your system setup and your personal preferences.

- Use the Start button on the Windows taskbar, select Microsoft Office PowerPoint 2003.

- Use the Start button on the Windows taskbar, select the All Programs menu, then select Microsoft Office, Microsoft Office PowerPoint 2003.

- Double-click the PowerPoint shortcut icon if one appears on your Windows desktop.

E X E R C I S E   **1-1**   **Start PowerPoint**

When you start PowerPoint, a new blank presentation automatically appears, ready for you to start inserting text, graphics, or multimedia elements.

NOTE: If you are unfamiliar with Windows, refer to the "Windows Tutorial" at the Professional Approach Online Learning Center at www.mhteched.com/pas.

1. Turn on your computer to load Windows.
2. Click the Start button on the Windows taskbar and point to Programs.

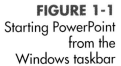
FIGURE 1-1
Starting PowerPoint
from the
Windows taskbar

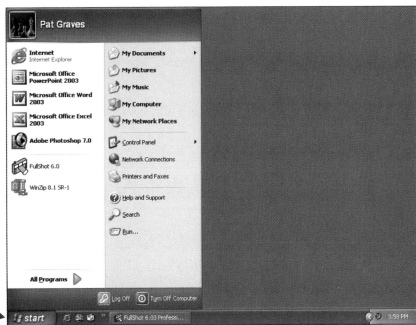

Start button

NOTE: Windows provides many ways to start applications. If you have problems, ask your instructor for help.

3. On the <u>P</u>rograms submenu, click Microsoft PowerPoint. In a few seconds, the program is loaded and the PowerPoint window appears.

FIGURE 1-2
PowerPoint
opening window

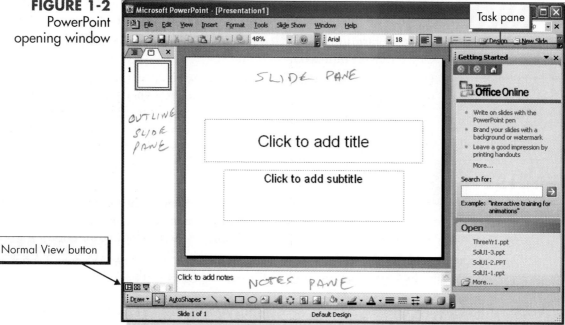

Normal View button

 NOTE: The pane on the right of the screen is the task pane. The task pane is designed to save you time by bringing options you regularly need close to your workspace so you can be more efficient. The next exercise will give you more information on the task pane.

4. If your screen does not look like Figure 1-2, click the Normal View button in the lower-left corner of the window or ask your instructor for assistance.

EXERCISE   **1-2**   **Work with Task Panes**

When you choose certain commands as you are working, specialized task panes appear on the right side of your window. They provide commonly used commands related to the action you are currently performing.

 NOTE: If the task pane is not displayed on the right of the screen, from the <u>V</u>iew menu choose Tas<u>k</u> pane.

FIGURE 1-3
Working with
task panes

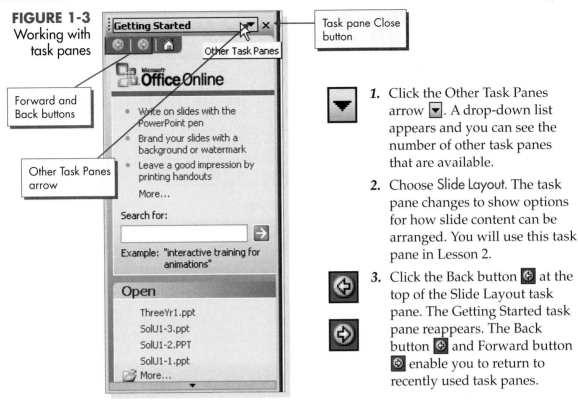

1. Click the Other Task Panes arrow ▼. A drop-down list appears and you can see the number of other task panes that are available.

2. Choose Slide Layout. The task pane changes to show options for how slide content can be arranged. You will use this task pane in Lesson 2.

3. Click the Back button ⊕ at the top of the Slide Layout task pane. The Getting Started task pane reappears. The Back button ⊕ and Forward button ⊕ enable you to return to recently used task panes.

4. Click the task pane's Close button ⊠. This removes the task pane from the screen.

5. Click View on the menu bar, and then click Task Pane. The last task pane you used is displayed again.

EXERCISE   1-3   Open an Existing Presentation

The opening PowerPoint window displays a blank slide, ready for you to add text, images, and additional slides. In Lesson 3 you will create a presentation using this blank slide.

In this exercise you open an existing PowerPoint presentation. The presentation was created especially for this lesson to give you an overview of many of PowerPoint's features.

1. From the Getting Started task pane in the Open section, choose More to display the Open dialog box.

TABLE 1-1 Buttons in the Open Dialog Box

BUTTON	NAME	PURPOSE
⊕	Back	Enables you to return to a folder or place you previously opened while working in this dialog box.
	Up One Level	Moves up one level in the hierarchy of folders or drives on your computer or on computers connected to your computer.
Q	Search the Web	Opens the Search page of your Internet browser (if you are online) so that you can search the Web for information.
×	Delete	Deletes a file or folder.
	Create New Folder	Enables you to create a new folder to organize your files.
	Views	Opens a menu of view options for displaying files and file icons.
Tools ▾	Tools	Opens a menu of other file utilities, such as finding a file, renaming a file, and adding a file or folder to the Favorites folder.

2. Click the down arrow next to the Look in box and choose the appropriate drive and folder for your student files according to your instructor's directions.

FIGURE 1-4
Files listed in the Open dialog box

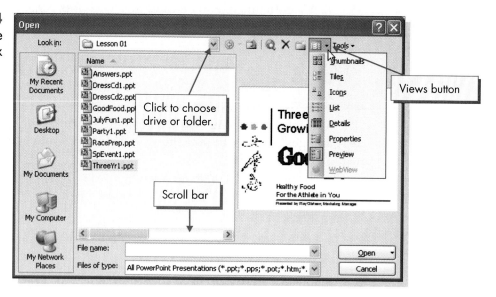

NOTE: Your instructor will advise you where to locate the files for this course. For more information about working with files, folders, and directories in Windows, refer to "File Management" at the Professional Approach Online Learning Center at www.mhteched.com/pas.

3. When you locate the student files, click the arrow next to the Views button in the Open dialog box to display a menu of view options.

4. Choose List to list all files by name.

5. Click the Views button again and choose Preview to get a quick look at a presentation's first slide before opening it.

6. Locate the file **ThreeYr1** (use the scroll bar if you need to) and click once to select the file.

7. Click Open. (You can also double-click the file's name to open it.) PowerPoint opens the file in Normal view.

 NOTE: The presentations you create in this course relate to the Case Study about Good 4 U, a fictional restaurant (see pages 1 through 4).

Exploring PowerPoint

If you are already familiar with other Microsoft Office programs, you'll feel right at home with PowerPoint. Although a number of new buttons appear in the PowerPoint window, it's easy to recognize similarities to Microsoft Word and Microsoft Excel.

FIGURE 1-5 Main features in PowerPoint's Normal view

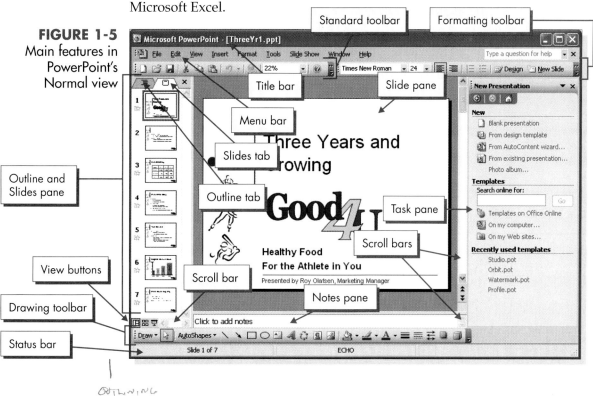

TABLE 1-2   Main Parts of the PowerPoint Window

PART OF WINDOW	PURPOSE
Title bar	Contains the name of the presentation.
Menu bar	Displays the names of menus you use to perform various tasks. You can open menus by using the mouse or the keyboard.
Toolbars	Rows of buttons that give instant access to a wide range of commands. Each button is represented by an icon and accessed by using the mouse. PowerPoint opens with the Standard and Formatting toolbars displayed in abbreviated form on one line at the top of the window.
Drawing toolbar	The drawing toolbar is displayed at the bottom of the window and gives access to buttons to add shapes, clip art, WordArt, change colors, and design aspects of objects.
Outline and Slides pane	The area that can display either an outline of the presentation's text or *thumbnails*—miniature pictures—of the presentation's slides. You choose either Outline or Slides by clicking the appropriate tab. (If this pane is not displayed, click the Normal View button.)
Slide pane	The area where you create, edit, and display presentation slides.
Notes pane	The area where you can add presentation notes for either the presenter or the audience.
Task pane	An area that can appear on the right side of the PowerPoint window, displaying a list of commands that are relevant to the task on which you are currently working.
Scroll bars	Used with the mouse to move a slide view or outline text right or left and up or down. You can also use the vertical scroll bar to move from slide to slide.
View buttons	Three buttons located in the lower-left corner of the window. You use these buttons to switch between Normal view (the default), Slide Sorter view, and Slide Show.
Status bar	Displays information about the presentation you're working on.

EXERCISE   **1-4**   **Identify Parts of the PowerPoint Window**

The first step to getting familiar with PowerPoint is to identify the parts of the window you'll be working with in this course, such as menus, toolbars, buttons, tabs, and panes. There are many different objects in the PowerPoint window. ScreenTips help you identify these objects. A *ScreenTip* is the box displaying an object's name that appears under a button or other object when you point to it.

1. Use the mouse to point to the Normal View button in the lower-left corner of the window. PowerPoint displays the button's ScreenTip. If this button is not already selected, click it with the left mouse button.

FIGURE 1-6
Identifying a button

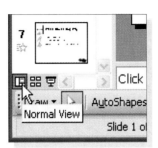

2. Point to other buttons in the window to identify them by name.

3. If the Office Assistant is displayed, click it with the right mouse button to display a shortcut menu. Choose <u>H</u>ide on the shortcut menu.

TIP: If you'd prefer to display the Office Assistant, click <u>H</u>elp on the menu bar and choose Show the <u>O</u>ffice Assistant. When the Office Assistant is displayed, you can also right-click it and use the shortcut menu to choose another animated character.

EXERCISE **1-5** **Work with Menus and Toolbars**

You access PowerPoint commands through many different methods:

- Choose from a menu.
- Use toolbar buttons.
- Choose from task pane items.

1. Point to <u>V</u>iew on the menu bar and click the left mouse button to open the menu. PowerPoint displays a short version of the <u>V</u>iew menu with the most commonly used <u>V</u>iew menu commands.

2. Expand the menu either by keeping it open for a few seconds or by pointing to the arrows at the bottom of the menu. Notice the additional commands on the expanded menu.

NOTE: PowerPoint's short menus are adaptive—they change as you work, listing the commands you use most frequently.

3. To close the menu, click <u>V</u>iew or a blank area of the window, or press [Esc].

4. Open the <u>V</u>iew menu again and point to <u>T</u>oolbars. On the <u>T</u>oolbars submenu, the Task Pane and three toolbars should be selected: Standard, Formatting, and Drawing. If one of these does not have a check mark, click it on the <u>T</u>oolbars submenu to select it. (See Figure 1-7 on the next page.)

5. Close the <u>V</u>iew menu. Open the <u>T</u>ools menu and expand it. Without clicking the mouse button, move the pointer left to <u>F</u>ormat on the menu bar. Continue moving the pointer left on the menu bar until you display the <u>E</u>dit menu. Close the <u>E</u>dit menu.

FIGURE 1-7
Displaying
menu options

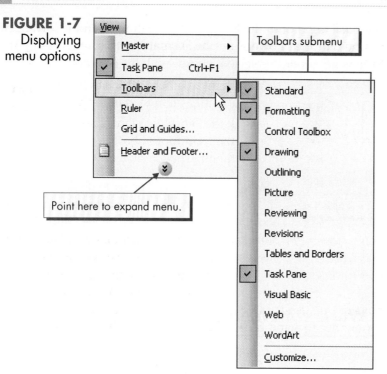

Point here to expand menu.

TIP: PowerPoint provides several ways to complete tasks: a menu shows which commands have corresponding toolbar buttons or keyboard shortcuts. For example, you can save a document by choosing File on the menu bar and then clicking Save, by clicking the Save button 🔲 on the Standard toolbar, or by holding down Ctrl and pressing S (this is shown as Ctrl+S).

6. Point to several buttons on the Standard toolbar and identify them by using the ScreenTip feature.

7. Click the Toolbar Options button 🔳 at the end of the Standard toolbar to see the rest of this toolbar's buttons. Move the mouse pointer over any button to identify it.

FIGURE 1-8
Side-by-side
toolbars

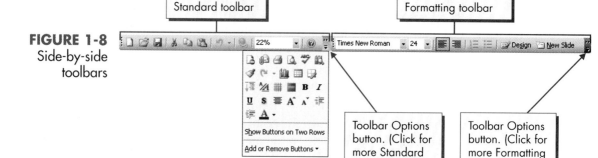

8. Click the Toolbar Options button ⬝ at the end of the Formatting toolbar to see additional toolbar buttons for the Formatting toolbar. Press (Esc) to hide the additional buttons.

> **NOTE:** When you click the Toolbar Options button ⬝ and use one of these "hidden" toolbar buttons, the button will move off the "More Buttons" list and onto the regular toolbar. PowerPoint's toolbars are adaptive—they change as you work, displaying the buttons you use most frequently.

EXERCISE | **1-6** | **Work with Docked and Floating Toolbars**

Sometimes it's convenient to move a toolbar to another location in the window—so you don't need to move your mouse back and forth when you're using the same tool repeatedly. Toolbars are either docked or floating. A *docked toolbar* is attached to one of the edges of the program window. A *floating toolbar* is not attached; you can drag its title bar to freely move it wherever you want. You *drag* a title bar by pointing to it and then holding down the left mouse button while you move the mouse.

1. Point to the move handle ⦚ on the left end of the standard toolbar. When the four-pointed arrow ✥ appears, drag the toolbar down until it appears to be in the middle of your window. The Standard toolbar is now a floating toolbar.

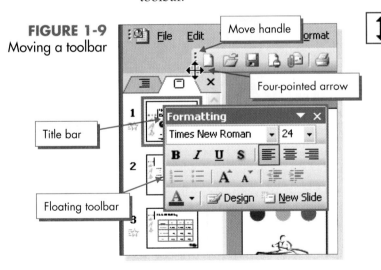

FIGURE 1-9
Moving a toolbar

Move handle

Four-pointed arrow

Title bar

Floating toolbar

2. Point to the bottom edge of the floating toolbar. When a vertical two-pointed arrow ↕ appears, drag it up or down to change the shape of the toolbar.

3. Point to the Standard toolbar's title bar and drag it to a new location on your window.

4. Double-click the Standard toolbar's title bar. The toolbar returns to its original place next to the Formatting toolbar. It is once again docked.

> **TIP:** To display both the Standard and Formatting toolbars on separate rows, right-click the Toolbar Options arrow and choose Customize (or from the View menu choose Toolbars and then Customize). From the Options tab, select Show Standard and Formatting toolbars on two rows. Click Close. Now all the buttons are easier to use.

EXERCISE **1-7** **Move from Slide to Slide**

PowerPoint provides several ways to move from slide to slide in a presentation:

- Use the mouse to drag the scroll box.
- Use the mouse to click the Previous slide or Next slide buttons.
- Use the Page Up and Page Down keys on the keyboard.

FIGURE 1-10
Moving from
slide to slide

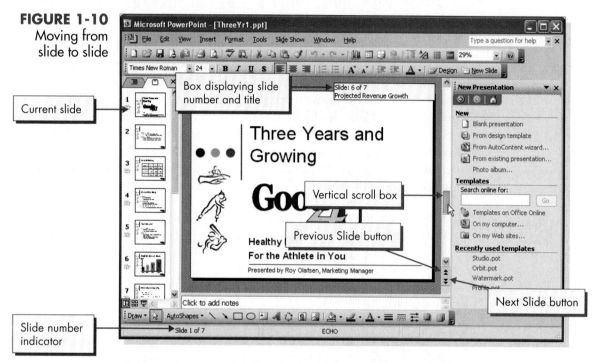

Current slide

Slide number
indicator

1. Drag the vertical scroll box on the Slide pane to the bottom of the scroll bar. Notice the box that displays slide numbers and slide titles as you drag. When you release the mouse button at the bottom of the scroll bar, slide 7 appears in your window. Notice the heavy border around the slide 7 thumbnail in the Slide pane. This identifies it as the current slide.

2. Drag the scroll box up to display slide 6. Notice that the slide number is indicated on the left side of the status bar.

3. Click the Previous Slide button ⬆ at the bottom of the vertical scroll bar several times to move back in the presentation. Use the Next Slide button ⬇ to move forward.

4. As an alternative to clicking the Next Slide button ⬇ and the Previous Slide button ⬆, press Page Down and Page Up on your keyboard several times. Use this method to move to slide 2. Check the status bar for the slide number.

Using Text Placeholders

Editing text in PowerPoint is very similar to editing text in a word processing program. You click an *I-beam* to position the *insertion point* where you want to key new text. An I-beam is a mouse pointer in the shape of an uppercase "I." An insertion point is a vertical blinking bar indicating where text you key will be placed. You can also drag the I-beam to select existing text. The keys Enter, Delete, and Backspace work the same way as in a word processing program.

NOT ACTIVE
ACTIVATE ONLY TEXT
SELECT - IS WHOLE PLACE HOLDER

It is important to understand that you *activate* a placeholder when you click the I-beam in it, making it ready to accept text.

EXERCISE **1-8** **Edit Text on a Slide**

PLACE HOLDER TEXT

Text on the slide is contained in text *placeholders*. Placeholders are used for *title text* (the text that usually appears at the top of a slide), *body text* (text in the body of a slide), and other objects, such as pictures. Placeholders help keep design layout and formatting consistent within a presentation.

Body text often contains *bullets* and is sometimes called "bulleted text." Bullets are small dots, squares, or other symbols placed to the left of each item in a list or series of paragraphs to add emphasis and readability.

1. With slide 2 displayed, click anywhere on the line of text that begins "Gus Irvinelli."

   Notice the box that surrounds the text. The wide border made up of tiny diagonal lines indicates that the text box is activated and in edit mode, meaning you can edit and insert text.

2. Without clicking, move the mouse pointer outside the border to the right and then back inside.

   Notice that the pointer changes from an I-beam ⟨I⟩ inside the border to an arrow pointer ⟨⟩ outside the border. When the pointer rests on top of the border, it becomes a four-pointed arrow ⟨⊕⟩, which can be used to move the text placeholder.

3. Drag the I-beam across the text "an avid" to select it. (Click to the left of "an avid," hold down the left mouse button, drag the I-beam across the two words, and then release the mouse button.) (See Figure 1-11 on the next page.)

4. Key **a professional** to replace the selected text. (You don't need to delete selected text before keying new text.)

5. To place the insertion point, click the I-beam to the right of the words "healthy eating" near the bottom of the slide.

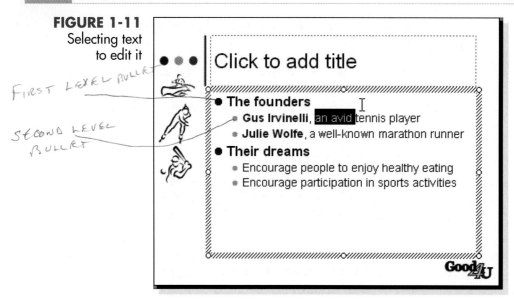

FIGURE 1-11
Selecting text
to edit it

FIRST LEVEL BULLET

SECOND LEVEL BULLET

6. To insert a new line, press Enter. Notice that a new dimmed bullet appears at the beginning of the new line.

NOTE: Bulleted text lists the points being made in a slide presentation. This presentation uses open circle and solid dot bullets. Later in this course, you will learn how to change bullet shapes and colors.

7. On the new blank bullet line, key **Make their financial investment grow**

8. Instead of a title, slide 2 contains an empty text placeholder. Click the placeholder containing the text "Click to add title." Then key **Where We Came From**

9. Click a blank part of the slide area to deactivate the text box. To make sure you're clicking a blank area, click when the pointer is a simple arrow, not an I-beam or a four-pointed arrow.

EXERCISE   1-9   Promote and Demote Bulleted Text

When you want to expand on a slide's main points, you can insert indented bulleted text below a main point. This supplemental text is sometimes referred to as a sub-bullet or a level 2 bullet. PowerPoint body text placeholders can have up to five levels of indented text, but you will usually want to limit your slides to two levels.

You can *demote* body text by increasing its indent level, or *promote* body text by decreasing its indent level. These changes can be made in two ways:

● Use the promote and demote text buttons.

● Move the insertion point before the text and press Tab to demote or Shift + Tab to promote.

1. With slide 2 displayed in the Slide pane, move your insertion point after "Gus Irvinelli" and delete the comma and the blank space after it, then press Enter. Notice that the rest of the line is turned into another bullet point. Click the Increase Indent button on the Formatting toolbar to demote text by one level. The text is reduced in size and indented to the right, and the bullet shape changes.

2. Move your insertion point after "Julie Wolfe" and delete the comma and the blank space after this text, then press Enter. With the insertion point before "a well-known marathon runner," click the Increase Indent button to demote the text.

3. Click the Decrease Indent button to return the text to its original size and placement even with Julie Wolfe, then press Tab to demote the text back to the level under Julie Wolfe. Notice the change in the Outline and Slides pane as you promote and demote text.

NOTE: If you press Tab when the insertion point is within the text, you insert a tab character instead of demoting text.

4. Leave the presentation open for the next exercise.

Using Tabs and Views

PowerPoint provides a selection of panes and views to help streamline your work. Using these various views, you can choose to work on presentation text in outline format, rearrange slides in Slide Sorter view, or work on an individual slide in the Slide pane. You can change the way you work by doing any of the following:

● Display or hide the task pane or the Outline and Slides pane.

● Change the information being displayed in the task pane or the Outline and Slides pane.

● Drag borders to change the size of panes.

● Switch between Normal and Slide Sorter views.

EXERCISE 1-10 **Use the Outline and Slides Pane**

1. Point to the right border of the Outline and Slides pane. When the splitter bar appears, drag it about an inch to the right. The tabs area becomes wider, and the tab labels change from icons to text.

2. Click the Outline tab. The Outline pane displays the presentation's text in outline format.

3. Drag the right border of the Outline pane area to the right so that you can see more of the text. Notice that the changes you made in the Slide pane are reflected in the outline.

4. Scroll down in the outline until you see the text for slide 4.

FIGURE 1-12
Working with the
Outline and
Slides pane

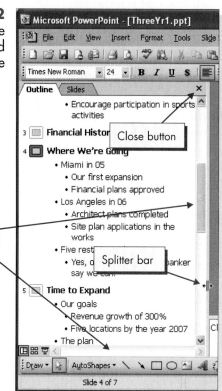

5. Working in the Outline pane, change each of the years (05, 06, and 07) to 2005, 2006, and 2007. The first line, for example, should read **Miami in 2005**. Notice that as you work, your changes are reflected in the Slide pane.

NOTE: When you have several bulleted lists, you can key them all in outline format if that's the way you like to work. You will learn more about outlines in Lesson 4.

6. Click the Close button ⊠ on the Outline and Slides pane to hide it. The Slide pane expands to fill the space.

7. Click the Normal View button ⊞ in the lower-left corner of the window. The Outline and Slides pane is displayed again.

8. Click the Slides tab. The Outline and Slides pane becomes smaller and the size of the Slide pane increases.

EXERCISE 1-11 **Use Slide Sorter View**

Slide Sorter view displays a window of presentation slide thumbnails, which are miniature versions of the slides. In this view you can easily rearrange slides or apply special slide show effects.

1. Click the Slide Sorter View button 🏢, located in the lower-left corner of the window to the right of the Normal button.

FIGURE 1-13
Slide Sorter view

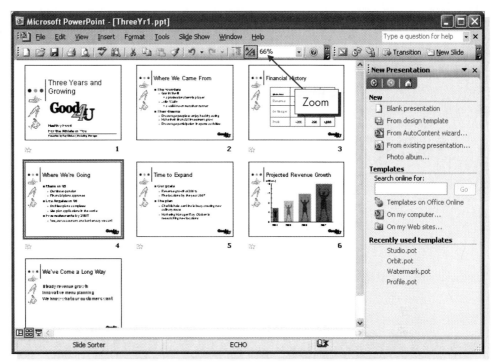

2. On the Standard toolbar, click the down arrow next to the Zoom box and choose 66%. This should enable you to see all seven slides in this presentation at the same time.

 TIP: Experiment with the zoom percentage. Depending on your screen resolution, a different percentage might be needed to show all seven slides at once.

3. Double-click slide 1 to return to Normal view.

TIP: The Zoom box is also available in Normal view. If the Slide pane is active, Zoom changes the magnification of the slide within the Slide pane. If the Outline and Slides pane is active, Zoom changes that area instead.

Naming and Saving a Presentation

In PowerPoint, presentations are saved as files. When you create a new presentation or make changes to an existing one, you must save the presentation to make your changes permanent. Until your changes are saved, they can be lost if there's a power failure or a computer problem.

The first step in saving a document is to give it a *filename*. Filenames can be up to 255 characters long.

Throughout the exercises in this book, your document filenames will consist of two parts:

- *[Your initials]*, which might be your initials or an identifier your instructor asks you to use, such as **rst**
- The number of the exercise, such as **3-1**

When you're working with an existing file, choosing the S̲ave command (or clicking the Save button on the Standard toolbar) replaces the file on the disk with the file on which you're working. After saving, the old version of the file no longer exists and the new version contains all your changes.

You can give an existing presentation a new name by using the Save A̲s command. The original presentation remains on the disk unchanged and a second presentation with a new name is saved on the disk as well.

TIP: The New Presentation task pane has an option labeled From existing presentation. If you click this link, locate a presentation you want to use, then click the C̲reate New button, your existing presentation becomes a new presentation and you can safely save it by using the Save command without fear of overwriting the presentation on which it is based.

EXERCISE **1-12** **Create a Folder for Saving Your Files**

Before saving a file, you need to decide where you want to save it: in a folder on your fixed disk drive, on a floppy disk or other removable medium, or on a network drive.

When you save a file, it's a good idea to create separate folders for specific categories to help keep your work organized. For example, you might want to create folders for different projects or different customers. In this course, you will follow these steps to create a new folder for each lesson's work before you begin the lesson.

NOTE: Your instructor will advise you of the proper drive or folder to use when creating your lesson folders.

1. Click F̲ile to open the F̲ile menu and choose Save A̲s. The Save As dialog box appears. (See Figure 1-14 on the next page.)

2. Using the Save i̲n list box, follow your instructor's directions to navigate to the location where you should create your folder. If you will be using a floppy disk, insert a disk into your floppy drive.

3. Click the Create New Folder button on the dialog box toolbar. The New Folder dialog box opens.

4. In the N̲ame box, key **Lesson 1**. Click OK. A yellow folder icon with the name "Lesson 1" appears in the Save i̲n box.

5. Click C̲ancel to close the Save As dialog box.

FIGURE 1-14
Creating a
new folder in
the Save As
dialog box

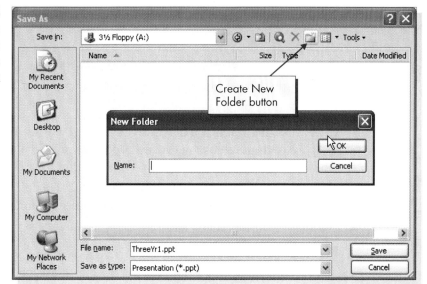

NOTE: Even though you clicked Cancel to close the Save As dialog box, your new folder has been created. You could have saved your presentation before closing the Save As dialog box, but you will do that in the next exercise instead.

EXERCISE   **1-13**   **Name and Save a Presentation**

To name files, you can use uppercase letters, lowercase letters, or a combination of both. Filenames can also include spaces. For example, you can use "Good 4 U Sales Report" as a filename.

1. Click File to open the File menu and choose Save As to reopen the Save As dialog box.

2. Navigate to the drive and folder where you created your new Lesson 1 folder.

3. Double-click the Lesson 1 folder to open it.

4. In the File name text box, key *[your initials]*1-13.

5. Click Save. Your document is saved and named for future use. Notice that the title bar displays the new filename.

Running a Slide Show

Usually the goal of creating a PowerPoint presentation is to present it as a slide show with computer projection equipment. One of the advantages of running a slide show from your computer is that you can use special animation effects. However, if this equipment is not available in the location where you present, you can use PowerPoint to prepare 35 mm slides or overhead transparencies.

EXERCISE 1-14 Run a Slide Show

One way to start a slide show is to click the Slide Show button . After you begin running a slide show, PowerPoint provides navigation tools to move from slide to slide.

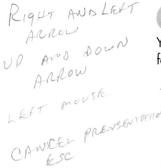

1. Move to slide 1 if it is not currently displayed. Click the Slide Show button at the bottom left of the PowerPoint window (next to the Slide Sorter View button). The first slide in the presentation fills the screen.
2. Click the left mouse button to move to slide 2. The left mouse button is one of many ways to move forward in a slide presentation.
3. Press N on the keyboard to move to the next slide, slide 3.

TIP: As an alternative to clicking the left mouse button, you can press N to move forward through the slides. N means "Next" and P means "Previous." You can also use the right and left arrow keys and Page Down and Page Up to move forward and backward in a slide show.

4. Press N again to move to slide 4, which is titled "Where We're Going."
5. Using the left mouse button, click anywhere to see a sample of a PowerPoint text animation. Click twice more to see the remaining text on this slide.
6. Press Esc or − (Minus) to end the slide show.

EXERCISE 1-15 Start a Slide Show from Any Slide

If you had to interrupt a slide show, or you only want to show specific slides, you can begin a slide show from any slide.

1. In Normal view, move to slide 5.
2. Click the Slide Show button to resume the slide show from slide 5.
3. Click the left mouse button twice to display the text animations on this slide.

Printing Slides and Handouts

Although the primary way of viewing a presentation is usually as a slide show, you can also print PowerPoint slides, just as you print Word documents or Excel worksheets. PowerPoint provides a variety of print options, including printing each slide on a separate page or printing several slides on the same page.

Throughout this course, to conserve paper and speed up printing, you usually print a *handout* instead of full-size slides. A handout contains several scaled-down slide images on each page (1, 2, 3, 4, 6, or 9 to a page), and is often given to an audience during a presentation.

EXERCISE 1-16 Preview a Presentation

The PowerPoint *Print Preview* feature lets you see what your printed pages will look like before you actually print them. You can view preview pages in black and white, grayscale, or color.

1. From the File menu, choose Print.
2. In the Print range option box, choose All.
3. Click Preview in the lower-left corner of the dialog box. The Preview window opens, showing you how the printed slide will appear on paper. The Print Preview toolbar is displayed at the top of the window.

FIGURE 1-15
Print Preview
toolbar

TABLE 1-3   Print Preview Toolbar Buttons

TOOLBAR BUTTON	NAME	PURPOSE
	Previous Page	Display the previous page to be printed.
	Next Page	Display the next page to be printed.
Print...	Print	Open the Print dialog box.
Print What:	Print What	Choose between printing slides, handouts, notes pages, or an outline.
100%	Zoom	Change the magnification in the Preview window.
	Landscape	Set the printed page orientation to landscape.
	Portrait	Set the printed page orientation to portrait.
Options ▾	Options	Choose from a variety of options and preview them before printing.
Close	Close Preview	Close the Preview window.

4. On the Print Preview toolbar, click the Next Page button . Page 2 of the printout is displayed.

5. Move your pointer to the middle of the slide. Notice that the pointer is in the shape of a magnifying glass .

6. Click the magnifying glass pointer in the center of the slide. The display is magnified.

7. Click again. The display returns to its regular size.

8. Close the Preview window.

EXERCISE **Print a Slide**

You can start printing in one of the following ways:

- From the File menu, choose Print Preview. After previewing, click the Print button from the Print Preview window.
- From the File menu, choose Print.
- Press Ctrl + P.
- Click the Print button.

The first method opens the Print Preview window, which you learned in Exercise 1-16. The next two methods open the Print dialog box, where you can choose printing options. The last method, the Print button, should be used with caution. It prints a presentation with the most recently used print options and does not open the print options dialog box. Usually this will result with one slide on a page for your whole presentation.

FIGURE 1-16
Print dialog box

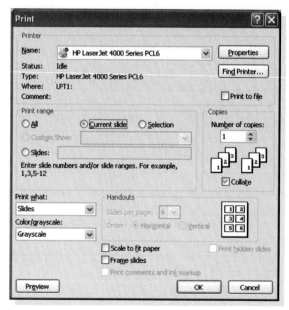

1. To print the first slide in your presentation, display slide 1, open the File menu, and then choose Print. The Print dialog box displays PowerPoint's default settings and indicates the designated printer.

2. In the Print range option box, choose Current Slide.

3. From the Print what drop-down list box, choose Slides.

4. From the Color/grayscale list box, choose Grayscale.

This setting optimizes color slides for a black-and-white printer. (If you have a color printer, you could choose Color instead.)

5. Click OK to start printing.

EXERCISE 1-18 Print a Presentation Handout

Printing several slides on a single page is a handy way to review your work and to create audience handouts. It's also a convenient way to print class assignments. You can create handouts in the Print Preview window or in the Print dialog box.

1. From the File menu, choose Print Preview. Click the arrow next to the Print What list box and then choose Handouts (2 slides per page). Two slides are displayed on the preview page.

2. Open the Print What list box again and choose Handouts (9 slides per page). Now the entire presentation is displayed on one page.

3. Click the Landscape button ⒜ to orient your slides sideways on the page.

4. Click the Options button Options ▾. Make sure the Frame Slides option is selected to put a line around each slide. Click Scale to Fit Paper to make each slide slightly larger than if this option was not selected.

FIGURE 1-17
Choosing printing
options

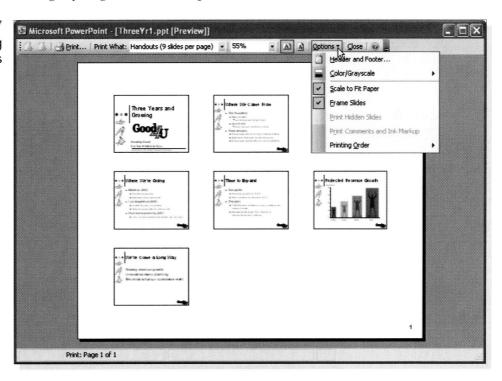

DEFAULT - PRINT 6 SLIDES PER PAGE
BUT CAN PRINT 9 ON PAGE
WHEN PRINTING USE (HANDOUTS)

5. Click the Print button . The Print dialog box opens. You can change print settings here as well as in the Print Preview window. No further changes are required now.

6. Click OK to print your handout page. After printing, the Preview window reappears because it was open before the Print window opened.

7. Click Close on the Preview toolbar to close the Preview window.

EXERCISE 1-19 Choose Print Options

In addition to the options covered previously, there are two options for printing in black and white. The Grayscale option converts the presentation colors to shades of gray. The Pure Black & White option converts all colors to either black or white, eliminating shades of gray. In complex presentation designs, this setting can be useful.

 NOTE: Because the Pure Black & White option simplifies your presentation graphics, it can sometimes speed up printing time.

The Print dialog box is divided into several areas: Printer, Print range, Copies, Print what, and Handouts. Each area presents choices that let you print exactly what you want in a variety of layouts.

1. With *[your initials]*1-13 presentation displayed, click File on the menu bar and choose Print to open the Print dialog box.

2. At the top of the Print dialog box, click the down arrow in the Name box. This is where you choose another printer, if one is available.

3. Follow your instructor's directions to choose an appropriate printer from the list.

NOTE: The information below the Name box applies to the selected printer. For example, "Status" indicates if the printer is idle or currently printing other documents.

4. Under Print range, click Slides and key **1,2** in the text box to print only slides 1 and 2.

TIP: To print consecutive slides, you can use a hyphen. For example, enter **2-4** to print slides 2 through 4. To print a combination of slides, you can key the range **1,3, 5-9,12** to print slides 1, 3, 5 through 9, and 12.

5. Under Copies, in the Number of copies box, key **2**. The Collate check box is selected by default to print the slideshow from beginning to end two times.

6. Choose Slides from the Print what drop-down list box.

7. If you have a black-and-white printer, choose Grayscale from the Color/ grayscale list box. If you have a color printer, you can choose Color from the list box.

8. Click OK. In the printouts, notice that only slide 2 is numbered.

TIP: You can create a presentation that uses overhead transparencies by printing your slides on transparency film. Before printing, insert transparency sheets directly into your printer (choosing the correct type for a laser or ink-jet printer).

9. Open the Print dialog box again and set the following options:
   - For Print range, choose <u>A</u>ll to print all slides.
   - For Num<u>b</u>er of copies, key **1**
   - In the Print <u>w</u>hat list box, choose Handouts.
   - Under Handouts, set the Slides pe<u>r</u> page to **3**.
   - From the Color/grayscale list box, choose Grayscale.
   - Click the Fra<u>m</u>e slides check box.

10. Click OK to print the presentation handout and close the Print dialog box.

11. Click the Save button ⊞ to resave the presentation, and then close it.

Closing Presentations and Exiting PowerPoint

After you have finished working on a presentation and saved it, you can close it and open another file or you can exit the program.

To close a presentation and exit PowerPoint, you can:

- Use the <u>F</u>ile menu and choose to close or exit.
- Use keyboard shortcuts. [Ctrl]+[W] closes a presentation and [Alt]+[F4] exits PowerPoint.

- Use the Close button ☒ in the upper-right corner of the window.

EXERCISE **1-20** **Close a Presentation and Exit PowerPoint**

1. From the <u>F</u>ile menu, choose <u>C</u>lose to close the presentation.

2. After printing a presentation, you are usually prompted to save it before closing. On the message prompt, click <u>Y</u>es to save the presentation again.

3. Click the Close button ☒ in the upper-right corner of the window to Exit PowerPoint.

USING ONLINE HELP

Microsoft Office PowerPoint Help is an excellent reference tool for reinforcing skills presented in a lesson and for finding more information on any PowerPoint feature.

There are several ways to open the Help window. You can:

- Click <u>H</u>elp on the menu bar and then choose Microsoft Office PowerPoint Help.
- Press F1 on your keyboard.
- Key a question or topic in the Ask a Question box on the right side of the menu bar.

 TIP: If you choose one of the first two options, the Microsoft Office Assistant might appear. If you like the Office Assistant, you can key your question in the Office Assistant balloon. If you don't like the Assistant, right-click it and choose <u>H</u>ide from the shortcut menu. To permanently turn off the Assistant, choose <u>O</u>ptions in the Assistant's balloon; then deselect <u>U</u>se the Office Assistant from the dialog box and click OK.

Get acquainted with PowerPoint Help:

1. Start PowerPoint, if it's not already open.
2. Click the Ask a Question box on the right side of the menu bar.

 NOTE: If this is the first time you are using Help, the Ask a Question box contains the text "Type a question for help."

3. Key **Views** and then press Enter. A list of Help topics appears.
4. Scroll down the list, and then select About PowerPoint views. (See Figure 1-18 on the next page.)
5. Drag the Help window's left border to the left until the Help window fills about half your screen.
6. In the paragraph with the heading "Normal View," point to the blue text notes pane. Notice the hand pointer and the underline that appear. This indicates a link to more information.
7. Click notes pane. A definition of the term appears in green text.
8. Click anywhere in the green text to make it disappear.
9. Scroll down until the blue numbered list of topics appears in the middle of the Help window. Click any topic to expand it. To compress the topic, click it again.
10. Scroll through and read the entire Help window, expanding all topics and defined terms as you go. Click the Hide all link at the top of the window to remove the definitions. Clicking Show all will display them again.

FIGURE 1-18
Using PowerPoint
Help

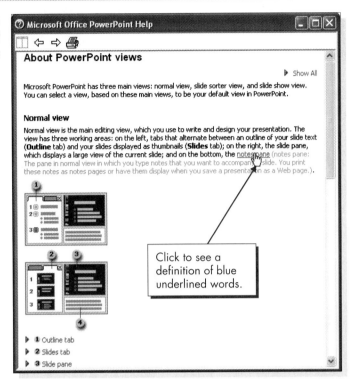

11. When you have finished, click the Close button ☒ in the upper-right corner of the Help window to close it and return to PowerPoint.

LESSON 1 Summary

➤ Microsoft PowerPoint is a powerful graphics program used to create professional-quality presentations for a variety of settings.

➤ To start PowerPoint, click Start on the Windows taskbar, point to Programs, and then select Microsoft PowerPoint from the submenu.

➤ When you perform certain tasks, a task pane with related commands appears automatically. Display other task panes by clicking the arrow next to the Other Task Panes button ▼. Hide a task pane by clicking its Close button ☒.

➤ Identify buttons on the PowerPoint window by pointing to them and waiting for their ScreenTips to appear.

➤ Menus and toolbars do not always show all the available commands. To see more menu options, point to the menu and wait for it to expand. To see more toolbar buttons, click the Toolbar Options button ▪.

➤ Toolbars can be docked or floating. To float a docked toolbar, drag its move handle ⋮ . To dock a floating toolbar, double-click its title bar. View, Toolbars, Customize, Options tab, Show Standard and Formatting toolbar on two rows.

➤ Key and edit text on a slide in the same way as you would in a word processing program.

➤ Promoting and demoting text on a slide is similar to working with an outline in a word processing program. When you demote text, you increase its indent. When you promote text, you decrease its indent.

➤ Use the Slide Show button 🖵 to run a slide show. A slide show always starts with the slide that is currently selected.

➤ Choose one of the options in the Print what box in the Print dialog box or in the Print Preview window to print handouts that contain more than one slide per page.

➤ Printing options provide a variety of ways to print your presentation: as slides, handouts, notes pages, and other page formats. Printing options are available in the Print dialog box and in the Print Preview window.

LESSON 1   Command Summary

FEATURE	BUTTON	MENU	KEYBOARD
Open a presentation	📂	File, Open	Ctrl + O
Display Outline and Slides pane	▣	View, Normal	
Display Task pane		View, Task Pane	
Promote Text	🔼		Shift + Tab
Demote Text	🔽		Tab
Zoom	100% ▾	View, Zoom	
Normal view	▣	View, Normal	
Slide Sorter view	▤	View, Slide Sorter	
Next Slide	▼		Page Down
Previous Slide	▲		Page Up

continues

LESSON 1   Command Summary   *continued*

FEATURE	BUTTON	MENU	KEYBOARD
Slide Show		View, Slide Show	F5
Save		File, Save	Ctrl + S
Save with a different name		File, Save As	
Next (Slide Show)	Left mouse button	Right-click, Next	N , Page Down
Previous (Slide Show)		Right-click, Previous	P , Page Up
End a slide show		Right-click, End Show	Esc or -
Print Preview		File, Print Preview	
Print		File, Print	Ctrl + P
Close a presentation		File, Close	Ctrl + W or Ctrl + F4
Exit PowerPoint		File, Exit	Alt + F4

Concepts Review

Each of the following statements is either true or false. Indicate your choice by circling T or F.

(T) F **1.** When you start PowerPoint, it automatically displays a blank presentation.

(T) F **2.** Editing text in PowerPoint is similar to editing text in a word processing program.

T (F) **3.** You can ~~demote~~ PROMOTE text by pressing [Shift]+[Tab].

(T) F **4.** In the Outline and Slides pane, you can display either slide thumbnails or outline text, but not both.

(T) F **5.** You can edit text in Normal view or in the Outline pane.

(T) F **6.** You can display multiple slides as thumbnails in Slide Sorter view.

T (F) **7.** When viewing a slide show, pressing the plus sign moves to the next slide.

T (F) **8.** If you click the Print button 🖨, you can choose exactly which items to print.

Write the correct answer in the space provided.

1. Where on the PowerPoint window are the view buttons located?

Bottom LEFT

2. What are the names of the three view buttons?

NORMAL   SLIDE SORTER   SLIDE SHOW

3. If the Outline and Slides pane is not displayed, what button can you click to make it appear?

NORMAL

4. What shape is the mouse pointer when you move it over a text box?

I - BEAM

5. Which menu and menu option would you use to save a copy of your presentation under a different filename?

FILE SAVE AS

6. Name all the ways to use the keyboard for moving to the previous slide during a slide show.

ARROW LEFT   PG DOWN   P   LEFT MOUSE

7. Which keys can you press to stop a slide show?

ESC — MINUS SIGN

8. What is the maximum number of slides you can print on a handout page?

9

DEFAULT IS 6

CRITICAL THINKING

Answer these questions on a separate page. There are no right or wrong answers. Support your answers with examples from your own experience, if possible.

1. In this lesson you learned how to display slide thumbnails in the Outline and Slides pane and also in Slide Sorter view. Which way do you prefer to view thumbnails and why? What advantages and disadvantages do you think there are for each option?

2. You can produce screen shows, printouts, 35 mm slides, overhead transparencies, and other presentation media with PowerPoint. Why would you choose one medium over another? What factors would influence your decision?

Skills Review

EXERCISE 1-21

Start PowerPoint, open a file, identify parts of the PowerPoint window, key and edit text, and save, print, and close the file.

1. If PowerPoint is already open, skip to step 2. Otherwise, start PowerPoint by following these steps:
   a. Click the Start button ⊞ start on the Windows taskbar.
   b. Point to Programs and then point to Microsoft PowerPoint and click it.

2. Open a presentation by following these steps:

   a. Click the Open button on the Standard toolbar.
   b. Choose the appropriate drive and folder, according to your instructor's directions.
   c. Double-click the file **Answers**.

3. Click anywhere on the text "Click to add subtitle" and key your full name.

4. Select the two question marks in the text "Exercise 1-??" by dragging the I-beam across them. Key the number of this exercise.

5. To move to slide 2, click the Next Slide button at the bottom of the vertical scroll bar.

6. Key the answers to the questions on slide 2 by following these steps:

   a. Click to position the insertion point after the word "Answer:" and press [Spacebar].
   b. Key the answer.

   c. Key the answers to the next two questions. Remember, to identify a toolbar button by name, point to the button. If the button does not appear on the toolbar, click the Toolbar Options button to locate the button.

   d. Promote each Answers space by one level. Place the insertion point before the word Answers and press the Decrease Indent button . Do this for all three of the answer bullet points.

7. Save the presentation as *[your initials]*1-21 in your Lesson 1 folder by following these steps:

   a. From the File menu, choose Save As to open the Save As dialog box.
   b. Choose your Lesson 1 folder from the appropriate drive and folder, following your instructor's directions.
   c. Key the filename *[your initials]*1-21 in the File name text box.
   d. Click Save.

8. Print the presentation by following these steps:

   a. From the File menu, choose Print.
   b. Choose All in the Print range option box.
   c. Choose Handouts from the Print what drop-down list.
   d. Because this is a two-slide presentation, change the Slides per page setting to 2.
   e. Choose Grayscale from the Color/grayscale drop-down list.
   f. Click the Frame slides check box to select it. Click OK.

9. Close the presentation by clicking the lower Close button in the upper-right corner of the PowerPoint window.

EXERCISE 1-22

Edit text on a slide, save a presentation, run a slide show, then preview and print it.

1. Open the file **GoodFood**.

2. Notice on the status bar and on the Outline and Slides pane that this is a three-slide presentation (slide 1 of 3 now appears). Move to slide 3 by dragging the vertical scroll box.

3. Make corrections to the slide's text as shown in Figure 1-19.

NOTE: Before making the changes indicated in Figure 1-19, refer to "Proofreaders' Marks" at the Professional Approach Online Learning Center at www.mhteched.com/pas. *Proofreaders' marks* are special notations used to mark up a printed draft with changes to be made before final printing. Some proofreaders' marks might be confusing if you are unfamiliar with them. For example, a hand-written "=" indicates that a hyphen is to be inserted.

FIGURE 1-19

Just Sweet Enough

    Carob Pecan Yogurt Cream Pie

        This light and fluffy des^sert has an all-natural grah^am cracker crust, great flavor, and very little sugar.

    Key Lime Soufflé

        The ~~striking~~ *intense* lime flavor is *chef* Michelle's secret. Made from organic key limes, sweetened with white grape juice, and thickened with organic egg whites.

4. Notice on slide 2 that the description of each dish would be more attractively displayed if they were demoted by one level. Demote the descriptions by placing the insertion point before the description and clicking the Increase Indent button 🔳.

5. Run the presentation as a slide show by following these steps:

    a. Display slide 1. Click the Slide Show button 🔳.
    b. After slide 1 appears, click the left mouse button to advance to the next slide.
    c. Click the left mouse button twice more to return to Normal view.

6. Save the presentation as *[your initials]***1-22** in your Lesson 1 folder.

7. Print slides 1 and 3 only by following these steps:

    a. Open the Print dialog box.

    b. In the Print range area, click Slides and key **1,3** in the text box.

    c. Choose Slides from the Print what drop-down list, choose Grayscale, and click OK.

8. Close the presentation.

EXERCISE 1-23

Work with views and tabs; edit text; run a slide show; and save, preview, and print a presentation.

1. Open the file **DressCd1**.

2. View the presentation's text in outline format by following these steps:

    a. If the Outline and Slides pane is not displayed, click the Normal View button .

    b. Click the Outline tab.

    c. Point to the Outline pane's right vertical border.

    d. When you see the splitter bar , drag to the right to the center of the screen to see the text on these slides. Move the splitter bar back to its original position.

3. Click the Slide Sorter View button to view the presentation in Slide Sorter view.

4. Double-click slide 1 in Slide Sorter view to change back to Slide view.

5. Create a subtitle on slide 1 by following these steps:

    a. Click the text placeholder containing the text "Click to add subtitle."

    b. Key your name.

    c. Press (Enter) to start a new line; then key today's date.

6. Run a slide show and navigate within the show by following these steps:

    a. Click the Slide Show button .

    b. Advance through the slides by pressing (Page Down) several times.

7. Save the presentation as *[your initials]***1-23**.

8. Preview the presentation before printing by following these steps:

    a. From the File menu, choose Print Preview.

    b. In the Print What drop-down list, choose Handouts (4 slides per page).

    c. In the Options drop-down list box, point to Color/Grayscale and then choose Grayscale.

    d. Click the Print button .

    e. In the Print dialog box, make sure the Frame slides option is selected. Click OK.

9. Click Close to close the Print Preview window and then close the presentation.

EXERCISE 1-24

Key text on a slide, save it, and print.

1. Open the file **SpEvent1**.
2. Display slide 2.
3. Insert a new line of bulleted text by following these steps:
    a. Click the I-beam to the right of the word "team" at the end of the line "National In-Line Skate demo team."
    b. Press (Enter) to start a new line with an automatic bullet.
    c. Key **Autograph session with Marsha Miles**
4. Edit the text you keyed by following these steps:
    a. Click the I-beam between the words "with" and "Marsha" to position the insertion point.
    b. Key **aerobic video star** and insert any necessary spaces.
5. Save the presentation as *[your initials]***1-24** in your Lesson 1 folder.

NOTE: When you print slides and handouts, colored backgrounds and some graphics are not usually shown on the printout because they can interfere with the legibility of the text. In a later lesson you learn how to control what gets printed by using grayscale settings.

6. Print the slides full-size by following these steps:
    a. From the File menu, choose Print.
    b. In the Print what drop-down list box, choose Slides.
    c. Click Preview.

    d. Click the Next Page button 🔽 to preview slide 2.
    e. Click Print and then click OK.
    f. Click Close to close the Preview window.
7. Close the presentation.

Lesson Applications

Edit text, change presentation views, and save, print, and close a presentation.

1. Open the file **Party1**.
2. Using the Slide pane, make the changes to slides 2 and 3 as shown in Figure 1-20.

FIGURE 1-20

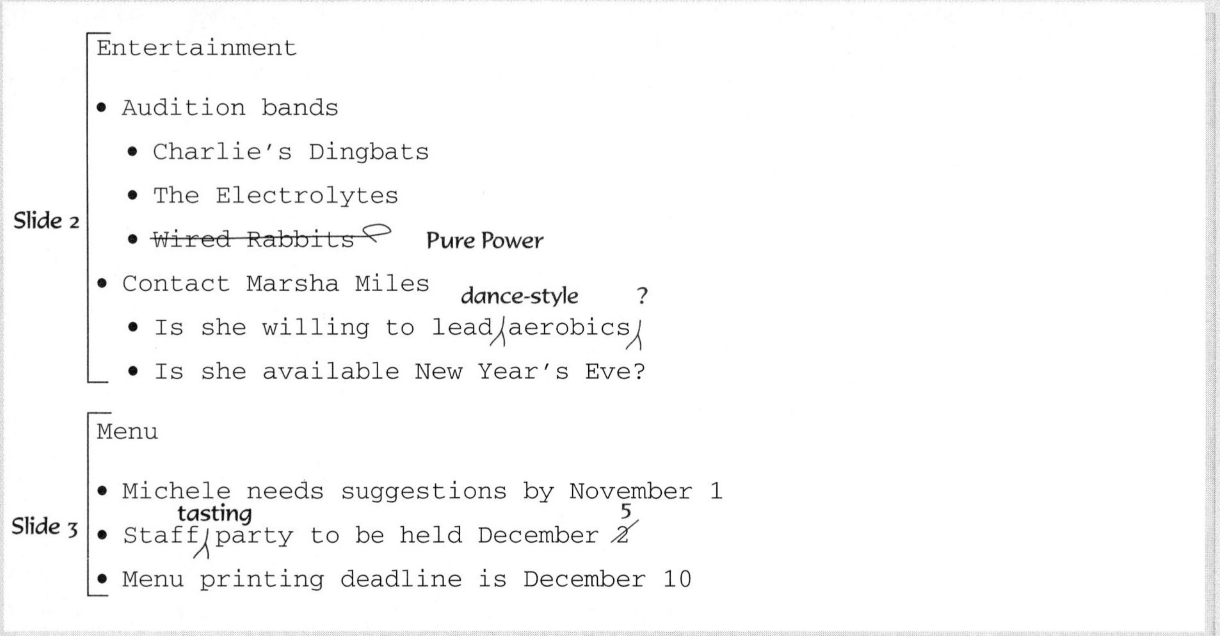

Slide 2
```
Entertainment

• Audition bands
  • Charlie's Dingbats
  • The Electrolytes
  • Wired Rabbits      Pure Power
• Contact Marsha Miles    dance-style    ?
  • Is she willing to lead aerobics
  • Is she available New Year's Eve?
```

Slide 3
```
Menu

• Michele needs suggestions by November 1
            tasting              5
• Staff party to be held December 2
• Menu printing deadline is December 10
```

3. Save the presentation as *[your initials]***1-25**.
4. View each slide in the presentation.
5. Preview the presentation as handouts, 3 slides per page, grayscale, framed, and then print it.
6. Close the presentation.

Edit text in Normal view and Slide view, run a slide show, and save, print, and close a presentation.

1. Open the file **JulyFun1**.

2. Move to slide 2. Change "am" in the first and second bullets to **a.m.** Change the date in the last bullet to **June 25**.

3. Click the Outline tab and drag the Outline pane's right border to make it wider.

4. Working on slide 3 in the outline area, change the age in the second bullet from "21" to **18**.

5. Save the presentation as *[your initials]***1-26**.

6. Click the Slides tab and display slide 1. Run a slide show of the presentation, clicking to display each new slide and text animation.

7. Preview and then print the presentation as handouts, 6 slides per page, grayscale, framed.

8. Close the presentation.

EXERCISE 1-27

Edit text, change presentation views, and save, print, and close a presentation.

1. Open the file **DressCd2**.

2. On slide 1, key the word **Personnel** to the left of "Training" so the title reads "Personnel Training Session."

3. Locate the last line of text on slide 2 (which begins "Under no circumstances"). Position the insertion point at the end of that line and key **while on the job**

4. Locate the last line of text on slide 3. Position the insertion point between "Good 4 U" and "test" and key **proficiency** (the phrase should read "Good 4 U proficiency test").

5. Click the Outline tab and make the Outline pane wide enough to work comfortably. Scroll down to display the outline text for slide 4.

6. Working on slide 4 in the Outline pane, delete the periods at the ends of the two sentences that begin "Guests."

7. Below the third bullet, change "Shirts are" to **T-shirts will be**

8. Save the presentation as *[your initials]***1-27**.

9. Preview and then print the presentation as handouts, 4 slides per page, grayscale, framed.

10. Close the presentation.

EXERCISE 1-28 *Challenge Yourself*

Edit text, print a slide and handouts, and close a presentation.

1. Open the file **RacePrep**.

2. Using whichever view you choose, edit slide 2 and slide 3 as shown in Figure 1-21.

FIGURE 1-21

Slide 2

Entertainment

• The Electrolytes will be here ~~for~~ on marathon eve, ~~injecting mental~~ charging up the runners ~~energy for all~~

• Julie will again lead her famous pre-marathon "Pump-you-up" chant

Slide 3

Pre Marathon

Carbo Loading Menu

• Marathon Angel

• A ~~huge pile~~ mountain of angel hair with fat-free tomato sauce and ~~sprinkled~~ pasta served ~~with~~ tiny bite-sized meat balls

• Bagel Bonanza

• Bagels brushed with a mixture of olive oil, garlic, and delicate herbs

3. Save the presentation in your Lesson 1 folder as *[your initials]*1-28

4. View the presentation in Slide Sorter view.

5. Run a slide show of the presentation, beginning with slide 1.

6. Preview and then print all slides in grayscale, framed.

7. Print the presentation as handouts, 3 slides per page, grayscale, framed.

8. Close the presentation.

On Your Own

In these exercises you work on your own, as you would in a real-life work environment. Use the skills you've learned to accomplish the task—and be creative.

EXERCISE 1-29

Open the file **SpEvent1**. Change slide 2 so that its title is **Summer Events**. Edit the slide's bullets by changing the events to be for June and July, describing activities relating to summer sports such as swimming, softball, sand volleyball, or others. Save the presentation as *[your initials]*1-29. Preview and then print the presentation as handouts, 2 slides per page.

EXERCISE 1-30
Open the file **GoodFood**. On slide 2, replace the text describing the pasta dishes with pasta creations from your imagination. On slide 3, replace the text describing the desserts with your own combination of sweet delights. Be sure the desserts you describe use healthy ingredients.

Save the presentation as *[your initials]*1-30. Preview and then print the presentation as handouts, 3 slides per page.

EXERCISE 1-31
Open the file **DressCd1**. On slides 2 and 3, replace the text under the "Uniform" bullet with a dress code you think would be appropriate for employees at the Good 4 U restaurant in New York City as described in the Case Study. Replace the second main bullet "Skates" with **Hair and Nails** and change the bullet under it to talk about what kind of rules may apply to the way that the employees must wear their hair and nails. On slide 4, upgrade the guest dress code to fit this restaurant scenario. Save the presentation as *[your initials]*1-31. Preview and then print the presentation as handouts, landscape orientation, 4 slides per page.

Basic Presentation Tools

OBJECTIVES

**MICROSOFT OFFICE
SPECIALIST
ACTIVITIES**
In this lesson:
PPO3S-1-1
PPO3S-1-2
PPO3S-2-5
PPO3S-2-7
PPO3S-4-1

See Appendix.

After completing this lesson, you will be able to:

1. Use the AutoContent Wizard.
2. Select, rearrange, and delete slides.
3. Edit and revise text.
4. Add slide transitions.
5. Add headers and footers.

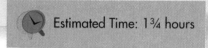 Estimated Time: 1¾ hours

This lesson introduces you to basic presentation tools, starting with the AutoContent Wizard. A *wizard* is a software feature that guides you through a task. The AutoContent Wizard provides step-by-step help for creating a presentation. It creates a complete presentation with sample text on each slide. *Sample text* provides content suggestions for your presentation.

After creating the presentation, you can change the sample text provided by the wizard to suit your needs. Then you can rearrange slides, delete slides, check the presentation for spelling errors, and find and replace text. You can further enhance your presentation by applying headers and footers, text animation, slide transitions, and a variety of print options.

Using the AutoContent Wizard

Using the AutoContent Wizard is a convenient way to create a presentation. The wizard asks a series of questions and uses your answers to develop the framework for your presentation.

EXERCISE **2-1** **Use the AutoContent Wizard**

1. Start PowerPoint.

FIGURE 2-1
New Presentation
task pane

2. In the New Presentation task pane on the right, choose the From AutoContent Wizard option (the third choice under New).

The AutoContent Wizard opening dialog box appears. The "road map" on the left side of the dialog box uses a green square to indicate where you are in the process.

REVIEW: If you don't see the New Presentation task pane, choose New from the File menu. If the Office Assistant appears, right-click it and choose Hide from the shortcut menu.

FIGURE 2-2
AutoContent
Wizard opening
screen

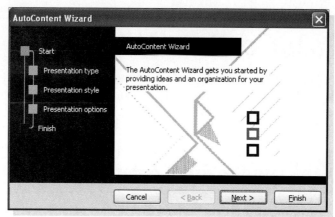

3. In the AutoContent Wizard opening dialog box, click Next. The second window appears. The green square moves to Presentation type.

FIGURE 2-3
Choosing a
presentation type

4. Click Sales / Marketing to view the types of presentations available in this category.

5. Click General and choose Recommending a Strategy from the list. Click Next. The third window appears. The green square moves to Presentation style. This is where you tell the wizard what format you plan to use when presenting your slide show.

6. Choose On-screen presentation and click Next.

7. In the fourth window, Presentation options, key **Selling to Corporations** in the Presentation title text box. Press Tab to move to the Footer text box and key your name. Clear the option for Date last updated by clicking its checkbox.

8. Click Next to move to the last dialog box. Click Finish. PowerPoint creates a seven-slide strategy presentation for you. Notice the presentation design and the sample text.

FIGURE 2-4
Presentation created
by using the
AutoContent
Wizard

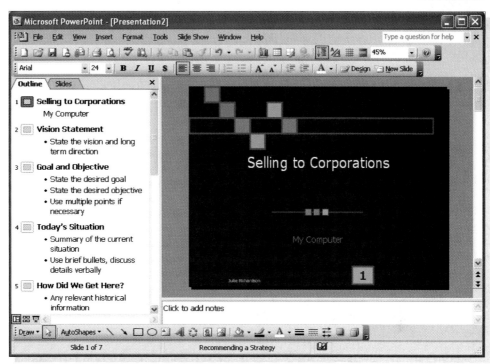

NOTE: The subtitle on slide 1 might have different text than that shown in Figure 2-4. The subtitle text is usually the name that was used to register the PowerPoint software. You change this text in the following exercises.

EXERCISE **2-2** **Edit Placeholder Text**

In a wizard-generated presentation, all the slides contain sample text, some in title placeholders and some in body text placeholders. For example, slide 2 is titled "Vision Statement" and slide 3 is named "Goal and Objective." You can select and then edit this sample text, and you can also add additional bullets.

1. In the Slide pane, click the Next Slide button at the bottom of the vertical scroll bar to view slide 2. Notice the sample text for the title and body text.

2. Display the slides one at a time, examining the sample text as you go. Then move back to slide 2.

REVIEW: To move to other slides, you can drag the scroll box, click the Next Slide button or the Previous Slide button , or press [Page Down] or [Page Up].

3. On slide 2, move the pointer over the title ("Vision Statement") until it becomes an I-beam and click to activate the title placeholder.

4. Drag the I-beam over the sample title text to select it. Key the new title **Corporate Market is Growing** in place of the selected text.

5. Click outside the title placeholder to deactivate it.

 REVIEW: After you edit placeholder text, deactivate the placeholder by clicking elsewhere on the screen. Be sure you see the white arrow pointer when you click.

TABLE 2-1

Selecting Text	
METHOD	**RESULT**
Click and drag	Selects text with the mouse
Double-click a word	Selects the entire word
Ctrl+click text	Selects the sentence
Triple-click text	Selects the paragraph or bulleted item
Click a bullet	Selects all the text for that bullet (in a body text placeholder)

NOTE: When you select bulleted text, the bullet character is not highlighted.

6. Working on slide 2, click the I-beam pointer on the bulleted text beginning with the words "State the vision." The body text placeholder is activated.

7. Position the I-beam to the right of the first bullet and drag to select all the text in the line. Key **Employee events** in place of the selected text.

8. Press Enter to add a new bullet. A dark bullet appears on the new line. It will change to a normal bullet when you key text on the line.

9. Key **Promotional events**

10. Press Enter to add a third bullet and key **Community event sponsorships**

11. Move to the next slide and click the I-beam on any bulleted text to activate the body text placeholder.

 12. Move the I-beam onto the first bullet. When you see a four-pointed arrow ⊕, click the bullet. The entire line is selected.

13. Key **Increase awareness of our corporate services** Notice how the text wraps to a new line.

14. Triple-click the text in the second bullet to select it. Then key **Increase corporate sales by 30%**

15. Press Enter to insert a blank bulleted line after the second bullet. Then key **Increase facility utilization to 85%**

16. Click the last bullet (beginning "Use multiple points") with the four-pointed arrow ⊕ and press Delete to remove it.

FIGURE 2-5
Editing sample text
on slide 3

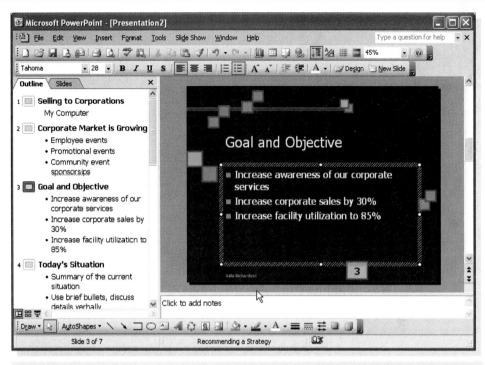

TABLE 2-2   **Editing Text**

METHOD	RESULT
Arrow key	Moves insertion point right, left, up, or down within the text
Ctrl+Arrow key	Moves insertion point to the next word or paragraph (bulleted item)
Backspace	Deletes characters to the left of the insertion point
Ctrl+Backspace	Deletes word to the left of the insertion point
Delete	Deletes characters to the right of the insertion point
Ctrl+Delete	Deletes word to the right of the insertion point

17. Change the title of slide 3 from "Goal and Objective" to **What We Want to Accomplish**

18. Move to slide 4 and change the title to read **Corporate Sales Today**

19. Still working on slide 4, select and delete both bulleted items. Key the following three bulleted lines, pressing Enter to start each new bullet:

● **Account for only 1% of revenues**

● **Only two corporations use our services regularly**

● **Our facilities are underutilized during mid-week periods**

20. Skip slide 5. Edit the text on slides 6 and 7 to match the text shown in Figure 2-6.

FIGURE 2-6

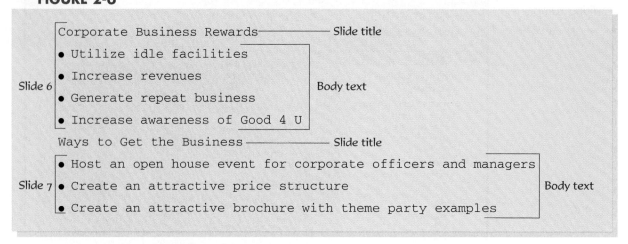

Slide 6
- Corporate Business Rewards —— Slide title
- Utilize idle facilities
- Increase revenues — Body text
- Generate repeat business
- Increase awareness of Good 4 U

Slide 7
- Ways to Get the Business —— Slide title
- Host an open house event for corporate officers and managers
- Create an attractive price structure — Body text
- Create an attractive brochure with theme party examples

EXERCISE **2-3** **Edit Text Using the Outline Pane**

1. In Normal view, click the Outline tab to display the Outline pane.

2. If necessary, scroll up until you can see the first slide. The AutoContent Wizard automatically inserted the subtitle text on slide 1. It might contain the name of your computer or some other text.

3. Using the Outline pane, edit the subtitle text on slide 1 to read **Developing a Strategy**

Selecting, Rearranging, and Deleting Slides

Just as you frequently rearrange paragraphs or sentences in a word processing document, you will often need to rearrange or delete slides in a PowerPoint presentation. You can change the arrangement of slides by dragging them to a new position in the Slides pane, in the Outline pane (covered in Lesson 4), or in Slide Sorter view.

You can delete selected slide thumbnails by pressing (Delete) on your keyboard.

EXERCISE **2-4** **Select Multiple Slides**

If you select multiple slides, you can move them to a new position all at one time. You can also delete several selected slides at one time. In addition, you can apply transitions, animation schemes, and other effects to a group of selected slides.

There are two ways to select multiple slides:

- To select *contiguous slides* (slides that follow one after another), click the first slide in the selection and then hold down (Shift) while you click the last slide in the selection.

- To select *noncontiguous slides* (slides that do not follow one after another), click the first slide and then hold down (Ctrl) while you click each slide you want to add to the selection, one at a time.

1. In the Outline and Slides pane, click the Slides tab to display slide thumbnails.

2. Without clicking, point to each thumbnail one at a time and notice that a ScreenTip appears displaying the title of the slide.

3. Click the thumbnail for slide 2 ("Corporate Market is Growing") to select it.

4. Hold down (Shift) and click the slide 4 thumbnail ("Corporate Sales Today"). Release (Shift).

FIGURE 2-7
Selecting
contiguous slides

Selected slides

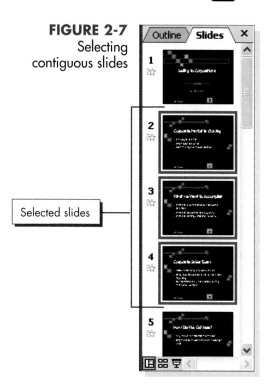

Slides 2, 3, and 4 are all selected, as indicated by the heavy borders around their thumbnails. This is a contiguous selection.

NOTE: You can change the number and size of slides displayed in the Slides pane by dragging its border to the right or to the left.

5. With (Shift) released, click slide 3. Now it is the only slide selected.

6. Hold down (Ctrl) and click slide 1. Slide 1 and slide 3 are both selected. This is a noncontiguous selection.

7. While holding down (Ctrl), click slide 5.

8. Now three noncontiguous slides are selected. You can add as many slides as you want to the selection if you hold down (Ctrl) while clicking a slide thumbnail.

EXERCISE   **2-5**   **Change the Order of Slides by Using the Slides Pane**

The Slides pane is a convenient place to rearrange slides. You simply drag selected slide thumbnails to a new position.

1. Click the slide 6 thumbnail to select it.

2. Position the arrow pointer within the selected slide's border, press the left mouse button, and drag the pointer above the fifth slide.

FIGURE 2-8
Moving a slide in the Slides pane

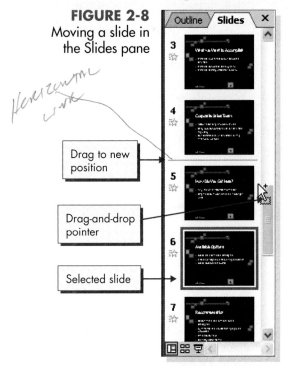

Drag to new position

Drag-and-drop pointer

Selected slide

 NOTE: While you are dragging, be sure not to release the left mouse button until it is pointing where you want the selection to go. Otherwise, you might either cancel the selection or drop the slides in the wrong place.

Notice the horizontal line and the drag-and-drop pointer as you drag. The horizontal line indicates where the slide will go.

3. Release the mouse button. Slide 6, titled "Corporate Business Rewards," becomes slide 5. Notice the change in the slide number in the Slides pane.

4. Using (Shift), make a contiguous selection of slides 2 ("Corporate Market is Growing") through 4 ("Corporate Sales Today").

5. Point to any slide in the selection and drag the selection below the fifth slide. All three slides move to the new position.

EXERCISE 2-6 **Change the Order of Slides in Slide Sorter View**

Slide Sorter view enables you to see more thumbnails at one time and is convenient if your presentation contains a large number of slides. You select slides in Slide Sorter view in the same way as in the Slides pane.

1. Click the Slide Sorter View button in the lower-left corner of the window.

2. Click slide 2 ("Corporate Business Rewards") and then hold down (Ctrl) and click slide 7 ("Ways to Get the Business") to make a noncontiguous selection of the two slides.

3. Release (Ctrl) and drag the selection until the drag-and-drop pointer rests between slides 5 and 6. A vertical line indicates where the two slides will be inserted.

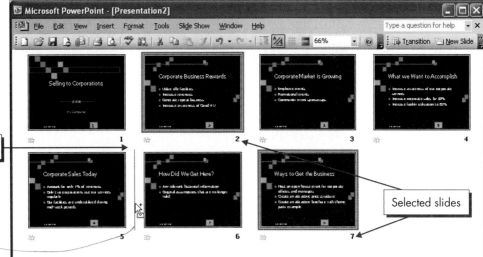

FIGURE 2-9
Moving a selection of noncontiguous slides in Slide Sorter view

Drag to new position.

VERTICAL LINE

Selected slides

4. Check to make sure your slides are in the following order. If not, rearrange your slides to agree.

   Slide 1: Selling to Corporations
   Slide 2: Corporate Market is Growing
   Slide 3: What We Want to Accomplish
   Slide 4: Corporate Sales Today
   Slide 5: Corporate Business Rewards
   Slide 6: Ways to Get the Business
   Slide 7: How Did We Get Here?

5. Double-click slide 6 ("Ways to Get the Business") to display it in Normal view.

EXERCISE **2-7** **Delete Slides**

When you want to delete slides, you first select them (in the Slides pane or in Slide Sorter view) the same way you select slides you want to move. You delete them by pressing ⌨Delete on your keyboard or by clicking the ~~View~~ menu and selecting the Delete Slide command.   *EDIT*

1. Working in Normal view, display the Slides pane if it is not already showing.

2. Click the slide 7 thumbnail to select it. The slide 7 title should be "How Did We Get Here?"

3. Press ⌨Delete on your keyboard. Slide 7 is deleted and slide 6 becomes selected.

 4. Move to slide 1 and click the Slide Show button 🖳 to start a slide show.

DOUBLE CLICK TO RETURN TO NORMAL VIEW FROM SLIDE SORTER VIEW

5. Advance through the slides (using any method), reading the text and observing the built-in animation effects.

 REVIEW: To advance through a slide show, click the left mouse button, press Page Down, or press N.

6. Create a new folder for Lesson 2. Save the presentation as *[your initials]*2-7 in the Lesson 2 folder. Do not print the presentation at this point, and do not close it.

Editing and Revising Text

PowerPoint provides many tools to edit and revise text, and improve the overall appearance of a presentation:

- Spelling checker, which corrects spelling by comparing words to an internal dictionary file.
- AutoCorrect, which corrects common spelling and capitalization errors automatically as you key text.
- Style checker, which automatically checks a presentation for visual clarity and consistency of case and punctuation.
- Thesaurus, which offers new words with similar meanings to the word you are looking up.
- Find and Replace, which allows you to find a certain word or phrase and replace it with a different word or phrase.

EXERCISE **2-8** **Use the Spelling Checker**

The spelling checker in PowerPoint works much the same as it does in other Microsoft Office applications. It flags misspelled words with a red wavy underline as you key text. It can also check an entire presentation at once. The spelling checker is an excellent proofreading tool, but it should be used in combination with your own careful proofreading and editing.

1. Without closing the current presentation, open the file **JulyFun2**. (You'll need to navigate from your Lesson 2 folder to the folder that stores the student files for this course.)

 TIP: You can open an existing presentation by clicking More presentations in the New Presentation task pane, if it is displayed.

2. On slide 1, a word in the title has a red wavy underline indicating a spelling error. Right-click the word. Choose the correct spelling ("Celebration") from the shortcut menu.

3. Notice the spelling of "Forth" in the title. This is an example of a word that is correctly spelled but incorrectly used. The spelling checker can't help you with this kind of mistake. Change the spelling to **Fourth**

4. To run the spelling checker for the entire presentation, click the Spelling and Grammar button on the Standard toolbar or press F7.

   PowerPoint highlights "Registraton," the first word it doesn't find in its dictionary. It displays the word in the Spelling and Grammar dialog box and suggests a corrected spelling.

   NOTE: You might need to click the Toolbar Options button 🔻 to find the Spelling button.

FIGURE 2-10
Using the spelling checker

5. Click Change to apply the correct spelling of "Registration."
6. When the spelling checker locates "slurpee," click Ignore because this word is spelled correctly.

   NOTE: If the Spelling dialog box is hiding a misspelled word, move the dialog box to a different position by dragging its title bar.

7. At the next spelling error, click Change to apply the corrected spelling of "raspberries."
8. At the next spelling error, click Change to apply the first suggested spelling, "guardian." Click OK when the spelling check is complete.

EXERCISE **2-9** **Use AutoCorrect**

If you key "teh" instead of "the" or "can;t" instead of "can't," *AutoCorrect* corrects the word automatically as you key. The correction takes place after you press Spacebar or Enter or enter punctuation, such as a period or comma. The AutoCorrect

AuTo CoRRect

Options button appears whenever the AutoCorrect feature changes text that you key. AutoCorrect automatically changes the word and places a *smart tag* symbol below the word. A smart tag is a button that appears after certain actions to give you a convenient way of making choices related to that action. For example, the AutoCorrect Options button enables you to undo the change that was automatically made.

Other smart tags will be discussed as they occur in this course.

1. Display slide 3 of the active presentation (**JulyFun2**).

2. From the Tools menu, choose AutoCorrect Options (you might need to expand the menu), and then click the AutoCorrect tab in the AutoCorrect dialog box.

3. If it's not already checked, click the checkbox for Replace text as you type. This turns on the AutoCorrect feature.

FIGURE 2-11
AutoCorrect
dialog box

4. Still in the AutoCorrect dialog box, scroll through the list box to see the changes AutoCorrect makes automatically. Click OK to close the AutoCorrect dialog box.

5. Under the first bulleted item on slide 3, select the text "Generously laden with." Key **Amde from** (including the misspelling). "Amde" is automatically corrected to "Made" as soon as you finish keying the word. Click on a blank area of the slide to deselect the bulleted list placeholder.

> **TIP:** You can add your own common keying mistakes or abbreviations to the AutoCorrect dialog box. For example, you can add "asap" and have it expand to "as soon as possible."

6. Point to the smart tag from where the computer corrected to "Made." The AutoCorrect Options button appears.

7. Click the AutoCorrect Options button to display its drop-down list.

FIGURE 2-12
Using the
AutoCorrect
Options button

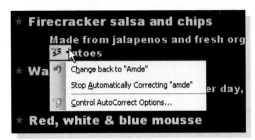

8. Choose Change back to "Amde" from the menu.

9. Fix "amde" back to "made" and then save the presentation as *[your initials]2-9* in the Lesson 2 folder. Do not close the presentation.

EXERCISE 2-10 Use the Style Checker

When the style checker is turned on and the Slide pane is active, the *style checker* automatically looks for consistency, balance, and overall readability of your presentation. For example, if your presentation has a bulleted item that ends with a period or a title that is uppercase when all other titles are in title case, it will mark the problem with a light bulb . You click the light bulb and then choose an appropriate option from the Office Assistant balloon that appears.

Even when the style checker is turned on, the light bulb appears only when the Slide pane is active. For that reason, it is best to use the slide navigation tools, rather than clicking slide thumbnails, to move from slide to slide when checking for style errors.

Sometimes the style checker light bulb can be distracting. Fortunately you can turn it off easily and then turn it back on again when you want to use it.

Even when you turn off the style checker, the Office Assistant stays in the background ready to pop up during other tasks. You can turn off the Assistant permanently by displaying it, right-clicking it, choosing Options from its shortcut menu, and deselecting the Use Office Assistant option.

1. From the Tools menu, choose Options and then click the Spelling and Style tab.

2. Under Style, make sure the Check style option is checked.

3. If an information box appears telling you that the style checker uses the Office Assistant, click Enable Assistant.

4. Click OK to close the Options dialog box.

5. In the active presentation (**JulyFun2**), click in the Slide pane to display slide 2 ("In-Line Skating Race in the Park").

6. Click the light bulb. The style checker detects a capitalization problem and provides options in an Office Assistant balloon.

FIGURE 2-13
Office Assistant
balloon indicating
a possible
capitalization error

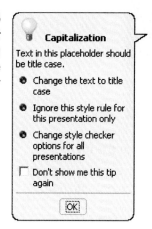

 NOTE: The style checker is questioning the uppercase "L" in "In-Line." In a sentence, a hyphenated word such as "in-line" would be lowercase, but in a title, heading, or name, it is correct as "In-Line."

7. Click OK because you don't want to change to title case, ignore the rule, or change style checker options.

8. Scroll down to slide 5 and click the light bulb. There's another capitalization problem. This is the only slide in the presentation with an all-uppercase title.

9. Click the first option to change the text to title case. The title text "ENTERTAINMENT" becomes "Entertainment."

10. Check each slide in the presentation. When you see a light bulb, click it, and then click OK. The other items the light bulb finds do not need to be corrected.

TIP: Remember to use the Slide pane's navigation tools and not thumbnails when moving from slide to slide to find light bulbs.

11. Return to slide 1.

12. Turn off the style checker by choosing the Tools menu, choose Options and then click the Spelling and Style tab. Under Style, deselect the Check Style check box. Click OK.

13. Click Help to open the Help menu and then choose Show the Office Assistant.

14. Right-click the Office Assistant and choose Options from the shortcut menu.

15. In the Office Assistant dialog box, deselect the Use the Office Assistant check box. Click OK. This action prevents the Office Assistant from popping up as you work.

NOTE: If you choose Hide from the Office Assistant's shortcut menu, it disappears only temporarily and reappears the next time you take an action where it can provide information.

EXERCISE **2-11** **Use the Thesaurus**

The Thesaurus is a tool used to find words with similar meanings. This tool is extremely helpful when you use the same word over and over and it becomes repetitious, or if you are looking for a more appropriate word with the same meaning.

1. On slide 1 of the **JulyFun2** presentation, put your insertion point on the word "Celebration." From the Tools menu choose Thesaurus to open the Research task pane. The word "Celebration" is automatically placed in the Search for box, a search has already been performed, and the results displayed.

FIGURE 2-14
Thesaurus window

2. Right-click the down arrow beside festival, and choose Insert. Notice that the word "Celebration" is replaced by the word "Festival," and the slide now reads "Fourth of July Festival."

 TIP: If you double-click on any word in the Thesaurus list, you will see another list of words related to that word.

EXERCISE ｜ **2-12** ｜ **Use Find and Replace**

When you create presentations—especially long presentations—you often need to review or change text. In PowerPoint, you can do this quickly by using the Find and Replace commands.

The *Find command* locates specified text in a presentation. The *Replace command* finds the text and replaces it with a specified alternative.

1. With slide 1 displayed in the presentation **JulyFun2**, click Edit on the menu bar and choose Find (or press ⌨Ctrl+⌨F) to open the Find dialog box.

2. Key & in the Find what text box.

FIGURE 2-15
Find dialog box

3. Click Find Next. PowerPoint locates and selects the text.

4. Close the Find dialog box.

5. Key **and** in place of "&" to be consistent with the first bulleted item on this slide.

6. From the Edit menu, choose Replace (or press ⌨Ctrl+⌨H) to open the Replace dialog box.

7. In the Find what text box, key **am**; in the Replace with text box, key **a.m.** (including the periods).

8. Check Match case and Find whole words only to ensure that you find only the lowercase text "am" and not words that contain these letters (such as "America" or "ramp").

FIGURE 2-16
Replace dialog box

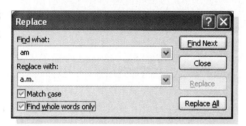

9. Click Find Next. PowerPoint finds the first occurrence of "am." Click Replace. Click Replace again at the next occurrence. A dialog box appears to tell you the search is completed. Click OK.

10. Click Close to close the Replace dialog box.

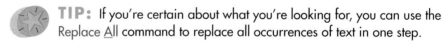

TIP: If you're certain about what you're looking for, you can use the Replace All command to replace all occurrences of text in one step.

11. Return to slide 1 and save the presentation as *[your initials]*2-12 in your Lesson 2 folder. Leave the presentation open for the next exercise.

Adding Slide Transitions

A *slide transition* is an effect that appears between two slides during a slide show. You can choose to make one slide blend into the next in a checkerboard pattern or fade pattern or choose from many other effects. A slide transition is often included as part of an animation scheme.

EXERCISE **2-13** **Add a Slide Transition to an Individual Slide**

Transitions can be applied to individual slides, to a group of slides, or to an entire slide show. The following steps will apply a transition to an individual slide.

1. Move to slide 1 and from the Slide Show menu, choose Slide Transition. (Or, if the task pane is displayed, click the down arrow next to the Other Task Panes button ▼ and choose Slide Transition from the drop-down list.) The Slide Transition task pane appears on the right side of the window.

2. In the list of transitions, choose Blinds Vertical. A preview of the transition effect appears in the Slide pane.

FIGURE 2-17
Choosing the Blinds
Vertical transition

3. Under Modify transition, choose Slow for the Speed and No Sound for the Sound.

4. Under Advance slide, select On mouse click, if it is not already checked.

5. Move to slide 2. Notice in the Slide pane that under slide 1 there is a star logo. This indicates that there is a slide transition for slide 1.

EXERCISE **2-14** **Add a Slide Transition to All Slides in a Presentation**

Transitions can have an effect like turning pages of a book; therefore, a movement can be applied to all slides in a presentation to control how they enter and exit display on the screen.

1. Move to slide 1 and from the Slide Show menu choose Slide Transition. (Or if the task pane is not displayed, click the down arrow next to the Other Task Panes button ▼ and choose Slide Transition from the drop-down list.) The Slide Transition task pane appears on the right side of the window.

2. In the list of transitions, choose Checkerboard Across. A preview of the transition effect appears in the Slides pane.

3. Under Modify transition, choose Medium for the Speed and Chime for the Sound.

4. Under Advance slide, select On mouse click, if it is not already checked.

5. Click Apply to All Slides near the bottom of the Slide Transition pane.

FIGURE 2-18
Adjusting slide
transition effects

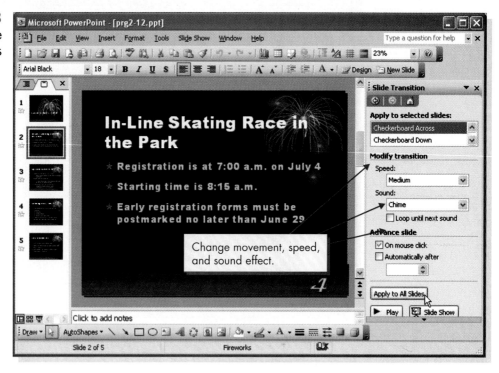

6. Click Slide Show to run a slide show. Advance through each slide and then return to Normal view.

7. Move to slide 1. Select the Box Out transition because this effect will better emphasize the fireworks graphic on the slide background. (Do not click Apply to All Slides.) The transition is applied only to the selected slide.

8. Move to slide 5 and apply the Newsflash transition.

9. Save the presentation as *[your initials]*2-14 in your Lesson 2 folder. Do not print it and do not close it.

10. View the presentation as a slide show, starting with slide 1. Notice that slide 1 and slide 5 have different transitions than the other slides.

11. When you are finished with the slide show, return to Normal view.

TIP: Try not to apply transition effects randomly. You might choose one transition for most of your presentation and then choose one or two other effects to better emphasize the slide content as it appears.

Adding Headers and Footers

You can add identifying information to your presentation, such as header or footer text, the date, or a slide or page number. A *header* is text that appears at the top of each notes page or handouts page. A *footer* is text that appears at the bottom of each slide, notes page, or handouts page. Header and footer text appears in special header and footer placeholders.

As is true in Word and Excel, you find the Header and Footer command on the View menu. In PowerPoint, this command opens the Header and Footer dialog box, which has two tabs: the Slide tab and the Notes and Handouts tab.

TABLE 2-3   Adding Identifying Information to Presentations

INFORMATION	DESCRIPTION
Date and Time	Current date and time—can be updated automatically or keyed
Header	Descriptive text printed at the top of the page on notes and handout pages only
Page Number	Number placed in the lower-right corner of notes and handout pages by default
Slide Number	Number you can place on slides, usually in the lower-right corner
Footer	Descriptive text printed at the bottom of slides, notes pages, and handout pages

EXERCISE **2-15** **Add Headers, Footers, Dates, and Page Numbers**

Using the Slide tab in the Header and Footer dialog box, you can add information to the footer of all slides in a presentation by clicking Apply to All, or you can add footer information to only the current slide by clicking Apply. Using the Notes and Handouts tab, you can insert both header and footer information on handouts and other types of printouts.

1. Working on the presentation *[your initials]*2-12, click View on the menu bar and choose Header and Footer. Note the tabs in the Header and Footer dialog box, one for adding information to slides and one for adding information to notes and handouts.

FIGURE 2-19
Header and Footer dialog box, Slide tab

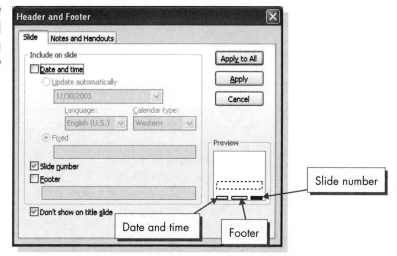

2. In the Preview box, notice the positions for the elements you can place on a slide. As you enable each element by selecting its checkbox, PowerPoint indicates where the element will print with a bold outline.

3. Click the Slide number check box to select it.

4. Click the checkbox labeled Don't show on title slide. When this box is checked, footer and page number information does not appear on the first slide.

5. Clear the Date and Time and Footer checkboxes.

6. Click Apply to All. The presentation now has slide numbers at the bottom right of each slide except the title slide.

7. Open the Header and Footer dialog box again (click View on the menu bar and choose Header and Footer) and display the Notes and Handouts tab.

8. Under the Date and Time option, click Update Automatically to add today's date. Each time you print the presentation handout, it will include the

current date. You can choose different date and time formats from the drop-down list.

FIGURE 2-20
Header and Footer
dialog box, Notes
and Handouts tab

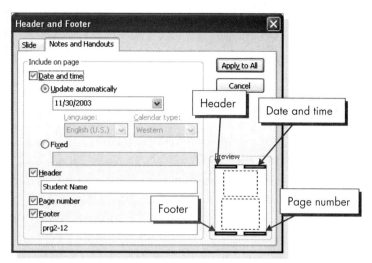

9. Make sure <u>H</u>eader is checked and key your name in the header text box. The header is printed in the upper-left corner of a notes or handouts page.

10. Make sure the <u>P</u>age number option is checked. Page numbers are printed at the bottom right of the page.

11. Make sure the <u>F</u>ooter check box is selected. Then key the filename *[your initials]*2-12 in its text box.

12. Click Apply to All to add this information to all handout pages you print (but not to individual slides).

13. Save the presentation as *[your initials]*2-12 in your Lesson 2 folder.

USING ONLINE HELP

PowerPoint's online Help feature is like an interactive teaching tool. One way to explore online Help is to display a list of Help topics. After you choose a topic, PowerPoint displays information or provides a demonstration.

Learn more about getting Help in PowerPoint:

1. Click the Ask a Question box in the upper-right corner of your window.

2. Key **transition** in the text box and press (Enter). A list of related topics appears.

3. Click Add transitions between slides from the list. The Add transitions between slides Help window opens.

4. Click on the first item listed to expand the topic, and review the information.

5. Expand the other topic in the window.

6. In the upper-right corner of the Help window, click the **Show all** link to display definitions of highlighted words.

7. Review the information and close the Help window when you finish.

LESSON 2 Summary

➤ A wizard is an online guide that helps you complete a task.

➤ The AutoContent Wizard provides step-by-step guidance to help you create a presentation. It creates a complete presentation with sample text that suggests appropriate content.

➤ You can edit the sample text in an AutoContent-generated presentation by using any normal editing methods.

➤ Before keying text in a placeholder, activate it by clicking inside it.

➤ To change the order of slides in a presentation, use either the Outline pane or Slide Sorter view. Select the slides you want to move; then drag them to a new location. You can also delete selected slides.

➤ Right-clicking a word flagged with a red wavy line provides a shortcut list of suggested spelling corrections. You can spell-check an entire presentation at one time by using the Spelling and Grammar dialog box.

➤ When AutoCorrect is activated, PowerPoint's AutoCorrect feature automatically changes common errors that it detects. A smart tag—the AutoCorrect Options button 🖅 ▾—alerts you of the change and enables you to undo it.

➤ When the Style Checker feature is activated, a light-bulb icon 💡 alerts you to possible style errors. To make sure you see all possible light-bulb alerts, navigate through your presentation by using the Slides pane's navigation tools.

➤ Use the Thesaurus to find words with similar meanings.

➤ The Find feature and the Replace feature search your entire presentation for specified text. The Replace feature enables you to automatically make changes to matching text it finds.

➤ Slide transitions add visual interest to slide shows. They can be applied to individual slides, a group of slides, or an entire slide presentation.

➤ Headers and footers can appear at the top and bottom of notes and handout pages. Footers can also appear at the bottom of slides. They are commonly used to provide page numbers, dates, and other identifying information common to an entire presentation.

LESSON 2 Command Summary

FEATURE	BUTTON	MENU	KEYBOARD
AutoContent Wizard		File, New, From AutoContent Wizard (on the task pane)	
Position an insertion point		Click the I-beam or use arrow keys	
Select text			Drag the I-beam across the text
Select a word			Double-click the word
Select a sentence			Ctrl+click left mouse button on the sentence
Select a paragraph			Triple-click the paragraph
Delete selected text			Delete
Select contiguous slides			Shift+click left mouse button
Select noncontiguous slides			Ctrl+click left mouse button
Delete selected slides		Edit, Delete Slide	Delete
Turn on or off spelling checker	ABC✓	Tools, Spelling and Grammar	F7
AutoCorrect		Tools, AutoCorrect Options, AutoCorrect tab, Replace text as you type	
Turn on or off style checker		Tools, Options, Spelling and Style tab, Check style	
Thesaurus		Tools, Thesaurus	
Find		Edit, Find	Ctrl+F
Replace		Edit, Replace	Ctrl+H
Slide transition		Slide Show, Slide Transition	
Header and footer		View, Header and Footer	

Concepts Review

TRUE/FALSE QUESTIONS

Each of the following statements is either true or false. Indicate your choice by circling T or F.

 1. The AutoContent Wizard begins a presentation with the title slide.

 2. The title slide in a presentation is limited to one line.

 3. Before editing text in a placeholder, you must click the placeholder to activate it.

 4. The only way to change the order of slides is to drag them to a new position in Slide Sorter view.

 5. You can activate the spelling checker by pressing F1. F-7

 6. The <u>F</u>ind command is located on the <u>E</u>dit menu.

 7. Slide transitions appear when you move from one slide to the next while presenting a slide show.

 8. You can put headers on slides, but not on handouts.

SHORT ANSWER QUESTIONS

Write the correct answer in the space provided.

1. When using the mouse, what method other than dragging the I-beam or using Shift+click can you use to select an entire paragraph?

TRIPLE CLICK

2. In the Slides pane, what displays when the pointer is placed on the thumbnail of a slide?

WHITE ARROW

3. How do you select two noncontiguous slides at the same time?

HOLD CTRL + CLICK

4. Which feature in PowerPoint, if turned on, replaces typos and commonly misspelled words with the correct spelling as you key?

AUTO-CORRECT

5. When the style checker is turned on and you want to find all the light-bulb flags, what method of slide navigation should you avoid using?

    AVOID   THUMBNAIL IN OUTLINE SLIDE PANE

6. What menu do you use to access the Thesaurus?

    TOOLS

7. How would you apply a transition to all of the slides in a presentation?

    APPLY TO ALL SLIDES

8. When you use the Header and Footer dialog box to add slide numbers to a presentation, where do the numbers usually appear on the slides?

    LOWER RIGHT HAND CORNER

CRITICAL THINKING

Answer these questions on a separate page. There can be more than one correct answer. Support your answers with examples from your own experience, if possible.

1. What is an advantage of using the AutoContent Wizard to create a PowerPoint presentation? How can the style checker help with uniformity of slide content? How can transition effects help to emphasize slide content?

2. You can use headers and footers to identify your slides, handouts, and notes. What information is most important to include? Why?

Skills Review

EXERCISE 2-16

Create a new presentation by using the AutoContent Wizard. Change sample text in the presentation and delete slides.

1. Use the AutoContent Wizard to create a new presentation by following these steps:

    a. Start PowerPoint. If the New Presentation task pane is not displayed, click <u>F</u>ile on the menu bar and choose <u>N</u>ew. In the task pane under New, choose From AutoContent wizard.

    b. In the AutoContent Wizard dialog box, click <u>N</u>ext.

    c. Click <u>G</u>eneral for type of presentation and pick Generic from the list at the right of the dialog box. Click <u>N</u>ext.

    d. Choose On-<u>s</u>creen presentation for type of output and click <u>N</u>ext.

    e. Key **Advertising Analysis** in the P̲resentation title text box and key your name in the F̲ooter text box. Click N̲ext.

    f. In the last dialog box, click F̲inish.

2. Change the sample title text by following these steps:

    a. Use ⌞Page Down⌟ or ▼ to go to slide 4. In the Slides pane, click the title text placeholder, select the text "Topic One," and key in its place **Newspaper Advertising**. Click outside the text box to deselect it.

    b. Change the title text on slide 5 from "Topic Two" to **Yellow Pages**

    c. Change the title text on slide 6 from "Topic Three" to **Radio Advertising**

3. Change the sample body text on slide 6 ("Radio Advertising") by following these steps:

    a. In the Slides pane, click the body text to activate the placeholder.

    b. Drag to select all bulleted text, from "Details" through "audience." Press ⌞Delete⌟.

    c. Key the following text, pressing ⌞Enter⌟ to start a new bulleted item:

      • **Drive-time spots**

      • **3 major stations**

      • **Delivers 10% of customers**

4. Change the sample body text on slide 3 ("Topics of Discussion") to the following bulleted items:

    • **Quality**

    • **Frequency**

    • **Effectiveness**

5. Change the sample body text on slide 4 ("Newspaper Advertising") to the following:

    • **4 x 4 display ad on entertainment page**

    • **One daily and two weekly newspapers**

    • **Delivers 5% of customers**

6. Change the sample body text on slide 5 ("Yellow Pages") to the following bulleted items:

    • **Attractive display, prominent placement**

    • **Ad appears in all metro editions**

    • **Delivers 6% of customers**

7. Delete slides by following these steps:

    a. Click the Slides tab in the Outline and Slides pane.

    b. Click the slide 9 thumbnail ("Next Steps") in the Slides pane.

    c. Press ⌞Delete⌟.

    d. Click the slide 2 thumbnail ("Introduction").

e. Hold down Ctrl and, without releasing it, click the thumbnails for slides 7 ("Real Life") and 8 ("What This Means").

f. Press Delete.

8. Move to slide 1 and delete the subtitle text (if there is any).

 NOTE: Do not be concerned with the subtitle placeholder that appears after you delete the text. It will not show in a slide show or a printout.

9. Save the presentation as *[your initials]*2-16 in your Lesson 2 folder.

10. Preview and then print the presentation as handouts, 6 slides per page, grayscale, framed. Close the presentation.

EXERCISE 2-17

Check spelling, find and replace text, use the style checker and Thesaurus.

1. Open the file **Ads1**.

2. Run the spelling checker by following these steps:

 a. Click the Spelling and Grammar button 🦜 on the Standard toolbar.

b. Click Change to correct the spelling of "advertising."

c. Click Change to correct the spelling of "humorous."

d. Click OK when the spelling check is complete, and return to slide 1.

3. Find and replace text by following these steps:

a. From the Edit menu, choose Replace.

b. In the Find what text box, key **Ads**. In the Replace With text box, key **Advertising**

c. Click Match case and then click Find Next.

d. Click Replace to replace "Ads" with "Advertising" in each slide title.

e. Click OK when complete and close the dialog box.

4. Turn on the style checker by following these steps:

a. From the Tools menu, choose Options.

b. Click the Spelling and Style tab.

c. Click the Check style checkbox to select it.

d. If the information box appears, click Enable Assistant.

e. Click OK to close the Options dialog box.

5. Use the style checker by following these steps:

a. Use the Slide pane's scroll bar to move to slide 1, which is the only slide with an all-uppercase title.

 b. Click the light bulb 💡.

c. In the Office Assistant balloon, choose Change the text to title case.

6. Turn off the style checker by following a, b, c, and e in step 4, but this time deselect the Check style checkbox.

7. Turn off the Office Assistant by following these steps:

     a. From the Help menu, choose Show the Office Assistant.

     b. Right-click the Office Assistant.

     c. Choose Options from the shortcut menu.

     d. Deselect the Use the Office Assistant checkbox at the top of the Options tab. Click OK.

8. On slide 1, change "Student Name" to your name.

9. Delete slide 8 ("What This Means").

10. Use the thesaurus to find a synonym for "upbeat" on slide 5. Highlight "upbeat" and then from the Tools menu, choose Thesaurus. The Thesaurus dialog box will appear with other words that have a similar meaning. Click on Positive and choose Replace.

11. Save the presentation as *[your initials]*2-17 in your Lesson 2 folder.

12. Preview and then print the presentation as handouts, 9 slides per page, grayscale, framed. (The entire presentation should fit on one page.)

13. Close the presentation.

EXERCISE 2-18

Edit slide text, rearrange slides, and delete slides.

1. Open the file **Resort**.

2. On slide 1, replace "Student Name" with your name.

3. On slide 2, change the title "Customer Requirements" to **Vacationer's Expectations**

4. On slide 3, insert a new bullet line by following these steps:

     a. Click your I-beam at the end of the first bullet to place the insertion point after the word "activities."

     b. Press Enter to insert a new line.

     c. On the new line, key **Our name associated with gourmet dining**

5. On slide 4, insert text in a blank body text placeholder by following these steps:

     a. Click your I-beam pointer anywhere on the text "Click to add text."

     b. Key **Miami Beach** and press Enter.

     c. Key **Palm Springs** and press Enter.

     d. Key **Niagara Falls**

6. Reverse the position of slides 2 and 3 by following these steps:

     a. Click the Slides tab on the Outline and Slides pane to display the Slides pane.

  NOTE: If the Slides pane or Outline pane is not displayed, click the Normal View button to display it.

b. Position your pointer on the right border of the Slides pane and drag the splitter bar to the right to enlarge the slide thumbnails.

  c. Click slide 3 to select it.

  d. Drag slide 3 up until the drag-and-drop pointer 🔨 and the horizontal line are between slides 1 and 2.

  e. Release your mouse button. Slide 3 should now be in the slide 2 position.

 7. Reverse the position of slides 5 and 6.

 8. Delete slide 7 ("Key Benefits").

 9. Move to slide 1 and save the presentation as *[your initials]***2-18** in your Lesson 2 folder.

 10. Preview and then print the presentation as handouts, 9 slides per page, grayscale, framed.

 11. Close the presentation.

EXERCISE 2-19

Apply a slide transition and add headers and footers to a presentation.

 1. Open the file **Takeout**.

 2. On slide 1, replace "Student Name" with your name.

 3. Add a transition effect by following these steps:

  a. Click the Other Task Panes arrow 🔽 on the task pane title bar to display the drop-down list.

  b. From the drop-down list, select Slide Transition to display the Slide Transition task pane.

  c. In the list of slide transitions, select Box Out.

  d. Under Modify Transition, choose Medium for the speed and Cash Register for the sound.

  e. Click Apply to All Slides (at the bottom of the task pane).

 4. Add a footer and slide numbers by following these steps:

  a. From the View menu, choose Header and Footer.

  b. Click the Slide tab.

  c. Check Slide number.

  d. Check Footer and key your name as a footer.

  e. Click Don't show on title slide so that the footer and slide number do not print on slide 1.

  f. Click Apply to All.

 5. Scroll through the presentation to check the footer and slide numbers.

 6. Add a date and footer to handout pages by following these steps:

  a. Open the Header and Footer dialog box.

  b. Click the Notes and Handouts tab.

c. Check <u>D</u>ate and Time and then select the <u>U</u>pdate automatically option.

d. Check <u>F</u>ooter and key *[your initials]*2-19 in the <u>F</u>ooter text box.

e. Make sure <u>P</u>age number is checked.

f. Click Apply to All.

7. Save the presentation as *[your initials]*2-19 in your Lesson 2 folder.

8. View all slides as a slide show.

9. Print all the slides as handouts, 6 slides per page (under Print range, select <u>A</u>ll), grayscale, framed. Close the presentation.

Lesson Applications

Create a presentation by using the AutoContent Wizard, edit sample text, move and delete slides, and check spelling.

1. Start the AutoContent Wizard to create a presentation. When choosing a presentation type, click Corporate and choose Company Meeting from the list at the right of the dialog box. Click Next.

2. Complete the rest of the steps in the wizard, choosing On-screen Presentation and keying **Good 4 U Power Bars** as the Presentation title and your name as the Footer. Include the slide number and date. Click Finish when you get to the last step of the wizard.

3. On slide 1, text has automatically been placed in the subtitle placeholder. Change this text to **Brainstorming Session**

4. Go to slide 2 and key the following text in the body text placeholder:

   Discuss how Good 4 U can develop and market a power snack (healthy "candy" bar).

5. On slide 4, change the title from "How Did We Do?" to **Product Development**. Replace the current body text with the following four bulleted items:

   - **Features of the product**
   - **Packaging**
   - **Naming**
   - **Promotion**

6. On slide 7, change the title from "Review of Prior Goals" to **Marketing Overview**. Change the bulleted text to:

   - **Customer profile**
   - **Market research**
   - **Advertising budget**

7. Switch to Slide Sorter view and make a noncontiguous selection of slides 3 ("Review of Key Objectives & Critical Success Factors"), 5 ("Organizational Overview"), and 6 ("Top Issues Facing Company").

8. Delete the selected slides.

9. Move slide 10 ("Summary") to the slide 5 position.

10. Make a contiguous selection of slides 6 through 10 and delete them.

The following slides should remain in the presentation: "Good 4 U Power Bars," "Agenda," "Product Development," "Marketing Overview," and ("Summary").

11. Check spelling in the presentation.

12. Move to slide 1 and save the presentation as *[your initials]*2-20 in your Lesson 2 folder.

13. View the presentation as a slide show, clicking the left mouse button to advance through the text and slides.

14. Preview and then print the presentation as handouts, 6 slides per page, grayscale, framed. Close the presentation.

EXERCISE 2-21

Use the AutoContent Wizard, delete and reorder slides, check spelling and style, find and replace text, and add a footer.

1. Use the AutoContent Wizard to create a presentation. For the presentation type, choose Training from the General category. The output will be an on-screen presentation. The presentation title is **Customer Relations Training**. Do not include any footer text, the date, or the slide number.

2. On slide 1, change the subtitle text to your name.

3. Delete slide 5 ("Vocabulary") and then delete slide 4 ("Overview"). If an Information box appears, click OK.

4. Change the sample text for existing slides 2 through 5 as shown in Figure 2-21.

FIGURE 2-21

Slide 2

Overview
- How you greet and seat people is critical
- Effective handling of parties guarantees success

Slide 3

Agenda
- Receiving customers
- Handling parties

Slide 4

Parties
- Usher celebrities to their tables
- Direct reporters to their station
- Consult with event planner for details

Slide 5

Receiving Customers
- Be professional, courteous
- Guide skaters and cyclists to equipment storage area
- Practice now by role playing

NEW DOCUMENT
NEW PRESENTATION - FROM DOWN ARROW ON TASK PANE

5. Delete remaining slides 6 and 7.

6. Reverse the positions of slides 4 and 5 so that "Receiving Customers" comes before "Parties."

7. Check spelling in the presentation.

8. Turn on the style checker. Correct any style inconsistencies to be sure all titles are in title case.

9. Turn off the style checker and the Office Assistant.

10. Use the Replace command to replace "parties" with "special events" (clear the Match case check box to find both "Parties" and "parties").

 TIP: Before using the Replace command, make sure the Match case option is turned off.

11. Add slide numbers and a slide footer that contains the text **Good 4 U** to each slide except the title slide.

12. Move to slide 1. Save the presentation as *[your initials]*2-21 in your Lesson 2 folder.

13. View the presentation as a slide show.

14. Preview and then print the presentation as handouts, 6 slides per page, pure black and white, framed.

15. Close the presentation.

EXERCISE 2-22

Change slide text, rearrange a slide, check spelling, add slide transitions, and add headers and footers.

1. Open the file **SpEvent2**. Change "Student Name" to your name.

2. Using the Find command, find the text "21st century." Close the Find dialog box and key **21st Century** over the selected text. (The "st" should appear as superscript automatically as you key the text.)

 3. If the style checker light bulb [ ] appears, turn it off.

4. Move slide 2 to the end of the presentation (the slide 6 position).

5. On the new slide 2 ("Objective"), create a line break before the word "Good" by pressing Shift + Enter.

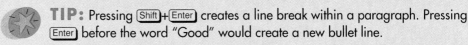 **TIP:** Pressing Shift + Enter creates a line break within a paragraph. Pressing Enter before the word "Good" would create a new bullet line.

6. Change the title of slide 2 to **Objectives** and add the following bullet point after the existing one:

   • **Increase bookings of special events from entertainment and sports industries**

7. Change the title of slide 3 from "Customer Requirements" to **What Does Everyone Want?**

8. On slide 4 ("Good 4 U Provides"), change the third bulleted item to:
   - **Award-winning service and cuisine**

9. Add a new first bullet to slide 4 that reads:
   - **High-energy, high-profile atmosphere**

10. Change slide 5 ("Next Steps") to read as shown in Figure 2-22.

FIGURE 2-22

Next Steps ——Title

Body text
- Develop list of ideas for special events
- Target sports-promotion companies and press agents
- Contact professional sports organizations and public relations firms
- Ask investors to call on sports-star and celebrity friends

11. Add slide numbers to all slides. Add a handout footer that contains the completed filename, *[your initials]*2-22. Add a handout header that contains your name.

12. Move to slide 1 and save the presentation as *[your initials]*2-22 in your Lesson 2 folder.

13. Preview and then print the presentation as handouts, 6 slides per page in vertical order, grayscale, framed.

14. Close the presentation.

EXERCISE 2-23 *Challenge Yourself*

Use the AutoContent Wizard, check spelling, find and replace text, add transitions, and delete and reorder slides.

1. Use the AutoContent Wizard to create a Generic presentation from the General category for output as an on-screen presentation. The presentation title is **Premium Items**. Add the footer **Good 4 U**, and include the slide number, but not the date.

2. On slide 1, change the subtitle text to the following:
   Item 1: Water bottle
   Item 2: Visor
   Item 3: Knee pads

3. Make a noncontiguous selection that includes the thumbnails for slides 2 ("Introduction"), 7 ("Real Life"), and 8 ("What This Means").

4. Delete the selected slides.

5. Use the Replace command to replace each occurrence of the word "Topic" with the word "Item." Use the Match case and Find whole words only options so that you replace only "Topic" and not "Topics" or "topic."

6. Edit slides 2 ("Topics of Discussion") through 6 ("Next Steps") so they contain only the text shown in Figure 2-23.

FIGURE 2-23

Slide 2

```
Topics of Discussion ——Title

        • Introduce new premium items to give away at
          special events
        • All premium items will contain the Good 4 U logo
```

Slide 3

```
Item 1: Water Bottle ——Title

        • Made of durable plastic
        • Excellent for outdoor sports and indoor workouts
```

Slide 4

```
Item 2: Knee Pads ——Title

        • Made of durable vinyl/foam
        • Essential protection for skaters
```

Slide 5

```
Item 3: Visor ——Title

        • Made of white cotton blend
        • Adjustable, one size fits all
        • Ideal for tennis, running, walking
```

Slide 6

```
Next Steps ——Title

        • Create designs
        • Produce prototype items
        • Analyze production costs
```

7. Reverse the order of slide 5 ("Item 3: Visor") and slide 4 ("Item 2: Knee Pads").

8. Edit the titles of slides 4 and 5 so the item numbers are consecutive. The slide 4 title should read **Item 2: Visor** and the slide 5 title should read **Item 3: Knee pads**.

9. Check spelling in the presentation.

10. Add a slide transition of your choice. Then view the presentation as a slide show.

11. Add your name to the handout header and the filename *[your initials]*2-23 to the handout footer, and set the date and time to update automatically.

12. Move to slide 1 and save the presentation as *[your initials]*2-23 in your Lesson 2 folder.

13. Preview and then print the presentation as handouts, 6 slides per page, grayscale, framed.

On Your Own

In these exercises you work on your own, as you would in a real-life work environment. Use the skills you've learned to accomplish the task—and be creative.

EXERCISE 2-24

Choose an automobile that you are interested in—for example, a specific sports utility vehicle, or sedan. Imagine you are a salesperson for this automobile.

Open the file **Selling1**. This presentation contains content suggestions similar to those a wizard would provide. On each of the presentation's slides, substitute information aimed at potential buyers of this vehicle. Create a handout header and footer that include the date and your name as header and the page number and filename *[your initials]*2-24 as footer.

Spell-check the presentation and save the presentation as *[your initials]*2-24. Preview and then print the presentation as handouts, 6 slides per page, grayscale, framed. Close the presentation.

EXERCISE 2-25

Think of a community service project that would benefit people from your community—for example, Adopt-a-Family at Christmas, a children's craft booth at a community festival, or a day out with senior citizens at a local nursing home.

Use the AutoContent Wizard's Brainstorming Session from the General category to help you create an on-screen presentation for a planning session for this project. Use six or more of the slides the wizard creates. You may rearrange the slides if you think it is appropriate. Create a handout header and footer that include the date and your name as header and the page number and filename *[your initials]*2-25 as footer.

Save the presentation as *[your initials]*2-25. Preview and then print the presentation as handouts, choosing an appropriate number of slides per page, grayscale, framed. Close the presentation.

EXERCISE 2-26

Imagine you are planning to start a small business—for example, a restaurant, a book store, or a bridal shop. To obtain financing from your local bank, you need to create a simple business plan.

Use the AutoContent Wizard's Business Plan from the Corporate category to help you create your own plan. Use at least 8 slides from the wizard's presentation, substituting information about your imagined business in place of the suggested content text. Create a handout header and footer that include the date and your name as header and the page number and filename *[your initials]*2-26 as footer. Add a transition to all of the slides in the presentation.

Spell-check and save the presentation as *[your initials]*2-26. Preview and then print the presentation as handouts, 4 or 6 slides per page, grayscale, framed. Close the presentation.

Unit 1 Applications

Copy and delete slides, edit slide text, check spelling, add header and footer information to handouts, and choose print options.

1. Open the file **1ThreeYr2**.

2. Use Slide Sorter view to move slide 2 ("Projected Growth Revenue") after slide 7.

3. Delete the newly numbered slide 2 ("Presenting Good 4 U").

4. Move slide 4 ("Financial History") after slide 5.

5. On slide 2, add the title **Who We Are** and delete the text "Their dreams" and the subtext below it.

6. Move to slide 3, which contains blank placeholders, and add the title **What We Want** and key these bulleted items:

   - **To encourage healthy eating**
   - **To promote participation in sports activities**
   - **To expand our market base**

7. Check spelling in the presentation (assume that all proper names are spelled correctly).

8. View the presentation as a slide show, starting on slide 1.

9. Create a header and footer for handouts that includes today's date as a fixed date (remember to key today's date in the Fixed text box), your name as the header, and the filename *[your initials]*u1-1 as the footer.

10. Using the Header and Footer dialog box, add a slide number to all slides, including slide 1.

11. Move to the first slide and save the file as *[your initials]*u1-1 in a new folder for Unit 1 Applications.

12. Preview and then print the presentation as handouts, 4 slides per page with landscape orientation, pure black and white, framed.

  TIP: Use the Landscape button on the Print Preview toolbar to change orientation of the handout pages.

13. Close the presentation.

Rearrange slides, edit text, find and replace text, check spelling and style, add slide transitions, add slide numbers, and add handout headers and footers.

1. Open the file **NewFood1**.

2. Find the word "desert" and replace it with **dessert**

3. On slide 5 ("Just Sweet Enough"), delete just the sentence that begins "The striking lime flavor."

4. On slide 3 (the first "Pasta Delights" slide), change the title to **Salad Delights**

5. Select all the bulleted text on slide 3 and delete it, leaving a blank body text placeholder. In the placeholder, key the text shown in Figure U1-1.

FIGURE U1-1

- Julie's Spinach Salad
- Michelle's Cobb Salad
- Grilled Chicken Salad
- Wild Rice and Smoked Turkey Salad
- Corn, Black Bean, and Mango Salad

6. Move slide 2 with the subtitle text "A New Dining Event" to the end of the presentation. (It will become slide 6.)

7. Move the new slide 5 ("Appetizer Specials") after slide 1 so that it becomes slide 2. Increase the size of the body text placeholder slightly so the size of the text will match the other body text.

8. Check spelling in the presentation.

9. Move to slide 1 and turn on the style checker. Click each light bulb you see and take appropriate action. (The light bulb will appear twice on slide 2.) Be sure to remove any periods the light bulb finds. When you have finished, turn off the style checker.

10. Use the Thesaurus to replace the word "Event" on slide 6. Choose "experience" to replace it from the Thesaurus window.

11. Add a slide transition to all slides.

12. Add slide numbers to all slides except slide 1. Add a handout header that contains your name, add a handout footer that contains the filename *[your initials]*u1-2, and add today's date as a fixed date.

13. Save the presentation as *[your initials]*u1-2 in your Unit 1 Applications folder.

14. Preview and then print the entire presentation as handouts, 6 slides per page, grayscale, framed.

15. Print slide 2 of the presentation in full size, grayscale, framed.

16. Close the presentation.

UNIT APPLICATION 1-3

Use the AutoContent Wizard to create a new presentation, edit slide text, rearrange slides, add handout headers and footers, and check spelling.

1. Use the AutoContent Wizard to start a new on-screen presentation. For presentation type, choose Generic from the General category. In the last wizard dialog box, do not include a presentation title or footer, but do include the date and slide number.

2. On slide 1, key the title **Special Events Planning** and the subtitle **Progress Report**

3. On slide 2, change the title to **Status Summary** and change the body text to the following:

- **Currently have at least one special event scheduled per month**
- **Some events are dependent on weather and other factors**

4. Delete slides 8 ("What This Means") and 3 ("Topics of Discussion").

5. Edit the new slides 3 through 7 as shown in Figure U1-2.

FIGURE U1-2

```
1st Quarter Events ——— Slide title

Slide 3    • January: New Year's Day power walk

           • February: Westchester Girls' Gymnastics demonstration and lunch

           • March: National In-line Skaters' warm-up party


2nd Quarter Events ——— Slide title

           • April: Health Expo brunch

Slide 4    • May:

           • June:
```

continues

```
        3rd Quarter Events───── Slide title

                • July: Autograph session with aerobic video star Marsha Miles
Slide 5
                • August: Marathon runner Steve Forbo

                • September:


        4th Quarter Events───── Slide title

                • October: Kick-boxing demonstration
Slide 6
                • November:

                • December: Holiday party for Special Olympics

        Next Steps───── Slide title

                • Confirm dates

Slide 7          • Make necessary schedule shifts

                • Draft ad copy schedule

                • Post schedule on the Internet
```

6. Using the Outline pane, edit the event schedule so the gymnastics event is moved from February to May and the brunch from April to June.

7. Change the first bullet on slide 2 to read **Currently have two special events scheduled per quarter**

8. Edit the August event to read **Autograph session with marathon runner Steve Forbo**

9. Add the Wedge slide transition effect to all slides.

10. Check the slide footer to be sure all slides have slide numbers. Remove the date from the slide footer. To the handouts, add a header that contains your name, add a footer that contains the filename *[your initials]*u1-3, and add today's date as a fixed date.

11. Check spelling in the presentation.

12. Move to slide 1 and save the presentation as *[your initials]*u1-3 in your Unit 1 Applications folder.

13. Preview and then print the presentation as handouts, 9 slides per page, landscape orientation, grayscale, framed.

14. Close the presentation.

Use the AutoContent Wizard to write your own presentation.

Use the Internet to research the company culture of a company of personal interest to you. As part of your research, gather information on the following:

- What product or service does this company provide?
- What are the values and beliefs of the company?
- Does the company support the community?
- Does the company support any causes, for example, breast cancer awareness, recycling, etc.?
- Is there any other information that would be useful for a presentation on this company?

Use the AutoContent Wizard and the material you researched to create an on-screen presentation of your company. Use the presentation type Generic (under General). As part of your presentation, apply a slide transition.

In the slide footer, include the text **Prepared by** followed by your name. Include the slide number on all slides, but not the date. In the handout footer, include the completed filename *[your initials]*u1-4. In the handout header, key **Presented to** and then identify to whom you would be giving this presentation. Include in the handout the date you would be delivering the presentation.

Spell-check the presentation and save it as *[your initials]*u1-4 in your Unit 1 Applications folder. Practice delivering the presentation as a slide show, clicking to advance the slides. Print the presentation handouts in pure black and white.

Developing a Presentation

Creating a Presentation

MICROSOFT OFFICE
SPECIALIST
ACTIVITIES
In this lesson:
PPO3S-1-1
PPO3S-1-2
PPO3S-2-3
PPO3S-4-1

See Appendix.

OBJECTIVES

After completing this lesson, you will be able to:

1. Create a new presentation.
2. Change slide layouts.
3. Work with design templates
4. Use the clipboard.
5. Work with multiple open presentations.
6. Work with speaker's notes.

 Estimated Time: 1½ hours

The AutoContent Wizard is a great tool for creating standard presentations, but you will soon find that you want the freedom to design your own slides and layouts. In this lesson you transform a blank presentation into a finished presentation by inserting text and slides, choosing *slide layouts* (arrangements of text and object placeholders for slides), and applying PowerPoint design templates.

You also create *speaker's notes*, which assist a speaker in delivering a presentation or can be included as additional information with presentations published on the Web.

Creating a New Blank Presentation

To create a new blank presentation, you can begin with either:

- A *design template,* which adds a uniform color scheme and design background to each slide in the presentation
- A blank presentation (simple text on a plain background), to which you can later apply a design template

You build each slide by choosing a slide layout and keying slide text.

EXERCISE **3-1** **Start a New Blank Presentation**

One way to create a presentation is to start with a blank slide, focusing first on content, and then adding color and other design elements later.

1. Start PowerPoint. A blank title slide appears, ready for your text input.

 NOTE: If PowerPoint is already open and a blank title slide is not displayed, click the New button 🗋 on the Standard toolbar or choose Blank Presentation in the New Presentation task pane.

FIGURE 3-1
Title slide

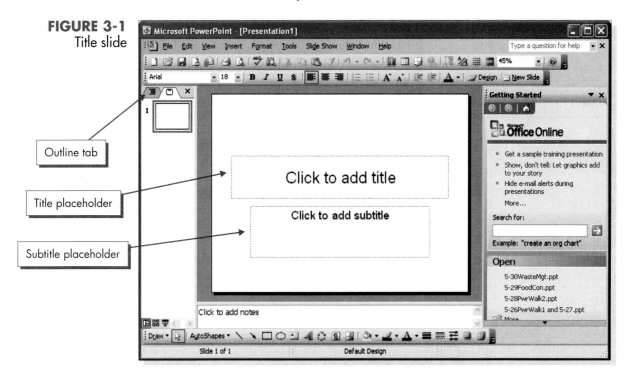

2. Click the title placeholder to activate it and key **For the Pleasure of Your Company**

3. Click the subtitle placeholder and key **Plan Your Next Event with Good 4 U**

 NOTE: The documents you create in this course relate to the Case Study about Good 4 U, a fictional restaurant business (see pages 1–4).

4. Click the Outline tab on the left side of your screen to display the Outline pane. Notice that both the Slides pane and the Outline pane show the text you key.

  REVIEW: If the Outline tab and Slides tab are not displayed on the left side of your screen, click the Normal View button.

5. Position the insertion point after the word "Event" in the subtitle; then press Shift+Enter. The subtitle is now split into two lines. Delete the space before "with" on the second line of the subtitle.

6. Split the title text into two lines so that "Your Company" appears on the second line. Notice that the changes you made are reflected in the Outline pane.

TABLE 3-1 **Using the Keyboard to Navigate on a Slide and in a Presentation**

KEYSTROKES	RESULT
Ctrl+Enter	Selects and activates the next text placeholder on a slide. If the last placeholder (subtitle or body text) is selected or activated, pressing Ctrl+Enter inserts a new slide after the current slide. Pressing Ctrl+Enter never selects other objects on a slide (including text boxes) that are not placeholders.
Esc	Deactivates the currently activated text placeholder or text box and selects the entire text box instead. If a text box is selected but not activated, pressing Esc deselects the text box.
Tab	If a text placeholder or text box is activated, inserts a tab character at the insertion point; if not activated, selects the next object on the slide. If the insertion point is between a bullet and the first text character on a line, pressing Tab demotes the bulleted text. Pressing Tab repeatedly when no objects are activated cycles through all objects on a slide but never moves to another slide.
Shift+Tab	If a text box or text placeholder is not activated, selects the previous object on a slide. If the insertion point is between a bullet and the first text character on the line, promotes the bulleted text.
Esc, Tab	This key sequence always moves to the next object on a slide, regardless of whether a text box is activated. It never inserts a new slide.

continues

TABLE 3-1   Using the Keyboard to Navigate on a Slide and in a Presentation   *continued*

KEYSTROKES	RESULT
Shift + Enter	If a text box or text placeholder is activated, inserts a new line (but not a new paragraph) at the insertion point.
Enter	If a text box or text placeholder is activated, inserts a new paragraph, including a bullet if in a body text placeholder. If a text box or text placeholder is selected but not activated, selects all the text in the object.
Ctrl + M	Inserts a new slide after the current slide.

EXERCISE 3-2 Insert New Slides

To insert a new slide after the current slide in a presentation, you can do one of the following:

- Click New Slide on the Formatting toolbar.
- From the Insert menu, choose New Slide or press Ctrl + M.
- Press Ctrl + Enter one or more times until a new slide appears.
- Point to a layout thumbnail on the Slide Layout task pane; then click its down arrow and choose Insert New Slide from the drop-down list.

When a new slide first appears on your PowerPoint window, you don't need to activate a placeholder to start keying text. When no placeholder is selected, as long as your Slides pane is active the text you key automatically goes into the title text placeholder. Knowing this can speed up the process of inserting new slides.

1. Click New Slide on the Formatting toolbar. A new slide appears, containing a title text placeholder and a body text placeholder. The Slide Layout task pane appears on the right side of your screen.

   NOTE: If the Slide Layout task pane does not appear, open the Format menu and choose Slide Layout. To make sure the Slide Layout task pane appears each time a new slide is inserted, check the Show when inserting new slides box at the bottom of the task pane.

2. Key **Excellent Service**. The text appears automatically in the title placeholder. (See Figure 3-2 on the next page.)

3. Press Ctrl + Enter or click the body text placeholder to activate it and key the following text, pressing Enter at the end of each line:

   - **We put your employees and guests at ease**
   - **We make your company look good**
   - **We adhere to promised schedules**
   - **We provide a professional and courteous staff**
   - **We guarantee customer satisfaction**

FIGURE 3-2
Keying text
on a slide

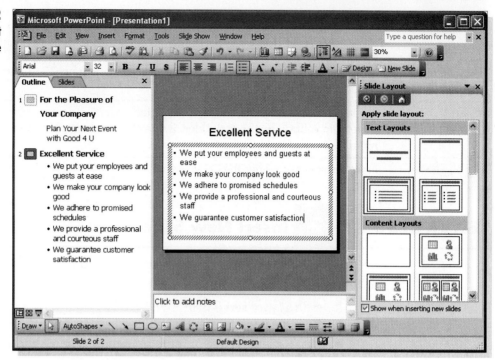

4. Press Ctrl+M to create a new text slide.

FIGURE 3-3
Inserting a new slide
by using the Slide
Layout task pane

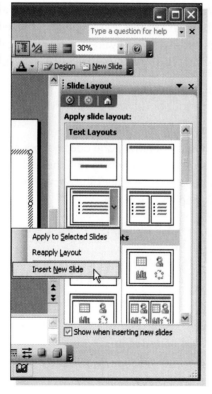

TIP: When you insert a new slide in a presentation, it uses the same layout as the previous slide (unless the previous slide was the title slide). You learn how to change slide layouts later in this lesson.

5. Key **A Delightful Menu** as the title and then key the following body text:

- **High-quality, healthy food**
- **Variety to appeal to a broad range of tastes**

6. In the Slide Layout task pane, point to—but don't click—the first layout thumbnail in the second row. The ScreenTip Title and Text appears below the thumbnail and a down arrow button appears on its right edge.

7. Click the down arrow button; then select Insert New Slide from the drop-down list.

8. Key **High-Energy Fun** as the title and then key the following body text:
   - **Athletic décor**
   - **Sports promotions**

   Notice that the AutoCorrect feature automatically adds the accent mark to the word "décor."

9. Change the word back to "decor" using the smart tag feature discussed in Lesson 2.

10. Press Ctrl+M to insert another slide; then key **A Healthy Atmosphere** as the title and key the following body text:
    - **Smoke-free**
    - **Alcohol optional**
    - **We sell none**
    - **We'll gladly serve your own**

Changing Slide Layouts

The Slide Layout task pane enables you to choose a layout when you insert a new slide and to change the layout of a slide at a later time if needed. For example, some bulleted text might look better with a two-column layout.

In this lesson you work with *text layouts* that include only text placeholders. In subsequent lessons you work with *content layouts* that include placeholders for pictures, tables, and charts.

E X E R C I S E   **3-3**   **Insert a New Slide with a Different Layout**

1. Move to slide 4 ("High-Energy Fun") and click New Slide on the Formatting toolbar. The Slide Layout task pane appears, and a blank slide is inserted after slide 4. (See Figure 3-4 on the next page.)

2. In the Slide Layout task pane, point to and then click the Title and 2-Column Text layout. The new layout has two body text placeholders.

3. Key the slide title **Events That Are Good 4 U** and then key the following bulleted text in the left body text placeholder:
   - **High-energy meetings**
   - **Productive lunches**
   - **Company celebrations**
   - **Celebrity promotions**

FIGURE 3-4
Choosing a
slide layout

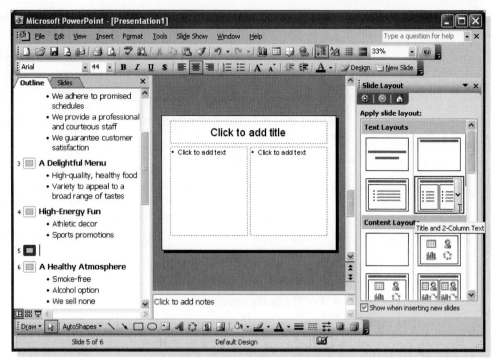

4. Key the following bulleted text in the right body text placeholder:
   - **Entertaining customers**
   - **Demonstrating products**

5. Click the Outline tab to display the Outline pane if it is not already displayed. Notice how each body text placeholder is numbered in the Outline pane.

EXERCISE 3-4 Change the Layout of an Existing Slide

1. Move to slide 4 ("High-Energy Fun") and then click the Title and 2-Column Text layout. The existing body text now appears in the left body text placeholder.

2. Click in the right column placeholder and add the following items to the column:
   - **Energetic staff**
   - **Special event tie-ins**

3. Create headers and footers for notes and handouts: include the date and your name at the top of the page, and the page number and the text *[your initials]*3-4 at the bottom.

4. Add the footer **Good 4 U Restaurant** on every slide except the title.

5. Move to slide 1, and spell-check the presentation.

6. Create a folder for Lesson 3. Save it as *[your initials]*3-4 in your Lesson 3 folder.

7. Preview and then print the presentation as handouts, 9 slides per page, grayscale, landscape, framed. Keep the presentation open for the next exercise.

Working with Design Templates

The presentation you are creating contains no special formatting, colors, or graphics. Sometimes it's convenient to work without design elements so that you can focus all your attention on the presentation's text. Before the presentation is completed, however, you will usually want to apply a design template to create a theme or add visual interest to help capture your audience's attention. You can apply or change a design template before, during, or after you create your presentation.

EXERCISE   3-5   **Apply a Design Template**

You select a design template from the Slide Design task pane. To display the Slide Design task pane, do one of the following:

- From the F**o**rmat menu, choose Slide **D**esign.
- Click De**s**ign on the Formatting toolbar.
- Double-click the current design template name on the status bar.

1. Click De**s**ign on the Formatting toolbar to display the Slide Design task pane.

2. Use the vertical scroll bar in the task pane to view the many design template thumbnails. They are grouped by "Used in This Presentation," "Recently Used," and "Available For Use."

3. Point to one of the design template thumbnails. A ScreenTip indicates the template's name. The templates are arranged alphabetically by name.

4. Click any design template thumbnail. The design you selected is applied to all the slides in your presentation. Sample several other design templates.

5. Locate the Cascade design in the list of design thumbnails and click it. (If Cascade is not available on your computer, use a different template.)

Notice that each thumbnail on the Slides tab shows the new template design. Note also that the name of the template appears in the center of the status bar below the slide.

FIGURE 3-5
Applying a design
template

Design template
name in status bar

6. Move to slide 1 and view the presentation as a slide show; then return to slide 1 in Normal view.

 REVIEW: To view a slide show, move to the slide with which you want to start, then click the Slide Show button 🖳. Advance through the show by clicking the left mouse button or pressing [Page Down].

EXERCISE **3-6** **Choose a Template Color Scheme**

You can apply different preset colors to the current design template by changing the template's color scheme. To display preset color schemes for the current design template, display the Slide Design task pane and choose Color Schemes.

You can also customize color schemes, as you'll learn in Lesson 7: "Working with Lines, Fills, and Colors."

1. Near the top of the Slide Design task pane, click Color Schemes. Color scheme samples, appropriate for the current template, are displayed.

2. Click any color scheme to apply it to your presentation and then try some other schemes.

FIGURE 3-6
Slide Design task
pane with color
schemes displayed

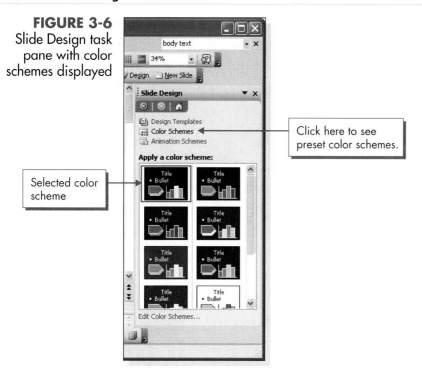

3. Apply the first color scheme on the first row with the black background.

NOTE: When referring to color scheme thumbnails, this course assumes that the thumbnails are displayed two across. If your display does not match Figure 3-6, drag the left border of the Slide Design task pane left or right until the thumbnails are displayed two across.

4. View the presentation as a slide show; then return to Normal view.

EXERCISE   **3-7**   **Change the Color Scheme for Selected Slides**

Sometimes, changing the color of just one or a few selected slides can add emphasis to those slides.

1. With the Slides tab displayed, select the thumbnails for slide 1 ("For the Pleasure of Your Company") and slide 4 (High-Energy Fun") by using the [Ctrl]+click method.

2. Point to—but do not click—the color scheme with the red-brown background and gold-tan accent colors (fourth row on the left). Notice the gray button with the arrow that appears on the thumbnail's right side.

3. Click the thumbnail's arrow button. A drop-down list of options is displayed.

4. Choose Apply to Selected Slides. The color scheme for slides 1 and 4 changes, but all other slides remain unchanged.

5. View the presentation as a slide show, starting with slide 1.

6. Move to slide 1 and save the presentation as *[your initials]*3-7. Do not close it.

EXERCISE **3-8** **Apply a Design Template to Selected Slides**

In the same way that you can apply more than one color scheme to a presentation, you can apply more than one template.

1. Select the thumbnails for slides 2 ("Excellent Service") through 6 ("A Healthy Atmosphere") by using [Shift]+click. (Four slides should be selected.)

2. On the Slide Design task pane, click Design Templates.

3. Point to the Pixel slide design thumbnail and click its down arrow.

 NOTE: Design template thumbnails are arranged alphabetically by name. You need to scroll down to find the Pixel template.

4. Choose Apply to Selected Slides from the drop-down list.

5. With slides 2–6 still selected, click Color Schemes. Click on the first thumbnail on the third row with the dark brown background.

6. View the presentation as a slide show, starting with slide 1. Now the first slide has bright colors that help to distinguish it as a title slide, while the other slides are more muted with the darker background. You will learn much more about design templates and customizing them in Lesson 9.

7. Move to slide 1 and save the presentation as *[your initials]*3-8. Do not close it.

EXERCISE **3-9** **Create a New Presentation from a Template**

Rather than start a new presentation with a blank white slide, you might prefer to choose a design template first. Some ways to do this are:

● Display the New Presentation task pane. Click the From design template link, and choose from the design templates shown as thumbnails. To access additional designs that may not be displayed as thumbnails, click Browse at the bottom of the Slide Design task pane and then choose a design template from the list.

● If a new blank presentation is already displayed on the screen, click Design on the Formatting toolbar to display the Slide Design task pane; then choose a design template from the thumbnails displayed.

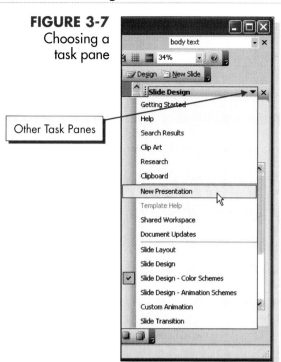

FIGURE 3-7
Choosing a
task pane

Other Task Panes

1. With the presentation *[your initials]*3-8 still open, click the Other Task Panes down arrow ▼ on the right side of the task pane title bar; then choose New Presentation.

   The New Presentation task pane is displayed. Click the From design template link. (If your task pane is not displayed, choose Tas̲k Pane from the V̲iew menu.)

2. As you did in the previous lesson, you could choose from the design templates shown as thumbnails in the Slides pane. If you want to check to see if more templates are on your computer that are not displayed as thumbnails, click Browse. The Apply Design Template dialog box opens.

FIGURE 3-8
Using the Apply
Design Template
dialog box

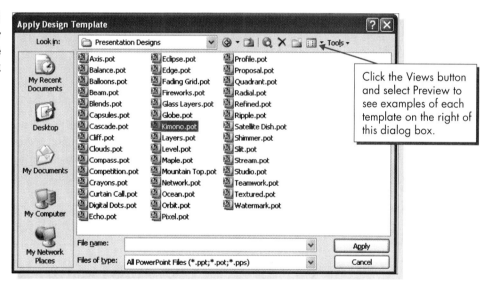

Click the Views button and select Preview to see examples of each template on the right of this dialog box.

3. Click to open the Presentations Designs folder.

4. Click on a template name to see a preview shown on the right side of the dialog box. Examine several different templates.

5. Select the template named Kimona (with a decorative graphic on the right of the background) and click OK. A new blank presentation opens with the chosen template design applied. You now have two presentations open and you are working in the second one.

6. Key the title on three lines as shown:

**Introducing
the Good 4 U
Sunday Brunch**

7. Key the subtitle on two lines:

**Every Sunday
from 10 a.m. to 2 p.m.**

Check to see if the AutoCorrect feature changed the "f" in "from" to uppercase.

8. If the "F" is capitalized, click the smart tag under "From" and choose Undo Automatic Capitalization from its drop-down list.

9. Click New Slide on the Formatting toolbar to insert a new slide.

10. On the new slide, key **Sample Menu** as the title with the following as bulleted body text:

- **Pineapple/grapefruit fizz**
- **Multigrain pancakes**
- **Tofu fajitas**
- **Western omelet**

11. Move to slide 1 and save the presentation as *[your initials]*3-9. Choose Close from the File menu to close this presentation. You will access it later in this lesson. The presentation *[your initials]*3-8 should still be displayed on your screen.

Using the Clipboard

The *Cut, Copy,* and *Paste* commands are almost universally available in computer programs. When you cut selected text or a selected object, it is removed from the presentation and placed on the clipboard. When you copy text or an object, it remains in its original place and a copy is placed on the clipboard. When you paste a clipboard item, a copy of the item is placed at the location of the insertion point and remains on the clipboard to use again if needed.

Each item you cut or copy is stored on the Office *Clipboard,* which can hold up to 24 items at a time. Clipboard items can be viewed and managed by using the Clipboard task pane. When working with the Office Clipboard, it is important to understand that unlike the Cut command, Delete does not save items to the clipboard.

The following cut, copy, and paste keyboard shortcuts are big time-savers when you do extensive editing:

- Ctrl+C   Copy
- Ctrl+X   Cut
- Ctrl+V   Insert (paste) the most recent item stored on the clipboard

If you press Ctrl+C twice, PowerPoint displays the Clipboard task pane.

EXERCISE 3-10 Use Cut, Copy, and Paste to Copy and Rearrange Slides

In Lesson 2 you learned how to rearrange slides by dragging their thumbnails. This exercise presents another way to arrange slides by using the clipboard. You can open the Clipboard task pane by choosing Office Clipboard from the Edit menu.

1. With the *[your initials]*3-8 presentation open, go to the Edit menu, and choose Office Clipboard to display the Clipboard task pane.

 REVIEW: If the Outline tab and Slides tab are not visible, click the Normal View button.

2. Display the Slides tab, and then click the thumbnail of slide 5 ("Events That Are Good 4 U").

 3. Click the Cut button on the Standard toolbar. This removes the slide and stores it on the clipboard.

4. Select the thumbnail for slide 3 ("A Delightful Menu").

 5. Click the Paste button on the Standard toolbar. The cut slide (on the clipboard) is inserted (or pasted) after slide 3. This accomplishes the same thing as if you moved the slide by dragging its thumbnail. If the slide does not have the correct color scheme, you will learn how to correct this in Exercise 3-12.

6. Select the slide 1 thumbnail ("For the Pleasure of Your Company"); then click the Copy button on the Standard toolbar. Notice that two slides are stored on the Clipboard task pane.

FIGURE 3-9
Using the Clipboard task pane

7. Move to slide 6 ("A Healthy Atmosphere"); then click the first item on the Clipboard task pane ("For the Pleasure of Your Company"). A copy of the slide is inserted at the end of the presentation to use for making a concluding comment. If the slide does not have the correct color scheme, you will learn how to correct this in Exercise 3-12.

8. Move to slide 7, the copied slide.

9. Delete the subtitle text and key the following text in its place on three lines:

Make Your Event Special
Call Good 4 U at
800-555-1234

10. Move to slide 1 and save the presentation as *[your initials]*3-10. Keep the presentation open for the following exercises.

EXERCISE **3-11** **Use Copy and Paste to Rearrange Text**

Just as you cut, copy, and paste slides, you can cut, copy, and paste text, and store it on the Office Clipboard.

1. In the Slides pane, select the thumbnail of slide 1, and press Ctrl+M to create a new text slide.

2. Key the title **Fun Is Good 4 U**. Click the ⊙ button twice at the top of the task pane to return to the Slide Design task pane and select the color scheme to match the first slide. Click the ⊙ button to return to the Clipboard task pane.

3. Display slide 5 ("High-Energy Fun").

4. Activate the first body text placeholder; then click the first bullet to select all its text.

5. Press Ctrl+C to copy the selected text to the clipboard. The selected text appears at the top of the Clipboard task pane. Notice the difference in appearance from the slides on the clipboard.

6. Click the second bullet in the first body text placeholder to select its text; then press Ctrl+X to cut the text from the slide. It too appears on the Clipboard task pane.

FIGURE 3-10
Text and slides stored on the Office Clipboard

7. Move to slide 2 ("Fun Is Good 4 U").

8. Activate the body text placeholder.

9. Click the first item on the Clipboard task pane ("Sports promotions").

   The bullet style is different from the bullet that first appeared in the placeholder because its appearance is controlled by the particular bullet used in the Pixel template. The color, however, is adapted for the Cascade color scheme being used. Notice the Paste Options button 📋 ▾ that appears. Paste Options is addressed in the next exercise.

10. Click the second item on the Clipboard task pane ("Athletic decor"). The text is inserted as a new bullet.

EXERCISE 3-12 Use the Paste Options Button

The Paste Options button appears near a pasted item if the item's *source* formatting is different from the formatting of similar elements in its *destination* presentation. A clipboard item's source is the presentation or other document from which it was cut or copied. Its destination is the presentation or other document in which it is pasted.

1. Click the thumbnail for slide 6, and click the first bullet in the second body text placeholder. Press Ctrl+X to cut the text from the slide.

2. Click on the thumbnail for slide 2, put your insertion point before "Athletic decor," and click the first item on the Clipboard task pane ("Energetic staff").

3. Click the Paste Options button that appears underneath the new bulleted item.

4. Choose Use Design Template Formatting from the drop-down list.

   Notice that the new bulleted item changes to the design and font size from the slide from which it was copied and is now the particular bullet used in the Cascade template. This change is sometimes desirable, for example, in a very complicated layout.

5. Click the Paste Options button again. This time choose Keep Source Formatting. The bullet design changes to match the other slides in the presentation.

   NOTE: The paste options can be very useful when working with multiple presentations, which will be discussed later in this lesson.

6. Repeat this process for any slides in this presentation with colors that do not blend with the current color scheme.

7. Add a handout header to the presentation that contains your name. Add a handout footer that contains the text *[your initials]*3-12.

   REVIEW: To add handout headers and footers, open the View menu and choose Header and Footer.

8. Delete slide 6 ("High-Energy Fun").

9. Move to slide 1, spell-check the presentation, and then save it as *[your initials]*3-12 in your Lesson 3 folder.

10. Preview and then print the presentation as handouts, 4 slides per page, grayscale, framed, landscape orientation, and leave it open for the next exercise.

11. Close the task pane on the right, since you will not use it for the next exercise.

EXERCISE **3-13** **Use the Undo and Redo Commands**

The Undo button ⤺ on the Standard toolbar reverses the last action you took. You can undo a series of editing actions, including keying or deleting text, promoting or demoting items, or deleting slides. By using Undo more than once, you can undo multiple actions. The Redo button ⤻ reapplies editing commands in the order you undid them.

In PowerPoint, unlike Word, Undo and Redo are cleared when you save a presentation. In other words, you cannot undo or redo actions performed prior to saving a presentation. Therefore, in PowerPoint, don't save if you think you may want to undo an action.

TIP: By default, PowerPoint can undo the last 20 actions. You can increase or decrease this number by choosing Tools, Options, Edit tab, and changing the Maximum number of undos. Increasing the number uses up more RAM memory on your computer.

1. Move to slide 3 ("Excellent Service"). Select the bulleted text "We make your company look good" and the two items below.

2. Click the Increase Indent button ⇥ three times. The items are indented three levels and the text is reduced in size.

3. From the Edit menu, choose Undo Increase Indent. The last indent is undone to return to a second-level bullet.

FIGURE 3-11
Demoted text at the second-level bullet

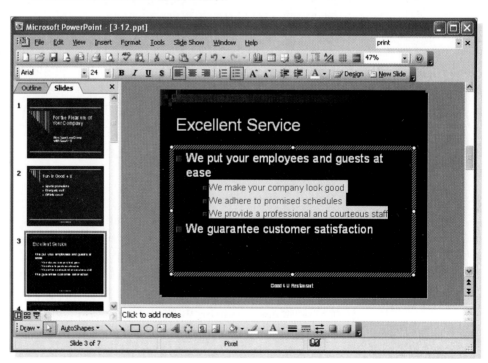

4. Click the Undo button 🔄 on the Standard toolbar. Another indent level is undone.

5. Press Ctrl+Z, the keyboard shortcut for Undo. The bullets are restored to their original level.

6. Press Ctrl+Y, the keyboard shortcut for Redo. The most recent indent is redone.

7. Click the Redo button 🔄. The previous indent is redone.

8. Open the Edit menu and choose Redo Increase Indent. The deepest indent level is redone.

9. Press Delete. The selected text is removed from the slide.

10. Press Ctrl+Z to restore the deleted text.

> **TIP:** It's fairly common to make unintentional deletions and unintentional text moves. The Ctrl+Z key combination is very handy to use when the unexpected happens.

11. Press Ctrl+Z three more times to restore the bullets to all the same level. Deselect the selected text.

Working with Multiple Open Presentations

Many times you want to adapt a presentation or use part of one presentation and part of another presentation to create a new presentation. To do this, you must be able to work with more than one open presentation.

EXERCISE 3-14 Insert Slides from Another Presentation

On occasion you might want to insert a slide from a presentation that you or someone else created previously. You can easily insert slides from other presentations by opening the Insert menu and choosing the Slides from Files command. This action opens the Slide Finder dialog box.

The Slide Finder dialog box enables you to select slides from thumbnails or from a list of slide titles. You can insert all the slides in a presentation by clicking Insert All. (See Figure 3-12 on the next page.)

1. With *[your initials]*3-12 still open, choose Open from the File menu. Open *[your initials]*3-9.

> **NOTE:** You should have two presentations open on your computer at this time (*[your initials]*3-9 and *[your initials]*3-12). The names of the open presentations are displayed on the Windows taskbar at the bottom of your screen, and they are also listed in PowerPoint's Window menu.

20 CHANCES

FIGURE 3-12
Switching between
open presentations

Open presentations
listed on the
Window menu

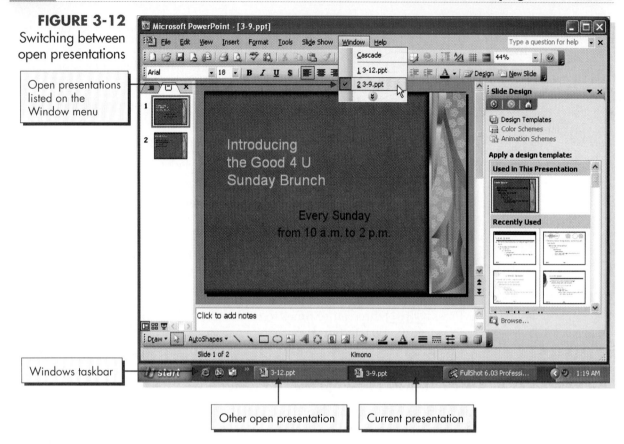

Windows taskbar

Other open presentation   Current presentation

2. Open the <u>W</u>indow menu and choose *[your initials]*3-12. PowerPoint switches to your other open presentation ("For the Pleasure of Your Company").

3. On the Windows taskbar at the bottom of your screen, click *[your initials]*3-9 to switch back to the new presentation ("Introducing the Good 4 U Sunday Brunch").

 TIP: Ctrl + F6 cycles through all open presentations.

4. Use either method to switch to *[your initials]*3-12 (red/brown backgrounds).

5. Move to slide 4.

6. Open the <u>I</u>nsert menu and choose Slides from <u>F</u>iles. The Slide Finder dialog box opens.

7. Click <u>B</u>rowse to open the Browse dialog box, and then navigate to the drive and folder where your student files are stored.

8. Select the file *[your initials]*3-9 and click <u>O</u>pen. Slide thumbnails appear in the lower half of the dialog box.

FIGURE 3-13
Inserting a slide
from another
presentation

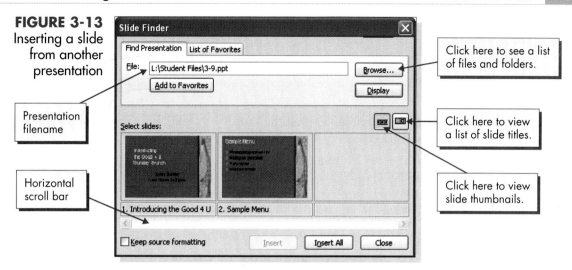

Presentation
filename

Horizontal
scroll bar

Click here to see a list
of files and folders.

Click here to view
a list of slide titles.

Click here to view
slide thumbnails.

 TIP: If you are frequently reusing slides from a particular presentation, navigate to it and then click Add to Favorites. The next time you want to insert a slide from that presentation, click the List of Favorites tab to find it quickly.

9. Locate the two buttons on the right side of the dialog box, just above the slide thumbnails. Click the button farthest to the right. A list of slide titles appears with a thumbnail of the current slide.

10. Select slide 2, "Sample Menu." Its thumbnail appears on the right.

11. Click the left button just above the thumbnail. The view changes to show two slide thumbnails and enough space to show a third one if it existed in the slide show. You can select slides in either the list view or the thumbnail view.

12. At the lower-left corner of the dialog box, make sure that the Keep source formatting check box remains unchecked. If this box is checked, the style and colors as well as the text will be copied to your presentation.

13. Click Insert. The selected slide (slide 2) is inserted after slide 4 in the current presentation.

TIP: If you want to insert all the presentation's slides, you don't have to select them. Instead, click Insert All.

14. Click Close to close the Slide Finder dialog box.

EXERCISE **3-15** **Copy Slides to Another Presentation**

Another way to insert slides from another presentation is to copy and paste the slides by using the Clipboard task pane.

When beginning a new cut, copy, and paste procedure, it's usually a good idea to clear the Clipboard task pane first by clicking Clear All.

1. If your Clipboard task pane is not open, choose the <u>E</u>dit menu and then Office Clip<u>b</u>oard. With *[your initials]*3-12 still open, click Clear All at the top of the Clipboard task pane to empty the clipboard.

2. With the Slides tab displayed, copy one at a time slide 2 ("Fun Is Good 4 U") and slide 3 ("Excellent Service").

3. Click *[your initials]*3-9 on the Windows taskbar to switch to your other open presentation.

4. Display slide 1; then click the second slide on the Clipboard task pane ("Fun Is Good 4 U"). The slide is inserted after slide 1, formatted with the current presentation's design template. The Paste Options button appears below the inserted slide's thumbnail in the Outline and Slides pane.

5. Choose <u>K</u>eep Source Formatting from the drop-down arrow on the Paste Options button. Notice that slide 2 has the Cascade design template background of the presentation from which it was copied, while the other slides still have the Kimono design template background.

> **NOTE:** The Paste Options button appears after pasting slides one at a time into a presentation. It does not appear if you use the Paste All button on the Clipboard task pane.

6. Switch to *[your initials]*3-12 and save the presentation and close it. Save the *[your initials]*3-9 presentation as *[your initials]*3-15 and leave it open for the next exercise.

Working with Speaker's Notes

Speakers often use notes to guide their presentations. In PowerPoint, you can create notes pages for your slides. A printed *notes page* contains a small image of the slide above text about the slide that was keyed in using the Notes pane. The text can include reminders or facts that you need for a reference during a presentation. Notes pages could be distributed as handouts, too, or included with presentations published on the Web.

E X E R C I S E   3-16   **Create Speaker's Notes**

You key notes directly into the Notes pane, which you can make larger, if needed. Text that is wider than the Notes pane automatically wraps to a new line.

1. Display slide 2 and click the Notes pane to activate it.

2. Resize the Notes pane by placing the mouse pointer on the horizontal splitter bar between the Slides and Notes panes. The pointer changes to a resize pointer ⬍. Drag the border up, enlarging the Notes pane until it fills approximately half the window.

3. Key the following text:

> **Good 4 U focuses on fun and service:**
>> **to keep customers happy**
>> **present an upbeat image**
>> **attract many organizations**
> **Some things we do to make the atmosphere fun are:**

FIGURE 3-14
Resizing the
Notes pane

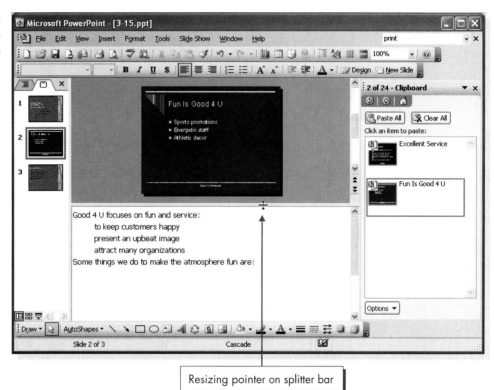

| Resizing pointer on splitter bar |

 NOTE: You can customize the size of each pane (Slides, Notes, and Outline) by dragging the pane splitter bar.

4. Key the following numbered note under the text in the expanded Notes pane:

1. Conducting sports promotions

 5. Press (Enter). The AutoCorrect Options button 🔏 ▾ appears on the right side of the Notes pane because the next item is automatically numbered.

6. Key the following numbered notes under the first one.

2. Utilizing energetic staff with a positive attitude to provide quick, efficient service

3. Decorating with a theme that fosters a relaxed atmosphere

7. Move to slide 3 and key the following in the Notes pane.

   Describe the sample menu

   Point out healthy beverages

   Point out vegetarian and meat dishes

8. Using the resize pointer ⬍, drag the upper border of the Notes pane down to make it approximately 1 inch tall to display all three lines of text.

9. Check spelling in the presentation.

 NOTE: The spell-checker checks for errors in note text, header and footer text, and slide text.

10. Change the notes and handouts footer text to *[your initials]***3-16**.

11. Move to slide 1 and save the presentation as *[your initials]***3-16** in your Lesson 3 folder.

EXERCISE 3-17 Print Notes Pages

You print notes pages by choosing options in either the Print dialog box or the Print Preview window.

1. Open the Print dialog box. From the Print what drop-down list, choose Notes Pages.

2. Under Print range, select Slides. Key **2-3** in the text box to print notes pages for slides 2 and 3 only.

3. Choose Grayscale.

4. Click Preview.

 5. In the Print Preview window, if the display is landscape oriented, click the Portrait button ⬛.

6. Click Print to return to the Print dialog box and click OK. Click Close to close the Print Preview window. Close the presentation.

USING ONLINE HELP

In this lesson you worked with many keyboard shortcuts to help navigate text placeholders and to insert slides. PowerPoint Help has numerous lists of keyboard shortcuts that can speed up your work. It's not necessary to memorize them all, but you should search for shortcuts for operations that you find you are frequently performing.

Exploring keyboard shortcuts:

1. Key **keyboard shortcuts** in the Ask a Question box and press ⟨Enter⟩.

2. Select Keyboard shortcuts from the list.

3. Under Common Microsoft PowerPoint tasks, choose the fourth topic, Select text and objects. Maximize the Help window to see the list below the selected topic.

FIGURE 3-15
Using Help to find keyboard shortcuts

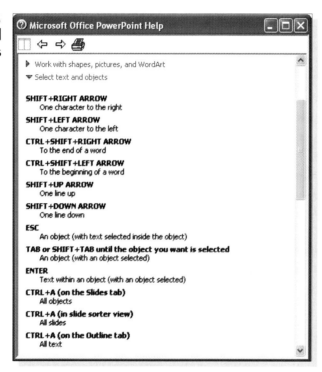

4. Review the list of keyboard shortcuts displayed and then click some other topics.

5. Close the Help window when you finish.

LESSON 3 Summary

➤ Creating a blank presentation lets you concentrate on textual content without the distraction of design elements. Any time during the process, you can choose a design and color scheme.

➤ Keyboard shortcuts are a big time-saver when creating a presentation. For example: ⟨Ctrl⟩+⟨Enter⟩ moves to the next text placeholder; ⟨Ctrl⟩+⟨M⟩ inserts a new slide.

➤ When you insert a new slide, you can choose a slide layout. Slide layouts can be either text layouts or content layouts. They contain various arrangements of text and content placeholders.

➤ After a slide is inserted, you choose its slide layout from the Slide Layout task pane. If you change your mind later, you can change the layout of the current slide or of a group of selected slide thumbnails.

➤ Another way to create a new blank presentation is to start with a design template and then insert slides and key text. Choose a design template from the Slide Design task pane.

➤ Each design template has several predefined color schemes associated with it. You choose color schemes by first clicking Color Schemes on the Slide Design task pane.

➤ Design templates and color schemes can be applied to individual slides, to a group of selected slides, or to an entire presentation. To apply to a group of slides, first select their slide thumbnails.

➤ The clipboard can store up to 24 items that you cut or copy from a presentation. The items can be text, entire slides, or other objects. Insert a clipboard item at the current location in your presentation by clicking the item.

➤ Slides can be rearranged by using drag-and-drop or by using the Cut, Copy, and Paste commands. Text can also be moved or copied by using these commands.

➤ The Paste Options button 📋▾ enables you to choose between a pasted item's source formatting and its destination formatting. The source is the slide or placeholder from which the item was cut or copied, and the destination is the location where it will be pasted.

➤ PowerPoint enables you to undo—and if you change your mind, redo—multiple editing actions. The default number of available undos is 20. When you save a presentation, the list of undos is cleared.

➤ Working with multiple open presentations is made easy with the clipboard. Open both presentations; then switch between them by clicking the filename on the Windows taskbar or by choosing the file from the Window menu.

➤ Slides from another presentation can easily be inserted into your presentation by using the Slide Finder dialog box or by using the Cut, Copy, and Paste commands.

➤ Speaker's notes are keyed in the Notes pane, below the Slides pane in Normal view. They can be used as a script for the presenter or as supplemental information for the audience.

➤ Notes pages contain an image of a slide at the top of the page and the speaker's notes associated with that slide at the bottom of the page. Notes pages are printed by using the Print dialog box.

LESSON 3   Command Summary

FEATURE	BUTTON	MENU	KEYBOARD
Create new presentation		File, New	Ctrl + N
Insert new slide	New Slide	Insert, New Slide	Ctrl + M
Change slide layout		Format, Slide Layout	
Apply design template	Design	Format, Slide Design	
Choose color scheme		Format, Slide Design, Color Schemes	
Apply color scheme	Design	Slide Design task pane, Color Schemes	
Activate placeholder			Ctrl + Enter
Deactivate placeholder			Esc
Insert line break			Shift + Enter
Move to next placeholder			Ctrl + Enter
Display Clipboard task pane		Edit, Office Clipboard	
Clear the Clipboard task pane		Clipboard task pane, Clear All	
Cut selected object or text	✂	Edit, Cut	Ctrl + X
Copy selected object or text		Edit, Copy	Ctrl + C
Undo	↶	Edit, Undo	Ctrl + Z
Redo	↷	Edit, Redo	Ctrl + Y
Paste (insert) cut or copied object or text		Edit, Paste	Ctrl + V
Paste options	▾		
Switch to another open file		Window, [filename]	Ctrl + F6
Insert slides from other files		Insert, Slides from Files	
Print notes pages		File, Print, Print what	

Concepts Review

TRUE/FALSE QUESTIONS

Each of the following statements is either true or false. Indicate your choice by circling T or F.

(T) F **1.** You can start a new presentation with a blank template or a design template.

T (F) **2.** You can add a new slide by pressing Ctrl+Y.

(T) F **3.** You can choose a slide layout in the Slide Layout task pane.

T (F) **4.** You can change a presentation's overall design in the Slide Layout task pane.

(T) F **5.** The clipboard can store up to 24 items that you cut or copy from a presentation.

(T) F **6.** The keyboard shortcut for undoing a task is Ctrl+Z.

T (F) **7.** The only way to insert a slide from another presentation is to use Cut and Paste.

(T) F **8.** You can print notes pages in either grayscale or color.

SHORT ANSWER QUESTIONS

Write the correct answer in the space provided.

1. Name three ways to insert a new slide.   NEW SLIDE BUTTON
INSERT NEW SLIDE   CTRL M

2. Which task pane do you use to change a slide from a Title slide to a Title and 2-Column Text slide?
SLIDE LAYOUT

3. How do you change the color scheme of just one slide in a presentation?
SELECT A SLIDE
COLOR SCHEME DROPDOWN

4. How do you clear the Office clipboard of all its contents?
CLEAR

5. Name three ways to copy a selection of text.

CTRL C   COPY BUTTON   EDIT MENU

6. What is the default number of actions that you can undo using the undo feature in PowerPoint?

20

7. Name two ways to switch from one of several open presentations to another.

ALT TAB / TASK / CTRL F6

8. Which drop-down list in the Print dialog box contains the option to print notes pages?

PRINT WHAT

CRITICAL THINKING

Answer these questions on a separate page. There are no right or wrong answers. Support your answers with examples from your own experience, if possible.

1. Review PowerPoint's design templates. In what kinds of presentations might you use the different templates?

2. What are some advantages of starting with a blank presentation instead of using the AutoContent Wizard? Which method do you prefer and why?

Skills Review

EXERCISE 3-18

Create a new presentation, add new slides, and insert a new slide with a different layout.

1. Start PowerPoint. (If PowerPoint is already running, click the New button on the Standard toolbar.)

2. Complete the title slide by following these steps:

    a. Key **Healthy Eating** as the first line of the title (you don't have to click the text "Click to add title" to begin keying the title slide text).

    b. Press [Enter] to start a new title line.

    c. Key **for Young Athletes** to complete the title.

      d. Press Ctrl+Enter.

      e. Key the subtitle **A Good 4 U Seminar**

3. Add a new slide with the Title and Text layout by following these steps:

      a. Press Ctrl+M.

      b. Key **Basic Food Groups** as the title.

      c. Key the following bulleted text:

- **Fats, oils, and sweets**
- **Dairy products**
- **Meat, poultry, fish, eggs, beans, and nuts**
- **Fruits and vegetables**
- **Rice, bread, and pasta**

4. Click New Slide on the Formatting toolbar to insert a third slide.

5. Key **Elements of a Healthy Diet** as the title of the slide and the following bulleted text:

- **Choose a variety of foods**
- **Eat moderate amounts**
- **Choose low-fat foods**
- **Choose fresh, unprocessed foods**
- **Avoid candy and junk foods**

6. Check spelling in the presentation.

7. Create a handout header and footer: include the date and your name as the header, and the page number and text *[your initials]*3-18 as the footer.

8. Move to slide 1 and save the presentation as *[your initials]*3-18 in your Lesson 3 folder.

9. Preview and then print the presentation as handouts, 3 slides per page, grayscale, framed. Close the presentation.

EXERCISE 3-19

Add new slides, change the slide layout, use the Cut and Paste commands, and insert a slide from another presentation.

1. Open the file **EatGuide**.

2. Add a new slide with the Title and Text layout by following these steps:

      a. Press Ctrl+M.

      b. Key **More Healthy Proportions** as the title.

3. Move to slide 4 ("Healthy Proportions") and cut the text from the second body text placeholder:

a. Click the I-beam pointer before "Vegetables" and drag through "6 to 11 servings."

b. Click the Cut button 🔪 on the Standard toolbar.

4. Move to slide 2, and click in the body text placeholder and paste the copied text:

a. Click the I-beam pointer in the body text placeholder.

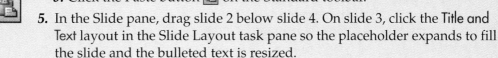

b. Click the Paste button 📋 on the Standard toolbar.

5. In the Slide pane, drag slide 2 below slide 4. On slide 3, click the Title and Text layout in the Slide Layout task pane so the placeholder expands to fill the slide and the bulleted text is resized.

6. Insert a slide from another presentation after slide 2 by following these steps:

a. Display slide 2 ("Basic Food Groups").

b. From the Insert menu, choose Slides from Files.

c. Click Browse.

d. In the Browse dialog box, navigate to the folder where your student files are stored.

e. Select Balance2. Do not check the Keep source formatting option.

f. Using the horizontal scroll bar in the Slide Finder dialog box, locate slide 5 ("Good Eating Habits").

g. Click slide 5 to select it and then click Insert. If the font on this slide does not match the other slides, click the down arrow on the Title and Text layout in the Slide Layout task pane and choose Reapply Layout.

h. Click Close to close the Slide Finder dialog box.

7. Check spelling in the presentation.

8. Create a handout header and footer: include the date and your name as the header, and the page number and text *[your initials]*3-19 as the footer.

9. Move to slide 1 and save the presentation as *[your initials]*3-19 in your Lesson 3 folder.

10. Preview and then print the presentation as handouts, 4 slides per page, landscape, grayscale, framed. Close the presentation. Also close the Balance2 presentation.

EXERCISE 3-20

Start a new presentation by using a design template, add new slides, insert new slides with different layouts, change design templates and color schemes, and use the Undo command.

1. Start a new presentation using a design template by following these steps:

a. From the File menu, choose New.

b. In the New Presentation task pane, click From Design Template.

c. In the Apply a design template list box, locate the thumbnail for the design template Capsules, the fourth template in the left column under the heading Available for Use.

d. Click the Capsules template to apply it.

2. On the first slide, key **Smart Diet Options** for the presentation title. Key **Choosing Low-Fat Foods** for the subtitle.

3. Insert a new slide with the Title and 2-Column Text layout by following these steps:

a. Click New Slide on the Formatting toolbar.

b. In the Slide Layout task pane, click the Title and 2-Column Text layout (the second layout in the right column).

 TIP: If the Slide Layout task pane is not showing, click the Other Task Panes button ▼ on the task pane title bar and choose Slide Layout from the drop-down list.

4. Key the title for slide 2 (on two lines) and bulleted text for slide 2 shown in Figure 3-16, demoting the bulleted text below "Under" and "Over" as shown. Repeat the process for slide 3.

FIGURE 3-16

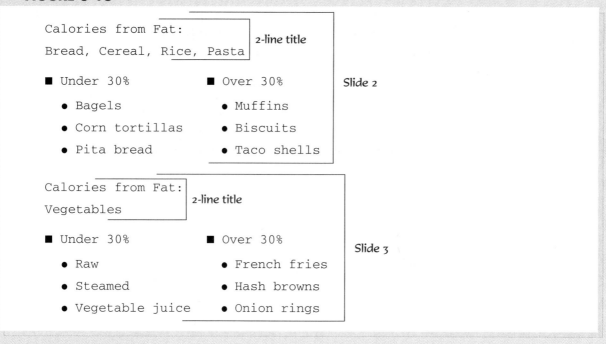

5. View the presentation as a slide show starting on slide 1. Return to Normal view when you're finished.

6. Apply a different design template by following these steps:

a. Click Design on the Formatting toolbar to display the Slide Design task pane.

     b. In the Apply a design template list box, click the design template Blends.

     c. Scroll through the presentation to view the applied design.

7. Change the presentation's color scheme by following these steps:

     a. Choose Color Schemes on the Slide Design task pane.

     b. Under Apply a color scheme, choose the sample with the black background; then scroll through all your slides to view the change.

     c. Select one of the three color schemes at the bottom of the task pane that have white backgrounds; then view the slides again.

8. Click the Undo button to compare the new color scheme with the previous one. If you prefer the white background, click the Redo button to reapply the color change.

9. Check spelling in the presentation.

10. Create a handout header and footer: include the date and your name as the header, and the page number and text *[your initials]*3-20 as the footer.

11. Move to slide 1 and save the presentation as *[your initials]*3-20 in your Lesson 3 folder.

12. Preview and then print the presentation as handouts, 3 slides per page, grayscale, framed. Close the presentation.

EXERCISE 3-21

Change slide layout, change the design template, use the Office Clipboard, and add speaker's notes.

1. Open the file **Balance2** and display slide 3.

2. Change the layout of slide 3 by following these steps:

     a. From the Format menu, choose Slide Layout to display the Slide Layout task pane.

     b. In the Slide Layout task pane, click the Title and 2-Column Text layout.

3. Use Cut and Paste to move the last two bulleted items to the second body text placeholder by following these steps:

     a. Position your I-beam pointer between the third bullet and the word "Eat."

     b. Drag the I-beam down and to the right to select all the text for the third and fourth bullets ("Eat moderately" and "Limit fat").

     c. Click the Cut button on the Standard toolbar (or press Ctrl+X).

     d. Click anywhere in the right body text placeholder.

     e. Click the Paste button on the Standard toolbar (or press Ctrl+V).

     f. If you see a dark bullet after the last line of text, click the insertion point to the right of the dark bullet and then press Backspace to remove the extra bullet.

4. Use the Clipboard task pane to copy slide 1 to the end of the presentation by following these steps:

   a. From the <u>E</u>dit menu, choose Office Clip<u>b</u>oard.

   b. If the Clipboard currently has items displayed, click the Clear All button.

   c. On the left side of your screen, click the Slides tab to display the thumbnails.

   d. Click the thumbnail for slide 1 and then click the Copy button.

   e. Move to the end of the presentation, displaying slide 5 ("Good Eating Habits").

   f. Click the first item on the Clipboard task pane (the slide thumbnail with the text "The Food Guide Pyramid").

5. Move to the new slide (slide 6) and change the subtitle text to read **A Healthy Way to Eat**

6. Return to slide 1; then enlarge the Notes pane by following these steps:

   a. Position the mouse pointer on the horizontal splitter bar between the Slides pane and the Notes pane.

   b. When you see the resizing pointer, drag the border up to about the middle of the screen.

7. Key the following text in the slide 1 Notes pane:

   Remind staff about Good 4 U's mission to serve healthy food.

   Our menu items balance food proportions according to USDA guidelines.

8. Key the following notes for the remaining slides:

   Slide 2: The USDA has classified foods into five basic groups.

   Slide 3: Emphasize whole grains and whole foods as opposed to processed foods.

   Slide 4: A good diet consists of foods from each of the five main groups and may contain a little fat, oil, and sweetener.

9. Resize the Notes pane to its original size.

10. Change the design template to Layers (which has a yellow background).

11. Check spelling in the presentation.

12. Create a handout header and footer: include the date and your name as the header, and the page number and text *[your initials]*3-21 as the footer.

13. Move to slide 1 and save the presentation as *[your initials]*3-21 in your Lesson 3 folder.

14. Preview and then print the presentation as handouts, 6 slides per page, grayscale, framed. Close the presentation.

Lesson Applications

Create a new blank presentation, add slides, change a slide layout, apply a design template, change the color scheme, and cut and paste text.

1. Start a blank presentation.
2. Create a title slide with the text **First in Food Safety** as the title and **Good 4 U Employee Training** as the subtitle.
3. Using the Title and Text layout, create three new slides, as shown in Figure 3-17.

FIGURE 3-17

Slide 2
Our Food Safety Programs ———— Title
- Food handler training
- Management inspections
- Safety supervisors on-site
- Reports to USDA

Slide 3
Safe Food-Handling Practices ———— Title
- Wear gloves, hair nets, and beard nets
- Wash hands before and after handling food
- Wear clean uniforms
- No smoking

Slide 4
Food Procurement ———— Title
- Know your suppliers
- Prefer local growers
- Prefer organic food
- Insist on freshness
- Insist on cleanliness
- Test for pesticides

4. Change slide 4 to the Title and 2-Column Text layout.
5. Cut the last three bullets in column 1 and paste them into column 2.
6. Check both body text placeholders for extra blank lines and remove them.
7. Apply the design template Eclipse to the presentation (use ScreenTips to find it).

8. Change the color scheme to the first one in the second row (white background with red, yellow, and blue accents).

9. Change the first slide only to the color scheme with the black background and red, yellow, and green accents.

REVIEW: To change the color scheme for just one slide, select the slide and then point to the color scheme sample, click the down arrow button, and choose Apply to Selected Slides.

10. Check spelling in the presentation.

11. View the presentation as a slide show, noting that the first slide is a different color than the others.

12. Create a handout header and footer: include the date and your name as the header, and the page number and text *[your initials]*3-22 as the footer.

13. Move to slide 1 and save the presentation as *[your initials]*3-22 in your Lesson 3 folder.

14. Preview and then print the presentation as handouts, 4 slides per page, grayscale, framed, landscape. Close the presentation.

EXERCISE 3-23

Add slides, change slide layouts, change the color scheme, cut and paste text, and insert a slide from another presentation.

1. Open the file **SafeFd1**.

2. Change the layout of slide 4 to the Title and Text layout.

3. Change the color scheme to the last color scheme sample—with the black background. (Use the scroll bar to locate it.)

4. On slide 4, cut the bulleted items in column 2 and paste them at the bottom of column 1. Ignore the Paste Options button that appears; the text is formatted correctly.

5. Edit text in slide 4 and demote bullets as shown in Figure 3-18.

6. Add a new slide 5, using the text shown in Figure 3-19.

7. Without closing **SafeFd1**, open the file **SafeFd2**.

8. Display the Clipboard task pane and clear all items in the Clipboard. Copy slide 2 ("Should We Be Safe?").

9. Close **SafeFd2**; then use the Clipboard task pane to insert the copied slide after slide 1 in **SafeFd1**.

 10. Click the Paste Options button and check to be sure that Use Design Template Formatting is selected.

11. Check spelling in the presentation.

FIGURE 3-18

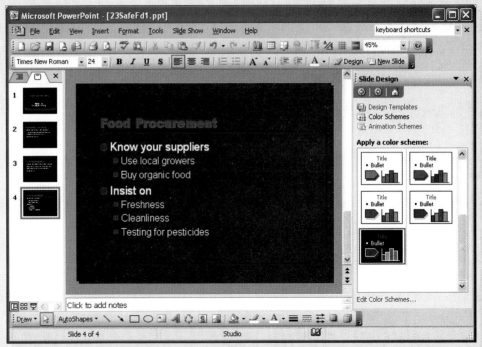

12. Create a handout header and footer: include the date and your name as the header, and the page number and text *[your initials]*3-23 as the footer.

13. Move to slide 1 and save the presentation as *[your initials]*3-23 in your Lesson 3 folder.

14. Preview and then print the presentation as handouts, 6 slides per page, grayscale, framed. Close the presentation.

FIGURE 3-19

```
Inspections

• Training inspections
    • Scheduled
    • Cooperative
• Internal evaluation inspections
• USDA inspections
```

Start a new presentation, add slides, apply a template, and change the color scheme.

1. Create a new presentation, using the text shown in Figure 3-20.

FIGURE 3-20

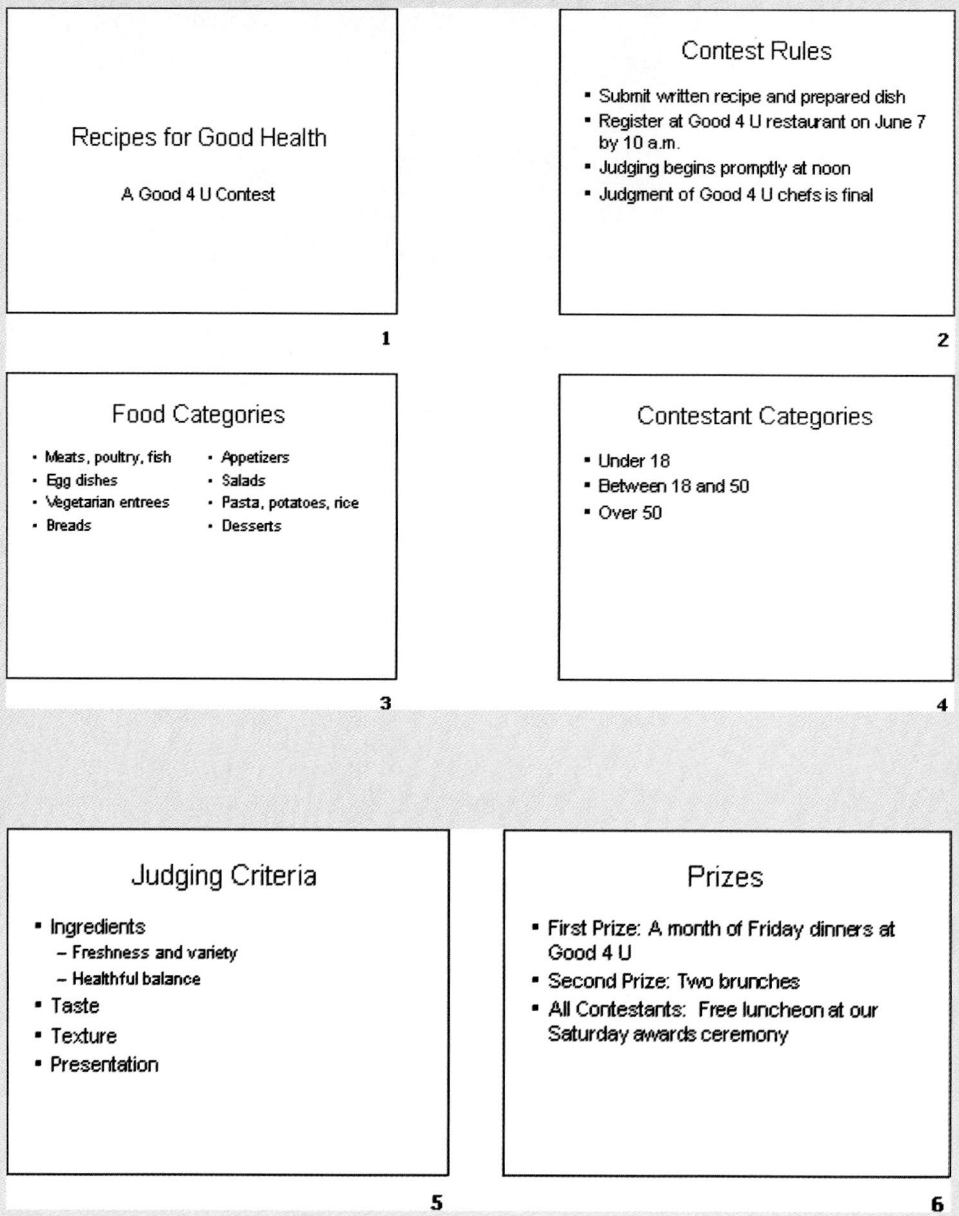

Recipes for Good Health

A Good 4 U Contest

1

Contest Rules

- Submit written recipe and prepared dish
- Register at Good 4 U restaurant on June 7 by 10 a.m.
- Judging begins promptly at noon
- Judgment of Good 4 U chefs is final

2

Food Categories

- Meats, poultry, fish
- Egg dishes
- Vegetarian entrees
- Breads
- Appetizers
- Salads
- Pasta, potatoes, rice
- Desserts

3

Contestant Categories

- Under 18
- Between 18 and 50
- Over 50

4

Judging Criteria

- Ingredients
  - Freshness and variety
  - Healthful balance
- Taste
- Texture
- Presentation

5

Prizes

- First Prize: A month of Friday dinners at Good 4 U
- Second Prize: Two brunches
- All Contestants: Free luncheon at our Saturday awards ceremony

6

2. Apply a template and color scheme of your choice.

3. Reverse the positions of slides 2 and 3.

4. Check spelling in the presentation.

5. Add a slide transition to all slides.

6. Add slide numbers to all slides.

7. Create a handout header and footer: include the date and your name as the header, and the page number and text *[your initials]*3-24 as the footer.

8. Move to slide 1 and save the presentation as *[your initials]*3-24 in your Lesson 3 folder.

9. Preview and then print slide 3 in full size in grayscale or in color if available.

10. Preview and then print the entire presentation as handouts, 6 slides per page, grayscale, framed. Close the presentation.

EXERCISE 3-25 ✚ *Challenge Yourself*

Add a new slide, choose a slide layout, insert slides from another presentation, and add speaker's notes.

1. Open the file **CookCon1**.

2. On slide 1, key the subtitle **Rules, Judging, and Prizes**

3. Add a new slide after the title slide, using the text shown in Figure 3-21.

FIGURE 3-21

```
Contest Rules

• Submit an original written recipe and dish
    • Good 4 U Restaurant, Saturday, June 7
    • 10 a.m. to noon
• Judging is from noon to 2 p.m.
• Judges' decisions are final
• Anyone may enter except Good 4 U employees and their families
```

4. Using either the Clipboard task pane or the Slides from Files command, insert slide 2 ("Ingredients to Use") and slide 3 ("Awards") from the presentation **CookCon2** at the end of the presentation.

5. Change slide 5 ("Ingredients to Use") to a Title and 2-Column Text layout; then cut the body text from slide 3 and insert it in the second column of slide 5.

6. Change the title of slide 5 to **Recipe Ingredients**. Insert a new line at the top of the first column. Key **Use** on the new line and demote all the text below it. Insert **Avoid** at the top of the second column and demote all the text below it.

7. Key a speaker's note on slide 1 stating that local businesses are sponsoring this event.

8. Key a speaker's note on slide 2 stating that three volunteer taste testers will be chosen from the entrants.

9. Delete slide 3 ("Ingredients to Avoid"); then rearrange the remaining slides where needed so that they appear in the following order:
   - Slide 1   ("Recipe Contest")
   - Slide 2   ("Contest Rules")
   - Slide 3   ("Recipe Ingredients")
   - Slide 4   ("Awards")
   - Slide 5   ("Judging Criteria")

10. Check spelling in the presentation.

11. Review the presentation as a slide show.

12. Create a handout header and footer: include the date and your name as the header, and the page number and text *[your initials]***3-25** as the footer.

13. Move to slide 1 and save the presentation as *[your initials]***3-25** in your Lesson 3 folder.

14. Preview and then print slides 1 and 2 as notes pages in grayscale.

15. Preview and then print the presentation as handouts, 6 slides per page, grayscale, framed. Close the presentation. Also close the **CookCon2** presentation.

On Your Own

In these exercises you work on your own, as you would in a real-life work environment. Use the skills you've learned to accomplish the task—and be creative.

EXERCISE 3-26
Imagine that you are organizing a contest for your local high school to raise money for new band equipment. Local businesses have donated interesting products and band students will sell tickets for a drawing to determine who will receive the products. Decide how you might organize such an event and prepare a slide show to promote it. Insert some slides from the student files used in this lesson and edit them to work for your contest. Apply a design template of your

choice to the first and last slides in your presentation and apply a different but complementary design template to the other slides. Add transition effects. Save the presentation as *[your initials]*3-26. Preview and then print the presentation as handouts.

EXERCISE 3-27

Create a presentation describing briefly your personal autobiography, including your family, interesting occupations or other facts about yourself, hobbies, and cultural, educational, or athletic achievements. Create at least six slides by using design templates, color schemes, and slide transitions. Copy and paste as necessary to put the text and slides in a logical sequence. Add speaker's notes detailing what you would say when showing the presentation to introduce yourself. Save the presentation as *[your initials]* 3-27. Preview and then print the presentation as handouts.

EXERCISE 3-28

Choose a children's story, for example, a Dr. Seuss classic, or the Berenstain Bears or Frog and Toad's Adventures. Create a presentation that includes a title slide with the subject title being the title of the book and the author's name for the subtitle. After the title slide, insert multiple slides describing the characters in the book using the title placeholder for each character's name and the body text placeholder for four or five important points about each character. Choose a design template and a color scheme that conveys the mood of the book. Add transition effects. Save the presentation as *[your initials]* 3-28. Preview and then print the presentation as handouts.

LESSON 4

Outlines, Hyperlinks, and HTML

OBJECTIVES

After completing this lesson, you will be able to:

1. Work with the Outline pane.
2. Rearrange outline text.
3. Move text and slides in the Outline pane.
4. Import and export outlines.
5. Work with hyperlinks.
6. Save a presentation as a Web page.

 Estimated Time: 1½ hours

MICROSOFT OFFICE SPECIALIST ACTIVITIES

In this lesson:
  PP03S-1-2
  PP03S-4-1
  PP03S-4-6
  PP03S-4-7
  PP03S-4-8

See Appendix.

Outlining helps you create and organize a presentation by focusing on content and flow rather than slide appearance. Working in the Outline pane, you can key text for your slides and then easily rearrange the text. You can also import a Word outline to create a PowerPoint presentation automatically, and you can export PowerPoint outline text to Word.

In addition to outlining, this lesson also introduces you to hyperlinks and to the HTML file format, which is used to save PowerPoint presentations as Web pages.

Working with the Outline Pane

The Outline pane appears in Normal view. To display the pane, click the Outline tab on the upper-left side of your PowerPoint window. To give yourself plenty of room for keying text, you can drag the Outline pane's right border to the right.

EXERCISE   **4-1**   **Use Zoom to Adjust the Size of Outline Text**

Lesson 1 introduced you to using *Zoom* in Slide Sorter view. You can also use Zoom to change the magnification of text in the Outline pane, change the size of slide thumbnails, or change the magnification of a slide in the Slide pane. Zoom does not change the actual size of objects, only the size at which you view them while working. When you use Zoom, first click the pane that you want to magnify.

1. Start a new presentation by using the design template Crayons. (This design template provides an interesting background for the message we will be sending about posters.)

2. Click the Outline tab to display the Outline pane. In the Outline pane, the blank title slide is represented as a numbered slide icon.

  REVIEW: If the Outline tab and Slides tab are not visible, click the Normal View button .

3. Enlarge the Outline pane by dragging its right border about 1 inch to the right (by using the ↔ pointer).

 4. To gain even more room, close the task pane by clicking its Close button ☒ on the right end of the task pane title bar.

FIGURE 4-1
Closing a task pane

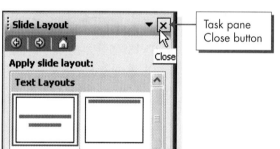

5. To activate the Outline pane, click anywhere inside it. Notice the insertion point to the right of the slide icon.

6. Key **Promotional Posters** as the slide title. The title line appears next to the slide icon. It also appears as red text in the Slide pane. (See Figure 4-2 on the next page.)

7. Click anywhere in the Slide pane, then click the arrow next to Zoom on the Standard toolbar and choose 100% from the list box. The slide is enlarged and the objects on the slide appear much larger.

8. Click the Zoom arrow again and choose Fit at the bottom of the list box to reduce the slide size so that all of the slide displays in the space available for it.

9. Click the Slides tab on the Outline and Slides pane to display the slide thumbnail. Click the slide thumbnail and then change the zoom to 100%. The slide thumbnail has enlarged.

10. Click the Outline tab to redisplay the Outline pane. Click anywhere in the Outline pane, and then change the zoom to 50%.

FIGURE 4-2
Creating a
presentation by
using the
Outline pane

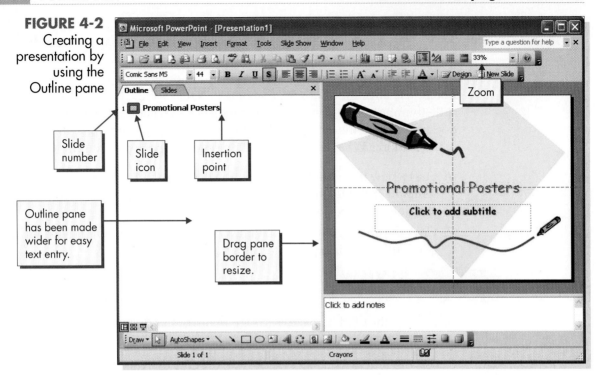

11. Key **45%** in the Zoom box and press Enter. You can key any percentage between 20% and 400% in the Zoom box. Adjust the zoom level so that you can comfortably key text in an easy-to-read size.

TIP: Notice that the font in the Crayons design template is Comic Sans. This font has a relaxed, informal tone and is appropriate for the message we are sending through this presentation. The background graphics and fonts you use should complement your message.

EXERCISE 4-2 Add New Slides in the Outline Pane

After a title slide is created, any new slide you insert will be formatted with the Title and Text layout by default. As you learned in a previous lesson, when working in the Slide pane you can insert a new slide by using these methods:

● Click New Slide on the Formatting toolbar.
● From the Insert menu, choose New Slide or press Ctrl+M.

These methods can be used when you are working in the Outline pane, too. But in the Outline pane, you can use another quick method:

● Place your insertion point at the end of a slide's title text and press Enter to insert a new slide.

For outline pane only

When the insertion point is at the end of the slide title text, pressing (Enter) inserts a new slide; when the insertion point is at the end of a bulleted text line, pressing (Enter) inserts a new bulleted line at the same level as the previous line.

1. Now in the Outline pane place your insertion point after the **Promotional Posters** text on slide 1 and press (Enter). A new slide icon for slide 2 appears.

2. Key **Poster Purpose** as the title and press (Enter). A new slide icon appears.

3. Press (Tab). The new slide icon changes to a bulleted line for slide 2.

4. Key **Inform customers** and press (Enter). A second bullet appears.

5. Key the following bulleted items, pressing (Enter) to start each new line:
   - **Promote our image**
   - **Design suggestions**
   - **Keep it simple**
   - **Limit the number of text items**

6. Press (Ctrl)+(M). A new slide icon appears. Notice in the Slide pane that the slide has the same layout (Title and Text) as the previous slide.

7. Key the title **Themes** for slide 3.

8. Click New Slide on the Formatting toolbar. Slide 4 is inserted. Choose the Title and 2-Column Text layout from the Slide Layout task pane. Notice the two body text placeholders in the Slide pane.

9. With the insertion point in the Outline pane (next to the slide 4 icon), key the title **Suggested Subjects**

10. Press (Ctrl)+(Enter) to insert a bulleted line for this two-column layout. Key **Menu items** and press (Enter) to insert a new bulleted line. Notice the small numbered box to the left of the bullet. This indicates that the bullet is in the first of two body text placeholders on the current slide.

11. Key **Price specials** and press (Ctrl)+(Enter) to move to the first bullet in the second column.

NOTE: When working in the Outline pane and using a two-column layout, you must use (Ctrl)+(Enter) to move to the second column. Lesson 3 showed you how to use (Ctrl)+(Enter) in the Slide pane to move from one text placeholder to the next. Pressing (Ctrl)+(Enter) does exactly the same thing when you are working in the Outline pane.

12. Key **Holiday events** and press (Enter). Key **Sports events** as the second bullet.

13. Press (Ctrl)+(M) and insert a new slide with the Title and Text layout. Key the title **Readability**. You should have five slides listed in the Outline pane.

FIGURE 4-3
Creating a slide
with the Title and
2-Column Text
layout

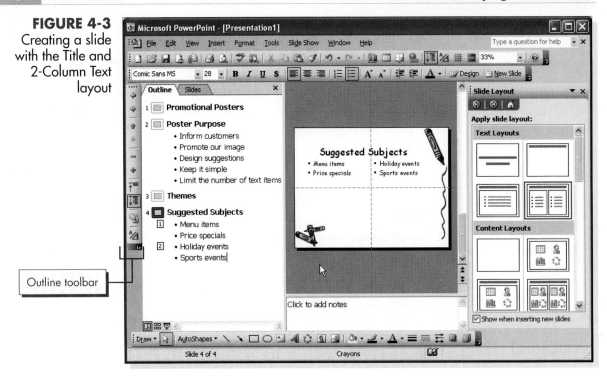

Outline toolbar

14. Press Enter then Tab and add the following bulleted items on slide 5:

- **Use large, simple titles**
- **Use color and graphics**
- **Limit the number of high-contrast colors**

15. Choose View, Header and Footer, Notes and Handouts tab. Remove the check for Date and time. Key your name in the Header box and in the Footer box key *[your initials]*4-2. Click Apply to All.

16. Create a new folder for your Lesson 4 files. Move to slide 1 and save the presentation as *[your initials]*4-2 in a new folder for Lesson 4. Do not close the presentation.

EXERCISE 4-3 Print a PowerPoint Outline

In previous lessons you printed either slides or handouts. Using the Print dialog box or the Print Preview window, you can also print a PowerPoint outline.

1. Open the File menu and choose Print.

2. In the Print what list box, choose Outline View.

3. Click Preview. The outline is displayed. Notice that the handout headers and footers are printed on outlines as well as on handouts.

4. Print the outline and close the preview window. Keep the presentation open for the next exercise. *CHANGE TO LANDSCAPE IN PRINT PREVIEW*

Rearranging Outline Text

The Outline pane allows you to complete many text editing tasks: you can promote or demote text to change slide level; join or split slides by demoting or promoting text; and delete slides or slide text.

When you work in the Outline pane, it is helpful to display the Outlining toolbar, which provides tools to help organize your text. To display the Outlining toolbar:

- Open the View menu, and choose Toolbars.
- From the submenu, choose Outlining. (You can also right-click a toolbar and choose Outlining.)

If the Outlining toolbar appears by itself as a floating toolbar, then drag it to the left side of your application window so that it will dock vertically on the left side of your Outline pane as shown in Figure 4-3.

EXERCISE   **4-4**   **Promote and Demote Text to Change Slide Level**

To promote or demote a bulleted item in the Outline pane, you may use one of the methods previously covered in the text, or the Outline pane allows you to use two new methods to promote or demote:

- Click the Promote button or the Demote button on the Outlining toolbar.
- Select an item and drag it to the right to demote it or to the left to promote it.

To demote or promote by dragging, point to a bullet, and when you see the four-pointed arrow ⊕ drag the bullet left or right. As you're dragging, a two-pointed horizontal arrow ↔ should appear, indicating that you can move left or right.

If you drag a selection up or down instead of left or right, the four-pointed arrow ⊕ changes to a two-pointed vertical arrow ↕, indicating that you might be changing the order of the lines or dragging the material to a different slide. If this happens unintentionally, release your mouse button, click Undo ↺, and start again.

1. On the Outline pane in slide 1, place the insertion point at the end of the text and press Enter. Click the Demote button on the Outlining toolbar (or press Tab) to move to the subtitle placeholder.

2. Key **Good 4 U Public Relations Training** as the subtitle text.

3. Working on slide 2 in the Outline pane, position the insertion point anywhere in the line "Design suggestions."

4. Click the Demote button [→] on the Outlining toolbar (or press [Tab]). The bullet becomes a sub-bullet of the line above it.

NOTE: In Outline view, you can click anywhere in a text item or select the item before demoting or promoting with [Tab] or [Shift]+[Tab]. When you're working in the Slide pane, be sure your insertion point is at the beginning of the text item. If the insertion point is placed inside the text, pressing [Tab] or [Shift]+[Tab] inserts a tab space within the text.

5. Click the Promote button [←] to restore the original position.

6. Select the last two bulleted items on slide 2 by dragging the I-beam across the text.

7. Demote the selected bulleted items by using any method. In outline terminology, slide 2 now has three levels: the title "Poster Purpose" is at level 1, "Inform customers" is at level 2, and "Keep it simple" is at level 3.

8. Position the pointer over the bullet to the left of "Design suggestions." Notice that the pointer changes to a four-pointed arrow [✛].

9. Click the "Design suggestions" bullet. Notice that this bullet and its sub-bullets are selected.

10. Click the Demote button [→] twice. The selected items are demoted two more levels.

11. Click the Promote button [←] twice to restore to the previous position.

12. Move the arrow pointer over the slide icon for "Poster Purpose" until it becomes a four-pointed arrow [✛].

FIGURE 4-4
Demoting by
dragging

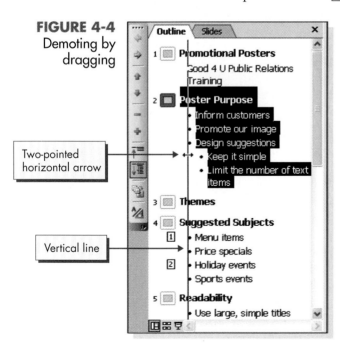

Two-pointed
horizontal arrow

Vertical line

13. Click the slide icon. The slide title for slide 2 and its bulleted items are selected.

14. Drag the icon to the right. The pointer becomes a two-pointed arrow [↔], and a vertical line appears.

15. Drag until the vertical line aligns with the bullets and then release. The material is all demoted to the subtitle of the title slide.

16. Click Undo.

17. Position the pointer over the "Design suggestions" bullet, drag the selected material to the right, and release. The items are demoted a level.

18. Drag the selected material back to the left until the vertical line aligns with the edge of the other bullets, and release. The material is promoted back one level.

TABLE 4-1   **Outlining Toolbar Buttons**

BUTTON		PURPOSE
⬅	Promote	Raises item one outline level
➡	Demote	Lowers item one outline level
⬆	Move Up	Moves selection up one line
⬇	Move Down	Moves selection down one line
➖	Collapse	Displays only titles for selected slides
➕	Expand	Displays details for selected slides
⬆☰	Collapse All	Displays only titles for entire outline
⬇☰	Expand All	Displays detail lines for entire outline
▦	Summary Slide	Creates a new slide from titles of selected slides
ᴬ⁄A	Show Formatting	Turns display of character formatting on and off

 NOTE: At the end of this lesson, the Command Summary lists keyboard shortcuts for Outlining toolbar buttons.

EXERCISE   **4-5**   **Split and Join Slides**

If you have too many bulleted items on one slide, you can divide the items into two slides by promoting a selected item to level 1 (the slide title level). The promoted item becomes the title of a new slide.

You can also join two slides by demoting the title of a slide. The demoted title and its body text are then added to the bottom of the previous slide. If you click the bullet for an item, the bulleted line and its sub-bullets below it are selected and can be promoted or demoted all at the same time.

1. Use the vertical scroll bar on the right side of the Outline pane to display slides 4 and 5.

2. Position the pointer over the slide 5 icon. Notice that the pointer changes to a four-pointed arrow ⊕.

3. Click the slide 5 icon. The entire slide and all its bullets are selected.

4. Click the Demote button ➡. All of the slide's text is added to the end of slide 4—slide 5 has been joined with slide 4. In the Slide pane, notice that the text is at the bottom of the right column.

5. Click the Promote button ⬅. The selected text becomes slide 5 again.

6. Scroll up in the Outline pane so that slide 2 is displayed.

7. On slide 2, click the bullet to the left of "Design suggestions" to select the bullet and the sub-bullets under it.

8. Click the Promote button ⬅. The selected text becomes slide 3 with the title "Design Suggestions" and two bulleted items, "Keep it simple" and "Limit the number of text items."

FIGURE 4-5
Joining and splitting slides

9. Capitalize the word "suggestions" in the slide 3 title to make it consistent with other slide titles.

10. Compare the outline text in your presentation with Figure 4-5. If necessary, promote and demote items to match the figure.

11. Move to slide 1 and save the presentation as *[your initials]*4-5 in your Lesson 4 folder. Do not close the presentation.

EXERCISE 4-6 **Delete Slides and Slide Text**

To delete a slide or a bulleted item, you simply click the slide icon or bullet to select it and press Delete. In the Outline pane, you can select multiple contiguous items by using the (Shift)+click method or dragging the insertion point, but you cannot select noncontiguous items.

1. Point to the bullet in the last line of the outline, "Limit the number of high-contrast colors."

2. Click the bullet to select the line and then press (Delete).

3. Assume that this was a mistake and click the Undo button 🔄 to restore the text.

4. Click the slide icon for slide 4 ("Themes") and press (Delete). The slide is deleted, and the remaining slides are renumbered.

Moving Text and Slides in the Outline Pane

In the Outline pane, you can move selected bulleted items or entire slides in several different ways:

- Click the Move Up button 🔼 or the Move Down button 🔽 on the Outlining toolbar.
- Drag selected bullets up or down.
- Use Cut and Paste.

If you click the Move Up button 🔼 or the Move Down button 🔽 without first selecting an item, only the item that contains the insertion point is moved.

If you want to move entire slides to a new position, first click the Collapse All button 🔼 to *collapse* the outline. When an outline is collapsed, only the slide icons and the slide titles are displayed. This makes it easier to move an entire slide without accidentally dropping the slide in the middle of another slide. When you want to see the details of the outline, click the Expand All button 🔽 to *expand* the outline again.

EXERCISE 4-7 **Move Bulleted Items**

1. On slide 5, select the "Use color and graphics" text item by clicking its bullet.

2. Click the Move Up button 🔼 on the Outlining toolbar. The selected bulleted item moves up one line.

3. Click the Move Up button 🔼 several more times until "Use color and graphics" is the last bulleted item on the "Design Suggestions" slide.

4. Select the second bulleted item on the "Design Suggestions" slide ("Limit the number of text items").

5. Click the Move Down button 🔽 several times until the selected bulleted item is the first bulleted item in slide 5 ("Readability").

6. Point to the last bulleted item on slide 5 ("Limit the number of high-contrast colors").

7. When you see the four-pointed arrow ⊕, click the bullet and drag it up. The pointer becomes a two-pointed vertical arrow ↕, and a horizontal line appears.

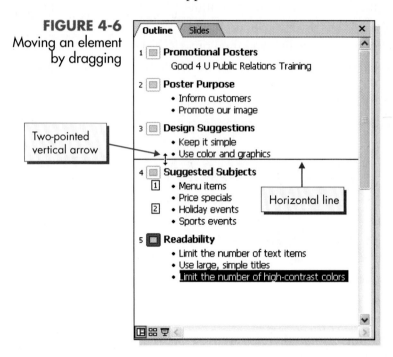

FIGURE 4-6
Moving an element by dragging

Two-pointed vertical arrow

Horizontal line

8. Continue to drag up, positioning the horizontal line under "Use color and graphics" on slide 3, and then release.

9. On slide 4, drag the I-beam pointer over the two bulleted items "Holiday events" and "Sports events." Click the Cut button to cut the text.

10. On the same slide, click to the left of the "M" in "Menu items" to position the insertion point and click the Paste button. All four bulleted items are now in the first column.

NOTE: You can select more than one bullet or slide and drag the selection to a new position. First, drag the I-beam pointer over the text to select it. Next, move the pointer over the selection and use the white drag-and-drop arrow pointer to drag it to a new position. A dotted insertion point guides your placement rather than a horizontal line.

11. Change the layout of slide 4 to the Title and Text layout (one column of bulleted text).

12. On slide 5, move "Use large, simple titles" to the first bullet position on the slide.

EXERCISE 4-8 **Change How the Outline Pane Displays Text**

By default, the Outline pane displays text in an unformatted style. You can change it to display the text formatting that is used on the actual slides if you prefer. You can also control how much text is displayed by collapsing or expanding the outline.

1. Click the Collapse All button 📄 on the Outlining toolbar to display only the slide titles in the Outline pane.
2. Click anywhere on the title text for slide 3 ("Design Suggestions").

3. Click the Expand button ➕. The text for slide 3 is expanded, but the other slides remain collapsed.

4. Click the Collapse button ➖. Now all the slides are collapsed again.
5. Click the Expand All button 📄 to redisplay all the text in the outline.

6. Click the Show Formatting button ⅍ on the Outlining toolbar. The outline text is now displayed with the same text formatting as in the Slide pane.
7. Click the Show Formatting button ⅍ again to turn it off.

EXERCISE 4-9 **Rearrange Slides in the Outline Pane**

When you use the Move Up button 🔼 or the Move Down button 🔽, the selected text moves up or down one line at a time. If you are moving an entire slide, be careful to position the slide between two slides and not in the middle of another slide.

If you collapse an outline before moving slides, all of a slide's text will stay together, and there is no danger of dropping a slide in the middle of another slide.

1. Click the slide 4 icon so that the title text and two bulleted items are selected.
2. Click the Move Up button 🔼 twice. Notice that the last two bullets from slide 4 are now part of slide 5.
3. Click the Move Down button 🔽 twice to restore slide 5 to its original position.

FIGURE 4-7
Using the
Move Up button

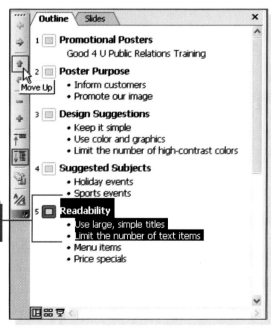

Slide 5 moved to the middle of slide 4.

4. Click the Collapse All button [≡]. Only the slide titles and slide icons are now displayed.

5. With slide 5 ("Readability") still selected, drag it up and position it between slides 3 and 4. When you select (or move) a collapsed slide, you select (or move) all its hidden text.

FIGURE 4-8
Dragging in a
collapsed outline

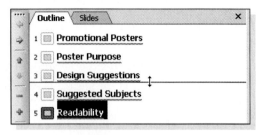

6. Click the Expand All button [≡] to display the entire outline.

7. Revise the Notes and Handouts header and footer: include the date and select Update automatically. Type your name as the header, and the page number and text *[your initials]*4-9 as the footer. Click Apply to All.

8. Move to slide 1 and save the presentation as *[your initials]*4-9 in your Lesson 4 folder. Leave the presentation open for the next exercise.

Importing and Exporting Outlines

You can import an outline created in another application (such as Microsoft Word) into a new presentation or an existing one. To *import* means to use a file in one application that was created in a different application. PowerPoint uses your outline's structural formatting (tab characters, indents, or heading styles) to create slide titles and bulleted items.

You can also export a PowerPoint outline in the standardized *Rich Text Format (RTF)* file type (with the file extension .rtf). To *export* is to save a file in a format that can be read by a different application. The Rich Text Format preserves text formatting in a way that can be read by other Microsoft Office programs as well as numerous programs that are not part of the Microsoft Office suite. Note that the Rich Text Format saves a presentation's text only, and not its graphics.

EXERCISE   **4-10**   **Export a Presentation as a Rich Text Format (RTF) Outline**

To save a presentation as an outline in the Rich Text Format, use the Save As command and choose the file type Outline/RTF.

1. With the presentation *[your initials]*4-9 open and displayed, open the File menu and choose Save As.

2. In the Save As dialog box, navigate to your Lesson 4 folder.

3. In the Save as type list box, choose Outline/RTF.

FIGURE 4-9
Saving a
presentation
as a Rich Text
Format outline

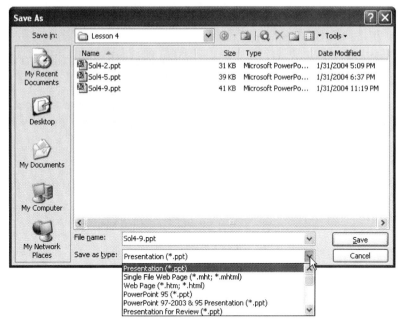

4. In the File name box, key *[your initials]***4-10**. Click Save. The presentation is saved in your Lesson 4 folder as an outline in Rich Text Format.

5. Close *[your initials]***4-9** (but do not close PowerPoint), and start Word.

6. Open the RTF file *[your initials]***4-10** from your Lesson 4 folder. All the text from your PowerPoint presentation appears in the Word window with the text formatting preserved.

NOTE: You can save a presentation as an outline in Word format by choosing File, Send To, Microsoft Office Word. The Send To dialog box lets you choose from many options, one of which is Outline only.

7. Print the outline. Close the document but leave Word open for the next exercise.

EXERCISE 4-11 Create an Outline in Word

To create an outline in Word, key the text in Word's Outline view, using the Promote ⬇ and Demote ➡ buttons on Word's Outlining toolbar in much the same way as you key an outline in PowerPoint's Outline pane.

An alternative way to create the Word outline is to assign heading styles to the outline levels. Use the style Heading 1 for the title, Heading 2 for the first level of bulleted text, and so on.

NOTE: If you will be using a word processor other than Microsoft Word, check with your instructor to be sure that the appropriate text converters have been installed on your computer.

1. Working in the Word window, open the <u>F</u>ile menu and choose <u>N</u>ew. In the new document task pane, choose Blank Document.

2. Click the Outline View button in the lower-left corner of your Word window to switch to Outline view.

 NOTE: Follow your instructor's directions for creating an outline if you're using a different word processing program.

3. Key the material shown in Figure 4-10. To create level 2 and level 3 entries, use the Demote and Promote buttons on Word's Outlining toolbar in the same way you would in the PowerPoint Outline pane. Or use Tab and Shift + Tab.

FIGURE 4-10

```
Poster Ideas
    Good 4 U Public Relations Training ——Level 2
Restaurant Topics
    Menu items
    Contests                        Level 2
    Ingredient profiles
        Exotic ingredients
        Organic ingredients    Level 3
Vendor Profiles
    Local organic farmers
    Herb farms                      Level 2
    Fisheries
Special Event Announcements
    New Health Marathon ——Level 2
        Pasta party
        Awards dinner    Level 3
    July 4th celebration ——Level 2
        In-line skating race
        Bike race               Level 3
```

4. Save the outline as *[your initials]*4-11 in your Lesson 4 folder.

5. Print the outline and close Word.

EXERCISE 4-12 Create PowerPoint Slides from a Word Outline

To create PowerPoint slides from a Word outline, use one of these methods:

- Open the outline file from within PowerPoint.
- Choose Slides from Outline from the Insert menu.
- Open the outline file in Word, choose Send To from the File menu, and then choose Microsoft PowerPoint from the submenu.

1. Working in PowerPoint, click the Open button 📂 on the Standard toolbar to display the Open dialog box.

2. In the Files of type list box, choose All Outlines.

3. Navigate to your Lesson 4 folder and notice that the files in the list box have a Word file icon 📄 near the filename. Choose the Word document *[your initials]*4-11 from the list of files (the outline you created in the previous exercise).

4. Click Open. PowerPoint interprets the structure of your outline and creates new slides, creating titles from the level 1 headings and body text from the level 2 and level 3 headings. All the slides use the Title and Text layout.

5. Change the layout of the new slide 1 ("Poster Ideas") to Title Slide.

REVIEW: To display the Slide Layout task pane, open the Format menu and choose Slide Layout, or click the Other Task Panes button ▼ on the task pane's title bar and then choose Slide Layout from the list box.

6. Apply the design template Layers and use the color scheme with the black background.

7. Display the Outline pane and enlarge it to see all the text. Close the task pane.

8. If necessary, make adjustments to the text in your Outline pane so that it matches Figure 4-11 on the next page.

9. Move to slide 1 and save the presentation as *[your initials]*4-12 in your Lesson 4 folder. Leave the presentation open for the next exercise.

Working with Hyperlinks

Earlier in the lesson you learned how to use a Word outline to create a presentation. Hyperlinks provide another way to get outside information into a presentation.

Hyperlinks are links from a particular place in your presentation to other slides, other PowerPoint presentations, other applications, or to a Web site on the

FIGURE 4-11
Presentation
created from
imported outline

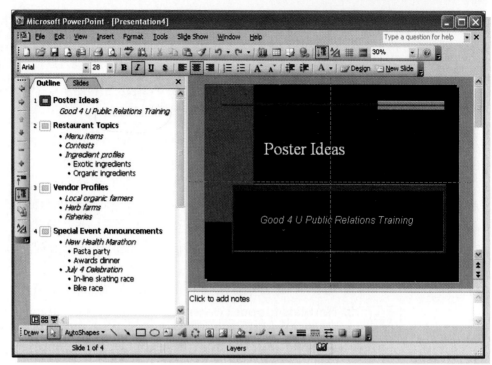

Internet. Hyperlinks can be created from text, Action buttons, or objects. This exercise will focus on text links.

EXERCISE 4-13 Insert a Hyperlink to Another Slide

By default, PowerPoint shows each slide in your presentation in sequential order. Creating hyperlinks to other slides is a convenient way to move to certain slides within your presentation. For instance, if you are discussing five major points, you could create a menu with the text of each major point linked to the first slide in a series that explains each point. Or you might want to quickly move to a supplemental slide related to your current content.

1. Working on *[your initials]*4-12, display slide 4 ("Special Event Announcements") and click after the last bulleted item "Bike race," and press Ctrl+M to insert a new slide.

2. For the title of slide 5 key **Pasta Party** then key the following text as bulleted points below it.

   ● **Choice of spaghetti or fettuccine**

   ● **Choice of iced tea or water**

   ● **Purpose: to give the runners energy to complete the marathon**

3. Save the file as *[your initials]*4-13 in your Lesson 4 folder.

4. Display slide 4 ("Special Event Announcements") and place your I-beam before the second-level bulleted item, "Pasta party," and select the text. Open the Insert menu and choose Hyperlink (or press Ctrl+K). The Insert Hyperlink dialog box opens.

FIGURE 4-12
Inerting a hyperlink to a slide in the same presentation

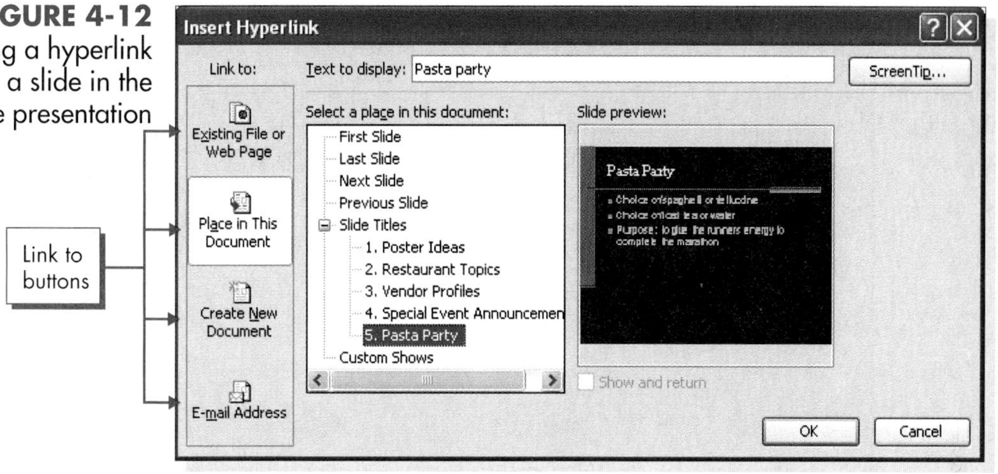

Link to buttons

5. In the Link to box on the left side, choose Place in This Document.

6. In the Select a place in this document box, choose 5. Pasta Party and click OK.

7. From the File menu, choose Save. Since you have already saved it as the correct filename, you can just choose Save to update your file with these recent changes. You will use this file in the next exercise.

EXERCISE   4-14   Insert a Hyperlink to Another Presentation

When you want to create a hyperlink to another file (for example, to another PowerPoint presentation), it is a good idea to first copy or save the file to the same directory as the presentation containing the hyperlink. If you move the presentation to another location, be sure to move the hyperlinked file as well. Otherwise, the hyperlink will no longer work after the move.

There are many ways to insert hyperlinks. As you learned in the previous exercise, you need to select text that relates to the hyperlink; then choose Insert, Hyperlink. You may also click the Hyperlink button or press Ctrl+K to open the Insert Hyperlink dialog box.

1. Open the file **CookCon2**. Without making any changes, save the file in your Lesson 4 folder with the same filename, **CookCon2**.

2. Close **CookCon2**.

3. Working on *[your initials]*4-13, display slide 2 ("Restaurant Topics") and select the second bulleted item, "Contests."

4. Open the Insert menu and choose Hyperlink (or press Ctrl+K). The Insert Hyperlink dialog box opens.

5. In the Link to box on the left side, choose Existing File or Web Page.

FIGURE 4-13
Inserting a hyperlink
to a different
document or
presentation

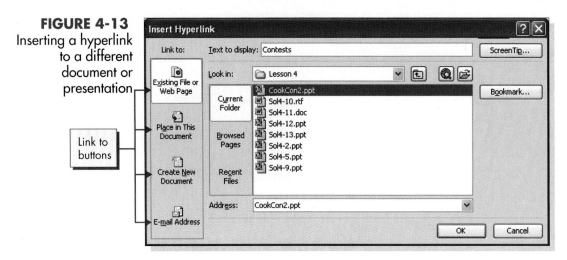

6. In the Look in box, navigate to your Lesson 4 folder.

7. From the list of files, select **CookCon2**. Notice the PowerPoint icon to the left of the filename, indicating that the file is a PowerPoint presentation.

8. Click ScreenTip in the upper-right corner. The Set Hyperlink ScreenTip dialog box opens.

9. In the ScreenTip text box, key **Recipe contest details**. This is the ScreenTip text that will appear when you point to the hyperlink during a slide show.

FIGURE 4-14
Setting the
hyperlink ScreenTip

10. Click OK to close the Set Hyperlink ScreenTip dialog box; then click OK again to close the Insert Hyperlink dialog box.

11. Deselect the text "Contests." The text is now in a contrasting color and underlined, indicating that it is a hyperlink.

12. Save the presentation as *[your initials]*4-14 in your Lesson 4 folder. Leave the presentation open for the next exercise.

EXERCISE 4-15 **Insert a Hyperlink to an Excel Worksheet**

1. Start Excel and open the file **VendExp**.
2. Save the file as **VendExp** in your Lesson 4 folder; then close Excel.
3. Working in PowerPoint, display slide 3 ("Vendor Profiles").
4. Select the title text "Vendor Profiles."
5. Press Ctrl+K to open the Insert Hyperlink dialog box.
6. Under Link to, click Existing File or Web Page.

7. Navigate to your Lesson 4 folder and select **VendExp** from the list of files. Notice the Excel icon to the left of the filename, indicating that this is an Excel file.
8. Click ScreenTip, and then key **Vendor Expenses Chart**. Click OK.
9. Click OK again to close the Insert Hyperlink dialog box.

EXERCISE 4-16 **Insert a Hyperlink to a Web Site**

 NOTE: Internet access is needed to complete this exercise. If you do not have Internet access, you can still do most of the exercise, but you will not be able to test the hyperlink.

1. The computer you are using may be connected to the Internet. If you have access to the Internet, make a connection now.
2. Following your instructor's directions, open your browser and search for a Web site related to organic food. Make a note of the Web address (or copy it to the clipboard) and then close your browser. If this is not possible, use the Web address provided in step 5 below or one provided by your instructor.
3. Working on slide 3, select the text "Local organic farmers" and then press Ctrl+K to open the Insert Hyperlink dialog box.
4. Under Link to, click the Existing File or Web Page icon.
5. In the Address box at the bottom of the dialog box, key the address for the Web site you found in step 2 above (or paste it from the clipboard). For example, key **http://www.mofga.org/**

NOTE: Web addresses often change. The Web address provided might not exist at the time that you do this exercise.

6. Click ScreenTip and key descriptive text appropriate to the Web site you are using. For example: **Maine Organic Farmers Association**
7. Click OK to close the Set Hyperlink ScreenTip dialog box. Click OK again to close the Insert Hyperlink dialog box.

8. Create a handout header and footer: include the date and your name as the header, and the page number and text *[your initials]*4-16 as the footer.

9. Move to slide 1 and open the Save As dialog box. In the Save as type list box, change the file type to Presentation if necessary. Save the presentation as *[your initials]*4-16 in your Lesson 4 folder.

10. View the entire presentation as a slide show and return to Normal view.

11. Preview and then print the presentation as handouts, 4 slides per page, grayscale, landscape, framed. Close the presentation.

12. If you made an Internet connection earlier in this exercise, close the connection.

EXERCISE **4-17** **Using a Hyperlink During a Slide Show**

1. Click the Slide Show button 🖵 to start a slide show on slide 2.

2. In the slide show, point to the hyperlink ("Contests"). The pointer changes to a pointing hand shape 👆. Notice that the ScreenTip displays the text you specified.

FIGURE 4-15
Hyperlink created on a slide

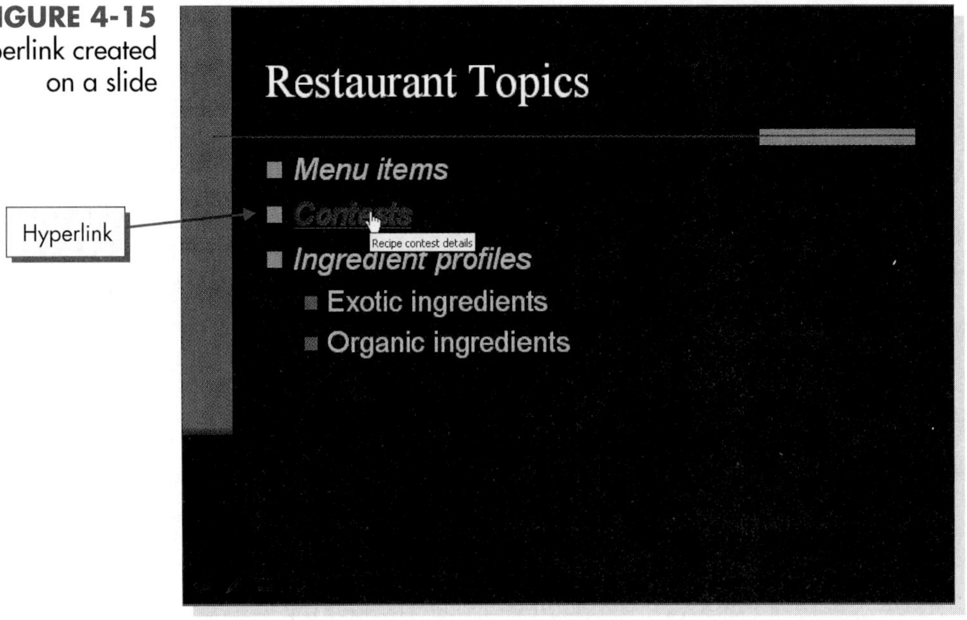

Hyperlink

Restaurant Topics

- Menu items
- Contests
  Recipe contest details
- Ingredient profiles
  - Exotic ingredients
  - Organic ingredients

3. Click the hyperlink. The "Cooking Contest" presentation opens.

4. Advance through the "Cooking Contest" slides, pressing Enter when you get to the end. The display returns to slide 2 of the original presentation. Notice that the hyperlink color changed from red to yellow, indicating that the hyperlink location has been visited.

5. Advance through the presentation and click each hyperlink to test it. When you open the Excel file or the Web site, explore it for a few moments and then close your browser by clicking the Close button ☒ in the upper-right corner. When the slide show is complete, return to PowerPoint's Normal view. If Excel's Web toolbar has appeared, you also have a Back button you can use to return to PowerPoint but then Excel will still be open when you close PowerPoint after your presentation.

Saving a Presentation as a Web Page

Ordinarily you will be displaying a PowerPoint presentation file on a computer that has PowerPoint installed. But you may encounter a situation where the software is not available for the people who need to view your presentation. This exercise focuses on one of the two methods that PowerPoint provides to handle a situation like this. You will learn the other method in a future lesson.

When you save a presentation file by using the *HTML (Hypertext Markup Language)* file format, anyone can open and view it by using a *browser* on their local computer such as Internet Explorer or Netscape Navigator. If you want the file to be accessible over the Internet, then the presentation HTML file must be saved on a file server connected to the Internet.

EXERCISE 4-18 Save in HTML File Format

1. Open the File menu and choose Save as Web Page. The Save As dialog box opens. Notice that in the Save as type list box, you can select Web Page.

2. Using the Save In box, navigate to your Lesson 4 folder.

3. In the File name box, notice that the filename of your presentation is already entered for you. Change the filename to *[your initials]*4-18.

NOTE: PowerPoint creates a folder of supporting files when you save in HTML format. This folder is saved in the same location as the HTML file and is necessary to display the HTML file in a browser. If you move the HTML file to another location, you need to make sure that the supporting file folder moves along with it.

4. Click Save. The file is saved in HTML format. It can now be read by using the browser Microsoft Internet Explorer 4.0 or a later version.

5. To preview the presentation in your Web browser, open the File menu and choose Web Page Preview. (You might have to expand the menu to locate this command.) The presentation appears in your browser window.

6. Close the browser window by clicking the window's Close button ☒.

USING ONLINE HELP

When using PowerPoint, there might be times when the actions you take do not create the results you expected. Help is available to guide you through the process of troubleshooting actions in the Outline pane.

Use Help for information about troubleshooting the Outline pane:

1. Click the Microsoft Office PowerPoint Help button on the Standard toolbar.

2. If the Office Assistant appears, turn it off permanently: click Options, clear the Use the Office Assistant check box, and click OK.

3. Click the Microsoft Office PowerPoint Help button again. In the Help task pane Assistance section Search for: text box, key **troubleshoot outlines** and click the Start Searching button.

4. In the list of topics, click Troubleshoot working on the Outline tab.

5. Click Show All in the upper-right corner of the Help window to expand the Help topics. Click Hide All to show only the help topics.

FIGURE 4-16
Help window about the Outline pane

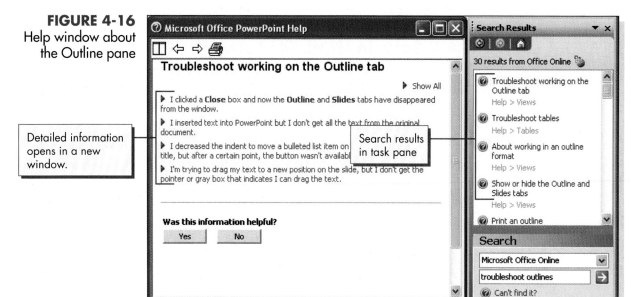

6. Review the information in the Help window. Select another entry from the list of topics if you want.

7. Close the Help window when you finish.

8. Close the presentation.

LESSON 4 Summary

➤ Use the Outline pane to help you organize and create a presentation by focusing on the content and flow rather than the appearance.

➤ Use Zoom to enlarge text for easy viewing without affecting its actual size.

➤ Widen the Outline pane to make a larger work area by dragging its border.

➤ Add new slides and work with slide layouts in the Outline pane by using the same commands as when working in the Slide pane or with slide thumbnails.

➤ When working in the Outline pane on a new slide with the Title and 2-Column Text layout, press [Ctrl]+[Enter] to move to the second column placeholder.

➤ An alternative to using the Promote 🔽 and Demote ▶️ buttons or keyboard shortcuts for changing outline text levels is to drag a bullet to the left or right.

➤ Use the Outline pane to join two consecutive slides into one by demoting the title of the second slide. Split a slide into two by promoting one of the slide's bullets to the title level.

➤ Delete selected slides or text in the Outline pane by pressing [Delete].

➤ Move selected slides or selected bullets up or down in the outline by using the Move Up 🔼 and Move Down 🔽 buttons or by dragging the selection up or down.

➤ Collapse the outline before moving a slide to avoid dropping it in the middle of another slide.

➤ To move more than one slide or more than one bullet at a time, use the drag-and-drop pointer 🖑, or cut and paste. Select multiple items by using the I-beam instead of the four-pointed arrow 🔶.

➤ The Outline pane can display either plain text or text formatted in the same way as it appears on a slide. Turn formatting on and off by using the Show Formatting button 🅰️.

➤ PowerPoint outlines can be saved (exported) in the Rich Text Format (RTF) for use with word processing and other programs. Rich text file format preserves text formatting but does not save any associated graphics.

➤ Outlines made in a word processing program can be inserted (imported) into a PowerPoint presentation.

➤ Creating an outline in Word is very similar to creating an outline in PowerPoint.

➤ Hyperlinks enable you to jump to supplemental material during a slide show presentation. Hyperlinks can link to other slides in your slide shows, other presentations, documents created in other programs, and Web sites on the Internet.

➤ To use a hyperlink, start a slide show and then click the hyperlinked text. You can distinguish hyperlinked text by its contrasting color and its underline.

➤ Save the files you plan to use as hyperlinks in the same directory as your presentation before creating the link. If you move your presentation to another location, be sure to move the linked files as well. Any changes in the file locations will cause the link to not work.

➤ PowerPoint presentations can be saved in Hypertext Markup Language (HTML) format. Using this format, the file can be opened as a Web page in a browser or viewed over the Internet when the file is placed on an accessible file server.

LESSON 4 Command Summary

FEATURE	BUTTON	MENU	KEYBOARD
Display Outline pane		Outline tab, View, Normal, click Outline tab	
Print outline		File, Print, Print what, Outline View	
Promote	or		Shift + Tab or Alt + Shift + Left Arrow
Demote	or		Tab or Alt + Shift + Right Arrow
Collapse All			Alt + Shift + 1
Expand All			Alt + Shift + 1
Expand			
Collapse			
Move Up			Alt + Shift + Up Arrow
Move Down			Alt + Shift + Down Arrow
Show Formatting			
Save as outline		File, Save As, Save as type, Outline/RTF	
Insert outline		Insert, Slides from Outline	
Create hyperlink		Insert, Hyperlink	Ctrl + K

Concepts Review

TRUE/FALSE QUESTIONS

Each of the following statements is either true or false. Indicate your choice by circling T or F.

T (F)   **1.** To display the Outline pane, you can choose Outline from the Insert menu.

T (F)   **2.** You can display slide thumbnails and the Outline pane at the same time.

(T) F   **3.** You can use Ctrl+Enter both to activate the next slide placeholder and to insert a new slide.

T (F)   **4.** The Demote button ➡ on the Outlining toolbar has the same effect as the Decrease Indent button 📑 on the Formatting toolbar.

(T) F   **5.** You can drag and drop bulleted items from one slide to another.

(T) F   **6.** You can use the Move Up button ⬆ on the Outlining toolbar to change the positions of slides in your outline.

T (F)   **7.** After you create a slide, you cannot split it into two slides.

T (F)   **8.** You can insert a hyperlink on a slide by pressing Ctrl+M.

SHORT ANSWER QUESTIONS

Write the correct answer in the space provided.

1. Which key do you press to insert another bullet at the same level?

ENTER

2. Which toolbar contains the Demote and Promote buttons?

OUTLINING TOOLBAR

3. What happens when you demote the title of slide 3 in a presentation?

BECOMES A BULLET ON SLIDE

4. If a slide has five bullets (and no sub-bullets), what happens when you promote the third bullet?

TITLE FOR NEW SLIDE

2 BULLETS BELOW

5. A slide has several bullets. If you select the title with the four-pointed arrow in Outline view and press [Tab], what happens?

SLIDE AND BULLETS ARE

DEMOTED AND BECOME PART OF previous
                                                          SLIDE

6. How can you turn character formatting on and off in Outline view?

OUTLINE TOOL BAR

7. What happens to hyperlink text after you click it during a slide show?

CHANGING COLOR

8. On what menu do you find a command for saving a presentation as a Web page?

FILE

CRITICAL THINKING

Answer these questions on a separate page. There are no right or wrong answers. Support your answers with examples from your own experience, if possible.

1. Do you prefer creating slides in the Slide pane or in the Outline pane? Why?

2. When would you want to create your outline in PowerPoint? In Word? What are some advantages of developing an outline in Word?

Skills Review

EXERCISE 4-19

Work with the Outline pane, add slides, and demote outline entries.

1. Start a new presentation using the Pixel design template. Choose the bright blue background with light blue and teal accent colors (on the second row of the color scheme samples).

2. Display and expand the Outline pane by following these steps:
   a. Click the Normal View button.
   b. Click the Outline tab.
   c. Drag the right border of the Outline pane to the right to increase the width of the pane.
   d. Click anywhere in the Outline pane to make it the active pane.
   e. Click the down arrow next to the Zoom box and select a zoom setting that enables you to comfortably read outline text.

3. Display the Outlining toolbar by following these steps:
   a. Right-click any existing toolbar.
   b. On the shortcut menu, locate Outlining.
   c. If Outlining is not checked, click it. If Outlining is already checked, press Esc to close the shortcut menu.

4. Enter a slide title and subtitle in the Outline pane by following these steps:
   a. Position the insertion point to the right of the slide 1 icon.
   b. Key **Advertising Campaign** as the slide title and press Enter.
   c. Press Tab and then key **Good 4 U Restaurant**

5. Add a new slide by following these steps:
   a. Press Ctrl+M.
   b. Key **Types of Media**
   c. Press Ctrl+Enter.
   d. Key the following bulleted items, pressing Enter to start each new line:
   - **Print**
   - **Newspapers**
   - **Magazines**
   - **Broadcast**
   - **Radio**
   - **Television**

6. Add the two new slides shown in Figure 4-17.

FIGURE 4-17

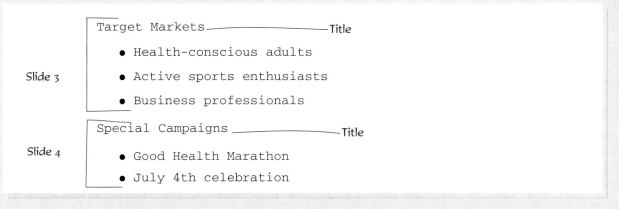

7. On slide 2, demote the bullets "Newspapers" and "Magazines" to sub-bullets under "Print" by following these steps:

   a. Position the insertion point anywhere in the "Newspapers" bulleted item.
   b. Click the Demote button on the Outlining toolbar.
   c. Position the insertion point anywhere in the "Magazines" bulleted item and press Tab.

8. Using the I-beam, select the bulleted text "Radio" and "Television." Click the Increase Indent button on the Formatting toolbar to demote the text as sub-bullets under "Broadcast."

9. Check spelling in the presentation.

10. View the presentation as a slide show.

11. Create a handout header and footer: include the date and your name as the header, and the page number and text *[your initials]*4-19 as the footer.

12. Move to slide 1 and save the presentation as *[your initials]*4-19 in your Lesson 4 folder.

13. Preview and then print the presentation as handouts, 4 slides per page, grayscale, landscape, framed. Close the presentation.

EXERCISE 4-20

Adjust the size of outline text using zoom, add slides, promote and demote bulleted items, and join slides.

1. Open the file **AdMedia1**. Change the design template to Fading Grid and choose the color scheme with the dark red background.

2. Display the Outline pane. Adjust the size and zoom setting of the pane so that you can comfortably read the outline text.

FIGURE 4-18

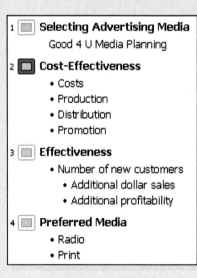

3. Using the Outline pane, key three new slides as shown in Figure 4-18. (This figure displays formatting.)

4. Join slides 2 and 3 by following these steps:
   a. Position the insertion point in the slide 3 title. (Do not select the slide.)
   b. Press Tab (or click the Demote button).

5. Promote the last two bullets in slide 3 by following these steps:
   a. Point to the bullet for "Additional dollar sales."

b. When you see the four-pointed arrow , drag the bullet to the left until the vertical line aligns with the previous bullet, and then release.

c. Repeat steps a and b for the last bullet on the slide ("Additional profitability").

6. Demote the last three bullets on slide 2 by following these steps:

a. Position the insertion point anywhere within "Number of new customers."

b. Drag the I-beam pointer down and across until the three lines are selected.

c. Press Tab.

7. Demote by one level each of the three bullets "Production," "Distribution," and "Promotion" by using any method.

8. Change the layout for slide 2 ("Cost-Effectiveness") by following these steps:

a. Move your insertion point anywhere in slide 2.

b. Display the Slide Layout task pane.

c. In the task pane, select the Title and 2-Column Text layout.

d. Press Ctrl+Enter to display a column 2 icon in the Outline pane.

e. Select the bullet "Effectiveness" and its sub-bullets; then click the Cut button.

f. Position the insertion point on the blank bulleted line beside the column 2 icon, and click the Paste button.

g. If a blank bullet appears at the end of the slide, delete it.

9. Check spelling in the presentation.

10. Create a handout header and footer: include the date and your name as the header, and the page number and text *[your initials]*4-20 as the footer.

11. Move to slide 1 and save the presentation as *[your initials]*4-20 in your Lesson 4 folder.

12. View the presentation as a slide show.

13. Preview and print the presentation's outline by following these steps:

a. From the File menu, choose Print Preview.

b. From the Print what list box, choose Outline View.

c. Click Print and then click OK.

14. Print the presentation as handouts, 3 slides per page, grayscale, landscape, framed. Close the Preview window and close the presentation.

EXERCISE 4-21

Promote and demote text, create an outline in Word and import it into PowerPoint; export a PowerPoint outline to Word.

1. Create an outline in Microsoft Word by following these steps:

a. Start Word and switch to Outline view.

b. Key the text shown in Figure 4-19, using the Demote and Promote buttons on Word's Outlining toolbar to create level 2 and level 3 entries in the same way you demote and promote text in PowerPoint.

FIGURE 4-19

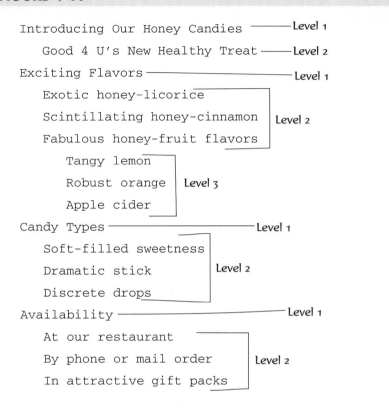

```
Introducing Our Honey Candies ——— Level 1
    Good 4 U's New Healthy Treat ——— Level 2
Exciting Flavors ——————————————— Level 1
    Exotic honey-licorice
    Scintillating honey-cinnamon    Level 2
    Fabulous honey-fruit flavors
        Tangy lemon
        Robust orange    Level 3
        Apple cider
Candy Types ——————————————— Level 1
    Soft-filled sweetness
    Dramatic stick    Level 2
    Discrete drops
Availability ——————————————— Level 1
    At our restaurant
    By phone or mail order    Level 2
    In attractive gift packs
```

c. Save the Word outline as *[your initials]*4-21a in your Lesson 4 folder.

d. Print the outline, close the document, and close Word.

2. Create a PowerPoint presentation from the Word outline by following these steps:

a. Start PowerPoint.

b. Click the Open button on the Standard toolbar.

c. In the Open dialog box, navigate to your Lesson 4 folder.

d. In the Files of type list box, choose All Outlines.

e. In the list of files, choose *[your initials]*4-21a. Click Open.

3. Change the first slide to the Title Slide layout. Check that your presentation has a total of four slides.

4. Apply the design template Textured and use the color scheme with the dark green background.

5. Check spelling in the presentation.

6. Create a handout header and footer: include the date and your name as the header, and the page number and text *[your initials]*4-21b as the footer.

7. Move to slide 1 and save the presentation as *[your initials]*4-21b in your Lesson 4 folder.

8. Preview and then print the presentation as an outline and as handouts, 4 slides per page, grayscale, framed. Do not close the presentation.

9. Save the presentation as a Rich Text Format (RTF) file by following these steps:

   a. From the File menu, choose Save As.
   b. Navigate to your Lesson 4 folder.
   c. In the Save as type list box, choose Outline/RTF.
   d. In the File name box, key *[your initials]*4-21c. Click Save.
   e. Close the PowerPoint presentation.

10. Start Word; then open the file *[your initials]*4-21c from your Lesson 4 folder.

11. Print the Word document; then close Word.

EXERCISE 4-22

Move bullets and slides in the Outline pane, create hyperlinks, and save the presentation as a Web page.

1. Open the file **AdMedia2**. Apply the design template Competition and use the color scheme with the blue background.

2. Display the Outline pane, adjusting it so you can read the outline text.

3. Move the "Newspapers" bullet from slide 3 to the end of slide 5 by following these steps:

   a. Position the insertion point in the text or click the bullet for "Newspapers."

   b. Click the Move Down button ![down arrow] (or press Alt+Shift+↓) several times until the bullet is positioned below "Magazines" on slide 5.

4. Move the "Electronic" bullet from slide 4 to the end of slide 3 (below "Print").

5. Drag the "Fliers" bullet on slide 5 to a new position on the slide by following these steps:

   a. Position the pointer over the "Fliers" bullet until the four-pointed arrow ⊕ appears.
   b. Drag the bullet up, making sure you see a two-pointed vertical arrow ↕ and a horizontal line.
   c. Position the horizontal line just under the slide 5 title, "Print Media," and then release.

6. Select the "Evaluate costs" bullet and its sub-bullets on slide 2 and move them above the "Evaluate effectiveness" bullet on the same slide.

7. Click the Collapse All button (or press Alt+Shift+1) to display only slide titles.

8. Move slide 4 ("Electronic Media") after slide 5.

9. Move slide 2 ("Return on Investment") to the slide 5 position (between "Electronic Media" and "Marketing Training: Next Steps").

10. Create a hyperlink to another presentation by following these steps:

    a. Open the presentations **Market3** and **Market4** from the drive and folder where your student files are stored.

    b. Without making any changes, save the files with the same names in your Lesson 4 folder. Close **Market3** and **Market4**.

    c. Select slide 6 ("Marketing Training: Next Steps") and then click the Expand button.

    d. Select the bullet "Marketing Strategy" and then choose Hyperlink from the Insert menu (or press Ctrl+K).

    e. Under Link to, choose Existing File or Web Page.

    f. Navigate to your Lesson 4 folder; then select the presentation **Market3**.

    g. Enter an appropriate screen tip. Click OK.

    h. Using the steps outlined above, select the second bullet on slide 6 ("Marketing Our Business") and create a hyperlink to the presentation **Market4**.

11. Check spelling in the presentation.

12. Create a handout header and footer: include the date and your name as the header, and the page number and text *[your initials]*4-22a as the footer.

13. Move to slide 1 and save the presentation as *[your initials]*4-22a in your Lesson 4 folder.

14. View the presentation as a slide show. When you come to slide 6, click each of the hyperlinks to jump to the linked presentations.

15. Preview and then print the presentation as handouts, 6 slides per page, grayscale, framed. Do not close the presentation.

16. Save the presentation in your Lesson 4 folder as a Web page by following these steps:

    a. From the File menu, choose Save as Web Page.

    b. In the File name box, key *[your initials]*4-22b

    c. Save as type, choose Web Page.

    d. Click Save.

17. Close the presentation.

Lesson Applications

Work with the Outline pane, add slides, promote and demote text, and move bullets and slides.

1. Start a new presentation.
2. In the Outline pane, create the two slides shown in Figure 4-20.

FIGURE 4-20

1. Marketing Our Restaurant
   Good 4 U Employee Training
2. Our Products
   - Food services
     - In-restaurant meals
     - Take-out meals
     - Delivered meals and catering
     - In-restaurant parties and meetings
   - Merchandise
     - Caps
     - T-shirts
     - Honeys and confections

3. Make the following changes in the Outline pane:
   - Make "Food services" and its sub-bullets a separate slide. (Remember to change the new slide's title to title case.)
   - Make "Merchandise" and its sub-bullets a separate slide.
   - Add the following bullets to the "Our Products" slide:
     - **Merchandise**
     - **Food services**
4. Change the order of bullets on the "Merchandise" slide to the following:
   Honeys and confections
   T-shirts
   Caps
5. Collapse the outline and move the "Merchandise" slide before the "Food Services" slide.
6. Expand the outline.
7. Apply the Network design template and use the color scheme with the purple background.
8. Check spelling in the presentation.

9. Create a handout header and footer: include the date and your name as the header, and the page number and text *[your initials]*4-23 as the footer.

10. Move to slide 1 and save the presentation as *[your initials]*4-23 in your Lesson 4 folder.

11. Preview and then print the presentation as handouts, 4 slides per page, grayscale, landscape, framed. Close the presentation.

EXERCISE 4-24

Promote outline items and move bullets in the Outline pane; save a presentation as a Web page.

1. Open the file **Market4** and display the Outline pane.

2. Select and delete slide 2 ("Elements of Marketing").

3. Revise the bullets in the new slide 2 ("Marketing Is About People"), as shown in Figure 4-21.

FIGURE 4-21

```
2 [  ]  Marketing Is About People
          • Respect
              • Co-workers
              • Customers
              • Yourself
          • Expect the best from
              • Co-workers
              • Customers
              • Yourself
```

4. Promote each of the bulleted items on slide 3 ("What Are We Marketing?") to three new slides. Delete the slide "What Are We Marketing?" Correct the capitalization on the new slide titles, and then insert bulleted text on slides 3 and 4 as shown in Figure 4-22.

FIGURE 4-22

```
          Our Food

              • Eat in
Slide 3       • Take out
              • Delivered and catered

          Our Merchandise

Slide 4       • Food products
              • Apparel and accessories
```

5. Move the three bulleted items in slide 6 ("Marketing Our Staff") and position them in slide 5 ("Our Service").

6. Delete slide 6.

7. View the presentation in the Slide pane and correct the capitalization of titles where necessary.

8. Change the layout of slide 2 to Title and 2-Column Text, moving the second bullet and its sub-bullets to the right column.

9. Check spelling in the presentation.

10. Create a handout header and footer: include the date and your name as the header, and the page number and text *[your initials]*4-24 as the footer.

11. Move to slide 1 and save the presentation as a Web page in your Lesson 4 folder. Use the filename *[your initials]*4-24.

12. Use the Web Page Preview command on the File menu to view the presentation.

13. Preview and then print the presentation as handouts, 6 slides per page, grayscale, framed. Close the presentation.

EXERCISE 4-25

Promote, demote, and move bulleted items in the Outline pane; move slides; and insert a hyperlink to a Word document.

1. Open the file **HonProd1**.

2. Display the Outline pane and adjust it so that you can easily read the text. Try clicking the Show Formatting button to see if you like the text formatting on or off.

3. Working in the Outline pane, promote, demote, and move bullets and slides as shown in Figure 4-23. Correct the case of title slides as necessary.

FIGURE 4-23

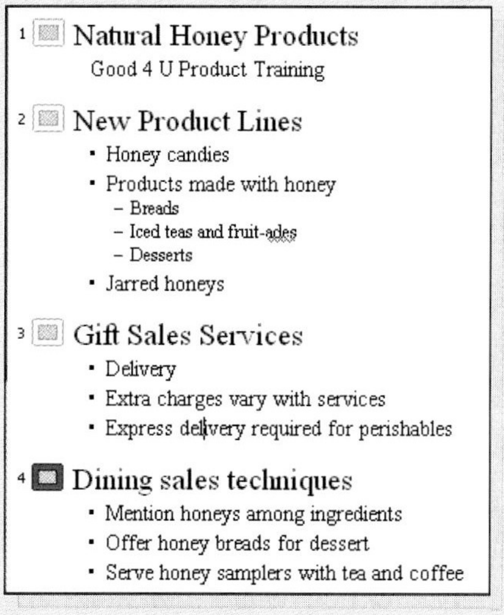

1. Natural Honey Products
   Good 4 U Product Training

2. New Product Lines
   - Honey candies
   - Products made with honey
     - Breads
     - Iced teas and fruit-ades
     - Desserts
   - Jarred honeys

3. Gift Sales Services
   - Delivery
   - Extra charges vary with services
   - Express delivery required for perishables

4. Dining sales techniques
   - Mention honeys among ingredients
   - Offer honey breads for dessert
   - Serve honey samplers with tea and coffee

4. On slide 3, move and add text as shown in Figure 4-24:

FIGURE 4-24

```
Gift Sales Services ——————Title
    • Gift-wrapping
    • Protective packaging
                               Level 2
    • Gift certificates
    • Delivery
      -Extra charges vary with services
                                          Level 3
      -Express delivery required for perishables
```

5. Apply the Kimono design template.

6. Open the Word document **Foods1** and save it with the same name in your Lesson 4 folder. Close Word.

SAVE TO BACK·UP

7. On slide 2, create a hyperlink that will display the Word file **Foods1** when you click the text "Products made with honey." Give it the ScreenTip **Foods and Beverages Made with Honey**

8. Check spelling in the presentation. (Leave the spelling of "fruit-ades" unchanged.)

9. Create a handout header and footer: include the date and your name as the header, and the page number and text *[your initials]***4-25** as the footer.

10. Move to slide 1 and save the presentation as *[your initials]***4-25** in your Lesson 4 folder.

11. View the presentation as a slide show and click the hyperlink on slide 2.

12. Preview and then print the presentation as handouts, 4 slides per page, grayscale, framed. Close the presentation.

EXERCISE 4-26 *Challenge Yourself*

Move bullets and slides, insert an outline from a word processing program into a presentation, and export an outline to Word.

1. Create a new presentation by opening the outline file **Foods2** in PowerPoint and put your insertion point below slide 3.

2. Choose Insert, Slides from Files, then use the Slide Finder dialog box to insert all the slides from the presentation **HonProd2** at the end of the presentation.

3. Working in the Outline pane, collapse the outline and then rearrange the slides so that they are in the order shown in Figure 4-25.

FIGURE 4-25

1. Natural Honey Products
2. New Product Lines
3. Honey Beverages
4. Breads and Desserts with Honey
5. Jarred Honeys
6. Dining Sales Techniques

4. Add a new slide after slide 5 with the title **Good 4 U Honey Promotion** and the following bullets:
   - **Honey-tasting contest**
   - **Bread and honey samples at take-out counter**
   - **Complimentary honey candies after meals**

5. Change the slide 3 layout ("Honey Beverages") to Title and 2-Column Text, moving the second main bullet ("Fruit-ades") and its sub-bullets to the second column placeholder. Delete any blank lines in the Outline pane.

6. On slide 7, move "Offer honey breads for dessert" so that it is the last bullet on the slide.

7. Open **HonProd1** and copy the text from slide 3 ("Gift Sales Services") then close **HonProd1**. Paste this text below slide 7.

8. Apply the design template Quadrant and use the color scheme with the black background.

NOTE: If an Internet connection is not available, follow your instructor's directions on how to execute steps 9 and 10 below.

9. If you have a connection to the Internet, search for a Web site that relates to honey products and make a note of its Web address.

10. Using the first bullet on slide 2 ("Products made with honey"), create a hyperlink to the Web site you found in step 9.

11. Check spelling in the presentation.

12. Create a handout header and footer: include the date and your name as the header, and the page number and text *[your initials]*4-26 as the footer.

13. Move to slide 1 and save the presentation as *[your initials]*4-26 in your Lesson 4 folder.

14. View the presentation as a slide show. While viewing the show, be sure to click on your hyperlink.

15. Preview and then print the presentation as handouts, 9 slides per page, grayscale, landscape, framed. Close the presentation.

On Your Own

In these exercises you work on your own, as you would in a real-life work environment. Use the skills you've learned to accomplish the task—and be creative.

EXERCISE 4-27
Locate a recipe for a dish that you enjoy. Organize the recipe steps to make it easy to teach someone to make it. Put the steps into an outline with at least four main points suitable for slide titles. Create the outline by using any method that is comfortable for you (index cards, Word, PowerPoint, etc.). From the outline, create a PowerPoint presentation with a title slide. Choose a suitable design template, color scheme, and transition pattern. Save the presentation as *[your initials]*4-27. Preview and then print the presentation as an outline and as handouts.

EXERCISE 4-28
Create instructions describing a process. For example: making lemonade, changing a tire, registering for a course, or completing a task at work. Translate the process into a PowerPoint presentation with a title slide and five slides with step-by-step procedures. Create at least six slides and use a design template, color schemes, and slide transitions of your choice. Save the presentation as *[your initials]*4-28. Preview and then print the presentation as an outline and as handouts.

EXERCISE 4-29

Imagine that you work at a car dealership where the computer system needs to be replaced. Research computer systems online, and give a recommendation on what brand and options would be appropriate. Be sure to include a slide describing the costs and a slide with the benefits of choosing this system. Create a hyperlink to one or more sites where you found the information. Starting in the Outline pane, create a presentation aimed at your boss, recommending this system. Create at least six slides and use a design template, color schemes, and slide transitions of your choice. Save the presentation as *[your initials]*4-29. Preview and then print the presentation as an outline and as handouts.

LESSON 5

Working with Text

OBJECTIVES

MICROSOFT OFFICE SPECIALIST ACTIVITIES

In this lesson:
  PP03S-1-2
  PP03S-2-1
  PP03S-2-3
  PP03S-2-7

See Appendix.

After completing this lesson, you will be able to:

1. Work with fonts.
2. Apply text formatting to placeholders.
3. Change the size and position of text placeholders.
4. Work with bullets.
5. Modify a design template's text placeholders
6. Work with text boxes.

 Estimated Time: 1½ hours

Y ou can add interest to a PowerPoint presentation by varying the appearance of text—that includes changing the font, text style, bullet shape, or position of text. You can change text appearance before or after you key it, or apply changes to the entire text in the presentation at once by applying changes to a master slide. When you make changes, always strive for readability and continuity within your presentation.

Working with Fonts

One way to change the appearance of text in your presentation is by changing the font. A *font* is a set of characters with a specific design. You can change the font face (such as Times New Roman or Arial) and the font size. Fonts are measured in *points* (with 72 points in an inch) indicating how tall a font is.

It is useful to understand that different fonts can take up different amounts of horizontal space, even though they are the same size. For example, a word formatted as 20-point Arial will be wider than a word formatted as 20-point Garamond, as shown in Figure 5-1.

FIGURE 5-1
Comparing fonts

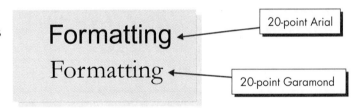

Another way to change the appearance of text is by applying *text attributes*. For example, you can apply a text style (such as bold or italic) and an effect (such as underline or shadow). You use the Formatting toolbar or the Font dialog box to change selected text.

FIGURE 5-2
Expanded
Formatting toolbar

TABLE 5-1   Text Formatting Buttons on the Formatting Toolbar

BUTTON	PURPOSE
Arial ▾ Font	Enables you to choose a font face for selected text or for text to be keyed at the insertion point
42 ▾ Font Size	Enables you to choose a font size for selected text or for text to be keyed at the insertion point
B Bold	Applies the bold attribute to text
I Italic	Applies the italic attribute to text
U Underline	Applies the underline attribute to text
S Shadow	Applies a text shadow
≣ Align Left	Left-aligns text in a text placeholder or text box

continues

TABLE 5-1   Text Formatting Buttons on the Formatting Toolbar   *continued*

BUTTON	PURPOSE
☰ Center	Centers text in a text placeholder or text box
☰ Align Right	Right-aligns text in a text placeholder or text box
Numbering	Turns numbering on or off
Bullets	Turns bullets on or off
A↑ Increase Font Size	Increases the size of selected text by one font size *ALL*
A↓ Decrease Font Size	Decreases the size of selected text by one font size *ALL*
Decrease Indent	Promotes text; removes one indent level, moving text to the left
Increase Indent	Demotes text; adds one indent level, moving text to the right
A Font Color	Changes text color

EXERCISE 5-1   **Change the Font Face and Font Size for Selected Text**

Times New Roman

A convenient way to apply text formatting is to first key the text, focusing on content, and then select the text and apply formatting, such as by changing the size or font. When working with fonts, keep in mind that you should limit the number of different fonts used in a presentation to no more than two or three. Also remember that the font size should be at least 18 points if the presentation is going to be viewed on a computer or projected on a screen.

Another thing to be aware of is the type of font you choose. The Font list box on the Formatting toolbar displays all the fonts available for your computer. On the left side of each font is a symbol indicating the font type. TrueType fonts have the following symbol: 𝕋. Fonts that work specifically with the currently selected printer have the symbol 🖨. If you plan to show your presentation on a different computer or print it with a different printer, it is best to choose a TrueType font.

The Increase Font Size A↑ and Decrease Font Size A↓ buttons change the size of all the text in a selected placeholder by one font size increment as shown in the font size box on the Formatting toolbar. If there are several sizes of text in the placeholder, each size is changed proportionately. For example, if a text placeholder contains both 24-point text and 20-point text, clicking the Increase Font Size button A⁺ will change the sizes to 28 points and 24 points at the same time.

Many of the buttons used to format text and text placeholders are toggle buttons. A *toggle button* switches between on and off when you click it. The Shadow button S is an example of a toggle button: click it once to apply a shadow, once again to remove it. Other examples of toggle buttons are Bold **B**, Italic *I*, and Underline U.

1. Open the file **Health1**.

2. Expand the Formatting toolbar and then locate the toolbar buttons listed in Table 5-1.

NOTE: To expand or shrink a toolbar, place your pointer on the vertical bar at the left end of the toolbar. When you see the four-pointed arrow ⊕, drag to the left to expand the toolbar or to the right to shrink the toolbar (the pointer changes to a two-pointed arrow ↔ as you drag). You can also drag the Formatting toolbar down slightly so it will dock below the Standard toolbar.

3. On slide 1, click the title placeholder to activate it and key **Heart**

4. Select the word you just keyed.

5. Click the down arrow next to the Font box on the Formatting toolbar.

FIGURE 5-3
Font drop-down list

FIGURE 5-4
Font Size
drop-down list

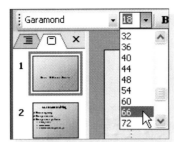

6. From the drop-down list, choose Arial (scroll up near the top of the list). As you can see, text formatting in PowerPoint is similar to text formatting in a word processing program.

7. With "Heart" still selected, click the down arrow next to the Font Size box. Choose 66. The text size increases to 66 points.

8. Click the Decrease Font Size button A⁻. The font size decreases by one size increment. Notice the number "60" displayed in the Font Size box.

9. Click the Increase Font Size button A⁺ twice. The font size increases by two size increments, to 72 points (the equivalent of 1 inch tall).

EXERCISE **5-2** **Apply Bold, Italic, and Text Color**

Sometimes it's convenient to apply text formatting as you key. This is particularly true with bold, italic, and underline if you use the following keyboard shortcuts:

- Ctrl+B for bold
- Ctrl+I for italic
- Ctrl+U for underline

1. Position the insertion point to the right of "Heart" and press Spacebar. Click the Bold button **B** (or press Ctrl+B) and then the Italic button *I* (or press Ctrl+I) to turn these attributes on.

2. Key **Smart!** The word is formatted as bold italic as you key. Notice that this word is also 72-point Arial, like the previous word.

3. Double-click the word "Heart" to select it.

4. Locate the Font Color button **A** on the Formatting toolbar. Click its down arrow to open the Font Color menu.

NOTE: If you click the Font Color button and not its down arrow, the color indicated on the button is automatically applied to the selected text. You use the down arrow to choose a different color.

5. Position your pointer on the gray bar at the top of the Font Color menu. When you see the four-pointed arrow, drag it down and to the left. Many of PowerPoint's submenus can be converted to floating toolbars in this manner. Unlike menus, floating toolbars stay open and available until you close them.

FIGURE 5-5
Font Color menu

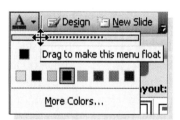

6. Click the bright red box on the Font Color floating toolbar. The selected text appears light blue because the text is still selected. You don't see the color you applied until you deselect the text.

7. Click in the word "Smart" to deselect "Heart." "Heart" is now red.

8. Close the Font Color toolbar by clicking its Close button **X**. Notice that the color bar on the Font Color button is now red. If you click this button instead of the down arrow, selected text will be changed to red.

EXERCISE **5-3** **Use the Font Dialog Box**

The Font dialog box is a convenient place to apply several font attributes all at one time. In addition to choosing a font, font style, and font size, this dialog box enables you to choose various effects, such as underline or shadow, and a font color.

1. Select the words "Diet and Exercise" in the subtitle.

2. Right-click the selected text to display the shortcut menu. Choose Font to open the Font dialog box.

3. Choose the following options in the Font dialog box:

- From the Font list box, choose Arial.
- From the Font style list box, choose Bold Italic.
- From the Size list box, choose 48.
- Under Effects, check Underline.

Notice the additional options available in this dialog box.

FIGURE 5-6
Font dialog box

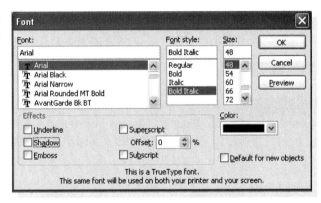

4. Click Preview and drag the Font dialog box to the side so that you can see your choices applied to the selected text.

5. Drag the dialog box back to the center of the screen. Click OK to accept the formatting and close the dialog box.

6. Select the word Heart and click the Underline button 🅤 on the Formatting toolbar to turn on underlining. Click the Underline button again to turn off this attribute.

TIP: Underlining is not the best way to emphasize text. It is not as easy to read as regular text because the line cuts through the bottom of letters (the descenders). And because underlining is used so much for hyperlinks on the Internet, underlining seems to have that connotation. So emphasize your text in different ways, such as by using a larger font size, more dramatic color, or bold.

7. With the word Heart still selected, change the size to 80 points and click the Bold button.

8. Create a handout header and footer: include the date and your name as the header, and the page number and text *[your initials]*5-3 as the footer.

9. Create a slide footer for all slides. Include the date, and in the <u>F</u>ooter text box key your name followed by a comma and your filename *[your initials]*5-3.

10. Create a folder for Lesson 5. Save the presentation as *[your initials]*5-3 in your new folder for Lesson 5.

11. Preview and then print the title slide only, grayscale, framed.

 NOTE: You can change text attributes in the Outline pane in the same way as in the Slide pane.

E X E R C I S E   5-4   Change the Case of Selected Text

If you find that you keyed text in uppercase and want to change it, you don't have to re-key it. By opening the <u>F</u>ormat menu and choosing the Change Case command, you can change any text to <u>S</u>entence case, <u>l</u>owercase, <u>U</u>PPERCASE, <u>T</u>itle Case, or <u>t</u>OGGLE cASE. You can also cycle through uppercase, lowercase, and either title case or sentence case (depending on what is selected) by selecting text and pressing Shift+F3 one or more times.

UPPERCASE, LOWER CASE, TITLE

FIGURE 5-7
Change Case dialog box

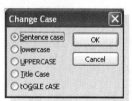

1. Move to slide 3.

2. Use the I-beam pointer to select the title "Walk to good health," which has only the first word capitalized.

3. Press Shift+F3. The case changes to uppercase. Press Shift+F3 again to change the text to lowercase. Press it a third time to change the text to title case.

4. Select the word "To" in the title. Press Shift+F3 one or more times to change it to lowercase.

5. Select the first item in the body text placeholder by clicking its bullet. This text was keyed with Caps Lock accidentally turned on.

6. From the <u>F</u>ormat menu, choose Change Cas<u>e</u>. Choose Toggle Case and click OK. This option reverses the current case, changing uppercase letters to lowercase, and lowercase letters to uppercase.

7. Select the two bullets under "Walking" (beginning with "reduces" and "lowers") by dragging your I-beam across all the words. Open the Change Case dialog box, choose <u>S</u>entence case, and click OK.

E X E R C I S E   5-5   Replace Presentation Fonts

After you finish a presentation, you might decide that a different font would look better. You can change the font for the entire presentation easily and quickly with the <u>R</u>eplace Fonts command.

1. Display slide 1. The slide contains the fonts Arial and Garamond. The rest of the presentation is in Garamond.

2. From the Format menu, choose Replace Fonts to display the Replace Font dialog box.

3. Drag the dialog box to a corner of the slide so that you can see the text.

FIGURE 5-8
Replace Font
dialog box

4. Open the Replace drop-down list and choose Arial. (This list contains the fonts currently used in the presentation.)

5. Open the With drop-down list to display the available fonts. Choose Impact and click Replace. The Arial font used in the title and subtitle is replaced with Impact. The dialog box remains open so that you can replace another font.

6. From the Replace list, choose Garamond and from the With list, choose Arial. Click Replace and then click Close. Notice the change in the last line of the subtitle and on the other slides, which are now in Arial instead of Garamond.

Applying Text Formatting to Placeholders

[handwritten: SELECT IS CHANGING EVERYTHING IN PLACE HOLDER]

[handwritten: ACTIVATE IS PINPOINTING WITH INSERTION pni]

You can change formatting features for an entire placeholder by first selecting the placeholder and then choosing the formatting. For example, you can change the text size, color, or font.

You can select placeholders several ways:

● Click the border of an active placeholder with the four-pointed arrow ⊕.

● Press Esc while a placeholder is active (when the insertion point is in the text).

● Press Tab to select the next placeholder on a slide (only when a text box or text placeholder is not active).

You can deselect placeholders several ways:

● Press Esc to deselect a placeholder or other object. (Press Esc twice if a text placeholder or text box is active.)

● Click an area of the slide where there is no object.

EXERCISE **5-6** **Select a Text Placeholder**

1. On slide 3, click anywhere in the title text to make the placeholder active. Notice that the border is made of tiny diagonal lines and small white circles.

FIGURE 5-9
Selecting a text
placeholder

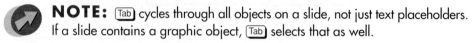

[handwritten: SELECTED]

2. Point to any place on the border between two small circles. When you see the four-pointed arrow , click the border. Notice that the insertion point is no longer active and the border's appearance has changed slightly— it is now made up of small dots instead of diagonal lines. This indicates that the placeholder is selected.

3. Press [Tab]. Now the body text placeholder is selected.

> **NOTE:** [Tab] cycles through all objects on a slide, not just text placeholders. If a slide contains a graphic object, [Tab] selects that as well.

4. Press [Esc] to deselect the body text placeholder. Now nothing on the slide is selected.

5. Still working on slide 3, click inside the title placeholder text and then press [Esc]. This is another way to select an active placeholder.

6. Click the Increase Font Size button [A] on the Formatting toolbar twice. The font size increases to 60 points.

7. Click the Decrease Font Size button [A] two or more times until the font size is 48 points. (The Font box on the Formatting toolbar indicates the size.)

8. Press [Tab] to select the body text placeholder. Notice the 32+ in the Font Size box. This indicates that there is more than one font size in the placeholder, and the smallest size is 32 points.

[handwritten: 32+]

9. Click any text in the first bullet. Notice that its font size is 36 points. Notice also that when you click text inside a placeholder, its border is no longer selected. (The diagonal lines return to the border.)

10. Click the first sub-bullet below it, which is 32 points.

11. Press [Esc] to reselect the entire placeholder.

12. Click the Decrease Font Size button [A] once so that 28+ appears in the Font Size box.

> **TIP:** Another way to increase or decrease font size is to press [Ctrl]+[Shift]+[>] or [Ctrl]+[Shift]+[<]. *[handwritten: KEYBOARD WAY]*

13. Click the down arrow on the Font Color button [A] and choose dark blue (the color sample farthest to the right), making all the body text on this slide dark blue.

[handwritten: SHADOW]

14. Click the Shadow button [s] on the Formatting toolbar. Now all the text has a shadow, but with the colors being used, the text looks blurred. Remove the Shadow by clicking the Shadow button [s] again.

15. Move to slide 1 and save the presentation as *[your initials]***5-6** but do not print it. Leave the presentation open for the next exercise.

EXERCISE   **5-7**   **Change Text Alignment**

Bulleted items, titles, and subtitles are all considered paragraphs in PowerPoint. Just as in a word processing program, when you press Enter, a new paragraph begins. You can align paragraphs with either the left or right placeholder borders, center them within the placeholder, or justify long paragraphs so that both margins are squared off. However, the last alignment option should be reserved for longer documents such as reports when you want a formal appearance. Fully justified text is not appropriate for presentation slides.

You can change text alignment for all the text in a placeholder or for just one line, depending on what is selected.

1. Move to slide 5 and select the body text placeholder.

2. Position the insertion point in the first line, "Earn Good 4 U discounts."

3. From the Format menu, choose Alignment; then choose Align Right from the submenu. The text in the first line aligns to the right.

 NOTE: Notice the keyboard shortcuts listed on the Alignment submenu for aligning paragraphs.

 4. Click the Align Left button 📄 on the Formatting toolbar. The paragraph aligns to the left.

 5. Select the placeholder border and click the Center button 📄 on the Formatting toolbar. Both lines are centered horizontally within the placeholder. Because the lines are centered, remove the bullets by clicking on the Bullet list button 📄.

 6. Make the title text bold.

EXERCISE   **5-8**   **Use the AutoFit Feature**

Earlier in the lesson, changing the font from Garamond to Arial expanded the width of the text. As a result, the text on slide 4 ("Walkers Breakfast with Good 4 U") expands beyond the bottom edge of the text placeholder.

AutoFit can be turned on or off in the AutoCorrect dialog box. To turn the feature on, click the AutoFormat As You Type tab and then check the AutoFit title text to placeholder and the AutoFit body text to placeholder options. To turn the feature off, uncheck these options.

TOOLS MENU
AUTO CORRECT OPTIONS
DIALOG BOX

When you activate a placeholder that has a text size problem or has had the text resized by AutoFit, the AutoFit Options button ✛▾ appears near the text, usually in the lower-left corner of its text placeholder. You access AutoFit options by clicking the button. This button is similar to the AutoCorrect Options and the Paste Options buttons discussed in Lesson 3: "Creating a Presentation."

1. From the <u>T</u>ools menu, choose <u>A</u>utoCorrect Options. The AutoCorrect dialog box appears.
2. Click the AutoFormat As You Type tab to check your current settings.

FIGURE 5-10
Turning on
AutoFit options

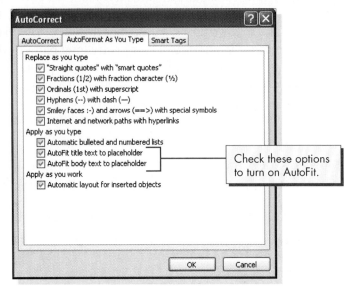

Check these options to turn on AutoFit.

3. Under Apply as you type, the AutoFit title text to placeholder and AutoFit body text to placeholder options should both be checked.
4. Click OK.

5. Move to slide 4; then click anywhere in the first bullet beginning "Half-hour." Notice the AutoFit Options button ⊥ that appears at the lower-left corner of the body text placeholder.

FIGURE 5-11
Working with
the AutoFit
Options button

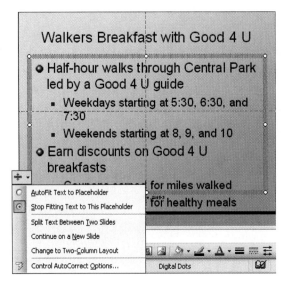

6. Click the AutoFit Options button ⊥. The AutoFit Options menu appears.

7. Notice that <u>S</u>top Fitting Text to This Placeholder is now selected and the text is too large for the placeholder.

8. Click the AutoFit Options button ⊥ again and select <u>A</u>utoFit Text to Placeholder. Now the text is reduced to an appropriate size to fit the placeholder. The bulleted text changes to 32 and 28 points.

9. Move to slide 1 and save the presentation as *[your initials]*5-8 but do not print it. Leave the presentation open for the next exercise.

Changing Size and Position of Text Placeholders

At times you will want to change the way text is positioned on a slide. For example, you might want to make a text placeholder narrower or wider to control how text wraps to a new line, or you might want to move all the text up or down on a slide.

You can change the size and position of text placeholders several ways:

- Drag a *sizing handle* to change the size and shape of a text placeholder. Sizing handles are the eight small circles along the border of a selected text placeholder or other object.
- Drag the placeholder border to move the text to a new position.
- Change placeholder size and position settings by using the Format Placeholder command.

EXERCISE **5-9** **Change the Size of a Placeholder by Dragging a Sizing Handle**

To change the size or shape of a placeholder, you must first select it, displaying the border made up of tiny dots and sizing handles. It is important to make sure that you're dragging a sizing handle when you want to change a placeholder's size.

Dragging a corner sizing handle changes both the height and width of a placeholder at the same time.

1. Display slide 5 and select the body text placeholder. Notice the small white circles around the border. These are the sizing handles.

2. Position the pointer over the bottom center sizing handle.

3. When the pointer changes to a two-pointed vertical arrow ⬍, hold down your left mouse button and drag the bottom border up until it is just below the second line of text.

As you drag, a dotted border shows the changing shape of the placeholder, and the pointer turns into a crosshair ✛. When you release the mouse, notice that the position of the text on the slide is unchanged. (See Figure 5-12 on the next page.)

4. Drag the bottom border of the placeholder down just enough so that all the text fits inside the placeholder.

5. Position your pointer over the lower-left corner-sizing handle; then drag it toward the center of the text. Both the height and width of the placeholder change.

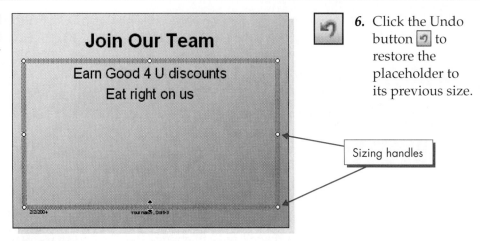

6. Click the Undo button 🔄 to restore the placeholder to its previous size.

Sizing handles

EXERCISE | **5-10** | **Move a Placeholder by Dragging Its Border**

As with changing the size of a placeholder, to change a placeholder's position you must first select it. It is important to make sure that you drag the placeholder border (any part of the border except the sizing handles) when you want to change its position.

1. Select the body text placeholder on slide 5.

2. Position the pointer over the placeholder border anywhere except on a sizing handle. The pointer changes to the four-pointed arrow ⊕.

3. Drag the four-pointed arrow ⊕ down until the placeholder appears vertically centered on the slide.

FIGURE 5-13
Moving a
placeholder

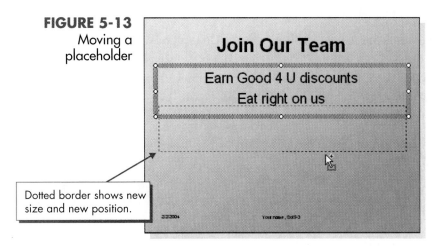

Dotted border shows new size and new position.

TIP: To fine-tune the position of an object, hold down [Alt] while dragging. Another way to adjust the position of a selected object is to press the arrow keys to "nudge" an object.

4. Deselect the placeholder. The text is now attractively placed on the slide.

EXERCISE **5-11** Use the Format Placeholder Command

TOP LEFT CORNER

The Format Placeholder command opens a dialog box, which offers, among other things, a way to change the size and placement of objects by using exact measurements. You'll learn more about other options in this dialog box throughout this course.

1. Move to slide 2.

2. Right-click anywhere in the body text placeholder and choose Format Placeholder from the shortcut menu. The Format AutoShape dialog box appears. Notice the different tabs. (You can also open this dialog box by displaying the Format menu and choosing Placeholder.)

FIGURE 5-14
Format AutoShape
dialog box,
Position tab

3. Click the Position tab and key **2** in the Horizontal text box. This places the placeholder 2 inches in from the left edge of the slide.

4. Click Preview and drag the dialog box out of the way to see the new position of the text. Notice that the placeholder moved to the right and its border now extends beyond the right edge of the slide.

5. Click the Size tab. Key **4** in the Height box and **6** in the Width box, making the placeholder 4 inches tall and 6 inches wide.

6. Click Preview to see the results and then click OK to close the AutoFormat dialog box. The placeholder is now sized appropriately for the text inside it and is centered on the slide.

7. Change the handout footer to show the text *[your initials]***5-11**.

8. Check spelling in the presentation; then move to slide 1 and save the presentation as *[your initials]***5-11** in your Lesson 5 folder.

9. Preview and then print the presentation as handouts, 6 slides per page, grayscale, framed. Close the presentation.

Working with Bullets

When you work with body text placeholders, each line automatically starts with a bullet. You can, however, turn bullets off when the slide would look better without them. You can remove bullets, add new ones, change the shape and color of bullets, and create your own bullets from pictures.

EXERCISE **5-12** **Turn Bullets On and Off**

[handwritten margin note: CHANGE BULLETS FOR A SLIDE OR INDIVIDUAL BULLET]

As you learned in Exercise 5-7, by using the Bullets button ⊞, you can turn on and off all the bullets in a selected text placeholder. You can also turn off just the bullets for text selected within the placeholder. The Bullets button is another example of a toggle button.

1. Display slide 2. Click within the body text to activate the placeholder. Press Esc to select the entire placeholder.

2. Click the Bullets button ⊞ on the Formatting toolbar. This turns bullets off for the entire placeholder and moves the text to the left.

3. Click the Bullets button ⊞ again to reapply the bullets.

4. Click within the first bulleted item, "Exercise regularly," and click the Bullets button ⊞ to turn off the bullet.

5. Click the Bullets button ⊞ again to reapply the bullet.

EXERCISE **5-13** **Change the Color and Shape of a Bullet**

You use the Bullets and Numbering dialog box to change the color and shape of a bullet. To change the bullet shape, you can choose a character from another font. Fonts that contain potential bullet characters include Symbol, Wingdings, and Webdings. Another source of bullet characters is the Geometric Shapes subset available for most other fonts.

1. Working on slide 2, select the body text placeholder.

2. Right-click the placeholder border to display the shortcut menu and choose Bullets and Numbering.

3. In the Bullets and Numbering dialog box, click the Bulleted tab.

4. Choose the check bullet option.

FIGURE 5-15
Bullets and
Numbering
dialog box

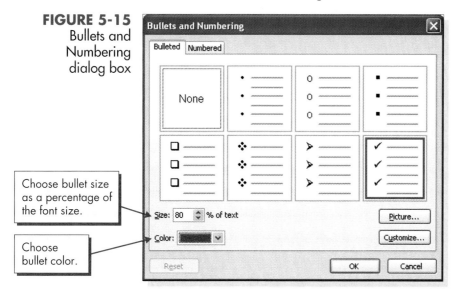

Choose bullet size as a percentage of the font size.

Choose bullet color.

(handwritten note in left margin) BULLETS MEASURED IN POINTS 72 per INCH

5. In the Color box, choose red.

6. In the Size box, click the down arrow several times until 80 is displayed. Click OK. All bullets on slide 2 are now red arrowheads, sized at 80% of the font size.

7. Using your I-beam, select the first three lines of bulleted text; then open the Format menu and choose Bullets and Numbering.

8. Click Customize to open the Symbol dialog box.

9. In the Font drop-down list (upper-left corner of the dialog box), scroll to the top and choose (normal text).

10. In the Subset drop-down list (upper-right corner), choose Miscellaneous Dingbats (near the bottom of the list). Several characters suitable for bullets appear in the dialog box grid. (See Figure 5-16 on the next page.)

11. Click the heart bullet to select it; then click OK. The Symbol dialog box closes, and the Bullets and Numbering dialog box reappears.

12. Change the Size to 110%. Click OK. The first three bullets on the slide change to red hearts. While the percentage you use is related to the size of the font for that bulleted item, symbols vary in size. So you may need to try more than one adjustment before you accept a size that is pleasing to you.

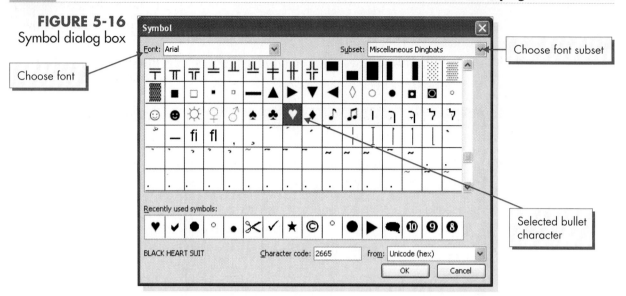

FIGURE 5-16
Symbol dialog box

Choose font

Choose font subset

Selected bullet character

E X E R C I S E   **5-14**   **Create a Bullet from a Picture**

A picture bullet can add a unique or creative accent to your presentation. A picture bullet is made from a graphic file and can be a company logo, a special picture, or any image you create with a graphics program or capture with a scanner or digital camera.

1. Display slide 3 and select the first two bullets (but not the sub-bullets).

2. Open the Bullets and Numbering dialog box, click the Bulleted tab, and then click Picture. The Picture Bullet dialog box displays a variety of colorful bullets. You can choose from one of these bullets or you can import a picture file of your own.

FIGURE 5-17
Inserting a picture bullet

Imported picture

3. Click Import. In the Add Clips to Organizer dialog box, navigate to the location of your student files.

4. Choose the file **Walker** and click Add. The selected picture file is added to the samples shown in the Picture Bullet dialog box.

NOTE: You learn more about using pictures and clip art in Lesson 6: "Working with PowerPoint Objects."

5. Click the picture of the person walking to select it and then click OK. The bullets are replaced with picture bullets, but they are too small.

6. With the two bullet items still selected, reopen the Bullets and Numbering dialog box. In the Size box, change the size to 200%. Click OK.

7. Using the steps just outlined, change the bullet for the last bullet item ("Walking is a mood elevator") to the picture of the walker and size it to match the other bullets.

 NOTE: If the AutoFit Options button ⬍▾ appears near the placeholder, click it and choose AutoFit Text to Placeholder.

8. Change the handout footer to show the text *[your initials]***5-14**. Move to slide 1 and save the presentation as *[your initials]***5-14** in your Lesson 5 folder.

EXERCISE   5-15   Create Numbered Paragraphs

Instead of using bullet characters, you can number listed items. A numbered list is useful to indicate the order in which steps should be taken or to indicate the importance of the items in a list.

Using the Numbered tab in the Bullets and Numbering dialog box, you can apply a variety of numbering styles, including numbers, letters, and Roman numerals. You can also create a numbered list automatically while you key body text.

1. Display slide 5 and select the body text placeholder.

2. Click the Left alignment button ▤ on the Formatting toolbar.

3. Select all the text in the placeholder and delete it.

4. With the placeholder activated, key **1.** and press Tab. Key **Walk with us**

5. Press Enter. The second line is automatically numbered "2."

6. Key **Eat with us** and press Enter.

7. Key **Do what's Good 4 U**. The slide now has three items, automatically numbered 1 through 3.

8. Press Esc to select the placeholder; then open the Bullets and Numbering dialog box and click the Numbered tab. Notice that there are several different numbering styles to choose from.

9. In the Color box, choose red. Click OK.

10. Change the handout header and footer to include the date and your name as the header, and the page number and text *[your initials]***5-15** as the footer.

11. Move to slide 1 and save the presentation as *[your initials]***5-15** in your Lesson 5 folder.

12. Preview and then print the presentation as handouts, 6 slides per page, grayscale, framed. Leave the presentation open for the next exercise.

 TIP: You can control the numbering style that is applied automatically by keying your first item with the style you want, such as **1.** or **A.**

Modifying a Design Template's Text Placeholders

A *master slide* contains formatted text placeholders and background items that are designed to appear on all slides in a presentation. Changes that you make on a master slide appear on all slides in the presentation that are based on that master. There are two masters you can use for slides:

- Title master, which includes text placeholders for the title and subtitle text of the title slide   *HAS TO HAVE 2 PLACEHOLDERS*
- Slide master, which includes text placeholders for the title and body text

In general, the *title master* and the *slide master* contain the same design elements (such as background color, graphics, and text formatting). However, the title master is arranged differently to accommodate title and subtitle text. The slide master is often less elaborate, leaving room for body text and other information. You can change the formatting and design of the masters and thus set the tone for the entire presentation.

EXERCISE **5-16** **Change Text Formatting on Master Slides**

There are two ways to display the slide and title masters:

- Use the <u>V</u>iew menu.
- Use [Shift]+ the Normal View button.

1. Display slide 2. Notice that this is the only slide with heart-shaped bullets. You'll use the masters to change all first-level bullets to hearts, to change the text color, and to make some additional changes.

Display title master + slide

 2. To display the slide master, open the <u>V</u>iew menu, choose <u>M</u>aster, <u>S</u>lide Master (or hold down [Shift] and click the Normal View button). Dotted placeholders indicate the position for title text, body text, and footer information. You can change the size, shape, position, and text attributes for any of these text placeholders. (See Figure 5-18 on the next page.)

NOTE: An easy way to tell whether you're viewing the slide master or title master is to check the indicator on the left side of the status bar.

FIGURE 5-18
Slide master

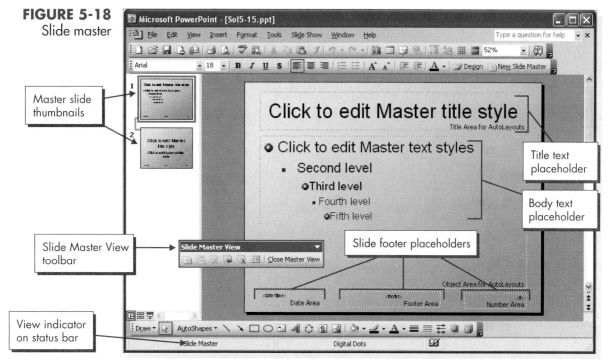

3. Select the title placeholder by clicking its dotted border with the four-pointed arrow .

4. Change the font for the title placeholder to Impact by using the Font box on the Standard toolbar.

5. With the title placeholder still selected, change the font size to 44 points and change the font color to red.

6. Click within the first-level bullet on the body text placeholder. Change the bullet character to a red heart from the (normal text), Miscellaneous Dingbats category. Make it 110% of the font size.

7. Format the second-level bullet as a red check mark from the Webdings font sized at 100%.

8. Press Page Down or use the vertical scroll bar to display the title master.

TIP: You can switch between the title and slide masters by pressing Page Down and Page Up, using the vertical scroll bar, or clicking each master's thumbnail.

9. Review the elements on the title master. Some of the changes you made to the slide master are reflected on the title master (the title text is red, Impact). PowerPoint does this automatically to help you judge how the formatting changes will appear on your slides.

FIGURE 5-19
Title master

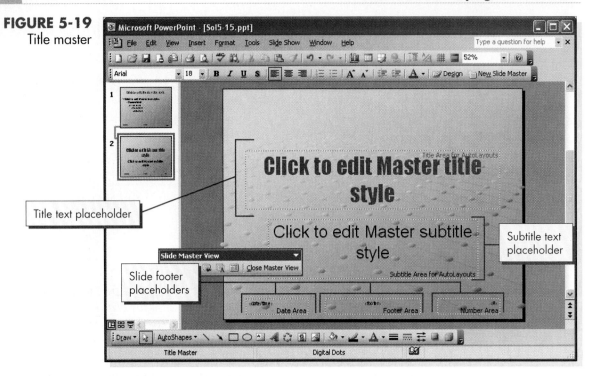

10. Click <u>C</u>lose Master View on the Slide Master View toolbar or click the Normal View button. Slide 2 is displayed.

11. Move to slide 1 and scroll through the presentation. Notice that most (but not all) the changes you made to the masters are reflected in the presentation. You correct this in the next exercise.

EXERCISE | **5-17** | **Reapply a Slide Layout**

Changing a master does not override formatting changes you made to individual slides. If you change a slide master after formatting individual slides, you can re-apply the slide layout to those slides to make them conform to the new master.

1. From the F<u>o</u>rmat menu, choose Slide <u>L</u>ayout to display the Slide Layout task pane.

2. Display slide 1; then right-click the Title Slide layout in the Slide Layout task pane and choose Reapply <u>L</u>ayout from the shortcut menu. The title master's formatting replaces the formatting you applied earlier.

3. Display slide 2. You changed the size and position of slide 2's body text placeholder.

4. Reapply the Title and Text layout to slide 2. The placeholder size and position change back to the master's layout.

5. Reapply the Title and Text layout to slides 3 and 5. Leave slide 4 as is. If the AutoFit Options button appears, click it and choose <u>A</u>utoFit Text to Placeholder.

6. Move to slide 1. Move the title and subtitle up. Change the notes and handouts footer to show the text *[your initials]***5-17**. Remove the date information from the Slide footer.

7. Move to slide 1 and save the presentation as *[your initials]***5-17** in your Lesson 5 folder.

8. View the presentation as a slide show. Preview and then print it as handouts, 6 slides per page, grayscale, framed. Keep the presentation open for the next exercise.

Working with Text Boxes

Until now, you have worked with text placeholders that automatically appear when you insert a new slide. Sometimes you'll want to put text outside the text placeholders or create free-form text boxes on a blank slide.

You create text boxes by clicking the Text Box button 🖺 on the Drawing toolbar and then dragging the pointer to define the width of the text box. You can also just click the pointer, and the text box adjusts its width to the size of your text. You can change the size and position of text boxes the same way you change text placeholders.

E X E R C I S E 5-18   **Add Text by Using a Text Box**

When you use the Text Box button 🖺 to create a single line of text, you are free to place that text anywhere on a slide, change its color and font, and rotate it. This type of text is sometimes called *floating text*.   *ONCE you CREATE*

1. Display slide 5.

🖺 2. Click the Text Box button 🖺 on the Drawing toolbar.

3. Place the pointer below the "G" in "Good 4 U" and click. A small text box containing an insertion point appears.

FIGURE 5-20
Creating
floating text

4. Key **Join Our Team Today!** Notice how the text box widens as you key text.

🡲 **NOTE:** If you accidentally drag as you click the text tool pointer, PowerPoint will think you want to restrict the width of the text box and the text you key will wrap within a tall and narrow text box. If this happens, click Undo 🔄 and try again.

EXERCISE `5-19` **Change Font and Color**

You can select the text box and change the font and color of text in a text box using the same methods as you did with text placeholders.

1. Click the text box border to select it. Change the text to 48-point, bold, shadowed.

FIGURE 5-21
Placement for floating text

2. With the text box selected, choose an attractive script font such as Monotype Corsiva or Script MT Bold.

3. Using the Font color button, change the text color to red.

4. Using the four-pointed arrow ⊕, move the floating text box to the bottom-right corner of the slide. See Figure 5-21 for placement guidelines.

EXERCISE `5-20` **Wrap Text in a Text Box**

When you drag the pointer to define the width of a text box, word wrapping is automatically turned on. As you key, your insertion point automatically jumps to a new line when it gets to the right side of the box. The height of the box automatically adjusts to accommodate additional text lines.

1. Move to slide 2, "Heart Smart Living."

2. Click the Text Box button ▣.

3. Position your pointer to the right of "Exercise regularly"; then drag to the right to create a rectangle that is about 4" wide. The Ruler is helpful in judging this measurement. If it is not displayed, from the View menu, choose Ruler.

4. In the text box, key **Be consistent wherever you are!**

5. Click the text box border to select it; then increase the font size to 28 points, bold, and red; and then right-align the text.

6. Position the text box as shown in Figure 5-22.

FIGURE 5-22
Text wrapped
in a text box

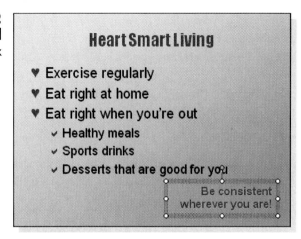

NOTE: If you want precise positioning, right-click the text box and choose Format Text box, click the Position tab of the dialog box, and make the Horizontal setting 5.6 inches and the Vertical setting 6 inches measured from the Top Left Corner. However, if your box is wider, you may need to adjust these numbers.

EXERCISE 5-21 Rotate a Text Box

You can rotate almost any PowerPoint object—including text boxes, placeholders, and clip art—by dragging the green *rotation handle* that appears at the top of a selected object. You can also control rotation of text boxes and placeholders by using the Format Text Box and Format AutoShape dialog boxes.

To constrain the rotation of an object to 15-degree increments, hold down Shift while rotating.

When text is in a rotated position, it can be awkward to edit. Fortunately, when you select a rotated text box for editing, it conveniently returns to a horizontal position while you revise the text.

1. On slide 5, click "Join Our Team Today!" and drag the text box up slightly so that you will have enough space to make it angle on the slide.

2. Point to the green rotation handle at the top of the text box and drag it to the left. Notice the circling arrow pointer that appears while you drag.

FIGURE 5-23
Rotating a text box

Circling arrow pointer

Dashed box indicates degree of rotation.

3. Position the text box as shown in Figure 5-23.

TIP: You can key a precise angle of rotation measurement on the Size tab of the Format Text Box dialog box.

4. Change the handout footer text to read *[your initials]*5-21. Save the presentation as *[your initials]*5-21 in your Lesson 5 folder but do not print it. Leave the presentation open for the next exercise.

USING ONLINE HELP

Working with the slide and title masters helps you create consistent and professional-looking presentations. In later lessons you learn how to place art on a slide master so that it appears throughout your presentation.

Use Help to learn more about master slides:

1. Key **slide master** in the Ask a Question box and press `Enter`.

2. Select the topic **About the slide master**.

FIGURE 5-24
About the slide master help screen

3. Review the information displayed for the topic. Expand each of the subtopics and read them also. Notice that glossary terms appear in blue text. If you see a term you are not sure of, click it to read a definition.

4. Close Help when you finish. Close your presentation.

LESSON 5 Summary

➤ A font is a set of characters with a specific design, for example, Arial or Times New Roman.

➤ Font size (the height of a font) is measured in points, with 72 points to an inch. Fonts of the same size can vary in the width, some taking up more horizontal space than others.

➤ Many formatting buttons are toggle buttons, meaning that the same button is clicked to turn an effect on and clicked again to turn it off.

➤ Change text attributes and effects such as bold, italic, and text color by first selecting the text and then clicking the appropriate buttons on the Formatting toolbar. Or, apply formatting as you key text.

➤ The Font dialog box enables you to apply multiple formatting attributes and effects all at one time. Using the Font dialog box is another way to apply text formatting.

➤ One or more fonts can be changed for an entire presentation by using the Replace Fonts command.

➤ When a text placeholder is selected, formatting that you apply affects all the text in the placeholder.

➤ Text in placeholders can be aligned with the left or right side of the placeholder, centered, or justified.

➤ When AutoFit is turned on, text is automatically resized to fit its placeholder. You can turn AutoFit features on or off by using the AutoCorrect Options dialog box.

➤ When a text placeholder with a size problem is selected, the AutoFit button ▣ appears near the placeholder. Click the AutoFit button to control how AutoFit affects the text.

➤ Body text placeholders are preformatted to have bulleted paragraphs. Bullets for selected paragraphs or placeholders are turned on or off by clicking the Bullets button ▤.

➤ Use the Bullets and Numbering dialog box to change the shape, size, and color of bullets or numbers.

➤ Graphics files can be imported and used as picture bullets.

➤ Format text placeholders on master slides in the same way as text placeholders on presentation slides. Making changes to master slides affects all the slides in a presentation.

➤ Switch between the title master and the slide master by pressing (Page Up) and (Page Down) or clicking a thumbnail on the left side of the screen.

➤ Changes made to master slides do not override formatting changes previously made to individual slides. To update a slide to agree with its master, reapply its slide layout.

➤ Text boxes enable you to place text anywhere on a slide. Using the Text Box button ▣, click anywhere on a slide or draw a box and then start keying text.

➤ Text in a text box can be formatted by using standard text-formatting tools. Change the width of a text box to control how it will word-wrap.

➤ When you select a text box on a slide, a green rotation handle appears slightly above the top-center sizing handle. Drag the rotation handle left or right to rotate the object.

LESSON 5 Command Summary

FEATURE	BUTTON	MENU	KEYBOARD
Increase Font Size	A▲	Format, Font, Size	Ctrl + Shift + >
Decrease Font Size	A▼	Format, Font, Size	Ctrl + Shift + <
Bold	B	Format, Font, Font style, Bold	Ctrl + B
Italic	I	Format, Font, Font style, Italic	Ctrl + I
Underline	U	Format, Font, Effects, Underline	Ctrl + U
Text Shadow	S	Format, Font, Effects, Shadow	
Text Color	A	Format, Font, Color	
Apply a font	Arial ▼	Format, Font, Font	Ctrl + Shift + F
Change font size	42 ▼	Format, Font, Size	Ctrl + Shift + P
Change case		Format, Change Case	Shift + F3
Replace fonts		Format, Replace Fonts	
Align Left	≡	Format, Alignment, Align Left	Ctrl + L
Center	≡	Format, Alignment, Center	Ctrl + E

continues

LESSON 5 Command Summary *continued*

FEATURE	BUTTON	MENU	KEYBOARD
Align Right	≡	Format, Alignment, Align Right	Ctrl + R
Justify		Format, Alignment, Justify	Ctrl + J
Turn bullets on or off	≔	Format, Bullets and Numbering	
Turn numbering on or off	≔	Format, Bullets and Numbering	
Display master slide	Shift + ▣	View, Master, Slide Master	
Text Box	▣	Insert, Text Box	

Concepts Review

TRUE/FALSE QUESTIONS

Each of the following statements is either true or false. Indicate your choice by circling T or F.

(T) F   **1.** You can apply text attributes before you key text.

(T) F   **2.** You can change selected text from uppercase to lowercase by using the [Shift]+[F3] keyboard shortcut.

T **(F)**   **3.** Sentence case capitalizes the initial letter of all words in a paragraph.

(T) F   **4.** To search for and replace one font with another throughout a presentation, use the Replace Font dialog box.

T **(F)**   **5.** You can drag a sizing handle to reposition a placeholder. *RESIZE*

(T) F   **6.** The Bullets button :≡ can turn bullets on or off.

(T) F   **7.** To move a text box, the pointer must remain on the border and not touch a sizing handle.

T **(F)**   **8.** Changes on the slide master automatically override changes you make to individual slides.

SHORT ANSWER QUESTIONS

Write the correct answer in the space provided.

1. Which toolbar buttons change font size?

INCREASE + DECREASE FONT SIZE

2. What must you do before you can change an attribute for existing text?

SELECT IT

3. Which dialog box enables you to change the color of text?

FONT

4. What does the Center button ≡ do to selected text?

CENTER IT

5. Which commands do you need to choose to change bullet color?

BULLETS + NUMBERING DIALOG BOX

6. How can you display the slide master without using the View menu?

SHIFT + CLICK - NORMAL VIEW

7. How do you create a text box that adjusts its width to the width of the text you key?

TEXT BOX BUTTON CLICK OVER ON SLIDE

8. How can you rotate a text box in 15-degree increments?

SHIFT + ROTATING HANDLE

CRITICAL THINKING

Answer these questions on a separate page. Support your answers with examples from your own experience, if possible.

1. Explain how font faces can affect a presentation. Can you use too many fonts in a presentation? Explain your answer.

2. Describe some advantages of using the Title Master and the Slide Master. How can this feature contribute to consistency of design within a presentation?

Skills Review

EXERCISE 5-22

Change font size, apply text attributes to selected text, and change the case of selected text.

1. Open the file **ComWalk**.

2. On slide 1, change font size and color and apply bold and shadow effects for the title by following these steps:

   a. Select the title text "Power Walking" by dragging the I-beam pointer across the text.

   b. Choose 54 from the Font Size drop-down list on the Formatting toolbar.

   c. Choose red from the Font Color button drop-down list on the Formatting toolbar.

   d. Click the Bold button and the Shadow button on the Formatting toolbar.

3. On slide 3, increase the font size for the title by following these steps:

   a. Move to slide 3 and select the title text.

   b. Click the Increase Font Size button several times until 36 appears in the Font Size box.

4. On slide 5, use the Font dialog box to change the title text formatting by following these steps:
   a. Select the title text.
   b. From the Format menu, choose Font.
   c. From the Font style list box, choose Bold.
   d. From the Size list box, choose 36.
   e. Under Effects, check the Shadow check box.
   f. In the Color drop-down list, choose red. Click OK.

5. Change the case of the text on slide 5 by following these steps:
   a. Select the last bulleted item by clicking its bullet.
   b. From the Format menu, choose Change Case.
   c. Choose tOGGLE cASE and click OK.

6. Using step 4 above as a guide, change the title text formatting on slides 2, 3, 4, and 6 to match slide 5. On slide 6, resize the placeholder slightly on the right side so that the title fits on one line.

7. Check spelling in the presentation.

8. Create a handout header and footer: include the date and your name as the header, and the page number and text *[your initials]*5-22 as the footer.

9. Move to slide 1 and save the presentation as *[your initials]*5-22 in your Lesson 5 folder.

10. Preview and then print the presentation as handouts, 6 slides per page, grayscale, framed. Close the presentation.

EXERCISE 5-23

Change a font face, apply text attributes to text placeholders and selected text, and work with bullets.

1. Open the file **PwrWalk1**.

2. Apply formatting to the slide 1 title text placeholder by following these steps:
   a. Click anywhere in the title text to activate the placeholder.
   b. Press Esc to select the border.
   c. Click the arrow next to the Font box on the Formatting toolbar and choose Arial Black.
   d. Click the Shadow **s** button on the Formatting toolbar.

   S

3. Change the color of the title text on slide 1 to a cream color.

   B

4. Press Tab to select the subtitle placeholder. Click the Bold button **B**.

5. On slides 2, 3, and 4, change the font for the title text to Arial Black; then make it a cream color, and shadowed to match the title text on slide 1. (Don't change the font size.)

6. Change the bullets for slide 2 by following these steps:

   a. On slide 2, select the body text placeholder.
   b. From the Format menu, choose Bullets and Numbering.
   c. Click Customize.
   d. From the Font drop-down list, choose Wingdings 3.
   e. Choose a right-pointing arrow bullet and click OK.
   f. In the Bullets and Numbering dialog box, click the arrow next to Color and choose bright green for the bullet color. Click OK.

7. Remove bullets from selected text on slide 2 by following these steps:

   a. Drag the I-beam to select the two second-level bulleted items under "When."
   b. Click the Bullets button ⁝☰ on the Formatting toolbar.
   c. Following steps a and b above, remove the bullets from the two second-level items under "Where."

8. In the last bullet on slide 2, select the word "Free" and make it bold and italic.

9. Change the bullets for slides 3 and 4 to the same arrow bullet and bullet color that you used on slide 2.

10. Create a handout header and footer: include the date and your name as the header, and the page number and text *[your initials]*5-23 as the footer.

11. Move to slide 1 and save the presentation as *[your initials]*5-23 in your Lesson 5 folder.

12. Preview and then print the presentation as handouts, 4 slides per page, grayscale, framed. Close the presentation.

EXERCISE 5-24

Change font size, apply text attributes, change text alignment, and change size and position of placeholders.

1. Open the file **PwrWalk1** and apply the Capsules design template.

2. On slide 1, increase the title size to 44 points and change the font to Impact.

3. Change the alignment of the title by following these steps:

   a. Select the title text placeholder (or click within the title text).
   b. Click the Align Left button ▤ on the Formatting toolbar.

4. Right-align the subtitle text by opening the Format menu and choosing Alignment, and then Align Right. (Or press Ctrl+R.)

5. Resize the subtitle placeholder by following these steps:

   a. Position the pointer over the top-center sizing handle on the border.
   b. When you see the two-pointed vertical arrow ↔, drag the sizing handle down, making the placeholder just tall enough to fit the text. (If you see the AutoFit Options button, you made the box too small.)

6. Move the subtitle placeholder to a new position by following these steps:

   a. Select the placeholder border (if it is not already selected).

   b. Position the pointer on the border between two sizing handles.

   c. Using the four-pointed arrow ⊕, drag the placeholder down so that its right border is aligned with the right end of the dark blue horizontal shape.

7. Drag the Good 4 U logo into position above the dark blue bar. Make the right edge of the logo aligned with the subtitle placeholder and the right end of the blue bar.

8. On slide 2, change the title placeholder font to Impact, 44 points, remove bold (this font is already very thick), and click right-align.

9. Adjust the width and position of the title text placeholder so that the right edge of the text in the placeholder aligns with the right edge of the dark blue shape below it.

10. On slides 3 and 4, format the slide titles to match the title of slide 2.

11. Create a handout header and footer: include the date and your name as the header, and the page number and text *[your initials]*5-24 as the footer.

12. Move to slide 1 and save the presentation as *[your initials]*5-24 in your Lesson 5 folder.

13. Preview and then print the presentation as handouts, 4 slides per page, grayscale, landscape, framed. Close the presentation.

EXERCISE 5-25

Work with the presentation master slides and work with text boxes.

1. Open the file **PwrWalk2**. Scroll through all the slides to view the text formatting. Notice three major design problems:

   ● The text placeholders are not positioned effectively in relationship to the background graphics.

   ● The text colors are not easily readable because they lack sufficient contrast with the background colors.

   ● The center alignment used for the Title and Subtitle placeholders does not fit the background graphics.

2. Apply formatting to the slide master by following these steps:

   a. Access Slide Master View by pressing Shift and then clicking the Normal View button 🖻.

   b. If the slide master is displayed, drag the scroll bar down to display the title master (or press Page Down).

3. Change the formatting on the title master by following these steps:

   a. Select the title placeholder and change its text attributes to Tahoma font, 54 points, bold, shadow, left alignment, and white. Position the left edge of the placeholder about 1" from the left edge of the slide on the blue rectangle.

b. Select the subtitle placeholder and change its text attributes to Tahoma, 36 points, bold, italic, left alignment, light gray. Resize this placeholder to fit two lines of text and move it to the right off the yellow rectangle. (See Figure 5-25 for placement guidelines.)

FIGURE 5-25

4. Change the formatting on the slide master by following these steps:

   a. Press [Page Up] to display the slide master.

   b. Select the title placeholder and change the text attributes to Tahoma, 40 points, bold, left alignment, shadow, blue. Position placeholder on the larger yellow rectangle aligned near the small blue rectangle.

   c. Select the bulleted list placeholder and change the text attributes to Tahoma and white. Reposition this placeholder by moving it to the right away from the narrow blue rectangle and then lowered slightly.

5. Change the Number Area text placeholder in the lower-right corner of the slide master.

   a. Zoom to 75%.

  REVIEW: Click the Zoom box arrow on the Standard toolbar and select 75%. You might need to click the Toolbar Options button to locate the Zoom box.

   b. Change the font to 18-point italic and the color to red.

   c. Position the insertion point in front of the <#> symbols.

   d. Key **Slide** and press [Spacebar]. (The completed text should be "Slide <#>.")

6. From the Zoom box drop-down list Choose Fit to return the zoom setting to its normal size.

7. Click the Normal View button to close Master view.

8. Using the Slide tab in the Header and Footer dialog box, apply slide numbers to all slides except the title slide.

9. On slide 5, create an interesting arrangement of soft drink names by using text boxes that angle on the slide. Follow these steps:

   a. Move to slide 5 and notice that the Title Only layout is used with a clip art image that matches the slide color scheme on the left.

   b. Click the Text Box button on the Drawing toolbar.

   c. Place the pointer on the slide, and click. (Be careful not to drag the mouse when you click.)

10. Create a text box for each of the concession products, following these steps:

    a. Key **Choco Max**

    b. Click the border to select the text box and then change the font to 32-point Tahoma, bold.

    c. With the text box still selected, press Ctrl+D to duplicate the box and edit the text of the second box for Electro Fizz. Do not be concerned about positioning until all five text boxes are prepared.

    d. Repeat step c for Hydro Cooler, Laser Lime, and Power Punch.

    e. Rotate each text box by using the green rotation handle and then drag the box by its border—not by a sizing handle—to position it attractively. (See Figure 5-26 for placement guidelines.)

FIGURE 5-26

11. Check spelling in the presentation.

12. Create a handout header and footer: include the date and your name as the header, and the page number and text *[your initials]***5-25** as the footer.

13. Move to slide 1 and save the presentation as *[your initials]***5-25** in your Lesson 5 folder.

14. View the presentation as a slide show, and then print the presentation as handouts, 6 slides per page, grayscale, framed. Close the presentation.

Lesson Applications

Apply text attributes to selected text and placeholders, work with bullets, resize and reposition placeholders, and make changes to the slide master.

1. Open the file **FoodCon**.

2. On the title master, left-align the text in the title placeholder; then make it bold and yellow. Increase the title text to 54 points. Change the subtitle placeholder to 32 points, left-align the text, resize it slightly, and move it to the right.

3. On the slide master, left-align the title text; then make it bold and brown. Change the first-level bullet to a solid square shape in brown from the Wingdings font. Make the bullet 90% of the text size.

4. On slide 1, edit the date to the current month and year.

5. Move to slide 4 and change the title to simply "Concession Products" on one line.

6. Change the layout of slide 4 to two columns. Click the increase font size bullet to make the first-level bulleted items the same size as on other slides. Rearrange the text as shown in Figure 5-27.

FIGURE 5-27

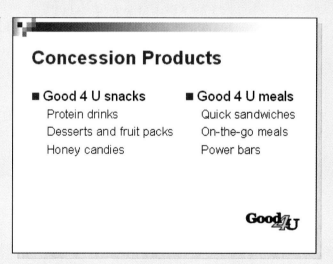

7. Widen the first column placeholder so that "Desserts and fruit packs" appears on one line without word wrapping.

8. View the presentation's text in the Outline pane and remove any extra blank lines that you find.

9. Check spelling in the presentation.

10. Create a handout header and footer: include the date and your name as the header, and the page number and text *[your initials]*5-26 as the footer.

11. Move to slide 1 and save the presentation as *[your initials]*5-26 in your Lesson 5 folder.

12. Preview and then print the presentation as handouts, 6 slides per page, grayscale, framed. Close the presentation.

EXERCISE 5-27

Apply text attributes to selected text and text placeholders, replace fonts, work with bullets, and the slide master.

1. Open the file **WasteMgt**.

2. Make the following changes to the slide master:
   - Remove the text shadow from all placeholders because the colors used make the text look blurred.
   - On the title master, change the title placeholder to 60 points.
   - Change second-level bullets to dark blue check marks (Wingdings 2 font).
   - Italicize the second-level text.

3. Edit slide 1 so that the title reads **Recycling Program** and the subtitle reads **Management Training**. Change the font color of the subtitle to red and make it bold. Move the title placeholder up slightly.

4. On slide 2, make the following words bold: "waste," "costs," and "landfill overloads" plus make each of these words 36 points to emphasize them more.

5. Add the following speaker's notes:

   Slide 2 **Discuss how waste reduction is cost-effective.**

   Slide 3 **Mention our targeted percentages for the coming year.**

6. Use the Replace Fonts command to replace the Arial, Arial Black, and Times New Roman fonts with Tahoma.

7. Modify the title master and the slide master to make the title placeholders bold because the regular appearance of Tahoma is not as bold as Arial Black.

8. Insert a new slide with the Title Only layout as slide 4 with the title **Local Recyclers**. Create a text box (Tahoma, 32 points) for the first local recycler listed next. Then duplicate the text box and edit the contents for each of the other three recyclers. See Figure 5-28 for text box placement:

   Frampton Paper
   800-555-9876
   Marion Mills
   800-555-1234

Cannon Box Company
800-555-5432
Andy's Scrap Metal
800-555-6565

FIGURE 5-28

Local Recyclers

Frampton Paper
800-555-9876

Cannon Box Company
800-555-5432

Marion Mills
800-555-1234

Andy's Scrap Metal
800-555-6565

9. Check spelling in the presentation.

10. Create a handout header and footer: include the date and your name as the header, and the page number and text *[your initials]5-27* as the footer.

11. Move to slide 1 and save the presentation as *[your initials]5-27* in your Lesson 5 folder.

12. Preview and then print the presentation as handouts, 6 slides per page, grayscale, framed. Print the notes pages for slides 2 and 3. Close the presentation.

EXERCISE 5-28

Apply text attributes to selected text and text placeholders, align text, work with bullets, resize and reposition placeholders, and work with the slide master.

1. Create a new presentation by opening the Word outline **PwrWalk3** from within PowerPoint.

  REVIEW: To open a Word outline in PowerPoint, click the Open button and then choose All Outlines in the Files of type drop-down list.

2. Apply the Eclipse design template to the entire presentation. Change the color scheme to the one with the black background and red, yellow, and green accents.

3. Apply the Title Slide layout to slide 1. Move the second line of the title to the subtitle placeholder and center it.

4. Make the following changes to the title master:
   - Change the title text placeholder font to Arial Black at 48 points and make it yellow.
   - Change the subtitle placeholder to Arial Narrow, 36 points, bold. Resize the placeholder slightly and indent it to the right.

5. Make the following changes to the slide master (make sure you're not working on the title master):
   - Change the title text placeholder font to Arial Black and make it yellow.
   - Change the bulleted list placeholder to Arial Narrow and make the first-level bullet 32 points and bold.
   - Change all first-level bullets to an X (Wingdings font, end of third row). Change the bullet size to 140% of text size and change its color to yellow.

6. Return to Normal view and apply slide layouts for each slide to make sure the slide master changes are reflected on all slides.

7. On slide 2, move the text "(fitness and health participants)" to a new line by pressing Shift+Enter before the parentheses.

8. On slide 3, change the case of the body text placeholder to sentence case.

9. On slide 4, resize the body text placeholder so the X bullets are under the "t" in Participants.

10. Check spelling in the presentation.

11. Create a handout header and footer: include the date and your name as the header, and the page number and text *[your initials]*5-28 as the footer.

12. Move to slide 1 and save the presentation as *[your initials]*5-28 in your Lesson 5 folder.

13. View the presentation as a slide show. Then preview and print the presentation as handouts, 4 slides per page, grayscale, framed. Close the presentation.

EXERCISE 5-29 Challenge Yourself

Apply text attributes to text and text placeholders, work with bullets, change alignment, resize and reposition placeholders, and work with the slide master.

1. Open the file **Sponsor1**.

2. Scroll through the slides, noticing the inconsistent formatting because the slide master and the title master have not been used effectively to control text sizes, placeholder positioning, and bullet use.

3. On the title master, make the following changes:

- Change the font color for the title placeholder to a cream color (Title Text Scheme color). Make the text bold.
- Change the title placeholder to left alignment and move it up.
- Increase the font size for the subtitle placeholder by one increment, making it bold and left aligned, also.
- Move the subtitle placeholder up and slightly to the right.

4. On the slide master, make the following changes:
   - Change the font color to the same cream color that was used for the title master and make the text bold.
   - Decrease the font size for the body text placeholder by one increment to make the first-level bullet text 28 points.
   - Change the first- and second-level bullets to shapes and colors of your choice.

5. Return to Normal view and then reapply the slide layouts for each slide; then scroll through the slides again.

6. At the end of the presentation, insert two new slides using the text shown in Figure 5-29.

FIGURE 5-29

7. On slide 2, edit the first bullet to read **Increase Good 4 U name recognition**

8. On slide 2, insert line breaks (Shift+Enter) before the parentheses in the second and third bullets. Italicize the text in parentheses.

9. On slide 3, edit the second bullet to read **Organize training seminars**

10. On slide 5, edit the bulleted items to read as follows:

FIGURE 5-30

```
• Lectures in Good 4 U banquet room

  - Conducted by local marathon winners

• Training walks in Central Park

  - Free bananas and Good 4 U sports drinks
```

11. On slide 3, move the first bulleted item ("Advertise Power…") to the last line on the slide. Change this last bullet to sentence case.

12. Move slide 4 ("Advertising") to the end of the presentation so that it becomes slide 8.

13. Check spelling in the presentation.

14. Create a handout header and footer: include the date and your name as the header, and the page number and text *[your initials]*5-29 as the footer.

15. Move to slide 1 and save the presentation as *[your initials]*5-29 in your Lesson 5 folder.

16. Preview and then print the presentation as handouts, 9 slides per page, grayscale, landscape, framed. Close the presentation.

On Your Own

In these exercises you work on your own, as you would in a real-life work environment. Use the skills you've learned to accomplish the task—and be creative.

EXERCISE 5-30

Pick a room (such as a residence hall lobby or a reception area at work) that you would like to renovate and refurnish. Create a PowerPoint presentation with at least six slides to inform others of the upcoming improvements such as the style of floor covering, the style of furniture and wall coverings, and other furnishings that you recommend for purchasing. Include desirable features and other information that you think would be helpful. Include a hyperlink to at least one Web site that displays the type of furnishings you are recommending. Format the presentation by using a design template (modify it in some way through your color scheme and text formatting) that you think are effective in conveying your information. Be sure to use a text box to emphasize some point in the presentation. Save the presentation as *[your initials]*5-30. Preview and then print the presentation as an outline and as handouts.

EXERCISE 5-31
Open the file **AdMedia2**. Apply a template and color scheme of your choice; then change the text formatting on the slide master and the title master. Use two different fonts in the presentation and be sure the titles are more bold than the body text. Change bullet shapes and colors; and apply bold, underline, or shadow formatting to individual words where you think it would be effective. Change the size and position of placeholders if you think it improves the look of a slide. Add a slide transition of your choice. Be prepared to explain your choices. Save the presentation as *[your initials]*5-31. Preview and then print the presentation as handouts.

EXERCISE 5-32
Assume you are on a planning committee for a student organization or for your employer that has the responsibility to plan a holiday banquet. Create a slideshow to guide discussion at your first meeting as your group starts planning this project. Identify all the tasks that must be accomplished before the event and plan for the various courses of the meal, such as salad, main dish, side items, and dessert. Using the skills that you have learned up to this point, format the presentation attractively. Include a transition effect. Save the presentation as *[your initials]*5-32. Preview and then print the presentation as handouts.

Unit 2 Applications

UNIT APPLICATION 2-1

Create a new blank presentation, apply a design template, insert slides, change a slide layout, apply text formatting, change text alignment, resize placeholders, change bullets, and work with the slide master.

1. Begin a new presentation that uses the Cliff design template. Change the color scheme to the one with the dark blue background.

2. Working in either the Slide pane or the Outline pane, key the presentation shown in Figure U2-1. Use the Title Slide layout for slide 1 and the Text layout for slides 2 through 4.

FIGURE U2-1

Slide 1
Power Walk and Breakfast
   Good 4 U Promotional Strategy

Slide 2
Objectives
● Encourage morning power walkers to breakfast at G4U
● Make G4U a social center for power walkers

Slide 3
Strategies
● Guided walks
● Seminars
● G4U merchandise
● Advertising

Slide 4
Cost/Benefits Analysis
● Costs
   – Walk guides' salaries
   – Seminar leaders' salaries
   – Merchandise costs
   – Advertising costs
● Benefits
   – Increase breakfasts served
   – Increase repeat business
   – Increase merchandise sales
   – Increase general sales

3. If the AutoFit button appears when you key slide 4, click it and choose the A̲utoFit Text to Placeholder option.

4. On the title slide, make the "Good 4 U" text resemble the company logo that has been used on other presentations by formatting those words in the slide 1 subtitle as follows:

- Make "Good 4 U" bold.
- Make "4 U" italic.
- Increase the font size of "4" three font size increments.
- Position "Promotional Strategy" so that it is on the second line of the subtitle.
- Left-align the title text and move the placeholder to the left slightly.
- Right-align the subtitle text.

5. Use copy and paste to replace all instances of "G4U" with the text you just formatted in step 4. If the Paste Options button appears, click it and choose Use D̲esign Template Formatting.

6. Make the following changes on the slide master:

- Increase the title text font size by one increment.
- Change the slide title font to Arial Black.
- Change the first-level bullet to a star shape of your choice, sized appropriately, in the same color as the original bullet.

7. On slide 4, make the following changes:

- Increase the body text size by one increment.
- Resize the body text placeholder on the right to fit the text.

8. On slide 4, do the following:

- Change the slide layout to Title and 2-Column Text.
- Move the "Benefits" bullet and all its second-level bullets into the right column.
- Center-align "Costs" and "Benefits" and turn off their bullets.
- Change the second-level bullets on this slide to the same shape and color you chose in step 6 above, but make them 80% of the text size.
- Adjust the width and horizontal position of the two bulleted text placeholders so they fit attractively on the slide.

TIP: Use the left and right arrow keys to "nudge" (move slightly) the placeholders without changing their vertical position.

9. Check spelling in the presentation.

10. View the presentation as a slide show.

11. Create a handout header and footer: include the date and your name as the header, and the page number and text *[your initials]*U2-1 as the footer.

12. Move to slide 1 and save the presentation as *[your initials]*U2-1 in a new folder for Unit 2 Applications.

13. Preview and then print the presentation as handouts, 6 slides per page, grayscale, framed. Close the presentation.

UNIT APPLICATION 2-2

Apply a design template, insert slides from another presentation, rearrange text and slides, apply text attributes to text placeholders, resize and position placeholders, change bullets, and work with the slide master.

1. Open the file **Fish1** and apply the Ocean design template.

2. After slide 2, insert slides 2 through 5 from the file **Fish2**. (Remember to use the Insert menu so you don't have to open the file.)

3. View the changes to the presentation.

4. Working in the Slide Sorter, rearrange slides 3 through 6 so that they are in the following order:

Slide number	Title
3	Saltwater Fish
4	Freshwater Fish
5	Shellfish
6	Specialties

    TIP: Display the Outlining toolbar and then collapse the outline before moving the slides.

5. Return to Normal View then use the Clipboard task pane or drag and drop to move the following text to a different slide:

Text to move	From	To
Catfish	slide 3	slide 4, first bullet position
Swordfish	slide 4	slide 3, second bullet position
Trout	slide 6	slide 4, second bullet position

Bass	slide 6	slide 4, third bullet position
Sushi	slide 4	slide 6, first bullet position
Sashimi	slide 4	slide 6, second bullet position

6. On slide 5 ("Shellfish"), promote all the bulleted text one level to first-level bullets.

7. Make the following changes to the slide master:

   - Change the font for both the title placeholder and the body text placeholder to Comic Sans MS.
   - Make the title text placeholder bold.
   - Increase the text size of both placeholders by two increments.
   - Make both placeholders exactly 6.5 inches wide. (Tip: Choose Format, Placeholder.) The title text will appear to wrap outside the placeholder box, but the text that goes here will be shorter than the master slide text.
   - Position both placeholders so that they are exactly 2.5 inches from the left edge of the slide.
   - Change the first-level bullet to the double wavy line shape (Wingdings, center of the fifth row) and change its color to white and 100% of text size.
   - Change the second-level bullet to a small white bullet of your choice, 70% of text size.

8. Display the title master. Check that the title font is Comic Sans MS, bold, and shadowed, and change the size to 66 points. Change the size of the subtitle text to 44 points, and make it Comic Sans MS if it is a different font. Resize the placeholders to fit these new sizes if necessary.

9. Return to Normal View and change the slide 2 bulleted text to sentence case. Make the title placeholder larger by dragging the right resizing handle so the text will fit on one line to match the other slides.

10. Create a handout header and footer: include the date and your name as the header, and the page number and text *[your initials]*U2-2 as the footer.

11. Move to slide 1 and in the subtitle placeholder make Server Training appear on the second line. Save the presentation as *[your initials]*U2-2 in your Unit 2 Applications folder.

12. View the presentation as a slide show. Preview and then print the presentation as handouts, 6 slides per page, grayscale, framed. Close the presentation.

Create slides from a Word outline, apply a design template, insert a new slide in the Outline pane, change a slide layout, apply text attributes, work with text boxes, and add speaker's notes.

1. Create a new presentation from the word-processed outline file **PwrWalk4**. (Use the Slides from Outline command on the Insert menu.) You should have five slides. If there are more, delete the blank slides.

2. Apply the design template Glass Layers and use the color scheme with the gold background.

3. Apply the Title Slide layout to slide 1.

4. On slide 2, make the following changes:
   - Promote the third-level bullets under "Healthy diet" to second-level bullets.
   - Move "Customer convenience" above "Sensible exercise."
   - Move "Healthy diet" above "Sensible exercise."

5. Reverse the positions of slide 4 and slide 5.

6. Make the following changes to the slide master:
   - Format the title placeholder as Verdana, bold, 44 points, and shadowed. (The shadow effect should have already been applied.)
   - Format the bulleted list placeholder as Verdana and change first-level bullets to a diamond shape, 75% of the text size, and make them a non-green color of your choice.
   - Change the second-level bullets to white boxed check marks, 75% of text size (Wingdings, bottom row).

7. Make the following changes to the title master:
   - Format the title placeholder as Verdana, bold, 54 points, and shadowed. (The shadow effect should have already been applied.)
   - Format the subtitle placeholder as Verdana, bold, 36 points, and shadowed. (The shadow effect should have already been applied.)

8. Return to Normal View. On each slide, reapply the layout to update to the master slide changes.

9. On slide 1, delete the word "Restaurant" and make Sports Promotions display on the second line. Add the following speaker's note to slide 1:
   Read first paragraph from mayor's press release on power walk event

10. On slide 2, change the case of the body text placeholder to sentence case.

11. Open the Excel file **Calories1** and save it in your Unit 2 Applications folder; then create a hyperlink to the Excel file by using the text "Sensible exercise" on slide 2. Give the hyperlink the ScreenTip **Calories burned by walking**

12. Create a text box on the lower part of slide 5. Key the text **We hope to see you here!** Make the text Verdana, 28 point, bold, and italic. Rotate the text box slightly.

13. Create a handout header and footer: include the date and your name as the header, and the page number and text *[your initials]*U2-3 as the footer.

14. Move to slide 1 and save the presentation with the filename *[your initials]*U2-3 in your Unit 2 Applications folder. Save it again as a Web page.

15. If possible, view your presentation as a Web page. If not, view it as a slide show.

16. Preview and print the presentation as handouts, 6 slides per page, grayscale, framed. Print the notes page for slide 1. Close the presentation.

UNIT APPLICATION 2-4   *Using the Internet*

Create a Word outline and use it to create a presentation.

Use the Internet to research a self-help topic. Choose something that interests you, such as weight loss, anti-aging, body toning, personality improvement, etc. The following is a list of suggested information to gather:

- Background on the topic
- Who might be interested in this topic
- Main points to begin the process of self-help in this area
- Any other information that you think would be useful for a presentation
- Be sure to cite where you found the information

Use the material you researched to create a Word outline suitable for an informative presentation on your subject; then use the outline to create a PowerPoint presentation. Choose any design template and format the presentation attractively.

Be sure to include in the presentation at least five slides and one hyperlink. The hyperlink can be either to a Word document, an Excel spreadsheet or chart, or a Web site.

In the slide footer, include the text **Prepared by** followed by your name. Include the slide number on all slides but not the date. In the handout footer, include the text *[your initials]*U2-4. In the handout header, key **Presented to** and then identify to whom you would be giving this presentation. Include in the handout the date you would be delivering the presentation.

Check spelling in the presentation and save it as a Web page with the file-name *[your initials]*U2-4 in your Unit 2 Applications folder. Practice delivering the presentation as a Web page by using the browser installed on your computer. Preview and then print the presentation handouts, choosing an appropriate number of slides per page, grayscale, framed. Close the presentation.

UNIT 3

Customizing a Presentation

LESSON 6

Working with PowerPoint Objects

OBJECTIVES

After completing this lesson, you will be able to:

1. **Work with drawing tools.**
2. **Use AutoShape tools.**
3. **Insert clip art.**
4. **Adjust clip art size and image settings.**
5. **Use WordArt for special text effects.**

 Estimated Time: 1½ hours

MICROSOFT OFFICE
SPECIALIST
ACTIVITIES
In this lesson:
   PP03S-1-4
   PP03S-2-2

See Appendix.

An effective slide presentation uses more than text alone. Although text carries most of the information, you can use several types of objects to emphasize your message and draw attention to the presentation. For example, you can add chart objects, free-floating text objects, clip art objects, and scanned photographs to a presentation.

After you add an object to a slide, you can change its size and position. In this lesson, you concentrate on basic changes that can be made to clip art and objects created with PowerPoint's drawing tools. In a later lesson, you learn how to manipulate objects further by applying colors and textured fills, and by rearranging elements within objects.

Working with Basic Drawing Tools

The PowerPoint Drawing toolbar provides you with a variety of tools you can use to create your own drawings. In this lesson, you learn basic drawing skills. In later lessons, you learn how to enhance simple objects and create more complex drawings.

The ruler can be helpful when drawing a specific sized object using the drawing tools. When the rulers are displayed, a dotted line on each ruler indicates the horizontal and vertical position of your mouse pointer, measured from the center of the slide. You can use these ruler indicators to help you draw, size, and position objects.

TABLE 6-1   Drawing Toolbar

BUTTON	PURPOSE
Draw ▾	Opens the Draw menu, which contains tools for aligning, grouping, rotating, flipping, and other manipulations of PowerPoint objects.
Select Objects	Selects an object. This tool is automatically in effect when no other tool is in use.
AutoShapes ▾ AutoShapes	Opens the AutoShapes menu, which contains predefined shapes you can draw.
Line	Draws a straight line.
Arrow	Draws an arrow.
Rectangle	Draws a rectangle or square.
Oval	Draws an oval or circle.
Text Box	Inserts text anywhere on a slide.
Insert WordArt	Creates a Microsoft WordArt object on a slide.
Insert Diagram or Organization Chart	Creates an Org chart or a diagram on a slide.
Insert Clip Art	Inserts a clip art object.
Insert Picture	Inserts a bitmap or photo image.

continues

TABLE 6-1 Drawing Toolbar *continued*

BUTTON	PURPOSE
Fill Color	Fills an object with colors, patterns, or textures.
Line Color	Changes the color of an object's outline.
Font Color	Changes the color of selected text. The Font Color button also appears on the Formatting toolbar.
Line Style	Chooses a line style and thickness for the outline of a selected object or a straight line that you draw.
Dash Style	Applies dotted or dashed line styles to an object.
Arrow Style	Applies arrowheads to selected lines.
Shadow Style	Applies shadow effects to an object. This is not the same as the Shadow button on the Formatting toolbar, which works only on text.
3-D Style	Applies 3-D effects to an object.

EXERCISE **6-1** **Draw Simple Lines and Shapes**

In this exercise, you practice drawing rectangles, ovals, and straight lines on a blank slide. To draw an object, click the appropriate Drawing toolbar button (Line ◣, Rectangle ▢, or Oval ◯); then drag the crosshair pointer ⊞ on your slide until the object is the size you want.

You can draw multiple objects by double-clicking a Drawing toolbar button. Double-clicking keeps the button activated, so you can draw as many shapes as you want without the need to reclick. When you finish drawing, click the button again to deactivate it.

1. Open the presentation file **Opening1**.

NOTE: Two of the slides in this presentation were created by using the Blank slide layout. The blank layout contains no text placeholders. The text that appears on the slides is placed in text boxes, instead of placeholders as you learned in Lesson 5.

2. Insert a new slide after slide 2 and use the Blank layout (the first layout under the Content Layouts heading). You will use this slide to practice drawing.

3. If the rulers are not showing, right-click a blank area of the slide and choose Ruler from the shortcut menu.

4. While watching the horizontal ruler at the top of the slide, move your mouse pointer back and forth, observing the dotted line on the ruler indicating the pointer's position. While moving your mouse pointer up and down, observe the dotted line on the vertical ruler. Click the Rectangle button ▢ on the Drawing toolbar. The mouse pointer changes to a crosshair pointer ⊞.

5. Move the crosshair pointer to the 3-inch mark to the left of the zero on the horizontal ruler (at the top of the slide) and to the 2-inch mark above the zero on the vertical ruler (at the side of the slide).

6. Click and hold the left mouse button. Drag diagonally down and to the right until you reach the 2-inch mark below the zero on the vertical ruler and the 3-inch mark to the right of the zero on the horizontal ruler. Release your mouse button. A white rectangle with a dark blue outline appears. (You learn how to change colors and line styles in the next lesson.) See Figure 6-1 to compare the size and placement of the completed rectangle.

NOTE: The green handle just above the rectangle is a rotation handle. It can be used to rotate a shape in the same way it was used to rotate a text box in the previous lesson.

FIGURE 6-1
Drawing objects
on a slide

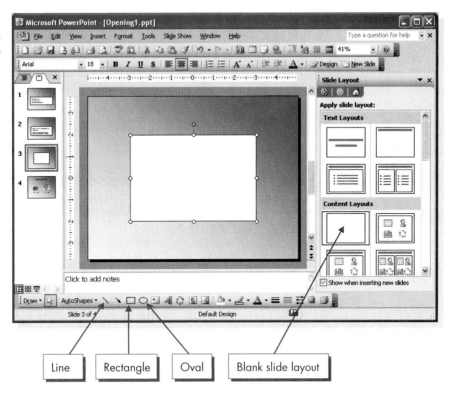

7. Click the Oval button ⬭.

8. Draw an oval on the inside of the rectangle that you previously drew, using the same method that you used to draw the rectangle.

9. Click the Line button ◥; then drag your pointer diagonally from the left corner of the rectangle to the edge of the oval to create a line.

10. Double-click the Line button ◥, and then draw another line from another corner of the rectangle to the edge of the oval. Notice that the mouse pointer still has the crosshair pointer ➕ and the Line button ◥ is still selected.

11. Without clicking the Line button, draw two more lines from the other two corners to the oval in the middle of the rectangle. Your screen should look similar to the back of an envelope with a seal.

12. Click the Line button ◥ again to deactivate it.

EXERCISE ▧ **6-2** ▧ **Delete Objects**

If you don't like an object that you created, you can easily remove it from your slide. Simply select the object by clicking it, and then press ⎗Delete⎘ on your keyboard.

1. Click one of the lines to select it. Notice the white sizing handles on each end of the line indicating that it is selected.

2. Press ⎗Delete⎘ on your keyboard. The selected line disappears.

3. Press ⎗Tab⎘ one or more times until another one of the lines is selected. (This is another way of selecting an object.)

4. Press ⎗Delete⎘ to delete the line; then delete the remaining lines. The slide should now contain one rectangle with one oval inside it.

EXERCISE ▧ **6-3** ▧ **Draw Horizontal, Vertical, and Other Constrained Lines**

You use ⎗Shift⎘ to *constrain* an object as you draw it on a slide. For lines, constraining enables you to make perfectly straight horizontal, vertical, or angled lines. With this feature, lines are limited to angles in increments of 15 degrees.

When using ⎗Shift⎘ to constrain an object, it's important to release your mouse button before releasing ⎗Shift⎘. Otherwise, you might accidentally move the mouse when ⎗Shift⎘ is no longer in effect, resulting in an object that is no longer constrained.

1. Still working on slide 3, zoom to 66 percent by using the Zoom box on the Standard toolbar; then scroll to display the rectangle. Zooming in on the area will make it easier to see what you're doing when you work on detailed objects.

2. Double-click the Line button ◥. You're going to draw several constrained lines without needing to reclick the Line button each time you draw.

3. Position the pointer on the left side of the rectangle on the ruler's zero marker, hold down Shift, and drag straight across to the right side of the rectangle. (As you drag, notice that the line remains straight, even if you move the mouse up or down a little.)

4. Release the mouse button first, and then release Shift.

5. With the Line button ◥ still activated, position the crosshair pointer ➕ at the left end of the rectangle again about ½ inch above where you drew the last line. Hold down Shift and drag to the right edge of the rectangle. Release the mouse button, and then release Shift. Continue this process until the rectangle is full of horizontal lines ½ inch apart.

6. Click on the oval to select it. Notice the white sizing handles on each end of the line indicating that it is selected. Press Delete on your keyboard. The selected oval disappears.

7. Change the zoom setting to Fit to display the entire slide.

8. Move the crosshair pointer to an open space on the slide. While pressing Shift, draw a diagonal line. Without releasing either the mouse or Shift, move your pointer up, and then down. Notice how the line "jumps" in 15-degree increments.

FIGURE 6-2
Drawing constrained lines at 15-degree increments

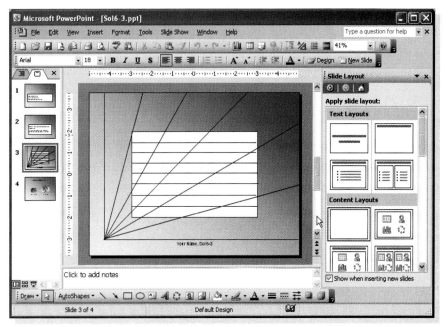

9. Now double-click the line tool so you can make a series of constrained lines. Starting at about ½ inch from the lower left of the slide, draw a

vertical line extending to the top of the slide. Then start at the same point and move the crosshair slightly to the right, so a second line moves 15 degrees. Repeat this process to draw additional lines for each of the next 15-degree increments until the final line is a horizontal line. Refer to Figure 6-2 for the approximate line placement and the angle.

10. Insert a footer only on slide 3 that contains your name, a comma, and the text *[your initials]***6-3**. (Do not include the date.)

 REVIEW: To insert a footer on one slide only, be sure the current slide is where you want the footer. Then open the Header and Footer dialog box and click <u>A</u>pply instead of Apply to All. The footer will appear only on that slide.

11. Create a new folder for Lesson 6. Save the presentation as *[your initials]***6-3** in the new Lesson 6 folder. Print only slide 3, full size, grayscale, and framed. Keep the presentation open for the following exercises.

NOTE: The documents you create in this course relate to the Case Study about Good 4 U, a fictional restaurant business (see pages 1–4).

EXERCISE `6-4` **Create Squares and Circles**

When you constrain other objects, such as rectangles or ovals, they grow at an equal rate horizontally and vertically as you draw, creating symmetrical objects such as squares and circles.

1. Insert a new slide after slide 3; use the Blank layout.

2. On the new slide 4, click the Rectangle button ▣.

3. Position the crosshair pointer on the left of your slide.

4. Press and hold (Shift) and drag diagonally down and to the right, ending near the center of the slide. Release the mouse button first, and then release (Shift). See Figure 6-3 for the approximate size and placement of the completed square.

FIGURE 6-3
Drawing a circle
and a square

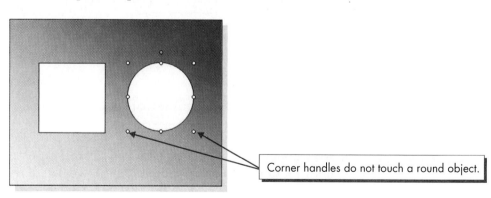

Corner handles do not touch a round object.

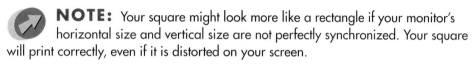

NOTE: Your square might look more like a rectangle if your monitor's horizontal size and vertical size are not perfectly synchronized. Your square will print correctly, even if it is distorted on your screen.

5. Click the Oval button 🔘.

6. Position your pointer to the right of the square.

7. While pressing (Shift), drag diagonally down and to the right to create a circle about the same size as the square. Your screen should resemble Figure 6-3. Notice that with a circular shape, the corner handles do not touch the shape.

EXERCISE 6-5   Change the Size and Position of Objects You Draw

You resize an object that you draw in the same way that you resize a text place-holder: select it, and then drag one of its sizing handles. Holding down (Shift) and/or (Ctrl) while dragging a sizing handle has the following effects on an object:

- (Shift) preserves an object's *proportions*, meaning that its height grows or shrinks at the same rate as its width, preventing objects from becoming too tall and skinny or too short and wide.

- (Ctrl) causes an object to grow or shrink from the center of the object, rather than from the edge that's being dragged.

- (Ctrl)+(Shift) together cause an object to grow or shrink proportionately from its center.

You reposition an object by dragging it with the four-pointed arrow ✛. Simply point anywhere in the object. When you see the four-pointed arrow, drag the object to another place on your slide.

1. Select the circle by clicking anywhere inside it, and then point to its bottom center sizing handle. Your pointer changes to a two-pointed vertical arrow [↕].

2. Drag the handle down. As you drag, the pointer changes to a crosshair ⊞. The circle has changed into an oval and is now larger.

3. Drag the bottom-left corner handle diagonally up and to the left. The oval is now wider and flattened, taking on an entirely new shape.

4. Click the Undo button 🔄 twice to restore the circle to its original size and shape.

5. Point to the circle's lower-left corner sizing handle. While holding down (Shift), drag diagonally out from the circle's center, making it larger. (Don't worry if the circle overlaps the rectangle.) The circle retains its original shape.

6. While holding down both (Ctrl) and (Shift), drag the lower-left corner sizing handle toward the center of the circle. The circle becomes smaller, shrinking evenly from all edges. (See Figure 6-4 on the next page.)

FIGURE 6-4
Resizing an object
from its center

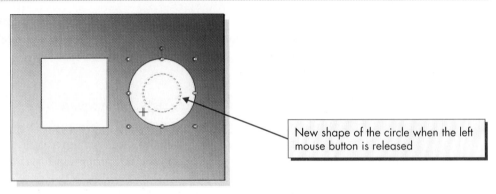

New shape of the circle when the left
mouse button is released

7. Point to the center of the circle. When you see the four-pointed arrow ⊕, drag the circle down, so that it is at the lower right of the slide.

NOTE: Whenever you drag to move an object or text, make sure you are not dragging a sizing handle by mistake. You must see the four-pointed arrow, and not the two-pointed arrow.

8. Save the presentation as *[your initials]*6-5 in your Lesson 6 folder, but do not print it. Leave it open for the next exercise.

EXERCISE **6-6** **Resize Objects by Using the Format AutoShape Dialog Box**

Just as you can resize text placeholders, you can use the Format AutoShape dialog box to resize objects that you draw. When the selected object is either a circle or a square, both the Height and Width settings on the Size tab will have the same measurement.

FIGURE 6-5
Resizing an object by using the Format AutoShape dialog box

Format AutoShape

Colors and Lines | Size | Position | Picture | Text Box | Web

Size and rotate
Height: 2.76" Width: 2.76"
Rotation: 0°

Scale
Height: 100 % Width: 100 %
☑ Lock aspect ratio
☐ Relative to original picture size
☐ Best scale for slide show
Resolution: 640 x 480

Original size
Height: Width: Reset

OK Cancel Preview

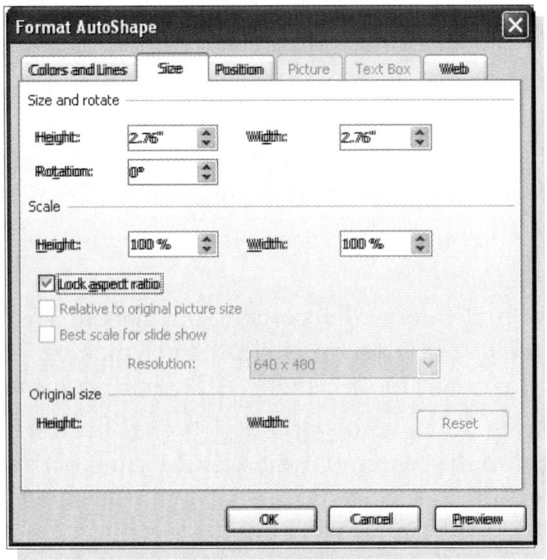

1. Still working on slide 4, right-click the square object, choose Format AutoShape from the shortcut menu, and click the Size tab. Notice that the height and width are the same measurement.

2. Under Scale, check the Lock aspect ratio check box. This will force the height and width of an object to change size at the same rate.

3. In the Size and rotate section, key **1.75** in the Height box; then press ⌨Tab to move to the next box. Notice that the measurement in the Width box automatically changes to 1.75 because the aspect ratio (relationship between height and width sizes) is locked. Click OK.

4. Select the circle, and then click the Cut button ✂ (or press Ctrl+X) to remove the circle from the slide and send it to the clipboard.

5. Insert two new slides after slide 4 that use the Blank slide layout (creating slides 5 and 6).

6. Paste the circle on the new slide 5.

7. Move to slide 6. (You return to slides 4 and 5 later in this lesson to add text and other elements.)

8. Draw a 4.5-inch square in the approximate center of slide 5. Using the Format AutoShape dialog box, make the square exactly 4.5 inches wide and 4.5 inches high. Under the position tab of the Format AutoShape dialog box, change the position of the square to be exactly 2.75 inches from the Top Left Corner (Horizontal setting) and exactly 1.75 inches down from the Top Left Corner (Vertical setting).

TIP: If you like working with the ruler indicators, you can precisely size and position objects without the need to open the Format AutoShape dialog box, but keep in mind that the rulers measure distances from the center of the slide. So, if you point to the 2-inch mark to the right of the zero mark on the horizontal ruler, you need to do some math to figure out how far you are from either edge of the slide. The Position tab on the Format AutoShape dialog box lets you choose to measure either from the center of the slide or from its top and left edges.

Creating Basic AutoShapes

PowerPoint provides an assortment of predefined shapes called *AutoShapes*. You can use AutoShapes to draw perfectly shaped arrows, stars, flowchart objects, callouts, and other shapes.

You resize these shapes the same way you resize other objects. Many shapes include an additional yellow diamond handle, called an *adjustment handle*, which you use to reshape the object after it is drawn.

EXERCISE   **6-7**   **Create AutoShapes**

The rectangles, ovals, and lines that you created by using the Drawing toolbar buttons are basic AutoShapes. To access a large assortment of basic and special-ized AutoShapes, click AutoShapes on the Drawing toolbar and choose from a menu of AutoShape categories. You can change this menu into a floating toolbar, as you did with the Font Color menu in Lesson 5. In addition, each AutoShape category has its own menu that can be floated.

1. Working on slide 6, click AutoShapes on the Drawing toolbar to display the AutoShapes menu.

2. Point to each option on the AutoShapes menu to view the shapes on the submenus.

FIGURE 6-6
Making the
Stars and Banners
menu float

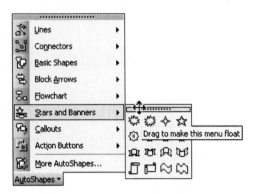

3. Point to Stars and Banners; then position your pointer over the thin bar at the top of the Stars and Banners submenu. When you see the four-pointed arrow ⊕, drag it to the upper-left corner of your screen. The Stars and Banners submenu is now a floating toolbar.

4. Point to the various shapes on the Stars and Banners floating toolbar and read their ScreenTips.

5. Double-click the 5-Point Star shape ☆, and then draw several stars in different sizes positioned randomly on the slide with some stars overlapping. Place stars on the square and on the blank area of the slide. You draw an AutoShape by dragging the crosshair pointer, just as when you draw a rectangle or oval.

 TIP: Use SHIFT to create a symmetrical AutoShape in the same way that you use SHIFT when you draw a circle or square.

6. Click the Close button ✕ on the title bar of the Stars and Banners floating toolbar to close it.

7. Move to slide 5, click AutoShapes on the Drawing toolbar to display the AutoShapes menu, and choose the Basic Shapes menu. Make this submenu a floating toolbar and position it at the upper left of the slide.

FIGURE 6-7
Drawing and
adjusting
an AutoShape

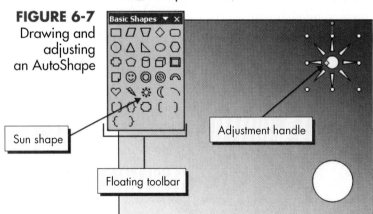

Sun shape

Floating toolbar

Adjustment handle

8. From the floating Basic Shapes menu, click the Sun ☼ object. Draw a sun, about two inches in diameter, in the upper-right corner of the slide.

9. Drag the yellow diamond-shaped adjustment handle ◇ toward the center of the Sun AutoShape to lengthen its points.

10. Click the Close button ☒ on the title bar of the Basic Shapes floating toolbar to close it.

EXERCISE **6-8** **Change an AutoShape**

If you draw an AutoShape, and then decide you want a different shape, you can delete it just as you deleted other objects earlier in this lesson, and then draw a new shape.

If you took the time to carefully size and place the AutoShape (and perhaps even key text inside it), you will find that it is more convenient to change the shape instead of deleting, and then re-creating it. You change an AutoShape by clicking Draw on the Drawing toolbar, and then choosing Change AutoShape from the menu.

1. Select the Sun shape on slide 5.

2. Click Draw on the Drawing toolbar to display the menu.

3. Choose Change AutoShape, and then choose Stars and Banners from the submenu. Choose Change Shape to 16-Point Star ⚙.

4. Select the circle shape on slide 5 and change its shape to a square. With the square selected, right-click to access the Format AutoShapes menu. Make the height and width exactly 4.5 inches. Move the square to the center of the slide.

FIGURE 6-8
Changing an
AutoShape

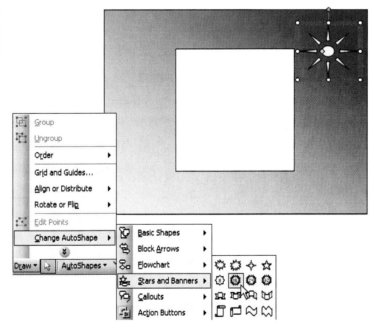

EXERCISE 6-9 **Place Text in an AutoShape**

You can easily transform an AutoShape into an attention-getting background for text. Simply select the AutoShape and key the text (or paste it from the clipboard). You can format and edit the text in the same way as in a text placeholder. The text in an AutoShape is centered by default.

1. Select the 16-Point Star 🔘 AutoShape.

2. Key **Grand Opening!** The text automatically appears in the center of the star in the same color as the AutoShape border. Notice the diagonal-line border similar to a text placeholder border.

3. Click the AutoShape's border anywhere between two sizing handles to select it.

4. Using the Font Size box on the Formatting toolbar, change the size from 18 points to 28 points and apply bold. The text becomes too large for the 16-Point Star AutoShape.

FIGURE 6-9
Inserting text in an AutoShape

5. Drag the center sizing handle on the left side to make the AutoShape wide enough to contain the text. Part of the star shape will be over the square shape.

6. Drag the top-center sizing handle down to flatten the AutoShape.

7. Save the presentation as *[your initials]*6-9 in your Lesson 6 folder, but do not print it. Leave the presentation open for the next exercise. You continue with slide 5 in the next exercise.

EXERCISE 6-10 **Rotate an AutoShape**

You rotate an AutoShape (or any other object) the same way that you rotate a text box. If the AutoShape contains text, the text also rotates.

1. Still working on slide 5, select the 16-Point Star AutoShape containing the text "Grand Opening!"

2. Hold down Shift and drag the green rotation handle one increment to the left. The AutoShape and its text are now rotated 15 degrees.

FIGURE 6-10
Edited text in
a rotated object

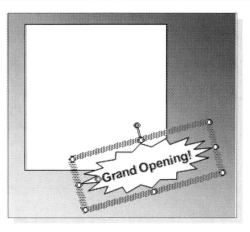

3. Drag the AutoShape down until it overlaps the lower-right corner of the square.

4. Compare slide 5 with Figure 6-10 and make any necessary adjustments.

5. Create a handout header and footer: include the date and your name as the header, and the page number and text *[your initials]*6-10 as the footer.

6. Move to slide 1 and save the presentation as *[your initials]*6-10 in your Lesson 6 folder.

Inserting Clip Art

Included with Microsoft Office is a collection of ready-to-use images known as *clip art* that you can insert on PowerPoint slides. The clip art collection includes *vector drawings*—images made up of lines, curves, and shapes that are usually filled with solid colors. It also includes *bitmap pictures*—photographs made up of tiny colored dots that are made from scanned photographs or a digital camera. These photographs can be accessed from the Insert Clip Art task pane.

You can insert clip art and picture images into a PowerPoint presentation in several ways:

- Click the Insert Clip Art button 🖾 on the Drawing toolbar to display the Insert Clip Art task pane.

- Use the Insert menu (Picture, Clip Art) to display the Insert Clip Art task pane.

- Use the Insert Picture button 🖾 on the Picture toolbar to insert picture files stored on a hard drive, floppy disk, or network drive. This method is useful for inserting your own images that you have stored on your computer and that are not part of the Microsoft Clip Organizer collection.

If your slide uses a content layout that includes a content placeholder, double-click the Insert Clip Art button 🖾 in the content placeholder to insert clip art.

E X E R C I S E `6-11` **Find and Modify a Clip Art Search**

Each clip art image that Microsoft provides has keywords associated with it. These keywords describe the subject matter of the picture. You search for the keywords to find the art you need for your presentation.

Clip art (and other media such as photographs, sound, and movie files) is organized into collections and media types. You can choose to search all collections

FIGURE 6-11
Insert Clip Art
task pane

[handwritten annotations: VECTOR DRAWING SHAPES; BIT-MAPS PHOTO QUALITY]

FIGURE 6-12
Search results

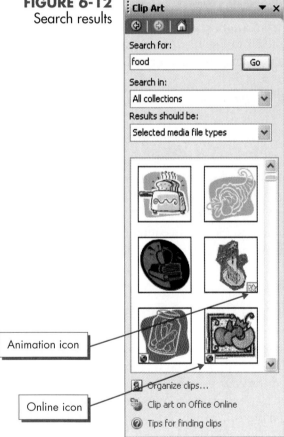

Animation icon

Online icon

and types or to select a particular type. If you know that you want a photograph only, be sure to select that type of media only to make the search faster and more efficient.

If you search for a keyword and don't find any pictures, or you don't find one you like, you can modify your search and look for something different.

1. If you have Internet access, but are not connected, make a connection now (unless your instructor tells you otherwise).

2. Move to slide 2, and then click the Insert Clip Art button 🖼 on the Drawing toolbar. The Insert Clip Art task pane is displayed.

3. If the Add Clips to Organizer dialog box appears, click Later.

4. In the Insert Clip Art task pane, click the list box arrow for Search in. Notice that Everywhere is checked, meaning that all categories in the Microsoft Clip Organizer will be searched and, if you are connected to the Internet, the Microsoft Office Online will be searched, too.

5. Close the list box; then click the list box arrow for Results should be. In this list box, you can choose to search all media types or limit your search to specific types. These options are helpful if you have a large number of media files stored on your computer, or you are searching on the Internet. Uncheck all categories except Clip Art.

6. Key **food** in the Search for text box at the top of the Clip Art task pane, and then click Go. The Results box shows thumbnails (miniature images) of clips that match the search word.

NOTE: Clips from the Microsoft Office Online collection have an online icon 🔘 in the lower-left corner of the image thumbnail. Some of these clips also contain a musical note, indicating that they are sound files. Some clips have an animation icon 🔲 displayed in the lower-right corner, indicating that they are movies.

7. Use the scroll bar to review some of the thumbnails.

8. Key **apple** in the Search text box, and then click Search. Thumbnails of pictures with apples in them should appear in your Results box. If you do not find a picture you like, modify again.

EXERCISE 6-12 Preview and Insert Clip Art

You can preview images in a larger format, so you can see more detail before choosing a picture.

1. Without clicking, point to a clip art thumbnail in the task pane. Notice the gray bar with the arrow on the right side of the thumbnail.

2. Click the gray bar to display a menu of options. You can also display this menu by right-clicking a thumbnail.

3. Choose Preview/Properties. In addition to displaying an enlarged picture, this dialog box also shows you the filename and location of the picture, its size, and other helpful information. See Figure 6-13.

FIGURE 6-13
Preview/Properties
dialog box

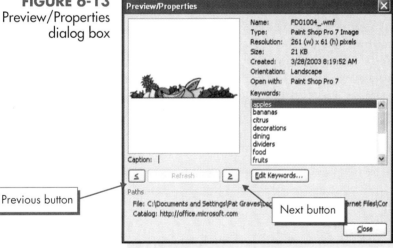

4. Click the Next button ≥ below the picture. The next picture in the search results pane is displayed.

5. Click the Next button ≥ several times more; then click the Previous button ≤. When you find a picture of health conscious food that you like, such as

the one in Figure 6-13, click Close. Notice that the last picture you previewed has a box around it.

6. With your left mouse button, click the thumbnail for the image you chose. The clip art image is inserted on the current slide.

 TIP: You can also drag the image directly from the task pane onto your slide or select Insert from the drop-down arrow next to the thumbnail.

7. Drag the image above the text box and resize it as necessary for a pleasing appearance. The image in Figure 6-13 was increased in size to fit across the width of the text box. If you found a different image, then decide how to position it attractively on the slide.

8. On slide 1, search for another image that would be appropriate for Miami Beach. So, for this slide, search for a palm tree and choose the Photograph media option in the Results should be: box. When you find a photograph of a palm tree that you like, insert it on slide 1.

EXERCISE **6-13** **Insert a Picture from File**

If you have a scanner or a digital camera that connects to your computer, you can insert images directly from those devices onto a slide. There are two ways to work with bitmap (digital) images:

● To insert an image directly onto a slide, set up the picture in the scanner (or set up your camera), open the Insert menu, and choose Picture, From Scanner or Camera. If you have both a camera and a scanner attached to your computer, choose the device from the drop-down list, and then choose Web Quality or Print Quality. Click Insert or Custom Insert. You can then use the tools on the Picture toolbar to adjust the image.

● To insert a digital image that is stored on a disk drive, open the Insert menu and choose Picture, From File (or click the Insert Picture button 🖼 on the Drawing toolbar). In the Insert Picture dialog box, locate the picture file and click Insert.

In this exercise, you insert a previously scanned photograph from your student data disk.

1. Display slide 5.

 2. Click the Insert Picture button 🖼 on the Drawing toolbar.

3. In the Insert Picture dialog box, locate the file **Miami1.jpg** on your student data disk and click Insert.

4. Use the Size tab on the Format Picture dialog box to lock the picture's aspect ratio, and then change its height to 4 inches.

EXERCISE **6-14** **Rearrange and Delete Clip Art Images**

You can easily rearrange or delete clip art. Moving clip art is similar to moving a text placeholder or an AutoShape.

1. Still working on slide 5, click on the photograph to select it and when you see the four-pointed arrow ⊕, drag the photograph to the center of the square, and then resize the square to fit the picture as though it is framed.

2. Move to slide 2 and point to the image on top. When you see the four-pointed arrow ⊕, drag the picture to the bottom of the slide to consider how the image would look there.

3. Although this image looks nice on the bottom of the slide, in this case, it looks better above the text box. So, click Undo to return the image to its previous location.

FIGURE 6-14
Repositioning
a picture

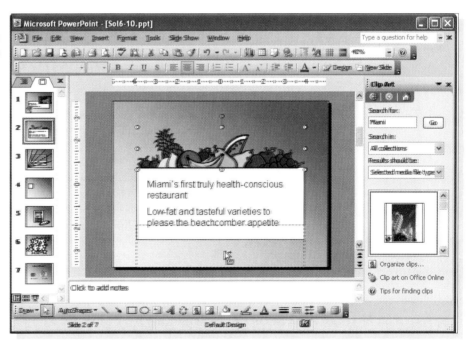

4. Move to slide 7. This slide has four images that have been previously inserted. Select the clip art beach scene on the lower left and press `Delete` to remove it from your slide.

5. Save the presentation as *[your initials]*6-14, but do not print it. Keep the file open for the next exercise.

EXERCISE **6-15** **Copy a Clip Art Image from Another Slide**

Sometimes you might insert a picture on a slide and later decide to move it to a different slide. You can cut, copy, and paste pictures in the same way as you cut, copy, and paste text.

1. On slide 7, click the palm tree image on the right to select it.
2. Click the Copy button 🔳 to copy the picture to the clipboard.
3. Move to slide 1 and click the Paste button 🔳. Make the palm tree smaller and position it in the lower-left corner. With this image selected, press Ctrl +D to duplicate the image, and then position it beside the first palm tree at the bottom of the slide. Repeat this process until the bottom of the slide is lined with palm trees.

EXERCISE **6-16** **Add a Picture to a Slide Master**

You can add pictures, AutoShapes, and other objects to a slide master in the same way as you add objects to a presentation slide. Images can be inserted directly, or you can paste them from the clipboard.

1. On slide 1, select one of the palm tree clip art images and click the Copy button 🔳.
2. Display the slide master.
3. Click the Paste button 🔳. Move the image to the upper left-hand corner of the slide. The image hides part of the title placeholder. Because this presentation uses only the Blank slide layout, the hidden placeholder is not a problem.
4. Close the Master view; then scroll through all the slides to see the effect of the new background.
5. Save the presentation as *[your initials]*6-16 in your Lesson 6 folder, but do not print it. Leave it open for the next exercise.

NOTE: Pictures or other objects that you want on the background of all slides of a presentation should be positioned on the slide master because it controls the background, fonts, and placeholder positioning for the slide layouts that make up the body of a presentation. The title master controls the title slide design only, so pictures or other objects placed there will appear only on slides created with the title slide layout.

Adjusting Clip Art Size and Image Settings

You can change the look of clip art images in many ways, including changing the size, contrast, and brightness. The Picture toolbar helps you accomplish this.

EXERCISE **6-17** **Resize a Clip Art Image**

Resizing a clip art image is similar to resizing a text placeholder or an AutoShape. The one difference is that with a clip art image, you can drag a corner handle without distorting proportions, even if you forget to hold down Shift.

1. Move to slide 7, choose the palm tree image you have already used with the dark green color and press Delete to remove it. Select the text box for Palm tree and move it to the bottom of the slide.

2. Select the remaining image of the palm tree; then place the pointer on the bottom-center sizing handle. The pointer changes to a vertical two-pointed arrow ↕.

3. Drag the handle down. The object becomes taller, distorting the image.

4. Press Ctrl+Z to undo the resizing.

5. With the palm tree still selected, drag a corner handle diagonally away from the center of the picture until the picture is about twice its original size. Dragging the corner handle preserves the image's proportions, without the need to hold down Shift.

6. Right-click the picture and choose Format Picture from the shortcut menu. Click the Size tab.

7. Make sure that Lock aspect ratio is checked. In the Height box, under Size and rotate, key **4.0**. Click OK.

8. Drag the image down and adjust the text box positioning below the image. You can use the arrow keys or Ctrl+the arrow key to fine-tune the picture's position. This permits small movements called *nudging*.

9. Select both the photo image and the text box for the Beach scene and move those two objects down by nudging.

10. Save the presentation as *[your initials]***6-17** in your Lesson 6 folder, but do not print it. Leave it open for the next exercise.

EXERCISE 6-18 Change Clip Art Image Settings

When a picture on a slide is selected, the Picture toolbar usually appears. You can use the Picture toolbar to control various aspects of an image's appearance, such as size, brightness, contrast, and color.

1. Delete slides 3 and 5 with the lines and stars you practiced earlier in this lesson. On the new slide 3, delete the white square.

2. Move to slide 5 and copy the picture labeled "Beach scene" to the clipboard; then paste it on slide 3. This is a photograph image that was previously inserted for you.

3. Select the beach scene picture that you copied onto slide 3 and move it to the center of the slide. If the Picture toolbar is not displayed, right-click the picture and choose Show Picture Toolbar from the shortcut menu.

FIGURE 6-15
Picture toolbar

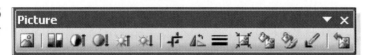

TABLE 6-2   Picture Toolbar

BUTTON	PURPOSE
Insert Picture	Opens the Insert Picture dialog box.
Color	Enables you to change a picture's color to grayscale, black-and-white, or washout.
More Contrast	Increases a picture's contrast.
Less Contrast	Decreases a picture's contrast.
More Brightness	Makes a picture lighter and brighter.
Less Brightness	Makes a picture less bright.
Crop	Enables you to cut away the edges of a picture.
Rotate Left	Turns a picture on its side.

continues

TABLE 6-2 Picture Toolbar *continued*

BUTTON	PURPOSE
≡ Line Style	Enables you to put a frame around a picture.
Compress Pictures	Strips unnecessary information from a picture file to make the file size smaller.
Recolor Picture	Enables you to change individual colors in a vector drawing. This button does not work for bitmaps.
Format Picture	Opens the Format Picture dialog box.
Set Transparent Color	Enables you to select one color on an image to make it disappear. This is best used with a simple vector image when you want to make its background disappear.
Reset Picture	Restores a picture's original attributes if changes were made by using the Picture toolbar buttons.

4. With the picture selected, click the Format Picture button on the Picture toolbar, and then click the Size tab.

5. Uncheck the Lock aspect ratio box (you want to deliberately distort this picture slightly).

6. Under Size and rotate, change the Height to 7.5 inches and the Width to 10 inches. Click OK. This makes the picture the same size as the slide.

7. Using the four-pointed arrow ⊕, reposition the picture so its edges align with the edges of the slide. The picture now fills the entire slide.

8. With the picture selected, click the More Contrast button on the Picture toolbar five times. The contrast is much more pronounced.

9. Click the Color button on the Picture toolbar; then choose Automatic from the drop-down menu. The picture's colors are restored to their original state.

10. Click the Less Brightness button four times. Now the picture has changed to a nighttime scene.

11. Restore the picture to its original colors.

12. Click the Color button and choose Grayscale. Now adjust the brightness and contrast slightly, until the picture is more clear as a black and white image.

13. Restore the picture to its original colors.

FIGURE 6-16
Image-adjusted
picture

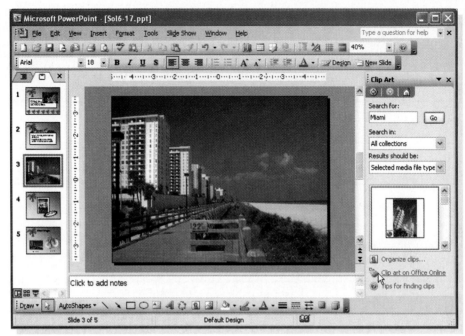

EXERCISE 6-19 Crop an Image

The Picture toolbar contains a tool you can use to *crop* (trim) parts of a picture, just as you might do with a page from a magazine by using a pair of scissors.

When you click the cropping tool, a picture's sizing handles change to *cropping handles*—heavy black lines and corners that you drag to trim a picture.

1. On slide 4, select the Miami1 picture.

2. Click the Crop button 📐 on the Picture toolbar. The pointer changes to a cropping tool 📐, and cropping handles appear around the edges of the picture.

3. Position the cropping tool on the top center handle and drag the handle down until the dotted cropping line is positioned at the top of the tower (see Figure 6-17 on the next page).

   TIP: Try holding down [Alt] as you crop. This enables you to make very fine adjustments.

4. Hold down [Ctrl] and drag the left-center cropping handle to the right slightly. Release the mouse button, and then release [Ctrl]. Both the left side and the right side are cropped at the same time. If you hold down [Ctrl] while dragging a corner cropping handle, all four sides of the picture will be cropped the same amount.

FIGURE 6-17
Cropping a picture

5. Crop the bottom of the picture to the sidewalk.

6. Click the Crop button on the Picture toolbar to turn it off.

7. Resize the picture to make it slightly larger.

> **TIP:** If necessary, click on the 16-point star, and then cut and paste it to get it to appear on top of the photograph.

8. Use the arrow keys to nudge the picture to position it approximately in the center of the white box. Or, you can hold down Alt while dragging to fine-tune the picture's position. If necessary, nudge the star shape, too.

FIGURE 6-18
Picture after cropping and positioning

> **TIP:** If you crop too far, use the cropping tool to drag the handle in the opposite direction to restore that part of the picture, or click the Undo button .

9. Save the presentation as *[your initials]*6-19 in your Lesson 6 folder, but do not print it. Leave the presentation open for the next exercise.

Using WordArt for Special Effects

WordArt can create special effects with text that are not possible with standard text-formatting tools. You can stretch or curve text, and add special shading effects, dramatic 3-D effects, and much more. And, because WordArt creates drawn objects, you can use drawing tools to modify and enhance WordArt objects.

EXERCISE **6-20** **Create and Modify a WordArt Object**

In this exercise, you create a WordArt object, and then modify it by changing its shape and size. It's important to note that WordArt objects are not checked by the spell-checker. PowerPoint treats them as drawing objects, not text. Make sure you key and proofread WordArt objects carefully.

1. Display slide 3 with the beach scene photograph.

2. Click the Insert WordArt button on the Drawing toolbar. The WordArt Gallery dialog box appears.

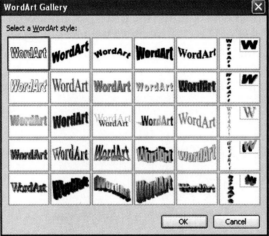

FIGURE 6-19
WordArt Gallery
dialog box

3. Choose the light blue WordArt style (third row, fifth column). Click OK. The Edit WordArt Text dialog box appears.

4. Key **Good for You** and click OK. The WordArt text object is added to the slide. Notice that the object is selected and the WordArt toolbar appears.

TABLE 6-3 WordArt Toolbar

BUTTON		PURPOSE
	Insert WordArt	Creates a drawing object that uses text effects.
Edit Text...	Edit Text	Opens the Edit WordArt Text dialog box, where you can revise the text of the selected WordArt object.

continues

TABLE 6-3 WordArt Toolbar *continued*

BUTTON	PURPOSE
WordArt Gallery	Opens the WordArt Gallery dialog box, where you can change the style for the selected WordArt object.
Format WordArt	Opens the Format WordArt dialog box, where you can work with a variety of WordArt properties.
WordArt Shape	Displays a menu of shapes that you can apply to the selected WordArt object.
WordArt Same Letter Heights	Makes all the letters in the selected WordArt object the same height.
WordArt Vertical Text	Stacks the text in the selected WordArt object vertically, so that it reads from top to bottom.
WordArt Alignment	Aligns the WordArt text left, center, right, or justified.
WordArt Character Spacing	Enables you to adjust the space between characters in the selected WordArt object.

5. Click the WordArt Shape button ⓐ on the WordArt toolbar.

6. On the WordArt Shape menu, choose Wave 2.

FIGURE 6-20
WordArt
Shape menu

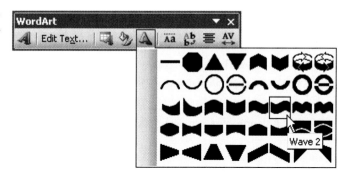

TIP: Many colors and shapes are displayed in the WordArt Gallery. Choose a color that works with your presentation colors, even if you don't like the WordArt shape. Changing the shape of WordArt is sometimes faster than changing the color.

7. Drag the WordArt text to the sky area on the right side of the slide. Use the sizing handles to increase its size by stretching it to the left near the buildings.

EXERCISE 6-21 **Edit WordArt Text**

WordArt text can be edited only in the Edit WordArt Text dialog box. You open the Edit WordArt Text dialog box by clicking Edit Text on the WordArt toolbar, or by double-clicking the WordArt object.

1. Select the WordArt object.
2. Click Edit Text on the WordArt toolbar.
3. Change the text "Good for You" to **Good 4 U**
4. When a shadow is used like this, it generally looks better with a thicker font. Therefore, select Arial Black. The font size does not matter, because you will stretch the WordArt to fit in the available space. Click OK.
5. Adjust any necessary spacing so your slide resembles Figure 6-21.

FIGURE 6-21
Completed
WordArt object

EXERCISE 6-22 **Adding WordArt to a Slide Master**

If you want a WordArt object to appear on each slide, you can place it on a slide master, just like you placed a picture on a slide master previously in this lesson.

1. Right-click the WordArt object and choose Copy from the shortcut menu. The WordArt object is copied onto the clipboard.
2. Display the slide master. Resize the body text placeholder by dragging the bottom up about 1 inch.
3. Click on a blank area on the slide master and choose Paste from the shortcut menu. The WordArt object is pasted into the slide master.
4. Resize the WordArt object to make it much smaller and position it on the lower left of the slide, just above the Date Area placeholder. Close the Master view.
5. Scroll through the presentation to check that the WordArt object appears on every slide in the same location. It appears too high for slide 2 and palm trees cover it on slide 1. So you need to make some adjustments.
6. Display the slide master. Select the Data Area placeholder and press (Delete) because you are not using it for this presentation. Now you have enough space to move the Good 4 U WordArt object down more.

7. Close the Master view.

8. Move to slide 1 and delete one or more palm trees until the Good 4 U WordArt object is visible.

9. Delete slide 5.

10. Move slide 3 before slide 1 to position it as the title slide for this presentation. Scroll through the presentation again to make sure that all slide elements are nicely positioned.

11. Select slide 1 and save the presentation as *[your initials]***6-22** in your Lesson 6 folder. View the presentation as a slide show, and then print the presentation as handouts, six slides per page, grayscale, landscape, framed. Close the presentation.

USING ONLINE HELP

PowerPoint and other Office programs can accept graphics files in many different formats. These formats are for both vector drawings and bitmaps.

Use Help to learn about the type of pictures you are using:

1. Key **pictures** in the Ask a Question box on the left side of the menu bar and press Enter.

2. In the drop-down list, choose **About pictures**.

3. Expand each topic and read about bitmaps and drawn pictures.

FIGURE 6-22
Help screen
about pictures

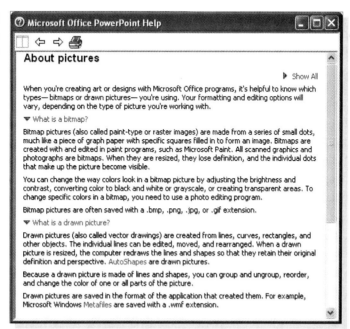

4. Expand any terms that you encounter if you are not familiar with them.

5. Close the Help window when you are finished.

LESSON Summary

➤ In addition to text placeholders, PowerPoint provides a variety of objects that you can use to enhance the visual appearance of your slides. These include AutoShapes, text boxes, clip art, and photographs. You can also insert your own pictures.

➤ PowerPoint's basic drawing tools enable you to create squares, circles, rectangles, ovals, and straight lines drawn at any angle.

➤ You draw a shape by first selecting it on the Drawing toolbar, and then dragging diagonally on your slide to define the size of the shape.

➤ If you don't like a shape you drew, select it and press Delete to remove it from your slide, or click Undo.

➤ Hold down Shift while drawing a line or other shape to constrain it. Constraining a shape makes it perfectly symmetrical, for example, a circle or a square, or it can make a line perfectly straight.

➤ Hold down Ctrl while drawing a shape to make it grow from the center instead of from one edge.

➤ Change the size of a drawn object by dragging one of its sizing handles (small white circles on its border) with a two-pointed arrow.

➤ To preserve an object's proportions when resizing it, hold down Shift while dragging a corner sizing handle.

➤ Move a drawn object by pointing to it and dragging the four-pointed arrow when it appears.

➤ AutoShapes are predefined shapes that are organized into several categories. To draw an AutoShape, select the shape you want, and then drag the crosshair pointer. After an AutoShape is drawn, you can change it to a different shape.

➤ When an AutoShape is selected, text that you key appears inside the shape.

➤ Use the Clip Art task pane to search for clip art. If you are connected to the Internet, the task pane's Search command will automatically search the Microsoft Office Design Gallery Live.

➤ To see a menu of clip art options, point to a clip art thumbnail in the Clip Art task pane, and then click the vertical gray bar that appears on the right side of the thumbnail (or right-click the thumbnail).

➤ Using the Cut, Copy, and Paste commands, you can easily move or copy clip art or other images from one slide to another or from one presentation to another.

➤ Pictures and drawn objects can be inserted directly into slide masters or can be copied from another location and pasted onto slide masters.

➤ Resize a clip art image by dragging one of its sizing handles. If you want to preserve proportions, drag a corner handle. If you want to distort the proportions, drag one of the side handles.

➤ Use the Picture toolbar to adjust a picture's brightness, contrast, color depth, and other picture attributes.

➤ Clip art images (vectors, bitmaps, or scanned images) can be cropped. Cropping is trimming away edges of a picture, much like using scissors to cut out a picture from a newspaper or magazine.

➤ WordArt enables you to create special effects with text that are not possible with standard text-formatting tools.

➤ WordArt is modified by using the WordArt Gallery to change its style, by changing its shape, and by editing its text. All these options and many more are available on the WordArt toolbar.

LESSON 6   Command Summary

FEATURE	BUTTON	MENU	KEYBOARD
Rectangle	□		
Oval	○		
Line	╲		
Constrained line	Shift + ╲		
Square	Shift + □		
Circle	Shift + ○		
AutoShapes	AutoShapes ▾	Insert, Picture, AutoShapes	
Change AutoShape		Draw, Change AutoShape	
Format Picture	🖼	Format, Picture	

continues

LESSON 6 Command Summary *continued*

FEATURE	BUTTON	MENU	KEYBOARD
Search for Clip Art		Search (on the Insert Clip Art task pane)	
Insert Clip Art		Insert, Picture, Clip Art	
Adjust contrast		Format, Picture, Picture tab, Contrast	
Adjust brightness		Format, Picture, Picture tab, Brightness	
Adjust color		Format, Picture, Picture tab, Color	
Crop a picture		Format, Picture, Picture tab	
Insert WordArt		Insert, Picture, WordArt	
Edit WordArt text	Edit Text...	Edit Text	
Change WordArt shape			
Change WordArt style			
Format WordArt		Format, WordArt	

Concepts Review

TRUE/FALSE QUESTIONS

Each of the following statements is either true or false. Indicate your choice by circling T or F.

(T) F   **1.** Anything placed on a PowerPoint slide is considered an object.

T (F)   **2.** You can type text only in an existing placeholder. *TEXT BOX*

(T) F   **3.** Use Shift with ☐ to create a square.

T (F)   **4.** Every AutoShape includes an adjustment handle. *YELLOW*

(T) F   **5.** A green handle on a PowerPoint object indicates that the object can be rotated.

T (F)   **6.** ⊞ is found on the AutoShapes toolbar.

T (F)   **7.** When you want to change the height of an object, but not the width, press Shift while dragging a corner sizing handle.

(T) F   **8.** WordArt enables you to create special effects with text.

SHORT ANSWER QUESTIONS

Write the correct answer in the space provided.

1. How do you draw a perfect circle?

OVAL TOOL AND HOLD SHIFT

2. What kind of handle is the yellow diamond?

ADJUSTMENT HANDLE

3. How can you change an object to a different AutoShape without deleting and redrawing it?

DRAW CHANGE AUTO SHAPE

4. What happens when you press Ctrl while you drag a corner sizing handle toward the center of an object?

SMALLER EVENLY ON ALL SIDES

5. Which task pane is used to bring a photograph into a presentation?

INSERT CLIP-ART

6. If you use the Format Picture dialog box, what option should you check to resize a picture proportionately?

LOCK ASPECT RATIO

7. How do you resize an object using the mouse?

SIZING HANDLE

8. How do you edit the text in a WordArt object?

EDIT TEXT BUTTON. Word Art Tool BAR

CRITICAL THINKING

Answer these questions on a separate page. There are no right or wrong answers. Support your answers with examples from your own experience, if possible.

1. Use the Clip Art task pane to select three pieces of clip art, and then explain the type of presentation in which you might use them.

2. In this lesson, you placed some text directly in an AutoShape and, in Lesson 5, you placed some text in a text box that could be then placed on top of an AutoShape. Think of reasons why you might place the text in a separate text box, instead of directly in an AutoShape.

Skills Review

EXERCISE 6-23

Use drawing tools to create simple and constrained AutoShapes, key text in an AutoShape, and use the Format AutoShape dialog box.

FIGURE 6-23
Drawing
AutoShapes

1. Open the file **Seminar1**. Move to slide 3.

2. Use the drawing tools to create the shapes shown in Figure 6-23. First, create the wide rectangle that appears on top of the triangle by following these steps:

a. Click the Rectangle button 🔲 on the Drawing toolbar.

b. Position the crosshair pointer ⊞ on the left of the slide.

c. Drag the pointer diagonally down and to the right, creating a wide rectangle, like the one shown in Figure 6-23. Release the mouse button. (Don't worry about the exact size or position. You size and place it in the next step.)

3. Precisely size and position the rectangle by following these steps:

   a. Right-click the rectangle, and then choose Format AutoShape from the shortcut menu.

   b. Click the Size tab. Key **0.75** in the Height text box and **8** in the Width text box.

   c. Click the Position tab. Key **1** in the Horizontal text box and **4.5** in the Vertical text box. Click OK.

4. Key text in the rectangle by following these steps:

   a. Select the rectangle.

   b. Key **Perfect Planning Requires Balance**

   c. Change the font to Arial Narrow, the size of the text to 36 points and the text color to white.

5. Create the triangle shown in Figure 6-23 by following these steps:

   a. Click AutoShapes on the Drawing toolbar.

   b. Choose Basic Shapes; then click the Isosceles Triangle shape △ .

   c. Position the pointer at the bottom center of the new rectangle.

   d. Drag diagonally down and to the right to create a triangle similar to the one in Figure 6-23.

   e. Position the pointer in the center of the triangle; then drag with the four-pointed arrow ✦ to position the triangle, so it appears centered under the rectangle.

6. Draw a circle by following these steps:

   a. Click the Oval button ◯.

   b. Position the crosshair pointer ✛ above the left end of the rectangle, hold down (Shift), and drag diagonally to draw a circle approximately the same size as the one in Figure 6-23.

   c. Hold down (Ctrl) while using the arrow keys on your keyboard to fine-tune the circle's position.

7. Copy the circle to the clipboard, and then paste it. Drag the copy to the other end of the rectangle, positioning it appropriately.

8. Create a horizontal line on slide 3 by following these steps:

   a. Click the Line button ◥ on the Drawing toolbar.

   b. Position the pointer below the title text even with the left edge of the rectangle below.

   c. Hold down (Shift) and drag to the right to draw a straight line across the slide to end even with the right edge of the rectangle below. Release the mouse button first, and then release (Shift).

   d. Adjust the position of the line, if necessary.

9. Check spelling in the presentation.

10. Create a footer for slide 3: include the slide number, date, and your name, followed by a comma and the text *[your initials]*6-23.

11. Create a handout header and footer: include the date and your name as the header, and the page number and text *[your initials]*6-23 as the footer.

12. Move to slide 1 and save the presentation as *[your initials]*6-23 in your Lesson 6 folder.

13. Print slide 3 in full size, framed. Preview and print the presentation as handouts, 4 slides per page, grayscale, landscape, framed. Close the presentation.

EXERCISE 6-24

Insert and size a picture from a file, work with slide masters, adjust its contrast and brightness, and create a WordArt text object.

1. Open the file **Seminar2**.

2. Replace the title on slide 1 with a WordArt text object by following these steps:

    a. Delete the title text and the title placeholder.

    b. Click the Insert WordArt button on the Drawing toolbar.

    c. Select the rainbow-colored WordArt style in the third row, fourth column. Click OK.

    d. In the Edit WordArt Text dialog box, key **Franchise Training** and click OK.

3. Change the formatting of a WordArt object by following these steps:

    a. Select the WordArt object, if it is not already selected.

    b. Double-click the WordArt object.

    c. Change the font to 60-point Impact. Click OK.

    d. Using the four-pointed arrow ⊕, drag the WordArt object to the position where the title placeholder would go.

4. Change the shape of a WordArt object by following these steps:

    a. Select the WordArt object.

    b. Click the WordArt Shape button 🅰 on the WordArt toolbar.

    c. Select the Chevron Up shape (fifth shape in the first row).

    d. Hold down Ctrl and drag the bottom center sizing handle down slightly to increase the height of the WordArt shape.

5. Add the Good 4 U logo to the slide master by following these steps:

    a. To display the slide master, open the View menu, and then choose Slide Master from the submenu.

    b. Be sure the title master is selected. Click the Insert Picture button on the Drawing toolbar.

    c. Navigate to the drive and directory where your student data files are stored and select the file **Logo1**. Click Insert.

    d. Drag the logo to the bottom of the subtitle placeholder in the center of the slide.

6. Copy the logo to the clipboard, select the slide master, and then paste the logo. Reduce its size by dragging a corner handle, and position it in the lower-right corner of the slide over the slide number placeholder. Close the Master view.

7. Review each slide to make sure the logo does not interfere with any slide text or objects. If necessary, resize and/or reposition the logo on the slide master.

8. Create a handout header and footer: include the date and your name as the header, and the page number and text *[your initials]*6-24 as the footer.

9. Move to slide 1 and save the presentation as *[your initials]*6-24 in your Lesson 6 folder.

10. Preview, and then print the presentation as handouts, four slides per page, grayscale, landscape, framed. Close the presentation.

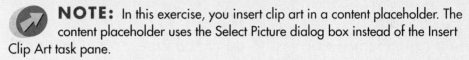

EXERCISE 6-25

Insert clip art, adjust picture image settings, and crop a clip art image.

1. Open the file **Seminar3**.

2. On slide 1, insert the picture file **Logo1** (from your student data disk) and position it at the bottom of the slide overlapping the white graphic shape.

3. Insert clip art in a content placeholder by following these steps:

   NOTE: In this exercise, you insert clip art in a content placeholder. The content placeholder uses the Select Picture dialog box instead of the Insert Clip Art task pane.

   a. If you have Internet access and you are not connected, make a connection now.

   b. Move to slide 2 and click the Insert Clip Art button 🖼 in the content placeholder.

   c. Scroll through the thumbnails in the Select Picture dialog box.

   d. In the Search text box, key **refrigerator**, and then click Search.

   e. Look for an image that most closely resembles a commercial-grade refrigerator, and then select it by clicking its thumbnail. Click OK.

4. Resize the picture proportionately from the center (to preserve its position) by following these steps:

   a. Select the picture.

   b. Hold down Ctrl while dragging a corner handle.

   c. When the picture is the size you want, release Ctrl first, and then release the mouse button.

5. Crop clip art by following these steps:

   a. Move to slide 3. Select the picture on the right side of the slide.

   b. Click the Crop button ╬ on the Picture toolbar.

   c. Drag the top cropping handle down to just above the square containing the chef's hat.

   d. Drag each of the side cropping handles in, so that only the squares containing the chef's hat and the rolling pin remain.

e. Click the Crop button ⊞ again to deactivate it.

f. Increase the size of the cropped image and position it beside the list with balanced spacing above and below the image.

6. On slides 4 and 6, insert clip art images appropriate to the slide text content and the overall presentation design. Crop and/or resize the pictures and adjust the contrast and brightness, if necessary.

7. On slide 2, at the bottom, insert a text box and key **Ask for our list of wholesale appliance dealers** and change the font to 24-point Arial Narrow, italic. Position the text box on the lower left.

8. Check spelling in the presentation.

9. Create a handout header and footer: include the date and your name as the header, and the page number and text *[your initials]*6-25 as the footer.

10. Move to slide 1 and save the presentation as *[your initials]*6-25 in your Lesson 6 folder.

11. Preview, and then print the presentation as handouts, six slides per page, grayscale, framed. Close the presentation.

EXERCISE 6-26

Create AutoShapes, add text to an AutoShape, rotate text and AutoShapes, and adjust image settings on a photograph.

1. Open the file **Seminar4**. Replace the word "Date" on slide 1 with today's date.

2. Create a left arrow AutoShape by following these steps:

   a. Move to slide 3 and click AutoShapes on the Drawing toolbar.
   b. Choose Block Arrows on the AutoShapes menu and choose Left Arrow (the second shape in the first row).
   c. Position the crosshair pointer ⊞ at the top of the brown bar in the fourth quarter of the chart, and then click and drag to create an arrow.

FIGURE 6-24

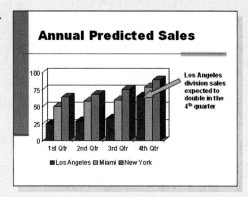

3. Rotate an AutoShape by following these steps:

   a. Select the arrow AutoShape.
   b. Drag the green rotation handle above the arrow to the left until the arrow points down at about a 45-degree angle. Reposition the arrow, so it points to the top of the brown bar, as shown in Figure 6-24.

4. Draw a text box in the space to the right of the arrow. Change the font to 20-point Arial, bold, and left-align the text. Key **Los Angeles division sales expected to double in the 4th quarter**

5. Adjust the position, size, and rotation of the arrow and text box, so they appear as shown in Figure 6-24.

6. On slide 2, insert the Restaurant1 picture from your student data files. Resize the picture as necessary and position it on the right side of the slide. Adjust the contrast and brightness, if necessary.

7. On slide 4, the picture that is already positioned on this slide is very dark. Adjust the contrast and brightness to clarify the image.

8. Below the picture on slide 4, insert a text box with the words **Only the finest produce!** Format the rotated text in a size, font, and color to match slide 3.

9. On slide 5, draw a 5-Point Star AutoShape (Stars and Banners submenu) in the upper-right corner. Position and size the star, so that it covers the light green rectangle on the right side of the brown horizontal line.

10. Place text in the star by following these steps:
    a. Select the star.
    b. Key **Star**, press Enter, and key **Team**. Make the text Arial Black in 32 points.
    c. Adjust the size of the star, if necessary, to fit the text.

11. Check spelling in the presentation.

12. Create a handout header and footer: include the date and your name as the header, and the page number and text *[your initials]*6-26 as the footer.

13. Move to slide 1 and save the presentation as *[your initials]*6-26 in your Lesson 6 folder.

14. Preview, and then print the presentation as handouts, six slides per page, grayscale, framed. Close the presentation.

Lesson Applications

Work with lines, AutoShapes, and clip art.

1. Open the file **Market1**.

2. On the slide master, draw a thin horizontal rectangle below the text in the title placeholder that extends completely across the slide. Remove the border line and change the fill color to a gradient with one color. Color 1 should be the teal accent color. Set the transparency for To: at 100 percent so the color blends to the background color on the right part of the slide. Set the shading style to be vertical, and then select the first variant on the top row with the color going from light to dark.

3. Copy the diamond shape on the title master and paste it over the thin rectangle. Give it a more horizontal shape and reduce the thickness of the border line to be more appropriate for this smaller size.

4. Select the title placeholder and change the font to Arial Black to match the title slide. Right-click to access the Format Placeholder menu. Select the Text Box tab and set the Text anchor point to be Bottom. Click OK. Move the placeholder up slightly, so the second line is directly above the rectangle you made. Also, move it to the right slightly, so it does not overlap the diamond shape.

5. Move the body placeholder to the right, below the slide title, and change the first bullet to a diamond shape. Choose Format, Bullets and Numbering, Custom, and then click the Customize button. Go to the Wingdings symbol set and choose a diamond shape in a green color at 70 percent size.

FIGURE 6-25

6. Close the Master view.

7. On slide 1, delete the subtitle placeholder. Draw a rectangle, approximately 3 inches wide. Position it attractively on the lower right side of the slide. Increase the border width to 6 points.

8. Use the Insert Clip Art task pane to search for a photograph image by using the search word **meeting**. Choose a picture that is appropriate in style, content, and color for this slide and insert it.

9. Resize and crop the picture, if necessary, and add a border that blends with the slide color scheme. Make the picture border width 3 points. Position the picture on the rectangle. Adjust the size of the picture and rectangle, if necessary, to create a picture-frame effect.

10. Copy the rectangle. On slide 2, paste the rectangle below the body text placeholder. Find a picture similar to the one you used on slide 1, size and/or crop it as needed, add a border line, and place it on top of the rectangle (just as you did on slide 1 to create a frame around the picture).

11. Depending on how you cropped your picture, position it below the bulleted list or move it (and the rectangle) beside the list on the right. If you move this image to the right, then resize the bulleted list placeholder, so this text remains on the left.

12. Move slide 5 before slide 4.

13. Check spelling in the presentation.

14. Create a handout header and footer: include the date and your name as the header, and the page number and text *[your initials]*6-27 as the footer.

15. Move to slide 1 and save the presentation as *[your initials]*6-27 in your Lesson 6 folder.

16. Preview, and then print the presentation as handouts, six slides per page, grayscale, framed. Close the presentation.

EXERCISE 6-28

Create a presentation from a Word outline, add an image to the title master, create and rotate a text box, and create an AutoShape containing text.

1. Create a presentation from the Word document **Cooking1** by opening the Word outline file from within PowerPoint. Change the slide layout of Slide 1 to Title Slide.

2. Apply the design template Profile with the original color scheme showing a white background and pinstripe effect.

3. Access the slide master and insert the Good 4 U logo, Logo1.jpg, on the lower-left corner of the title master. On the title master, change the title text to Verdana, bold at 54 points. Change the slide title text to 40-point Verdana bold.

4. On the title master, make the subtitle placeholder bold. Close the slide master.

5. On slide 1, the title slide, insert an appropriate clip art image of fruit. Move the placeholder text directly under the thin red line.

6. On slide 2, create a text box and key the following text: **Low fat, low carb selections available**. Change the text to bold and red; apply a white file color for the text box. Rotate the text box on the lower right area of the slide.

7. On slide 4, change the layout to Title Only. Below the title, draw a large, 24-Point Star AutoShape, placing it in the center of the slide. Key the following two lines of text in the star:

   The Good 4 U
   Seal of Approval

8. Format the text as 32-point Verdana bold. Adjust the height and width of the star to fit the text.

9. For the star, select a two-color gradient fill with yellow and gold. Select a center gradient with the lighter color in the middle. Add a black border line at 4½ points.

10. Check spelling in the presentation.

11. Create a handout header and footer: include the date and your name as the header, and the page number and text *[your initials]*6-28 as the footer.

12. Move to slide 1 and save the presentation as *[your initials]*6-28 in your Lesson 6 folder.

13. View the presentation as a slide show.

14. Preview, and then print the presentation as handouts, four slides per page, grayscale, landscape, framed. Close the presentation.

EXERCISE 6-29

Insert and rotate a picture from a file, add photo images to the slide master, and insert WordArt.

1. Open the file **Recruit1**.

2. On the title master, increase the title text placeholder font size to Georgia, 54 points, bold, left alignment, brown. Change the body text placeholder font to Arial. For the subtitle, use Georgia, 32 points, bold, left alignment, black.

3. Search for photograph images using the word "dining." Insert three photograph images that are 2.5 inches wide with a 6-point brown border line. Stack these pictures to completely fill the left side of the slide.

4. Copy these images and paste them on the slide master. Make them much smaller and position them in the upper left. Draw a brown 6-point line below the slide title placeholder. Close the Master view.

5. Adjust placeholder positions as needed. On slide 1, insert the picture file **Logo1** from your student data disk. Rotate it, so that it slants up and place it in the lower-right corner of the slide.

6. In the subtitle placeholder, key **New Hires** and today's date.

7. On slide 2, break the second bulleted item into two bulleted items and revise wording:
   - **Company History**
   - **Company Vision**

8. Insert two new slides at the end of the presentation; use the Text slide layout. Key the text in Figure 6-26 on the slides indicated.

FIGURE 6-26

```
        ┌─  Who's Who
        │
        │    • Julie Wolfe and Gus Irvinelli are the co-owners of the restaurant
Slide 4 │    • Michele Jenkins is the head chef
        │
        └─   • Roy Olafsen is the marketing manager

        ┌─  Summary
        │
        │    • Good 4 U is growing rapidly with our new franchising philosophy
Slide 5 │    • Our healthy living message has worldwide appeal
        │
        └─   • We are relying on you, our new employees, to help us grow
```

9. After the last slide, insert a new slide with a blank layout. Insert WordArt for the words **Welcome to Good 4 U**. Select an appropriate WordArt shape and adjust WordArt colors to be appropriate for the presentation color scheme. Use the same Georgia font and apply a black shadow.

10. Check spelling in the presentation.

11. Scroll through the presentation and check each slide to make sure the apple picture does not interfere with any text. If necessary, readjust the size and/or position of the picture on the slide master and the title master.

12. Create a handout header and footer: include the date and your name as the header, and the page number and text *[your initials]*6-29 as the footer.

13. Move to slide 1 and save the presentation as *[your initials]*6-29 in your Lesson 6 folder.

14. Preview, and then print the presentation as handouts, six slides per page, grayscale, framed. Close the presentation.

EXERCISE 6-30 ✚ *Challenge Yourself*

Use drawing tools, AutoShapes, insert pictures, and WordArt.

1. Open the file **Funding1**.

2. Using the Outline pane, insert the body text for each slide, as shown in Figure 6-27 (on the next page).

3. On the title master, create a thin rectangle across the top of the slide with a white, one-color gradient fill going from transparent on the left to white on the right. Insert the file **Logo1**, reduce its size, and then position it on the white area of the rectangle on the right.

FIGURE 6-27

1. Attracting Investors

2. Objective
   - Obtain investors to establish Good 4 U as a franchise
   - Revisit the current business plan
   - Hire a marketing consulting firm

3. Our Specialties
   - Organic fruit and vegetables
   - Fresh juices
   - Innovative cuisine

4. Investors Want:
   - High-profile location
   - Hotel or storefront
   - City with tourism, such as Miami or New York
   - "Curb appeal"

5. Next Steps
   - Target health-conscious areas
   - Target high-profile areas
   - Study traffic patterns in selected areas

4. On slide 1, delete the title text and its placeholder. Use the title text shown in Figure 6-27 to create a WordArt title. Use the WordArt style in the second row, fourth column (shaded silver color). Resize the WordArt to stretch across the slide and move it up slightly from the center of the slide.

5. On slide 2, resize the body text placeholder to make it fit on the left of the slide.

6. Still working on slide 2, draw a **Bevel** AutoShape (from the **Basic Shapes** submenu) under the text placeholder and approximately the same width as the placeholder. Key **Investors are our building blocks** in the AutoShape, format it as 28-point Arial bold, and change the text color to dark blue. If necessary, use the Format AutoShapes dialog box to make the text wordwrap in the shape. Drag the adjustment handle to make the bevel effect narrow.

7. On slide 3, remove the bullets from the body text placeholder and center its text. Insert a picture of fruit in one of the content placeholders and a picture of a vegetable in the other. Adjust the size and image settings of the pictures, if necessary.

8. On slide 4, insert the picture **Miami1** from your student data disk. Crop and resize the picture, so that it fits within the turquoise rectangle and appears to be framed.

9. On slide 5, draw a 15-degree line to help judge your angle, and then draw a **Block Arrow** AutoShape angled to fit on the line. Duplicate this arrow by pressing Ctrl+D and position the second arrow on the line. Repeat for a third arrow. Once the arrows are aligned on the angled line, as shown in Figure 6-28, delete the line.

FIGURE 6-28

Next Steps
- Target health-conscious areas
- Target high-profile areas
- Study traffic patterns in selected areas

10. Review each slide, and make changes to the size and position of any objects you want to make a pleasing composition.

11. Check spelling in the presentation.

12. Create a handout header and footer: include the date and your name as the header, and the page number and filename *[your initials]*6-30 as the footer.

13. Move to slide 1 and save the presentation as *[your initials]***6-30** in your Lesson 6 folder.

14. Preview, and then print the presentation as handouts, six slides per page, grayscale, framed. Close the presentation.

On Your Own

In these exercises, you work on your own, as you would in a real-life work environment. Use the skills you've learned to accomplish the task—and be creative.

EXERCISE 6-31

Open the file **Seminar1**. Choose another design template and color scheme. Insert a suitable clip art image on the title slide and a complimentary image on the slide master. Change the size, shape, and position of text placeholders and other objects, and change font sizes to create a pleasing composition. Use your own creativity to design a lively presentation, remembering to maintain a clear and unified look throughout. Save the presentation as *[your initials]***6-31**. Preview, and then print the presentation as handouts.

EXERCISE 6-32

Create a presentation entitled "Gift Suggestions for *[choose occasion or person]*." Select five or more suitable items from mail order catalogs and create a separate slide describing each item, including the price and why you selected it. If you have access to a scanner, scan each item's picture from the catalog and insert it on the appropriate slide. If a scanner is not available, insert a suitable clip art image on each slide. Use your own creativity and the tools learned in this and previous lessons to add interest to the slides. Save the presentation as *[your initials]***6-32**. Preview, and then print the presentation as handouts.

EXERCISE 6-33

Imagine that you are about to open a new retail store or restaurant. Using the content and layout of the Miami Beach presentation from this lesson as a general guide, create a presentation with at least five slides announcing the opening of your business. Use clip art, text boxes, AutoShapes, WordArt, and, if possible, scanned photos to illustrate your presentation. Include a transition effect. Save the presentation as *[your initials]***6-33**. Preview, and then print the presentation as handouts.

LESSON

7

Working with Lines, Fills, and Colors

MICROSOFT OFFICE
SPECIALIST
ACTIVITIES
In this lesson:
PP03S-1-4
PP03S-2-2
PP03S-4-7

See Appendix.

OBJECTIVES

After completing this lesson, you will be able to:

1. Change the line color and line style of AutoShapes.
2. Change the fill color of objects.
3. Work with an extended range of colors.
4. Add patterns, gradient fills, and textures.
5. Use the Format Painter tool to copy formatting.
6. Adjust presentation color settings.

 Estimated Time: 1½ hours

In Lesson 6, you learned how to create shapes and add clip art images and photographs to your presentation. In that lesson, most of the shapes in a presentation were the same color, but you made a few changes to the fill colors and line colors. This lesson shows you how to make even more changes to enhance your presentation by applying color, patterns, shading, and line styles to shapes you draw, text placeholders, and pictures.

Changing the Line Color and Line Style of AutoShapes

To emphasize or separate text, clip art, or other objects from the rest of your slide, you can create a border by using a variety of color and line options. Borders can be applied to any PowerPoint object, including text boxes, text placeholders, AutoShapes, clip art, and pictures.

EXERCISE 7-1 Apply a Border

The fastest way to add a border to an object is to select the object, and then click the Line Style button ▤. *Line style* refers to the type of border or outline that an object has. Options include single, double, and triple lines of varying *line weights.* The weight of a line is its thickness, measured in points.

For more line style options, open the Format AutoShape, Format Text Box, or Format Picture dialog box in one of the following ways:

- Double-click the object.
- Right-click the object; then choose Format AutoShape, Format Text Box, or Format Picture from the shortcut menu.
- From the Format menu, choose Placeholder, AutoShape, Text Box or Picture.

1. Open the file **SanFran1** and move to slide 2.
2. Press [Tab] one or more times to select the body text placeholder.
3. Click the Line Style button ▤ on the Drawing toolbar to display a menu of options.

FIGURE 7-1
Line styles

4. Click to select the 3-point double line. A double line now frames the body text.
5. Deselect the text box and change the Zoom to 150% to see the double line clearly. The color of the line is the template's default line color. (You will change the line color later in this lesson.)

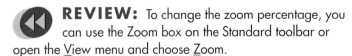

REVIEW: To change the zoom percentage, you can use the Zoom box on the Standard toolbar or open the View menu and choose Zoom.

6. Select the body text placeholder again and apply the 1-point single-line style to its border.
7. Change the Zoom setting back to Fit.

EXERCISE 7-2 Change the Border Line Style

PowerPoint offers a variety of dash styles to apply to lines and borders. A *dash style* is the pattern of dashes and dots that make up a line. Styles include solid line, square dot, dash, and combinations of dashes and dots.

When used sparingly, a dash style can add interest to a presentation. You can apply dash styles to lines, arrows, and object borders. They can be any color and any line weight.

1. Move to slide 3 and select the star object.

2. Apply the 6-point single-line style. A thicker border now surrounds the star.

3. With the star still selected, click the Dash Style button on the Drawing toolbar.

FIGURE 7-2
Dash styles

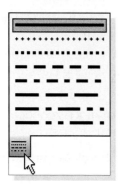

4. Apply the Round Dot style, which is the second style on the menu. A dash-style line or border can produce a dramatic effect.

EXERCISE 7-3 Change the Border Line Color

You can change the color of a border in one of two ways:

- Click the Line Color button on the Drawing toolbar.
- Use the Format AutoShape dialog box (Colors and Lines tab).

The color sample on the Line Color button shows the last color you applied. If you click a color button (such as Line, Fill, or Text) without clicking its arrow, you'll apply the color shown on the button's color bar.

1. Still working on slide 3, select the star shape.

2. Click the arrow for the Line Color button on the Drawing toolbar to display the line color choices. The gray bar at the top of the menu indicates that you can float the menu if you want.

FIGURE 7-3
Line colors

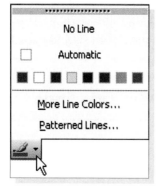

3. Without clicking, move the mouse pointer over each color sample and notice the ScreenTips. These tips identify the automatic colors for the PowerPoint objects that make up a presentation.

4. Click the dark pink color on the right to select it. The ScreenTip indicates that this color is used as an accent color (and as a followed hyperlink if you're creating links to other slides, files, or Web pages).

EXERCISE   7-4   Draw and Format Arrows

Besides drawing arrow AutoShapes, you can draw lines with attached arrow-heads by using the Arrow button on the Drawing toolbar, or you can add arrowheads to existing lines by using the Arrow Style button ⇄ or the Format AutoShape dialog box (Colors and Lines tab).

Arrow style options include several varieties of arrowheads, dots, and diamonds. By using the Format AutoShape dialog box, you can control whether to put an arrowhead on either end or on both ends of a line.

1. Move to slide 4.

2. Click the Arrow button and draw a diagonal line that slants down from the right, pointing toward the tallest bar on the chart.

3. Deselect the line. Notice the small arrowhead on the end of the line.

4. Select the arrow; then use the Line Style button ≡ to change the arrow to a three-point single-line style. (If you like, you can increase the zoom to see the change more clearly.)

5. Click the Arrow Style button ⇄ on the Drawing toolbar.

FIGURE 7-4
Arrow styles

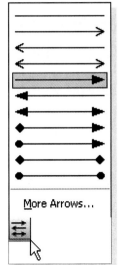

6. Select Arrow Style 3, a left-pointing arrow. The arrow points away from the chart.

NOTE: The placement of the arrow is determined by where you started drawing the line. The left arrowhead appears at the beginning of the line, and the right arrowhead appears at the end of the line.

7. Click the Arrow Style button ⇄ again. Select Arrow Style 2, a right-pointing arrow.

8. Adjust the length and angle of the arrow by dragging the sizing handle on the end of the arrow, as shown in Figure 7-5 (on the next page). No rotation handle is required to make lines angle on the slide.

FIGURE 7-5
Adjusting the arrow

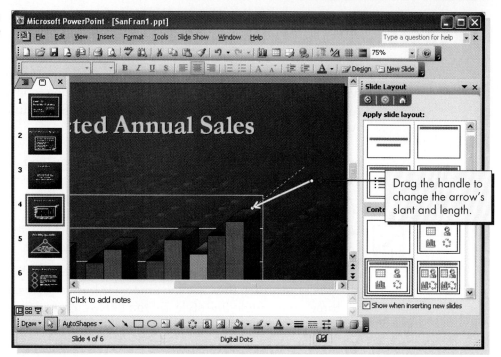

FIGURE 7-5
Adjusting the arrow

> Drag the handle to change the arrow's slant and length.

EXERCISE   7-5   Using the Format AutoShape Dialog Box

The Format AutoShape dialog box is a convenient place to apply many different types of formatting to all types of PowerPoint objects. Besides letting you change multiple attributes at one time, the Format AutoShape dialog box offers many options that are not available on toolbars.

1. Double-click the arrow to open the Format AutoShape dialog box.

2. Click the Colors and Lines tab.

3. In the Line section, open the Color drop-down list. The first line of color samples represents the colors for the current presentation's color scheme.

4. Point to the first sample on the first line (a blue/gray color). The ScreenTip identifies this sample as the color scheme's background color.

5. Click the blue/gray background color to select it.

6. Click Preview in the lower-left corner of the dialog box, and then drag the dialog box out of the way to see the new color of the arrow. The arrow fades into the background.

7. Change the color to dark pink, the Accent and Followed Hyperlink Scheme color on the right end of the first line of colors. Preview the change.

8. In the Weight box, click the up arrow several times until 8 pt appears. Click Preview. The arrow is thicker.

9. On the End style drop-down list, choose the first arrow style on the second row (Stealth Arrow).

10. On the End size drop-down list, choose the third arrow on the second row (Arrow R Size 6).

FIGURE 7-6
Format AutoShape
dialog box, Colors
and Lines tab

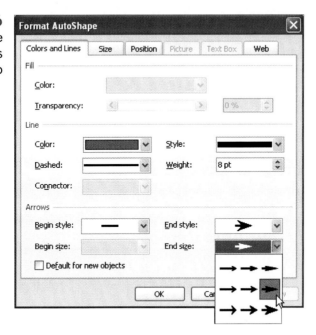

11. Click Preview. The arrow is now much wider and has a larger arrowhead.

12. Click OK to accept the changes and close the Format AutoShape dialog box. If you zoomed in on the arrow, change your zoom setting to Fit, so your entire slide is displayed.

 NOTE: You use the same technique to change the color of an object border or a line as you use to change the color of an arrow.

Changing the Fill Color of Objects

When you draw an object on a slide, the color of the object—its *fill color*—is determined by the presentation's color scheme. You can easily change the fill to another color from the presentation's color scheme or to any color you want.

EXERCISE   **7-6**   **Change the Fill Color of AutoShapes**

You change the fill color by using one of two options:

- Use the Fill Color button on the Drawing toolbar.
- Use the Format AutoShape dialog box (Colors and Lines tab).

1. Move back to slide 3 and right-click the star. From the shortcut menu, choose Format Aut**o**Shape to open the Format AutoShape dialog box.

2. Click the **Colors and Lines** tab.

3. In the Fill section of the dialog box, click the arrow next to **C**olor. Choose the gold sample (Accent and Hyperlink Scheme) color. Click **OK**.

4. With the star still selected, click the arrow next to the Fill Color button 🖌 on the Drawing toolbar. Click the purple sample, the accent scheme color.

FIGURE 7-7
Changing an object's fill color

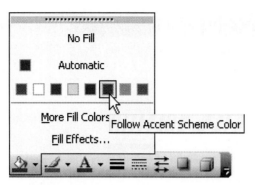

E X E R C I S E   **7-7**   **Remove Fill Colors and Borders from AutoShapes**

If you apply a fill or border to an object, and later decide you don't want it, it's easy to remove. The first Fill Color option is No Fill, and the first Line Color option is No Line.

1. Move to slide 5 and select the large triangle AutoShape.

2. On the Drawing toolbar, click the arrow for the Fill Color button 🖌 and choose No Fill. The color disappears, but the line remains.

3. With the triangle still selected, use the Line Color button 🖌 to choose No Line. The triangle's border disappears. Although it looks like the object disappeared, it is still there.

4. Click the text containing the names of cities, and then press Esc to select the object (the invisible triangle).

5. Choose purple (accent scheme color) for the fill. The triangle is once again visible.

TIP: The border is always present on an AutoShape. If you do not want a contrasting color, then choose no line. If you want to emphasize the border, then choose a contrasting color that blends with your color scheme and make the line thicker, so it is easily visible on your slide.

EXERCISE **7-8** **Use Recolor to Color an Image**

The *recolor* feature is an excellent tool that can be used to change a clip art image's colors to match the color scheme of your presentation.

This feature can only be used with Microsoft Windows Metafiles (a vector image format used mostly for clip art in Windows), and not with bitmapped images such as .jpg, .gif, or .png. You need to use an image editing program to edit such images.

Recoloring can be done by two methods:

● Click the Recolor Picture button on the Picture toolbar, and click Colors to change any color in the picture.

● Click the Recolor Picture button on the Picture toolbar, and click Fills to change only background or fill colors in the picture.

1. Move to slide 2. Select the image in the lower right-hand corner of the slide.

2. On the Picture toolbar, click the Recolor Picture button.

3. Choose Colors in the Change box at the lower left-hand corner of the dialog box. This will enable you to change any color in the picture.

4. Select the check box for several of the colors and change them to match the colors used in the presentation. (These colors come up automatically on the palette when you click on the drop-down arrow beside each color.)

FIGURE 7-8
Recoloring a
Microsoft Windows
Metafile image

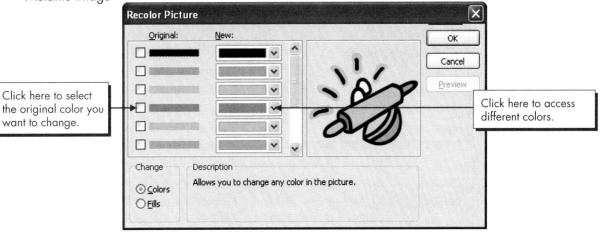

Click here to select the original color you want to change.

Click here to access different colors.

Working with an Extended Range of Colors

So far, you have been instructed to choose from only the eight colors that make up the presentation's color scheme. An infinite number of other colors are also available.

It's usually best to stick with the eight colors that make up the color scheme but, at times, one or two additional colors can enhance the look of a slide. Be careful when choosing extra colors because too many colors can spoil a presentation.

EXERCISE 7-9 Choose a Standard Color

Extra colors are available from the Colors dialog box. This dialog box has two tabs—Standard and Custom. *Standard colors* are premixed colors that you choose by clicking a sample on the Standard tab. *Custom colors* are colors that you mix yourself on the Custom tab. You can create an infinite variety of custom colors.

You open the Colors dialog box by choosing More Fill Colors from the Fill Color button's drop-down list or by choosing More Line Colors from the Line Color button's drop-down list.

FIGURE 7-9
Working with
standard colors

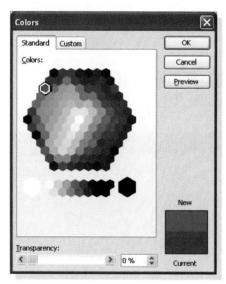

1. With the triangle on slide 5 selected, click the arrow for the Fill Color button 🖊.

2. Select More Fill Colors to display the Colors dialog box.

3. Click the Standard tab. A honeycomb of colors is displayed.

4. Click a dark green/blue color in the upper-left corner of the honeycomb. Notice the color sample on the right side of the dialog box, showing you the Current color and the New one you just selected.

5. Click Preview and drag the dialog box out of the way to see the result. Click OK.

EXERCISE 7-10 Create a Custom Color

The Custom tab on the Colors dialog box enables you to create any color you desire. Drag a crosshair to choose the color you want; then use a scroll bar to choose the brightness level for the color. It is important for you to remember the color terms for the RGB color model a computer uses to mix all colors that you see:

- Hue—the actual name of the color that you select.

- Saturation—the intensity of the color. Colors you select from the top of the Custom color palette are strong colors that are highly saturated; colors at the bottom seem muted because their saturation level is low.

- Luminance—the brightness of the color. When you drag the arrowhead up on the vertical bar, you are increasing the amount of white in a color; therefore, the luminance level has increased and the color is brighter. When you drag the arrowhead down, you are decreasing the amount of white in the color and adding black. Therefore, the color has a lower luminance level and is less bright.

CROSS HAIR

ARROW ADJUSTMENT

After you choose a custom color, it appears on the second line of the Fill Color and Line Color buttons' drop-down lists, so you can use it again without having to re-create it.

1. Working on slide 5, select the circle on top of the triangle.
2. Click the arrow for the Fill Color button 🔲 and choose More Fill Colors.
3. Click the Custom tab on the Colors dialog box. This dialog box contains a color palette and a vertical bar for choosing brightness.

FIGURE 7-10
Working with custom colors

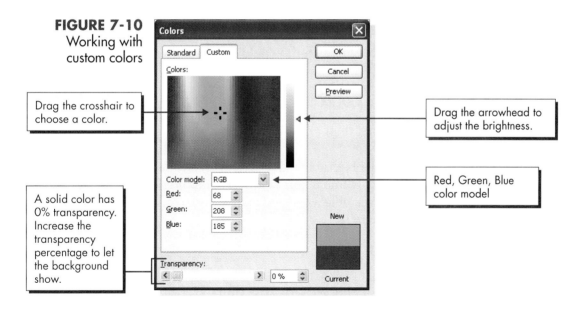

Drag the crosshair to choose a color.

Drag the arrowhead to adjust the brightness.

Red, Green, Blue color model

A solid color has 0% transparency. Increase the transparency percentage to let the background show.

4. Drag the crosshair straight up. Notice in the sample on the lower-right corner that the New color is much brighter than the Current color.

5. Drag the crosshair across the top of the palette. All the colors at the top are bright and the colors change horizontally like a rainbow.

IN COLORS (LIGHT — MORE COLOR IS WHITE
— ABSENCE OF COLOR IS BLACK

6. Drag the crosshair across the bottom of the palette. The colors are subdued.

7. Choose a fairly bright color; then drag the black arrowhead on the vertical bar up and down to see how the color becomes lighter and darker.

8. Experiment with the color palette and the brightness bar until you find a color you like. Click OK.

EXERCISE 7-11 Adjust Transparency Settings

Making colors transparent can enhance many PowerPoint color settings. For example, you can make an AutoShape's fill transparent, so that a slide's background shows through. Line color can also be made transparent. You can change transparency in the Color dialog box that you used in the previous two exercises.

1. Working on slide 5 with the circle selected, click the arrow for the Fill Color button 🖎 and choose More Fill Colors. Notice the Transparency slider at the bottom of the dialog box.

2. Drag the Transparency slider to the right, until you see 40% (more or less) in the spin box. Click OK.

3. Using the previous steps, change the transparency of the green/blue triangle to 60%. Notice that the slide's background shows through transparent colors.

4. Save the presentation as *[your initials]*7-11 in a new folder for Lesson 7, but do not print it. Keep it open for the following exercises.

Adding Patterns, Gradient Fills, and Textures

To add more interest to objects on your slides, you can add special effects such as fill patterns, gradient fills, and textures. PowerPoint provides many patterns, including textures that resemble wood and marble surfaces. You can also fill objects with pictures and clip art.

EXERCISE 7-12 Apply a Gradient Fill to an AutoShape

A gradient fill can add interest and dimension to PowerPoint objects. When you apply a *gradient fill,* the object contains colors that blend (or shade) into one another. A gradient fill can consist of one color blending to black, two colors that blend to each other, or a preset combination of multiple colors that are built into PowerPoint.

Besides choosing colors for gradient fills, you can specify the direction of the gradual color change, such as horizontal or diagonal. You can also add transparency effects. When using single-color gradients, you adjust the degree of light and dark by using a slider.

1. Move to slide 3 ("Sample Menu") and select the star AutoShape.
2. Click the arrow for the Fill Color button 🔲 and choose <u>F</u>ill Effects at the bottom of the menu. The Fill Effects dialog box appears.
3. Click the Gradient tab.
4. In the Colors options box, click Pre<u>s</u>et. The Preset colors list box appears, containing specially created gradient fills. Select some of these preset colors, and then look at the display in the V<u>a</u>riants box.

FIGURE 7-11
Fill Effects
dialog box

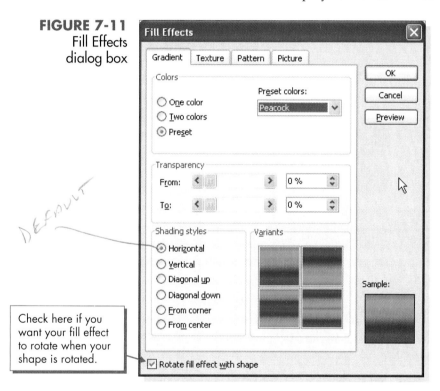

DEFAULT

Check here if you want your fill effect to rotate when your shape is rotated.

5. Choose Late Sunset from the Pre<u>s</u>et colors list box.
6. In the Shading Styles options box, choose <u>F</u>rom corner. Notice that the Sample box changes as you choose different effects.
7. Under V<u>a</u>riants, click the option in the upper-left corner. Click the <u>P</u>review button and drag the dialog box out of the way, so you can see the effect on the slide.
8. In the Transparency options section, drag the F<u>r</u>om slider to the right until you see 50% in the spin box. Move the T<u>o</u> slider to 50% also.

NOTE: Changing transparency settings does not activate Preview. If you want to preview the results of changing transparency settings, temporarily change one of the other settings in the dialog box.

9. Under Va̱riants, change to the sample in the upper-right corner.

10. Click P̱review to see the results of the transparency settings. Notice that because of the transparency, the Late Sunset colors are now subdued.

FIGURE 7-12
Setting transparency for a gradient fill

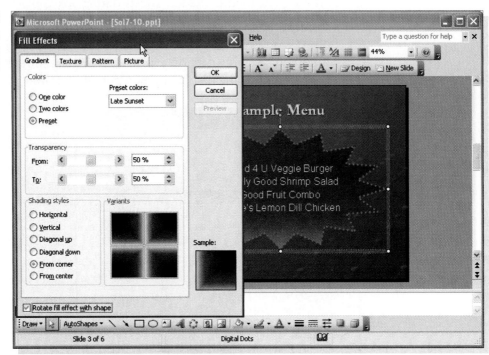

11. Click OK to accept the gradient fill settings and close the dialog box.

EXERCISE **7-13** **Apply a Gradient Fill to Add Dimension**

Applying a one- or two-color gradient fill to a circle can give it the appearance of a sphere.

1. Move to slide 5 and select the circle on top of the triangle.

2. Remove the circle's border.

3. Use the Fill Color button 🔲 to open the Fill Effects dialog box and display the Gradient tab.

4. Choose the O̱ne color option.

5. In the Color 1̱ list box, choose the dark pink color on the right end of the scheme colors.

6. Move the Dar<u>k</u>/Light slider a short distance to the right (still keeping it left of the center) until the Sample shades from very dark gray to dark pink.

7. Move the transparency sliders all the way to the left, for 0% transparency.

8. In the Shading styles options box, choose Fro<u>m</u> center.

9. Choose the left V<u>a</u>riants option (the one with the lightest color in the center).

10. Click <u>P</u>review. The circle now looks like a sphere.

11. If necessary, adjust the circle's shading, so that it stands out from the background. Click OK to close the dialog box.

12. Select the triangle and remove the border line. Apply the same gradient fill you used for the star AutoShape in Exercise 7-12 (Late Sunset preset, 50% transparency, shading from corner, upper right variant).

FIGURE 7-13
Using gradient fills

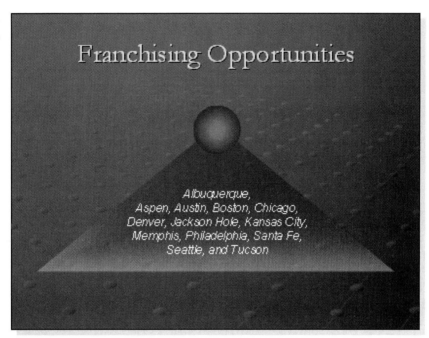

E X E R C I S E   **7-14**   **Apply a Gradient Fill to a Text Placeholder**

You apply fills to text placeholders in the same way that you apply fills to AutoShapes. All the options, including gradient fills and transparency settings, can be used.

When working with gradient transparency settings, you will notice that there are two transparency sliders. The F<u>r</u>om slider controls Color <u>1</u> and the T<u>o</u> slider controls Color 2.

1. Move to slide 2 and select the body text placeholder.

2. From the Format menu, choose Placeholder to open the Format AutoShape dialog box.

3. On the Colors and Lines tab, Fill section, click the Color list box arrow and choose Fill Effects.

4. In the Fill Effects dialog box, click the Gradient tab and click the Two colors option.

5. Keep Color 1 as dark blue/gray (fills scheme color), and change Color 2 to the dark pink color on the right end of the color samples.

6. Choose the Horizontal shading style and the upper right variant (which is darkest at the bottom).

7. Under Transparency, drag the From slider to the right, all the way to 100%. Drag the To slider to 20%.

8. Click OK to accept the shading. Click OK again to close the Format AutoShape dialog box.

9. Remove the outline from the text placeholder. Notice how the gradient fill fades into the background.

10. Move to slide 6. Apply the same shading to the text placeholder that you applied on slide 2.

11. Save the presentation as *[your initials]*7-14 in your Lesson 7 folder, but do not print it. Leave the presentation open for the next exercise.

EXERCISE **7-15** **Add a Fill Pattern to an AutoShape**

When you click the Pattern tab on the Fill Effects dialog box, you can choose from 48 two-color patterns to apply to PowerPoint objects. You can choose any foreground color and any background color to create an endless variety of pattern effects.

1. On slide 6, right-click the top diamond shape and choose Format AutoShape from the shortcut menu. Select the Colors and Lines tab.

2. In the Line section, click the Color drop-down list box and choose No Line.

3. In the Fill section, click the Color drop-down list box and choose Fill Effects.

4. Click the Pattern tab.

5. Click the Solid Diamond Pattern, which is the last pattern in the last row. Notice that when you click the pattern, its name appears in the box below the pattern samples. (See Figure 7-14 on the next page.)

6. Change the Background color to gold and click OK.

7. Click Preview to view the changes.

8. Click OK to close the Format AutoShape dialog box.

FIGURE 7-14
Adding a pattern fill
to an object

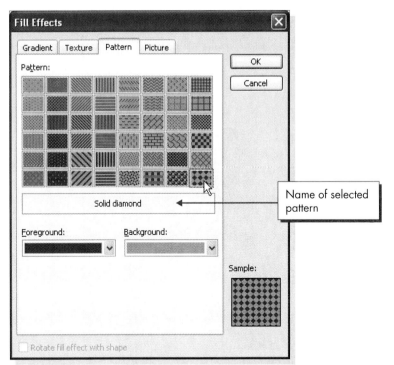

EXERCISE 7-16 Add a Textured Fill to an AutoShape

In addition to gradient fills and patterns, you can apply textured fill effects, such as marble and wood grain.

1. On slide 6, right-click the middle diamond and open the Format AutoShape dialog box. Click the Colors and Lines tab.

2. In the Fill section, choose Fill Effects from the Color drop-down list and click the Texture tab.

3. Click several different textures, one at a time. Notice the name of the texture and its appearance in the Sample box.

> **TIP:** You are not limited to the textures shown on the Textures tab. If you click Other Texture, you can navigate through your disk drives and network drives to choose graphics files from other sources that you can use as textures.

4. Click Bouquet, the last option in the third row.

5. Click OK to accept the texture and close the Fill Effects dialog box. (See Figure 7-15 on the next page.)

6. Click OK to close the Format AutoShape dialog box.

FIGURE 7-15
Choosing a
textured fill

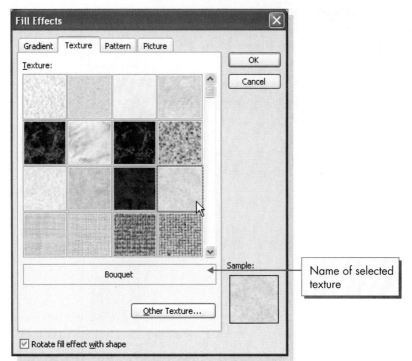

EXERCISE **7-17** **Add a Picture Fill to an AutoShape**

You can further customize your slides by using a picture file as an object fill.

1. Select the last diamond on slide 6. Change its border color to black (use More Line Colors).

2. Use the Fill Color button to open the Fill Effects dialog box. Click the Picture tab.

3. Click the Select Picture button. The Select Picture dialog box opens.

4. Navigate to the folder where your student files are stored.

5. Select the file **Emp1** and click Insert.

6. To make sure that the picture's proportions are not distorted, check Lock picture aspect ratio at the bottom of the dialog box. (See Figure 7-16 on the next page.)

7. Click OK. The diamond shape is now filled with an employee picture.

8. Save the file as *[your initials]***7-17**, but do not print it. Leave the presentation open for the next exercise.

FIGURE 7-16
Picture tab on
the Fill Effects
dialog box

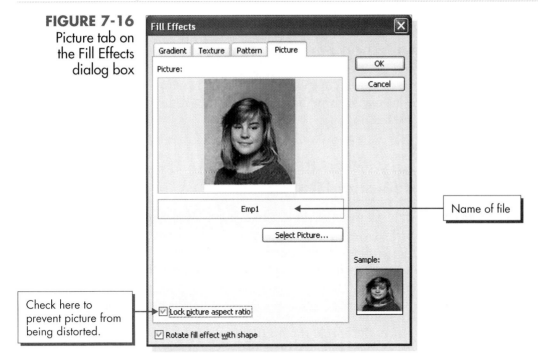

Name of file

Check here to
prevent picture from
being distorted.

EXERCISE 7-18 Apply a Pattern to a Border

In the same way that you apply a pattern to fill an object, you can apply one to the border of an object, a line, or an arrow. Depending on the colors you choose, a pattern can soften the effect of a line or accent it.

1. Move to slide 1.
2. Right-click the picture of a San Francisco street and select Format Picture from the shortcut menu.
3. In the Format Picture dialog box, click the Colors and Lines tab.
4. In the Line options section, change the Color to white.
5. Change the line weight to 10 points by keying **10** in the Weight spin box.
6. Click Preview to view the results. (Don't close the dialog box.)
7. Open the Color list in the Line section and choose Patterned Lines.

FIGURE 7-17
Picture with small
diagonal-patterned
border

8. Choose Black for the Foreground color, and the first gray/blue color sample (shadows scheme color) for the Background color.
9. For the pattern, choose the third sample in the third row, named Dark downward diagonal.
10. Click OK to close the Patterned Lines dialog box. Click OK again to close the Format Picture dialog box.

Using the Format Painter Tool

If you use Word or Excel, you're probably familiar with the *Format Painter* tool. This tool makes it easy to copy the formatting, for example, the fill pattern, from one object to another object.

EXERCISE **7-19** **Copy Formatting from One Object to Another Object**

When you copy the format of an object, many default settings associated with that object are copied as well. For example, when you copy the formatting of an AutoShape, the default text formatting associated with that AutoShape is copied, too (even if there is no text in the AutoShape). If you apply that formatting to a text box, the text formatting might change along with the fill and outline formatting. The Undo command can be handy when using the Format Painter tool.

1. On slide 6, select the checkerboard diamond.

2. Click the Format Painter button ▨ on the Standard toolbar. The Format Painter picks up the checkerboard formatting, and the mouse pointer has a paintbrush attached to it.

3. Click within the title text. The text appears in a tiny size with a checkerboard background. Click the Undo button ▨.

4. Select the third diamond (with the picture fill) and double-click the Format Painter button ▨. Double-clicking keeps the Format Painter active, so you can copy the formatting to more than one object.

5. Click the top diamond, and then click the middle diamond. All diamonds now contain the employee picture fill and are outlined in black. Notice that the Format Painter button is still turned on.

6. Click the Format Painter button ▨ again or press (Esc) to restore the standard mouse pointer.

7. Double-click the top diamond to open the Format AutoShape dialog box, and then in the Fill section click the Color drop-down menu to choose Fill Effects. When the Fill Effects dialog box appears, the Picture tab is automatically displayed.

8. Click Select Picture. The Select Picture dialog box opens to the folder where you selected the previous picture.

9. Choose **Emp2**; then click Insert and click OK twice.

10. Change the picture in the middle diamond to the file **Emp3**.

EXERCISE   **7-20**   **Copy Object Formatting to a Different Slide**

Just as you can copy objects from one slide to another, you can copy formatting from one slide to another by using the Format Painter.

1. Click the body text placeholder on slide 6; then double-click the Format Painter button 🖌.

2. Move to slide 1 and click the large rectangle with the white outline. The rectangle takes on the transparent gradient fill of the copied text box format.

3. Click the Format Painter button 🖌 to turn it off.

4. Click Undo twice to return the fill color and the text to its previous settings.

5. On slide 4, change the color of the arrow you created earlier to a color that contrasts with its background.

6. Check spelling in the presentation.

7. Create a handout header and footer: include the date and your name as the header, and the page number and text *[your initials]*7-20 as the footer.

8. Move to slide 1 and save the presentation as *[your initials]*7-20 in your Lesson 7 folder.

9. View the presentation as a slide show; then preview and print the presentation as handouts, six slides per page, grayscale, framed. Leave the presentation open for the next exercise.

Notice in your printout that the slides are dark and some of the detail is lost. You correct that in the following exercises.

Adjust Presentation Color Settings

In many cases, slides look great in color, but the text becomes difficult or impossible to read when you print in grayscale (shades of gray) to a black-and-white printer.

Fortunately, you can display the grayscale view of your presentation in the Slide pane. When the grayscale view is displayed, you can change grayscale settings without affecting the color version of your presentation.

EXERCISE   **7-21**   **Choose the Grayscale Version**

To adjust the grayscale image of a presentation, first display the grayscale version of your presentation in one of the following ways:

● Open the View menu and choose Color/Grayscale, Grayscale.

● Click the Color/Grayscale button ▣ on the Standard toolbar and choose Grayscale.

When the grayscale version is in view, select an object on a slide or on a master slide, click Setting on the Grayscale View toolbar, and choose one of the options.

1. Move to slide 1. Click the Color/Grayscale button on the Standard toolbar and choose <u>G</u>rayscale. The slide changes to a grayscale image and the Grayscale View floating toolbar appears.

NOTE: You might need to click the Toolbar Options button ⌄ to find the Color/Grayscale button.

2. Display the slide master; then click one of the dots in the background picture to select the picture. The sizing handles for this picture extend beyond the slide's border, but you can tell when it is selected by the green rotation handle at the top of the dots.

3. Click Setting on the Grayscale View toolbar.

4. Choose <u>D</u>on't Show from the drop-down list. The dots are no longer visible on the slide master. Although the dots are interesting in the color version, they are too pronounced in the grayscale version, so it's better to hide them.

5. Using the same steps as the previous ones, hide the dots on the title master.

FIGURE 7-18
Changing grayscale settings

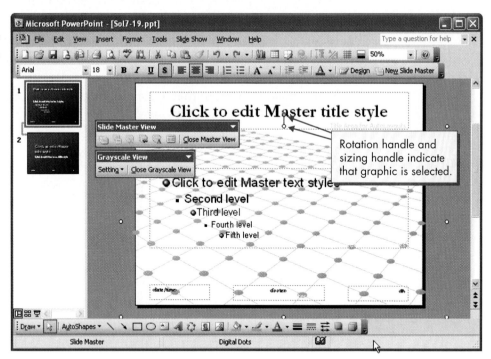

6. Close the Master view. Slide 1 looks better without the dots.

7. Move to slide 2. Slide 2 looks fine, but it will print better if the gradient fill is removed from the body text placeholder.

8. Select the body text placeholder, and then click Setting on the Grayscale View toolbar.

9. Choose Black with White Fill from the drop-down list. This setting displays all lines and text in black and eliminates fills.

10. On slides 1, 3, and 5, change the large rectangle, the star shape, and the triangle to the Black with White Fill setting in the same way that you changed the text placeholder on slide 2.

11. On slide 4, change the graph setting to Inverse Grayscale.

12. On slide 5, change the setting for the sphere on top of the triangle to Light Grayscale.

13. Click Close Grayscale View on the Grayscale View toolbar to view the presentation in color. Notice the color view has not changed.

FIGURE 7-19
Presentation after changing grayscale settings

14. Update the handout footer to show the text *[your initials]*7-21.

15. Move to slide 1 and save the presentation as *[your initials]*7-21 in your Lesson 7 folder.

16. Preview, and then print the presentation as handouts, six slides per page, grayscale, framed.

17. Compare your Exercise 7-20 printout to your Exercise 7-21 printout.

18. Close the presentation.

EXERCISE **7-22** **Choose the Black and White Version**

The black and white version of a PowerPoint presentation is available through the same Color/Grayscale button ▣ as used in the previous exercise.

The black and white option puts all objects in a pure black and white setting, which saves ink when printing and makes notes easy to read for handouts.

1. *Move* to slide 1. Click the Color/Grayscale button on the Standard toolbar and choose Pure Black and White. This displays only black and white.

2. Notice that the Grayscale View toolbar appears as in the previous exercise. Choose Settings, and Black. Notice the black and white inverts on the slide. This could be used to show contrast, but will use much ink in printing.

3. Click the Close Black and White View to return to the color presentation.

USING ONLINE HELP

In this lesson, you worked with colors that are not part of a presentation's color scheme. Understanding the fine points about scheme colors and non-scheme colors is useful when customizing a presentation.

Use Help to learn more about scheme colors and non-scheme colors:

1. Key **color scheme** in the Ask a Question box and press Enter.

2. Select **About color schemes** from the drop-down list.

FIGURE 7-20
About color schemes Help topic

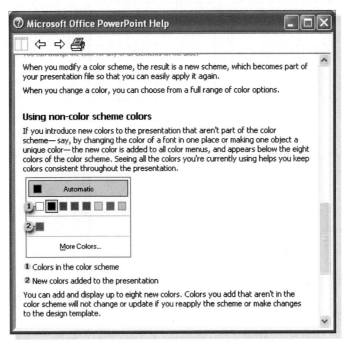

3. Read the information in the Help window, paying special attention to the last topic, Using non-color scheme colors.

4. Close the window when you're finished.

LESSON 7 Summary

➤ All PowerPoint objects—AutoShapes, text placeholders, text boxes, and WordArt—can be enhanced with the addition of border and fill effects.

➤ Border effects include solid lines, dashed lines, and patterned lines in any thickness (weight) or color you want.

➤ Apply border effects by using the Line Color 🖊, Line Style ▤, and Dash Style ▦ buttons. Or, use the Colors and Lines tab of the Format AutoShape dialog box.

➤ The Arrow button 🖺 draws a line with an arrowhead on its end. You can add or remove an arrowhead from any drawn line by using the Arrow Style 🖺 button.

➤ The Colors and Lines tab of the Format AutoShape dialog box offers additional ways to format an arrow, enabling you to choose the size and shape of the arrowhead and line formatting options.

➤ Fill effects include solid colors, patterns, gradients, textures, and pictures. In addition, solid colors and gradients can have varying degrees of transparency, enabling background objects and colors to show through.

➤ Remove a border from an object by choosing the No Line option from the Line Color button's drop-down list. Remove the fill effect from an object by choosing the No Fill option from the Fill Color button's drop-down list.

➤ It is usually best to use the eight standard colors that are part of a design template's color scheme but, occasionally, a few additional colors can enhance a presentation.

➤ The recolor picture button on the picture toolbar can be used to change the color of Microsoft Windows Metafile images to match the color scheme of your presentation.

➤ Additional colors are available by choosing More Fill Colors from the Fill Color button's drop-down list, More Line Colors from the Line Color button's drop-down list, or More Colors from the Font Color button's drop-down list.

➤ The Colors dialog box enables you to choose from a honeycomb of premixed colors on the Standard tab or to mix your own colors on the Custom tab.

➤ Gradient fills—the blending of colors into each other—have several options, including the direction and transparency of the effect.

➤ Pattern fills have 48 varieties, including vertical, horizontal, and diagonal lines; checks; and dots using any two colors that you choose.

➤ PowerPoint includes several textures that you can use for fill effects. In addition, you can use graphics files containing textures from other sources that are saved on your computer or network.

➤ Any picture—a scanned photograph or other image—can be used to fill an object. When using a picture, you have the choice of distorting the picture to fill the space or preserving its proportions.

➤ The Format Painter button ⬜ enables you to copy formatting from one object to another. This is a great time-saver if you applied several effects to an object and want to duplicate the effects.

➤ Double-clicking the Format Painter button ⬜ keeps it active, so that multiple objects can receive the copied format. Click the Format Painter button again to turn it off.

➤ Be careful using the Format Painter because all formatting associated with the object is copied, including default text formatting, even if the object does not contain any text.

➤ The grayscale version and the black and white version of a presentation can be adjusted for clearer printing on black-and-white printers. Adjusting the grayscale settings has no effect on the color version of the presentation.

LESSON 7   Command Summary

FEATURE	BUTTON	MENU	KEYBOARD
Format line style	⬜	Format, AutoShape (or Placeholder, or Text Box), Lines and Colors tab	
Change line color	⬜	Format, AutoShape (or Placeholder, or Text Box), Lines and Colors tab	
Change a line's dash style	⬜	Format, AutoShape (or Placeholder, or Text Box), Lines and Colors tab	
Draw an arrow	⬜		
Format arrowheads	⬜	Format, AutoShape (or Placeholder, or Text Box), Lines and Colors tab	
Apply fill color, texture, pattern, gradient	⬜	Format, AutoShape (or Placeholder, or Text Box), Lines and Colors tab	
Copy formatting of an object	⬜		
Switch from Color to Grayscale or Black and White view	⬜	View, Color/Grayscale, Grayscale	

Concepts Review

TRUE/FALSE QUESTIONS

Each of the following statements is either true or false. Indicate your choice by circling T or F.

T F   *1.* When you draw an object, it appears in a color that is available from the color scheme of the current template.

T **F**   *2.* A transparency effect can be applied only to solid fill colors.

T **F**   *3.* A gradient fill can have only two colors.

T F   *4.* A fill pattern can have only two colors.

T F   *5.* Granite and marble are examples of textured fills.

T F   *6.* You can use the Format Painter tool to copy formatting from one slide to another.

T **F**   *7.* The Format Painter doesn't copy text formatting.

T **F**   *8.* You must be careful when making changes in Grayscale view, because they can affect the colors of your presentation.

SHORT ANSWER QUESTIONS

Write the correct answer in the space provided.

1. Which button can be used to recolor a Microsoft Windows Metafile?

RE COLOR   PICTURE TOOLBAR

2. What dialog box can you use to change line and fill colors for an AutoShape?

FORMAT AUTO SHAPE DIALOG BOX

3. What gradient fill option should you choose if you want to shade from a color to a very light shade of that same color?

ONE COLOR GRADIENT

4. How do you create a patterned line or border?

SELECT → CHOOSE PATTERN LINES FROM LINE COLOR DROP DOWN

5. How do you remove a fill effect from an object?

FILL COLOR → NO-FILL

6. What button can you use to copy fills and colors to another object?

FORMAT PAINTER

7. How do you switch the screen display of your presentation from color to grayscale?

COLOR GRAYSCALE BUTTON

8. How do you change grayscale settings for PowerPoint objects?

SWITCH TO GRAYSCALE VIEW
CLICK SETTINGS

CRITICAL THINKING

Answer these questions on a separate page. There are no right or wrong answers. Support your answers with examples from your own experience, if possible.

1. Think of the way you used a gradient fill to add dimension to a simple circle. What other objects could you change by using a gradient fill to add dimension?

2. Which objects in a presentation are most suited to borders? What types of border styles and colors work best against what types of backgrounds?

Skills Review

EXERCISE 7-23

Create borders, change line colors and styles, and change fill colors.

1. Open the file **Funding2**.

2. Add a border to all body text placeholders in the presentation by following these steps:

   a. Display the slide master and select the body text placeholder.
   b. Click the Line Color button 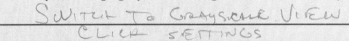 on the Drawing toolbar.
   c. Choose the fourth color from the left, the title text scheme color.

3. Format the border by following these steps:

   a. With the body text placeholder on the slide master selected, click the Line Style button ▤ on the Drawing toolbar.
   b. Choose the 6-point line style.
   c. Click the Dash Style button ▦ on the Drawing toolbar.
   d. Select the second style (Round Dot).

4. Apply a fill to a text placeholder by following these steps:

   a. With the body text placeholder on the slide master selected, click the down arrow next to the Fill Color button [img]．

   b. Select the third color from the left, the shadows scheme color. Select More Fill Colors to access the Colors dialog box and the Custom tab. Change the transparency setting to 30 percent.

   c. Close the Master view.

5. Draw and format an arrow by following these steps:

   a. On slide 3, click the Arrow button [img] on the Drawing toolbar.

   b. Drag the cross pointer from the word "Specialties" in the title to the word "fat" in the first line of the body text placeholder.

6. Use the Format AutoShape dialog box to format the arrow by following these steps:

   a. Right-click the arrow and choose Format Auto Shape from the shortcut menu.

   b. Click the Colors and Lines tab.

   c. In the Style list box (in the Line options section) select the **6 pt** solid line.

   d. In the End style drop-down list, choose the first arrow style in the second row (Stealth Arrow).

   e. In the End size drop-down list, choose the third arrow in the second row (Arrow R Size 6). Click OK.

7. On slide 1, add a dark brown 4 ½-point double-line border (either one) to the subtitle text placeholder. Resize the placeholder, so that the border surrounds both the subtitle text and the Good 4 U logo. Increase the title text to 54 points and add a shadow. Align the title and the box surrounding the subtitle and logo on the right.

8. Check spelling in the presentation.

9. Create a handout header and footer: include the date and your name as the header, and the page number and text *[your initials]*7-23 as the footer.

10. Move to slide 1 and save the presentation as *[your initials]*7-23 in your Lesson 7 folder.

11. Preview, and then print the presentation as handouts, six slides per page, grayscale, framed. Close the presentation.

EXERCISE 7-24

Use a color from the extended color palette, apply a transparent gradient fill, and use the Format Painter.

1. Open the file **Owners1**.

2. Apply a gradient fill to an object by following these steps:

a. Move to slide 2 and select the body text placeholder.

b. Click the arrow for the Fill Color button 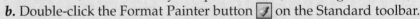 and choose **Fill Effects.**

c. In the Fill Effects dialog box, click the **Gradient** tab.

d. Choose **Two** colors.

e. Change **Color** 1 to purple and **Color** 2 to dark gray (the background scheme color).

f. Under **Transparency**, drag the **From** slider to approximately 25% and drag the **To** slider to 25%.

g. Choose the **From corner** shading style and the bottom left **Variants** option (with purple in the lower left and dark gray in the upper right).

h. Click **Preview**; then drag the dialog box out of the way so you can view the results. Leave the dialog box open.

3. Choose a custom color by following these steps:

a. With the Fill Effects dialog box still open, click the list box arrow for **Color** 1 and choose **More colors.**

b. In the Colors dialog box, click the **Custom** tab.

c. On the **Colors** palette, drag the crosshair near the bottom of the blue section up a little to create a color that is brighter.

d. Drag the black arrowhead up the vertical bar to make the color a little lighter.

e. Compare the **Current** and **New** colors in the sample box in the lower-right corner of the dialog box. When you like the new color, click **OK.**

f. Click **Preview.** If you like the result, click **OK.** Otherwise, adjust the custom purple color. When you are finished adjusting the color, click **OK** to close the Fill Effects dialog box.

4. Remove the white border from the text placeholder.

5. Use the Format Painter button to copy the gradient fill to the subtitle placeholder on slide 1, and the body text placeholders on slides 3 and 4, by following these steps:

a. On slide 2, select the body text placeholder (with the gradient fill).

b. Double-click the Format Painter button on the Standard toolbar.

c. With the paintbrush pointer, move to slide 3, and then click each body text placeholder.

d. Click the paintbrush pointer on the body text placeholder on slide 4; then click the paintbrush pointer on the subtitle text placeholder on slide 1.

e. Click the Format Painter button once to turn it off.

6. Add dimension to circles by following these steps:

a. Use the Format Painter button to copy the formatting of the subtitle text placeholder.

b. Display the title master and click one of the purple circles in the center of the title master to apply the copied formatting.

c. With the circle selected, click the arrow for the Fill Color button, choose **Fill Effects,** and click the **Gradient** tab.

      d. Under Transparency, change the T<u>o</u> setting to 50%.

      e. Change the shading style to <u>From</u> center and select the variant on the left. Click OK to accept the gradient effect and click OK to close the Format AutoShape dialog box.

  7. Use the Format Painter button 🖋 to copy the circle's formatting to the other two circles on the title master and to the three circles on the slide master.

  8. Add a clip art that relates to the presentation to the Master Slides and recolor it to match the presentation. Resize and rearrange the placeholders for an attractive design.

  9. Close the Master view.

10. Check spelling in the presentation.

11. Create a handout header and footer: include the date and your name as the header, and the page number and text *[your initials]*7-24 as the footer.

12. Move to slide 1 and save the presentation as *[your initials]*7-24 in your Lesson 7 folder.

13. View the presentation as a slide show; then preview and print the presentation as handouts, four slides per page, grayscale, landscape, framed. Close the presentation.

EXERCISE 7-25

Copy formatting by using Format Painter, add a patterned border, apply a transparent gradient fill, and work with grayscale settings.

  1. Open the file **MiamBch1**.

  2. On the master slides, remove the shadow on the body text and subtitle placeholders because it looks blurred. To be effective, shadows must contrast with the text color. Change the placeholder fonts to Tahoma on both the slide master and the title master. Close the master slide.

  3. On slide 3, increase the size of the body text placeholder, so the text does not wordwrap. Apply a patterned border by following these steps:

      a. Right-click the body text placeholder on slide 3 and choose Format Plac<u>e</u>holder from the shortcut menu.

      b. Click the Colors and Lines tab.

      c. In the Line options section, click the C<u>o</u>lor arrow and choose <u>P</u>atterned Lines.

      d. In the Patterned Lines dialog box, choose dark brown (text and lines scheme color) for the <u>F</u>oreground color and pink for the <u>B</u>ackground color.

      e. Choose Sphere for the pattern (second pattern from the right on the bottom row). Click OK.

      f. Change the <u>W</u>eight to 20 pt.

      g. Click <u>P</u>review to view the border, and then click OK.

4. Use the Format Painter button to copy the border from the placeholder on slide 3 to the picture on slide 1.

5. Apply a transparent gradient fill to an object by following these steps:

   a. On slide 3, select the body text placeholder.
   b. Click the arrow for the Fill Color button and select Fill Effects.
   c. In the Fill Effects dialog box, choose Preset.
   d. Choose Early Sunset from the Preset colors drop-down list.
   e. Choose the Diagonal down shading style, and choose the lower left Variants option (with the brightest yellow stripe in the center).
   f. Click Preview to view the results. Keep the Fill Effects dialog box open.
   g. In the Transparency options section, drag the From slider to 75% and the To slider to 75%.
   h. To reactivate Preview, select a different variant, and then reselect the lower-left corner variant.
   i. Click Preview again and click OK.

6. Still working on slide 3, copy the formatting of the star on the right to the other stars on the slide.

7. Copy the formatting of the text placeholder on slide 3 to the chart on slide 2.

8. Adjust grayscale settings by following these steps:

   a. Move to slide 1.
   b. Click the Color/Grayscale button and choose Grayscale.
   c. Select the picture on slide 1.
   d. Click Setting on the Grayscale View toolbar. Choose Grayscale.
   e. Click Close Grayscale View on the Grayscale View toolbar.

9. Check spelling in the presentation.

10. Create a handout header and footer: include the date and your name as the header, and the page number and filename *[your initials]7-25* as the footer.

11. Move to slide 1 and save the presentation as *[your initials]7-25* in your Lesson 7 folder.

12. Preview, and then print the presentation as handouts, three slides per page, grayscale, framed. Close the presentation.

EXERCISE 7-26

Add fill and outline effects to slide master objects and change grayscale settings.

1. Open the file **Opening2**.

2. On the slide master, select the body text placeholder (banner shape) and change its border and fill effects by following these steps:

   a. Using the Line Color button , select No Line.

b. Using the Fill Color button , display the Gradient tab of the Fill Effects dialog box.

    c. Click Preset and choose Early Sunset from the Preset colors list box.

    d. Choose the Diagonal down shading style and the upper right variant (with the red color in the upper-right corner). Click OK.

    e. Without using the Format Painter, apply the same formatting to the subtitle placeholder on the title master. Close the Master view.

3. Switch to grayscale view by clicking the Color/Grayscale button on the Standard toolbar and choosing Grayscale. Scroll through the presentation.

4. Change the grayscale settings by following these steps:

    a. While still in Grayscale view, display the slide master.

    b. Select the body text placeholder.

    c. Click Setting on the Grayscale View toolbar.

    d. Choose Light Grayscale.

    e. On the title master, repeat this setting for the subtitle placeholder. Change the grayscale setting for the title text placeholder to Black.

5. Close the Master view, but keep the Grayscale view open. Scroll through all the slides to view the changes to grayscale settings.

6. Click Close Grayscale View on the Grayscale View toolbar.

7. Check spelling in the presentation.

8. Create a handout header and footer: include the date and your name as the header, and the page number and text *[your initials]*7-26 as the footer.

9. Move to slide 1 and save the presentation as *[your initials]*7-26 in your Lesson 7 folder.

10. Preview, and then print the presentation as handouts, four slides per page, grayscale, landscape, framed. Close the presentation.

Lesson Applications

Work with gradient fills, create and format an arrow, change grayscale settings, and use the Format Painter.

1. Open the file **Recruit1** and apply the design template Edge. Use the color scheme with the dark brown background (the first sample in the second row if your task pane is wide enough to show two samples across).
2. Insert two new slides after slide 3. Use the text in Figure 7-21 to create bulleted lists.

FIGURE 7-21

Slide 4

Who's Who
- Julie Wolfe, Co-owner
- Gus Irvinelli, Co-owner
- Michele Jenkins, Head Chef
- Roy Olafsen, Marketing Manager

Slide 5

Summary
- Six-month probation period
- Annual salary increases
- Quarterly stock purchase options
- Annual profit sharing

3. On slide 1, select the title text placeholder, and then click the WordArt button on the Drawing toolbar. Create a WordArt title by using the WordArt Gallery sample in the bottom row, fifth column.
4. Delete the title text placeholder and position the WordArt in its place.
5. Using the same WordArt style, substitute WordArt titles for the title text on the remaining slides. Adjust the size of the WordArt titles to make them slightly smaller, so you have some space between the WordArt and the body text placeholders. Make the sizing consistent for each of the titles.

6. Select the WordArt on slide 1. Use the Fill Color button to change the gradient fill to the following:
   - Wheat preset
   - Horizontal shading style
   - Upper left variant

7. Use the Format Painter button to copy the gradient fill from the WordArt on slide 1 to the WordArt on all the other slides.

8. On slide 1, select the subtitle text placeholder and change its fill to gradient with white, transparency To: 50%, and a vertical shading style blending from white to black. Insert the picture file **Logo1** from your student data disk on the white area (left) of this placeholder.

9. Insert a suitable clip art picture in the lower-right corner of the slide. Position and size it appropriately.

10. Copy the clip art and paste it on the slide master. Resize it to be smaller and place it in the upper right of the slide, so it does not conflict with the body text placeholder.

11. On slide 5, draw a 16-point star at the bottom center of the slide. Key the text **Substantial!** inside the star. Format the star as follows:

- Make it 1.75 inches high and 4 inches wide.
- Change the text size to 32 points, change its color to dark brown, and make it bold.
- Rotate it slightly to the left (about –10 degrees)
- Use Format Painter to copy the formatting from the WordArt title and apply it to the star.
- Adjust the star's position to make a pleasing composition.

12. Using the Arrow button , draw an arrow pointing from the star to the text "Annual profit sharing." Change the arrow's line thickness to 4.5 points.

13. Review all the slides, resizing the WordArt titles if needed to improve the appearance. Resize the body placeholders on slides 2 and 3 if the image on the slide master overlaps the text. View the presentation as a slide show.

14. View slide 1 in Grayscale view.

15. Check spelling in the presentation.

16. Create a handout header and footer: include the date and your name as the header, and the page number and text *[your initials]*7-27 as the footer.

17. Move to slide 1 and save the presentation as *[your initials]*7-27 in your Lesson 7 folder.

18. Preview, and then print the presentation as handouts, six slides per page, grayscale, framed. Close the presentation.

Change line colors, line styles, and fill colors of objects; change an AutoShape; add an arrowhead; adjust grayscale settings.

1. Open the file **TrainPt3**.

2. On slide 2, make the green color of the dollar sign clip-art image darker to better blend with the slide color scheme.

3. On slide 3, insert a text box near the upper-right corner of the graph with the text **Estimating over $89,000** on two lines. Change the font to 20-point Arial bold.

4. Add a 3-point dark green border to the text box; then change its AutoShape to Line Callout 3.

REVIEW: To change the text box to a callout AutoShape, select the AutoShape and choose Draw, Change AutoShape, Callouts. The Line Callout 3 shape is the third shape in the second row.

5. Use the callout shape's yellow adjustment handles to make the callout line point to the tallest green column on the graph.

6. With the callout shape selected, apply Arrow Style 6, so that an arrowhead appears on the end of the callout line, pointing to the tallest column.

7. On slide 4, delete the text placeholder. In its place, draw a text box. In the text box, key **10% discount off the lunch menu, Monday through Thursday**

8. Format the text box as follows to give it a blackboard effect:
   - Change the fill color to black.
   - Change the text to white 32-point Tahoma.
   - Apply an 8-point patterned border; use black as the Foreground and white as the Background. Choose the Wide upward diagonal pattern (third from left, last row).
   - Change its AutoShape to a rounded rectangle.

9. Resize and reposition the clip art and the text box if needed to create a pleasing composition.

10. On slide 4, change the grayscale setting for the AutoShape to Light Grayscale. Review all the slides in Grayscale view and make any other necessary adjustments.

11. Check spelling in the presentation.

12. Create a handout header and footer: include the date and your name as the header, and the page number and text *[your initials]*7-28 as the footer.

13. Move to slide 1 and save the presentation as *[your initials]*7-28 in your Lesson 7 folder.

14. Preview, and then print the presentation as handouts, six slides per page, grayscale, framed. Close the presentation.

EXERCISE 7-29

Apply a textured fill, apply patterned lines, and use custom colors.

1. Open the file **Seminar2**. Apply the design template Default Design (the first design template in the Available for Use section of the Slide Design task pane) and use the color scheme with the dark gray background.

2. On slide 1 below the subtitle, draw a Horizontal Scroll AutoShape (Stars and Banners, second shape on the bottom row). Make the shape slightly wider than the subtitle and about 2 inches high.

3. Key the text **Good 4 U** in the scroll AutoShape and format the text as 40-pt Arial bold shadowed. Change the text color to dark gray (background scheme color).

4. Apply the following formatting to the scroll:
   - Drag the yellow adjustment handle to the right as far as it will go.
   - Change the border to a 3-pt dark gray line (background scheme color); then use the Custom tab of the Colors dialog box to make the line color a noticeably darker shade.
   - Apply a textured fill using the Stationery texture (last selection on the first row).

5. On the slide master, draw a rectangle slightly larger than the body text placeholder and position it on top of the placeholder. Use the Colors and Lines tab of the Format AutoShape dialog box to format the rectangle as follows:
   - Remove the fill color.
   - Under Line, change the Style to a 6-pt triple-line.
   - Change the Weight of the line to 10 points.
   - For the Color of the line, choose a Wide downward diagonal pattern using gold as the foreground and a custom darker shade of gold for the background.

6. Insert a title master. Remove the gold-outlined rectangle from the title master. Change the title on the title master to 54 points, gold, bold, with a shadow. Repeat for the title on the slide master, but leave the font size 44 points. Close the master slide view.

  REVIEW: If a title master does not exist, insert one by displaying the slide master, and then clicking the Insert New Title Master button ▣ on the Slide Master View toolbar.

7. On slide 1, delete the subtitle placeholder and move the title placeholder to the top of the slide.

8. Search for an appropriate photograph image and resize it to fit between the title and the banner at the bottom of the slide.

9. After slide 4, insert a new slide with a blank layout. Insert WordArt. From the Gallery, select the first WordArt style on the third row. Type the text **Welcome**

10. Resize and reposition the WordArt for a pleasing appearance.

11. View the presentation as a slide show.

12. Check spelling in the presentation.

13. Create a handout header and footer: include the date and your name as the header, and the page number and text *[your initials]*7-29 as the footer.

14. Move to slide 1 and save the presentation as *[your initials]*7-29 in your Lesson 7 folder.

15. Preview, and then print the presentation as handouts, six slides per page, grayscale, framed. Close the presentation.

EXERCISE 7-30 ✚ *Challenge Yourself*

Work with master slides, gradient fills, patterned lines, and grayscale settings.

1. Open the file **Market3**.

2. Change the color scheme to the sample with the dark blue background (the last sample on the bottom row).

3. Working on the title master, click the medium blue area below the subtitle placeholder to select that area. (This is a rounded rectangle AutoShape with a dark blue rounded rectangle on top of it.)

4. Apply a two-color vertical gradient fill to the selected area with the following properties:
   - Color 1: Medium blue (fills scheme color)
   - Color 2: Light blue (title text scheme color)
   - Shading style: Vertical
   - Variant: Upper left, with darkest color on the left

5. Select the rounded rectangle that surrounds the subtitle text placeholder and apply a patterned border with the following properties:
   - Foreground: Medium blue (fills scheme color)
   - Background: Medium purple (accent and followed hyperlink scheme color)
   - Pattern: Large checkerboard—last pattern in the fourth row
   - Line weight: 10 points
6. Use Format Painter to copy the patterned border to the large rounded rectangle on the slide master.
7. Apply a two-color gradient fill to the rounded rectangle on the slide master; use dark blue (background scheme color) for Color 1 and medium blue (fills scheme color) for Color 2. Choose the vertical shading style and the variant that has the darkest color on the left.
8. Select the subtitle placeholder and change its fill color to teal (fills accent color). Close the Master view.
9. On slide 1, substitute a WordArt title for the title text. Use the upper left sample from the WordArt gallery. Apply a vertical gradient fill by using the Calm Water preset, upper left variant. Resize and position it appropriately.
10. Review the presentation in Grayscale view and make any necessary adjustments.
11. View the presentation as a slide show.
12. Check spelling in the presentation.
13. Create a handout header and footer: include the date and your name as the header, and the page number and text *[your initials]*7-30 as the footer.
14. Move to slide 1 and save the presentation as a Web page with the filename *[your initials]*7-30 in your Lesson 7 folder.
15. Preview, and then print the presentation as handouts, six slides per page, grayscale, framed. Close the presentation.

On Your Own

In these exercises, you work on your own, as you would in a real-life work environment. Use the skills you've learned to accomplish the task—and be creative.

EXERCISE 7-31

Plan a children's party for a church group or an elementary school class. Prepare a presentation to help explain the event. Using the Balloons template, create a title slide and separate slides listing activities or games and the rules or instructions for each one. For example, you could plan to carve pumpkins, take a hayride, and have a wiener roast, or you could plan a weekend at a hotel with a pool and playground, or a trip to an aquarium with plans to eat at a fun restaurant. If you have access to a scanner, include scanned pictures that relate to the activities. Otherwise, find clip art pictures to illustrate your presentation. Use your own creativity to format an attractive presentation that has some of the fill effects and border effects presented in this lesson. Save the presentation as *[your initials]*7-31. Preview, and then print the presentation as handouts.

EXERCISE 7-32

Imagine that you are organizing a family reunion for your extended family at a remote location where you can enjoy tourist activities (not at someone's house). For example, you could travel to South Dakota, and explore Mount Rushmore and other local attractions, or Colorado Springs and explore Seven Falls, Pikes Peak, and other local attractions. Create a presentation describing the reunion, including location, who is invited, activities that are planned, estimated costs, and a slide encouraging them to attend. Apply a design template of your choice to the slides in your presentation. Format the presentation by using fill effects and border effects. Add clip art and photographs (recolor the clip art to match the presentation where possible). Save the presentation as *[your initials]*7-32. Preview, and then print the presentation as handouts.

EXERCISE 7-33

Open the file **SanFran1** used in this lesson. Change to a different design template and color scheme of your choice. Customize the slide and title masters in some way. Change all the slide titles to WordArt, and apply fill effects and border treatments to all AutoShapes and body text placeholders in the presentation. Be careful to keep the look and style of each slide uniform throughout the presentation, and use good judgment to keep the design from looking too busy. Save the presentation as *[your initials]*7-33. Preview, and then print the presentation as handouts.

LESSON 8

Formatting Objects

After completing this lesson, you will be able to:

1. Work with multiple objects.
2. Align, distribute, and flip AutoShapes.
3. Work with layers of objects.
4. Group, ungroup, and regroup objects.
5. Apply object shadows and 3-D effects.
6. Use the Duplicate command.
7. Use advanced image editing techniques.

 Estimated Time: 1½ hours

In earlier lessons you learned how to add clip art, scanned images, text objects, and drawings to a presentation. This lesson shows you how to move or change a group of objects, layer objects, and align objects. These techniques help you create more effective presentations.

Working with Multiple Objects

When you want to treat several objects on a slide the same way, such as making them all the same color, you can select all the objects at the same time by using multiple selection techniques. There are two basic ways to select multiple objects:

- Select one object, hold down Shift, and click another object.

● Draw a selection rectangle around the objects you want to select by dragging the mouse.

You can also select all the objects on a slide by opening the Edit menu and choosing Select All or by pressing Ctrl+A. To deselect all items, simply click a blank area of the slide or press Esc.

EXERCISE | **8-1** | **Select Multiple Objects Using the Shift Key**

To select multiple objects one at a time, first click an object to select it and then add objects to the selection by pressing Shift as you click another object.

1. Open the file **Market2**.
2. With slide 1 displayed, open the Edit menu and choose Select All (or press Ctrl+A). Notice the multiple sets of sizing handles. Every item on slide 1 is selected.

FIGURE 8-1
Multiple
selected
objects

3. Click a blank area on the slide (or press Esc) to deselect the items.
4. Click the top line of the four thin lines. Notice its sizing handles.
5. Hold down Shift and click the next line. Notice that there are sizing handles around both objects, indicating that they are both selected.

6. With the two lines selected, use the Line Color button ⊿ to change their color to green (use the text and lines scheme color). Both selected lines change color.

7. With the two green lines selected, press Shift and click the next two lines. Now all four long thin lines are selected.

8. With all the lines selected, change to a patterned line with a two-color pattern using the following settings (with the Line Color button ◢):

- For Foreground, choose dark tan.
- For Background, choose maroon.
- From Pattern, choose Dark Horizontal. (This is on the bottom row, fifth from the left.)

EXERCISE 8-2 **Select Multiple Objects by Drawing a Selection Rectangle**

To draw a *selection rectangle,* start at a blank area of a slide and drag your mouse pointer diagonally to create a dotted box surrounding the objects that you want to select. Only objects completely enclosed in the selection rectangle are selected.

It takes a little practice to get the knack of where to start a selection rectangle, and it's easy to miss an object. If that happens, try drawing the selection rectangle again, or add a missed object to the selection by using the Shift+click method.

1. Move to slide 2.

2. Position the pointer in the lower-left corner of the slide.

3. Left-click the mouse and hold down the left mouse button while you drag the crosshair diagonally to the right and up to draw a dotted box—selection rectangle—surrounding all three rectangles with text.

FIGURE 8-2
Selection rectangle

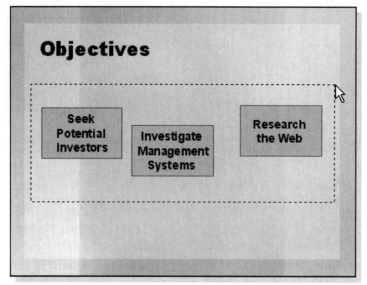

4. Release the mouse button. Notice the sizing handles surrounding each rectangle.

5. If one or more of the rectangles is not selected, try again, making sure that all rectangles are completely inside the selection rectangle.

6. Change the fill of the selected rectangles to a horizontal two-color gradient, using the Color 1 as the gold color and Color 2 as the custom light yellow color. Choose the From center shading style and the variant with the lightest color in the middle.

7. Remove the border line from the rectangles by choosing no line from the Line Color button ☑.

EXERCISE **8-3** **Remove an Item from a Group of Selected Objects**

You might want to change the composition of a group of selected items as you work. One way is to deselect all the objects by clicking a blank part of the slide. Another way is to hold down (Shift) and click the selected item to deselect it, leaving the remaining items in the group selected.

1. Move back to slide 1 and select all four lines.

2. To deselect the line at the top and leave the other three lines selected, hold (Shift) and click the top line. The remaining three lines are still selected.

3. Hold (Shift) and click the bottom line. The bottom line is deselected, leaving only the two center lines selected.

4. Keeping the same colors, change the pattern of the two center lines to Narrow Horizontal.

5. Create a new folder for Lesson 8, and save the presentation as *[your initials]*8-3 in the new folder but do not print the presentation. Leave it open for the next exercise.

Aligning, Distributing, and Flipping AutoShapes

PowerPoint has a number of tools that you can use to reorient objects on a slide. You can rotate and *flip* them, creating mirror images of the original. Selected objects can be aligned with each other, either vertically or horizontally. And you can *distribute* multiple objects, spacing them evenly across the slide either horizontally or vertically.

EXERCISE 8-4 Align Objects Horizontally and Vertically

When multiple objects are selected, you access the tools to accomplish alignment and distribution tasks by clicking D<u>r</u>aw on the Drawing toolbar, choosing <u>A</u>lign or Distribute, and then choosing an appropriate command from the submenu. Note that you can float the submenu.

1. Move to slide 2, select the three rectangles. Notice that the rectangles are not positioned evenly on the slide.

2. Display the Align or Distribute floating toolbar by doing the following: Click D<u>r</u>aw on the Drawing toolbar and point to <u>A</u>lign or Distribute. Point to the gray title bar on the submenu and drag it to a convenient place on your screen, out of the way of the selected arrows.

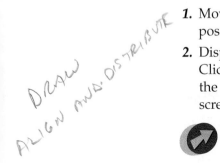

DRAW
ALIGN AND DISTRIBUTE

NOTE: If the Drawing toolbar is not in view, open the <u>V</u>iew menu and choose <u>T</u>oolbars, Drawing.

TABLE 8-1   Alignment Options

BUTTON		PURPOSE
⊫	Align Left	Vertically aligns the left edges of objects.
⊹	Align Center	Vertically aligns the centers of objects.
⊒|	Align Right	Vertically aligns the right edges of objects.
⊤|↑	Align Top	Horizontally aligns the top edges of objects.
⊣|⊢	Align Middle	Horizontally aligns the center points of objects.
⊥|↓	Align Bottom	Horizontally aligns the bottom edges of objects.
□-□-□	Distribute Horizontally	Spaces objects evenly in a horizontal direction.
⊟	Distribute Vertically	Spaces objects evenly in a vertical direction.
Relative to <u>S</u>lide	Relative to <u>S</u>lide	A toggle button. When selected, aligns or spaces objects relative to slide. When not selected, aligns or spaces objects relative to each other.

3. Point to each button on the Align or Distribute toolbar and read their ScreenTips. Notice that the first three buttons on the toolbar control vertical alignment and that the next three buttons control horizontal alignment.

4. Verify that Relative to Slide on the Align and Distribute toolbar is not selected. (A thin black outline indicates when it is turned on.)

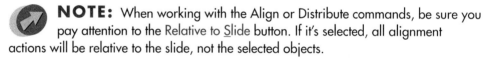 **NOTE:** When working with the Align or Distribute commands, be sure you pay attention to the Relative to Slide button. If it's selected, all alignment actions will be relative to the slide, not the selected objects.

5. Click the Align Top button ⬚. The objects line up with the top of the highest rectangle.

6. Deselect the rectangles; then if your rulers are not displayed, choose Ruler from the View menu to display a horizontal and a vertical ruler.

7. Drag the rectangle that is farthest to the right up about 1 inch; use the ruler to help you position the object. Drag the rectangle that is farthest to the left down to the bottom of the slide.

8. Draw a selection rectangle around all three rectangles.

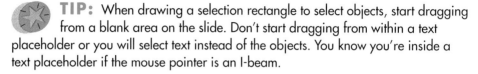 **TIP:** When drawing a selection rectangle to select objects, start dragging from a blank area on the slide. Don't start dragging from within a text placeholder or you will select text instead of the objects. You know you're inside a text placeholder if the mouse pointer is an I-beam.

9. Click the Align Bottom button ⬚. The objects align horizontally again, but this time they align with the bottom object.

10. Click the Undo button ⬚ several times to return the rectangles to their previous position where they are evenly aligned on the top.

11. With the three rectangles still selected, click the Align Left button ⬚. The objects are all aligned at the left, but two of the rectangles are hidden because they are under one rectangle.

12. Click the Undo button ⬚, with the rectangles still selected; click the Align Right button ⬚. The objects are all aligned on the right with two rectangles hidden again. Click the Undo button ⬚.

EXERCISE 8-5 **Distribute Objects Horizontally and Vertically**

---

1. Still working on slide 2, deselect the rectangles. Drag the top rectangle up about 1.5 inches, and the bottom rectangle down about 1 inch.

2. Reselect the three rectangles and click the Distribute Vertically button ⬚ again. Now the rectangles are evenly spaced vertically.

3. With the rectangles still selected, click the Distribute Horizontally button ⬚. Again, the rectangles are spaced evenly apart.

4. Reselect the rectangles; then click the Distribute Horizontally button ⬚ again. Now the rectangles are evenly spaced horizontally but they are not aligned.

5. Click the Align Middle button ⬚.

TIP: It is very quick to align objects by establishing one object in the left position and one in the right position and other objects between them. You don't have to worry about precise positioning because the Distribute Horizontally button can do that. Then while the objects are selected, click the top, middle, or bottom alignment option so all objects are evenly aligned from both directions.

EXERCISE **8-6** **Align Objects Relative to the Slide**

The Relative to Slide option makes it easy to center an object horizontally or vertically on a slide. For example, you can center a placeholder perfectly. You can also use the Relative to Slide option to distribute objects evenly across a slide from edge to edge.

1. Move to slide 3, select the body text placeholder.

2. Click Relative to Slide on the Align or Distribute toolbar to select that option.

3. Click the Align Center button ⬚. The placeholder is centered horizontally on the slide.

4. Click the Align Middle button ⬚. The placeholder is now also centered vertically on the slide. Click ⬚ twice to return the placeholder to its original position.

5. With Relative to Slide still selected, move to slide 2 and select all three rectangles.

6. Click the Distribute Horizontally button ⬚. Now the rectangles are evenly spaced across the entire width of the slide.

FIGURE 8-3
Objects horizontally
aligned and
distributed

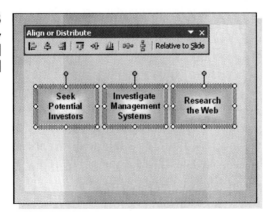

EXERCISE **8-7** **Flip and Rotate Objects**

Use the Rotate and Flip commands on a single object or a group of objects. You can rotate and flip any PowerPoint object, including text placeholders.

1. When you have an object selected, to display the Rotate or Flip toolbar, click Draw on the Drawing toolbar and point to Rotate or Flip, and drag the submenu's title bar to float the toolbar.

 2. Move to slide 1, select the picture. Click the Flip Horizontal button . The man is now pointing the bow and arrow to the right.

 3. Click the Rotate Right button four times. The picture rotates around and ends up in the previous position.

FIGURE 8-4
Rotating an object

4. Move to slide 5, select the WordArt title "Teamwork" and the banner behind it. With the objects selected, use the Down Arrow key on your keyboard to move the objects down right above the ClipArt image.

5. Select all of the objects on the slide. With Relative to Slide selected, click the Align Center button 🔲.

Working with Layers of Objects

Although objects appear to be drawn on one surface, each of a slide's objects actually exists as a separate layer. Imagine that the objects are drawn on individual sheets of transparent plastic stacked on top of one another. When you rearrange the sheets, different objects appear on the top, sometimes hiding parts of the objects beneath them. The most recently drawn object is added to the top of the stack.

Within a stack of objects, you can move an individual object backward and forward by using the buttons on the Order toolbar.

TABLE 8-2   Order Options

BUTTON		PURPOSE
	Bring to Front	Brings an object to the top of the stack
	Send to Back	Moves an object to the bottom of the stack
	Bring Forward	Brings an object up one layer in the stack
	Send Backward	Moves an object down one layer in the stack

EXERCISE 8-8 Change Forward/Backward Stacking Order

When you draw a new object on a slide, it automatically becomes the top object on the stack. To change its layer, select it and then from the Draw menu choose Order then one of the layering options. If you are making several changes, you might want to float the Order menu so each of the options is a button.

When you are working with layered objects, sometimes you want to change the stacking order by just one level to make one object appear on top of another object. To do this you select the object and use the Bring Forward or Send Backward buttons available from the order menu. If the object is not visible, you can press (Tab) several times until the desired object is selected and then bring that object to the front.

Using Bring to Front or Send to Back moves a selected object to the front of all other objects or behind all other objects. Using Bring Forward or Send Backward moves the object one layer at a time.

1. Move to slide 4. Draw a rectangle that hides the circle.

2. Change the fill color to the light tan and remove the border. Change the rectangle's fill color to 25% transparency. Now you can faintly see the circle behind the rectangle.

REVIEW: To change transparency settings, select the object, click the arrow for the Fill Color button [▼], choose <u>M</u>ore Fill Colors, and then drag the Transparency slider.

3. Press [Tab] several times until a small set of selection handles appears in the center of the circle. Pressing [Tab] is a good technique to use when layering because it is difficult to select an object with your mouse when it is under another object.

4. Click D**r**aw on the Drawing toolbar, choose O**r**der from the expanded menu. You may float the O**r**der submenu if you wish.

5. Click on the Bring Forward button to move the circle on top of the square.

FIGURE 8-5
Rectangle and circle

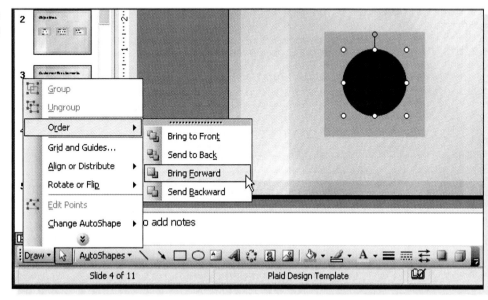

6. Still working on slide 4, draw an AutoShapes diamond about the size of the square then select a tan fill color with no line.

7. Click the Draw menu and select Order. Then click the Send Backward button on the Order Toolbar. The diamond moves behind the circle but is in front of the square.

8. Repeat this step to make the diamond go behind the square.

9. Leave the presentation open for the next exercise.

EXERCISE   **8-9**   **Bring to Front or Send to Back**

To manipulate an object that is located behind several other objects, you can send the top objects to the back, one at a time, until the desired object is on top.

1. Still working on slide 4, draw an AutoShapes square to cover the existing shapes on the slide and make it a different color.

2. Click the Draw menu and select Order. Then click the Send to Back button on the Order Toolbar. The new square moves behind all other objects.

3. Save the presentation as *[your initials]*8-9 in your Lesson 8 folder but do not print it. Leave the presentation open for the next exercise.

Grouping, Ungrouping, and Regrouping Objects

When you *group* objects, you combine two or more objects so they behave as one. If you then move one member of the group, all the other members move with it. Grouping assures that objects meant to stay together don't accidentally get moved individually or deleted. When you apply formatting to a group, all the members of the group receive the same formatting.

EXERCISE | 8-10 | **Group Objects**

To create a group of objects, first select the objects and then click Draw on the Drawing toolbar and choose Group.

1. Move to slide 1, select the four lines in the middle of the slide. Notice the four sets of sizing handles.

2. From the expanded Draw menu, choose Group. Now there is only one set of sizing handles, indicating that all four lines are grouped as a single object.

FIGURE 8-6
Objects after grouping

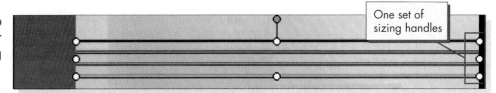

3. Deselect the object. Drag the first line up, just below the WordArt. All the lines move up.

4. Click Undo, so the lines are positioned in the previous place.

EXERCISE | 8-11 | **Ungroup and Regroup Objects**

If you want to delete a member of a group, change its position relative to the other members, or change its size, you must first *ungroup* the objects. When the objects are ungrouped, they once again become individual objects.

After working on individual members of an ungrouped object, you can easily *regroup* the objects by selecting any one of the group's original members. The Regroup command finds all the objects of the original group that remain on the slide and groups them again.

1. Right-click any of the grouped lines; then choose <u>G</u>rouping from the shortcut menu and <u>U</u>ngroup from the submenu. Each line now has its own set of sizing handles.

2. Click a blank area of the slide to deselect all the lines.

3. Click the bottom line to select it (the other lines should not be selected) and then press Delete. One line is deleted from the slide.

4. Select one of the remaining lines; then open the D<u>r</u>aw menu and choose Regr<u>o</u>up. The three remaining lines are grouped again.

5. Close both floating toolbars.

6. Save the presentation as *[your initials]***8-11** in your Lesson 8 folder but do not print it. Leave the presentation open for the next exercise.

EXERCISE 8-12 **Format Part of a Grouped Object**

You can easily select one member of a group of objects to make individual changes. First select the group; then click an object within the group. The object displays gray selection handles, indicating that you can change its fill, outline, and orientation without affecting the other objects in the group.

1. Move to slide 2, and select the three rectangles.

2. Group the rectangles together to make one object. One set of white sizing handles appears.

3. Click the edge of the middle rectangle. (When you click the middle of the rectangle, the rectangle border changes to diagonal lines indicating that the text can be edited. If this happens, click again.) Gray handles surround the rectangle.

FIGURE 8-7
Selecting a single object in a group

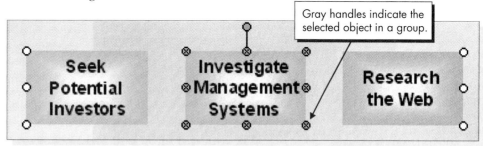

4. Click the Flip Vertical button 🔼. The selected rectangle turns upside down.

5. Click the Flip Vertical button 🔼 again to make the rectangle return to its previous position.

6. For the selected rectangle, change the gradient fill colors as follows: change the Gradient Fill Variant to the one with the lightest color on the outside of the center gradient.

7. Close the Rotate or Flip toolbar.

Applying Object Shadows and 3-D Effects

You can add interest and depth to an object by applying shadows or 3-D effects. Each of these effects has its own toolbar with buttons that enable you to change the color, depth, and other attributes.

EXERCISE 8-13 **Apply a Shadow Effect**

To apply a shadow to an object, select the object, click the Shadow Style button 🔲 on the Drawing toolbar, and choose a style from the drop-down menu.

1. Still working on slide 2. Select the group of rectangles (not just the center rectangle).

2. Click the Shadow Style button 🔲 on the Drawing toolbar to display a menu of shadow effects.

FIGURE 8-8
Shadow Style
options

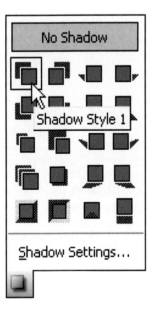

3. Choose **Shadow Style 1**, which is the first style in the first row. A pale gray shadow appears.

4. Click the Shadow Style button 🔲 again and choose **Shadow Style 3**. This shadow style looks quite different. Each style orients the position and the depth of the shadow in a different way as though light is shining on the object from different directions. Try several other shadow styles.

5. Change to **Shadow Style 5**.

EXERCISE `8-14` **Customize a Shadow**

You can customize an object shadow by displaying the Shadow Settings toolbar and using its buttons. To display the toolbar, click the Shadow Style button on the Drawing toolbar and click Shadow Settings from the drop-down menu.

1. Select the group of rectangles.

2. Click the Shadow Style button and choose Shadow Settings. The Shadow Settings toolbar is displayed.

3. Click the Nudge Shadow down button two times. Notice that each time you click the button, the shadow moves down slightly.

4. Click the Nudge Shadow Left button twice. The shadow gradually moves to the left each time you click the button.

5. Click the arrow on the Shadow Color button and choose brown (accent scheme color) for the shadow color. The shadow color is not as dark as the color sample.

6. Click the arrow next to the Shadow Color button again. Notice that Semitransparent Shadow is automatically selected. This setting can be used to soften the effect of the shadow if the color you have selected seems too dark.

7. Click Semitransparent Shadow to deselect this option. The shadow color is now brown.

TIP: You can control the degree of transparency for shadows. To do this, click the arrow next to the Shadow Color button, choose More Shadow Colors, and use the Transparency slider in the Colors dialog box.

FIGURE 8-9
AutoShape with shadow effects applied

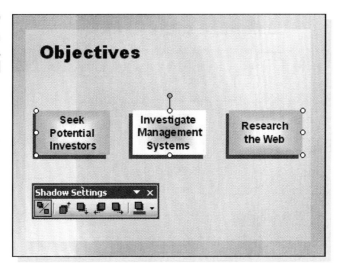

8. Close the Shadow Settings toolbar.

EXERCISE **8-15** **Choose a 3-D Effect**

To apply a 3-D effect to an object, select the object, click the 3-D Style button on the Drawing toolbar, and choose a style from the drop-down menu.

1. Move to slide 5, select the rectangle on top with the text "Share the credit."

2. Click the 3-D Style button on the Drawing toolbar to display a menu of 3-D effects.

FIGURE 8-10
3-D menu

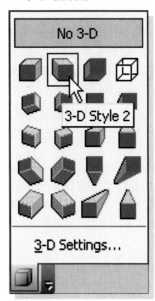

3. Choose 3-D Style 2. A 3-D effect that creates the illusion of depth is applied to the object and the fill color becomes darker. The rectangle looks more like a block.

4. Click the 3-D Style button again and choose 3-D Style 18. Notice that some 3-D styles rotate the object and create depth. In this case, this particular effect does not work well because the text does not rotate with the shape. Try other styles and note the differences. Like shadows, use these effects sparingly.

5. Reapply 3-D Style 2.

6. Select each of the remaining rectangles which are stacked and apply the same 3-D Style 2.

EXERCISE **8-16** **Customize a 3-D Effect**

In a manner similar to customizing shadow effects, you can customize a 3-D effect by using buttons on the 3-D Settings toolbar. To display the toolbar, click the 3-D Style button on the Drawing toolbar and select 3-D Settings from the drop-down menu.

You use the 3-D Settings toolbar to change the color, angle of rotation, depth, and other features of the 3-D effect. These tools are fun to use. Try them on all types of objects, not just AutoShapes.

1. Still working on slide 5, select all four rectangles by the shift and click methods then click the 3-D Style button and choose 3-D Settings.

FIGURE 8-11
3-D Settings toolbar

2. On the 3-D Settings toolbar, click the Tilt Up button twice. The angle of the objects is shifted up so the front moves up and the back moves down.

3. Click the Tilt Down button three times so the front moves down and the back moves up.

4. Press (Esc) to deselect the objects. Select the first rectangle. Click the arrow on the 3-D Color button . Choose brown and the top and side color changes. Click Undo to remove this color because it does not match as well as the automatic color.

5. Select all four rectangles again and click the Depth button and choose 72 pt.

6. Click the Lighting button ; then choose the center option in the top row (light shining down from the top). The rectangles should now look like Figure 8-12.

7. Close the 3-D Settings toolbar.

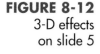
FIGURE 8-12
3-D effects
on slide 5

8. Save the presentation as *[your initials]*8-16 in your Lesson 8 folder but do not print it. Leave the presentation open for the next exercise.

Using the Duplicate Command

The Duplicate command is a convenient tool for making additional copies of an object on the same slide. In some ways, the Duplicate command is similar to Copy and Paste, but it does not place a copy on the clipboard. Duplicated objects can overlap one another or be spaced apart. After you position the first duplicated object, additional duplicates are positioned with the same spacing. So careful positioning of the first duplicate is important for efficiency.

EXERCISE | 8-17 | **Duplicate an Object**

To duplicate an object, select the object, open the Edit menu, and choose Duplicate or press Ctrl+D. While being careful to keep the duplicated object selected, reposition it if you want, then press Ctrl+D several times until you have the number of duplicates you want.

1. Move to slide 3. Select the arrow in front of "Target health-conscious areas."

2. From the expanded Edit menu, choose Duplicate or press Ctrl+D. A copy appears, slightly offset from the original.

3. Being careful not to deselect the arrow, use the arrow keys on your keyboard to move the arrow down and to the right so that it appears as though it is a bullet for the second line of text. (See Figure 8-14 on the next page for approximate positioning of the second arrow.)

> **NOTE:** The Duplicate command works only if the duplicate copy remains selected. As soon as it is deselected, the command is no longer in effect. If that happens, delete the duplicate and start again.

4. Press Ctrl+D. A second copy appears, which is offset the same amount as the first copy.

5. If necessary, reposition the arrow in front of the third line of text.

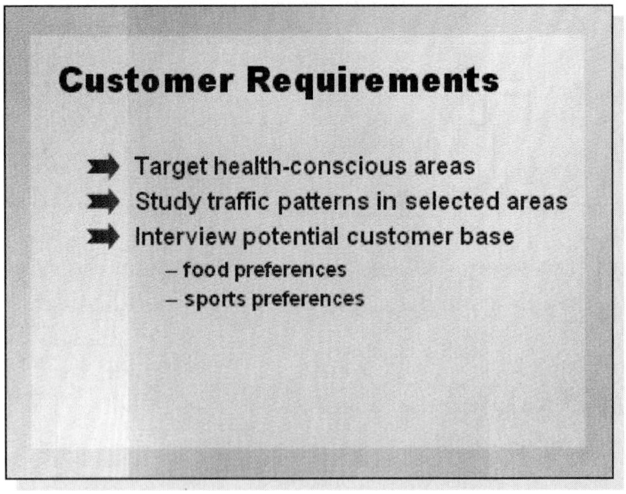

FIGURE 8-13
Creating duplicates

Customer Requirements

➡ Target health-conscious areas
➡ Study traffic patterns in selected areas
➡ Interview potential customer base
  – food preferences
  – sports preferences

6. Select all three arrows and align them on the left using the Align or Distribute menu (remove the option for Relative to Slide if it is selected).

This adjustment will correct any small errors in alignment you may have had.

7. With these arrows selected, group them.

8. Save the presentation as *[your initials]*8-17 in your Lesson 8 folder but do not print it. Leave the presentation open for the next exercise.

EXERCISE 8-18 Duplicate a Slide

When you are building presentations it is often helpful to duplicate a slide as a starting point for the next slide, especially if you have a few very similar slides, or if you would like to duplicate the opening slide for the closing slide. You can duplicate slides in Slide Sorter or in the Outline and Slides Pane.

1. Using the Outline and Slides Pane, select the thumbnail for slide 1.

2. From the expanded **E̲dit** menu, choose **Dupli̲cate** or press Ctrl+D. After the original slide 1, a copy of the slide appears as slide 2.

3. Click and drag slide 2 after slide 6. This slide now becomes slide 6, the closing slide.

4. Delete the photograph image on slide 6.

5. Insert a new photograph for the closing slide. Complete a search for the keyword **Time**. Try to find the photograph shown in Figure 8-14. If you are not able to locate this image, find one with the similar meaning.

FIGURE 8-14
Duplicate Slide

6. Resize the image to fit attractively on the slide.

Advanced Image Editing

You have already learned how to insert, resize, and crop pictures, and how to change image settings such as brightness and contrast.

PowerPoint enables you to perform additional editing on pictures that are vector-based drawings (for example, Windows Metafile drawings with the file extension .wmf). These pictures can be converted (ungrouped) into a collection of ordinary PowerPoint objects.

 NOTE: Unlike vector-based drawings, bitmap pictures cannot be ungrouped. To perform extensive editing on bitmap pictures, you need to use a paint-type program such as Imaging for Windows.

EXERCISE 8-19 **Ungroup and Change Fill Color for Parts of an Image**

When a vector-based drawing is ungrouped, it is converted into a collection of PowerPoint objects that you can delete, resize, and reposition, just like any objects that you draw. You can also change the fill color and border for parts of a picture that has been converted.

1. Move to slide 5 and select the clip art picture.
2. With the picture selected, change the Zoom setting to 100%.
3. From the D̲raw menu, choose U̲ngroup. A dialog box asks whether you want to convert this image to a Microsoft Office drawing object.
4. Click Y̲es to agree to the conversion.

FIGURE 8-15
Converting a picture to a Microsoft Office drawing object

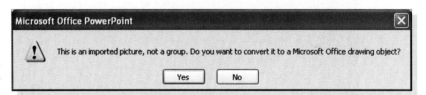

 NOTE: Not all clipart images can be ungrouped. It depends on how they are made.

5. From the D̲raw menu, choose U̲ngroup again. You will see many sets of selection handles. Notice that on this particular image you have two rotation handles and two corner selection handles at the top of the image. One of these sets is for the green background shape; the other is for a square behind the green shape that isn't needed. You'll remove these shapes in the next exercise.

FIGURE 8-16
Ungrouped object
showing handles on
all image parts

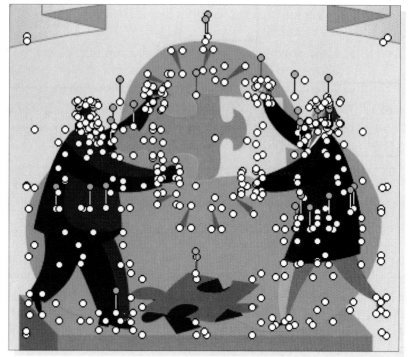

6. Press (Esc) (or click any blank area of the slide) to deselect all of the pieces of the clipart.

FIGURE 8-17
Selecting a
part of an
ungrouped image

Only one piece of the image, the puzzle piece, is selected.

7. Select the puzzle piece that the woman is holding and change the color to the maroon.

8. Hold down the Shift key while you carefully select the four small shapes above and below the puzzle pieces and change their color to maroon. Be careful not to select the green background shape.

EXERCISE 8-20 Delete Parts of an Image

If you want to delete pieces of an ungrouped image, you must select them and then press delete.

1. Select the green puzzle piece at the bottom of the image. Press Delete.

2. Select the brown puzzle piece at the bottom of the image. Press Delete.

3. Select the light-green shape that creates the background of the image. Because of its rounded shape, the selection handles seem far away from the image. Press Delete.

4. As mentioned in step 5 in the previous exercise, this image has a rectangle behind it that is currently the same color as the slide background. Click above the woman's head and you will see selection handles in a similar position as the shape you just removed. To confirm this, apply a different color and you can see where the rectangle is located. Press Delete.

NOTE: Because the rectangle in this situation blended with the background, it would have been okay to leave it on the slide. However, a background can affect the design you are trying to achieve when it is not colored with one of the design palette colors, so you need to know how to remove it if necessary.

5. Compare your picture with Figure 8-18. If too much of the picture was deleted, click the Undo button 🔄 and try again.

6. Draw a selection rectangle around the remaining parts of the picture and group them. (Do not use the Regroup command.)

7. Close any floating toolbars that you opened during this lesson and change the zoom setting to Fit.

8. If the ruler is displayed, hide it by opening the View menu and choosing Ruler.

9. Check spelling in the presentation.

10. Review the grayscale settings for all slides and make any changes that might be necessary.

11. Create a handout header and footer: include the date and your name as the header, and the page number and text *[your initials]*8-20 as the footer.

12. Move to slide 1 and save the presentation as *[your initials]*8-20 in your Lesson 8 folder.

FIGURE 8-18
The completed
picture, after editing

13. Preview and then print the presentation as handouts, six slides per page, grayscale, framed. Keep the presentation open for the next exercise.

EXERCISE   8-21   Optimize Photograph Images

When you use many photograph images in a presentation, the file size increases dramatically. So optimizing your pictures (clip art and photographs) can reduce your presentation's file size. However, you will only want to do this if the presentation is for viewing as a slide show or on the Web. A reduction in image quality will usually not be noticeable for on-screen viewing, but it will make a difference in printed output. You will also have the option to delete cropped areas of pictures, too.

To decrease the file size, use the Compress Pictures option from the Picture Toolbar.

1. Move to slide 1, select the picture.

2. Choose the Compress Pictures button 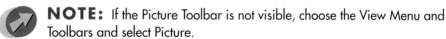 on the Picture Toolbar.

> **NOTE:** If the Picture Toolbar is not visible, choose the View Menu and Toolbars and select Picture.

3. Choose All pictures in document. Change the resolution to Web/Screen. Be sure you have checks in front of Compress pictures and Delete cropped areas of pictures. This will compress all images in the document, and make them

at a good quality for viewing on the Web or through a projection device such as an LCD Projector.

4. Click OK. A warning box will appear asking if you want to apply picture optimization. Click Apply.

5. Update your handout footer information to change it to *[your initials]*8-21.

6. Move to slide 1 and save the presentation as *[your initials]*8-21 in your Lesson 8 folder.

7. Just to test the difference in file sizes, access the storage location where your exercise files are saved and compare the file sizes of Exercise 20 with Exercise 21. In this case, only a small reduction resulted. However, the reduction can be dramatic depending on the type of images you are using.

 TIP: In presentations where you have more photographs, you will see a dramatic difference in file size.

USING ONLINE HELP

PowerPoint provides extensive help for all facets of working with objects. If you're unsure about when to use text shadows, object shadows, or 3-D effects on text, use Help for clarification.

Explore Help about text shadows, object shadows, and 3-D effects:

1. Key **3-D** in the Ask a Question box and press Enter.

2. In the drop-down list, click **About text shadows and 3-D effects**.

FIGURE 8-19
Help on shadows and 3-D effects

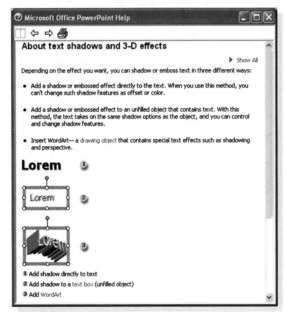

3. Review the Help screen and then close the Help window.

4. Click the Ask a Question box arrow and select 3-D from the list.

5. Choose a different topic from the drop-down list.

6. Review the topic. Close the Help window when you're finished.

LESSON 8 Summary

➤ Select multiple objects when you want to perform the same operation on all of them, for example, making them all the same color or moving all of them at the same time.

➤ Select multiple objects one at a time by holding down [Shift] while clicking each object.

➤ Select multiple objects all at once by drawing a selection rectangle around them (drag the standard mouse pointer). Be sure to start dragging on a blank area of the slide.

➤ Add items to the selection by using the [Shift]+click method. Remove an item from a group of selected items by [Shift]+clicking it.

➤ Selected objects can be aligned horizontally or vertically, relative to each other. They can be aligned by their tops, bottoms, middles, right sides, left sides, or centers. They can be aligned relative to the edges of a slide when the Relative to Slide option is selected.

➤ Selected objects can be distributed (evenly spaced) horizontally or vertically, relative to each other, by using Align or Distribute toolbar buttons. Objects can also be evenly distributed across the width or height of a slide when the Relative to Slide option is turned on.

➤ Flipping an object creates a mirror image of it. The Rotate Left and Rotate Right buttons rotate objects in 90-degree increments.

➤ When objects overlap, use the buttons on the Order toolbar to control which object appears on the top. The most recently drawn object will be on top until you change its order.

➤ Grouping two or more objects combines them in such a way that they behave as if they were one object.

➤ After grouping objects, an individual object within the group can be selected without ungrouping all the objects. First click the group to select it; then click an object in the group. The gray selection handles indicate which object is selected. The selected group object can have its fill and outline formatted and can be flipped, but it cannot be deleted, resized, or rotated.

➤ To delete, resize, or rotate an individual object within a group, first ungroup the objects. After you are finished working on individual items of a group, regroup them.

➤ Apply an object shadow or 3-D effect to emphasize an object. There are 20 shadow styles and 20 3-D styles to choose from, and each style can be customized by using the Shadow Settings toolbar or the 3-D Settings toolbar.

➤ The Duplicate command creates a copy of the selected item on the same slide, offset by a small amount. Using the Duplicate command multiple times creates an evenly spaced series of duplicated items.

➤ Vector-based pictures (for example, pictures with the .wmf file extension) can be converted into a group of PowerPoint objects by using the Ungroup command. Once ungrouped, the individual objects can be formatted and manipulated like any PowerPoint object.

➤ To reduce the file size of a presentation containing pictures, use the Compress Pictures button on the Picture Toolbar reduce the resolution, omit cropped areas, and compress the pictures.

LESSON 8   Command Summary

FEATURE	BUTTON	MENU	KEYBOARD
Select all objects		Edit, Select All	Ctrl+A
Deselect all selected objects			Esc
Deselect one object from a group of selected objects			Shift+click
Add to a selection of objects			Shift+click
Align or distribute objects		Draw, Align or Distribute	
Flip or rotate objects		Draw, Rotate or Flip	
Change the order of objects		Draw, Order	
Group objects		Draw, Group	Ctrl+Shift+G
Ungroup objects		Draw, Ungroup	Ctrl+Shift+H
Regroup objects		Draw, Regroup	
Apply an object shadow			
Apply a 3-D effect			
Duplicate an object		Edit, Duplicate	Ctrl+D
Display the ruler		View, Ruler	

Concepts Review

TRUE/FALSE QUESTIONS

Each of the following statements is either true or false. Indicate your choice by circling T or F.

T **(F)** **1.** You cannot use selection rectangles to select multiple objects.

T **(F)** **2.** Flipping an object makes it appear at a 45 degree angle.

(T) F **3.** If you continually click the Rotate Left button [⟳] while an object is selected, the object eventually returns to its original position.

(T) F **4.** To select multiple objects, press (Shift) while clicking each object.

T **(F)** **5.** The Duplicate command is available from the ~~Insert~~ menu.　*EDIT*

(T) F **6.** There are 20 different 3-D styles that you can apply to an object.

T **(F)** **7.** You cannot change the color of object shadows.

(T) F **8.** The keyboard command to select all objects on a slide is (Ctrl)+(A).

SHORT ANSWER QUESTIONS

Write the correct answer in the space provided.

CHAP 7
BORDERS　263
ARROWS　265

1. To select multiple objects with the mouse, which key do you press while clicking?

SHIFT

FORMAT
AUTOSHAPE　266
FILL COLOR　267

2. What appears when you drag the mouse to select multiple objects?

SELECTION RECTANGLE

RECOLOR　269
EXTENDED COLOR　270
TRANS GRADIENT　272

3. Which Align option do you select to line up objects side-by-side along their bottom edges?

ALIGN BOTTOM

FILL TO AUTO　276
FILL TO PICTURE　278
PATTERN TO BORDER　279

4. Which button do you use to flip an object from left to right?

FLIP HORIZONTAL

FORMAT PAINTER
GRAY SCALE
BLACK + WHITE 280

5. Which Order option do you use to place an object at the top of all the other objects on a slide?

BRING TO FRONT

CHAP 8
MULTIPLE OBJECTS　302
SELECTION RECTANGLE　304
ALIGN DISTRIBUTE FLIP　305
DISTRIBUTE HOR + VERT　307

STACKING ORDER　310
GROUPING　312
SHADOW 3-D　314
DUPLICATE　317
IMAGE EDITING　320

6. On what layer does the most recently drawn object appear?

<u>   TOP   </u>

7. What appears when you ungroup a clip art image?

<u>   SEVERAL SETS OF SIZING HANDLES </u>

<u>   </u>

8. What can you do to reduce the file size of a presentation that contains clip art and photographs?

<u>   COMPRESS PICTURE FEATURE   </u>

<u>   </u>

CRITICAL THINKING

Answer these questions on a separate page. There are no right or wrong answers. Support your answers with examples from your own experience, if possible.

1. In this lesson you learned how to work with layers of objects. Which objects might you place on top of each other? When would you find it useful to overlap them?

2. Think of the way you used the Duplicate command to add evenly spaced objects to your slide. In what other ways could you use this feature? Which objects would you duplicate?

Skills Review

EXERCISE 8-22

Select multiple objects; align, distribute, flip, rotate, and group objects.

1. Open the file **Cooking3**.

2. Select multiple objects by following these steps:

    a. On slide 1, click one of the small black diamonds below the title.
    b. Press and hold [Shift] while clicking the remaining two diamonds.
    c. With all diamonds selected, change the fill color to green.

3. Align and distribute the selected diamonds by following these steps:

    a. Click D<u>r</u>aw on the Drawing toolbar and point to <u>A</u>lign or Distribute.
    b. Float the <u>A</u>lign or Distribute submenu by dragging its gray title bar.
    c. If the Relative to <u>S</u>lide option is selected, deselect it by clicking it.

d. Click the Align Top button .

e. Click the Distribute Horizontally button.

4. Use a selection rectangle to select multiple objects by following these steps:

   a. Move the pointer to the upper-right corner of slide 1.

   b. Drag the pointer diagonally down and to the left, drawing a selection rectangle large enough to surround the cluster of red squares in the upper-right corner. (Don't include the single red square on the left side of the slide.)

   c. To add the last red square to the group, press and hold (Shift) while clicking the square on the left side of the slide.

5. Align and distribute objects relative to the slide by following these steps:

   a. Click Relative to Slide on the Align or Distribute toolbar to select it.

   b. Reselect all the red squares, if necessary.

   c. Click the Align Top button.

   d. Click the Distribute Horizontally button. You should have a series of evenly spaced red squares along the top edge of the slide. If not, click the Undo button several times and try again.

   e. If the squares do not seem to stay where you want to release them, your Snap to feature may be enabled. To turn it off, select Draw, Grid and Guides, remove the check in front of Snap objects to grid, and click OK.

6. With all the red squares still selected, copy and paste them. Using the four-pointed arrow, drag the pasted group of selected squares down and to the right to form a checkerboard pattern.

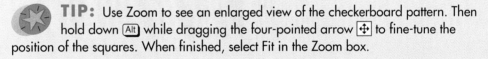

TIP: Use Zoom to see an enlarged view of the checkerboard pattern. Then hold down (Alt) while dragging the four-pointed arrow to fine-tune the position of the squares. When finished, select Fit in the Zoom box.

7. Deselect the squares. Copy just one square and paste it on the left end of the second row to complete the checkerboard pattern.

8. Group the red squares by following these steps:

   a. Use the selection rectangle method to select all the squares in both rows.

   b. Click Draw on the Drawing toolbar and choose Group.

9. Copy and paste the grouped squares, and move the pasted copy to the bottom of the slide. With Relative to Slide selected, click the Align Bottom button and then click the Distribute Horizontally button.

10. Flip an object by following these steps:

    a. Select the grouped squares at the bottom of the slide (be sure to select the group and not just one square).

    b. Click Draw on the Drawing toolbar and float the Rotate or Flip menu.

    c. Click the Flip Vertical button to reverse the position of the two rows of squares. (The checkerboard pattern at the bottom of the slide now mirrors the pattern at the top of the slide.)

11. Group the top and bottom checkerboard patterns on the slide; then copy the grouped checkerboard to the title master and to the slide master so all slides in the presentation have the checkerboard pattern.

12. Group the three green diamonds on the title slide; then copy and paste them to the slide master. Position the diamonds vertically between the title placeholder and the body text placeholder. Center them horizontally.

13. Flip and rotate an object by following these steps:

   a. Move to slide 3. Select the red arrow below the graph.

   b. Click the Flip Horizontal button on the Rotate or Flip toolbar to make the arrow point to the right.

   c. Click the Rotate Right button to make the arrow point up.

   d. Position the arrow on the right side of the chart and resize it to match the height of the chart. Use Figure 8-20 as a guide.

FIGURE 8-20

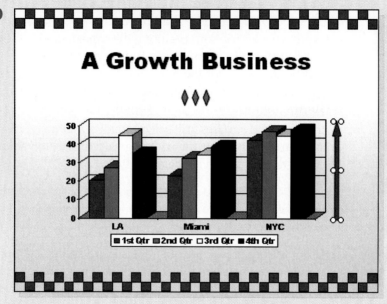

14. Check the grayscale settings for the presentation to see if any changes are needed.

15. Close all floating toolbars.

16. On the title slide, add a red fill color to the title placeholder. Increase the font size to 60 points and change the font color to white.

17. Create a handout header and footer: include the date and your name as the header, and the page number and text *[your initials]*8-22 as the footer.

18. Move to slide 1 and save the presentation as *[your initials]*8-22 in your Lesson 8 folder.

19. Preview and then print the presentation as handouts, four slides on a page, grayscale, landscape, framed. Close the presentation.

EXERCISE 8-23

Align and distribute objects relative to the slide and to each other and work with layers of objects.

1. Open the file **MiamBch2**.

2. On slide 1, draw a constrained Sun AutoShape (found in the sixth row of the Basic Shapes menu). Make it 2 inches high and 2 inches wide. Position it on top of the subtitle text.

3. Apply a two-color gradient fill to the sun with the following attributes:
   - For Color 1, choose peach (fills scheme color).
   - For Color 2, choose warm brown (title text scheme color).
   - From Shading styles, choose Horizontal.
   - From Variants, choose the lower-right sample (with peach in the middle and brown on the top and bottom).

4. Remove the border line from the sun.

5. Move the sun behind the subtitle text by following these steps:
   - *a.* From the Draw menu, choose Order. Float the submenu to display the Order toolbar.
   - *b.* Select the sun.
   - *c.* Click the Send to Back button .

6. Center the sun horizontally relative to the slide by following these steps:
   - *a.* Float the Align or Distribute toolbar (by using the Draw menu).
   - *b.* Select Relative to Slide (if it is not selected).
   - *c.* Select the sun AutoShape.
   - *d.* Click the Align Center button .

7. Center the sun vertically with the subtitle by following these steps:
   - *a.* Select both the sun AutoShape and the subtitle text.
   - *b.* On the Align or Distribute toolbar, deselect Relative to Slide.
   - *c.* Click the Align Middle button ⊕.

8. Copy the sun from slide 1 and paste it on slide 2.

9. Reduce the sun on slide 2 proportionately, to 1.5 inches wide. Move the sun so it covers the uppercase "G" in the title; then send the sun behind the text and fine-tune its position so that the "G" is centered over the sun.

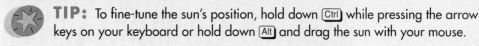

   TIP: To fine-tune the sun's position, hold down [Ctrl] while pressing the arrow keys on your keyboard or hold down [Alt] and drag the sun with your mouse.

10. Copy the sun from slide 2 and paste it on slide 3. Position it behind the "W" in "We."

11. On slide 3, resize the text placeholder, making it just large enough for the text to fit; then center it relative to slide both horizontally and vertically by using the Align and Distribute toolbar.

12. Close all floating toolbars.

13. Check the grayscale settings and make adjustments if needed.

14. Create a handout header and footer: include the date and your name as the header, and the page number and text *[your initials]*8-23 as the footer.

15. Move to slide 1 and save the presentation as *[your initials]*8-23 in your Lesson 8 folder.

16. Preview and then print the presentation as handouts, three slides per page, grayscale, scale to fit paper, framed. Close the presentation.

EXERCISE 8-24

Align, distribute, and group objects; work with layers; apply shadow and 3-D effects; and duplicate objects.

1. Open the file **AdMedia3**.

2. Move to slide 2. Duplicate the arrow four times by following these steps:

   a. Select the arrow and press Ctrl+D (or choose Duplicate from the Edit menu).

   b. Being careful not to deselect the duplicated arrow, drag or use the arrow keys to position it as shown in Figure 8-21. (Notice that the duplicate is quite close to the first arrow.)

FIGURE 8-21

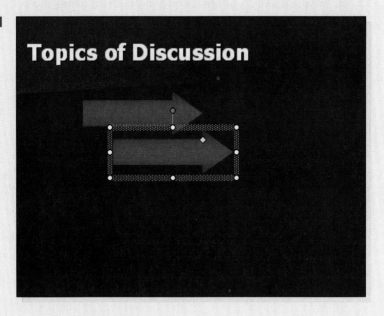

   c. Press Ctrl+D twice more so there are four arrows on the slide.

3. Key the following text inside the arrows:

    Arrow 1: Quality

    Arrow 2: Frequency

    Arrow 3: Effectiveness

    Arrow 4: Cost

4. Apply a 3-D effect to the arrows by following these steps:

    a. Select all four arrows.

    b. Click the 3-D Style button on the Drawing toolbar and choose 3-D Style 2.

    c. Click 3-D Style again and choose 3-D Settings.

    d. On the 3-D Settings toolbar, click the Direction button and choose Perspective.

    e. Click the Depth button and choose 144 pt.

5. Change the order of the arrows to reveal the hidden part of the arrowheads by following these steps:

    a. Deselect all the arrows and then select only the third one, which contains the text "Effectiveness."

    b. From the Draw menu, choose Order; then float the Order menu.

    c. Click the Bring to Front button .

    d. Click the arrow with the text "Frequency" and click the Bring to Front button again.

    e. Bring the arrow with the text "Quality" to the front.

6. Select all four arrows and group them.

7. Move the group of arrows diagonally down and to the right approximately 0.5 inches.

8. On slide 4, select the four bright red dots. Align their tops and distribute them evenly among themselves (not relative to the slide).

9. Group the four bright red dots.

10. Position the red dots after the word Steps so they appear to be part of the title.

11. Apply a shadow effect to the red dots by following these steps:

    a. Select both the red dots and the title placeholder.

    b. Click the Shadow Style button on the Drawing toolbar.

    c. Choose Shadow Style 6 (the second style in the second row).

12. Change the shadow color by following these steps:

    a. With the title and red dots still selected, click the Shadow Style button once again.

    b. At the bottom of the menu, choose Shadow Settings to display the Shadow Settings toolbar.

    c. Click the arrow next to the Shadow Color button and choose More Shadow Colors.

d. In the Colors dialog box, click the Standard tab and choose black. Move the Transparency slider all the way to the left. Click OK.

13. Still working on slide 4, center the body text placeholder horizontally.

14. Close all floating toolbars and check the slides in Grayscale view. If necessary, change the grayscale setting for the arrows on slide 2 to light grayscale. Repeat this adjustment for the diamond shape on slide 1.

15. Create a handout header and footer: include the date and your name as the header, and the page number and text *[your initials]*8-24 as the footer.

16. Move to slide 1 and save the presentation as *[your initials]*8-24 in your Lesson 8 folder.

17. Preview and then print the presentation as handouts, four slides per page, grayscale, landscape, framed. Close the presentation.

EXERCISE 8-25

Work with layers of objects, align and distribute objects, flip an object, group objects, and use advanced image editing tools.

1. Open the file **Opening3**.

2. On slide 1, edit the beach umbrella picture by following these steps:

a. Select the picture and then choose Ungroup from the Draw menu.

b. Click Yes in the dialog box that asks whether you want to convert the picture.

c. Display the Rotate or Flip toolbar and flip the image horizontally so the umbrella points in the opposite direction.

d. With the picture selected, zoom to 200%.

e. Click one of the white sections of the beach ball to select it with gray selection handles. Change its color to bright yellow.

f. Select each of the remaining two white sections of the beach ball and change them to bright yellow so you have alternating yellow sections.

g. For the remaining sections, change their color to red.

3. Change the Zoom setting to Fit; then copy the beach umbrella image to the lower-right corner of the slide master.

4. On slide 1, use the Align and Distribute toolbar to center the sun horizontally and vertically relative to the slide, and then send it to the back, behind the WordArt and subtitle text. Move the subtitle text up slightly.

5. On slide 2, align the middles of the sun and the text box relative to the slide and then group them.

6. Duplicate the group three times, allowing the copies to remain where they are inserted.

7. Drag down one copy of the sun, positioning it slightly below the top of the umbrella. Drag another copy up, so it is approximately 0.5 inches below the title.

8. Select all the sun/text combinations and distribute them vertically, relative to each other. If the spacing doesn't look correct, move the bottom line up or down a small amount and then vertically redistribute the combinations again. Left-align the sun/text combinations.

9. Edit lines 2 through 4 as shown in Figure 8-22.

FIGURE 8-22

10. Group all four lines; then center the group horizontally on the slide. Center the WordArt title horizontally on the slide and adjust the vertical position of the text grouping to make a pleasing composition.

11. Copy the grouped text and paste it on slide 3. Ungroup the copied text and delete the last line. Edit the three remaining lines to show the following text:

    Line 1: Beach front

    Line 2: Patio juice bar

    Line 3: Boardwalk

12. Group and then center the three lines horizontally, relative to the slide. Center the slide title horizontally.

13. Copy the sun AutoShape from slide 1 and paste it on slide 4. Center the sun relative to the slide and send it behind the WordArt and subtitle text.

14. Center the subtitle text horizontally, relative to the slide, and then move it up enough so that it does not overlap the beach umbrella.

15. Check the slides in Grayscale view and make any necessary adjustments.

16. Check spelling in the presentation.

17. Create a handout header and footer: include the date and your name as the header, and the page number and text *[your initials]*8-25 as the footer.

18. Move to slide 1 and save the presentation as *[your initials]*8-25 in your Lesson 8 folder.

19. Preview and then print the presentation as handouts, four slides per page, grayscale, landscape, framed. Close the presentation.

Lesson Applications

Select, align, and layer multiple objects; group and ungroup objects; and work with object shadows.

1. Open the file **InfoPak1**.

2. On the title master, select all the tiny diamonds. Align their tops relative to each other. Then distribute them evenly, relative to each other.

3. Select the third diamond from the right and change its color to gold. Group all the diamonds and center the group horizontally, relative to the slide.

4. Copy the group of diamonds and paste them on the slide master. Position the diamonds between the title placeholder and the body text placeholder.

5. Still working on the slide master, change the first-level bullet to the diamond from the Symbol font (sixth row to the bottom). Make it 100% of the font size and change its color to gold. Return to Normal view.

6. On slide 1, send the large diamond AutoShape behind the subtitle text, align its middle relative to the subtitle text, and center it and the subtitle text horizontally, relative to the slide. Center the diamond and subtitle text vertically, but not relative to the slide.

7. On slide 5, apply an object shadow (by using the Shadow button on the Drawing toolbar) to the text in the diamond. Choose Shadow Style 6, make the shadow color dark red (background scheme color), and adjust the nudge settings to bring the shadow closer to the text. Deselect the semitransparent setting for the object shadow.

8. Duplicate the diamond and increase its size. Change its color to the brown accent scheme color. Send it to the back and then make any necessary size adjustments so it is evenly spaced behind the first diamond.

9. Group the text box and the diamond, and center them horizontally on the slide. Adjust the vertical position of the group to make a pleasing composition.

10. View the presentation in Grayscale view and make any necessary adjustments to the grayscale settings.

11. Create a handout header and footer: include the date and your name as the header, and the page number and text *[your initials]*8-26 as the footer.

12. Move to slide 1 and save the presentation as *[your initials]*8-26 in your Lesson 8 folder.

13. Preview and then print the presentation as handouts, six slides per page, grayscale, framed. Close the presentation.

Align, distribute, and group objects; work with shadows and 3-D effects; and use the Duplicate command.

1. Open the file **Recruit2**.

2. Delete all graphic elements on the slide master and on the title master. Only the text placeholders should remain.

3. On the title master, draw a 0.25-inch circle, creating a small dot in the center of the slide. Make the dot purple and apply Shadow Style 8. Make the shadow color black and deselect the semitransparent setting.

4. Duplicate the dot you just created 15 times (without repositioning), so you have a total of 16 dots. Select all the dots; then align their tops relative to each other. Distribute the dots horizontally, relative to the slide.

5. Group the dots then align in the middle relative to the slide. You should now have a line of evenly spaced dots across the middle of the title master.

6. Select the title placeholder, the group of dots, and the subtitle placeholder, and distribute them vertically, relative to each other (not to the slide). This spaces the line of dots evenly between the two placeholders.

7. Copy the group of dots and paste it to the slide master, between the title placeholder and the body text placeholder. Center the group relative to the slide.

8. Move the body text placeholder down 0.5 inch to add some extra space for the dots.

9. Change the bullet shape for all the bullets in the body text placeholder to a solid, thick, right-pointing arrow from the Wingdings3 font. Change their size to 75% and their color to bright green (use More Colors).

10. Change the slide master's title text to Impact and 60 points. Apply Shadow Style 6 to the text. Make the shadow fit the text a little better by nudging it up twice and to the left twice. Change the shadow color to black and deselect the semitransparent setting.

11. On slide 1, replace the title text "New Employee Orientation" with a WordArt title (positioned where the title text would usually be). Use the fifth WordArt style on the second row (the dark blue one). Make the font 54-point Impact.

12. Change the fill color of the WordArt object to purple and the outline color to bright green. Change the WordArt shadow to Shadow Style 8 and change the shadow color to black, with the semitransparent setting not selected. Resize and reposition the WordArt so its shadow does not overlap the purple dots.

13. Copy the WordArt and paste it on slide 2. Edit the text of this WordArt for the title of this slide. Repeat this process for slides 3 and 4. Resize so the text size is the same on slides 2–4. Delete the original title text.

14. Repeat this procedure for the title on the title slide, too, but increase the text size for this slide. If the shadow overlaps the purple dots, then return to the master and move the grouped dots down.

15. Draw a rounded rectangle where the subtitle would appear. Make the rectangle 1 inch high and 3.5 inches wide. Apply a black, one-color, horizontal gradient fill with the darkest color at the top. Adjust the shading intensity so the bottom is the same dark gray shade as the bottom of the slide's background.

16. Inside the rectangle, key **Good 4 U** in bright green, 44-point Arial bold.

17. On slide 4, key the following text in the body text placeholder:

- **Reinforce our message of healthy living**
- **Describe our new franchising philosophy**
- **Encourage fresh ideas from new employees**

18. Adjust the Grayscale view settings in the presentation, as needed.

19. Check spelling in the presentation.

20. Create a handout header and footer: include the date and your name as the header, and the page number and text *[your initials]***8-27** as the footer.

21. Move to slide 1 and save the presentation as *[your initials]***8-27** in your Lesson 8 folder.

22. Preview and then print the presentation as handouts, six slides per page, grayscale, scaled to fit paper, framed. Close the presentation.

EXERCISE 8-28

Align and distribute objects, work with layers, group and ungroup objects, and use advanced image editing tools.

1. Open the file **Cooking4**.

2. Apply the Blends design template to the presentation. Change the template's color scheme to one with the black background.

3. On the title master, ungroup the graphic objects and delete the red and blue rectangles. Resize the gold rectangle to create a tall, narrow rectangle extending from the top to the bottom of the slide. Change the title font to 48 points, bold, and white. On the slide master, delete only the red and blue rectangles, allowing the gold one to remain. Change the title font to 40 points, bold, and white.

4. On slide 1, left-align the subtitle text in its placeholder.

5. Convert the carrot picture to PowerPoint objects. Then select just the orange part and change its fill color to a brighter shade of orange (create a custom color).

6. Increase the carrot's size proportionately, making it 3 inches tall, and rotate it to the right about 60 degrees. Position the carrot in the lower-right corner of the slide.

7. Move the apple from the upper-left corner to the middle of the carrot, hiding part of it. (Bring the apple to the front.)

8. Insert a picture of a cluster of grapes (or another fruit or vegetable) that works well with the apple and carrot. Size and rotate the picture appropriately and place it to the left or right of the apple, whichever makes the best grouping.

9. Group the three images and position the group attractively. Copy the group to the slide master. Decrease its size proportionately, making it approximately 75% of the original size, and place it in the lower-right corner.

10. On slide 3, resize and reposition the graph so that it does not overlap the fruit in the lower-right corner. Change the graph's grayscale setting to Inverse Grayscale.

11. On slide 4, increase the size of the body text placeholder and increase the font size to 32 points so it matches slide 2. Increase the picture, too, on the left side of the slide nicely balanced beside the text.

12. Reposition the picture and the text box to create an attractive layout. You may change the size of the picture and the text size if you want.

13. Review the presentation in Grayscale view and make adjustments where needed.

14. Create a handout header and footer: include the date and your name as the header, and the page number and text *[your initials]8-28* as the footer.

15. Move to slide 1 and save the presentation as *[your initials]8-28* in your Lesson 8 folder.

16. Preview and then print the presentation as handouts, four slides per page, grayscale, landscape, framed. Close the presentation.

EXERCISE 8-29 *Challenge Yourself*

Align, rotate, and flip objects, work with layers, apply 3-D effects, and use advanced image editing tools.

1. Open the file **WhoWeAre**.

2. Insert a picture in the lower-right corner of slide 1 that is appropriate to the content of the presentation. Size the image appropriately and change its color setting. Change the title text to 60-point Arial, bold.

3. Insert a different but related picture on the slide master. Choose a simple image and make it approximately 2 inches tall. Change its color setting to grayscale, and move it to the upper-right corner of the slide master. Send it to the back so that it is behind the title text placeholder and other graphics.

4. Change the slide master's title text to 44-point Arial, bold. Change the title master's title text to 60-point Arial, bold. Make the subtitle text bold and move it and the horizontal line up to make room for the picture at the bottom right of the slide.

5. Rotate or flip the images, if needed, to create better positioning. Adjust the contrast and brightness as necessary.

6. On slide 1, replace the "Good 4 U" title and its placeholder with a WordArt image by using the first choice in the first row of the WordArt Gallery. Adjust the WordArt width to make it approximately 5.5 inches wide, 1.25 inches high, and position it where the title placeholder usually goes.

7. Apply the 3-D Style 7 to the WordArt. Using the Direction button on the 3-D Settings toolbar, choose the Perspective option, and change the direction to the second choice in the bottom row (which places the perspective vanishing point directly behind and slightly above the WordArt image). Choose a color that works well with the colors in the photograph you selected.

8. On slide 2, resize the body text placeholder to fit the text and center the placeholder horizontally and vertically on the slide.

9. Draw a constrained Diamond AutoShape on slide 2. Make the shape 4.5 inches wide. Change the fill color to a light shade of gray (use More Colors). Remove the border line.

10. Select both the diamond and the body text placeholder and align their middles and centers relative to each other. Send the diamond behind the text.

11. Copy the diamond and paste it to slide 3. Send the diamond to the back and then position it behind the picture of people. Align the centers and middles of the clip art and diamond relative to each other; then move them slightly to the left.

12. Still working on slide 3, adjust the body text placeholder by increasing the font size to 30 points to match the text on slide 2. Adjust its vertical position so it is in balance with the image.

13. Format slide 5 in the same style as slide 3 but make the diamond more narrow to better fit the picture. Increase the font size to 30 points. Format slide 4 in the same style as slide 2.

14. Review the presentation in Grayscale view and make adjustments where needed.

15. Apply an animation scheme of your choice and then view the presentation as a slide show.

16. Create a handout header and footer: include the date and your name as the header, and the page number and text *[your initials]*8-29 as the footer.

17. Move to slide 1 and save the presentation as a Web page with the filename *[your initials]*8-29 in your Lesson 8 folder.

18. Preview and then print the presentation as handouts, six slides per page, grayscale, framed. Close the presentation.

On Your Own

In these exercises you work on your own, as you would in a real-life work environment. Use the skills you've learned to accomplish the task—and be creative.

EXERCISE 8-30

Imagine that you have invented a new product: a vacuum that runs itself, a new type of breathable waterproof fabric, a new type of golf ball, or whatever else you want. Create a persuasive presentation aimed at possible financial backers for the product. Explain the product's features and the benefits of its use. Identify its potential market. Include at least five slides in your presentation. Use the tools and features presented in this lesson and in previous lessons to create an attractive presentation. Save the presentation as *[your initials]*8-30. Preview and then print the presentation as handouts.

EXERCISE 8-31

Create a presentation to get donations for a charity event sponsored by a community organization, such as a blood drive, a heart walk, or bowl for kids' sake. In your presentation, describe the organization and the event activities, including dates and times. Also include one or two slides explaining to people why they should donate. Use the tools and features presented in this lesson and in previous lessons to create an attractive presentation. Save the presentation as *[your initials]*8-31. Preview and then print the presentation as handouts.

EXERCISE 8-32

Imagine that you are organizing a cook-off at a local community. Create a presentation describing the contest, rules, location, and categories. Recognize winners from the previous year. Format your presentation attractively and in keeping with the theme of your idea. Save the presentation as *[your initials]*8-32. Preview and then print the presentation as handouts.

Unit 3 Applications

Work with clip art; create and format WordArt objects; use gradient fills; align, rotate, and flip objects; and group and ungroup objects.

1. Open the file **FranOpt.**

2. Delete the title text placeholder. In its place insert a WordArt title by using the text **Good 4 U** and the following formatting:

   - WordArt style: Fourth column, third row (multicolor characters with shadow).
   - Font: 60-point bold Arial Black.
   - Fill: Gradient fill, one-color red, dark shading, vertical shading style, lower-left variant with darkest color in center.
   - Border: 2-point dark red (create a custom color).
   - Shadow style: Shadow Style 4.
   - Shadow color: Medium gray, non-transparent (choose from More Shadow Colors).
   - Position: Centered horizontally, approximately 1.5 inches from the top of the slide.

3. Insert two slides after slide 1; use the Title and Text layout. Delete the title text placeholders on both slides; then create WordArt with the same formatting as slide 1, but reduce the font size to 40 points. Use the text **Advantages** for slide 2 and **Objectives** for slide 3. Position the WordArt where the title placeholder would usually be.

    TIP: To save time, copy the WordArt from slide 1, edit its text and reduce the font size, and reposition it.

4. Using the text in Figure U3-1, key the subtitle text for slide 1 and the body text for slides 2 and 3.

5. On slide 1, convert the picture of the knife, fork, and spoon to PowerPoint objects. Ungroup the objects again; then delete all the parts that make up the spoon. Delete the transparent rectangle that is behind the objects.

6. Manipulate the remaining knife and fork parts by performing the following:
   - Select all the knife and fork parts and apply a horizontal gradient fill with the Silver preset and the first variant. Apply a medium gray line to show the detail of the knife and fork.

Slide 1
```
Good 4 U
• Restaurant Franchise Opportunities
```

Slide 2
```
Advantages
• Fast-growing market
• Excellent income potential
• Expert training and support
```

Slide 3
```
Objectives
• Help people achieve a healthy lifestyle
• Help you grow a healthy business
```

- Group all the knife parts as one group, and all the fork parts as a second group.
- Using the Format AutoShape dialog box, rotate the fork 45 degrees (to the right), and the knife 315 degrees (–45 degrees to the left).
- Align the knife and fork middles and centers relative to each other; then group them to form one object.
- Position the knife and fork behind the subtitle text and center it horizontally and vertically relative to the subtitle text, as shown in Figure U3-2 on the next page.

7. Copy the grouped fork and knife to the slide master. Reduce the size of the picture proportionately with a height of 2.5 inches high and place it near the bottom of the slide master, within the large yellow shape.

8. Review each slide. Adjust the position of the WordArt and the size and position of body text placeholders and other objects as needed to create a pleasing composition on each slide.

9. Change the grayscale setting for each WordArt object in the presentation to Light Grayscale. View each slide in Grayscale view, adjusting other settings where needed.

FIGURE U3-2

10. Check spelling in the presentation.
11. Create a handout header and footer: include the date and your name as the header, and the page number and text *[your initials]*U3-1 as the footer.
12. Create a new folder for Unit 3 Applications. Save the presentation as a Web page with the filename *[your initials]*U3-1 in this folder.
13. View the presentation as a slide show and then view it in your Web browser.
14. Preview and then print the presentation as handouts, three slides per page, grayscale, framed. Close the presentation.

UNIT APPLICATION 3-2

Work with WordArt, work with images, apply gradient fills, change the order of objects, group objects, and apply 3-D effects and object shadows.

1. Open the file **Runner1**. On the title master, increase the slide size to 75% so you can see the details of the runners. Rearrange, resize, and flip where necessary the four runners so they appear as shown in Figure U3-3 (on the next page). You also need to change the order of the runners and other elements so that they overlap as shown.
2. Adjust the contrast, brightness, and color settings (by using the Picture toolbar) so that all the runners stand out from the background. Change your zoom to Fit so you can see the entire slide.

FIGURE U3-3

3. When you are satisfied with the arrangement of the runners, group them and copy the group to the slide master.

4. Proportionately resize the group of runners on the slide master to be no more than 3 inches high, and place it in the lower-right corner.

5. On the slide master, draw a Right Arrow AutoShape, starting at the upper-left corner of the body text placeholder and dragging to the lower-right corner of the body text placeholder. Format the arrow as follows:

    • Drag the adjustment handle up a little to make the tail of the arrow thicker.

    • Apply a two-color vertical gradient fill with orange (fills scheme color) as Color 1 and brown (shadows scheme color) as Color 2. Use the variant with the lightest color on the right.

    • Apply 3-D Style 2 to the arrow, and change its 3-D color to dark brown (background scheme color). Change its direction to Perspective, and increase its depth to 144 pt.

    • Send the arrow backward several times so that the body text placeholder text and the runners appear on top of it.

    The completed arrow should appear as in Figure U3-4.

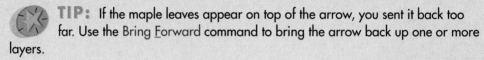 **TIP:** If the maple leaves appear on top of the arrow, you sent it back too far. Use the Bring Forward command to bring the arrow back up one or more layers.

6. Change the size and position of the slide master's text placeholders to agree with Figure U3-4.

7. Change the body text placeholder's font to Arial Narrow with a text shadow. Increase its font size by one increment.

8. Change the title placeholder's font to Arial Black **not bold**, 40 points, and apply an object shadow by using Shadow Style 1 so the shadow is in the same direction as the shade on the 3-D arrow shape. Change the shadow to a custom color that is very dark brown—almost black. Nudge the shadow down and to the right to make it fit the text better. Increase the font size by one increment.

9. Make any changes needed so that the text on the title master matches the text on the slide master; then increase the size of the title text to 72 points.

10. Working in the Outline pane, key the text shown in Figure U3-5, inserting new slides where needed. The shadow you applied in step 8 may not appear when you first see the slide, but it will appear after you have entered text in the placeholders.

11. On slides 2 and 4, remove the bullets from the body text placeholders and resize the placeholders to center the text vertically on the arrow.

12. On slide 3, allow the bullets to remain, decrease the font size by one increment, and resize the body text placeholder so the first bullet's text "before race" wraps to a second line. Raise the placeholder slightly so the text is centered vertically on the arrow.

13. Insert a new slide after slide 4 that uses the Blank layout. Insert a picture of a suitable landscape, fireworks, or a race. Resize the picture proportionately so it fills the entire slide. If the picture is an odd size, crop it where necessary so it is the same size and shape as the slide. Adjust the picture's brightness and contrast settings to soften the colors so WordArt will be readable when placed above the image.

14. Create a WordArt image by using the style in the upper-left corner. Key the following text on three lines:

Award Ceremony
6 p.m.
Central Park

15. Change the WordArt shape to Button (Curve), which is the fourth choice in the second row. Fill the WordArt with a diagonal gradient fill by using the Gold II preset, any variant. Apply a brown outline, and a shadow style and color of your choice.

16. Adjust the height and width of the WordArt shape so that it is rounder and larger. Adjust the character spacing to make the letters tight.

17. Adjust the grayscale settings for the elements on slide 5 (including the background) and for the rest of the presentation, as needed.

18. Check spelling in the presentation.

19. Create a handout header and footer: include the date and your name as the header, and the page number and text *[your initials]*U3-2 as the footer.

20. Move to slide 1 and save the presentation as *[your initials]*U3-2 in your Unit 3 Applications folder.

21. Preview and then print the presentation as handouts, six slides per page, grayscale, framed. Close the presentation.

Work with WordArt and images, align and distribute objects, group objects, and apply and customize 3-D effects.

1. Open the file **StaffTrn**.

2. Duplicate the clip art image on slide 1 and move the second image to the lower-left corner.

3. Crop the original image so only the lecturer and her lectern remain. Crop the copy (in the lower-left corner) so that only the three audience members remain.

4. Duplicate the audience members and position the second image evenly spaced to the right of the first image. Duplicate two more times.

5. Select the two audience member images (six people) on the right and group them. Flip this image horizontally and move it to the right of the slide to allow a little space between the people on the left and right. Group all of the people at the bottom of the slide.

6. Reduce the size of the grouped people slightly; then center the group horizontally at the bottom of the slide. Reduce the contrast and brightness settings so that the people are almost silhouetted.

7. Horizontally center the picture of the lecturer. Refer to Figure U3-6 for the final arrangement of the picture elements.

FIGURE U3-6

8. Copy the group of people to the slide master in the same position.

9. On slide 1, substitute a WordArt image for the title text by using the following formatting:

- From the WordArt Gallery, select the style in the second row, fourth column (with the gray and white horizontal gradient fill).
- Format the text as 60-point bold Arial Black and make the character spacing tight.
- Make the WordArt 9.25 inches wide, 2 inches tall, and center it horizontally above the picture of the lecturer.
- Apply the Deflate Bottom Up WordArt shape (fourth shape in the fourth row).
- Apply 3-D Style 20, change the 3-D color to dull purple (background scheme color), and change the lighting to shine up from the bottom (middle choice in the bottom row). Select the Bright lighting option.

10. Adjust the position of the WordArt so the top of the 3-D effect is at the top of the slide and centered horizontally, as shown in Figure U3-6. Move the subtitle up slightly, too.

11. On the slide master, make the title placeholder bold, make the body text placeholder bold, and remove the bullet on the first line in the list.

12. Create three new slides with the Title and 2-Column Text layout. Key the text shown in Figure U3-7. Right-align the text in the right-column placeholders on all three slides. Increase the font size by one increment. Resize and arrange the placeholders attractively on each slide. Be sure to align the tops of the column placeholders.

FIGURE U3-7

Slide 2

```
Training Presentation  ————— Title
Managers         8:30 a.m.
Servers          10:15 a.m.
Greeters         1:00 p.m.
Kitchen staff    3:15 p.m.
```

Slide 3

```
On-the-job Training  ————— Title
Managers         7:30 p.m.
Servers          5:30 p.m.
Greeters         8:15 p.m.
Kitchen staff    4:30 p.m.
```

continues

Slide 4

Food Services Training ———————— Title

Managers   January 17

Servers   January 18

Greeters   January 19

Kitchen staff   January 20

 TIP: To save time, create the 2-column text on slide 2 first, copy the slide twice, and then edit the copies for slides 3 and 4.

13. Adjust the grayscale settings for each slide in the presentation as needed.

14. Check spelling in the presentation.

15. Create a handout header and footer: include the date and your name as the header, and the page number and text *[your initials]*U3-3 as the footer.

16. Move to slide 1 and save the presentation as *[your initials]*U3-3 in your Unit 3 Applications folder.

17. Preview and then print the presentation as handouts, four slides per page, grayscale, landscape, framed. Close the presentation.

UNIT APPLICATION 3-4 *Using the Internet*

Write and design a presentation that uses WordArt, images, AutoShapes, fill effects, line styles, shadows, and 3-D effects and shadows.

Use the Internet to research a college or university that is at least 200 miles away from where you live. Gather information about the organizations on campus, sports teams, recreation facilities, libraries, degrees offered, and general information about the location of the campus. You can also find information about public transportation and weather.

Use the information you gathered to create a presentation that you could use to explain about this university to students at a nearby high school. Use a template and color scheme that complements your material. Include at least five slides, one or more WordArt objects, one or more pictures that have been edited in some way (cropped, altered brightness and contrast, flipped, etc.), and one or more AutoShapes. Be sure to include some of the following effects: gradient fills, pattern fills, picture fills, shadow effects, 3-D effects, patterned or dashed lines. Use these effects in a tasteful manner, making sure that all slides have a unified style. When the presentation is complete, review the slides in Grayscale view and make any grayscale adjustments that might be needed.

In the slide footer, include the text **Prepared by** followed by your name. Include the slide number on all slides but not the date. In the handout footer, include the completed filename *[your initials]*U3-4. In the handout header, key **Presented to** and then identify to whom you would be giving this presentation. Include in the handout the date you would be delivering the presentation.

Check spelling in the presentation and save it as *[your initials]*U3-4 in your Unit 3 Applications folder. Practice delivering the presentation. Preview and then print the presentation handouts as an appropriate number of slides per page, grayscale, framed. Close the presentation.

Advanced Techniques

LESSON 9

Customizing Templates

OBJECTIVES

MICROSOFT OFFICE SPECIALIST
A C T I V I T I E S

In this lesson:
PP03S-1-1
PP03S-2-1
PP03S-2-3
PP03S-2-6
PP03S-2-7
PP03S-4-6

See Appendix.

After completing this lesson, you will be able to:

1. **Work with backgrounds.**
2. **Customize an existing design template.**
3. **Create a new design template.**
4. **Apply design templates and color schemes from other presentations.**

 Estimated Time: 1 hour

Design templates make it easy to add visual interest to a presentation and at the same time ensure a consistent look for all slides. Besides applying the templates that PowerPoint provides, you can alter PowerPoint templates to create your own look, create your own templates from a blank presentation, and apply templates directly from other presentations.

Working with Backgrounds

One way to change a presentation's overall appearance quickly and easily is to change background effects and background colors by choosing Format, Background. You can change background effects for an entire presentation or for just one slide. Just as AutoShapes can have a variety of fill types applied, backgrounds can be solid colors, gradient fills, textures, or pictures.

Another way to change a background is to add an object or objects to the slide and title masters. If you size an object to cover the entire slide and then send it behind the text placeholders, it behaves in a way that is similar to using the Background command. Each method has its advantages and disadvantages. For example, you can use the Picture toolbar features on an object placed on a master slide, but not on one placed by using the Background command. It is sometimes easier to apply background effects to individual slides by using the Background command.

EXERCISE **9-1** **Change Background Color for an Entire Presentation**

The Background dialog box lets you choose from the design template's color scheme colors, other colors, or fill effects.

FIGURE 9-1
Background
dialog box

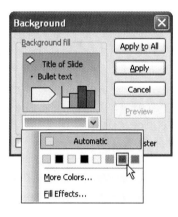

1. Open the presentation **Lecture1**.
2. Working on slide 1, open the Format menu and choose Background. The Background dialog box opens.
3. Click the down arrow on the color box and choose the brown color.
4. Click Apply to All. Scroll through the presentation to verify that the brown is now the background color of all slides.

EXERCISE **9-2** **Create a Picture Background for an Entire Presentation**

A picture that fills the whole screen can be a slide background. In this exercise you will apply a picture of vegetables.

1. Move back to slide 1, open the Format menu and choose Background. The Background dialog box opens.
2. Click the down arrow on the sample color box and choose Fill Effects. The Fill Effects dialog box opens.
3. Click the Picture tab and click Select Picture.
4. In the Select Picture dialog box, select the student disk and choose **Vegetable1** and click Insert. The picture you selected appears on the Picture tab of the Fill Effects dialog box.

TIP: The picture shown in Figure 9-2 is available in Microsoft Office Online. Search for photos by using the search word "onions." It is also available with your student data files with the filename of **vegetable1**.

FIGURE 9-2
Selecting a picture
for a background

5. Click OK to close the Fill Effects dialog box.

6. In the Background dialog box, click Apply to All. Scroll through the presentation to verify that the vegetable picture background appears on all slides. Notice that the background is not appropriate for slide 7 because the pictures of vegetables are not easy to see on top of the background vegetable picture.

EXERCISE 9-3 **Change the Background for an Individual Slide**

Although background consistency is important for a unified presentation theme, at times you will want a different background for one or more slides in a presentation. For example, slide 7 in the current presentation would look better with a plain background. By clicking Apply in the Background dialog box, you can change the background for one or a selected group of slides. Just be sure that the colors chosen blend with the overall color scheme and the tone of the presentation.

1. Move to slide 7 ("To Good Health!") and open the Background dialog box.

2. Click the down arrow on the sample color box and choose the green color used for body text placeholders on other slides so that the colors of this slide will blend with other slides.

 3. Click Apply. Check the slide thumbnails to verify that slides 1 through 6 still contain the vegetable background. If not, click the Undo button 🔄 and try again.

EXERCISE 9-4 **Omit Slide Master Graphics from an Individual Slide**

Sometimes the master slide graphics interfere with the design of one or more slides in your presentation. You can use the Background dialog box to eliminate master slide graphics on individual slides.

1. Display slide 7. Notice the Good 4 U logo that is partially hidden under a picture.
2. Open the Background dialog box.
3. Click the check box labeled Omit background graphics from master at the bottom of the dialog box.
4. Click Apply. The logo is removed from this slide, but it still appears on slides 1 through 6.
5. Using steps 2–4 above, remove the Good 4 U logo from slide 6, "Cost/ Accommodations," since the body text placeholder covers part of the logo.
6. Scroll through the slides to verify that the logo still appears on slides 1 through 5.

 NOTE: If you click Apply to All by mistake, you remove the master slide graphics from all slides. In that case, click the Undo button and try again.

7. Switch to Grayscale view. On the slide master, click anywhere on the background, click Setting, and choose Light Grayscale to make the vegetable background visible in Grayscale view.
8. Apply the Light Grayscale setting to the title master's background. Scroll through all slides and make additional grayscale setting changes if needed. Close Grayscale view.
9. Create a handout header and footer: include the date and your name as the header, and the page number and text *[your initials]*9-4 as the footer.
10. Create a new folder for Lesson 9. Move to slide 1 and save the presentation as *[your initials]*9-4 in a your new folder for Lesson 9.
11. Preview and then print the presentation as handouts, 4 slides per page, grayscale, landscape, framed. Close the presentation.

Customizing an Existing Design Template

PowerPoint offers a large variety of design templates, each with several color schemes you can apply. You can further customize these design templates to fit the needs of a presentation by changing the background graphics, placeholder positioning, and fonts on the slide master and the title master. Many more design templates are available in Microsoft's online collection and at other sites on the Internet.

EXERCISE   9-5   Change Presentation Background

In the previous exercise you learned how to add a picture to the entire background or cause the background graphics to not show on a particular slide. This exercise will focus on changing the background color on the title master. You will create a presentation to help explain the technology changes at Good 4 U.

1. Start a new presentation using the slide design template named **Layers**. Choose the slide color scheme with the green background. Display the slide title master.

2. From the F̲ormat menu, choose Background.

3. Choose F̲ill Effects from the drop-down menu, and change to a two-color gradient fill, with Color 1 the green background color and Color 2 the light yellow (Title Text Scheme) color. Click OK and choose A̲pply so that this gradient color treatment is applied only to the title master. See Figure 9-3 to compare your slide.

FIGURE 9-3
Changing the
background color
on a title master

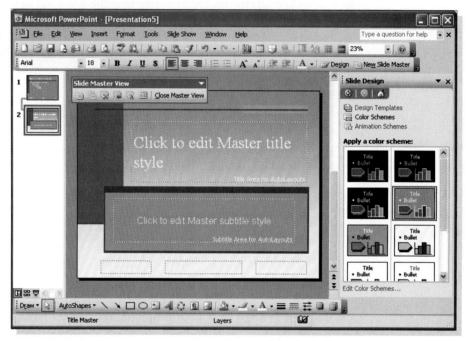

4. Keep this presentation open for the next exercise.

EXERCISE **9-6** **Rearrange Template Graphics**

To further customize the look of a design template, you can modify or delete existing objects (lines, shapes, images) plus add your own objects suitable for your particular topic. Remember to keep the presentations professional and fitting with the presentation topic.

1. Still working on the title master of the current presentation, click twice on the line at the top of the master. Notice that most of the slide has sizing handles around it and the line has subselection handles that shows it is part

of the grouped objects. You will change this line later. Choose Ungroup from the Draw menu.

2. Deselect the objects.

3. Notice where the handles are located for the subtitle placeholder. Click on the rectangle that is behind this placeholder. It appears to have a border line of dark green with a thicker line at the top of the rectangle. Press (Delete) to remove the rectangle but not the subtitle placeholder.

4. Select the blue rectangle at the top left of the slide, resize it to 3" tall by 2.5" wide. Change the fill color to dark green (Shadows Scheme). Be sure this rectangle does not have a line color.

5. With the same rectangle still selected, choose duplicate from the Edit menu. Change the fill color to blue (Fills Scheme). Duplicate this rectangle and change the third rectangle's color to green (Accent and Followed Hyperlink Scheme).

6. Stagger the rectangles as shown in Figure 9-4.

FIGURE 9-4
Rearranging
template graphics

7. Move the dark green horizontal line grouped with the thin green rectangle down below the staggered rectangles and title placeholder.

8. Ungroup the line and rectangle.

9. Stretch the rectangle out to be the length of the line, then select both of these objects, align them in the middle, and then group. Resize the grouped object to go across the slide.

10. Search for a clip art image of a computer similar to the one shown on top of the rectangles in Figure 9-5. Resize it to fit the top rectangle and recolor it, if necessary, using the colors in the design template color scheme.

11. Select the computer image and the three rectangles behind it and group them. Press (Ctrl)+(C) to copy.

12. Click on the slide master thumbnail.

13. On the slide master, click twice on the blue rectangle and notice that most of the slide is surrounded by sizing handles. Choose Ungroup. Deselect the objects.

14. Delete the blue rectangle. Delete the short horizontal line at the left of the slide. Press Ctrl+V to paste the computer and rectangles you grouped and copied from the slide master.

15. Resize this grouped object to be 2" high (lock aspect ratio) and position it in the upper left-hand corner of the slide to match the layout of the title master.

16. Close the Master Slide view.

17. Leave the presentation open for the next exercise.

EXERCISE 9-7 Reposition Template Placeholders

When you make changes to the layout of the graphics and the backgrounds of a template, many times you must reposition the template placeholders for all objects to fit attractively on the slide.

1. View the master title slide of the current presentation, and select the title placeholder.

2. Resize and move the placeholder to fit beside the rectangles in the upper left and above the dark green line that is grouped with the thin, green rectangle.

3. Move the subtitle placeholder down to fit under the grouped line and rectangle. See Figure 9-5 for placement.

FIGURE 9-5
Placeholder position on the title master

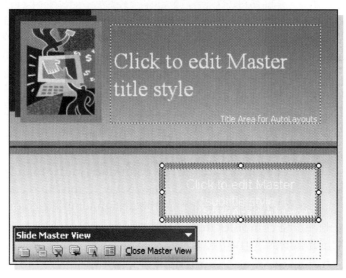

4. Move to the slide master, and move the placeholders to fit attractively on the slide. See Figure 9-6 (on the next page) for placement.

5. Save the presentation as *[your initials]*9-7 in a your folder for Lesson 9 and leave the presentation open for the next exercise.

 **FIGURE 9-6**
Placeholder position
on the slide master

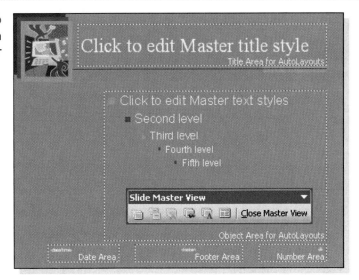

RJB 9-8

E X E R C I S E   **9-8**   **Change Template Placeholder Font**

Remember that text must be easy to read. So when you change text placeholder font colors, be sure to have a high contrast between the slide background colors and the text colors. For many fonts, a bold attribute will make the text easier to read, too. Sometimes a shadow can help to define letterforms, but again, contrast is needed so that the shadow outlines the text and does not make it look blurred.

The fonts you choose will affect the tone of your presentation. Some look very formal or traditional, while others seem more relaxed or modern. Use one or perhaps two fonts in a presentation. Be sure that slide titles are emphasized more than the text in the body of the slides.

1. Still working in the master slides for the current presentation, click the title placeholder on the title master.

2. Change the font to Tahoma, 54 point, bold, and shadow.

3. Select the subtitle placeholder and change the font to Tahoma, bold, left align, and dark green.

4. Move to the slide master, and change the title placeholder font to Tahoma, bold, and shadow.

5. Change the body placeholder font to Tahoma. Select the first two outline levels and make them bold. Change the first-level bullet to dark brown.

6. Close the Master Slide view.

7. On slide 1, key the title **Tremendous Technology** and the subtitle **By Your Name**

8. Insert a new slide using the Title and Text layout.

9. Key the text from Figure 9-7 into new slides.

FIGURE 9-7   Text for slides

Proposed Changes ————————Title and Text layout

Slide 2
- New PCs with the latest application software
- New laser printers to replace old dot matrix printers
- Order processing program upgrade

Training—Next 2 Weeks ————————Title, Text, and Content

Slide 3
- Supervisory
- Wait staff
- Accounting
- Kitchen staff
- Manager

Rewards for Learning ————————Title and Text

Slide 4
- Automatic $.25/hour wage increase when training sessions are complete
- Increased online capabilities
  - Complete training tests
  - Place supply orders
  - Conduct Internet research
  - Bonus—check e-mail on breaks

Slide 5 Let's Get Started! ————————Title Slide

10. On slide 3, increase the title placeholder size by dragging the right sizing handle so that the title text remains the same size as on other slides. Increase the body placeholder font size by one increment to match the first-level bulleted text on other slides. Insert a photograph similar to the one in Figure 9-8 (on the next page).

11. Move to slide 1, save the presentation as *[your initials]*9-8, then view the presentation as a slide show noting the changes that you made in the template.

12. Close the presentation.

FIGURE 9-8
Photograph
image for slide

Creating a New Design Template

In addition to altering a predesigned template to create your own design, you can create a new design using your own creativity or your company's design guidelines and logos.

EXERCISE **9-9** **Change Slide Master Background**

The new presentation default design is blank with no predesigned graphics. By working on the slide master and the title master, you can apply a background, AutoShapes, lines, and pictures. You can also change the size and position of text placeholders and change the font, color, and size of text to individualize your design.

1. Start a new blank presentation and display the slide master. When you begin, there is only a slide master. You will insert a title master later.
2. Using the Background dialog box, apply a two-color gradient fill to all slides: use light blue as Color 1, white as Color 2, the Horizontal shading style, and the variant that is white on the top. Click Apply.
3. Leave the Master view open for the next exercise.

EXERCISE **9-10** **Edit Color Scheme**

You change colors in a color scheme by first opening the Edit Color Scheme dialog box. To do this, display the Slide Design task pane, click Color Schemes, and then click Edit Color Schemes.

After the dialog box is open, double-click a color you want to change. You can then choose the Standard tab to select a premixed color or click the Custom tab and mix your own color.

1. Display the Slide Design task pane.
2. Click Color Schemes; then click Edit Color Schemes at the bottom of the task pane. The Edit Color Scheme dialog box opens, displaying the eight standard colors used for the current color scheme.
3. Under Scheme colors, select the dark blue Accent color, and then click Change Color. The Accent Color dialog box opens with the palette of standard colors arranged in a honeycomb pattern.

FIGURE 9-9
Editing a color scheme

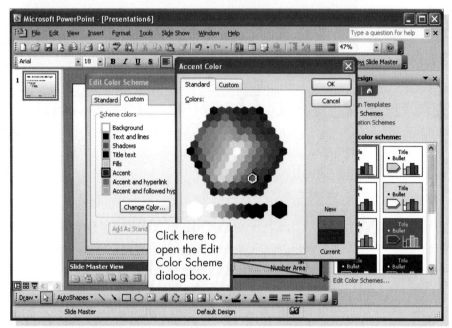

FIGURE 9-10
Creating a custom color for a new color scheme

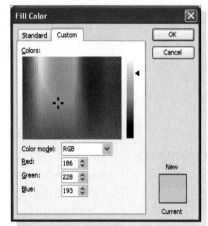

4. In the third row from the bottom of the palette, click the third color sample from the right (light red). The sample box in the lower-right corner displays the new color and current color.
5. Click OK to accept the new color.
6. On the Edit Color Scheme dialog box, double-click the light blue Fills color sample. The Fill Color dialog box opens. Click the Custom tab as shown in Figure 9-10 if it is not already selected.
7. In the Colors mixer box, drag the crosshair left, to the middle of the green area, to

give the original color a green tint. Then with the slider on the right that controls luminance, drag the arrow down just a little to make the color a little darker green. Click OK.

8. In the Edit Color Scheme dialog box, click Preview. The background changes to a light green gradient.

9. Click Add As Standard Scheme to preserve these colors as a standard color scheme for this design template. At this point, you could create another color scheme without losing the current one.

10. Click the Standard tab. Notice the sample box with your new color scheme displayed.

11. Click Apply. The Edit Color Scheme dialog box closes, and the new colors are applied to the presentation.

EXERCISE 9-11 **Insert a Title Slide Master**

When you are working in the Master view and have not entered text in the presentation yet, you can insert a Master Title Slide. This allows you to complete the master slide formatting even before there is any text or slides in the presentation.

You can do this by clicking the Insert New Title Master button on the Slide Master View toolbar.

1. Still working in Master view from the previous exercise, use ScreenTips to locate the Insert New Title Master button on the Slide Master View toolbar.

FIGURE 9-11
Adding a
new title master

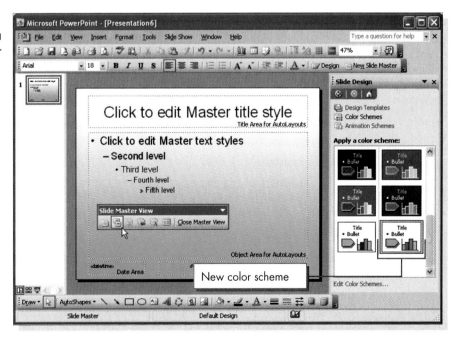

2. Click the Insert New Title Master button . A title master appears, formatted the same as the slide master.

> ★ **TIP:** You can also use these buttons to add multiple Title and Slide Master Slides. This can be used if you would like different formats on different sets of slides.

3. Leave the presentation open for the next exercise.

E X E R C I S E   **Use Drawing Tools to Create Background Graphics**

1. Working in the Title Slide Master, on the left side draw a Rectangle formatted as follows:
   - 7.5 inches tall and 1.5 inches wide
   - Two-color horizontal gradient fill using the same colors as the background and variant but with light green on the top
   - No border line
   - Aligned with the left side of the slide, extending from the top to the bottom of the slide
   - Layered underneath the text placeholders

2. Adjust the width of the title placeholder and the subtitle text placeholder so that they do not overlap the rectangle on the left side. See Figure 9-12 for the completed layout. You will make the text changes in step 5.

> ★ **TIP:** Use the Align and Distribute commands to help position the placeholders.

3. Draw a narrow vertical Rectangle that extends from the top of the slide to the bottom. Format it as follows:
   - 7.5 inches tall and 0.05 inches wide
   - Two-color horizontal gradient fill using bright green on top and light red Accent color on the bottom
   - No border
   - Positioned so that it aligns with the right edge of the rectangle you drew in step 1

4. Draw a narrow horizontal Rectangle that extends from the left side of the slide to the right side, formatted as follows:
   - 0.05 inches tall and 10 inches wide
   - Two-color vertical gradient fill using bright green on the left and light red Accent color on the right
   - No border
   - Positioned between the title placeholder and the subtitle placeholder

5. Make the following changes to title master placeholders:
   - Title placeholder: left aligned, Verdana font, bold, text shadow, dark red text color
   - Move the title placeholder up on the slide so the dark red text is on the lighter background color, and then move the horizontal thin rectangle up, too
   - Subtitle placeholder: Verdana font, bold, left align, resize to the right

FIGURE 9-12
Completed
title master

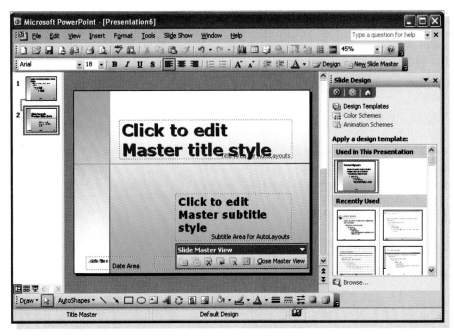

6. Copy the rectangle at the left and the two thin rectangles and paste them on the slide master. Adjust the position of the horizontal thin rectangle to fit under the title placeholder. Change the fonts to match the title master and make the title placeholder 40 points. Adjust the position of the placeholders to fit these new background graphics.

7. Return to Normal view and enter the following text so that you can see the effects of your design.

FIGURE 9-13
Text for slides

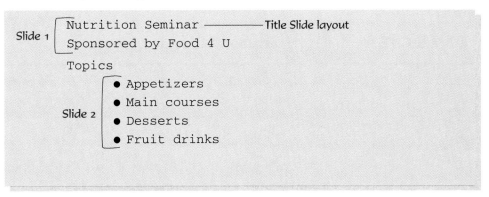

EXERCISE 9-13 **Insert Graphics on a Template**

To add interest to your design template and help to establish your presentation's theme, insert a clip art picture of an apple in the upper left of your title master. Repeat the same image in a smaller size on the slide master.

1. On the title master, insert a picture of an apple and resize as necessary. Position the apple as shown in Figure 9-14.

2. Apply an object shadow to the clip art; use Shadow Style 14. Change the shadow color to black and not semitransparent.

3. Position the apple on the rectangle at the left beside the title text.

4. Copy the apple, paste it on the slide master, resize, and position beside the slide title placeholder. Compare your finished slides to the example in Figure 9-14.

FIGURE 9-14
Completed slides

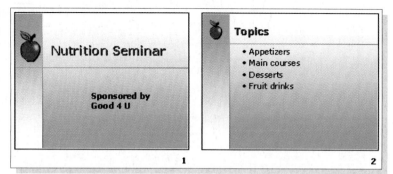

TIP: One or more images can be added to slide masters. Remember that you can recolor these images if they are Windows Metafile pictures (filename extension .wmf) to harmonize with your template's color scheme. Also, you can ungroup images, rearrange some or all parts of them, and use these modified images in your design. You can include other objects such as AutoShapes or photograph images. The effects for your background should be rather subtle so that your audience will focus on the information each slide contains.

EXERCISE 9-14 **Save a New Template**

You can save a new template in the default template directory, on your student disk, in your lesson folder, or in any other place that provides convenient access.

1. Click the Save button on the Standard toolbar to open the Save As dialog box.

2. In the Save as type drop-down list, choose Design Template. Notice that the Templates folder is displayed in the Save in box.

3. In the Save in box, navigate to your Lesson 9 folder.

4. In the File name box, key the filename **Nutrition**. Click OK. Your template is now ready to use. You can tell it is a template file because the file extension is .pot.

FIGURE 9-15
Saving a
design template

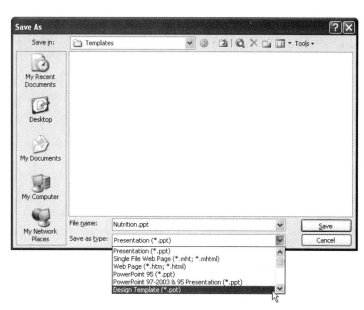

5. Close the template.

Applying Design Templates and Color Schemes from Other Presentations

If you have a presentation with a customized design template that you'd like to use again, you can apply the design from the presentation file just as if it were a design template file. The design can be applied to an entire presentation or to one or more selected slides.

If you are working with a design template that you like, but would rather use a color scheme from a different design template or a customized color scheme from a presentation, you can copy that color scheme to individual slides or an entire presentation.

EXERCISE **9-15** **Apply Templates from Other Sources**

Up to now, you have applied design templates by selecting them from the Slide Design task pane. If you have templates stored in a different location, for example, in your Lesson 9 folder, you use the **Browse** command at the bottom of the Slide Design task pane to locate them.

1. Start a new blank presentation.

2. On the Insert menu, use the Slides from Outline command to insert the Word outline **Lecture2** from your student disk.

3. If a blank slide appears at the beginning of the presentation, delete it.

4. Apply the Title Slide layout to the new slide 1, "Nutrition Seminar."

5. Display the Slide Design task pane and click Browse (at the bottom of the pane). The Apply Design Template dialog box opens.

6. In the Look in list box, navigate to your Lesson 9 folder.

7. In the Name box, choose Nutrition and click Apply. The template you created is applied to the new presentation.

8. Create a handout header and footer: include the date and your name as the header; and the page number and text *[your initials]*9-15 as the footer.

9. Move to slide 1 and save the presentation as *[your initials]*9-15.

10. Preview and then print the presentation as handouts, 6 slides per page, grayscale, framed. Keep the presentation open for the next exercise.

EXERCISE | **9-16** | **Apply a Customized Design from Another Presentation**

To apply the design from another presentation to the one on which you are currently working, click the **Browse** command at the bottom of the Slide Design task pane. This opens the Apply Design Template dialog box. Although the dialog box name implies that you should be choosing a design template, you can navigate to any folder available to your computer and choose either a design template file or a presentation file.

 NOTE: Another way to apply a presentation's design is to open the presentation and use the Format Painter button to copy the design from a slide thumbnail to selected slide thumbnails in the other presentation.

1. With the presentation *[your initials]*9-15 open, display the Slide Design task pane. You will see **Design Templates** at the top of the task pane and thumbnails are displayed.

TIP: Double-clicking the current template name in the center of the status bar (below the Slide pane) is another way to display the Slide Design task pane.

2. Click Browse at the bottom of the task pane. The Apply Design Template dialog box opens.

3. In the Look in box, navigate to your student disk. In the Files of type box, verify that either All PowerPoint Files or All PowerPoint Presentations is selected. Remember, you can choose either a presentation file or a template file in this dialog box.

FIGURE 9-16
Choosing a
presentation file to
apply its design

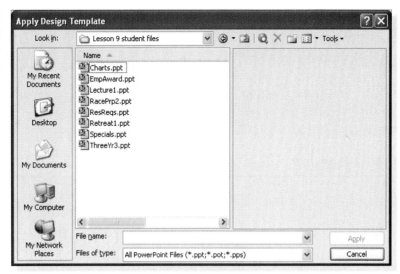

4. In the Name list box, choose **RacePrp2**. Click Apply. Scroll through the presentation. The entire look has changed.

EXERCISE **9-17** **Copy a Color Scheme from Another Presentation**

You might have a presentation with a great color scheme that you want to reuse in another presentation. You can use the Format Painter tool to copy just the color scheme (without copying the design template) from a master slide thumbnail in one presentation to a master slide thumbnail in another presentation.

1. Without closing the presentation *[your initials]*9-15, open the file **TrainPt3** from your student disk.

2. Display the slide master for the presentation **TrainPt3**.

3. Select the slide master thumbnail.

4. Double-click the Format Painter button 🖌 on the Standard toolbar.

5. Switch to *[your initials]*9-15 and display its slide master.

 6. With the Format Painter pointer ▷▲, click both the slide master and title master thumbnails.

7. Click the Format Painter button 🖌 to turn it off.

8. Scroll through the presentation. The green slides do not harmonize well with the blue ones. To correct this, you can copy the color scheme from one set of masters to the other.

NOTE: If you use the Format Painter with slide thumbnails instead of master thumbnails, the entire design template will be copied, replacing all the design elements of the original design template with the copied template elements.

9. Update the handout footer with the text *[your initials]*9-17.

10. Move to slide 1 and save the presentation as *[your initials]*9-17 in your Lesson 9 folder.

11. Preview and then print the presentation as handouts, 6 slides per page, grayscale, framed. Close the presentation. Close the **TrainPt3** presentation.

USING ONLINE HELP

When you start a new presentation, a new slide is displayed using the default blank design template. If you find that each time you start a new presentation you make the same changes to fonts, colors, or other design features, you can create a custom template that will be automatically applied to all new presentations.

Use Help to find out about changing the default design template:

1. Start a new presentation. From the Help menu, choose Microsoft Office PowerPoint Help.

 NOTE: If the Office Assistant appears, click Options and clear the Use the Office Assistant check box. Then repeat step 1.

2. In the PowerPoint Help task pane key **default design** in the Search for text box. Click the ➡ button or press Enter.

3. In the list of topics that appears, select the first topic, Change the default design for new presentations.

FIGURE 9-17
Help screen about the default design template

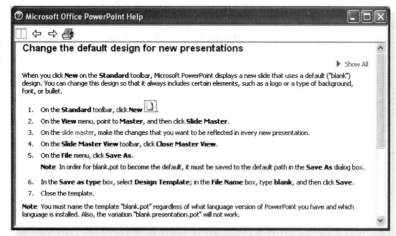

4. Read the information, then select and read other topics of interest that are displayed in the Search pane.

5. Close the Help window when you are finished.

LESSON *9* **Summary**

354
BACKGROUNDS

➤ Use the Background dialog box (F<u>o</u>rmat, Bac<u>k</u>ground) to apply a background effect to one or more slides in a presentation. Backgrounds can be solid colors, gradient fills, patterns, textures, or pictures.

➤ The Apply <u>t</u>o All command on the Background dialog box applies a background effect to all slides in a presentation. The <u>A</u>pply command applies a background effect only to slides that are currently selected.

➤ If graphic elements from a master slide interfere with the design of one or more slides, they can be hidden on those slides by selecting the Omit background graphics from master option in the Background dialog box.

➤ You can customize presentation color schemes to suit individual needs. On the Slide Design task pane, click Color Schemes and then click Edit Color Schemes. Double-click the color you want to change, and then choose a color from the Standard tab or create one by using the Custom tab.

➤ Customize a predesigned template by rearranging graphics, changing the background, repositioning placeholders, and changing font treatments.

➤ Create a new design template by changing and adding elements on the slide and title masters of a blank presentation. Save it as a template by choosing Design Template in the Save as <u>t</u>ype list box in the Save As dialog box.

➤ Presentation design templates can be applied directly from one presentation to another. Select the slide thumbnails to which you want to apply a design, click Browse in the Slide Design task pane, select the presentation you want to use, and click A<u>p</u>ply.

➤ When you use the Format Painter button ![icon] on a master thumbnail, it copies only the color scheme and background effect. Copy the color scheme to a different presentation by clicking its master thumbnails with the Format Painter pointer ↳♣.

LESSON 9	Command Summary		
FEATURE	BUTTON	MENU	KEYBOARD
Format background		F<u>o</u>rmat, Bac<u>k</u>ground	
Omit master graphics from a slide		F<u>o</u>rmat, Bac<u>k</u>ground, Omit background graphics from master	
Save a design template		<u>F</u>ile, Save <u>A</u>s, choose Design Template from Save as <u>t</u>ype box	
Customize a color scheme		F<u>o</u>rmat, Slide <u>D</u>esign, Color Schemes, Edit Color Schemes	

Concepts Review

TRUE/FALSE QUESTIONS

Each of the following statements is either true or false. Indicate your choice by circling T or F.

T F **1.** You can create gradient fills for slide backgrounds.

T **F** **2.** If you choose a picture for a background, it must be applied to only one slide.

T F **3.** You can omit background graphics from individual slides.

T F **4.** It is possible to modify an existing design template to fit a unique presentation theme.

T **F** **5.** A PowerPoint color scheme consists of 10 colors.

T F **6.** You can use both standard colors and custom colors in a color scheme.

T F **7.** You can save a design template on a floppy disk.

T **F** **8.** If you want to apply a design from a different presentation, you must first save the current presentation as a design template.

SHORT ANSWER QUESTIONS

Write the correct answer in the space provided.

1. How do you access the background dialog box?

FORMAT MENU

2. How do you apply a background to only slide 2 in a presentation?

SELECT SLIDE 2 - OPEN BACKGROUND DIALOG BOX
CHOOSE FILL APPLY

3. What must you use to rearrange a design template's graphics?

MASTER VIEW

4. How do you open the Edit Color Scheme dialog box?

SLIDE DESIGN TASK PANE CLICK COLOR SCHEME

5. When customizing a presentation's color scheme, what is the maximum number of colors that you can change?

_8_

6. How do you apply a design template that does not appear on the Slide Design task pane?

CLICK BROWSE

7. What are the four kinds of fill effects that you can apply to backgrounds?

GRADIENT   PATTERN -PICTURE   TEXTURE

8. If you are using the Format Painter button, what must you first select to copy a color scheme but not design template graphics?

MASTER   SLIDE   THUMBNAIL

CRITICAL THINKING

Answer these questions on a separate page. There are no right or wrong answers. Support your answers with examples from your own experience, if possible.

1. You can apply a background directly to master slides, or you can use the Background dialog box. Describe situations in which you would prefer one method over the other.

2. Describe a situation where it might be more productive to modify a current design template than to create a new one.

Skills Review

EXERCISE 9-18

Create background effects.

1. Open the presentation **Retreat1**.
2. Change the background for the entire presentation by following these steps:
   a. From the Format menu, choose Background.
   b. In the Background dialog box, click the down arrow on the sample color box and choose Fill Effects.
   c. Choose a one-color horizontal fill effect using dark green (shadows scheme color) with the shading slider slightly to the left of center. Use the shading style variant with the lightest color in the middle. Click OK to close the Fill Effects dialog box.
   d. Click Apply to All.
3. Change the background for just one slide by following these steps:
   a. Select slide 1.
   b. From the Format menu, choose Background.
   c. Click the down arrow on the sample color box and choose Fill Effects.

     d. Click the Picture tab and click Select Picture.

     e. In the Select Picture dialog box, navigate to your student disk and choose the file **Wtrfall1**. Click Insert.

     f. Check the box labeled Lock picture aspect ratio.

     g. Click OK to close the Fill Effects dialog box. Click Apply to apply the picture to only the selected slide.

4. To make the text more legible, draw a Rectangle AutoShape large enough to cover all the text and then send the rectangle to the back.

5. Right-click the rectangle and choose Format AutoShape to change the rectangle's color to dark green (shadows scheme color) with 30% transparency and remove its border.

6. Adjust the size and position of the rectangle so that it frames all the text attractively.

7. Change the grayscale setting for the background on slide 1 to Grayscale. Change the grayscale setting for the transparent rectangle to White.

8. Create a handout header and footer: include the date and your name as the header, and the page number and text *[your initials]*9-18 as the footer.

9. Move to slide 1 and save the presentation as *[your initials]*9-18 in your Lesson 9 folder.

10. Preview and then print the presentation as handouts, 4 slides per page, grayscale, landscape, framed. Close the presentation.

EXERCISE 9-19

Customize a design template and edit the presentation color scheme.

1. Open the presentation file **RacePrp2**.

2. Go to the presentation Master view by choosing the View menu, Slide master, and select the Title master thumbnail.

3. On the Slide master, select the rectangle filled with the checkerboard pattern, change its fill to a solid black, and move it down slightly below the center of the slide. Reduce its height slightly, too.

4. Modify the gradient fill shading style for the title slide background and choose From center with the darkest color in the center.

5. Create a rectangle with a white fill for the top half of the slide. Send this rectangle behind the title placeholder.

6. Move the subtitle placeholder down slightly.

7. On the clip art image of the runner, click to select the shirt and change it to red.

8. Search for a race flag with a black-and-white flag on a red shape and insert the image on the right side of the slide. Now it looks as if the runner is going toward the finish line.

9. Reduce the width of the title placeholder so that it fits between the two images. Change the title and subtitle placeholders to center alignment and then align both placeholders relative to the slide.

10. Edit a color scheme color by following these steps:
   a. Display the Slide Design task pane and then click Color Schemes.
   b. At the bottom of the Slide Design task pane, click Edit Color Schemes.
   c. Select the Title text color sample and click Change Color.
   d. In the Title Text Color dialog box, select a darker shade of blue that matches the blue color in the Good 4 U logo. Click OK.

11. Edit other color scheme colors by following these steps:
   a. Double-click the Shadows color sample.
   b. In the Shadow Color dialog box, click the Custom tab.
   c. Under Colors, drag the crosshair down and to the left a little until the color matches the gold color in the Good 4 U logo. Click OK.

12. Create a new standard color scheme from the new colors you chose above and then apply the new color scheme by following these steps:
   a. In the Edit Color Scheme dialog box, click Add As Standard Scheme.
   b. Click the Standard tab and verify that the new color scheme appears as one of the samples.
   c. Click Apply and then change the zoom setting to Fit.

13. Modify the title text on both the title master and the slide master to remove the current shadow and change the color to dark blue.

14. On the slide master, change the background to solid white. Change the runner's shirt to red to match the title master.

15. Create a handout header and footer: include the date and your name as the header, and the page number and text [your initials]9-19 as the footer.

16. Move to slide 1 and save the presentation as [your initials]9-19 in your Lesson 9 folder.

17. Preview and then print the presentation as handouts, 3 slides per page, grayscale, framed.

EXERCISE 9-20

Apply a background effect, create and save a custom template, and apply the template to a presentation.

1. Start a new blank presentation with the default template in effect. Choose the color scheme with the black background.

2. Create a custom template by following these steps:
   a. Display the slide master.

b. Apply a patterned background to the slide master that uses the Wide upward diagonal pattern, black for the <u>B</u>ackground color, and red (a custom color) for the <u>F</u>oreground color.

c. Change the font in both the title text placeholder and the body text placeholder to Comic Sans MS if it is available, or choose another informal sans serif font. Increase the font size of the title placeholder to 54 points and move it up slightly.

d. Draw a large, black, borderless, Rounded Rectangle with the dimensions 6.85 inches by 9.35 inches. Send it behind the text placeholders and center it both vertically and horizontally relative to the slide.

e. Move both placeholders down slightly. Change the title text to white and the body text to light gray.

f. Insert a small picture of a calendar or appointment book in the lower-right corner of the black rounded rectangle. Choose a picture that will stand out against the black background (or change its colors to work with the background).

g. In Grayscale view, change the settings to <u>W</u>hite for the rectangle with rounded corners. Change the background grayscale setting to <u>I</u>nverse Grayscale so that the pattern shows. Return to color view.

h. Click the Insert New Title Master button ▣ on the Slide Master View toolbar.

3. Save a presentation as a template by following these steps:

a. From the <u>F</u>ile menu, choose Save <u>A</u>s.

b. In the Save as type list box, choose Design Template.

c. In the Save <u>i</u>n list box, navigate to your Lesson 9 folder.

d. In the File name box, key **BlackBoard**. Click <u>S</u>ave. Close the design template file.

4. Open the presentation file **ResReqs**.

5. Apply the template you created by following these steps:

a. Display the Slide Design task pane and click Design Templates.

b. At the bottom of the task pane, click Browse.

c. Navigate to your Lesson 9 folder and select BlackBoard from the Name list. Click Apply.

6. Adjust placeholder positioning on the title master and slide master if needed. You may need to adjust your calendar position, too.

7. Create a handout header and footer: include the date and your name as the header, and the page number and text *[your initials]*9-20 as the footer.

8. Move to slide 1 and save the presentation as *[your initials]*9-20 in your Lesson 9 folder.

9. Preview and then print the presentation as handouts, 4 slides per page, grayscale, landscape, framed.

EXERCISE 9-21

Apply a design template and a color scheme from other presentations.

1. Start a new presentation and insert slides from an outline by using the Word document file **Lecture2**.

2. If the first slide is blank, delete it. Apply the Title layout to the new first slide ("Nutrition Seminar").

3. Apply a design template from another presentation by following these steps:

   a. Display the Slide Design task pane and click Browse at the bottom of the task pane.

   b. In the Files of type list box, verify that All PowerPoint Files or All PowerPoint Presentations is selected.

   c. Navigate to the location where your student files are stored and select the presentation file **Specials**. Click Apply.

4. Apply a color scheme from another presentation by following these steps:

   a. Without closing the new presentation, open the presentation file **Ads1** and display its slide master.

   b. Select the slide master thumbnail; then double-click the Format Painter button.

   c. Switch to the Nutrition Seminar presentation and display its slide master.

   d. With the Format Painter tool still active, click the slide master and the title master to transfer the copied color scheme.

   e. Click the Format Painter button (or press Esc) to turn off Format Painter.

   f. Close the presentation **Ads1** without saving it.

5. Working on the Nutrition Seminar presentation, replace the clip art on the title master and the slide master with an image of food that blends with the new color scheme. If the image has a background color, remove it using the Transparent color button on the Picture toolbar. Create a border by copying an image in a small size across the top of the title master.

6. On the slide master's body text placeholder, add bullets in a shape of your choice that are appropriately colored and sized. Copy the clip art image from the title master, make it smaller, and position it in the upper left. Change the title placeholder to left alignment. Add a 6-point line in an orange color.

7. Switch to the title master. If the subtitle has a bullet, remove it. Make both placeholders right aligned. Increase the title placeholder to 54 points and choose a softer yellow color for the subtitle placeholder. Move the box with the dotted line up slightly and move the subtitle placeholder down slightly.

8. Change the title color on both masters to orange.

9. On slide 6, remove the bullets from the body text placeholder and press `Enter` to add blank space between each item to emphasize them more.

10. Scroll through each slide, making adjustments necessary for a pleasing composition.

11. Create a handout header and footer: include the date and your name as the header, and the page number and text *[your initials]*9-21 as the footer.

12. Move to slide 1 and save the presentation as *[your initials]*9-21 in your Lesson 9 folder.

13. Preview and then print the presentation as handouts, 6 slides per page, grayscale, framed.

Lesson Applications

Create individual custom background colors for each slide in a presentation and make placeholder adjustments.

1. Open the presentation **AdMedia2** and apply the **Crayons** design template.

2. Working in the Outline pane, make the following changes to text:
   - Move the "Electronic" bulleted text from the middle of slide 4 to the bottom of slide 3 (which is titled "Media Categories").
   - Move the "Newspapers" bulleted text from the middle of slide 3 to the bottom of slide 5 (which is titled "Print Media").
   - Switch the order of slide 4 ("Electronic Media") and slide 5 ("Print Media").

3. Create a custom background for slide 2 only by using a horizontal gradient with white on the top and shading to light yellow on the bottom.

4. Create the same style gradient for the backgrounds of slides 3 through 6 with the bottom yellow gradient color for each slide getting progressively more saturated (more intense or a deeper color) until the color for slide 6 is the gold color used for the crayon.

5. On the title master, make the title placeholder text bold, 48 points, and center aligned. Move it down slightly. Make the subtitle text bold and reduce the size of the placeholder slightly so that the text will word wrap on the yellow area of the slide.

6. On the slide master, make the title placeholder text bold, shadow, left aligned, and red to match the title slide. Reduce the size of the body placeholder and move it down slightly and to the right.

7. Change the first-level bullet to a check mark from the Wingdings 2 Symbol set. Make it red and 130% of the text size.

8. View the presentation as a slide show. Make any final adjustments that are needed in placeholder positioning.

9. Check the presentation's grayscale settings and make any changes that might be necessary.

10. Create a handout header and footer: include the date and your name as the header, and the page number and text *[your initials]*9-22 as the footer.

11. Move to slide 1 and save the presentation as *[your initials]*9-22 in your Lesson 9 folder.

12. View the presentation as a slide show. Preview and then print the presentation as handouts, 6 slides per page, framed, in color if available, otherwise in grayscale. Close the presentation.

Customize a presentation, customize a color scheme, and insert slides from another presentation.

1. Open the file **ThreeYr3**.

2. Change the accent and followed hyperlink color to a medium shade of blue; then add the customized color scheme as a standard scheme. Apply the new scheme to the presentation.

3. On the slide master, draw a Rectangle the width of the slide and 2.75" tall. Position it at the bottom of the slide master. Apply a two-color horizontal gradient fill that shades from white at the top to medium blue at the bottom. Remove the rectangle's border and send it to the back.

4. To the blue semicircle on the slide master, apply a gradient fill that shades from white in the center to blue on the outside. To the yellow semicircle, apply the same style fill that shades from white in the center to yellow on the outside.

5. Copy the blue-and-white rectangle to the title master and send it to the back.

6. Use the Format Painter to copy the formatting of the blue and yellow shapes on the slide master to the title master.

7. Make the title placeholder text bold on both the title master and the slide master.

8. After the last slide of the **AdMedia2** presentation, insert two slides from the **Charts** presentation. Be sure to use the design template formatting when inserting the slides.

   REVIEW: To insert slides from another presentation, use the Slides from Files command on the Insert menu. To keep the source formatting, click the checkbox in the lower-left corner of the Slide Finder dialog box.

9. Working in the Outline pane, move slide 5 ("Past Performance") before slide 4 ("Time to Expand").

10. Check the presentation's grayscale settings and make any changes that might be necessary.

11. Create a handout header and footer: include the date and your name as the header, and the page number and text *[your initials]*9-23 as the footer.

12. Move to slide 1 and save the presentation as *[your initials]*9-23 in your Lesson 9 folder.

13. View the presentation as a slide show; then preview and print the presentation as handouts, 6 slides per page, grayscale, framed. Close the presentation.

Create a new design template, save it as a new template, and use the template to create a presentation.

1. Start a new blank presentation.

2. Copy the color scheme from the presentation file **EmpAward** to the blank presentation using the master slides and Format Painter. Make it a standard color scheme.

3. Insert a new title master.

4. On the title master, draw a Rectangle, 2.85 inches tall by 3.95 inches wide. Format it as follows:
   - One-color gradient fill using bright purple, shading to medium dark
   - 50% From transparency and 50% To transparency
   - Diagonal up gradient fill, darkest color in the upper-left corner
   - No border
   - Inverse Grayscale setting

5. Duplicate the rectangle three times (total of four rectangles); then distribute the rectangles horizontally and vertically relative to the slide. The rectangles should be arranged in an overlapping diagonal pattern from the upper-left corner to the lower-right corner of the slide.

6. Group the rectangles, send them to the back behind the text placeholders, and then copy the grouped rectangles to the slide master. (Do not send the rectangles to the back on the slide master.)

7. On the slide master, ungroup the rectangles, delete the third one from the top, and make the second rectangle larger by dragging its lower-right corner down and to the right. See Figure 9-18.

FIGURE 9-18
Layout for
slide master

8. Group the three rectangles and send them to the back. Adjust the size and position of the body text placeholder so that it coincides with the large purple rectangle.

9. Using the Replace Font command, change the font for the entire presentation to Tahoma.

10. On the slide master, make the following changes to the body text placeholder:

- Change the text color to white.
- Change the bullet to a square in light purple.
- Reduce the text by one font size.

11. Left-align the text in the title placeholder and use 36 points, bold.

12. On the title master, resize and rearrange the title placeholder so that its left edge aligns with the left edge of the second rectangle. Make the text bold and 44 points. Resize the subtitle placeholder so that its left edge aligns with the third rectangle. Left-align the subtitle text, make it bold and 32 points. Refer to Figure 9-19.

FIGURE 9-19
Arrangement
for title master

13. Save the presentation as a design template in your Lesson 9 folder with the filename **Boxes**. Close the file.

14. Start a new presentation and apply the **Boxes** template that you just created. Key the text for the slides shown in Figure 9-20 (on the next page). Use the Title Slide layout for slide 1 and the Title and Text layout for the other slides.

15. On the title slide, increase the size of the title placeholder slightly so that the text will fit in the 48 point size.

16. Check spelling and grayscale settings and make any necessary changes.

FIGURE 9-20

Slide 1
```
Staff Fitness Program ————Title

  A New Benefit

  for Employees
```

Slide 2
```
We Encourage Employee Fitness————Title

  ●  Strong, healthy employees enhance our image

  ●  A high level of fitness reduces accident rates

  ●  Healthy employees are happy employees
```

Slide 3
```
How the Exercise Program Works ————Title

  ●  A customized fitness program is created for each employee

  ●  A fitness professional is available for 2 hours prior to
     every work shift

  ●  An employee bonus program rewards consistent workouts
```

Slide 4
```
How the Nutrition Program Works ————Title

  ●  Staff nutritionists work individually with each employee

  ●  An individual healthy diet plan is developed

  ●  Monthly nutrition lectures are planned

  ●  Private monthly nutrition consultation available for each
     employee
```

17. Create a handout header and footer: include the date and your name as the header, and the page number and text *[your initials]*9-24 as the footer.

18. Move to slide 1 and save the presentation as a Web page in your Lesson 9 folder with the filename *[your initials]*9-24. View the presentation in your Web browser.

19. Preview and then print the presentation as handouts, 4 slides per page, landscape, grayscale, framed. Close the presentation.

Apply pictures to slide backgrounds, alter master slide graphics, and change a color scheme.

1. Open the file **Funding2** and apply the Radial design template. Choose the color scheme that has a black background with purple, blue, and pale yellow accents.

2. On the title master and slide master, make the following changes:
    *   On each master slide, delete the vertical rectangle on the right side of each master slide. Select the remaining graphic elements and ungroup them.
    *   On the slide master, select the rounded rectangle behind the body text placeholder and apply a white fill (use the title text scheme color, fourth sample from the left) with 30% transparency. Use Format Painter to apply this color to the rounded rectangle on the title master and the rectangle above the title on the title master.
    *   Edit the presentation color scheme to change the text and lines scheme color to black.
    *   Change the title placeholders for both masters to Arial Black. Change the title master subtitle text font to Arial Black, too.
    *   On the title master, position the Good 4 U logo at the bottom center of the rounded rectangle.

3. After slide 2, insert slide 3 ("Financial History," white background) from the presentation file **Charts** on your student disk. Do not keep the source formatting. Make the table text white and bold. Change the fill color to purple to match the shape behind the slide title text. Center the table on the rounded rectangle.

4. Locate a suitable picture for the background of the title slide. Be sure to lock the picture's aspect ratio.

5. If necessary, edit the color scheme for the presentation to harmonize with your title slide background picture.

6. Change the grayscale settings so that your background picture appears in grayscale shades, but still allowing enough contrast so that the text is legible.

7. Create a handout header and footer: include the date and your name as the header, and the page number and text *[your initials]*9-25 as the footer.

8. Move to slide 1 and save the presentation as *[your initials]*9-25 in your Lesson 9 folder.

9. Preview and then print the presentation as handouts, 6 slides per page, grayscale, framed. Close the presentation.

On Your Own

In these exercises you work on your own, as you would in a real-life work environment. Use the skills you've learned to accomplish the task—and be creative.

EXERCISE 9-26
Open the file **Funding2**. Change the design template and graphics. Use any tools you have learned about up to this point to create a unique design template expressing your own taste, but remember to keep a uniform look throughout that harmonizes with the presentation's subject matter. Save the presentation as *[your initials]*9-26. Preview and then print the presentation as handouts.

EXERCISE 9-27
Open the presentation **AdMedia2** and review the content, then close the presentation. Create a new design template and use your own creativity to make it interesting and attractive. Save the template as *[your initials]*9-27Design. Open the presentation **AdMedia2** again then apply the template you created. Save the presentation as *[your initials]*9-27. Preview and then print the presentation as handouts.

EXERCISE 9-28
Search the Web for information on your favorite music group or singer. Condense the information into major points and use these points to create a presentation of at least six slides. Using the tools you learned in this lesson and in previous lessons, create a template and format your presentation attractively and in keeping with the theme of your choice of music group. Save the presentation as *[your initials]*9-28. Preview and then print the presentation as handouts.

LESSON 10

Controlling Layout Options

OBJECTIVES

**MICROSOFT OFFICE
SPECIALIST
ACTIVITIES**

In this lesson:
 PP03S-2-1
 PP03S-2-3
 PP03S-4-1

See Appendix.

After completing this lesson, you will be able to:

1. Adjust indents by using the ruler.
2. Set tab stops, edit tab stops, and create a tabbed table.
3. Control line spacing and paragraph spacing.
4. Use grids and guides to control layout.
5. Work with text in AutoShapes.
6. Work with page setup options.
7. Customize handout masters and notes masters.

 Estimated Time: 1 hour

In earlier lessons you learned how to add text to a slide and change text attributes such as color, font, font style, and font size. In this lesson you learn how to change the indent settings, set tab stops and line spacing, and manipulate text in other ways.

Working with Indents

Each text placeholder has a ruler you can use to change paragraph indents and tab settings. These settings affect all text in a placeholder or text box. To apply different settings to some of the text, you put that text in a separate text box.

EXERCISE 10-1 **Remove Bullets and Adjust Paragraph Indents**

PowerPoint provides three types of paragraph indents:

- *Normal indent*—where all the lines are indented the same amount from the left margin
- *Hanging indent*—where the first line of the paragraph extends farther to the left than the rest of the paragraph
- *First-line indent*—where the first line of the paragraph is indented farther to the right than the other lines in the paragraph

An example of these paragraph indents is shown in Figure 10-1 with different colors behind the text so that you can better distinguish between the type of indents.

FIGURE 10-1
Paragraph indents

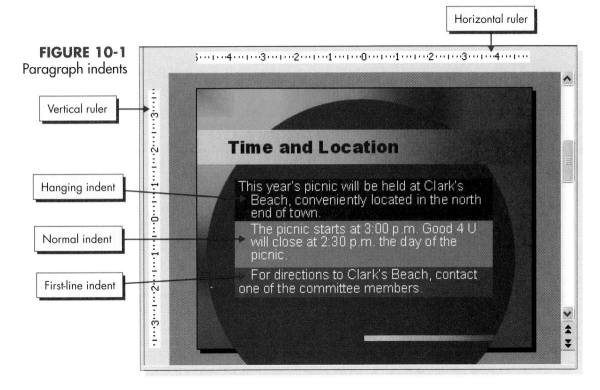

You set indents by using the ruler. If the ruler is displayed, you can see and manipulate *indent markers* when you activate a text object for editing. Indent markers are the two small triangles and the small rectangle that appear on the left side of the ruler.

1. Open the file **Outing1**.
2. From the <u>V</u>iew menu, choose <u>R</u>uler to display the ruler. The vertical and horizontal rulers appear.

NOTE: Ruler is a toggle command. Choose it once to display the rulers; choose it again to hide them.

3. Move to slide 2 and select the body text placeholder. Remove the bullets. The paragraphs now have hanging indents.

4. Click anywhere within the placeholder as if you were planning to edit some text. Notice the indent markers that appear on the horizontal ruler. Also notice that the white portion of the ruler indicates the width of the text placeholder.

 NOTE: You must have an insertion point somewhere inside a text box to change settings on the ruler. The appearance of the ruler reflects whether the entire placeholder is selected or the insertion point is active within the placeholder.

5. Point to the first-line indent marker on the ruler (the top triangle) and drag it to the right, to the 1-inch mark. The first line of each paragraph is now indented. Notice that each paragraph in the placeholder is indented the same way. To create different indents for different paragraphs, you must put them in separate text boxes.

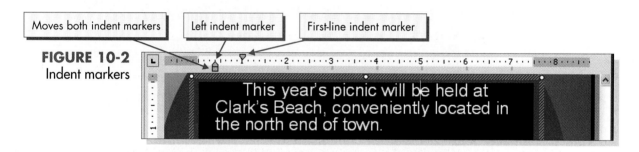

FIGURE 10-2
Indent markers

6. Drag the small rectangle (below the bottom triangle) to the zero mark on the ruler (the left edge of the white portion). Notice that both triangles move when you drag the rectangle.

7. Drag the left indent marker (bottom triangle) to the right until it aligns with the first-line indent marker (the top triangle). Now all the lines of the paragraphs are indented the same amount.

8. Drag the small rectangle to the zero mark on the ruler once again. Now there are no indents in this placeholder.

EXERCISE   10-2   Change Indents After Bullets

At times you might want to change the distance between the bullets and text in a text placeholder. For example, you may use a large bullet that causes the text that follows it to word-wrap unevenly. You can easily adjust this spacing by dragging one of the indent markers to the left or right.

1. Move to slide 3. Click within the left body text placeholder (containing "Veggie burgers"). Notice the position of the indent markers.

2. Point to the left indent marker (the bottom triangle, not the small rectangle) and drag it to the right, to the 1-inch mark on the ruler. The text is now indented 1 inch, but the bullet remains in its original position. Drag the left indent marker to the left, to the 0.5-inch mark.

3. Click within the right bulleted text placeholder and drag the left indent marker to the right, to the 0.5-inch mark.

TIP: Indents can be controlled through the slide master to keep a consistent look throughout the presentation. However, formatting that you apply to individual slides before you change the master is not changed by the master slide. To make master slide changes take effect on those slides, reapply the slide layout.

4. Create a new folder for Lesson 10 and save the presentation as *[your initials]***10-2** in your new folder for Lesson 10 but do not print it. Leave the presentation open for the next exercise.

Working with Tabs

You can set tabs to create simple tables in PowerPoint. You set tabs the same way you set tabs in Word, and they are left-aligned by default. In PowerPoint, however, default tabs are set at 1-inch intervals. To set your own tabs, click the Tab Type button ⬛ (in the upper-left corner of the Slide pane, where the two rulers meet) to choose the alignment style. Then click the ruler at the location where you want the tab.

EXERCISE   10-3   Set Tabs

1. Insert a new slide after slide 2 that uses the Title Only slide layout.

2. Key the title **Picnic Committee Award Winners** and extend the title placeholder to the right edge of the slide so that this text does not word-wrap.

3. Draw a text box at least 7 inches wide, positioning the upper-left corner about 1.5 inches below the word "Picnic."

4. Key the following, pressing (Tab) where indicated:

Darin Haley(Tab)**Sports Program**(Tab)**4798**(Tab)**112.76**

5. Select the text box and change the font to 20-point Arial.

6. Using the Format Text Box dialog box, make the width of the text box exactly 7 inches.

 REVIEW: Right-click the text box and choose Format Text B̲ox from the shortcut menu. Click the Size tab and set the Wi̲dth to **7**.

7. Click anywhere within the text box to activate the text box ruler.

 8. Click the Tab Type button [L] at the left end of the horizontal ruler. Each time you click the button, a different tab type icon appears, enabling you to cycle through the four tab type choices.

 NOTE: Tabs are set when the tab type symbol appears on the ruler. It might take some practice before you are comfortable with tab type selection and tab placement.

TABLE 10-1

Types of Tabs

TAB	PURPOSE
[L]	Left-aligns text at the tab setting
[⊥]	Centers text at the tab setting
[⌐]	Right-aligns text at the tab setting
[⊥]	Aligns decimal points at the tab setting

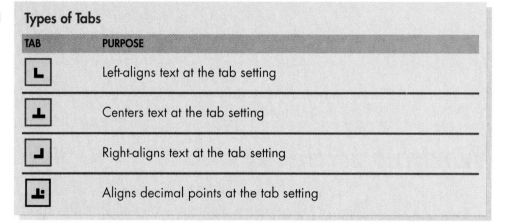

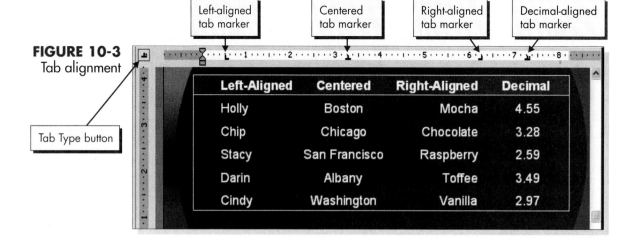

FIGURE 10-3
Tab alignment

Tab Type button

9. Click the Tab Type button one or more times until the center-aligned tab icon appears. Click the ruler at the 3-inch position. The text "Sports Program" moves so that it is centered under the tab marker.

10. Set a left-aligned tab marker at the 4.75-inch mark and a decimal-aligned tab marker at the 6.375-inch mark (the third tick mark after 6 inches). Note that the last number you keyed moves to align its decimal point with the tab.

TIP: When setting tabs, you might want to increase the zoom setting for an enlarged view of the ruler.

EXERCISE **10-4** **Edit Tabs**

After tabs are set, tabbed text that you key will automatically align under the tab markers you placed on the ruler.

You can change the position of a text column by dragging its tab marker to a new place on the ruler. To remove a tab marker, drag it down and off the ruler.

1. Working in the text box you created on slide 3, position the insertion point at the end of the line and press Enter to start a new line.

2. Key the balance of the table, shown in Figure 10-4, pressing Tab between columns and pressing Enter at the end of each line. The text you key might extend below the bottom border of the text box. You fix that in step 6.

FIGURE 10-4
Creating a
tabbed table

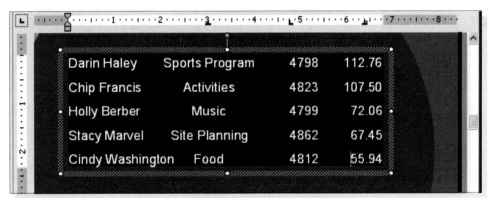

3. Click inside the text box. Drag the center-aligned tab marker from the 3-inch position on the ruler to 3.25 inches. The entire column moves to the right.

4. Drag the center-aligned marker down and off the ruler to remove it. The table realigns in an unattractive way.

5. Click the Undo button to restore the table's appearance.

6. Select the entire text box by clicking its border. Adjust its height to fit the text (you might need to make the text box taller) and add a 1.5-point white border.

EXERCISE **10-5** **Create Column Headings for a Tabbed Table**

Because tab and indent settings in PowerPoint affect all text in a placeholder, you might need to put column headings in a separate text box to align them independently from the table columns.

1. Still working on slide 3, create a second text box above the table, making it the same width as the table. You fine-tune the size and position later.

2. Key the following in the text box:

   Name⟨Tab⟩Responsibility⟨Tab⟩Extension⟨Tab⟩Points

3. Change the font to 20-point Arial and adjust the vertical position of the text box if it overlaps the table.

4. Set the following tabs in the heading text box:

   Center-aligned: 3.25-inch mark
   Center-aligned: 5.00-inch mark
   Right-aligned: 6.75-inch mark

5. Add a 1.5-point white border to the heading text box and add a purple fill color.

6. Adjust the position of the heading text box so that its bottom border touches the top border of the table. Left-align the text boxes in relation to each other.

FIGURE 10-5
Completed table with column headings

7. Adjust the width of the heading text box, if necessary, so that it is the same width as the table text box.

8. Adjust the tab marker positions in the heading text box, if necessary, so that the headings align above the table columns, as shown in Figure 10-5.

9. Select both text boxes and group them. Then position them attractively on the slide so that they appear centered in the large circle shape.

10. Save the presentation as *[your initials]*10-5 in your Lesson 10 folder but do not print it. Leave the presentation open for the next exercise.

Controlling Line Spacing

You can control line spacing by adding more space between the lines in a paragraph or by adding more space between paragraphs. Increased line spacing can make your text layout easier to read and enhance the overall design of a slide.

EXERCISE | **10-6** | **Change Line Spacing within Paragraphs**

To change spacing between lines within a paragraph, you can:

● Open the Format menu and choose Line Spacing.

● Click the Increase Paragraph Spacing button or the Decrease Paragraph Spacing button on the Formatting toolbar. These buttons increase or decrease the space between lines within a paragraph by increments of 0.1 lines.

 NOTE: The Increase Paragraph Spacing and Decrease Paragraph Spacing buttons might not appear on the toolbar. To find them, click the Toolbar Options button , click Add or Remove Buttons from the drop-down menu, choose Formatting, and then click the paragraph spacing buttons on the submenu to place them on the Formatting toolbar.

1. Move to slide 2. Click within the first paragraph in the placeholder.

2. From the Format menu, choose Line Spacing. The Line Spacing dialog box appears.

FIGURE 10-6
Line Spacing
dialog box

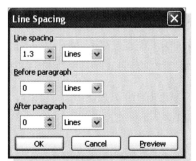

3. Under Line Spacing, key **1.3** or click the spin box up arrow until 1.3 appears. Click Preview to view the changes. The line spacing of the first paragraph has increased. Click OK to accept the changes.

NOTE: The default unit of measurement for line and paragraph spacing is lines. You can change the measurement to points, if you prefer, by clicking the arrow next to Lines and choosing Points.

4. Usually you will want to change the line spacing for an entire text placeholder. Select the placeholder, reopen the Line Spacing dialog box, and change the Line spacing to **0.9** lines. Click Preview to see the results and then click OK.

EXERCISE **10-7** **Change Spacing Between Paragraphs**

You have seen how to change line spacing in text placeholders. You can also change the amount of space before or after paragraphs by using options in the Line Spacing dialog box.

1. Still working on slide 2, click within the second paragraph and open the Line Spacing dialog box.

2. Under Before paragraph, change the line setting to **2** lines.

3. Click Preview to view the changes. Click OK. Notice that the AutoFit Options button appears. It automatically reduced the text size to accommodate the extra space before the paragraph.

4. To make all paragraph spacing uniform, select the entire text placeholder and open the Line Spacing dialog box. Change the Before paragraph spacing to **1** line and the After paragraph spacing to **0**. (The Line spacing setting should remain at 0.9 lines.) Click OK. The text is now evenly spaced in the placeholder.

5. Adjust the text placeholder font size to 24 points, if necessary.

  NOTE: If the AutoFit body text to placeholder feature is turned on, the text may automatically be resized. You can control this by clicking the AutoFit Options button that appears at the lower-left corner of the text box.

6. Save the presentation as *[your initials]***10-7** in your Lesson 10 folder but do not print it. Leave the presentation open for the next exercise.

Using Grids and Guides

Grids and guides can make the task of aligning objects easier for you by providing visible lines that help you judge where to place objects in relation to other objects and the slide as a whole.

Grids and guides are not visible during a presentation, but they are powerful tools for consistent positioning of slide objects when designing the presentation.

EXERCISE   10-8 Align Using Grid

The Grid and Guides dialog box enables you to set up a visible or invisible grid. Grid spacing can be adjusted from very fine up to two-inch spacing to suit a variety of drawing tasks. In general, you work with grid spacing of 1/16 inch or less (0.063 inches).

There are three ways to access the Grid and Guides dialog box:

- From the View menu, choose Grid and Guides.
- Click Draw on the Drawing toolbar and choose Grid and Guides.
- Press Ctrl + G.

If you set grids to a large increment—anything over 1/10 inch—it is a good idea to return the grid to its default setting when you are finished. Otherwise, objects will jump to positions where you might not want them to go.

1. Move to slide 5 ("The Entertainment Committee").

2. Click Draw on the Drawing toolbar and then choose Grid and Guides. The Grid and Guides dialog box opens.

3. If it is not already selected, check the box labeled Snap objects to grid.

FIGURE 10-7
Setting grid spacing

4. Under Grid settings, click the arrow next to the Spacing box and choose 0.5" from the drop-down list. Check the Display grid on screen option and click OK.

5. Working on slide 5, drag the clip art image diagonally up and to the left. Notice how it "jumps" instead of moving smoothly.

FIGURE 10-8
Working with a half-inch grid setting

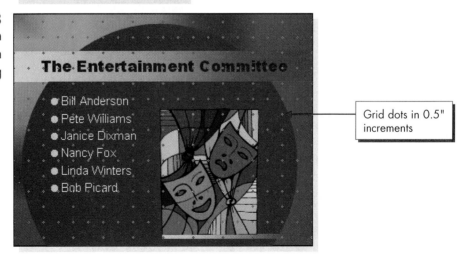

Grid dots in 0.5" increments

6. Drag the image to a different position, this time observing the dotted line indicators on the rulers. The indicators jump in half-inch increments.

7. Hold down [Alt] while you drag the image. The image now moves smoothly. [Alt] temporarily turns off the Snap objects to grid option.

8. Position the image so that the top of it aligns with the top of the text box.

9. From the View menu, choose Grid and Guides (this is another way to access the same dialog box).

10. From the Spacing drop-down list, choose 1/16" (0.063"). Leave the Display grid on screen option turned on. Click OK. The grid is now returned to its original setting and the dots are displayed.

EXERCISE 10-9 Remove Snap to Grid

When you want complete control for where objects are positioned, then you can turn off the Snap objects to grid feature. When this feature is disabled, you can also fine-tune object positioning by nudging with the arrow keys.

1. Still working on slide 5, from the View menu, choose Grid and Guides.

2. Click the box Snap objects to grid. This removes the Snap objects to grid feature and allows the object to move smoothly around the slide.

3. Click on the clip art image and drag the image. Notice that it moves without jumping from grid line to grid line.

4. Nudge the clip art image with the arrow keys to move in very small increments.

 REVIEW: If you just want to remove the Snap objects to grid feature temporarily, use the [Alt] key.

5. From the View Menu, choose Grids and Guides and uncheck the Display grid on screen box to remove the gridlines. Click OK to close the dialog box.

EXERCISE 10-10 Align Using Guide

Guides offer a great degree of flexibility. They can be added, removed, and repositioned without the need to open a dialog box. As with grids, they aid in the alignment and positioning of objects on a slide.

You move a guide by dragging it with your standard mouse pointer. Be careful: when moving a guide, make sure you are not dragging an I-beam or a two- or four-pointed arrow by mistake. If you do, you will instead either be selecting text or moving an object.

TABLE 10-2   Working with Guides

PRESS	TO DO THIS (WHILE DRAGGING A GUIDE)
Shift	Measure the distance from the guide's starting position to its new position
Ctrl	Add a new guide
Shift + Ctrl	Add a new guide at a measured distance from an existing guide

It is important to understand that guides are affected by grid settings in the same way as clip art or other objects. If a grid is set to 0.5 inches, for example, and Snap objects to grid is turned on, guides will jump in half-inch increments when you try to move them. For that reason, when working with guides you will usu-ally—but not always—want to work with a fairly fine grid setting or turn off the Snap objects to grid option.

1. From the View menu, choose Grid and Guides. Uncheck the Snap objects to grid and the Display grid on screen boxes. Under Guide settings, click the checkbox labeled Display drawing guides on screen. Click OK. Two guides, one vertical and one horizontal, appear centered on the slide.

2. To make the guides easier to see, switch to Grayscale view.

  REVIEW: Click the Color/Grayscale button ▣ on the Standard toolbar and choose Grayscale from the submenu.

3. Be careful where you attempt to select the guide that you don't click on one of the objects on a slide. Still working on slide 5, use your mouse pointer to touch the vertical guide above your title text at the center of the slide. Make sure your mouse pointer is a left-pointing white arrow.

FIGURE 10-9
Working with guides
in grayscale view

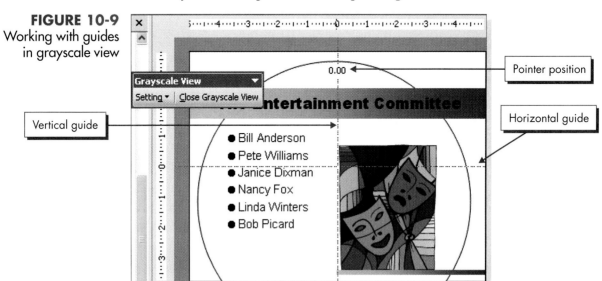

4. Press and hold the mouse button. The measurement 0.00 appears in place of the pointer, indicating that the guide is in the center of the slide and that you have it selected.

5. While pressing the mouse button, move to the left until the measurement 4.0 (or close to that number) appears, and then release the mouse button. The vertical guide moves to the left, 4.0 inches from the center of the slide.

FIGURE 10-10
Vertical guide moved
4.0" to the left
of the center

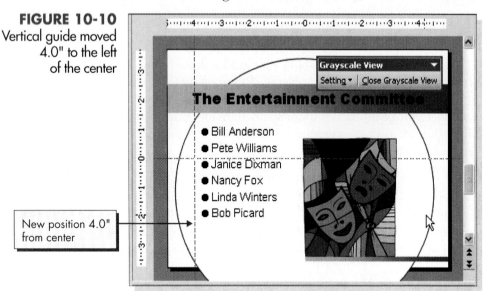

New position 4.0"
from center

6. To add a second vertical guide to the slide, point to the first guide and press and hold Ctrl while dragging the guide to the right. The plus sign below the indicator shows that you are adding an additional guide. Drag the guide 4.0 inches to the right of center. Notice that as you drag the guide, the indicator shows 0.00 as it passes the center of the slide and increases as you drag to the right.

7. Release the mouse button first and then release Ctrl.

 NOTE: If you release Ctrl before releasing the mouse button, the result will be moving the line, not adding a new one.

8. Align the clip art image with the guide on the right and then enlarge it to fit the space between the horizontal rectangles.

9. Remove the right vertical guide by dragging it to the right, off the edge of the slide.

 NOTE: You can add up to eight horizontal and eight vertical guides. When you no longer need them, simply drag them off the slide. You can remove all but one set of guides that way. You can hide the remaining set of guides, but you cannot remove them.

10. Switch back to Color View and save the presentation as *[your initials]***10-10** in your Lesson 10 folder. Keep the presentation open for the next exercise.

Working with Text in AutoShapes

You can change the position of text within its text box or AutoShape by changing its *text anchor point*. For example, you can position text at the top of an AutoShape, the bottom of an AutoShape, or the middle. You can also change the text box *margins* (the amount of space between the edges of an object and the text contained in it), the text box size, and the word-wrap options. These options are found on the Text Box tab of the Format AutoShape dialog box.

TABLE 10-3   **Text Box Options**

OPTION	PURPOSE
Text <u>a</u>nchor point	Specifies the position inside an AutoShape where text is attached
Internal margin	Adjusts the distance from the text inside an AutoShape to the shape's left, right, top, and bottom edges
<u>W</u>ord wrap text in AutoShape	Wraps text to fit within the width of an AutoShape
Resize AutoShape to <u>f</u>it text	Makes an object automatically adjust to the size of the text contained inside it
Rota<u>te</u> text within AutoShape by 90°	Turns text sideways inside an AutoShape

EXERCISE   **10-11**   **Change the Text Anchor Position in an AutoShape**

The text anchor point defines the position of text within a text box, text placeholder, or AutoShape. For example, in a body text placeholder, text usually starts at the top of the placeholder—or in other words, it is anchored at the top. When you key text in an AutoShape, its anchor point is usually the middle center of the shape. This anchor position remains fixed when text shrinks and grows during editing, or when the size of the AutoShape or placeholder is changed. You can set the anchor point to Top, Middle, Bottom, Top Centered, Middle Centered, or Bottom Centered.

FIGURE 10-11
Examples of text anchoring

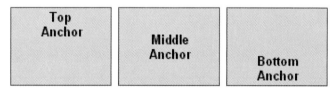

1. Move to slide 5. Select the body text placeholder containing the committee members' names.

2. Apply a dark purple fill (shadows scheme color) and remove the bullets. Notice that the text is positioned in the upper-left corner of the box.

3. Right-click the placeholder and choose Format Place<u>h</u>older from the shortcut menu.

4. When the Format AutoShape dialog box appears, click the Text Box tab. Drag the dialog box to the right so that you can see the text box.

5. Open the Text <u>a</u>nchor point drop-down list box, choose Bottom, and click <u>P</u>review. The text moves to the bottom of the placeholder.

6. Choose Middle Centered for the anchor point and click <u>P</u>review. The text is now centered vertically and horizontally in the placeholder, but in this case, it is behind the image.

7. Choose Middle for the anchor point and click <u>P</u>review again. The text is centered vertically and left aligned. Click OK.

FIGURE 10-12
Changing the text anchor position

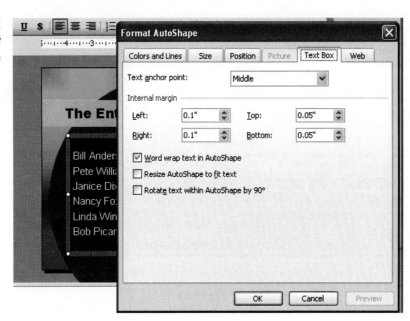

8. Change the text box AutoShape to a Rounded Rectangle.

 REVIEW: To change an AutoShape, click <u>D</u>raw on the Drawing toolbar and choose <u>C</u>hange AutoShape, <u>B</u>asic Shapes.

EXERCISE **10-12** **Resize an AutoShape to Fit Text**

When you choose the Resize AutoShape to <u>f</u>it text option (on the Text Box tab of the Format AutoShape dialog box), the text box or other AutoShape automatically shrinks or grows as you add or delete text and when you change the font size.

1. With the committee members placeholder still selected, reopen the Format AutoShape dialog box and display the Text Box tab. Drag the dialog box to the right so that you can see the placeholder.

2. Check the **Resize AutoShape to fit text** option and click **P**review. The placeholder shrinks in height, but not in width.

3. Clear the **W**ord wrap text in AutoShape checkbox and click **P**review again. Now the placeholder shrinks in width. Word wrap changes the way the Resize option works.

4. Click OK to apply the placeholder settings.

5. Increase the committee members text by one font size. Notice that the placeholder grows.

E X E R C I S E   10-13 Change AutoShape Internal Margins

In an AutoShape, you can change the space between the text and the border by changing the Internal margin settings on the Text Box tab of the Format AutoShape dialog box.

1. With the committee members placeholder still selected, reopen the **Text Box** tab of the Format AutoShape dialog box.

2. Under Internal Margin, change **L**eft to 0.5" and click **P**review. The left margin becomes wider.

3. Set the **R**ight margin to 0.5" inches and the **T**op and **B**ottom margins to 0.3" inches. Click OK. The size of the text placeholder increases to accommodate the wider margins.

4. Reduce the text by one font size. The placeholder shrinks to fit the new text size.

E X E R C I S E   10-14 Wrap Text in an AutoShape

When you key text in an AutoShape, the text is automatically anchored at the middle center position, word wrap is turned off, and the resize AutoShape feature is turned off. You can change these settings so that your text fits into the AutoShape.

1. Insert a new slide after slide 5 that uses the **Blank** slide layout (the first choice under **Content Layouts**).

2. In the center of the slide, draw a **Diamond** AutoShape approximately 1 inch wide and 1 inch tall.

3. Fill the diamond with a two-color gradient, choosing dark purple (shadows scheme color) for **Color 1** and light purple (accent scheme color) for **Color 2**. Choose the **From** center option and the variant with the lighter center. Remove the diamond's border line.

4. With the AutoShape selected, key **See you at the beach!** The text extends outside the diamond's border.

5. Change the text font to 48-point Arial, bold.

6. Open the Format AutoShape dialog box and click the Text Box tab. Check Resize AutoShape to fit text and click OK. The text fits inside the diamond, but the diamond is too large for the slide.

7. Resize the diamond by dragging the left-center sizing handle toward the center of the slide. The text automatically word-wraps even though the word wrap option was not chosen.

 TIP: In step 7, you might need to scroll left or right or reduce the zoom setting to see all the sizing handles for the AutoShape.

8. Adjust the width of the diamond so that the text wraps to three lines.

9. Using Figure 10-13 as a guide, position the diamond so that it appears horizontally centered within the large circle shape. (The circle is not precisely centered on the slide.)

FIGURE 10-13
Text word-wrapped inside an AutoShape

10. Check spelling in the presentation.

11. Review the grayscale settings for all slides and make any changes that might be necessary.

12. Create a handout header and footer: include the date and your name as the header, and the page number and text *[your initials]*10-14 as the footer.

13. Move to slide 1 and save the presentation as *[your initials]*10-14 in your Lesson 10 folder.

14. Preview and then print the presentation as handouts, 6 slides per page, grayscale, framed. Leave the presentation open for the next exercise.

Working with Page Setup Options

By using settings on PowerPoint's Page Setup dialog box and/or Print dialog box, you can distribute and deliver your presentation in many different ways:

- As an on-screen slide show by using either a computer screen or projection equipment attached to a computer
- As overhead transparencies
- As 35 mm slides
- As color or black-and-white printouts, either in *landscape* (horizontal) or *portrait* (vertical) page orientation

PowerPoint has built-in page settings for each option. You use the Page Setup dialog box to choose these settings.

Although you can change the way you want to deliver a presentation at any time, it's generally best to plan ahead and start with the one you intend to use for the finished product. Changing page settings can change the proportions or orientation of a page layout, making it necessary to make tedious adjustments to individual objects on each slide.

EXERCISE   10-15   Change Page Setup for Presentations

So far, you've worked with slides that are sized for an on-screen presentation in landscape orientation. In this exercise, you change the page setup to a paper presentation in portrait orientation. This sort of paper presentation might be placed in a binder and distributed at a meeting when no computer is available.

1. Continuing with the presentation you saved in Exercise 10-14, apply the Eclipse design template to your presentation. Use the color scheme with a white background and red, yellow, and bright green accents.

2. From the File menu, choose Page Setup. In the Page Setup dialog box, notice that the current presentation is sized for an On-screen show in Landscape orientation. Notice that notes and handouts use Portrait orientation.

3. Open the Slides sized for drop-down list and review the options. Choose Letter Paper (8.5x11in).

FIGURE 10-14
Changing page
setup options

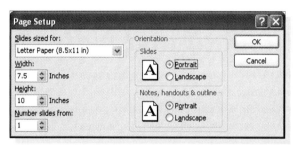

4. Under Slides, click Portrait and click OK. The slide proportions change to the new orientation.

5. Scroll through the presentation and notice the distortion in some of the graphics.

6. Make the following changes to fix the layout:

   - Slide 2: Make the body text placeholder font 24 points

   - Slide 3: Make the table's font two sizes smaller, make both text boxes wider, and adjust the tabs to make the text align correctly. Ungroup the text boxes, resize the bottom box so that the bottom of it is closer to the text. Resize the column heading box by dragging the top town so that the text is centered vertically in the space. Group the boxes again and move them up slightly. Reposition the page title so that the text appears above the horizontal line to match other page titles.

   - Slide 4: Correct the proportions of the clip art by reducing its height but preserving its width. Move it up slightly to allow about 0.25" of blank space on the left and bottom of the page. (This adjustment is important if your printer cannot print to the edge of your paper.) Move the text in the second column to the bottom of the first column and change the slide layout to Title and Text. Change the font to 24 points.

   - Slide 5: Change the fill color of the Rounded Rectangle to yellow and add a 6-point black border line. Change the font size to 24 points. Decrease the height of the clip art image and reposition both objects attractively.

   - Slide 6: Change the Diamond AutoShape to a 16-Point Star, change its fill color to yellow, and add a 6-point black border line to match slide 5. Reduce the font size twice. Adjust the width of the star so that the text wraps to three lines and reposition it appropriately.

7. View the presentation in Slide Sorter view and then view it as a slide show.

8. Review all slides in Grayscale view and make adjustments where needed.

9. Update the handout footer to show the text *[your initials]*10-15. On slide 3 only, include the date.

10. Save the presentation as *[your initials]*10-15 in your Lesson 10 folder.

11. Print slide 3 in full size, grayscale, framed.

12. Preview the entire presentation as handouts, 6 slides per page, landscape, grayscale, framed, scale to fit paper. Print and then close the presentation.

Customizing Handout and Notes Masters

Just as the slide master controls the appearance of the slides in your presentation, the notes master and handout master control the overall look and formatting of notes and handouts. You can customize these masters by using many of the same techniques you used with slide and title masters.

EXERCISE **10-16** **Work with the Notes Master**

On a notes master, you can format, resize, and reposition the notes text placeholder, the slide placeholder, and the header and footer placeholders in the same
way as you do on a slide master. You can also add pictures, text boxes, and other
AutoShapes.

Also, just as on a slide master, you can delete placeholders that you don't need.
To restore a deleted placeholder, click the Notes Master Layout button on the
Notes Master View toolbar and check the item you want to restore.

1. Reopen the file you saved as *[your initials]***10-14**.

2. From the <u>V</u>iew menu, choose <u>M</u>aster, <u>N</u>otes Master. Note the portrait
orientation of the notes master page.

3. Select the slide image and apply a 6-point black border line to it.

4. Select the notes text placeholder and increase the font size to 18 points.

5. Open the Page Setup dialog box. Under Slides sized for, change to Letter
Paper. Click OK.

6. Click <u>C</u>lose Master View on the Notes Master View toolbar to return to
Slide view.

7. Add the following notes to the slides indicated:

   ● Slide 2: Remind employees that they can also find directions on the
   employee Web site.

   ● Slide 5: Remind employees to bring their musical instruments for our
   sing-along.

EXERCISE **10-17** **Work with the Handout Master**

On a handout master, you can make the same kinds of changes as on the notes
master, except that you cannot alter the size or position of the slide placeholders.
Handout masters come with six different prearranged layouts, ranging from one
to nine slides per page. When placing pictures or other objects on a handout master, you must be careful to size and position them so that they do not overlap the
slide placeholders.

1. Copy the picture of food on slide 4 to the clipboard; then display the
Clipboard task pane. (You will insert this picture on the handout master.)

2. From the <u>V</u>iew menu, choose <u>M</u>aster, Han<u>d</u>out Master. Notice the landscape
orientation of this page. You changed the orientation in Exercise 10-15.

3. Click the second button on the Handout Master View toolbar , which
shows how handouts will print with two slides per page. The slides are
represented by dotted outlines.

4. Click the button that shows the positioning of three slides per page 📊; then click the button that shows nine slides per page 📊.

5. Select all four text placeholders on the handout (Header, Date, Footer, and Number) by using the Select All method (Ctrl+A). Change the font to 10-point Arial, bold italic.

FIGURE 10-15
Handout master with
text placeholders
selected

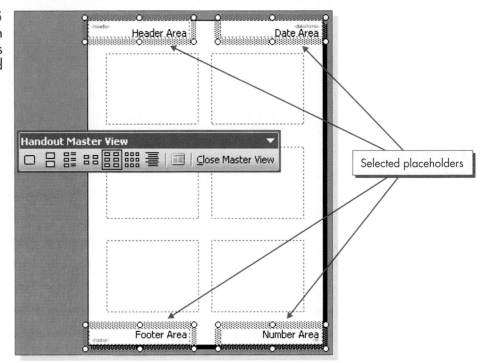

6. Increase the zoom setting so that you can see the placeholder formatting changes more clearly.

7. Select only the Date placeholder (upper right) and delete it. Select the Header placeholder. Right-align the text within the placeholder and move the placeholder to the right of the page.

8. Insert the food picture from the Clipboard task pane. Position it at the top left of the handout master. Resize it proportionately so that it is small enough to fit right above the slide placeholders for the 6-per-page layout.

9. Under the Header placeholder, create a text box with the text **Annual Picnic Presentation**. (The edges of this box will overlap the header area box, but the text will not overlap when it prints.) Right-align the text in the box, change the box font to 16-point Arial bold italic, and right-align the text box under the Header placeholder and with the right side of the slide.

10. Close Handout Master view and update the handout footer to show the text *[your initials]*10-17.

11. Save the presentation as *[your initials]***10-17** in your Lesson 10 folder.

12. Preview and then print notes pages for slides 2 and 5.

13. Preview and then print the presentation as handouts, 6 slides per page, grayscale, sized for fit paper, framed. Close the presentation.

USING ONLINE HELP

Just like master slides and handout masters, the notes master can be customized to meet specific needs.

Use Help to find out more about the notes master:

1. Choose Microsoft Office PowerPoint <u>H</u>elp to open the <u>H</u>elp task pane.

2. In the Search for box, key **master** and then click the Start Searching button.

3. In the Search Results pane, scroll down the list of topics to Reapply placeholders for headers and footers and select it.

FIGURE 10-16
Help screen about header and footer placeholders

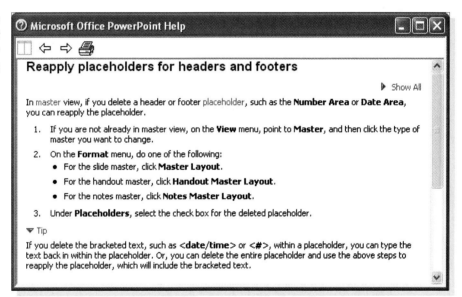

4. Read the topic, including the tip at the bottom of the screen.

5. Select and read other topics of interest displayed in the Search Results pane.

6. Close the Help window when you are finished.

LESSON Summary

➤ Paragraph indents can be applied to text placeholders, text boxes, and AutoShapes by dragging indent markers on the ruler when a text object is selected.

➤ To display the ruler for a text object, choose <u>V</u>iew, <u>R</u>uler, and then activate the text object as if to edit the text.

➤ Bulleted text always uses a hanging indent. Changing the distance between the top indent marker and the bottom indent marker on the ruler controls the amount of space between a bullet and its text.

➤ Indent settings can be applied to text placeholders on master slides as well as on individual slides.

➤ Indent and tab settings apply only to the selected text object and all the text in the text box. To create more than one type of indent or tab setting, you must create a new text object.

➤ To set tabs within a text object, activate the object, choose the type of tab you want, and then click the ruler at the point where you want to position the tabs.

➤ Click the Tab Type button [L] on the left edge of the ruler to change the type of tab. The button cycles through four tab types: left-aligned, centered, right-aligned, and decimal.

➤ Change the position of tab markers by dragging them across the ruler. Remove tab markers by dragging them off the ruler.

➤ Line spacing and the amount of space between paragraphs are controlled using the Line Spacing dialog box. Unlike tab and indent settings, line and paragraph spacing can be applied to one or more paragraphs in a text object, or to the entire object.

➤ PowerPoint's grid is a matrix of dots that can be used to help draw, align, and position objects. The spacing of grid dots can be adjusted from 1/24" (0.042") to 2".

➤ The Snap objects to grid feature automatically aligns the edges of objects to grid dots, making it easy to align objects relative to each other.

➤ When the Snap objects to grid feature is turned on, moving guides automatically aligns them with grid dots.

➤ Pressing [Alt] while drawing, moving, or resizing an object temporarily turns off the Snap objects to grid feature.

➤ Guides are horizontal and vertical dotted lines that are used to help align and position objects on a slide. Up to eight horizontal and eight vertical guides can be displayed on a slide. They can be moved freely while you work.

➤ Text object settings, such as the text anchor point, word-wrapping, automatically resizing a text object to fit its text, and text object margins are set by using the Text Box tab of the Format AutoShape dialog box.

➤ The text anchor point defines the position of text within a text object. Text can be anchored to the top, middle, bottom, top center, middle center, or bottom center of an object.

➤ Page setup options control the size of slides. They can be sized for 35 mm slides, overhead transparencies, on-screen display with a computer screen, or various paper sizes. Also, slides can have landscape or portrait page orientation.

➤ The method of delivering a presentation should be determined before creating the presentation. Changing the size or orientation of a presentation after the fact can sometimes require tedious changes to the layout of individual slides.

➤ Notes and handout masters can be customized in a way similar to customizing slide masters and title masters. The only difference is that slide placeholders on the handout master cannot be moved or resized.

➤ When placing text boxes or pictures on a handout master, care must be taken to make sure that the objects do not conflict with the slide placeholder layouts.

LESSON 10   Command Summary

FEATURE	BUTTON	MENU	KEYBOARD
Increase paragraph spacing		Format, Line Spacing	
Decrease paragraph spacing		Format, Line Spacing	
Display grid		View, Grid and Guides, Display grid on screen	Ctrl + G
Snap to grid		View, Grid and Guides, Snap objects to grid	
Display guides		View, Grid and Guides, Display drawing guides on screen	Ctrl + G
Change text box options		Format, AutoShape, Text Box	Tab
Change page setup options		File, Page Setup	
View handout master	Shift +	View, Master, Handout Master	
View notes master		View, Master, Notes Master	

Concepts Review

TRUE/FALSE QUESTIONS

Each of the following statements is either true or false. Indicate your choice by circling T or F.

T F   **1.** Each paragraph in a body text placeholder has its own set of tab stops.

T F   **2.** If you need to move the position of a tab marker, you must remove the marker and then set a new one.

T F   **3.** You can remove a tab marker by dragging it off the ruler.

T F   **4.** If the Snap objects to grid feature is off, it may feel as if objects do not move smoothly as you drag them across a slide.

T F   **5.** Top Centered, Middle Centered, and Bottom Centered are text anchor-point options.

T F   **6.** You can drag a text anchor point to position a block of text within a placeholder or text box.

T F   **7.** Unless you change page setup options, slides print in landscape orientation and handouts print in portrait orientation.

T F   **8.** You can customize a handout master by adding clip art, text boxes, and other objects to it.

SHORT ANSWER QUESTIONS

Write the correct answer in the space provided.

1. Which menu do you open to display the ruler?

2. How do you change the distance between bullets and text?

3. What is the difference between line spacing and paragraph spacing?

4. Which kind of tab do you use to align rows of dollars and cents?

_____

5. Where do you change indents, set tab stops, and move tab stops?

_____

6. From which two menus can you access the Grid and Guides dialog box?

_____

7. In which dialog box and tab do you find the option to automatically adjust an AutoShape's size to accommodate its text?

_____

8. Assuming that the Word wrap and Resize AutoShape to fit text options are applied, which settings do you change to modify the amount of space between text and the edge of an object?

_____

CRITICAL THINKING

Answer these questions on a separate page. There are no right or wrong answers. Support your answers with examples from your own experience, if possible.

1. Think of ways you might use indent markers. When would you want lines in a block of text to indent at different points?
2. There are many ways to control the size and position of objects on a slide. In what situations do you think guides are the best tools to use, and in what situations do you think the grid is a better tool?

Skills Review

EXERCISE 10-18

Adjust indents using the ruler.

1. Open the file **EmpAward2**.
2. Move to slide 2. If the ruler is not displayed, open the View menu and choose Ruler.
3. Create first-line indents by following these steps:
   a. Remove the bullets from the body text placeholder.
   b. Click within the text box to activate the ruler.

    c. Drag the first-line indent marker (top triangle) to the right, to the 1-inch mark on the ruler.

    d. Drag the small rectangle to the left, to the zero point on the ruler.

4. Move to slide 3 and change the bullet spacing by following these steps:

    a. Click within the body text placeholder.

    b. Drag the left indent marker (bottom triangle) to the right one tick mark, to the 0.5-inch position on the ruler.

5. On the slide master, change the first-level bullet to a star of your choice from the Wingdings font. Make the star dark blue (fourth sample from the left) and 100% of font size.

6. Move to slide 4 and increase the space between the bullets and text by one tick mark on the ruler. Move the oval shapes that emphasize the words week and paid slightly to the right.

7. Move to slide 6 and apply bold to the words Position, Years of Service, and Hobbies. For the two paragraphs, modify the line spacing: bold and remove the bullets and indents by following these steps:

    a. Select both paragraphs.

    b. Choose Format, Line Spacing and change the Before paragraph spacing to 0. Now the text will fit better on the slide.

8. Review all slides in Grayscale view and make adjustments where needed.

9. Create a handout header and footer: include the date and your name as the header, and the page number and text *[your initials]***10-18** as the footer.

10. Save the presentation as *[your initials]***10-18** in your Lesson 10 folder.

11. Print the presentation as handouts, 6 slides per page, grayscale, framed. Close the presentation.

EXERCISE 10-19

Set tabs, edit tabs, and create tabbed tables.

1. Open the file **Runner2**.

2. Move to slide 2 and add tabs to the table in the text box by following these steps:

    a. Display the ruler; then click anywhere within the table to activate the table's ruler.

    b. Click the Tab Type button ⎣ one or more times until it displays a right tab ⌐.

    c. Click the ruler at the 6-inch mark and then drag it to the 6.25-inch mark.

3. Center the table horizontally, relative to the slide. Add a 2-color horizontal gradient fill using green (background scheme color) and teal (fills scheme color) with the green color on top.

4. Insert a new slide after slide 2 and use the Title Only layout. Key **Station Assignments** in the title placeholder.

5. Create a tabbed table by following these steps:

    a. Draw a text box approximately 2 inches below the top of the slide and the same width as the title text placeholder. (The text box should be at least 7 inches wide.)

    b. Key the following table heading:
    Description[Tab]**Class**[Tab]**Station**

    c. Draw a second text box the same width directly below the table heading.

    d. Key the following, pressing [Tab] between columns.

Under 18	**A**	**10**
18-39	**B**	**30**
40-54	**C**	**40**
55 and Over	**D**	**20**

6. Format the table by following these steps:

    a. Select both text box objects and align their left edges.

    b. Change the heading text to 36-point Arial bold. Change the text color to bright green and apply a text shadow. Add a teal fill color.

    c. In the heading text box, set a center tab at 4 inches and a right tab at 7 inches.

     TIP: You might need to make the heading text box wider to set the 7-inch tab stop.

    d. Change the table text size to 28-point Arial bold and apply a text shadow. Apply a 2-color gradient fill to match the table on slide 2.

    e. In the table text box, set a left tab at 4 inches and a right tab at 6.25 inches.

    f. Left-align both text boxes relative to each other.

7. Indent the table text 0.25 inches by following these steps:

    a. Click within the body of the table (not the heading).

    b. Drag the small rectangle on the ruler to the 0.25-inch position. Both triangles should be aligned on top of the rectangle.

    c. Adjust the table text tab markers slightly to fine-tune the alignment of the columns under the heading.

8. Use the Format Text Box dialog box to change the width of both the header and table to exactly 7 inches.

9. Group the table and the table heading; then center-align it on the slide. Move it up slightly if necessary.

10. Review all slides in Grayscale view and make adjustments where needed.

11. Create a handout header and footer: include the date and your name as the header, and the page number and text *[your initials]*10-19 as the footer.

12. Save the presentation as *[your initials]*10-19 in your Lesson 10 folder.

13. Preview and then print the presentation as handouts, 3 slides per page, grayscale, framed. Close the presentation.

EXERCISE 10-20

Change line spacing and paragraph spacing, align using grids and guides, and customize the handout master.

1. Open the file **Specials2**.
2. On the title master, move the clip art image to the top-left corner with the title placeholder positioned to fit beside it. This adjustment will make more space on the slide so that you can add space in the body text placeholders of the slides for easier reading of menu items.
3. Change line spacing within paragraphs by following these steps:
   a. Move to slide 2 and click within the descriptive paragraph below the bold heading "Stuffed Spinach Bread."
   b. From the Format menu, choose Line Spacing.
   c. Change the After paragraph setting to 0.5 lines and click OK.
   d. Repeat this setting to add space between the descriptive paragraphs on the right.
   e. Select both text boxes and move them up by using the Format AutoShape dialog box with a 1.75" vertical from top-left corner setting.
4. On slide 3, repeat the adjustments you made for slide 2.
   a. Select both text boxes and move them up slightly by using the Format AutoShape dialog box with a 1.75" vertical from top-left corner setting.
   b. Drag the center sizing handle down for each text box to allow more space so that text can expand downward as space is added between paragraphs.
   c. Change the After paragraph setting for the first two descriptive paragraphs in both text boxes to 0.5 lines.
5. On slide 4, repeat the adjustments you made for slide 3 but change the After paragraph setting for the first two descriptive paragraphs in both text boxes to 1 line.
6. Align an image using guides.
   a. Under Guide settings, click the checkbox labeled Display drawing guides on screen. Click OK. Two guides, one vertical and one horizontal, appear centered on the slide.
   b. Viewing the title master, position your mouse pointer so that it touches the vertical guide shown on the slide. Make sure your mouse pointer is a left-pointing white arrow.
   c. Press and hold the mouse button. The measurement appears in place of the pointer, indicating the position of the guide. While pressing the mouse button, move to the guide until the measurement 1 on the left side of the slide (or close to that number) appears, and then release the mouse button. Release the mouse button first and then release Ctrl. The vertical line is 1 inch to the left of the center.
   d. Drag the horizontal guide down to 0.5 inches above the center.

7. Enlarge the clip art image proportionately in the upper-left corner so that it fills the space between the guides.

8. Drag the horizontal rectangle down so that it fits immediately below the horizontal guide. Resize the title and subtitle placeholders on the left so that they fit immediately to the right of the vertical guide.

9. On slide 1, move the logo slightly so that its left side aligns with the vertical guide.

10. Remove the guides by accessing the Grid and Guides dialog box and unchecking the Display drawing guides on screen box.

11. Customize the handout master by following these steps:

   a. From the View menu, choose Master, Handout Master.
   b. Zoom to a larger size so that you can see the Footer Area and Number Area placeholders clearly.
   c. Delete the Number Area placeholder in the lower-right corner.
   d. Position the insertion point after the text "<footer>" in the Footer placeholder.
   e. Key a comma, a space, and the text **Presentation on Lunch Specials**
   f. Center the Footer placeholder horizontally, center-align the text within the placeholder, and make the text Arial Narrow and bold. Close the handout master view.

12. Review all slides in Grayscale view and make adjustments where needed.

13. Create a handout header and footer: include the date and your name as the header, and the text *[your initials]*10-20 as the footer.

14. Save the presentation as *[your initials]*10-20 in your Lesson 10 folder.

15. Preview and then print the presentation as handouts, 4 slides per page, grayscale, landscape, scale to fit paper, framed. Close the presentation.

EXERCISE 10-21

Change text box settings and page setup options.

1. Open the file **Upgrade1**. Change the color scheme to the option with the white background and gold and magenta accents.

2. Assume you will be using this presentation as printed pages stapled together as a handout. Therefore, change the presentation to letter paper size with portrait orientation by following these steps:

   a. From the File menu, choose Page Setup.
   b. Open the Slides sized for drop-down list and choose Letter Paper (8.5x11 in).
   c. Under Slides, choose Portrait and click OK.

3. Change the presentation's font from Times New Roman to Bookman Old Style using the Replace Fonts feature in the Format menu.

4. On the title master, make these changes:
   - Title placeholder: Change to 36 points, shadow, and magenta (accent scheme color). Move the title placeholder up to 0.4" horizontally and 1.4" vertically from the top-left corner.
   - Arrow: Move the arrow up under the title placeholder. If the arrow does not seem to move smoothly as you drag it, remove the Snap objects to grid setting in the Grid and Guides dialog box.
   - Subtitle placeholder: Change to 24 points and left alignment. Position this placeholder 1.75" horizontally and 4" vertically from the top-left corner.

5. On the slide master, make these changes:
   - Title placeholder: Change to 32 points, shadow, and magenta (accent scheme color). Move the title placeholder up to 0.56" horizontally and 0.56" vertically from the top-left corner.
   - Arrow: Move the arrow up under the title placeholder. Resize the arrow to make it appear thinner (height = 0.5").
   - Change the body text placeholder's position to 1" horizontally and 2.5" vertically from the top-left corner. Change the first-level bullet text to 24 points, the second-level to 20 points, and the third-level to 18 points. Change the first-level bullet to purple.

6. On slide 2, make the following changes to the body text placeholder:
   - Remove the bullet and hanging indent from the body text placeholder.
   - Reduce the text box width to 5 inches.
   - Center the placeholder horizontally, relative to the slide.

7. On slide 2, select the text on the arrow AutoShape and change it to a rectangle. Make the text left aligned on two rows. Using the Format AutoShape dialog box, make these changes:
   - Change the color to a two-color vertical gradient using gold on the left to white on the right.
   - Make the shape 3.5" high and 5" wide.
   - Change the text anchor point to text fit on two lines.

8. Still working on slide 2, left align the three rectangles showing the equipment names, change the text to white and apply bold. Arrange these three rectangles attractively below the Equipment Categories text on the gradient rectangle.

9. On slide 4, make the following changes to the body text placeholder:
   - Delete the text of the first-level bullet. Select all the text and indent it to the left to promote the bullet levels.
   - Increase the After paragraph spacing of the second-level hyphen bullets to 0.5 lines.

- Adjust the size of the body text placeholder to by 6" × 6" and position it 1" horizontally and 2.5" vertically from the top-left corner.

10. On slide 5, delete the clip art image of a computer and insert a photo image of a computer that blends with the color scheme and tone of the presentation.

11. Review all slides in Grayscale view and make adjustments where needed.

12. Create a handout header and footer: include the date and your name as the header, and the page number and text *[your initials]*10-21 as the footer.

13. Save the presentation as *[your initials]*10-21 in your Lesson 10 folder.

14. Preview and then print the presentation as handouts, 6 slides per page, grayscale, landscape, framed. Close the presentation.

Lesson Applications

Work with indents, tabbed tables, and text box options.

1. Open the file **Tucson1**. Apply the Network design template and the color scheme with a white background and gold, rust, and gray accents.

2. Change the background for all slides to the Wheat preset gradient fill, using the horizontal option with the lightest color in the middle.

3. On the slide master, change the title text to 48-point bold Arial Narrow.

4. To the body text placeholder, apply a two-color gradient fill with the following settings:
   - Diagonal down shading style
   - Rust (accent scheme color) as the first color, and gold (shadows scheme color) as the second color
   - 25% From transparency and 75% To transparency settings
   - The variant with gold in the upper-right corner

5. In addition to the gradient fill applied above, make the following changes to the body text placeholder:
   - Apply a 3-point brown border (title text scheme color).
   - Remove the bullets and remove the hanging indents for all bullet levels.
   - Set all internal margins to 0.5 inches.
   - Turn on Resize AutoShape to fit text and turn off Word wrap.

6. On the title master, make the following changes to the subtitle placeholder:
   - Apply the same gradient fill and outline as the body text placeholder on the slide master.
   - Increase the font size to 36 points.
   - Set all internal margins to 0.5 inches.
   - Turn on Resize AutoShape to fit text and turn off Word wrap.

7. On slide 2, center-align the body text and center the body text placeholder horizontally on the slide. Move the placeholder down about 1 inch.

8. Insert a new slide after slide 2 and use the Title and Text layout. Key **Appetizers** as the title, and key the following in the body text placeholder, pressing (Tab) before each price:
   Wild Rice Soup(Tab)**5.25**
   Dill Cucumber Salad(Tab)**4.50**
   Four Bean Salad(Tab)**4.25**

9. Format the body text placeholder on slide 3 as follows:
   - Set a decimal tab at the 4.5-inch mark to align the prices.
   - Change the Line spacing to 0.9 lines, and the Before paragraph spacing to 0.3 lines.
   - Center the placeholder horizontally on the slide and move it down about 1 inch.
10. Working on slide 4, make the following changes to the indented text in the body text placeholder (change the descriptions, but not the names of the items):
    - Change Line spacing to 0.8 lines.
    - Change the Before paragraph spacing to 0 lines.
    - Change the font to 24-point Arial Narrow italic.
    - Adjust the tab to add space after the bullet.
11. Still on slide 4, make the following changes to the body text placeholder:
    - Set right tabs at 5 inches and 6.5 inches.
    - Change the top and bottom internal margins to 0.3 inches.
    - Center the text placeholder horizontally on the slide.
    - Reduce the text box font size by 1 increment.

 TIP: You can use right tabs instead of decimal tabs to align numbers if all the numbers in the list have the same number of decimal places.

12. Find an appropriate image for the upper left of the title slide.
13. Review all slides in Grayscale view and make adjustments if needed.
14. Create a handout header and footer: include the date and your name as the header, and the page number and text *[your initials]*10-22 as the footer.
15. Save the presentation as *[your initials]*10-22 in your Lesson 10 folder.
16. Preview and then print the presentation as handouts, 4 slides per page, grayscale, landscape, framed. Close the presentation.

EXERCISE 10-23

Work with indents, tabs, line spacing, and page setup options.

1. Open the file **Invent**.
2. Working on the slide master, apply the following formatting to the body text placeholder:
   - Increase the space between the bullet and text for the first-level bullet to 0.5 inches.
   - Change the first-level bullet to a large solid square from the Wingdings 2 font.

- Change the line spacing to 0.9 lines and the before-paragraph spacing to 0.4 lines.

3. On slide 2, make the following changes to the body text placeholder:
   - Change the bullets to a numbered list, formatting the numbering at 100% of text size.
   - Reduce the width to approximately 6.25 inches, making each numbered item wrap to two lines.
   - Center the placeholder horizontally, relative to the slide.

4. On slide 3, reduce the width of the body text placeholder so that the first bullet wraps to three balanced lines. Center the placeholder horizontally, relative to the slide.

5. On slide 4, remove the second-level bullets and indent the second-level text to the 1-inch mark. Italicize the second-level text and make it one font size smaller. Reduce the width of the placeholder so that it is just wide enough to accommodate the last text line without forcing it to wrap. Center the placeholder horizontally on the slide.

6. On slide 5, do the following:
   - Remove the bullets from the table.
   - Insert a left-aligned tab at the 3-inch mark on the ruler.
   - Increase the table text by one font size.
   - Turn off Word wrap and turn on Resize AutoShape to fit text.
   - Center the table horizontally and vertically, relative to the slide.

7. On slide 6, reduce the text box width so that all bullets except the last wrap to two lines. Center the placeholder horizontally, relative to the slide.

8. Review all slides in Grayscale view and make adjustments if needed.

9. Create a handout header and footer: include the date and your name as the header, and the page number and text *[your initials]*10-23a as the footer.

10. Save the presentation as *[your initials]*10-23 in your Lesson 10 folder.

11. Print as handouts, 6 slides per page, grayscale, landscape, framed. Close the presentation.

Work with indents, line spacing, grids, and text box settings.

1. Open the file **Party2**.

2. On slide 2, remove all the bullets and hanging indents from both body text placeholders. Center-align the text in the left placeholder, make it bold, change its font size to 36 points, and change its text color to gold (the title text scheme color). Format the text in the right text placeholder as 20-point Arial bold.

3. Resize the "Directions" text placeholder so that its text wraps on two lines and it is just high enough for the text to fit. Position the text placeholder at the bottom of the slide and center it horizontally.

4. Make the left text placeholder 8 inches wide. Change the font size of the line that begins "Festivities begin" to 32 points. Change the space before paragraphs in the text box to 0 lines. Adjust the height of the placeholder to fit, and then center it horizontally and vertically on the slide.

5. Display grids and set objects to snap to grid.
   a. From the View menu, choose Grid and Guides.
   b. Click so that there is a check mark in Snap objects to grid and Display grid on screen.
   c. Change the grid spacing to ½ or 0.5 and click OK.

6. Insert a new slide after slide 2 that uses the Title Only layout. Key **Evening Menu** in the title placeholder. Draw a 3-inch circle below and to the left of the title (there should be 6 grid marks across the center of the circle.) Using Figure 10-17 as a guide, key the "Appetizers" text as shown in the first circle.

FIGURE 10-17
Slide 3

7. Format the text in the circle as follows:
   - Make the word "Appetizers" in Comic Sans MS, 28-point, bold, shadowed, and burgundy (the accent scheme color).
   - Make the rest of the text 20-point, bold, shadowed, and dark pink (the fills scheme color).

8. Using the Format AutoShape dialog box, format the circle as follows:
   - Remove the circle's border.
   - Fill the circle with a two-color gradient that uses cream for Color 1 and gold for Color 2. Choose the From corner shading style and the variant with the darkest color in the lower-right corner.

- Change the size of the circle to 2.75 inches high and 3 inches wide.
- Change the text anchor point to Middle Centered.

9. Duplicate the circle three times. Use Figure 10-17 as a guide for positioning the circles in an overlapping fashion. Edit the text in the three duplicated circles as shown in the figure.

 TIP: To make the accent appear in the word "Sautéed," use the spell-checker.

10. Change the shading of the three copied circles as follows by using custom colors:
    - Main Course: cream to bright pink
    - Side Dishes: cream to orange
    - Desserts: cream to bright blue (custom color)

11. On slide 4, change the AutoShape of the body text placeholder to a Rounded Rectangle with a two-color gradient fill (cream to dark gold) to match the first circle from slide 3.

12. Continuing on slide 4, remove all the bullets and hanging indents. Make all the first-level text bold, pink, and with a text shadow. Make the second-level text bold and change the text color to black (use More Colors).

 TIP: If you have trouble seeing the text in the Rounded Rectangle on slide 4, try working in Grayscale view.

13. Change the line spacing for the second-level paragraphs to 0.8 lines.

14. Change the text anchor point to Middle Centered and turn on the Resize AutoShape to fit text option. Then adjust the vertical position and center the rectangle horizontally.

15. Check spelling in the presentation and adjust grayscale settings where needed.

16. Turn off the grid and snap to grid settings.

17. Create a handout header and footer: include the date and your name as the header, and the page number and filename *[your initials]*10-24 as the footer.

18. Save the presentation as *[your initials]*10-24 in your Lesson 10 folder.

19. Preview and then print the presentation as handouts, 4 slides per page, grayscale, landscape, scale to fit paper, framed. Close the presentation.

EXERCISE 10-25 *Challenge Yourself*

Create a tabbed table, change line spacing, change text box margins and anchor point settings, and customize the handout master.

1. Start a new blank presentation. Use the Blends template and the color scheme with the black background.

2. On the title master, find an appropriate image for softball similar to the one shown in Figure 10-18. Resize the image and position it as shown. If necessary, flip the image. Copy and paste the image on the top-left corner of the slide master.

FIGURE 10-18
Title master

3. Remove any graphics that are not needed on the title master and the slide master. Edit the slide color scheme to choose summer-like colors that blend with the image you found. If necessary, adjust the colors of the image to complement the design theme you are creating. Add horizontal lines (solid color or gradient colors).

4. Select appropriate fonts for placeholders. The examples in this exercise uses the font Cooper Black in blue with a black shadow for titles and Tahoma in dark blue for the body. If you do not have those fonts, then make appropriate substitutions.

5. On slide 1, key a two-line title with the text **Good 4 U** and **Softball Schedule**

6. Key **Spring/Summer 2004** for the subtitle.

7. Using the Title Only layout, create slide 2 as shown in Figure 10-19 (on the next page). Key the table and its heading all in one text box and format the table as follows:

   ● Change the font to 24-point Tahoma in dark blue for all the table text, and 24 point Cooper Black in black for the column heading text.

   ● Set appropriate tabs, paragraph spacing, and line spacing.

   ● Draw a 1.5-point line under the column headings.

   ● Position the table appropriately on the slide.

8. Using the Title and 2-Column Text layout, create slide 3 as shown in Figure 10-20 (on the next page). Format the body text placeholders as shown in the figure to remove bullets and indents. Make the text "Team A" and "Team B" 28-point Copper Black in black and the team member names as 24-point Tahoma in dark blue. Add blue lines to highlight the column headings and separate the columns as shown.

FIGURE 10-19
Slide 2

July/August Schedule

Date	Opponent	Location	Time
7/8	American Sports	Away	5:45
7/15	Jim Jones Pie Co.	Home	6:00
7/22	Smith's Shoes	Home	6:00
7/29	Ace Factory Supply	Away	5:45
8/5	American Sports	Home	6:00
8/12	Jim Jones Pie Co.	Away	6:15
8/19	Smith's Shoes	Away	6:15
8/26	Ace Factory Supply	Home	6:00

FIGURE 10-20
Slide 3

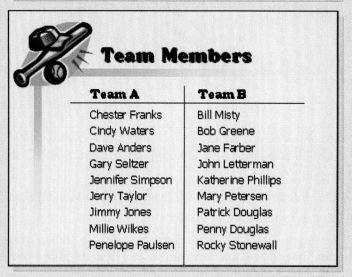

Team Members

Team A	Team B
Chester Franks	Bill Misty
Cindy Waters	Bob Greene
Dave Anders	Jane Farber
Gary Seltzer	John Letterman
Jennifer Simpson	Katherine Phillips
Jerry Taylor	Mary Petersen
Jimmy Jones	Patrick Douglas
Millie Wilkes	Penny Douglas
Penelope Paulsen	Rocky Stonewall

9. Using the Title Only layout, create slide 4 as shown in Figure 10-21 by using the Rounded Rectangle Callout AutoShape for the text box. Change the font to Cooper Black, 28 points, dark blue. Apply a 3-point blue border and a gradient fill. Disable Word Wrap, enable the Resize AutoShape to fit text option, and change all internal margins to 0.2 inches.

10. Check spelling in the presentation and adjust grayscale settings if needed.

11. Create a handout header and footer: include the date and your name as the header and the page number and filename *[your initials]*10-25 as the footer.

12. Save the presentation as *[your initials]*10-25 in your Lesson 10 folder.

13. Preview and then print the presentation as handouts, 4 slides per page, landscape, grayscale, scale to fit paper, framed. Close the presentation.

FIGURE 10-21
Slide 4

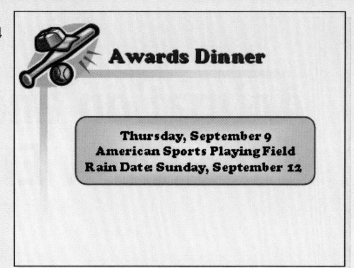

On Your Own

In these exercises you work on your own, as you would in a real-life work environment. Use the skills you've learned to accomplish the task—and be creative.

EXERCISE 10-26
Create a presentation giving information to third and fourth grade girls (plus their parents) about the girls' basketball league. Create at least four slides, including one that is a tabbed table (you could name teams, or use a table for scheduled games). On the other slides, change line spacing, internal margins, and word-wrap and resize options. Apply attractive formatting to the presentation and save it as *[your initials]*10-26. Preview and then print the presentation as handouts.

EXERCISE 10-27
Create a presentation that describes your favorite movies. Include at least one tabbed table in which you rate the movies from 1-5. Use the skills that you have learned up to this point to create an interesting presentation design with a movie theater theme. Save the presentation as *[your initials]*10-27. Preview and then print the presentation as handouts.

EXERCISE 10-28
Create a presentation describing your ideal romantic date. Create a table that lists the activities as a summary at the end of the presentation. The presentation should have at least five slides, but you can create more, detailing specific activities. Using the tools you learned about in this lesson and previous lessons, format your presentation attractively and in keeping with the romantic date theme. Save the presentation as *[your initials]*10-28. Preview and then print the presentation as handouts.

11

Animation and Slide Show Effects

MICROSOFT OFFICE
SPECIALIST
ACTIVITIES
In this lesson:
   PP03S-1-5
   PP03S-2-4
   PP03S-4-1
   PP03S-4-2
   PP03S-4-3

See Appendix.

OBJECTIVES

After completing this lesson, you will be able to:

1. Use animation schemes and custom animation.
2. Modify and enhance animation effects.
3. Add multimedia elements.
4. Control a slide show.
5. Work with custom shows.

 Estimated Time: 2 hours

In Lesson 2 you learned to apply transitions for interesting movements between slides as they change on a computer's display. PowerPoint provides another type of movement that provides many of the same effects, plus much more, for objects on slides. *Animation schemes* offer a quick and easy way to add interest to a presentation by animating text and adding other special effects, including transitions. By using PowerPoint's *custom animation* tools, you can create other types of text animation and animate objects, such as clip art, drawings, and video clips. *Custom animation* enables you to control the timing, speed, sound, and other aspects of how and when a slide's elements appear on the screen.

Using Animation Schemes and Custom Animation

To *animate* an object, text, or graphics means to apply visual and sound effects that control how the object behaves during a slide show. For example, you can make an object:

- Fly into the center of the screen accompanied by a sound effect
- Fade into the background when another object appears
- Blink when you click your mouse button
- Leave the screen in a spiral path

In the Slide Design task pane you can select from preset Animation Schemes that control placeholder movement and slide transitions. The Custom Animation task pane provides many tools that enable you to create a variety of interesting effects. If you enjoy using these tools, you will want to spend time on your own experimenting with custom animation's endless possibilities.

But remember, use animation carefully to enhance—not distract from—the message that your presentation needs to deliver.

EXERCISE `11-1` **Apply an Animation Scheme**

Animation schemes are displayed in the Slide Design task pane. The task pane's list box displays a list of recently used schemes (if any), followed by subtle schemes, moderate schemes, and exciting schemes.

When you choose an animation scheme, it is applied to all slides that are currently selected.

1. Open the file **Motion1** and display slide 1.

2. Click Sli_de Show on the menu bar and choose Animation S_chemes. The Slide Design task pane appears on the right side of the screen with a list of animation schemes displayed. (See Figure 11 on the next page.)

 NOTE: If the task pane is already open, you can also display the Slide Design task pane by clicking the Other Task Panes button ▼ on the task pane title bar and choosing Slide Design, Animation Schemes from the drop-down list.

3. In the list of animation schemes, under Subtle, choose Faded wipe. A preview of the animated text appears in the Slide pane. Click Apply to All Slides.

4. Click Slide Show (at the bottom of the task pane) and continue to left-click to progress through the slides. Notice the animation effect as slides are displayed.

FIGURE 11-1
Choosing the Faded
Wipe animation
scheme

5. Move to slide 1 and scroll down the list of animations until you see the Exciting heading. Under Exciting, choose Bounce and observe how the effect is displayed in the Slide pane. Click Apply to All Slides and then go through the slide show to see the effects on all slides.

6. Sample some other animation schemes from the list. Then choose the Elegant scheme, under Moderate, and click Apply to All Slides. This scheme is applied simultaneously to all the selected slides.

7. Now use a different animation scheme for two slides in the presentation. Click the slide 5 thumbnail in the Slides pane and then (Shift)+click the slide 6 thumbnail to select both slides. Choose the Big title scheme, under Exciting, and click Apply to All Slides. This scheme is applied only to the selected slides.

8. Move to slide 1 and click Slide Show; then notice the animation effects as you display the slides.

9. Return to Normal view.

REVIEW: Slide transitions are the effects between two slides during a slide show. Transitions can be applied to one or more slides through the Slide Transition task pane or in Slide Sorter view.

EXERCISE **11-2** **Apply Custom Animation**

You animate an object by using the Custom Animation task pane. You can display the task pane in one of two ways:

- From the Slide Show menu, choose Custom Animation.
- If a task pane is already displayed, click the Other Task Panes arrow ▼ on the task pane title bar and choose Custom Animation from the drop-down list.

To apply an animation to an object, select it in the Slide pane, click Add Effect at the top of the Custom Animation task pane, choose an effect type, and then choose an effect from the list that appears. There are four types of effects that you can apply:

- Entrance: An *entrance effect* is one that you apply to text or an object to control how it first appears on a slide.
- Emphasis: An *emphasis effect* is one that you apply to draw attention to an object that is already displayed on a slide.
- Exit: An *exit effect* is one that you apply to control how an object leaves (or disappears from) a slide.
- Motion Paths: A *motion path* defines the line of travel that an object can follow as part of an animation effect.

After you apply an effect, an *animation tag*—a small, numbered box—appears on the slide next to the animated object. The number in the box indicates the order in which the animation will play in relation to other animation effects on the slide. This number correlates with the list of animations in the *custom animation list*— a list on the Custom Animation task pane of all animations applied to the current slide. Items in this list can be reordered.

1. Continue with the Healthy Food presentation (**Motion1** file).
2. If the task pane is not displayed, click View on the menu bar and choose Task Pane.
3. On the task pane's title bar, click the Other Task Panes arrow ▼ and choose Custom Animation from the drop-down list.
4. On slide 1, select the "Healthy Food" WordArt object.
5. Click Add Effect at the top of the Custom Animation task pane. The drop-down list contains four general categories of effects.
6. Choose Entrance. A list of the most recently used entrance effects appears. Your list will be different from the one pictured in Figure 11-2 (on the next page).
7. Choose any effect from the list. A preview of the effect is displayed in the Slide pane, and an animation tag with the number "1" appears next to the animated object.

FIGURE 11-2
Choosing
an entrance effect

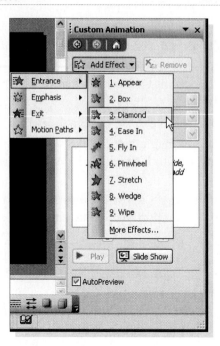

NOTE: If you did not see a preview of the animation, make sure AutoPreview is checked (at the bottom of the Custom Animation task pane) and then click Play.

8. Click Add Effect again, choose Entrance, and then choose the Pinwheel effect. A box with the number "2" appears next to the selected object. The two animation effects are listed with corresponding numbers on the Custom Animation task pane.

9. Still working on slide 1, select the blue text, "for the Athlete in You." Click Add Effect and choose Entrance, but this time choose More Effects at the bottom of the list of entrance effects. The Add Entrance Effect dialog box opens.

10. Use the scroll bar to view the complete list of entrance effects available in the categories of Basic, Subtle, Moderate, and Exciting.

FIGURE 11-3
Choosing from
more entrance
effects

11. From the group of Basic effects, choose Dissolve In and click OK. Now five effects are listed in the task pane because three have been added to the two that were created with the animation scheme.

12. To see how the effects will appear during a show, click Slide Show at the bottom of the task pane (or click the Slide Show View button). Slide 1 appears in Slide Show view, but the WordArt that you animated is not showing. Click four times through all the animation effects that you applied. You will remove some of these in Exercise 11-5.

13. Press (Esc) to return to Normal view.

EXERCISE `11-3` **Apply Emphasis and Exit Animation Effects**

In addition to entrance animation effects, you can use interesting emphasis effects to draw your audience's attention to an object on your slide. Or you can use exit effects to make objects leave. Of course, effects can be combined, too. While you are learning about animation, it is fun to try out different combinations. However, you ultimately want to select movements that seem logical and contribute to your audience's understanding of your information.

1. Move to slide 2 and select the small star to the right of the text "Gus Irvinelli."

    TIP: Make sure you see the four-pointed arrow ⊕ when you click the star, to avoid activating the text box behind it.

2. Apply the <u>E</u>ntrance effect Appear. (If needed, go to the More Effects option at the bottom of the menu to find the Appear effect.)

3. With the star still selected, click Add Effect and point to <u>E</u>mphasis.

4. Choose <u>M</u>ore Effects. From the Moderate category, choose Flicker. Click OK.

   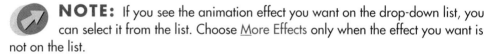 **NOTE:** If you see the animation effect you want on the drop-down list, you can select it from the list. Choose <u>M</u>ore Effects only when the effect you want is not on the list.

5. With the star still selected, click Add Effect and point to E<u>x</u>it.

6. Choose <u>M</u>ore Effects. From the Basic category, choose Disappear.

 7. With slide 2 selected, click Slide Show 🖳 Slide Show ; then click to advance through the title animation. Click three more times to see the star appear, flicker, and then disappear. Press (Esc) to end the show and return to slide 2.

EXERCISE `11-4` **Apply a Motion Path to an Object**

You have seen some ways to make objects appear on a slide. With a motion path, you can make an object enter a slide from any point and travel across the slide in a variety of paths, including diagonal, zigzag, or spiral paths.

1. Change the zoom to a low setting, for example, 33%, so that you can see a large amount of the gray desktop area.

2. Move to slide 1, and select the clip art runners and move them off the slide to the gray desktop area beside the title on the left.

3. With the runners selected, click Add Effect on the Custom Animation task pane and point to Motion <u>P</u>aths. Choose <u>M</u>ore Motion Paths. The Add Motion Path dialog box offers a large number of choices (see Figure 11-4 on the next page). You can add motion paths to any object, including text.

FIGURE 11-4
Choosing a preset
motion path

4. Under Lines & Curves, choose
S Curve 2 and click OK.

5. A curving line extends from the
runners to the left part of the slide
with triangles at each end of the line.
The green triangle indicates the start
of the path, and the red triangle
indicates the end.

6. Select the motion path only; then
drag its sizing handles to resize it,
extending across the slide. Use the
rotation handle to adjust the angle
slightly. Even if the rotation causes
the green beginning triangle to
move away from the runners, they
will begin movement from the
triangle position.

FIGURE 11-5
Working with a
preset motion path

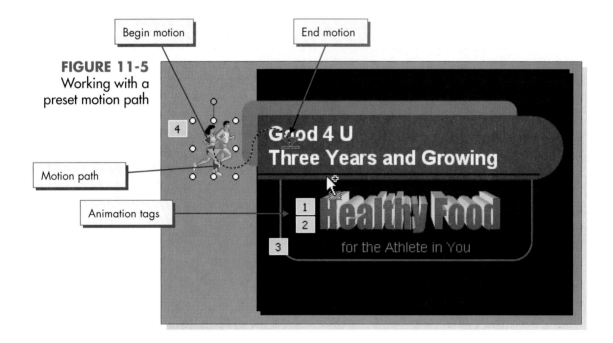

FIGURE 11-6
Motion path and the
Custom Animation
task pane

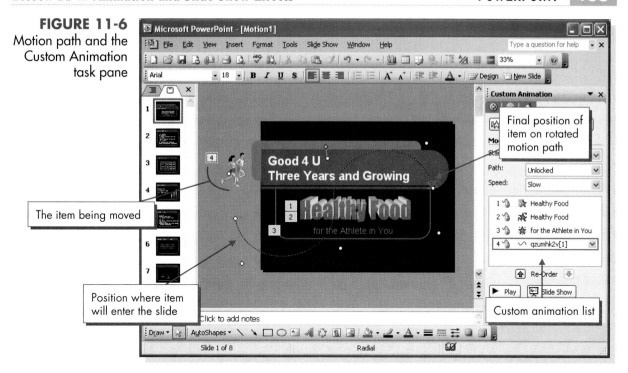

FIGURE 11-6
Motion path and the
Custom Animation
task pane

7. Click Play at the bottom of the task pane to test these movements in Slide view. Click Slide Show at the bottom of the task pane to test these movements in full-screen display.

8. Create a Lesson 11 folder. Save the presentation as *[your initials]***11-4** in your new Lesson 11 folder. Keep the presentation open for the next exercise.

EXERCISE 11-5 Remove Animations

If you want to remove an animation from an object, select it in the custom animation list, and click Remove at the top of the Custom Animation task pane or press Delete . You can select multiple items from the list in the same way that you select multiple slide thumbnails.

1. Working on slide 1 in the task pane, click the first item for Healthy Food. A box surrounding it indicates that it is selected. Click Remove at the top of the task pane.

2. Now only three numbered items appear in the list. They are renumbered, as are the animation tags on the slide.

3. Click the Master: Body item. Notice that this item has a yellow star indicating that this animation is controlled on the title master. Click the down arrow and select View Slide Master. Select both animation effects and remove them. Return to Normal view.

4. Click Slide Show; then click your mouse to see the three animations. Press (Esc) to end the show.

Modifying and Enhancing Animations

Animations can be modified in many ways. They can be made to appear faster or slower, dissolve or fly, be activated by a mouse click or play automatically. In addition, you can attach sound effects to them.

EXERCISE   11-6   Modify Animations

The animations you created up to this point don't appear during a slide show until you click your mouse. You can modify an animation so that it appears automatically, and you can change the speed at which the animation occurs.

1. Working on slide 1, click anywhere on the text "for the Athlete in You." Notice that the "Dissolve In" Entrance Effect has been applied to this text.

2. Click the arrow for the Start list box (near the top of the task pane) and choose After Previous. A clock icon replaces the mouse icon, indicating that the animation will start automatically after the first animation completes. The item number is removed, indicating that it is now considered part of the first animation.

3. With this item still selected, click the arrow for the Speed drop-down list. Choose Medium.

NOTE: When list items move to a different position, timing and start settings sometimes need to be changed. Experimentation is often the only way to determine the best settings for the effect you want.

4. Click the runners image. From the Start list box, choose After Previous. Change the Speed to Slow. Notice that all the animation tags now contain the number "1," indicating that they are the first events in the animation.

NOTE: Choosing After Previous when there is no previous event makes the animation start as soon as the slide is displayed. In this case, the previous event is the display of the slide, before any animation occurs.

5. Click Slide Show. One click will start the first animation, and then the other two appear automatically, one after the other, without a mouse click. Press (Esc) to end the show.

6. Move to slide 2 and select the star. To make the star flicker more than one time, click the list box arrow for item 2 and choose Timing from the drop-down list. The Timing tab for the Flicker dialog box appears. (If the dialog box title is not Flicker, click Cancel and choose another list item.)

7. From the Repeat list box, choose 3 and click OK. The star will now flicker three times.

8. Click the down arrow next to item 1 and choose Start After Previous and the animation tag changes to 0.

9. Change the start settings for item 1 (this was item 3 before the last step) to Start After Previous. Now the star will flicker and then disappear without the need for additional mouse clicks.

10. Save the presentation as *[your initials]*11-6. Keep it open for the next exercise.

EXERCISE 11-7 Add Sound Effects to Animations

You can add sound effects as part of an object animation or as an object by itself. If you add sound by using the Custom Animation task pane, the sound becomes part of an animation effect. Another way to add sound is by using the Clip Art task pane to insert a sound file. Sound files are covered later in this lesson.

Be careful to use sound in a way that does not distract from the presentation. Use it to draw attention to an object or as a subtle background. Always test sound effects on the equipment that you plan to use when presenting a slide show. You might need to turn down the volume to prevent a jarring effect.

1. Moving to slide 1, select the first item ("Healthy Food") in the custom animation list. A list box arrow appears.

2. Click the list box arrow and choose Effect Options. The Pinwheel dialog box opens. Each animation effect has its own dialog box. The options vary, depending on the animation.

3. Click the Sound list box arrow; then scroll down the list of sounds and select Chime.

4. Click the Speaker button to the right of the Sound list box. Move the Volume slider down, near the bottom, to lower the sound level. Click OK. The chime sound plays.

FIGURE 11-7
Adding a
sound effect

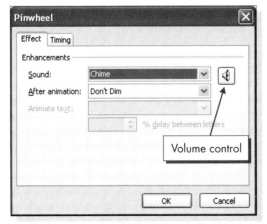

5. If necessary, access Effect Options again to adjust the sound up or down as needed to create a quiet sound.

TIP: If you have trouble adjusting the volume the way you want, click the speaker icon on the right side of the Windows task bar to adjust your system's sound. Some speakers have volume knobs as well.

6. Use the steps just outlined to add the same chime sound to the second text animation.

7. Click Play at the bottom of the Custom Animation task pane to preview the animations and sounds.

 NOTE: Sounds that you have recorded can be inserted using the same dialog box.

EXERCISE **11-8** **Modify the Order of Animations**

When animating a body text placeholder, you can control the order of how the text appears:

- All at once so text appears as one object
- All paragraphs (or bullet) at the same time
- Paragraphs (or bullet) entering by their level

To apply a consistent movement effect to all the bulleted lists in a presentation, the animation should be applied on the slide master. Then you can interweave additional animations on selected slides. For example, on slide 4 you can cause one of the three yellow arrows to appear with each text line. But to do this when slide master animations have been applied, you must first copy the slide master animation to the slide.

To make an animation appear at the same time as another animation, reposition its listing in the custom animation list so that it is directly below the other animation, and change its Start setting to With Previous.

1. First, go to the slide master to notice how the animation is set up there. In the animation list, the first item is the title and the second item is the text placeholder with the various list levels.

2. On the slide master, select the body placeholder. Apply the Entrance effect Stretch and use the default Direction setting (Across).

FIGURE 11-8
Choosing text
animation for a
bulleted list

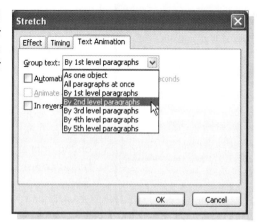

3. Move to slide 4 in Normal view. In the custom animation list, click the Master: Body list box arrow and choose Copy Effects to Slide. Below the object name is a chevron that shows the list can be expanded. Click the chevron and the three body text items are listed.

4. Select each of the three yellow arrows.

5. Apply the Entrance effect Fly In and use the default Direction setting (From Bottom).

6. In the Start drop-down list, choose With Previous.

7. Click Play to preview the effect. The arrows appear after the listed text. Notice that the rows are numbered from 1-3 in animation sequence 4-6.

8. Point to "Up arrow 3." When you see the two-pointed vertical arrow $\updownarrow$, drag the item up the list (or click the Re-Order arrow) and drop it below item 1 ("Miami in 2005"). Notice in the Slide pane that the first arrow's animation tag number changed to match the animation tag for the first text line.

FIGURE 11-9
Moving an item in
the custom
animation list

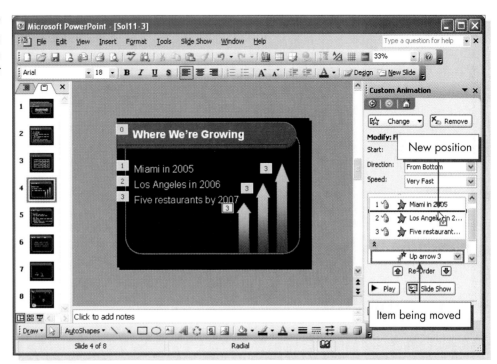

9. Drag the item labeled "Up arrow 4" and drop it below item 2 ("Up Arrow 3"). Now the arrows will appear on click from shortest to tallest to match the sequence of years.

10. Click Slide Show; then click your mouse to advance through the animations on the slide. Press (Esc) to end the show.

11. Save the presentation as *[your initials]*11-8 in your Lesson 11 folder. Leave the presentation open for the next exercise.

EXERCISE **11-9** **Modify an Animation's Timing**

You have already seen that you can make an animation start automatically with the display of a slide, start immediately after another animation has completed, or wait until you click your mouse. You can fine-tune the timing of an animation by specifying a delay before the animation begins.

1. Move to slide 1, select the second item in the custom animation list ("for the Athlete"), and click its list box arrow. Choose Timing.

2. In the Delay spin box, key **2** (for 2 seconds). Click OK. This delays the final animation a little for each one to have time to take effect.

3. Using steps 1 and 2 as a guide, add a 2-second delay to the first list item ("Healthy Food").

4. Move to slide 2 and select the star. Select item 1, click its list box arrow, and choose Timing. Key **0.5** (for 0.5 seconds) in the Delay box. Click OK.

5. Click Slide Show to see the effect of the delayed start. When the animations complete in slides 1 and 2, press (Esc) to end the show.

6. Save the presentation as *[your initials]*11-9 in a new folder for Lesson 11. Keep the presentation open for the next exercise.

EXERCISE **11-10** **Copy an Animated Object**

Sometimes you want two or more objects to have the same animation effect. If it is an elaborate animation that takes many steps to create, as is the case with the star in the previous exercise, you can save time by copying the object to a new position on the same slide or to a new slide. The animations are copied along with the object.

1. Working on slide 2, select the star on the slide, copy it to the clipboard, and then paste it on the same slide.

2. Use your arrow keys to nudge the copied star to the right of the name "Julie Wolfe." Three more animation items appear at the bottom of the custom animation list, referring to star 4.

FIGURE 11-10
Slide 2 with the
completed star
animation

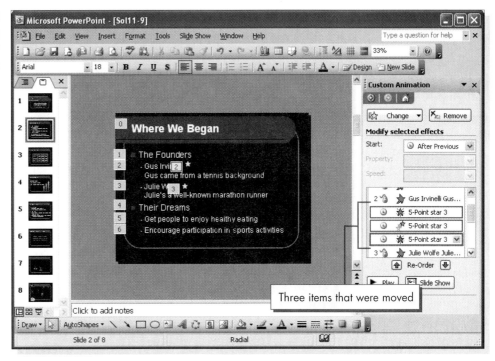

3. As you did in the previous exercise, copy the body placeholder effects to the slide. Then re-order the star effects to appear after each name in the list. Select all three star effects and use the re-order arrows to move them into position at one time.

4. Click Slide Show and use the mouse to advance through the text animations. The flickering star appears to the right of "Gus Irvinelli" and again to the right of "Julie Wolfe." Press (Esc) to end the show.

5. Save the presentation as *[your initials]***11-10** in your Lesson 11 folder. Keep it open for the next exercise.

Adding Multimedia Elements

Besides attaching sound effects to animations, you can add sound objects that stand on their own. Like most animations, sound objects can be set to play automatically when a slide appears or to wait for a mouse click. Like the chime sound you used with custom animation, many of the sounds are short "event" sounds like a door closing or glass clinking that are small files with the extension of .wav. However, some of the sounds are music sounds with the extension of .midi. You will learn to distinguish between these file types and to look at the file properties.

In PowerPoint, the term *movie* refers to any motion file, for example, a video clip or animated clip art file. Microsoft provides many animated files (sometimes called animated GIFs) and sound files within Office 2003 Professional. Additional material is available on the Web at Microsoft Office Online. You can also insert sound and movie files from other sources.

EXERCISE 11-11 Insert Sound Clips

Sounds, like other effects, should be chosen carefully to make sure that they enhance—not distract from—your presentation's message. You can play a short burst of music to accompany an effect, or you can set music to play for an entire slide or an entire presentation.

1. Move to slide 1 in Normal view.

2. From the Insert menu, choose Movies and Sounds, Sound from Clip Organizer. The Insert Clip Art task pane opens, displaying icons for sound files. When you mouse over the sound thumbnail, information about the file appears. You can see the file size and the type of file. Those marked with WAV are usually short sound effects, such as a drum roll, chimes, or applause. Those marked with MID or MIDI are music files that are usually longer in length.

3. In the Search text box, key **Sports**

4. Click the Results should be list box arrow and make sure Sounds is checked. Clear any other checkboxes that might be selected. Click the list arrow again to close the list box; then click Start Search. If Microsoft media content was installed on your computer or if your computer is connected to the Internet, a list of sound files relating to sports themes appears.

FIGURE 11-11
Sound files in the
Clip Art task pane

5. Right-click any sound file icon and choose Preview/Properties from the shortcut menu. The current sound file begins to play.

6. In the Preview/Properties dialog box, click the Next button ≥ to preview the next sound. Most (if not all) the sounds are short sound effects. Click Close to close the Preview/Properties dialog box.

7. Locate the music file Sports Drive and click it.

8. When the dialog box asking whether you want to play the sound automatically appears, click When Clicked. A small loudspeaker appears in the center of the slide.

9. Working in Normal view, make sure you're on slide 1 and switch to Slide Show view. Click the speaker object. The music starts to play. Click a blank area of the screen to turn off the music. Press (Esc) to end the slide show. You will make some adjustments to how this music plays in the next exercise.

E X E R C I S E 11-12 Control How Music and Sound Plays

By using the Custom Animation task pane, you can change a music object so that it plays automatically when a slide starts, with a mouse click, or after another animation. If the music object is set up so that it doesn't need a mouse click to start, you can hide it by dragging it off your slide onto the gray desktop area of the Slide pane.

1. Return to slide 1 in Normal view. Right-click the speaker object and choose Custom Animation from the shortcut menu. Depending on how you inserted your sound object, you might or might not see an item for the sound object in the custom animation list.

FIGURE 11-12
Custom animation list showing four items

2. If your custom animation list contains items not shown in Figure 11-12, delete the extra list items.

3. Select the music object name in the Custom Animation task pane; then change the sound item's Start setting to With Previous. Move the item to the top of the custom animation list.

4. Click the sound item's list box arrow and choose Effect Options. The Play Sound dialog box opens, displaying the Effect tab.

FIGURE 11-13
Setting sound options

5. Under *Start playing*, choose From b̲eginning.

6. Under *Stop playing*, choose After c̲urrent slide.

7. Under *Sound Settings* tab, click the Speaker button 🔊 and turn down the Sound v̲olume. Click OK.

TIP: To make a sound play for the duration of an entire presentation, right-click the sound object and choose Edit Sound Object from the shortcut menu. In the Sound Options dialog box, check the box labeled Loop until stopped and click OK.

8. Working on the Slide pane, select the speaker object and drag it off the slide onto the gray desktop area below the slide. This will hide the speaker during a show but still allow it to play.

FIGURE 11-14
Sound object moved off the slide

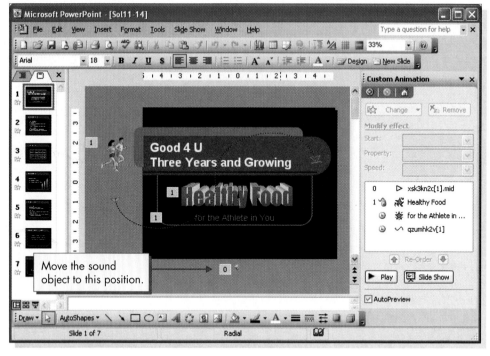

9. Select the second item in the list, "Healthy Food," and open its list box. Choose T̲iming. Change the Start setting to With Previous, and then reset the D̲elay to 2 seconds. Click OK.

NOTE: This change is necessary because the After Previous setting would cause this event to wait until the music stops playing. By adding the 2-second delay, the animation gives the appearance of starting after the music starts.

10. View the presentation as a slide show, starting on slide 1; then return to slide 1 in Normal view.

11. Save the presentation as *[your initials]***11-12**. Keep it open for the next exercise.

EXERCISE 11-13 Play Music from a CD

Music from a CD is often superior to what you will hear with either a .wav or .midi file. Therefore, you can achieve very professional results playing music from a CD. You might want to play music before a presentation as people are entering the room, or to energize your audience after an afternoon break. Inserting a CD music track is much like inserting any other sound.

1. Display slide 6.

2. Place a music CD in the CD drive of your computer.

3. Choose Insert, Movies and Sounds, Play CD Audio Track. From the dialog box that opens, set the options you want for how the CD will play.

FIGURE 11-15
Insert CD Audio

4. If you wanted the CD to play until stopped, you would select the Loop until stopped option. In this case, however, you will let the first track play until the song is completed and ready for the second track to begin. If you wish, you can indicate the specific seconds within a track when the music will begin and end playing.

5. Click Hide sound icon during slide show so that the CD icon will not appear. Click OK.

6. PowerPoint will ask how you want the sound to start in your slideshow. Click Automatically to have the music start when this slide appears. Click When Clicked if you want to control when the music starts playing.

7. Now start your slide show to make sure your CD audio track is working correctly.

8. Keep the presentation open for the next exercise.

EXERCISE 11-14 Insert and Play a Movie

Inserting a movie (or animated clip art file) onto a slide is similar to inserting a sound object. Once it's on the slide, you can add animation effects to control when and how it appears.

1. Working on slide 6, click the Insert menu, choose Movies and Sounds, and then choose Movie from Clip Organizer on the submenu. The Clip Art task pane appears. A small yellow star animation icon ▨ in the lower-right corner of the thumbnails identifies movie files.

2. In the Search for box, key **Sports**

3. In the Search in list box, check Everywhere so that the search will be performed not only on your computer but also on Microsoft Office Online if you are currently connected to the Internet.

4. In the Results should be list box, check Movies and clear all the other checkboxes.

5. Close the list box and click Go.

6. Preview some of the movies and then click one with suitable colors and theme to insert it onto the slide. Once it's on the slide, use your judgment to resize it proportionally to fit below the blue text on the slide.

NOTE: The size of most animated movies cannot be increased without making them become distorted, so be careful when you are trying to make these images larger.

7. Redisplay the Custom Animation task pane; then click Play to see the movie. It will play as soon as the slide appears and the CD will play after all the text is displayed.

8. Click Stop at the bottom of the Custom Animation task pane (or press Esc). Because the music is set to play for the duration of the slide, the preview will not stop by itself.

Controlling a Slide Show

If you want to create a self-running slide show, for example, a Web-based show, a show distributed to viewers on a disk or CD, or a show running at a trade show kiosk, you must set slide timings so that the animations and slides can advance automatically.

EXERCISE 11-15 **Use Rehearse Timings to Set Automatic Slide Timings**

PowerPoint's Rehearse Timings command offers a convenient way to set slide timings. When you start the Rehearse Timings procedure, the slide show begins with the Rehearsal toolbar displayed. You use its buttons to advance animations and slides, to pause, or to repeat a slide.

FIGURE 11-16
Rehearsal toolbar

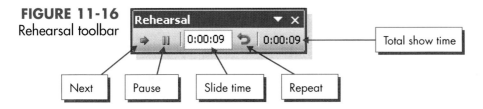

TABLE 11-1 Rehearsal Toolbar

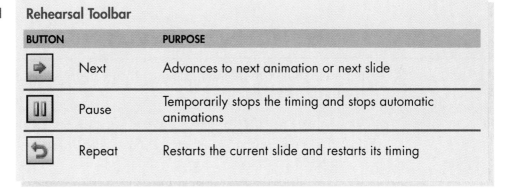

BUTTON		PURPOSE
	Next	Advances to next animation or next slide
	Pause	Temporarily stops the timing and stops automatic animations
	Repeat	Restarts the current slide and restarts its timing

The time it takes to advance from one animation or one slide to another is automatically recorded. These times are used when the slide show is set to run automatically. During a rehearsal procedure, make sure to allow enough time for each animation so that your viewer can read and absorb the information before moving on.

1. From the Slide Show menu, choose Rehearse Timings. A slide show begins, starting on slide 1. The Rehearsal toolbar appears in the upper-left corner of your screen.

2. When all the animation on slide 1 is complete, wait a moment or so; then click the Next button 🔀 on the Rehearsal toolbar to move to slide 2.

3. Wait for the title text to appear, click the Next button 🔀 to display the slide's first bullet, and then click Next 🔀 again to display the first sub-bullet.

4. Wait until the star for Gus Irvinelli finishes shimmering and allow enough time to read its text. Then click Next 🔀 again.

5. Continue clicking the Next button at appropriate times to advance through the entire show.

  If you make a mistake on a slide, click the Repeat button 🔄 to start the slide again. If you need to stop in the middle of a rehearsal for any reason, click the Pause button ⏸ to stop the timer temporarily. Click Pause ⏸ again to continue with the rehearsal.

6. When the information box appears, informing you of the show's total time, click Yes to keep the slide timings that were recorded during the rehearsal. Slide Sorter view is displayed, showing the timings underneath each slide.

7. Select slide 1; then click the Slide Show View button [🖳 Slide Show] to start an automatic show. The show progresses automatically without any mouse clicks. If you don't like the timings, you can rehearse timings again.

8. When the show is complete, press [Esc] to return to Slide Sorter view. Double-click slide 3 to display it in Normal view.

EXERCISE 11-16 Set Timings Manually

It is also possible to set timings manually if you can estimate how long each slide should be displayed.

1. From the Slide Sorter view, double-click slide 3 for Normal view.

2. Click the Slide Show menu and choose Slide Transition. The task pane will appear.

3. Under the Advance Slide section, select the Automatically after check box, and then manually enter 5 seconds.

4. View the slide show as a presentation and notice that slide 3 timings are set differently than before.

EXERCISE 11-17 Set Up a Slide Show

There are many different ways that you can run a slide show. Prior to this lesson, you viewed all slide shows as full-screen shows, advancing manually from one slide to the next. PowerPoint gives you tools to fine-tune the way you run a show. For example, you can:

- Run a show in a window or using the full screen
- Advance slides by using the mouse and keyboard or have slides advance automatically by using preset slide timings
- Run a show with or without preset animations
- Run a show with or without prerecorded voice narration

The Set Up Show command on the Slide Show menu gives you access to the various options you can use to customize your show. If your slide show does not run as expected, chances are that changing a setting in the Set Up Show dialog box will fix the problem.

1. From the Slide Show menu, choose Set Up Show. Notice the many options in this dialog box in addition to the Advance slides options.

2. Under Show type, click Browsed at a kiosk (full screen). This option makes a show loop continuously until you press Esc to stop it.

3. Click OK. The kiosk option is useful for a presentation that is set up to run unattended in a public place.

4. View the slide show. After slide 1 appears for the second time, press Esc to stop the slide show.

5. Reopen the Set Up Show dialog box. Under Show Type, choose Presented by a speaker (full screen).

6. Under Advance slides, choose Manually. Click OK. This option will override any slide timings that have been set. It gives a speaker flexibility in deciding when it's time to display the next text animation or the next slide. It's also the best choice if you plan to use hyperlinks during a show.

7. Create a handout header and footer: include the date and your name as the header, and the page number and text *[your initials]*11-17 as the footer.

8. Make any needed adjustments in Grayscale view; then move to slide 1 and save the presentation as *[your initials]*11-17 in your Lesson 11 folder.

9. Preview and then print the presentation as handouts, 6 slides per page, grayscale, framed. Keep the presentation open for the next exercise.

Working with Custom Shows

A *custom show* is a presentation within a presentation. It displays only specially selected slides instead of all the slides in a show. This is convenient if you have a large presentation that deals with several different topics. You can create a custom show for each topic that includes only related slides, but the entire presentation is still available to you if you want to switch to another topic.

EXERCISE 11-18 **Create and Run Custom Shows**

You create a custom show by selecting related slides within a presentation and giving the selected group a name.

1. From the Slide Show menu, choose Custom Shows. The Custom Shows dialog box opens.

2. Click <u>N</u>ew. The Define Custom Show dialog box appears. The slide titles in the presentation are listed in the Slides in presentation list box.

3. In the Slide show <u>n</u>ame box, key **Financial**

4. Using Ctrl+click, select slides 1, 2, 3, 4, and 6. Click <u>A</u>dd. The selected slides are added to the Slides in custom show list box on the right.

FIGURE 11-17
Define Custom
Show dialog box

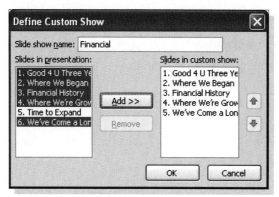

5. In the Slides in custom show list box select slide 2. Click <u>R</u>emove. Slide 2 is removed from the custom show list. Click OK. You have defined a custom show containing four slides.

6. With the Custom Shows dialog box still open, click <u>N</u>ew again to create a second show.

7. Name this show **Background**

8. Select slides 2, 4, and 6. Then click <u>A</u>dd.

9. Select slide 1 from the left list box and click Add again. Slide 1 is added to the bottom of the Slides in custom show list, meaning that it will be the last slide displayed in the custom show.

10. Select the last slide in the right list and then click the Move Up button several times until it is at the top of the list.

FIGURE 11-18
Repositioning a
slide in the custom
show list

11. Click OK. The Custom Shows dialog box is once again displayed, and two shows are listed in the Custom shows list box.

12. Select "Financial" from the list and then click <u>S</u>how. A slide show with four slides plays automatically.

13. When the show ends, return to Normal view.

From the Sli<u>d</u>e Show menu, choose Custom Sho<u>w</u>s to reopen the Custom Shows dialog box.

14. Select "Background" from the C<u>u</u>stom shows list and click <u>S</u>how. When the show ends, return to Normal view.

15. Save the presentation as *[your initials]***11-18**. Leave the presentation open for the next exercise.

EXERCISE 11-19 Create Action Button Links to Custom Shows

Interrupting a presentation to set up a custom show might not seem very professional. Instead, you can create an *action button*—a button with a link associated with it—or a hyperlink that you can click to discreetly choose the show that's right for your audience.

The action buttons you create in this exercise will be placed on slide 1. Because both custom shows start on slide 1 as well, this will create a conflict unless the custom show lists are edited.

1. Move to slide 1 in Normal view. From the Slide Show menu, choose Custom Shows.

2. Select "Financial" and then click Edit. In the Slides in custom show list box on the right, select the first item ("Good 4 U") and click Remove. Click OK.

3. Using step 2 above as a guide, remove the first slide from the "Background" custom show.

4. Click Close to close the Custom Shows dialog box.

5. From the Slide Show menu, choose Action Buttons. Float the Action Buttons submenu.

6. On the Action Buttons toolbar, click the first button—the one with the ScreenTip Action Button: Custom. Your pointer changes to a cross shape.

7. Use this point to draw a rectangle approximately 0.5 inches tall by 1.5 inches wide in the lower-left corner of slide 1. The Action Settings dialog box opens.

8. Click the Mouse Click tab. Under Action on click, choose Hyperlink to.

9. Open the Hyperlink to list box, scroll to the bottom of the list, and choose Custom Show.

10. In the Link to Custom Show dialog box, select "Background" (the name you gave to one of the custom shows) and click OK. Click OK again to close the Action Settings dialog box.

11. In the Slide pane, with the action button selected, key **Background** to identify the button.

12. To make the button less obvious on the slide, change its fill color to black and its text color to very dark red (a custom color). Adjust its size, if needed, so the text fits inside the button.

13. Duplicate the button and move the duplicate above the original. Change the text in the duplicate to **Financial**

14. Right-click the "Financial" button and choose Edit Hyperlink from the shortcut menu. From the Hyperlink to drop-down list, choose Custom Show; then choose "Financial." Click OK. Click OK again to close the Action Settings dialog box.

15. Arrange the two action buttons attractively in the lower-left corner of the slide.

16. Start a slide show from slide 1. As soon as all the animated text and the runners appear, click one of the action buttons. The custom show you selected should run automatically. Run the show again to test the other action button.

17. Save the presentation as *[your initials]*11-19 in your Lesson 11 folder. Leave it open for the next exercise. Leave the Action Buttons toolbar displayed—you use it again in another exercise.

EXERCISE | 11-20 Create a Summary Slide with Text Hyperlinks

A *summary slide* is a slide that contains the titles of some or all slides in a presentation. It can be used as an agenda slide or a table-of-contents slide. It could also be used for a wrap-up or summary slide at the end of a presentation. It can have hyperlinks to other slides, custom shows, other presentations, or files created by other programs.

Although you can create a summary slide in Normal view (if the Outlining toolbar is displayed), it is usually more convenient to use Slide Sorter view.

1. Switch to Slide Sorter view and select slides 2 through 6.

2. Click the Summary Slide button 🔲 on the Slide Sorter toolbar. A new slide is inserted before the first slide that you selected, in this case, before slide 2.

3. Double-click the summary slide (slide 2) to display it in Normal view.

4. Change the title "Summary Slide" to **Discussion Points**

5. To create a hyperlink for the first bullet in the body text placeholder, right-click the bullet, and choose <u>H</u>yperlink from the submenu (or press Ctrl+K).

6. In the Insert Hyperlink dialog box under Link to, choose P<u>l</u>ace in This Document. From the Select a pla<u>c</u>e in this document list box, choose "3. Where We Began." Click OK.

7. Create hyperlinks for the other bullets on slide 2.

FIGURE 11-19
Inserting a hyperlink
on a menu slide

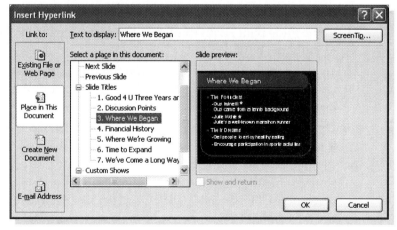

TIP: When creating hyperlinks for a menu slide, make sure that the slide to which you link matches the text in the text box at the top of the Insert Hyperlink dialog box.

EXERCISE **11-21** **Create Links That Return to the Menu Slide**

Setting up links on a summary slide to function like a menu enables you to jump to many different slides in a presentation. Chances are pretty good that after you get to a linked slide, you'll want to return to the summary slide and then link to another. This requires an action button or hyperlink on each slide to which you set up a link.

When you insert an action button or hyperlink on the slide master, it will appear on every slide (except the title slide) in the presentation, making the job of linking each slide back to the menu slide a small task.

1. Display the slide master.
2. If the Action Buttons toolbar is not displayed, click the Slide Show menu, choose Action Buttons, and float the Action Buttons toolbar.
3. Select the second button on the Action Buttons toolbar—with the ScreenTip Action Button: Home—and draw a small rectangle in any convenient blank area of the slide master.
4. In the Action Settings dialog box, click the Hyperlink to list box arrow and choose Slide.
5. In the Hyperlink to Slide dialog box, choose slide 2 ("Discussion points"). Click OK. Click OK again to close the Action Settings dialog box.
6. Change the button's fill color to dark red (the accent and followed hyperlink scheme color); then position the button to the left of the title text placeholder. (The button should be the same color as the red shape underneath it.) Return to Normal view.
7. Start a slide show beginning with slide 2 ("Discussion points"). Click your mouse several times until the five hyperlinks appear.
8. Click "Financial History." The show jumps to that slide. Click the action button in the upper-left corner of the slide. "Discussion points" reappears. Press (Esc) to end the slide show.

 NOTE: Usually you do not use automatic slide timings when you are using a summary slide with hyperlinks.

9. Save the presentation as *[your initials]*11-21 in your Lesson 11 folder and close the presentation.

USING ONLINE HELP

Inserting video and sound clips from other formats sometimes needs some special attention to make the clips work correctly.

Use Help to learn more about inserting videos:

1. Key **movie** in the Ask a Question box and press (Enter).
2. Select **Troubleshoot movies** from the list in the Search Results task pane.
3. Click the first topic to expand it and read it.
4. Expand and read some of the other topics in the Help window.
5. Close the Help window when you're finished.

LESSON Summary

> Custom animation enables you to control the timing, speed, sound and other aspects of how and when a slide's elements appear on the screen. Custom animation goes beyond animation schemes, allowing greater flexibility and variety.

> To animate an object means to apply visual and sound effects that control how an object behaves during a slide show. You can apply several animation effects to a single object.

> All animation effects are available from the Custom Animation task pane. There you can choose entrance, emphasis, and exit effects and vary the direction, timing, speed, and other options.

> A motion path can be used to control how an object moves across the screen. PowerPoint provides a large variety of predefined paths that you can resize, rotate, and reposition to suit your needs.

> To remove an animation from a slide, select its list item in the custom animation list and click Remove or press (Delete).

> Sound effects can be added to individual animations. The sound effect plays when the animation occurs. Be careful with sounds, making sure that they are appropriate and play at the proper volume.

> When multiple animations are used on a slide, the order of their appearance is determined by the order they are listed on the Custom Animation task pane. You change the order in the list by selecting and then dragging a list item up or down to a new list position.

➤ As part of the timing options, you can choose to have an animation appear when you click your mouse, appear when a previous animation appears, or be delayed a number of seconds that you specify.

➤ An animated object can be copied to the same slide, another slide, or another presentation. All the animation settings are copied along with the object.

➤ Animations can be applied to master slide items in the same manner as to individual slides. Animations on master slides play before animations on individual slides.

➤ Override master slide animations on an individual slide by copying them to the slide. Once copied, the animations behave as if they were originally placed on the slide instead of on the slide master. You can delete, rearrange, or modify the copied animations.

➤ Besides attaching sound effects to individual animations within a presentation, you can also add sound objects that stand on their own within a presentation. Sound objects can be set to play for the duration of a single slide, for an entire presentation, or until you click your mouse. Music can be played from an audio CD, too.

➤ Movies—animated clip art or videos—can be inserted on a slide. Once on a slide, they can be animated in the same way as any other object.

➤ Use the Rehearse Timings feature to set the timing of individual slides and animations on the slides for a self-running slide show.

➤ Use the Slide Transition task pane to set timings manually.

➤ Using the Set Up Show dialog box, slide shows can be set to run continuously with no manual intervention, to be run only on mouse clicks, or to be modified in many other ways.

➤ Another way to make a presentation adaptable to varying audiences is to create custom shows. Custom shows are subsets of a complete show, displaying only preselected slides.

➤ Creating action buttons or hyperlinks to custom shows makes it easy to manage a slide show during a presentation.

➤ Another way to manage a slide show is to create a summary or agenda slide listing the titles of each slide, each with hyperlinks to the actual slide.

LESSON 11   Command Summary

FEATURE	BUTTON	MENU	KEYBOARD
Custom Animation		Slide Show, Custom Animation	
Entrance animation effect		Add Effect, Entrance (Custom Animation task pane)	
Emphasis animation effect		Add Effect, Emphasis (Custom Animation task pane)	
Exit animation effect		Add Effect, Exit (Custom Animation task pane)	
Motion path		Add Effect, Motion Paths (Custom Animation task pane)	
Remove animation		Remove (Custom Animation task pane)	
Modify an effect		Select item, Effect Options (Custom Animation task pane)	
Add sound effect		Select item, Effect Options (Custom Animation task pane)	
Modify timing		Select item, Timing (Custom Animation task pane)	
Add music		Insert, Movies and Sounds, Sound from Clip Organizer	
Add movies		Insert, Movies and Sounds, Movie from Clip Organizer	
Rehearse Timings	🕦	Slide Show, Rehearse Timings	
Set Up Show	Shift + 🖥	Slide Show, Set Up Show	
Create a custom show		Slide Show, Custom Shows	
Action Button		Slide Show, Action Buttons	
Create a summary slide	📑		
Hyperlink		Insert, Hyperlink	Ctrl + K

Concepts Review

TRUE/FALSE QUESTIONS

Each of the following statements is either true or false. Indicate your choice by circling
T or F.

T (F) *1.* An emphasis effect controls how an animated object first *ENTRANCE*
appears on a slide.

T (F) *2.* Before adding a different animation effect to an object, you can
delete its existing animations by selecting the object on the slide
and pressing `Delete`.   *TASK PANE*

T (F) *3.* You add sound effects to animated objects by choosing
commands from the Insert menu.

(T) F *4.* You can change the order of animations on a slide.

(T) F *5.* You choose movies and sounds to add to your presentation
from the Clip Art task pane.

(T) F *6.* You can set different timings for each slide in a slide show.

T (F) *7.* You can create only one custom show per presentation.

(T) F *8.* Summary slides can be created automatically from existing slides.

SHORT ANSWER QUESTIONS

Write the correct answer in the space provided.

1. How do you add a sound to an animation effect?

    CHOOSE EFFECT OPTIONS FROM DROP DOWN

2. How do you change the order in which animations occur on a slide?

    CUSTOM ANIMATION LIST — CHANGE POSISTIONS

3. How do you copy an animated object?

    COPY + PASTE

4. How do you set an animation effect to start automatically without a mouse click?

   WITH PREVIOUS or AFTER PREVIOUS

5. Which two toolbars contain the Summary Slide button 🔲?

   SLIDE SORTER TOOLBAR AND OUTLINE

6. How do you display the Action Buttons toolbar?

   SLIDE SHOW — Action Buttons

7. What do you call an object that, when clicked, displays another slide?

   HYPERLINK LINK, ACTION BUTTON

8. Without using a hyperlink, action button, or the Set Up Show dialog box, how can you run a custom show?

   SLIDE SHOW CUSTOM SHOW

CRITICAL THINKING

Answer these questions on a separate page. There are no right or wrong answers. Support your answers with examples from your own experience, if possible.

1. Which animation effects are your favorites? How do you like to use them?
2. Adding sound effects, text and object animations, and slide transitions to a slide show allows for a great deal of variety. How can you avoid distracting from the presentation's message?

Skills Review

EXERCISE 11-22

Add entrance, emphasis, and exit animation effects; add a sound effect; and change timing.

1. Open the file **Promo1**.
2. On slide 1, animate the hat—but not its logo—by following these steps:
   a. Select the hat and ungroup it once. Deselect the grouping.
   b. Right-click the hat (not its red logo) and choose Custom Animation.
   c. In the Custom Animation task pane, click Add Effect, point to Entrance, and choose More Effects.
   d. Choose Dissolve In from the Basic category. Click OK.

3. Change the timing and speed for the animation by following these steps:

   a. Make sure the hat is selected.

   b. On the Custom Animation task pane, click the arrow next to Start and choose With Previous from its drop-down list.

   c. Click the arrow next to Speed and choose Medium from its drop-down list.

4. Animate the hat's logo by following these steps:

   a. Select the red logo on the front of the hat.

   b. Using steps 2c and 2d as a guide, apply the Entrance effect Spiral In from the Exciting category.

   c. Using step 3 as a guide, change the logo's Start setting to After Previous and make sure its Speed setting is Fast.

5. Apply a sound effect and delay the appearance of the logo by following these steps:

   a. Make sure the red logo is selected.

   b. In the custom animation list on the task pane, click the list box arrow for the second item (labeled "Group 40").

   c. Choose Effect Options from the list.

   d. Click the Sound list box arrow and choose Wind.

   e. Click the Speaker button ◀ and move the slider down near the bottom to lower the volume.

   f. Click the Timing tab in the dialog box.

   g. In the Delay spin box, key **1** (for 1 second). Click OK.

6. Move to slide 4 and animate the star on the T-shirt by following these steps:

   a. Select the T-shirt and zoom to 100% (so you can easily select the star).

   b. Select the star on the T-shirt's shoulder.

   c. Click Add Effect on the Custom Animation task pane, point to Emphasis, and choose More Effects.

   d. Choose Spin from the Basic category. Click OK.

7. Change effect options for the star's animation by following these steps:

   a. Make sure the star is selected. In the custom animation list box, click the drop-down arrow and choose Effect Options.

   b. On the Effect tab in the Settings area, for the Amount list box choose Half Spin.

   c. Click the Timing tab.

   d. In the Start list box, choose With Previous.

   e. In the Speed list box, key **0.25** (for 0.25 seconds).

   f. In the Repeat list box, choose 3. Click OK.

8. Add a second emphasis effect to the star by following these steps:

   a. Make sure the star is selected, click Add Effect, choose Emphasis, and then click More Effects. Choose Complimentary Color from the Subtle category. Click OK.

   b. Select the second item in the custom animation list, click its drop-down arrow and choose Timing.

    c. Set the following timing options:
       Start   With Previous
       Speed   0.5 seconds (Very Fast)
       Repeat 3
    d. Click OK.

9. Add an entrance and an exit effect for the star by following these steps:

    a. Make sure the star is selected. Click Add Effect, point to Entrance, and choose More Effects. Choose Dissolve In and click OK. Change the Speed to Very Fast.

    b. In the custom animation list, drag the last item (the Dissolve In entrance effect) to the top of the list so that it will play first.

    c. Make sure the star is selected; then click Add Effect again. This time point to Exit, and choose More Effects. Choose Dissolve Out and click OK.

    d. For the exit effect (the last one on the list), change the Start setting to After Previous and the Speed to Very Fast.

    e. Change the zoom setting back to Fit.

10. Create a handout header and footer: include the date and your name as the header, and the page number and text *[your initials]***11-22** as the footer.

11. Move to slide 1 and save the presentation as *[your initials]***11-22** in your Lesson 11 folder.

12. Move to slide 1 and view the presentation as a slide show. Use your mouse to advance from one slide to the next. When you reach slide 4, click your mouse once to run the star animation; then click again to complete the show. Return to slide 1.

13. Preview and then print the presentation as handouts, 4 slides per page, grayscale, landscape, framed. Close the presentation.

EXERCISE 11-23

Copy an animated object, add animation effects to a master slide, override master slide animations on a slide, and add music.

1. Open the file **Bevgs1** and display the title master.

2. Select the dotted arrow at the top of the slide. Add the Entrance animation effect Stretch from the Moderate category with the following timing and effect attributes:
With Previous, From Left, Medium.

3. To the title text placeholder, apply the same effect as in step 2.

4. To the subtitle placeholder, apply the Entrance effect Faded Zoom, starting After Previous with a 3-second delay.

5. Insert a music file that plays through the entire slide show by following these steps:

a. From the Insert menu, choose Movies and Sounds, Sound from Clip Organizer.

b. Preview some of the sound files; then click one of the files with the music icon ⊚. When the information box appears, click Automatically.

c. Right-click the sound object and choose Edit Sound Object from the shortcut menu. In the Sound Options dialog box, check Loop until stopped and Hide sound icon during slide show. Click OK.

d. Right-click the sound object again and choose Custom Animation from the shortcut menu.

e. Select the last item on the custom animation list—with the Play symbol—and click its drop-down list arrow. Choose Timing.

f. In the Start drop-down list box, choose With Previous.

g. Click the Effect tab. Under Start playing, make sure that From beginning is selected.

h. Under Stop playing, key **6** in the After spin box.

i. Click the Speaker button 🔊 and reduce the volume. Click OK.

j. In the Custom Animation dialog box, drag the last item to the top of the list.

6. Copy an animated object to another slide by following these steps:

a. On the title master, select the dotted arrow at the top of the screen and copy it to the clipboard.

b. Display the slide master; then paste the dotted arrow from the clipboard. Position the arrow below the title text placeholder.

7. Apply the same entrance effect to the slide master title text placeholder as you did to the title text placeholder on the title master—Stretch, With Previous, From Left, Medium speed.

8. Select the body text placeholder and apply the Entrance effect Faded Zoom, On Click, Very Fast speed.

9. Override a master slide animation on an individual slide by following these steps:

a. Move to slide 4.

b. In the custom animation list, select the item "Master: Body," click its drop-down arrow, and choose Copy Effects to Slide.

c. In the custom animation list, select the last item in the list ("Decaf coffee/tea").

d. Click Change at the top of the Custom Animation task pane; then choose the Entrance effect Dissolve In. Change its speed to Fast.

10. Animate an object to appear and then disappear after the slide master animations are completed by following these steps:

a. Move to slide 4 and select the picture in the lower-right corner.

b. Add the Entrance effect Wheel and change its Start setting to After Previous.

c. With the picture still selected, add the Exit effect Wheel from the Basic category and change its Start setting to After Previous.

    d. Click the Exit effect in the custom animation list (the last item) and click its drop-down list arrow. Click Timing.

    e. In the Delay spin box, key **3** to delay the effect's start for 3 seconds. Click OK.

11. Using step 10 as a guide, apply the same entrance and exit effects to the picture in the lower-left corner of slide 5.

12. Create a handout header and footer: include the date and your name as the header, and the page number and text *[your initials]***11-23** as the footer.

13. Move to slide 1 and save the presentation as *[your initials]***11-23** in your Lesson 11 folder.

14. View the presentation as a slide show.

15. Preview and then print the presentation as handouts, 6 slides per page, grayscale, framed. Close the presentation.

EXERCISE 11-24

Change animation settings, set slide timings, use Set Up Show options, create custom shows, and create action buttons and hyperlinks.

1. Open the file **Employ1**. Run a slide show to view the existing text animation.

2. Modify an existing animation scheme by following these steps:

    a. Display the slide master and the Custom Animation task pane.

    b. Select the second item in the custom animation list, which is the body placeholder.

    c. Click Change at the top of the Custom Animation task pane.

    d. Choose the Entrance effect Fly In.

3. Change the animation effect by following these steps:

    a. Click the list box arrow for the second item and choose Effect Options.

    b. Click the Text Animation tab.

    c. Change the Group text setting to By 2nd level paragraphs.

    d. Click the Timing tab.

    e. Change the Speed setting to 2 seconds (Medium). Click OK.

4. Move to slide 1. Copy the Master title slide effects to this slide.

5. Apply the Entrance effect Spiral In to the clip art image. Move its animation effect to the top of the list, above the title master animations so that the Spiral In effect occurs before the text animations. Make the effect appear automatically and at medium speed when the slide first appears.

6. Apply the Exit effect Spiral Out from the Exciting category to the clip art image. It should occur automatically at medium speed, with a 3-second delay after the title text appears.

7. Set up slide timings for a self-running slide show by following these steps:

   a. From the Slide Show menu, choose Rehearse Timings.

   b. Wait for the animations to complete on slide 1; then click the Next button ⬛ on the Rehearsal toolbar.

   c. When the next slide appears, allow enough time to read the title; then click the Next button ⬛ to advance to the next text line.

   d. Continue clicking the Next button ⬛ at the appropriate times until the slide show is finished.

   e. When the information box appears, click Yes to save your slide timings.

   f. Switch to Normal view.

8. View the presentation as a slide show to check your slide timings.

9. Create a custom show by following these steps:

   a. From the Slide Show menu, choose Custom Shows.

   b. In the Custom Shows dialog box, click New to open the Define Custom Show dialog box.

   c. In the Slide show name text box, key **Vision**

   d. In the Slides in presentation list box, use Ctrl+click to select slide 3 ("Our Vision") and slide 6 ("Why We're Successful").

   e. Click Add and then click OK.

   f. In the Custom Shows dialog box, click New again.

   g. Following steps c through e above, create a second custom show named **About Us** that includes slides 4 ("Who We Are") and 5 ("Where We're Going").

10. Create an action button that links to a custom show by following these steps:

   a. Move to slide 1.

   b. From the Slide Show menu, choose Action Buttons and drag the submenu title bar to float it.

   c. Click the first button on the Action Buttons toolbar (Action Button: Custom).

   d. Using the action button's cross pointer, draw a small rectangle in the lower-right corner of the slide.

   e. In the Action Settings dialog box, with the Mouse Click tab displayed, select Hyperlink to and choose Custom Show from its drop-down list.

   f. In the Link to Custom Show dialog box, choose "Vision." Click OK. Click OK again to close the Action Settings dialog box.

   g. Select the action button and key the label **Vision**. Adjust the size of the button to fit the text.

   h. Change the button color to deep rust (accent scheme color) and the text color to light rust (fills scheme color).

11. Create a second action button by following these steps:

   a. Copy the action button you created in step 10 and paste the copy on slide 1.

   b. Reposition the copied button above the original.

   c. Change the text label in the copied button to **About Us**

d. Select the "About Us" button; then right-click it and choose Edit Hyperlink from the shortcut menu.

e. In the Hyperlink to list box, choose Custom Show and then choose "About Us." Click OK. Click OK again to close the Action Settings dialog box.

12. Adjust the size and position of the two action buttons to give a neat and unobtrusive effect in the lower-right corner of the slide.

13. Set up a show to run manually by following these steps:

14. From the Slide Show menu, choose Set Up Show.

15. Under Advance slides, choose Manually. Click OK.

16. Run a slide show starting on slide 1. Click the action button for "About Us" to run a custom show. Run the show a second time, clicking the action button for "Vision." Run the show a third time, this time not clicking any action button.

17. Create a handout header and footer: include the date and your name as the header, and the page number and text *[your initials]*11-24 as the footer.

18. Adjust grayscale settings if needed; then move to slide 1 and save the presentation as *[your initials]*11-24 in your Lesson 11 folder.

19. Preview and then print the presentation as handouts, 6 slides per page, grayscale, framed. Close the presentation.

Lesson Applications

Create text animations, object animations, add a movie and music, and add action buttons.

1. Open the file **SpEvent3**. Apply the Blends template. Change the color scheme to the one with the royal blue background; then customize the color scheme by changing the pink Accent and hyperlink color to red.

2. Apply a one-color horizontal gradient fill to the background of all slides by using the existing blue background color and the darkest setting. Choose the variant with black at the top.

3. On the slide master and the title master, delete all the graphic elements, leaving only text placeholders. Then center the text placeholders horizontally on the masters. Center-align the text in the title master's title placeholder.

4. To the slide master body text placeholder, apply the Entrance animation effect Split, choosing Vertical Out for the Direction and On Click for the Start setting.

5. Apply the slide transition effect Split Vertical Out to all slides, at medium speed.

6. On the title master, draw a long, thin, right-pointing block arrow AutoShape as shown in Figure 11-20. Make the arrow the same length as the title placeholder, and position it between the title and the subtitle. Use the arrow's adjustment handle to make a smaller arrowhead. Apply a vertical

FIGURE 11-20
Arrow shape
and placement

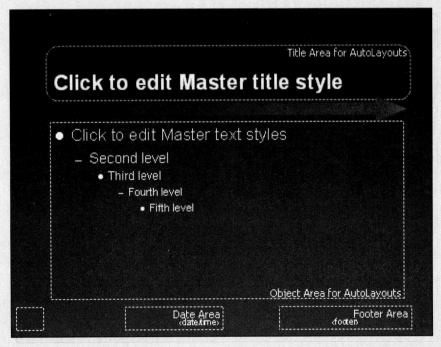

gradient fill to the arrow, using the Early Sunset preset. Choose the variant with the lightest color on the right. Remove the border line from the arrow.

7. Apply the Entrance effect Stretch to the arrow, making it stretch from the left at medium speed. Apply the Drum Roll sound effect at an appropriate volume. Make the effect happen automatically when the slide appears.

8. Copy the animated arrow to the slide master, and place it between the title and bullet placeholders. To make the arrow appear before the body text, move it to the top of the custom animation list.

9. On slide 1, at the bottom center of the slide, insert an appropriate movie from the Clip Organizer. If you cannot find an appropriate movie, use a copy of the cross-country skier from slide 5.

10. Insert a music clip of your choice on slide 1 and use the display options to hide it during the slide show. Make it play automatically for the duration of slide 1. If you cannot find an appropriate music clip, use a copy of the sound object on slide 5. Adjust its sound to an appropriate volume.

11. Insert a new slide after slide 3 that uses the Title, Text & Content layout. Key the slide text in Figure 11-21.

FIGURE 11-21

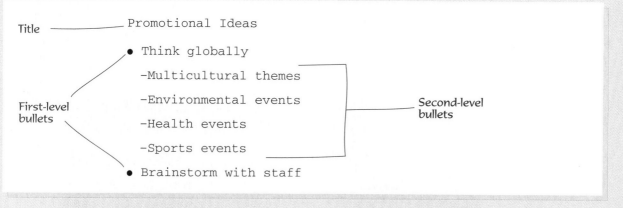

12. Insert a clip art image of a globe. If necessary, recolor the globe to harmonize with the presentation's color scheme. Apply the Entrance effect Swivel to the globe, and make it appear automatically with medium speed before the slide's text appears. Resize and reposition the body text box and the clip art as needed to create a pleasing composition.

13. On slide 2, create an action button that links to slide 3. Use the fourth button on the first row of the Action Buttons toolbar (Action Button: Information). Recolor it to suit your taste and change its depth by using its adjusting handle.

14. On slide 3, create an action button that links back to slide 2: use the first button on the third row of the Action Buttons toolbar (Action Button: Return).

15. Delete slide 6, the slide containing movie and sound samples.

16. Create a handout header and footer: include the date and your name as the header, and the page number and text *[your initials]*11-25 as the footer.

17. Move to slide 1 and save the presentation as *[your initials]*11-25 in your Lesson 11 folder.

18. View the presentation as a slide show. After all slide 2 text is displayed, click the action button to display slide 3. Use the action button on slide 3 to return to slide 2, and then continue viewing the slide show.

19. Preview and then print the presentation as handouts, 6 slides per page, grayscale, framed. Close the presentation.

EXERCISE 11-26

Animate text and objects, override master slide animations, and set up the slide show.

1. Open the file **Comp1**. Apply the Edge design template and use the color scheme with the brownish-red background. Change the background to a two-color gradient fill using brown (background scheme color) and rust (accent scheme color). Choose the From corner shading style and the variant with brown in the lower-left corner and apply to all slides.

2. On the slide master and the title master, change the title placeholder to Arial Black. Apply the Elegant animation scheme to all slides, and then apply the Wipe Right slide transition at slow speed to all slides.

3. On slide 4, copy the slide master body animation effects to the slide.

4. To the loaf of bread, apply the entrance effect Wheel and have it appear 1 second after the previous effect. To the same object, apply the exit effect Wheel and have it appear 2 seconds after previous. In the custom animation list, move the two bread animation items up so that they are inserted below item 1 ("Best bread").

5. Animate the plate of spaghetti and meatballs by using the same settings as for the loaf of bread. Move the spaghetti and meatball animation items up and insert them below item 2 ("Power-packed pasta").

6. Animate the soup tureen in the same manner and make it appear after "Healthy fast foods." Animate the piece of cake the same way and make it appear after "Fat-free desserts."

7. On slide 5, apply the same animation effects to the three clip art images, making them appear one after each of the first three bullets.

8. On slide 1, move the prize ribbon at the top left of the slide; then choose a motion path to animate it going diagonally down to the right. Adjust the position as needed and move this animation to the top of the custom animation list.

9. On slide 3, make the picture of people dissolve in on a mouse click after all the text appears.

10. On slide 2, find an appropriate clip art image to place below the text, and animate it in a way that you think would be effective.

11. Use the Rehearse Timings feature to add slide timings to the presentation; then set up the slide show to run continuously, as it would if it were being presented at a trade show kiosk. Run the show, making sure it repeats itself, and then stop it by pressing [Esc].

12. Create a handout header and footer: include the date and your name as the header, and the page number and text *[your initials]*11-26 as the footer.

13. Move to slide 1 and save the presentation as *[your initials]*11-26 in your Lesson 11 folder.

14. Preview and then print the presentation as handouts, 6 slides per page, grayscale, framed. Close the presentation.

EXERCISE 11-27 ➕ *Challenge Yourself*

Apply entrance, emphasis, and exit effects to objects; animate text; create a summary slide with hyperlinks; and insert an action button.

1. Open the file **Stratgy2**.

2. On slide 1, change the text emphasis. Make the Good 4 U title text smaller (32 points) and position it in the lower right of the slide. Increase the Marketing Strategy text to 48 points.

3. Ungroup the four arrows in the center of the slide and move them apart slightly. Position the Marketing Strategy subtitle in the middle. Move these elements up and resize the arrows for a more dramatic composition.

4. Make each arrow fly in from a corner of the slide, one after the other in a clockwise direction by applying the following entrance effects:
   - Light blue arrow: fly in from top left with previous, Push sound effect, fast speed.
   - Yellow arrow: fly in from top right after previous, Push sound effect, fast speed.
   - Royal blue arrow: fly in from bottom right after previous, Push sound effect, fast speed.
   - Red arrow: fly in from bottom left after previous, Push sound effect, fast speed.

5. On slide 2, make the clip art image of a man, woman, and light bulb zoom in from the center of the slide, starting with a mouse click, at medium speed. On top of the light bulb, draw a small star AutoShape. Color and animate the star in such a way that it twinkles or blinks several times. Have it appear by spiraling in with another mouse click after the clip art image appears.

6. On the slide master, animate the body text placeholder by using any effect that you like, making sure that the bullets appear one at a time with a mouse click.

7. Create a summary slide from slides 2, 3, and 4 and make sure it is positioned after slide 1. Give the summary slide the title **Agenda**. Create a hyperlink to the appropriate slide for each bullet on the "Agenda" slide.

8. Still working on the "Agenda" slide (slide 2), apply a fill pattern to the hyperlink text box, using dark blue (shadows scheme color) for the foreground and black for the background. Choose the first fill pattern in the fourth row. Change the margins of the text box to 0.5 inches all around, turn off the word-wrap option, and turn on Resize AutoShape to fit text. Turn off the bullets; then center the hyperlink text box both vertically and horizontally, relative to the slide.

9. Insert an action button on the slide master that will display the "Agenda" slide (slide 2) when clicked. Format the button to suit your taste.

10. Check grayscale settings and make any needed changes.

11. Create a handout header and footer: include the date and your name as the header, and the page number and text *[your initials]*11-27 as the footer.

12. Move to slide 1 and save the presentation as *[your initials]*11-27 in your Lesson 11 folder.

13. Preview and then print the presentation as handouts, 6 slides per page, grayscale, framed. Close the presentation.

On Your Own

In these exercises you work on your own, as you would in a real-life work environment. Use the skills you've learned to accomplish the task—and be creative.

EXERCISE 11-28
Create a presentation with at least six slides that describes your favorite movie. Identify the main characters, quotable lines, and the main idea of the movie. Animate the presentation to draw attention to key points and to help promote the movie to your audience. The slide show should advance by mouse clicks. Save the presentation as *[your initials]*11-28. Preview and then print the presentation as handouts.

EXERCISE 11-29
Create a presentation of at least six slides that is designed to run in a kiosk in a car dealership. The presentation should promote new models and features of vehicles. It could be a new SUV, car, truck, or the like that might draw the interest of

people entering the dealership. Apply eye-catching animations to the presentation, including sound, but make sure the animations do not obscure the presentation's message. Test and refine the presentation's animations as needed to make it run smoothly and professionally. Check spelling and grayscale settings. Save the presentation as *[your initials]*11-29. Preview and then print the presentation as handouts.

EXERCISE 11-30

Imagine that you are an artist or someone marketing the work of an artist. Choose an artistic theme and then design a four-slide presentation to run as a kiosk at an art gallery by using several animation sequences, making objects and text appear and disappear as you please, adding music, video, and sound effects. Play the animation and then fine-tune it. Set up the presentation to run continuously (so that it repeats automatically). Be prepared to run your presentation for your instructor and your classmates. Add a slide footer with your name and the text *[your initials]*11-30. Save the presentation as *[your initials]*11-30. Preview and then print the presentation as handouts.

Unit 4 Applications

Customize a design template, work with bullets and tabs, change paragraph spacing, add text and object animations, apply a slide transition, set slide timings, and customize a handout master.

1. Open the file **JobFair3**. Change the color scheme for this default design to the last choice (a white background and blue, green, and purple accents). Customize the color scheme by changing the Background color to dark navy blue; then apply a two-color gradient, blending from dark blue on the top to light blue on the bottom. Change the Text and lines color to white, and the Title text color to very bright neon green (chartreuse).

2. On the slide master, increase all text in the title placeholder and the body text placeholder by one size, change the font for all text to Arial Narrow, and make all text bold.

3. Apply the Entrance animation effect Dissolve In at medium speed to both the title text and the body text placeholders, making the title text appear automatically and the body text appear after the title text with a mouse click.

4. Still working on the slide master, change the first-level bullet to a slightly larger Wingdings 2 round bullet and make it bright green. Increase the spacing between the bullet and its text to 0.5 inches, and change the before-paragraph spacing to 0.5 lines.

5. After slide 2, insert a new slide with the Title Only layout. Key the title **Salary Ranges** and create a tabbed table using the following text:

   Wait staff `Tab` **$** `Tab` **8.00** `Tab` **plus tips**
   Assistant chefs `Tab` **$** `Tab` **12.50** `Tab` **to start**
   Experienced chefs `Tab` **$** `Tab` **17.50** `Tab` **and up**

6. Format the table text as 36-point bold Arial Narrow. Insert appropriate tab stops, and size and position the text box appropriately.

7. To the table, apply the Entrance animation effect Dissolve In at medium speed, making it appear on a mouse click. Make sure the table appears after the slide's title.

8. On slide 1, select the Great Jobs 4 U text and make it 60 points. Change its border to a 3-point bright green line.

9. Apply the Entrance animation effect Fly In from the bottom at medium speed. Adjust the animation order, if necessary, so that the logo is the last item to appear on the slide, appearing with a 1-second delay after a mouse click.

10. On slide 1, increase the subtitle text to 48 points. Arrange both text placeholders on the top half of the slide.

11. Still on slide 1, resize the Good 4 U logo proportionately to 6 inches wide; then center it horizontally on the bottom half of the slide.

12. Insert a music file of your choice on slide 1. Hide the sound object by dragging it off the slide. Make it start playing at the beginning of the slide show and loop continuously for the duration of the show.

 TIP: To make the sound loop until stopped, right-click the sound object, choose Edit Sound Object, check Loop until stopped, and click OK.

13. On slide 4, change the slide layout to Title Slide.

14. Move to slide 4. Select the picture in the middle of the slide and resize it disproportionately to be 7.5 inches high by 10 inches wide (the size of a slide). Reposition the picture so that it aligns with the slide; then use the Picture toolbar's brightness and contrast buttons to make it darker, so that the design fades into the background.

15. Copy the picture, paste it onto the slide master, and send it to the back. If necessary, adjust the contrast and brightness of the background picture so that it does not conflict with the text.

16. Apply the Wipe Left slide transition effect to all the slides in the presentation, using medium speed and no sound.

17. Use the Rehearse Timings feature to set automatic slide timings for all slides.

18. Review the slides, making adjustments to text size and text box placement as needed to make an attractive presentation. Run the slide show; then make any changes needed to the slides' timing and animation effects.

19. Adjust grayscale settings.

20. Customize the handout master by deleting the page number placeholder and adding the text **Job Fair Presentation** to the footer placeholder so that the text in the footer placeholder reads "<footer> Job Fair Presentation." Center the footer placeholder horizontally, center-align the footer text, and increase the font by one size increment. Move it up slightly.

21. Create a handout header and footer: include the date and your name as the header, and the text *[your initials]*U4-1 in the footer.

22. Move to slide 1 and save the presentation as *[your initials]*U4-1 in a new folder for Unit 4 Applications.

23. Preview and then print the presentation as handouts, 4 slides per page, grayscale, landscape, framed. Close the presentation.

Change page setup options, use drawing tools, set text box options, and set tabs.

1. Start a new blank presentation to create a printed menu. Choose the Title Only slide layout for the first slide. Set the page orientation to Portrait with slides sized for Letter Paper (8.5x11 in).

2. Apply the Edge design template. Change the color scheme to the last sample (white background with green, blue, and gray accents). Customize the color scheme by changing the Background color to pale yellow, the Fills color to medium blue, and the Accent color to red.

3. To the background, apply a one-color Diagonal down gradient fill, using pale yellow and shading to the lightest setting. Choose the variant with white in the upper-right corner.

4. Copy slide 1 and paste it as slide 2, keeping the source formatting (use the Paste Options smart tag if it appears). On the second slide, omit the background graphics from the slide master and change the gradient fill shading style to Diagonal up. Choose the variant with the lightest color in the upper left. The effect should be a mirror image of the gradient on slide 1.

5. Copy the slide master graphics (the angled horizontal line at the top and the horizontal line at the bottom) and paste them on slide 2. On slide 2, flip horizontally the line at the top. Slide 2 should now be an exact mirror image of slide 1.

6. Working on slide 1, key the title **July 4 Brunch Menu**. Decrease the font size to 32 points and make it bold.

7. Draw an Oval 0.75 inches high and 2.5 inches wide. Give the oval a white fill (custom color) and outline it in red. Key **Starters** in the oval. Format the text as 20-point Arial, red, bold, centered, and with a text shadow. Apply Shadow Style 6 to the oval. Change the shadow color to solid red (not semitransparent); then nudge the shadow up and to the left to make it slightly thinner.

8. Duplicate the oval. Format the copy as follows:
   - Resize to 1.5 inches high and 3.75 inches wide.
   - Set text box margins to 0.0 inches all around, turn on word-wrap, and set the text box anchor to Middle.
   - Reduce the font size to 14 points, remove the bold attribute and the text shadow, and change the text color to black (text and lines scheme color).
   - Left-align the text and set a decimal tab at the 2.5-inch mark.
   - Make sure line spacing is set at 1 line, and spacing before and after paragraphs is set to 0.

9. Change the text "Starters" in the second oval to Red, White, and Blue. After "blue," insert a tab and key 3.50. Press Enter and key **Raspberries and blueberries with a lightly sweetened vanilla yogurt topping**

10. Change the formatting of just the text "Red, White, and Blue" to 14 points, red, bold, and with a text shadow.

11. Duplicate the oval three times and change the text in each oval to match the Starter menu items shown in Figure U4-1. Arrange the ovals in an overlapping pattern at the top of the screen and change the order of the ovals as needed (for example, bring the "Starters" oval to the front).

FIGURE U4-1
Slide 1

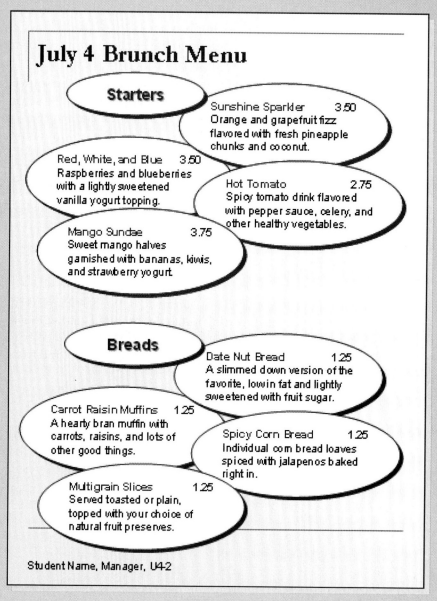

12. Select all the ovals and copy them to the bottom half of the slide. Change the red text, borders, and shadows of the copied ovals to medium blue.

13. In the copied ovals, key the Bread menu items shown in Figure U4-1, and rearrange them as needed so that all text is visible.

14. Select all the ovals on slide 1 and copy them to slide 2. Working on slide 2, group all the ovals, flip them horizontally, and then ungroup them, making a mirror image of the oval placement on slide 1.

15. Change the text in the slide 2 ovals to the Main Dish and Beverage menu items shown in Figure U4-2. Delete the title placeholder.

FIGURE U4-2
Slide 2

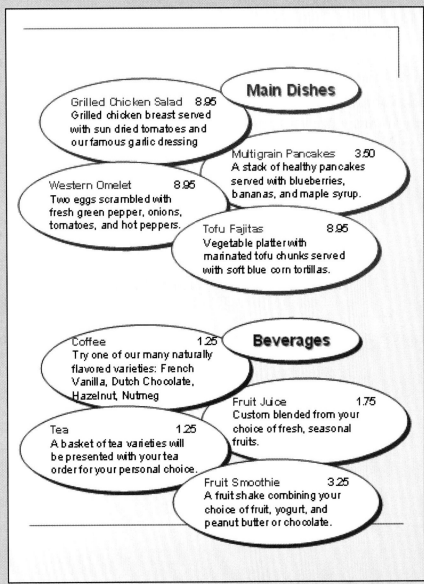

16. Adjust the height of individual ovals to accommodate all the text. Change the order of the ovals on slide 2 to agree with Figure U4-2. Rearrange and reorder the ovals as needed so that no text is hidden.

17. Insert a text box in the lower-left corner of slide 1 with the text *[Your Name]*, **Manager, U4-2**. Format the text as 14-point Arial, and make it black.

18. Check spelling in the presentation.

19. Check grayscale settings and make changes, if needed.

20. Save the presentation as *[your initials]***U4-2** in your Unit 4 Applications folder.

21. Print both pages of the presentation as full-sized slides. Close the presentation.

UNIT APPLICATION 4-3 *Using the Internet*

Write and design a presentation that uses text manipulation features, custom animation, freeform drawing, and action buttons.

Use the Internet to research a vacation destination, for example, Orlando, Florida; San Diego, California; Billings, Montana; Williamsburg, Virginia; or other location. Gather information on places to visit, unique restaurants and places to stay, and any other information that you find interesting.

Use the information you gathered to create a presentation. Use a template and color scheme that complements your material. Include at least six slides. Include text and object animations, music, and sound effects where appropriate. Create a summary slide with a suitable name and hyperlinks to each slide. Include a "Home" action button on each slide that links back to the summary slide. Check spelling and review all the slides in grayscale view, making grayscale adjustments if needed.

In the slide footer, include the text **Prepared by** followed by your name. Include the slide number on all slides but not the date. In the handout footer, include the completed filename *[your initials]***U4-3**. In the handout header, key **Presented to** and then identify to whom you would be giving this presentation. Include in the handout the date you would be delivering the presentation.

Save the presentation as *[your initials]***U4-3** in your Unit 4 folder. Practice delivering the presentation. Preview and then print the presentation handouts as an appropriate number of slides per page, grayscale, framed. Close the presentation.

Charts, Tables, and Diagrams

12

Creating a Chart

After completing this lesson, you will be able to:

1. Create a chart.
2. Format a column chart.
3. Use different chart types.
4. Work with pie charts.
5. Import charts from Excel.
6. Enhance chart elements.

MICROSOFT OFFICE SPECIALIST ACTIVITIES
In this lesson:
PP03S-1-3
PP03S-1-4
PP03S-1-5
PP03S-2-4

See Appendix.

Estimated Time: 2 hours

*C*harts, sometimes called *graphs,* are diagrams that display numbers in pictorial format. Charts can help you understand the significance of numeric information more easily than viewing the same information as a table or a list of numbers. The elements that make up a chart help you to judge size relationships between data or examine trends over time.

Creating a Chart

PowerPoint provides several ways to start a new chart. You can add a chart to an existing slide or you can select a slide layout with a chart placeholder at the time you create a new slide. Here are three methods:

- From the Insert menu, choose Chart.
- Click the Insert Chart button on the Standard toolbar.

- Choose one of the slide layouts that includes a **Content** placeholder, and then click the Insert Chart icon 🏛 in the center of the placeholder.

Any one of the previous actions opens Microsoft Graph, the program used by PowerPoint to create charts. When you start a new chart, a sample *datasheet* appears. A datasheet is a table in which you key the numbers and labels used to create a chart.

EXERCISE | **12-1** | **Choose a Slide Layout for a Chart**

When you create a new slide, the Slide Layout task pane offers several Content Layouts that are suitable for charts. Text and Content Layouts make it easy to combine a chart and body text on the same slide.

1. Open the file **Finance1**.

2. Insert a new slide after slide 1 that uses the **Title and Content** slide layout. Key the slide title **Sales Forecast**. This layout contains a placeholder suitable for charts. If you want to place more than one chart on a slide, use one of the other Content Layouts.

FIGURE 12-1
Choosing a slide
layout for a chart

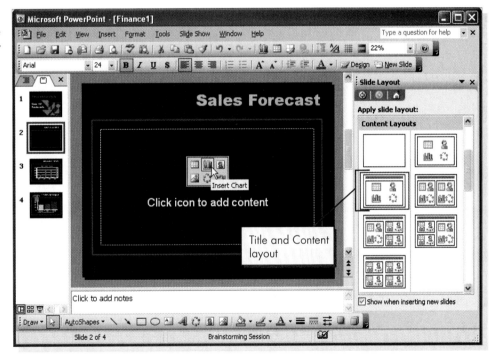

3. Click the Insert Chart icon 🏛 in the center of the content placeholder. Microsoft Graph opens within PowerPoint. A sample chart and sample data appear, along with chart-related buttons in the toolbars at the top of the screen.

EXERCISE 12-2 Make Changes to Sample Datasheet

The datasheet contains rows and columns. You key each number or label in a separate *cell*—the rectangle formed by the intersection of a row and a column—the same way that you would key information in a spreadsheet program such as Excel. The datasheet also contains gray column headings and row headings with a button-like appearance that indicates row numbers and column letters. If you like, you can move the datasheet by dragging its title bar, and you can resize it by dragging its borders.

As you enter data, you can monitor the results on the sample chart. You key new information by overwriting the sample data or by deleting the sample data and keying your own data.

NOTE: When working in Microsoft Graph, be sure to click your mouse pointer only inside the datasheet, within the sample chart, or on toolbar buttons and scroll bars. If you click anywhere else, Microsoft Graph closes and you return to Normal view. If that happens, double-click the chart displayed on the slide to reopen Microsoft Graph.

FIGURE 12-2
Creating a chart

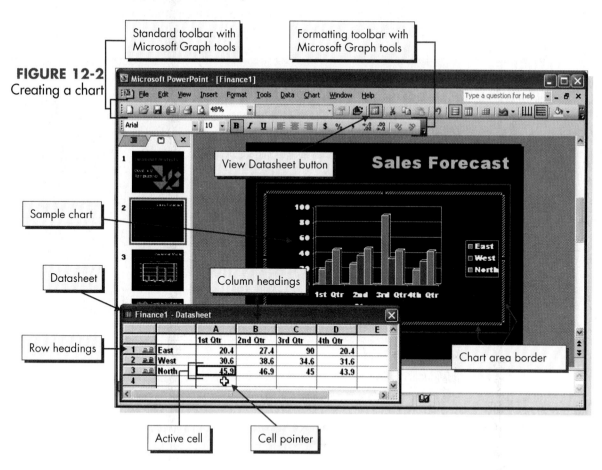

1. On the datasheet, click the word "East." A heavy black border surrounds the cell that contains "East." Notice that when working on the datasheet, your mouse pointer is a white cross , called a *cell pointer*.

2. Move around the datasheet by clicking on individual cells. Then try pressing Enter, Tab, Shift+Enter, Shift+Tab, and the arrow keys to get the feel for how to navigate in a datasheet.

3. Click cell A3 (the cell in column A, row 3 that contains the value 45.9).

4. Key **90** and press Enter. Notice on the chart that the blue column for the first quarter becomes taller automatically.

5. Click the Undo button to restore the blue column to its original height.

NOTE: Although you can perform multiple Undo actions elsewhere in PowerPoint and in other Microsoft Office programs, you get only one chance to undo an action when editing a chart. Be careful when making changes!

TABLE 12-1 Chart-Related Buttons on the Standard Toolbar

BUTTON	NAME	PURPOSE
Chart Area	Chart Objects	Selects an element of the chart
	Format	Formats the selected chart item
	Import File	Imports data from a spreadsheet or text file
	View Datasheet	Displays or hides the datasheet window
	By Row	Plots chart data series from data across rows
	By Column	Plots chart data series from data down columns
	Data Table	Displays the values for each data series in a grid below the chart
	Chart Type	Changes the chart type for the active chart or a selected data series
	Category Axis Gridlines	Shows or hides category axis gridlines
	Value Axis Gridlines	Shows or hides value axis gridlines

continues

TABLE 12-1 *continued*

BUTTON	NAME	PURPOSE
	Legend	Adds or removes a chart legend
	Drawing	Shows or hides the Drawing toolbar
	Fill Color	Changes the fill color or fill effect of the selected chart object

EXERCISE `12-3` **Delete Sample Data**

1. Click cell A1, the first-quarter cell for the East region, with the value "20.4."
2. Press ⌈Delete⌋ to delete the contents of cell A1. Notice that the first green column in the chart is no longer displayed.
3. Drag the pointer from cell A2 to cell D2 to select the four numbers in row 2.
4. Press ⌈Delete⌋. All the dark green chart columns for the West region are deleted along with their data.
5. Click the gray box in the upper-left corner of the datasheet. The entire datasheet is selected.

FIGURE 12-3
Editing the datasheet

Click here to select the entire datasheet.

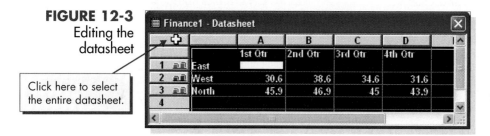

			A	B	C	D	
			1st Qtr	2nd Qtr	3rd Qtr	4th Qtr	
1		East					
2		West	30.6	38.6	34.6	31.6	
3		North	45.9	46.9	45	43.9	
4							

6. Press ⌈Delete⌋. The datasheet is now blank and ready for you to key new data. Notice that the chart column disappears.

EXERCISE `12-4` **Key New Chart Data**

The Microsoft Graph datasheet looks like an Excel spreadsheet with one exception: there is an unnumbered row above row 1 and an unlettered column to the left of column A. This is where you key chart labels that appear below columns or in a legend to identify chart content.

NOTE: If you key labels in other rows or columns or leave gaps between columns or rows as you enter data, your chart will not display correctly.

1. Click the first cell in the upper-left corner. All the cells in the datasheet are deselected. Now you can enter new data.

2. Key the numbers and labels shown in Figure 12-4. Be sure to put the labels in the top row and left-most column. Notice how the chart grows as you key data.

TIP: You don't need to be concerned about number formatting in the datasheet. But if you want to align decimals and add commas, use the Formatting toolbar, just as you would if you were working in Excel.

3. Click the cell with the label "Los Angeles." Notice that the label is truncated.

4. Move the pointer to the right border of the column heading—the gray box—at the top of the column containing "Los Angeles" (see Figure 12-4 for exact placement).

5. Drag the two-pointed cross pointer ↔ to the right so that the first column is wide enough to display all the text. (The chart will display properly even when datasheet columns are too narrow to show all text.)

FIGURE 12-4
Datasheet with new data

Drag here to change column width on datasheet.

Finance1 - Datasheet		A	B	C	D
		2005	2006	2007	
1	New York	920	1130	1450	
2	Miami	500	850	1210	
3	Los Angeles	350	760	990	
4					

EXERCISE 12-5 Switch Rows and Columns

When you key data for a new chart, Microsoft Graph interprets each row of data as a *data series*. On a column chart, each data series is usually displayed in a distinct color. For example, on the current chart, the New York row is one data series and is displayed in light green. Miami is a second data series, displayed in dark green, and Los Angeles is a third, displayed in blue.

Sometimes it's hard to predict if it's best to arrange your data in rows or columns. Fortunately, you can enter it either way and easily change the way it is displayed on the chart.

1. Continue working on the datasheet for the chart on slide 2.

2. Click the By Column button ⊞ on the Standard toolbar. The chart columns are now grouped by city instead of by year. The city names are displayed below each group of columns.

3. Click the By Row button ⊟ to group the chart columns by year again.

4. Click the By Column button ⊞ once again. Return to Normal view by clicking on a blank area of the chart. Your chart should look like the one shown in Figure 12-5.

5. Create a slide footer for the current slide (slide 2 only) containing today's date and the text *[Your Name], [your initials]*12-5.

6. Create a new folder for lesson 12. Save the presentation as *[your initials]*12-5 in your folder for Lesson 12.

7. Print the current slide (slide 2) in full size. If you have a color printer, print it in color.

FIGURE 12-5
Chart with new data

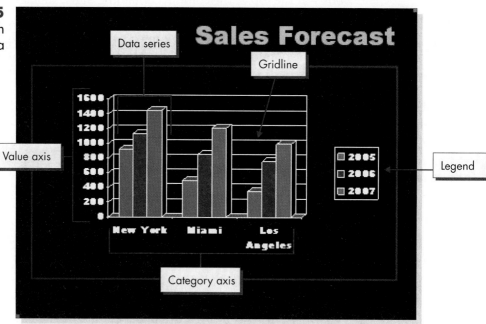

EXERCISE **12-6** **Hide the Datasheet and View the Chart**

While working on your chart, you can hide the datasheet by clicking its Close button ⊠ or by clicking the View Datasheet button ⊞ that is available on the Standard toolbar when you are using Microsoft Graph. To redisplay the datasheet, click the View Datasheet button ⊞ again (or choose Datasheet from the View menu).

1. Double-click the chart to open Microsoft Graph.

2. Click the View Datasheet button on the Standard toolbar to hide the datasheet.

3. Click the same button again to display the datasheet.

4. Click anywhere on the slide, outside the chart area border. Microsoft Graph closes, and PowerPoint's Normal view is displayed.

Formatting a Column Chart

You can apply a wide variety of format options to charts. The default chart type is a 3-D Column Chart. Other types include bar, area, line, pie, and surface. You can change the colors, patterns, fonts, and number formats of a chart.

You can alter the appearance of your chart's axes by changing text color, size, font, and number formatting. You can also change scale and tick mark settings. The *scale* indicates the values that are displayed on the value axis and the intervals between those values. *Tick marks* are small measurement marks, similar to those found on a ruler, that can show increments on the value axis (on the left for column charts) and the category axis (on the bottom for column charts).

To make these changes, use the Format Axis dialog box, which you display in one of the following ways:

- Double-click an axis.

- Select an axis and click the Format button on the Standard toolbar (or press (Ctrl)+(1)).

- Right-click an axis and choose Format Axis from the shortcut menu.

> **TIP:** (Ctrl)+(1) opens the formatting dialog box that is appropriate for whatever chart element is currently selected.

EXERCISE **12-7** **Explore Parts of a Chart**

PowerPoint provides several tools to help you navigate around the chart and ScreenTips to help you select the part of the chart on which you want to work.

1. Move the pointer over the words "New York." The ScreenTip identifies this part of the chart as the Category Axis.

2. Using the tip of the pointer, point to a horizontal white line (gridline) within the chart. The ScreenTip identifies this as Value Axis Major Gridlines.

3. Move the pointer around other parts of the chart and try to find the Plot Area, Chart Area, and Legend. Each of these areas can be formatted with fill colors, border colors, and font attributes.

4. On the Standard toolbar, click the Chart Objects list box arrow. A list of the various chart elements is displayed. (See Figure 12-6 on the next page.)

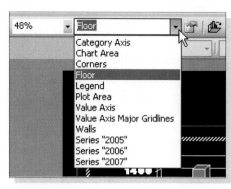

FIGURE 12-6
Chart Objects
list box

5. Choose Floor from the list to select the chart floor. Sometimes it's easier to select the chart's smaller elements this way.

6. Close the datasheet, but keep the chart open for the next exercise.

EXERCISE 12-8 Work with Solid Color Fills

You can change the colors of individual chart areas, columns, or an entire group of columns.

1. Working on the chart on slide 2, point to one of the blue columns and notice the ScreenTip that appears, identifying the data series.

2. Click any blue column. All the blue columns are selected, as indicated by the four handles that are displayed on each selected column.

3. Click the blue column for Los Angeles. Now the Los Angeles column is the only one selected. Clicking once selects all the columns in a series; clicking a second time (not double-clicking) changes the selection to just one column.

4. Click one of the light green columns to select all the light green columns.

5. Click the arrow next to the Fill Color button 🖎 on the Standard toolbar. (Use the Toolbar Options button ⬓ if necessary.) Float the menu by dragging its title bar.

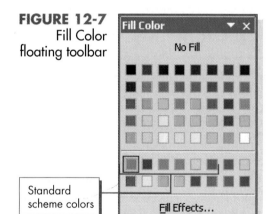

FIGURE 12-7
Fill Color
floating toolbar

Standard
scheme colors

6. On the Fill Color toolbar, move your pointer across the second row from the bottom, which contains the currently selected color. ScreenTips identify some of the colors as "Standard Colors," which means they follow the presentation color scheme. Usually, the first six colors in this row are standard colors.

7. Click the gold box (the fifth color in the second row from the bottom). The selected columns in the chart change to gold.

8. Click the gold column for Los Angeles, and then click a red color. The Los Angeles column is now a different color from the other columns in its series.

9. Click a blank area within the chart area border to deselect the Los Angeles column; then click Los Angeles again to select all the columns in its series and change it back to gold.

EXERCISE **12-9** **Work with Pattern and Gradient Fills**

Special fill effects, including textures and gradient fills, can be used the same way you use them for other PowerPoint objects. You can also change the border style of columns, bars, and other chart elements.

1. With the columns selected that contain the gold fill color, click Fill Effects on the Fill Color floating toolbar. Click the Pattern tab. Change the Background color to red, the first color in the bottom row (the Foreground color is gold).

2. Choose the Wide upward diagonal pattern in the third column and the last row of pattern samples. Click OK. The three columns are now gold with diagonal red stripes.

3. Select the dark green columns and reopen the Pattern tab in the Fill Effects dialog box. Change the background to bright green (third color on the bottom row) and choose the Dark horizontal stripe pattern in the fourth column and the bottom row (Foreground is dark green). Click OK.

4. Double-click a blue column to open the Format Data Series dialog box.

5. Click Fill Effects on the Patterns tab to open the Fill Effects dialog box. Then open the Pattern tab. Change the fill pattern to Wide downward diagonal, using dark blue as the background color (Foreground is light blue). Click OK to accept these changes, and then click OK to exit the Format Data Series dialog box.

6. Double-click the red/gold columns to open the Format Data Series dialog box. In the Patterns tab, notice the Border options on the left side of the dialog box. Click the Color list box arrow and change the column's border to gold. Click OK.

7. Using the Format Data Series dialog box, change the border of the green columns to light green, and the border of the blue columns to light blue.

8. Close Microsoft Graph and look at the graph in Slide Show view. Then return to Normal view.

NOTE: Pattern fills are a good choice when you print your slides in black and white or if you want to use the chart in a report that is printed in black only. However, this multicolor treatment might seem a little too colorful for a business presentation. In the next steps, you will apply another type of fill.

9. Double-click the chart to open Microsoft Graph. Double-click one of the red/gold columns to open the Format Data Series dialog box.

10. On the Patterns tab, click Fill Effects to open the Fill Effects dialog box. Then click the Gradient tab. Select a one-color gradient in gold and a Horizontal shading style with the dark color at the bottom. Click OK to accept the fill effects.

11. Still working on the Patterns tab, select the Border color and change it to gold. Click OK to close the Format Data Point dialog box.

12. Repeat this process for the green and blue columns using a one-color gradient for the fill color of each.

13. Create a slide footer for the current slide (slide 2 only) containing today's date and the text *[Your Name], [your initials]***12-9**. Then, update the notes and handouts footer for *[your initials]***12-9**.

14. Save the presentation as *[your initials]***12-9** in your new folder for Lesson 12.

15. Print the current slide (slide 2) in full size. If you have a color printer, print it in color.

E X E R C I S E 12-10 **Format the Value Axis**

1. With the datasheet closed for the chart on slide 2, point to one of the numbers on the left side of the chart. When you see the Value Axis ScreenTip, double-click to open the Format Axis dialog box. (You can also right-click and open it from the menu.)

2. Click the Font tab and change the font to Arial, Bold, 18 points.

3. Click the Number tab. In the Category box, choose Currency and change the decimal places to **0** because all numbers in the datasheet are even numbers.

4. Click the Scale tab. In the Maximum box, key **1500** to set the largest number on the value axis.

5. In the Major unit text box, key **500** to set wider intervals between the numbers on the value axis.

6. Click OK. The chart now shows fewer horizontal gridlines, and each value is formatted as currency with a dollar sign.

FIGURE 12-8
Formatting the
value axis

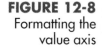
Value axis showing
new font, scale, and
currency format

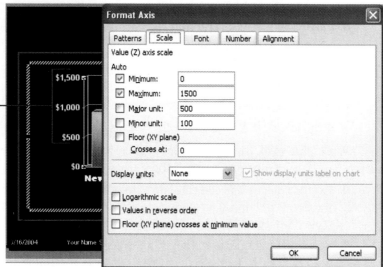

7. With the value axis selected, click the Italic button I on the Formatting toolbar. The value axis labels are italicized.

8. Click the Font Size list box arrow and choose 16.

EXERCISE 12-11 Format the Category Axis

You format the category axis in the same way as the value axis.

1. Right-click the text "New York" on the category axis and choose Format Axis from the shortcut menu.

2. In the Format Axis dialog box, click the Font tab and choose Arial, Bold Italic, 16 points. Click OK to close the dialog box.

EXERCISE 12-12 Insert Axis Titles

Axis titles are an important part of charts. Careful labeling ensures that your charts will be interpreted correctly.

1. Move the mouse pointer near the right edge of the chart until you see the Chart Area ScreenTip. Right-click the chart area and choose Chart Options from the shortcut menu.

2. In the Chart Options dialog box, click the Titles tab. In the Category (X) axis text box, key **Apparel Sales**

3. In the Value (Z) axis text box, key **(thousands)** and click OK. The new titles appear on the slide.

FIGURE 12-9
Rotating the
axis title

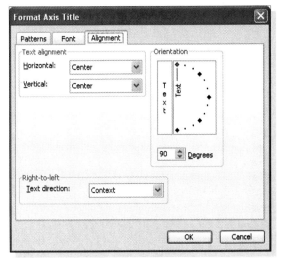

4. Right-click "(thousands)" and choose Format Axis Title.

5. Click the Alignment tab. Under Orientation, drag the red diamond up to 90 degrees to change the text to a vertical orientation.

6. Click the Font tab and choose Arial, Italic, 14 points. Click OK.

7. Click the category axis title ("Apparel Sales") to select it. Use the Formatting toolbar to change the font from Arial Black to Arial.

EXERCISE 12-13 Change or Remove the Legend

A *legend* is a box showing the colors and patterns assigned to the data series. You can customize a chart's legend by changing the border, background colors, and font attributes.

1. Right-click the legend box and choose Format Legend.
2. In the Format Legend dialog box, click the Font tab and change the font to Arial, Bold Italic, 16 points.
3. Click the Patterns tab and change the Border to None.

TIP: If the legend is to be the same color as the chart background, make sure that the legend's Area option on the Patterns tab is set to None. Choosing a fill color, even if it is the same as the background, can make it difficult to choose good grayscale settings for printing.

4. Click the Placement tab and choose Top. Click OK. The legend appears above the chart without a surrounding border. Note that sizing handles surround the legend.
5. Using a right or left sizing handle, resize the legend box to make it wider so there is more space between the legend items.
6. Point to the center of the legend. Using the arrow pointer, drag the legend down so it is below the top gridline and above the columns. Adjust the width of the legend if it overlaps any columns.
7. Close Microsoft Graph to view the completed chart.

FIGURE 12-10
Completed chart

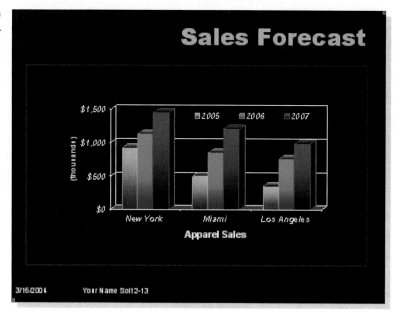

8. Update your slide footer for the current slide (slide 2 only) containing today's date and the text *[Your Name], [your initials]***12-13**. Then update the notes and handouts footer for *[your initials]***12-13**.

9. Save the presentation as *[your initials]***12-13** in your Lesson 12 folder.

Using Different Chart Types

In addition to the default 3-D Column Chart, PowerPoint offers a wide variety of chart types. Other types include bar, area, line, pie, and surface, in both two- and three-dimensional varieties. In addition, you can include more than one type on a single chart, for example, a combination of lines and columns.

If you are working on a two-dimensional (2-D) chart, you can add a secondary axis, so that you can plot data against two different scales. This feature makes it possible to work with two types of data on the same chart, for example, air temperature compared to wind speed, or number of customers compared to dollar sales. A secondary axis is also a good choice if you need to display numbers that vary greatly in magnitude, for example, comparing national sales trends with sales generated by a small local brand.

E X E R C I S E   12-14 Switch to Other Chart Types

Sometimes switching to a different chart type can make data easier to understand. You can change chart types in the following ways:

- From the Chart menu, choose Chart Type to open the Chart Type dialog box.
- Right-click the chart area; then choose Chart Type from the submenu.
- Click the list box arrow for the Chart Type button ![chart type icon], float the Chart Type menu, and then make a selection from the Chart Type toolbar.

1. Move to slide 3 and activate the chart. If the datasheet is showing, hide it. This chart compares dollar sales to number of customer visits. Because of the different types of data, the sales figures are not easy to understand.

2. Click the list box arrow for the Chart Type button ![chart type icon] and float its submenu. Many chart types are available on this toolbar.

3. Click the second chart type in the second row with the ScreenTip 3-D Bar Chart. The chart's vertical columns change to horizontal bars. (See Figure 12-11 on the next page.)

4. Click several different chart types on the Chart Type toolbar. Notice that some chart types display the data more effectively than others.

5. Close the Chart Type toolbar.

6. From the Chart menu, choose Chart Type. The Chart Type dialog box opens.

FIGURE 12-11
Changing to a
different chart type

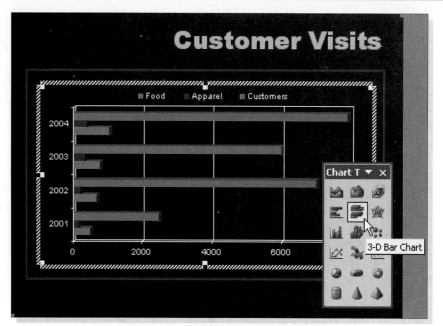

7. In the Chart type list box, choose Column (at the top of the list). Several varieties of column charts appear in the Chart sub-type box. The upper-left sample is selected.

8. Click one of the other subtypes. Notice the description that appears in the box below.

9. Reselect the upper-left sample. Its description is Clustered Column. Compare values across categories. Click OK. The chart changes to a 2-D column chart.

EXERCISE **12-15** **Add a Secondary Chart Axis**

The chart on slide 3 ("Customer Visits") contains dollar values for apparel and food sales, and also unit values for number of customer visits. Plotting customer visits on a secondary axis will improve the chart.

If you are working with a 3-D chart, you must change it to a 2-D chart (as you did in the previous exercise), before you can add a secondary axis.

1. Activate the chart on slide 3.

2. Right-click one of the blue columns and choose Format Data Series from the shortcut menu. Click the Axis tab.

NOTE: If the Format Data Series dialog box does not contain an Axis tab, your current chart type does not support a secondary axis. Make sure you are working with a 2-D chart.

3. In the Plot series on option box, select Secondary axis. Click OK. Now the red and green columns have become taller, the scale on the left has changed, and a new scale has been added on the right. Notice the secondary axis on the left side of the chart. You improve the appearance of this chart in the following exercises.

FIGURE 12-12
Adding a
secondary axis

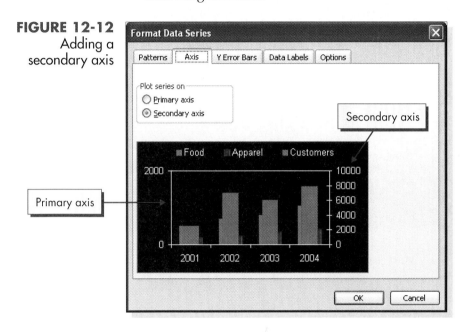

EXERCISE 12-16 Combine Chart Types

A good way to distinguish between different data types on a single chart is to assign different chart types. For example, with the current chart, the "Customers" data series can be shown as a line or an area, while the sales data remains as columns.

1. Float the Chart Type toolbar.
2. Click one of the blue columns to select the "Customers" data series.
3. Click Area Chart button, the first button on the Chart Type toolbar. A large blue area appears behind the sales columns. (See Figure 12-13 on the next page.)
4. Click the blue area to select it; then choose Line Chart from the Chart Type toolbar (the first sample in the fourth row). The area changes to a green line.
5. Double-click the green line representing "Customers." Click the Patterns tab.
6. In the Line section on the left, click the Color list box arrow and choose the standard color, medium blue (third color from the left in the second row from the bottom).
7. For the Weight, choose the heaviest weight in the list box. Click the Smoothed line check box to select it.

FIGURE 12-13
Area and column
combination chart

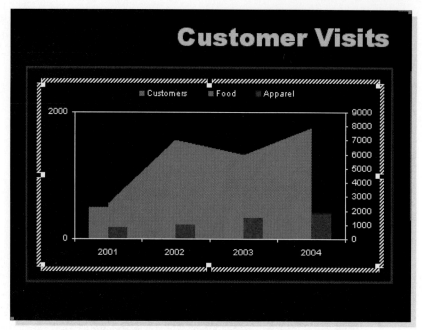

8. In the Marker section on the right, select N̲one. Click OK. A smooth blue line replaces the green line.

EXERCISE 12-17 Format a Primary and Secondary Axis

Proper formatting and labeling on a chart is always important to ensure that viewers understand the information you want to convey. This is even more important when you have both a primary and secondary axis on the chart.

1. From the C̲hart menu, choose Chart Opti̲ons and click the Titles tab.
2. In the V̲alue (Y) axis text box, key **Sales (thousands)**. The sample indicates the position of the text on the chart.
3. In the Second value (Y̲) axis text box, key **Customer Visits (hundreds)** and click OK. Descriptive titles now appear next to both the primary and the secondary axes.
4. Right-click Value Axis on the left (Sales) and choose F̲ormat Axis. Click the Scale tab.
5. In the M̲ajor unit text box, key **500**. This will insert tick marks and numbers on the axis.
6. Click the Number tab. In the C̲ategory list box, choose Currency. In the D̲ecimal places spin box, change the number to **0**. Click OK.

7. Right-click the Secondary Value Axis on the right (Customers) and choose Format Axis. Click the Scale tab.

8. Change the value in the Major unit text box to **1500** to reduce some of the tick marks and number labels. Click OK.

9. If the columns have white borders, remove them (right-click a column, choose Format Data Series, display the Patterns tab, and click None under Border).

10. Select the green columns and change the fill color to gold.

11. Click outside the chart area to return to Normal view.

 TIP: It is best to avoid red and green to distinguish between data on column and bar charts. Some individuals have difficulty distinguishing between those two colors.

FIGURE 12-14
Completed
combination chart

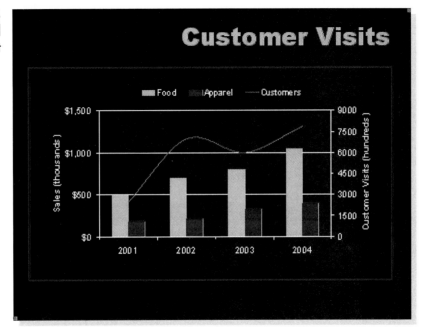

12. Create a slide footer for slide 3 that includes the date and the footer text *[Your Name]*, *[your initials]***12-17**, and also update the notes and handout footer. Save the presentation as *[your initials]***12-17**.

13. Print slide 3 in full size. Leave the presentation open for the next exercise.

Working with Pie Charts

A *pie chart* is a simple, yet highly effective, presentation tool that shows individual values in relation to the sum of all the values—it makes it easy to judge "parts of a whole." Each value is displayed as a "slice" of the pie.

A pie chart can show only one data series. To show more than one data series, use more than one pie chart.

EXERCISE 12-18 Create a Pie Chart

In this exercise, you create a pie chart to display the breakdown of the restaurant's sales by category.

If your datasheet contains more than one series, a pie chart uses the first row of numbers. You can change to a different row or column if you like.

1. Insert a new slide after slide 3 that uses the Title Only layout.

2. Key the title **2004 Sales Categories**

3. Click the Insert Chart button [image] on the Standard toolbar. The sample chart and datasheet appear.

4. Click the list box arrow for the Chart Type button [image] on the Standard toolbar.

5. Choose Pie Chart, the first option in the fifth row. A pie chart replaces the column chart, displaying numbers from the first row in the datasheet.

6. On the datasheet, click the gray box in the upper-left corner to select all the sample data, and then delete it.

7. Key the data shown in Figure 12-15.

FIGURE 12-15
Datasheet for
pie chart

Sol12-17 - Datasheet

		A	B	C	D	E
		Food	Beverages	Apparel	Other	
1	2004 Sales	3339	2933	1529	906	
2						
3						
4						

8. Close the datasheet to view the chart.

EXERCISE 12-19 Add Pie Slice Labels

You can add labels to the chart's data series and edit those labels individually.

1. Right-click one of the pie slices and choose Format Data Series.

2. Click the Data Labels tab. In the Label Contains section, select both Category name and Percentage. Click OK. Data labels appear next to the slices. Notice that with the addition of data labels, the legend is no longer needed and the pie is now very small.

NOTE: Depending on the pie chart, sometimes parts of the data labels might be hidden by the edges of the chart placeholder. In this case, you need to resize the pie by using the plot area sizing handles.

3. Select the legend box and delete it. The pie becomes a little larger.

4. Click any data label. All the data labels are selected. Change the font to 16-point Arial, bold italic. The pie becomes a little larger.

5. Click the data label "Other 10%" once to select just that label. As with columns, click once to select all labels, and click again to select just one. You can now edit the selected label's text.

6. Click within the text to display an insertion point. Delete the word "Other" (but not "10%"), and key in its place **Take-out**

FIGURE 12-16
Pie chart with
data labels

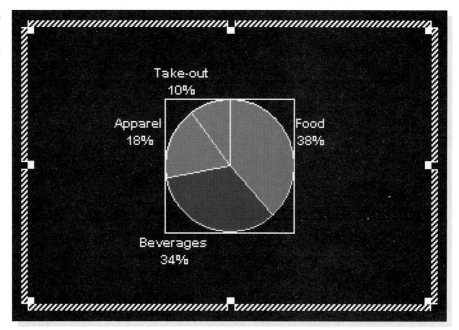

7. Click anywhere within the chart to deselect the label.

EXERCISE   **12-20**   **Format the Pie Plot Area**

The *plot area* of a chart is the area containing the actual columns, bars, or pie slices. It can be formatted with or without a border and a fill effect.

1. Move your mouse pointer over a corner of the pie chart border until the Plot Area ScreenTip appears; then right-click and choose Format Plot Area from the shortcut menu.

2. In the Format Plot Area dialog box, under Border, click <u>N</u>one. Click OK. The pie chart border is removed.

3. With the pie's plot area still selected, drag its lower-right corner sizing handle down to make the pie as big as possible without hiding the "Beverages" label and percentage. Drag the upper-left corner up as far as you can without losing the "Take-out" label. Deselect the plot area by clicking outside of it.

 NOTE: You cannot move the plot area to center it. However, if you resize the plot area from opposing corners, you can maintain its position within the chart area.

EXERCISE 12-21 Enhance a Pie Chart

You can enhance the appearance of your pie chart with additional effects, such as changing the color of a slice or *exploding* a slice (dragging it out from the center of the pie) for emphasis.

1. Click the center of the pie once to select all the slices. Notice that each slice has one selection handle.

2. Click the Food slice. Six selection handles appear around the slice.

3. Use the Fill Color button ![fill color icon] to change the color of the Food slice to the blue that is the sixth color in the Standard Colors row. Change the Apparel slice to gold and the Take-out slice to turquoise.

![tip icon] **TIP:** Use <u>F</u>ill Effects to apply gradient fills, patterns, or textures to individual slices.

4. Place the pointer in the middle of the Apparel slice and drag it slightly away from the center of the pie. This is called *exploding a slice*.

5. Return to Normal view. Create a text box below the pie with the text **Apparel includes revenue from trademark licensing**. Format the text as 24-point Arial bold and center the text box horizontally.

 NOTE: Although you can also insert text boxes in an active chart, you will sometimes want to do this in Normal view, so you can place the text outside of the chart area.

6. Make the chart slightly larger by using the corner sizing handles in Normal view. Arrange the chart so that it appears centered inside the green box. Note that because of the exploded pie slice, you will want to offset it a little to make it appear centered.

7. Change the grayscale setting for the pie chart to Inverse Grayscale, so that the pie slice labels will print.

FIGURE 12-17
Pie chart with
exploded slice and
text box

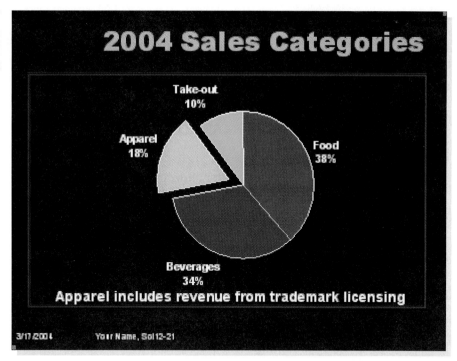

8. Create a slide footer for slide 4 that includes the date and the footer text *[Your Name], [your initials]***12-21**, and update the notes and handouts footer. Save the presentation as *[your initials]***12-21**.

9. Print slide 4 in full size. Leave the presentation open for the next exercise.

Importing Charts from Excel

Besides creating charts from within PowerPoint, you can also import charts created in Excel and other programs. You insert an Excel chart in one of two forms: as an *embedded object* or as a *linked object*.

An embedded Excel chart becomes part of the presentation (the destination) in which it is placed, and is saved as part of the file. When you make changes to an embedded chart, it does not affect the original file (the source) from which it came. Double-clicking the chart opens an Excel window from within PowerPoint, where you can make changes by using Excel commands and tools.

A linked Excel chart is a pointer to an external file (the source) that contains the data. Only the pointer is saved with the presentation (the destination) in which it is placed. When you make changes to a linked Excel chart, you are making changes to the actual file that was used to create it. Double-clicking a linked Excel chart starts Excel in a separate window and opens the linked file as an Excel workbook.

E X E R C I S E **12-22** **Embed an Excel Chart**

To embed an Excel chart, from the Insert menu choose Object. The Insert Object dialog box gives you several choices, including creating a new Excel chart or inserting a chart from a file.

After an object is embedded onto a slide, you can use the Recolor command on the Picture tab of the Format Object dialog box to make it match your presentation's color scheme.

1. Insert a new slide after slide 4 that uses the Title Only layout. Key the title **New York 2004**, and then click outside the title placeholder.

2. From the Insert menu, choose Object.

3. In the Insert Object dialog box, select Create from file.

4. Click Browse and navigate to the directory where your student files are stored. Choose the Excel file **Apparel1** and click OK. In a moment, the outline of a small worksheet appears on the slide.

FIGURE 12-18
Embedding an
Excel chart

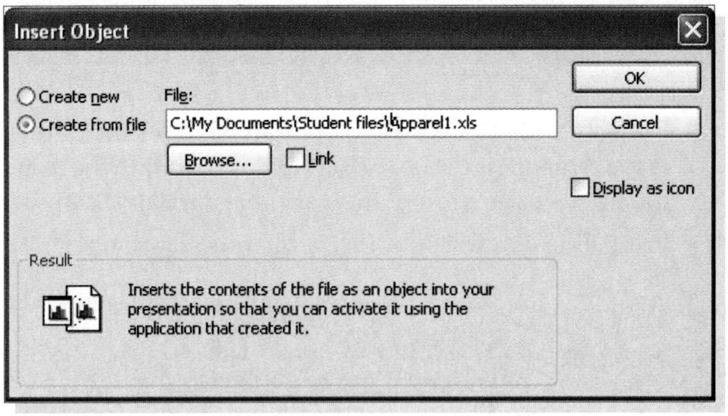

5. Double-click the worksheet object to open Excel from within PowerPoint. Notice that the PowerPoint toolbars and menu change to the ones Excel uses. You can use all the tools available in Excel to edit the chart.

6. Notice the three sheet tabs on the bottom of the Excel object named "Sheet1," "Sales Chart," and "NY Chart." Click the "NY Chart" sheet tab to display the New York Apparel Sales chart.

7. Click the chart's title, "New York 2004," and press Delete to remove it.

8. Click the slide anywhere outside the Excel chart to return to PowerPoint. The chart is now on the PowerPoint slide, but the colors and size are wrong for this presentation.

9. Click the chart to display its sizing handles. Size and position the chart so it fills the green frame on the slide.

FIGURE 12-19
Working with an
Excel workbook
from within
PowerPoint

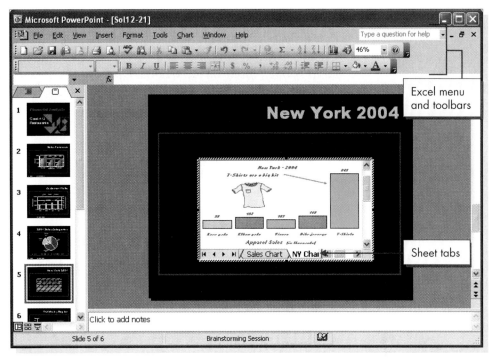

10. With the chart selected, open the Format Object dialog box, click the Picture tab, and then click Recolor. Change the gray text to white, change the gray arrow to white, and change the colors of the columns to colors appropriate for this presentation. Use the standard colors and other bright colors. You might also want to change the color of the T-shirt.

FIGURE 12-20
The embedded
Excel chart,
completed

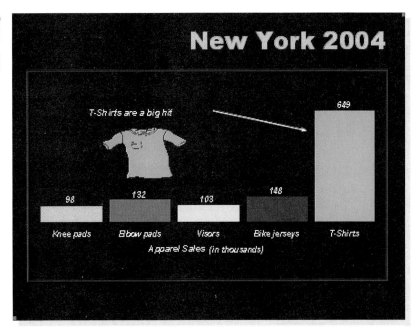

11. Change the grayscale settings for the Excel chart to Black with Grayscale Fill, so the labels show.

12. Create a slide footer for slide 5 that includes the date and the footer text *[Your Name], [your initials]***12-22**. Update the notes and handout footer for Exercise 12-22. Save the presentation as *[your initials]***12-22**.

13. Print slide 5 in full size. Leave the presentation open for the next exercise.

EXERCISE 12-23 **Insert a Linked Excel Chart**

When you link an Excel chart on a PowerPoint slide, it is a good idea is to first save the chart's file in the same directory where your presentation is saved. Then, if you need to move or copy your presentation, be sure to copy the Excel chart file along with it. Another alternative is to save your Excel file (before linking) on a shared network drive to which all potential viewers have access.

1. Without closing PowerPoint, start Excel. (On the Windows task bar, click Start, point to All Programs, and click Microsoft Office Excel—or follow your instructor's directions.)

2. Open the Excel file **Apparel3** from your student data disk. Save the workbook as *[your initials]***12-23a** in your Lesson 12 folder. Close Excel.

3. Insert a new slide after slide 5 that uses the Title Only slide layout. Key the title **Apparel Product Mix 2004**.

4. From the Insert menu, choose Object.

5. In the Insert Object dialog box, choose Create from file.

6. Click Browse, and then select the file *[your initials]***12-23a** from your Lesson 12 folder.

7. Click the Link check box under the File box. Click OK. In a moment or so, a chart with two pies appears. Don't worry about the color or size right now. (If you see a chart without the pie charts, right-click anywhere on the chart and choose Update Link from the shortcut menu.)

8. Double-click the chart. Excel opens with the linked chart displayed. Maximize the Excel worksheet. Click the Pie Charts tab and notice that the Miami pie has a large Elbow Pads slice.

9. Click the "Apparel Numbers" sheet tab in the lower-left corner of the window to display the chart data.

10. Select cell C7—the Elbow Pads number for Miami. With the cell selected, key **127**, overwriting "468." Press Enter.

11. Click the "Pie Charts" sheet tab. The Elbow Pads slice is smaller.

12. Resave the Excel workbook with the same name, and then close Excel.

13. If you do not see the change on your PowerPoint slide, right-click anywhere on the chart; then choose Update Link from the shortcut menu. The Miami Elbow Pads slice is now smaller.

14. Using the same method as you did on slide 5 in the previous exercise, recolor the chart to match the presentation's color scheme. Resize and reposition the chart as needed.

15. Change the chart's grayscale settings to Black with Grayscale Fill, so that the labels show.

16. Create a slide footer for slide 6 that includes the date and the footer text *[Your Name]*, *[your initials]***12-23b**. Update the notes and handouts footer for this exercise. Save the presentation as *[your initials]***12-23b**.

17. Print slide 6 in full size. Leave the presentation open for the next exercise.

Enhancing Chart Elements

You can add many interesting effects to your chart. For example, you can add objects that help you make a particular point or highlight one aspect of the data. You can also annotate your charts with text—an especially useful option when your presentation contains a series of related, but different, charts. In the same way that you animate text and graphic objects, you can also animate charts to make each data series, category, or pie slice appear one at a time, automatically, or with a mouse click.

EXERCISE **12-24** **Adding AutoShapes for Emphasis**

 The Drawing toolbar that you have used on slides in previous lessons is available from within Microsoft Graph. To display the Drawing toolbar, right-click any open toolbar and choose Drawing from the shortcut menu, or click the Drawing button 🖉 on Microsoft Graph's Standard toolbar.

1. Move to slide 7, titled "T-shirts by Region." Activate Microsoft Graph. If the datasheet is showing, hide it.

2. Right-click any toolbar; then choose Drawing from the shortcut menu.

 3. Click the Text Box button 🔲; then click above the Miami column, and key **LA may top NY in 2005**

4. With the text box selected, use the Formatting toolbar to change the text to 18-point Arial, bold, italic.

5. Use the AutoShapes menu on the Drawing toolbar to draw a small Left Arrow shape. Make it red with no border, and rotate it as shown in Figure 12-21 (on the next page).

FIGURE 12-21
Chart with arrow
and text box

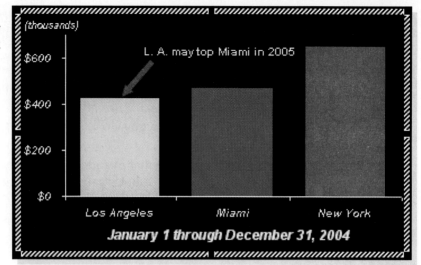

 TIP: If you cannot see the arrow's rotation handle, use Zoom to enlarge your view of the arrow.

6. Arrange the arrow and text box to match Figure 12-21. Close Microsoft Graph and return to Normal view.

 NOTE: You can also draw and add text boxes in Normal view.

7. In Normal view, click the chart once to select it. Notice it has sizing handles. Reposition and resize the chart appropriately for the slide. In Normal view, you can move and resize the chart, just as you do with any other object.

8. Insert the footer text on slide 7 for *[Your Name]*, *[your initials]***12-24** and update the notes and handouts footer. Save the file as *[your initials]***12-24** in your Lesson 12 folder.

9. Print slide 7 in full size. If you have a color printer, print it in color. Keep the presentation open for the next exercise.

EXERCISE 12-25 Animating Chart Elements

Some, but not all, animation effects enable you to make chart elements appear one at a time. Effects that work well with charts are Dissolve In, Split, Random Bars, Blinds, and Wipe.

1. On slide 7, right-click the graph and choose Custom Animation from the shortcut menu.

2. In the Custom Animation task pane, click Add Effect and choose <u>E</u>ntrance. Choose the Wipe effect.

3. Make sure the Start setting is On Click, and the Direction setting is From Bottom. Change the Speed to Medium.

4. In the custom animation list, click the list box arrow for "Chart 2;" then choose <u>E</u>ffect Options.

5. Click the Chart Animation tab. Click the list box arrow for <u>G</u>roup chart and choose By Category.

 NOTE: Some animation effects do not have options available in the <u>G</u>roup chart list box. If no choices are available, try a different animation effect.

6. Clear the check box for <u>A</u>nimate grid and legend. By turning off this option, the grid will appear when the slide is displayed.

7. Click the Effect tab. For the <u>S</u>ound, choose Cash Register and turn down the volume. Click OK.

8. View the presentation as a slide show, starting with slide 1. When you get to the animated chart, click the mouse to make each column appear, one after the other.

9. Update the handout header and footer: include the date and your name as the header, and the page number and text *[your initials]*12-25 as the footer.

10. Move to slide 1 and save the presentation as *[your initials]*12-25 in your Lesson 12 folder.

11. Preview, and then print, the presentation as handouts, nine slides per page, grayscale, landscape, scale to fit paper, and framed. Close the presentation.

USING ONLINE HELP

It's important to understand the difference between linking and embedding objects, such as the chart objects taught in this lesson.

Use Help for an overview of linking and embedding objects:

1. Key **linking** in the Ask a Question box and press Enter.

2. In the Search Results task pane, choose **About linked objects and embedded objects**.

3. Read the topic, expanding the definitions as you go.

4. Close Help when you are finished.

LESSON 12 Summary

➤ Charts are diagrams that display numbers in pictorial format. Charts can help you understand the significance of numeric information more easily than viewing the same information as a list of numbers.

➤ When you start a new chart, a sample datasheet appears. A datasheet is a table where you key the numbers and labels used to create a chart.

➤ The Slide Layout task pane offers several Content Layouts that are suitable for charts. Text and Content Layouts also make it easy to combine a chart and body text on the same slide.

➤ The datasheet contains rows and columns. You key each number or label in a separate cell—the rectangle formed by the intersection of a row and a column.

➤ On the datasheet, key labels in the unnumbered row above row 1 and in the unlettered column to the left of column A.

➤ When Microsoft Graph is closed, double-click a chart on the Slide pane if you want to edit it.

➤ A data series is a group of data that relate to a common object or category. Often, more than one data series is displayed on a single chart.

➤ Use the By Column button ▥ or the By Row button ▤ to switch how a data series is defined on a datasheet.

➤ A wide variety of chart types and chart format options are available. The default chart type is 3-D Column Chart. Other types include bar, area, line, pie, and surface.

➤ Use ScreenTips or the Chart Objects list box to select the part of a chart on which you want to work.

➤ Special fill and border effects, including textures and gradient fills, can be used in charts the same way you use them for other PowerPoint objects.

➤ Use the Format Axis dialog box to modify the scale, font, and number format of the value axis or secondary value axis. Modify the scale settings to specify the range of numbers displayed and increments between numbers.

➤ Axis titles are an important part of charts. Careful labeling ensures that your charts will be interpreted correctly.

➤ A legend is a box showing the colors and patterns assigned to the data series. Customize a chart's legend by changing the border, background colors, and font attributes.

➤ Use a secondary axis when you need to plot two dissimilar types of data on the same chart. A secondary axis is available only for a 2-D chart type.

➤ Proper formatting and labeling on a chart is important when your chart has both a primary and secondary axis.

➤ A good way to distinguish between different data types on a single chart is to assign different chart types. For example, use columns for one type of data and lines for the other type.

➤ A pie chart shows individual values in relation to the sum of all the values. Each value is displayed as a "slice" of the pie.

➤ A pie chart can show only one data series. To show more than one data series, use more than one pie chart.

➤ The plot area of a chart is the area containing the actual columns, bars, or pie slices. It can be formatted with or without a border and a fill effect.

➤ Exploding a pie slice (dragging it out from the center of the pie) emphasizes the slice.

➤ Excel charts can be either embedded or linked on a PowerPoint slide. An embedded chart becomes part of the presentation. A linked chart is a pointer to an external file that contains the data. Only the pointer is saved with the presentation.

➤ Use the Recolor command on the Picture tab of the Format Object dialog box to make an embedded or linked object match the presentation color scheme.

➤ Before linking an Excel chart on a PowerPoint slide, a good idea is to save the chart's file in the same directory where your presentation is saved.

➤ Use the Drawing toolbar to add AutoShapes and text boxes directly onto a chart. Use text boxes wherever needed to annotate your chart.

➤ Not all animation effects enable you to make chart elements appear one at a time. Effects that work well are Dissolve In, Split, Random Bars, Blinds, and Wipe.

LESSON 12   Command Summary

FEATURE	BUTTON	MENU	KEYBOARD
Insert a chart		Insert, Chart	
Display/hide datasheet		View, Datasheet	
Insert axis titles		Format, Selected Axis	Ctrl + 1
Insert or remove a legend		Chart, Chart Options, Legend tab	
Switch data series to rows		Data, Series In Rows	
Switch data series to columns		Data, Series in Columns	

continues

LESSON 12 Command Summary *continued*

FEATURE	BUTTON	MENU	KEYBOARD
Format a chart object		Format, Selected object	Ctrl + 1
Change the chart type		Chart, Chart Type	
Add a secondary axis		Format, Selected Data Series, Axis tab (must be a 2-D chart)	
Add data labels		Format, Selected Data Series, Data Labels tab	
Link or embed an object		Insert, Object	
Display the drawing toolbar		View, Toolbars, Drawing	

Concepts Review

TRUE/FALSE QUESTIONS

Each of the following statements is either true or false. Indicate your choice by circling T or F.

T (F)   **1.** PowerPoint offers only one slide layout choice for slides with charts.

T (F)   **2.** The sample datasheet for a new chart is always blank.

T (F)   **3.** You cannot see the chart while you are working on the datasheet.

(T) F   **4.** You can change the colors and patterns of columns in a column chart to whatever you find appealing.

T (F)   **5.** The scale on the value axis is set by PowerPoint and cannot be changed.

T (F)   **6.** Every chart must include a legend.

(T) F   **7.** You must use a two-dimensional chart if you want to include a secondary axis.

T (F)   **8.** Double-clicking a pie slice or column enables you to change its size.

SHORT ANSWER QUESTIONS

Write the correct answer in the space provided.

1. What do you do if you don't want to use the sample data in the datasheet?

DELETE

2. How do you change the grouping of the data series on a chart from columns to rows?

By ROW OR By COLUMN BUTTONS

3. While working on a chart, how do you display the datasheet if it is not visible?

VIEW DATASHEET

4. What type of number formatting do you apply to values to display dollar signs?

CURRENCY

5. In Microsoft Graph, what item on the Standard toolbar can you use to select different parts of a chart?

CHART OPTION DROP DOWN LIST

6. Which button can you click to change the color of a selected pie slice?

FILL COLOR

7. How can you change the font size for chart labels without opening a dialog box?

CLICK ON IT - USE FORMATTING TOOLBAR

8. On a column chart, how can you change one of the data series to an area?

CHART TYPE LIST BOX

CRITICAL THINKING

Answer these questions on a separate page. There are no right or wrong answers. Support your answers with examples from your own experience, if possible.

1. How do you decide if a chart is needed in your presentation? Do you think a presentation can have too many charts? Explain your answer.

2. Imagine that you are trying to explain to someone how you spend your waking hours during a typical day. Can you think of a chart that would break down your activities into different categories and show how much time you spend on each during the day? Describe the chart's appearance and the values that you would include.

Skills Review

EXERCISE 12-26

Create a new presentation that includes a simple column chart.

1. Open the file **FinSum1**.
2. Create a chart by following these steps:
   a. Insert a new slide after slide 2 that uses the Title and Content layout.
   b. Key **2004 Quarterly Earnings** for the title.
   c. Click the Insert Chart icon 📊 in the center of the content placeholder.

d. Click the upper-left gray box on the datasheet to select all the existing data and press (Delete).

e. Key the data shown in Figure 12-22.

FIGURE 12-22
Datasheet

▦ FinSum1 - Datasheet						☒
		A	B	C	D	E
		Q1	Q2	Q3	Q4	
1	New York	1888	2008	2116	1543	
2	Los Angeles	1743	1799	1844	1539	
3	Miami	1634	1439	1783	1469	
4						

3. View the new chart by following these steps:

a. Click the View Datasheet button ▦ on the Standard toolbar to hide the datasheet.

b. Click outside the chart border to return to Normal view.

4. Click the chart once in Normal view to select it; then use the chart's sizing handles to reduce the chart's height by approximately 0.5 inches and adjust the chart's position to make an attractive composition.

5. Edit the chart by following these steps:

a. Double-click the chart to activate it.

b. If the datasheet is not displayed, click the View Datasheet button ▦.

c. Click cell D2 (Q4 for Los Angeles) to select it.

d. Key **1849** to replace the value "1539." Press (Enter).

e. To switch the data series from rows to columns, click the By Column button ▦ on the Standard toolbar.

6. Return to Normal view.

7. Create a handout header and footer: include the date and your name as the header, and the page number and text *[your initials]***12-26** as the footer.

8. Move to slide 1 and save the presentation as *[your initials]***12-26** in your Lesson 12 folder.

9. View the presentation as a slide show; then preview and print it as handouts, three slides per page, grayscale, framed. Close the presentation.

EXERCISE 12-27

Edit and format an existing chart.

1. Open the file **Finance2**.

2. Edit the chart on slide 4 by following these steps:

    a. Double-click the chart to open Microsoft Graph.

    b. On the datasheet, click cell A2 containing the value "-2%."

    c. Key **2%** in the selected cell to overwrite the negative value with a positive value. Press Enter.

     d. Click the View Datasheet button to hide the datasheet.

3. Change the fill effect of the chart's columns by following these steps:

    a. With Microsoft Graph still open, click one of the green columns on the chart to select the "Gross Margin" data series.

     b. Click the list box arrow for the Fill Color button on the Standard toolbar and float the toolbar by dragging its gray title bar.

    c. Choose Fill Effects and click the Gradient tab.

    d. Change the Color 1 color to Sky Blue with a horizontal shading style and the darkest color on the bottom of the column. Click OK.

    e. Use the same steps to change the fill pattern of the blue columns to a one-color horizontal gradient fill with Gold using the darkest color on the bottom. Close the Fill Color floating toolbar.

4. Change the border color of a series of columns by following these steps:

    a. Right-click one of the columns in the "Gross Margin" series and choose Format Data Series from the shortcut menu.

    b. Click the Patterns tab.

    c. In the Border section, click the list box arrow for Color and choose dark blue. Click OK.

5. Change the outline color of the columns in the "Operating Margin" series to the same dark gray.

6. Change the font for the category axis labels by following these steps:

    a. Click the category axis label "1999" to select the category axis.

     b. From the Font drop-down list, choose Tahoma. Click the Bold button **B** to remove the bold attribute.

7. Format the value axis by following these steps:

    a. Right-click a number on the value axis and choose Format Axis from the shortcut menu.

    b. Click the Scale tab.

    c. Key **5%** in the Major unit text box.

    d. Click the Font tab and choose Tahoma, regular (remove the bold attribute). Click OK.

8. Format the legend by following these steps:

    a. Right-click the legend and choose Format Legend from the shortcut menu.

    b. Click the Placement tab and choose Bottom.

    c. Click the Patterns tab, choose None for Border, and click OK.

d. Use the Formatting toolbar to change the legend font to Tahoma, regular (not bold).

e. Adjust the width of the legend, so that it fits on one line.

9. Return to Normal view. Resize and reposition the chart appropriately.

10. Create a handout header and footer: include the date and your name as the header, and the page number and text *[your initials]*12-27 as the footer.

11. Move to slide 1 and save the presentation as *[your initials]*12-27 in your Lesson 12 folder.

12. View the presentation as a slide show; then preview and print the presentation as handouts, four slides per page, grayscale, landscape, framed. Close the presentation.

EXERCISE 12-28

Add data to a chart, format chart axes, and add a secondary axis.

1. Open the file **Finance3**.

2. Move to slide 4 and double-click the chart to open Microsoft Graph.

3. Apply a different color gradient fill to each column by following these steps:

a. Click the "1st Quarter" column to select the data series.

b. Float the Fill Color toolbar, and then choose Fill Effects.

c. Click the Gradient tab and set up a two-color horizontal gradient fill using the medium blue standard color, fading to pale blue at the top.

d. Click OK.

4. Add another data series to the chart by following these steps:

a. Click the View Datasheet button ▦ to display the datasheet if it is not showing.

b. Key the second row of data, as shown in Figure 12-23. The scale numbers will overlap with narrow gridlines until you fix the secondary axis in the next steps.

FIGURE 12-23
Datasheet

▦ Sol12-28 - Datasheet		A	B	C	D	⌃
		1st Quarter	2nd Quarter	3rd Quarter	4th Quarter	
1 ▟▌	Special Events	71	141	118	149	
2 ▟▌	Total Revenue	800	1076	1149	1207	
3						⌄

c. Close the datasheet.

5. Add a secondary axis to the chart by following these steps:

a. To change the chart to a 2-D chart, click the list box arrow for the Chart Type button , and then choose Column Chart (the first selection in the third row).

    b. Right-click one of the tall green "Total Revenue" columns and choose Format Data Series.

    c. Click the Axis tab and choose Secondary axis. Click OK.

6. Change the chart type for the green columns by following these steps:

    a. If the data series is not already selected, click one of the green columns to select it.

    b. Click the list box arrow for the Chart Type button.

    c. Choose Line Chart (the first selection in the fourth row).

7. Change the formatting of the line for the data series by following these steps:

    a. Right-click the line and choose Format Data Series. Click the Patterns tab.

    b. In the Line section, change the Color to red, and the Weight to the heaviest selection.

    c. In the Marker section, change the Foreground color to gray and the Background color to white. Change the size to 16 points and click the shadow. Click OK.

8. Format the secondary value axis by following these steps:

    a. Right-click one of the numbers on the right side of the chart (on the secondary value axis) and choose Format Axis.

    b. Click the Patterns tab. Under Lines, change the Color to yellow.

    c. Click the Scale tab and change the Major unit to **500**.

    d. Click the Font tab. Change the Font to Arial, the Font style to Regular, and the Color to yellow.

    e. Click the Number tab and choose Currency with no Decimal places. Click OK.

9. Except for the scale, apply the same formatting to the value axis (on the left side of the chart). Change the scale's Maximum to **250** and the Major unit to **50**.

10. Change the formatting of the category axis by following these steps:

    a. Double-click the category axis to open the Format Axis dialog box.

    b. On the Patterns tab, change the line Color to yellow.

    c. Change the Font, Font style, and Color to match the value axis.

    d. Click the Alignment tab. Drag the red diamond up to the 30-degree setting. Click OK.

11. Add chart titles and a legend by following these steps:

    a. Right-click the chart area and choose Chart Options.

    b. Click the Titles tab.

    c. In the Value (Y) axis text box, key **Special Events (thousands)**

    d. For the Second value (Y) axis, key **Total Revenue (thousands)**

    e. Click OK.

12. Using the Formatting toolbar, format text for the two axis titles as 16-point Arial, not bold, in black.

13. Resize the plot area by following these steps:

    a. On the Standard toolbar, click the Chart Objects list box arrow and choose **Plot Area.**

    b. Drag one or more sizing handles to enlarge the plot area to fill the chart area.

14. Close Microsoft Graph by clicking outside the chart border. Working in Normal view, resize and reposition the chart, so that it fills the space attractively.

FIGURE 12-24
Completed chart

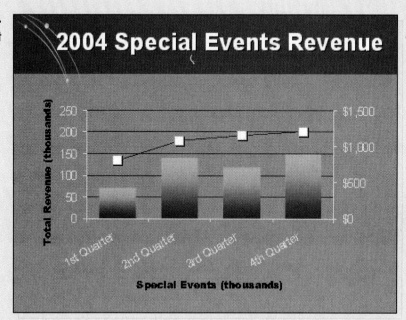

15. Create a handout header and footer: include the date and your name as the header, and the page number and text *[your initials]***12-28** as the footer.

16. Move to slide 1 and save the presentation as *[your initials]***12-28** in your Lesson 12 folder.

17. View the presentation as a slide show; then preview and print the presentation as handouts, four slides per page, grayscale, landscape, framed. Close the presentation.

EXERCISE 12-29

Create and format a pie chart; import an Excel chart; and add shapes, text boxes, and animation effects.

1. Open the file **Apparel2**.

2. Insert a new slide after slide 2 that uses the Title and Content layout. Key the title **Apparel Mix – 2004**.

3. Create a pie chart by following these steps:

a. Click the Insert Chart icon in the center of the content placeholder.
b. On the datasheet, key the information shown in Figure 12-25.

FIGURE 12-25
Datasheet for
pie chart

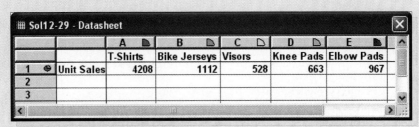

c. On the Standard toolbar, click the list box arrow for the Chart Type button and choose 3-D Pie Chart (the second sample in the fifth row).

4. Format a pie slice by following these steps:

a. Hide the datasheet.
b. Click the gold pie slice (T-shirts) once to select the entire pie.
c. Click the gold slice again to select the individual slice.
d. Click the list box arrow for the Fill Color button and choose Ice Blue, the last color on the second row from the bottom.
e. Click these slices and change the colors: Bike Jerseys, lime green; Visors, yellow; Knee Pads, gold; and Elbow Pads, red.

5. Delete the pie's legend.

6. Add data labels by following these steps:

a. Move the pointer along the outside edge of the pie until the Plot Area ScreenTip appears; then right-click and choose Chart Options from the shortcut menu.
b. Click the Data Labels tab. Check the Category name and the Percentage check boxes. Clear the Show leader lines check box (at the bottom of the dialog box). Click OK.

7. Change the font for the data labels by following these steps:

a. Right-click any data label; then choose Format Data Labels from the shortcut menu.
b. Click the Font tab. Change the font size to 20 points. Clear the Auto scale option in the lower-left corner of the dialog box. Click OK.

TIP: When the Auto scale option is set, font sizes change in proportion to the resizing of a chart. If you want the font size to remain unchanged when you resize a chart, clear this check box.

8. Resize the pie by following these steps:

a. Select the plot area (left-click).
b. Drag the upper-right sizing handle away from the center of the pie, making the pie as large as possible without hiding "Elbow Pads."
c. Drag the lower-left corner away from the center in the same manner.

9. Format the plot area by following these steps:
   a. Right-click the pie's plot area and choose F̲ormat Plot Area from the shortcut menu.
   b. Under Border, choose N̲one and click OK.

10. Explode a pie slice by following these steps:
    a. Select the gold Knee Pads slice.
    b. Drag the slice away from the center of the pie.

11. Adjust the position of the data labels by following these steps:
    a. Select just the "T-shirt" label.
    b. Move the pointer to any part of the label border. Drag the "T-shirt" label up and to the left a little, positioning it above its slice.
    c. In the same way, adjust the position of all the data labels to make a pleasing composition. If necessary, the chart area can be increased slightly if some of the label text is cut off.

12. Insert a text box and an arrow by following these steps:

    a. If the Drawing toolbar is not already displayed, click the Drawing button on the Standard toolbar.
    b. Click the Text Box button ⬚ on the Drawing toolbar.
    c. Click below the large blue T-shirt pie slice and key **T-shirts are still the best sellers**
    d. Change the text box font to 18-point Comic Sans MS, bold, blue.
    e. Click the Arrow button ⬚ on the Drawing toolbar and draw a black arrow from the text you keyed in the previous step c to the T-shirt pie slice.

13. Adjust the position of the chart placeholder in Normal view to balance the pie chart on the slide.

14. Animate the pie chart by following these steps:
    a. Working in Normal view, right-click the pie chart and choose Custo̲m Animation from the shortcut menu.
    b. In the Custom Animation task pane, click Add Effect. From the E̲ntrance effects list (or the Add Entrance Effect dialog box), choose Dissolve In.
    c. In the custom animation list, click the "Chart 2" list box arrow and choose E̲ffect Options.
    d. Click the Chart Animation tab. From the G̲roup chart list box, choose By Category. Deselect the A̲nimate grid and legend check box.
    e. Click the Timing tab. In the Spe̲ed list box, choose 2 seconds (Medium). Click OK.

15. Embed an Excel chart by following these steps:
    a. Insert a new slide after slide 3 that uses the Title Only layout. Key the title **Apparel Sales – 2004**
    b. From the I̲nsert menu, choose O̲bject to open the Insert Object dialog box.
    c. Select Create from f̲ile. Navigate to the folder where your student files are stored. Choose the Excel file **Apparel1** and click OK.

d. Double-click the spreadsheet image on the slide to open Excel. If necessary, zoom to enlarge the view of the Excel object.

e. Click the "Sales Chart" sheet tab to display a column chart.

f. On the chart, click the title "Apparel Sales - 2004" and press Delete to remove it.

g. Click anywhere outside the Excel object to return to PowerPoint.

16. Format the imported chart by following these steps:

a. Right-click the chart and choose Format Object from the shortcut menu. Click the Picture tab, and then click Recolor.

b. Change the gray color sample to black. Change the colors of the columns to colors from the template's color scheme and colors that match the pie chart. Close the Format Object dialog box when the color changes are completed.

c. Resize and reposition the chart object to fit the slide.

17. Create a handout header and footer: include the date and your name as the header, and the page number and text *[your initials]*12-29 as the footer.

18. Move to slide 1 and save the presentation as *[your initials]*12-29 in your Lesson 12 folder.

19. View the presentation as a slide show; then preview and print the presentation as handouts, six slides per page, grayscale, framed. Close the presentation.

Lesson Applications

Create a presentation containing a column chart and format the chart.

1. Start a new presentation using the Default design template and the color scheme with the white background and yellow, orange, red, and brown accent colors. Replace all the fonts with Tahoma.

2. Customize the color scheme by changing the Background to black, the Title text and Text and lines colors to white, and the Accent and followed hyperlink color to royal blue. Change the yellow, orange, and red colors to brighter shades of the same colors.

3. Using the text in Figure 12-26, create a three-slide presentation; use the Title Slide layout for slide 1, the Title and Text layout for slide 2, and the Text and Content layout for slide 3.

FIGURE 12-26

Slide 1 ———Three Years of Phenomenal Sales——— Title

Highlights——— Title

• New York revenue still increasing

Slide 2

• Miami and Los Angeles meeting goals

• Revenues reach 120% of budget

Slide 3 ———Sales by Region – 2002 to 2004 ——— Title

4. On slide 3, create a column chart by using the data shown in Figure 12-27.

FIGURE 12-27
Datasheet for chart

		A	B	C	D
		2002	2003	2004	
1	New York	5650	8753	11332	
2	Los Angel	4183	5892	9852	
3	Miami	3843	6388	8487	
4					

Presentation4 - Datasheet

5. Change the value axis Scale settings to have a Maximum of 12,000 and a Major unit of 2,000. Change its Number format to Currency with no decimals, its font size to 16 points, and its Font style to Regular (not bold).

6. For the category axis and legend, change the font to 16 points, not bold.

7. Apply a one-color horizontal gradient fill to each column. Choose a bright color from the standard scheme colors, and shade to a darker tone of the same color at the bottom of each column. Remove the white border from all the columns.

8. Change the floor color of the chart to black. (Use the Chart Objects drop-down list on the Standard toolbar to select the floor.)

9. Move the legend to the bottom and remove its border. Resize, if necessary.

10. In Normal view, reposition and resize the chart to create a pleasing layout. Check grayscale settings for all slides and make adjustments if needed.

11. On the title slide, delete the subtitle placeholder. Draw a rectangle .25" high and 10" wide in gold. Duplicate this rectangle four times and arrange the five rectangles to touch each other in alternating colors of gold and white. Group the rectangles and position them below the title.

12. Insert the picture file **Logo1** and position it on the rectangles.

13. To define the edge of the black slide, draw a rectangle that completely covers the slide. Apply a gold 10-point border and no fill. This should provide a thin distinctive gold edge on the slide.

14. Copy this rectangle with the gold border and paste it on the master slide, so each slide has this same treatment.

15. Create a handout header and footer: include the date and your name as the header, and the page number and text *[your initials]*12-30 as the footer.

16. Move to slide 1 and save the presentation as *[your initials]*12-30 in your Lesson 12 folder.

17. View the presentation as a slide show; then preview and print it as handouts, three slides per page, grayscale, framed. Close the presentation.

EXERCISE 12-31

Insert a chart; change the chart to a combination chart; format the chart text, data series, and legend; add a secondary axis; and add an AutoShape.

1. Open the file **Earnings2** and apply the Globe design template using the color scheme with the blue background. On the slide master, change the first-level bullet to a different bullet. Change the bullet color, if you like. Make the title text on both masters bold.

2. Insert a new slide between slides 2 and 3 that uses the Title and Content layout. Give the slide the title **Gross Income**.

3. Create a column chart on the new slide by using the data in Figure 12-28 (on the next page).

4. Change the chart type to a 2-D column chart.

5. Plot the "Year Total" data series on a secondary axis. Change the chart type for the series to Line Chart. Format the line in a bright color and add thickness.

6. Change the font for the value axis, category axis, the secondary value axis, and legend to 16-point Arial Regular (not bold).

7. For the value axis (on the left), change the number format to currency with no decimal places, change the scale to range from 0 to 10,000 displayed at

FIGURE 12-28

	2002	2003	2004
San Francisco	1246	2033	5432
Miami	2734	4630	6325
Los Angeles	2871	4126	7235
New York	3566	5135	7555
Year Total	10416	15924	26547

intervals of 2,000. On the Scale tab, set the Display units to Thousands and check the box labeled Show display units labeled on chart.

8. Format the secondary value axis (on the right) in the same way as in the previous step 7, with the scale ranging from 0 to 30,000 displayed at intervals of 5,000. Set the Display units to Thousands and check the box labeled Show display units labeled on chart.

9. Move the legend to the bottom of the chart and remove its border. Make the legend wider to provide some extra space between entries. Adjust the legend's position as needed.

10. Apply a one-color horizontal gradient fill to each column, shading from the column's original color at the top to a medium dark shade at the bottom. Remove the border from each column.

11. In Normal view, adjust the chart size and position relative to the slide, if needed.

12. Create a text box centered above the chart. Key **Impressive!** in the text box. Change the font to 24-point Arial. Draw a small, white, 5-Point Star and place it on the upper-left corner of the New York column for the year 2004. Draw a line from the text box to the star.

13. Create a handout header and footer: include the date and your name as the header, and the page number and text *[your initials]*12-31 as the footer.

14. Move to slide 1 and save the presentation as *[your initials]*12-31.

15. View the presentation as a slide show; then preview and print it as handouts, four slides per page, grayscale, landscape, framed. Close the presentation.

EXERCISE 12-32 *Challenge Yourself*

Customize a presentation design template, and create and format an animated pie chart with hyperlinks.

1. Open the file **Expense2**.

2. Create a custom color scheme by changing the current background scheme color to medium blue (third from the right in the top row of the standard

color honeycomb). Change the presentation's background to a one-color gradient fill, shading from the medium blue background scheme color at the title to a darker shade at the edges.

3. Replace all the presentation's fonts with Arial.

4. Cut the logo (WordArt) from slide 1 and paste it on the title master. Change the thin purple shape to white and resize it to fit behind the logo. Send the shape backward, adjust positioning if necessary, and group it with the logo. Position this group between the title and subtitle placeholders. Move the subtitle placeholder down. Make the title placeholder text bold.

5. Near the top of the title master, draw a constrained 5-Point Star that is 0.75 inches high. Apply a two-color vertical gradient fill using orange and blue, with orange on the left side. Remove the star's border line.

6. Move the star to the left end of the horizontal bar and use the Duplicate command to make a string of 12 stars across the top of the slide. Use the Align and Distribute commands to space the stars evenly and in a straight row.

 TIP: Make sure only the stars are selected (and not the bar) before you distribute the stars.

7. Insert a new slide after slide 1 that uses the Title and Content layout. Key the title **Expense Breakdown**

8. Create a 2-D pie chart on the new slide 2 by using the following data:

	Food	Payroll	Depreciation	Lease
2004 Expenses	2190	1813	577	1737

9. Change the pie slice borders to black; then add Percentage data labels to the chart. Select each percentage individually and drag it onto its pie slice.

10. Remove the pie's plot area border.

11. Increase the legend font to 22 points and remove its border.

12. Resize the pie as large as it can be and still fit inside the chart area border. Change the data label font size to 22 points.

13. In Normal view, adjust the position of the pie chart as needed.

14. Ungroup the pie chart, and then group each data label with its pie slice. Animate each pie slice to fly from the appropriate edge of the slide, one at a time, with the cash register sound. Make the slices appear in clockwise order, starting with the gold food slice. Make them appear with a click.

15. Turn each legend label into a hyperlink, linking Food to the "Food and Beverages" slide, Payroll to the "Payroll & Benefits" slide, etc.

16. To make the hyperlink text more readable, change the presentation's Accent and hyperlink scheme color to a lighter shade of pink.

17. On the slide master, create a Home button, formatting it as you like, that links to the slide with the pie chart.

18. Create a handout header and footer: include the date and your name as the header, and the page number and text *[your initials]***12-32** as the footer.

19. Check grayscale settings and make any needed adjustments.

20. Move to slide 1 and save the presentation as *[your initials]***12-32** in your Lesson 12 folder.

21. View the presentation as a slide show; then preview and print it as handouts, six slides per page, grayscale, scaled for paper, framed. Close the presentation.

On Your Own

In these exercises, you work on your own, as you would in a real-life work environment. Use the skills you've learned to accomplish the task—and be creative.

EXERCISE 12-33
Make a list of your monthly or yearly living expenses (or the expenses of a fictional person). Group the expenses into no more than eight categories, for example, Food, Clothing, Housing, Transportation, Entertainment, and Tuition. Total the items in each category, and then use your totals to create a slide with a pie chart. In addition, create a separate slide for each category, giving details about the category. On the pie chart slide, insert hyperlinks to each detail slide and, on the detail slides, insert a link back to the pie chart. Add a title slide and a conclusion slide. Format and animate the presentation in a way that will hold a viewer's attention. Save your presentation as *[your initials]***12-33**. Preview, and then print the presentation as handouts.

EXERCISE 12-34
Make a list of your activities during a typical weekday, including the *actual* time you spend on each activity. Group your activities into no more than eight categories. Make sure the times add up to 24 hours. Add a second set of times listing the amount of time you *should* be spending on each activity, and a third set of times listing the amount of time you would *prefer* to. (Don't be too serious about the times—make it fun.) Create a column or bar chart to represent these times, and then add three pie chart slides, one for each set of times (actual, should, prefer). Add a title slide and a conclusion slide. Use your creativity to make the charts interesting and fun to view, including animation effects. Save the presentation as *[your initials]***12-34**. Preview, and then print the presentation as handouts.

EXERCISE 12-35
Research the effects of stress in the workplace. Prepare slides to explain the problem using bulleted lists and diagrams. Find some statistics about absenteeism, turnover, health problems, illness, etc. and create at least two charts to display the statistics. Add a title slide and a conclusion slide. Format your presentation attractively, save it as *[your initials]***12-35**, and then print handouts.

Creating Effective Tables

OBJECTIVES

MICROSOFT OFFICE
SPECIALIST
ACTIVITIES
In this lesson:
   PPO3S-1-3
   PPO3S-1-5

See Appendix.

After completing this lesson, you will be able to:

1. Create a table.
2. Select a table, cells, and text.
3. Modify table structure.
4. Align text and numbers.
5. Apply fill colors and borders.
6. Insert a Microsoft Word table.

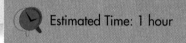 Estimated Time: 1 hour

Tables display information organized in rows and columns. Once a table is created, you can modify its structure by adding columns or rows, plus you can merge and split cells to modify your table's design. Table content can be aligned in different ways for easy-to-read layouts. And color can be applied to highlight selected table cells or to add table borders. If you are familiar with using tables in Microsoft Word, you will find that working with PowerPoint tables is similar.

Creating a Table

PowerPoint provides several convenient ways to create a table and, with each method you specify, the number of columns and rows that you need.

- Insert a new slide, choose Text and Content layout, and click the table button.
- Choose the Insert Table button on the Standard toolbar.

- Choose the Table button on the Tables and Borders toolbar.
- Draw a table using the Draw table pen tool on the Tables and Borders toolbar.

Because you have used Title and Content layouts in previous lessons, the first three exercises in this lesson will focus on the methods you have not used. Several tools on the Formatting and Drawing toolbar can be used when designing tables; however, you will find it convenient to float the Tables and Borders toolbar for easy access to those tools while you are working.

EXERCISE **13-1** **Insert a Table**

When you use the Insert Table button 🔳, you define a table's dimensions by dragging down and across a grid.

1. Open the file **Briefing**. Insert a new slide after slide 2 that uses the Title Only slide layout. Key the title **Employment Levels 2003**

FIGURE 13-1
Defining a table

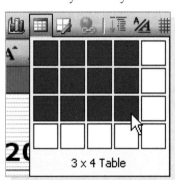

2. Click the Insert Table button 🔳 on the Standard toolbar. A grid appears for defining the size of the table.

3. Drag your pointer down three squares and across four squares to define a 3 x 4 Table (three rows by four columns). A table appears, filling the available space on the slide.

4. Click the Automatic Layout Options 🔲 smart tag button at the lower-right corner of the table. Choose Undo Automatic Layout from the drop-down list. The table becomes smaller, but it is not well positioned.

5. Point to the table's border and use the four-pointed arrow ✥ to move the table to a better position.

6. Key the text shown in Figure 13-2. Entering text in a table is similar to entering text in a chart's datasheet. Press Tab to move from cell to cell.

EXERCISE **13-2** **Navigate in a Table**

A *table* is composed of a series of rows and columns. The rectangle formed by the intersection of a row and a column is called a *cell*. There are many ways that you can move from cell to cell:

- Click the cell.
- Use the Arrow keys ←, →, ↑, or ↓.
- Press Tab to move forward or Shift+Tab to move backward.

FIGURE 13-2
Table with text

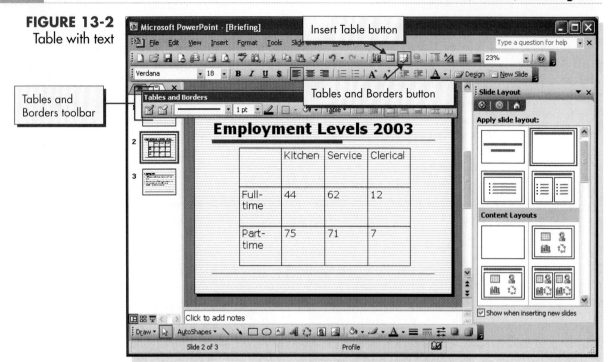

NOTE: When a cell is blank, pressing the left arrow key ⬅ or the right arrow key ➡ moves the insertion point left or right one cell. If text is in a cell, the left and right arrow keys move the insertion point one character to the left or right.

1. Click any table cell. Notice the insertion point in the cell you clicked.

2. Press ⌧Tab several times. The insertion point moves through cells from left to right. When you reach the end of a row, pressing ⌧Tab moves the insertion point to the beginning of the next row.

3. Press ⌧Shift+⌧Tab several times. The insertion point moves through cells from right to left.

4. Press each arrow key several times and observe the movement of the insertion point.

In the next several exercises, you will use many tools in the Tables and Borders toolbar.

TABLE 13-1   Buttons on the Tables and Borders Toolbar

BUTTON		PURPOSE
▨	Draw Table	Draws a table or adds rows and columns by dragging the pencil pointer. Splits rows, columns, or cells. Also, use it to color individual cell borders.

continues

TABLE 13-1   Buttons on the Tables and Borders Toolbar   *continued*

BUTTON		PURPOSE
	Eraser	Removes a table cell border and merges the two adjacent cells.
	Border Style	Indicates a line style to apply to borders.
	Border Width	Indicates a line width to apply to borders.
	Border Color	Indicates a color to apply to borders.
	Borders	Applies the selected border color, style, and line width options to the selected cell border. This is a dynamic button, based on the selection from its submenu.
	Fill Color	Applies a fill color or fill effect to selected cells.
	Table	Displays a menu of commonly used table options and commands.
	Merge Cells	Combines two or more selected adjacent cells and their contents into one larger cell.
	Split Cell	Splits a selected cell into two smaller cells.
	Align Top	Aligns the contents of selected cells with the top of the cells.
	Center Vertically	Centers the contents of selected cells between the top and bottom of the cells.
	Align Bottom	Aligns the contents of selected cells with the bottom of the cells.
	Distribute Rows Evenly	Makes all selected rows the same height.
	Distribute Columns Evenly	Makes all selected columns the same width.

EXERCISE   **13-3**   **Draw a Table Using the Pencil Pointer**

To draw a table, you first drag the pencil pointer 🖉 diagonally down and across to create a rectangle the approximate size of the table's outside border. Then you draw horizontal and vertical lines within the table to divide it into columns and rows.

1. Insert a new slide after slide 3 that uses the Title Only slide layout. Key the title **Employment Levels 2004**

2. Click the Tables and Borders button ![icon] on the Standard toolbar.

3. If your pointer is not a pencil pointer ![icon], click the Draw Table button ![icon] on the Tables and Borders toolbar.

4. Using the pencil pointer, drag from under the left edge to the title (down and to the right) to create a rectangle that fills the available space. See Figure 13-3 for size and placement. At this point, you have a one-cell table.

FIGURE 13-3
Using the
pencil pointer

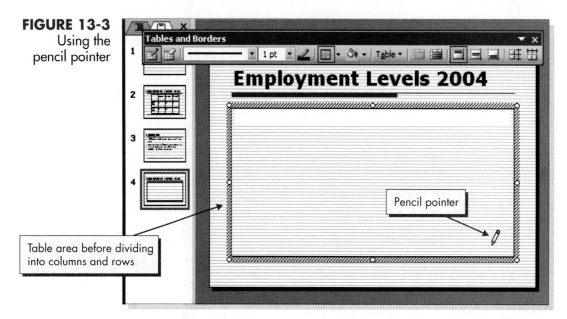

Table area before dividing into columns and rows

Pencil pointer

5. Using Figure 13-4 as a guide, allow enough space for where the table title will be placed and then draw a horizontal line all the way across the table. Because the table started as one cell, you have divided it into two cells.

NOTE: For now, don't worry if your table cell sizes do not perfectly match Figure 13-4. You will learn how to adjust cell sizes in Exercise 13-10.

6. Each time you draw a line, you split a table cell into two cells. Because you are drawing horizontal lines now, the cells you are splitting will become the table rows. Draw four more horizontal lines to create five rows.

7. Now, split the table with four vertical lines extending from the first horizontal line inside the table to the bottom of the table. You should have five columns.

8. Key the table text shown in Figure 13-4. If needed, adjust column widths so that text does not wrap, but don't worry about making them a uniform size.

FIGURE 13-4
Table with text

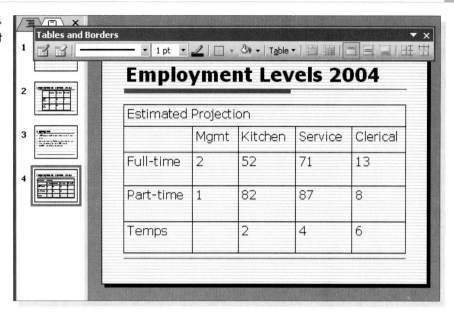

Selecting a Table, Table Cells, and Text

PowerPoint has many formatting features you can use to enhance your table. Before you can apply special formatting to table cells, you must first select those cells. You can select a single cell, a group of cells, or an entire table.

EXERCISE   **13-4**   **Select Groups of Cells and Text**

To select cells, you can use the following selection methods:

- Select a single cell by clicking it.
- Select the column or row containing the active cell by choosing T̲able on the Tables and Borders toolbar and then choosing Select C̲olumn or Select̲ Row from the menu.
- Select a rectangular group of cells by clicking a corner cell and dragging diagonally to the other corner.
- Click the starting cell in a selection; then (Shift)+click the ending cell.
- When the table is not selected, move your pointer just outside the table border above a column and then click when your pointer changes to a small, black, down-facing arrow ⬇.

When selecting a group of cells, be careful that you are dragging the I-beam pointer I and not the drag-and-drop arrow pointer ⬚. If you accidentally drag text to a new location, use Undo to correct the error.

1. On slide 2, click the cell that contains "Kitchen." The blinking insertion point indicates that the cell is active.

2. Press ⦋Tab⦌ once. "Service" is highlighted in a different color, indicating that the text "Service" is selected. Click once on the word "Service." Now there is a blinking insertion point. The cell is activated, but the text in the cell is not selected.

3. Click the "Service" cell and then drag down the column to the last row. The entire column is now selected.

4. Move your mouse pointer above the "Clerical" column, just above the table border. When you see the small, black, down-facing arrow ⬇, click to select the column.

FIGURE 13-5
Selecting a column

5. Click the cell that contains the number "44," and then ⦋Shift⦌+click the cell containing the number "7." The six cells containing numbers are now selected.

6. Use the Font Color button Ａ on the Drawing toolbar to change the font color to blue, the accent scheme color.

EXERCISE   **13-5**   **Select an Entire Table**

When the entire table is selected, you can change the formatting for the whole table at one time. A selected table has many similarities to a selected placeholder. To select the whole table, you can do one of the following:

- Select all the cells in the table by dragging diagonally across them.

- Click the table's selection border, so that the border changes from small diagonal lines to small dots.
- Right-click the table and choose S̲elect Table from the shortcut menu.
- When at least one table cell is activated or selected, press Ctrl+A.
- When the table is not active, press Tab one or more times to cycle through all the objects on the slide until the table's selection border is displayed.

1. Right-click any cell in the table and choose S̲elect Table from the shortcut menu. The table's selection border changes to the same small dot pattern that other PowerPoint objects display when they are selected.

2. Click the Shadow button s on the Formatting toolbar to apply a shadow to all the text in the table. Click outside the table to deselect it.

3. Click the upper-left cell and then drag to the lower-right cell to select all the cells in the table. Use the Formatting toolbar to make the selected cells bold and remove the text shadow. Change the font size to 20 points.

Modifying Table Structure

When you create a table, you decide how many rows and columns the table should have. After entering some data, you might discover that you have too many columns or perhaps too few rows. Or, you might want one row or column to have more or fewer cells than the others. You can modify your table structure inserting or deleting columns, merging a group of cells, or splitting an individual cell into two cells.

EXERCISE 13-6 Insert and Delete Rows and Columns

There are two ways to select cells when you want to insert or delete columns. You use a different menu depending on the way you select the cells.

- If you select an entire column, right-click the column and use commands on the shortcut menu.
- If you select one or more cells in a column, click Ta̲ble on the Tables and Borders toolbar, and choose a command from its menu.

Columns can be inserted either to the right or the left of the column that contains the active cell. The column formatting of the active column is copied to the new column. To insert more than one column at a time, select cells in as many columns as you want before using one of the Insert Column commands. The process of inserting and deleting rows is similar to inserting and deleting columns. In addition, you can insert a row at the bottom of the table by pressing Tab if you're in the last cell of the last table row. This is convenient if you run out of rows while you're entering data.

1. On slide 2, select the "Kitchen" column.

2. Right-click the selected column and choose <u>I</u>nsert Columns from the shortcut menu. A new column appears to the left of "Kitchen." It is the same size as the "Kitchen" column and has all the same formatting. The table is wider to accommodate the extra column.

3. Click the blank cell in the upper-left corner of the table.

4. Click T<u>a</u>ble on the Tables and Borders toolbar and choose Insert Columns to the <u>R</u>ight. A new column appears to the right of the selected cell, and it is the same size and format as the selected cell's column.

FIGURE 13-6
Inserting a column

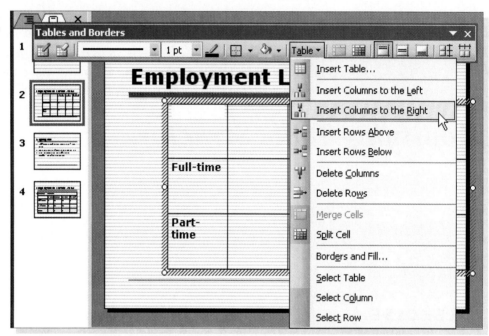

5. Click any cell in the second column (the last column that was inserted).

6. Click T<u>a</u>ble on the Tables and Borders toolbar, and choose Delete <u>C</u>olumns. The column that contained the selected cell is deleted. Your table should now have one blank column, to the left of the "Kitchen" column, and it should be the same size and format as the "Kitchen" column.

 NOTE: If more than one column is selected when you use the Delete <u>C</u>olumns command, all the selected columns will be deleted.

7. Select one or more cells in each of the first two table rows.

8. Click T<u>a</u>ble on the Tables and Borders toolbar and choose Insert Rows <u>B</u>elow. Two rows are inserted.

9. Click the last cell in the last row, containing the number "7."

10. Press (Tab). A new row is inserted at the bottom of the table. The table is now too big for the slide.

11. Select cells in the two blank rows below the text "Full-time."

12. Right-click the selected cells and choose Delete Columns from the shortcut menu.

13. Select the entire table and change the font size to 24 points.

14. Use a bottom sizing handle to make the table fit above the horizontal line at the bottom of the slide.

15. Position the table attractively on the slide by using the same method that you use to move text boxes or other objects.

16. Complete the table by keying the information shown in Figure 13-7 into the blank row and blank column.

FIGURE 13-7
Resized table

	Mgmt	Kitchen	Service	Clerical
Full-time	2	44	62	12
Part-time		75	71	7
Temps				2

Employment Levels 2003

3/18/2004   Your Name, So 13-6

17. Create a slide footer for the current slide (slide 3 only) containing today's date and the text *[Your Name], [your initials]*13-6.

18. Create a new folder for Lesson 13 and save the presentation as *[your initials]*13-6 in your new Lesson 13 folder.

EXERCISE 13-7 **Split Cells**

As you discovered when drawing the table, you can split cells by drawing a line through them with the pencil pointer ⟨✐⟩. You can also split a cell by using the Split Cell button ⟨▦⟩ on the Tables and Borders toolbar, or by clicking Table and choosing Split Cell from the menu.

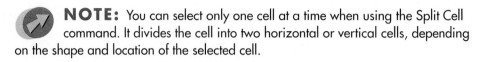

NOTE: You can select only one cell at a time when using the Split Cell command. It divides the cell into two horizontal or vertical cells, depending on the shape and location of the selected cell.

1. On slide 4, at the top of the table, click the cell containing the text "Estimated Projection."

2. Click the Split Cell button ▦ on the Tables and Borders toolbar. The selected cell becomes two cells.

3. In the new cell, key **Revised Figures**

EXERCISE 13-8 Merge Cells

There are several ways to merge cells. You can:

- Use the Eraser button ▦ on the Tables and Borders toolbar to remove a border between two adjacent cells.
- Select two or more cells and then click the Merge Cells button ▦ on the Tables and Borders toolbar.
- Select two or more cells, right-click the selection, and choose Merge Cells from the shortcut menu.

1. On slide 4, select the first three cells in the third row that begins "Full-time."

2. Click the Merge Cells button ▦ on the Tables and Borders toolbar. The three cells transform into one wide cell. The text and numbers from the merged cells all appear in one cell.

3. Click the Undo button ↺ to return the cells to their original state.

4. Click the Eraser button ▦ on the Tables and Borders toolbar. Your mouse pointer changes into an eraser pointer ✐.

5. Using the eraser, click the border between the first two cells in the bottom row. The two cells become one.

FIGURE 13-8
Using the eraser
to merge cells

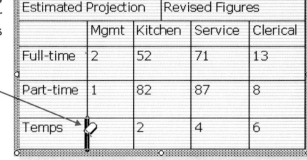

Estimated Projection		Revised Figures		
	Mgmt	Kitchen	Service	Clerical
Full-time	2	52	71	13
Part-time	1	82	87	8
Temps	2	2	4	6

Eraser

6. Click the Eraser button ![icon] on the Tables and Borders toolbar to turn off the Eraser tool. You may also press (Esc) to turn off the Eraser.

EXERCISE   **13-9**   **Use the Pencil to Split a Cell Diagonally**

You can split a cell diagonally. For example, if you are using a PowerPoint table to create a calendar, you might want to put two dates in the same square, separated by a diagonal line. Splitting a cell in this way does not create two separate cells, but is merely a line drawn within one cell. You can make it look like two cells by carefully placing text inside the cell.

1. On slide 4, select the two cells in the first row and then click the Merge button ![icon] to combine the two cells on that row. The text "Revised Figures" now appears on a separate line below "Estimated Projection" in one cell.

2. On the Tables and Borders toolbar, change the line style to a dashed line, 1½-point, medium blue line.

3. Click the Draw Table button ![icon] to change the pointer into a pencil.

4. Position the pencil tool near, but not touching, the lower-left corner of the cell in the first row. Draw a diagonal line across the cell to the upper-right corner.

FIGURE 13-9
Using the pencil
to split a cell
diagonally

Line style

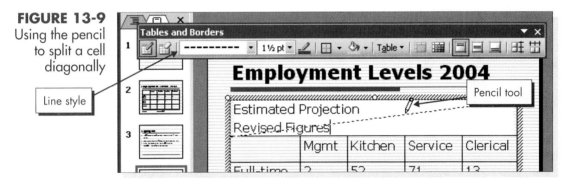

NOTE: Be careful where you start drawing. If you touch one of the cell borders with the pencil, the formatting of that border might change. If that happens, use Undo to restore it.

5. Click the Draw Table button ![icon] to turn off the pencil. Deselect the table to see the result.

6. To give the cell the appearance of being two cells, right-align the line containing the text "Revised Figures."

7. Create a slide footer for the current slide (slide 4 only) containing today's date and the text *[Your Name], [your initials]***13-9**. Notice that the table extends over the footer area. You will correct this in another exercise.

8. Save the presentation as *[your initials]***13-9** in your Lesson 13 folder.

EXERCISE **13-10** **Change the Height and Width of Rows, Columns, and Tables**

You may decide that a table is taking up too much space on your slide. If you decide to add rows or columns, or you decide to make a column wider, the table might no longer fit. You can make a table smaller or larger by dragging its sizing handles, and you can change the height of rows and the width of columns individually by dragging cell borders.

1. On slide 2, move your mouse pointer over the right border of the first column until the pointer changes to ⟨•⟩.

2. Using this pointer, drag the column border to the left. The column width decreases, and the adjacent column becomes wider.

FIGURE 13-10
Moving a
column border

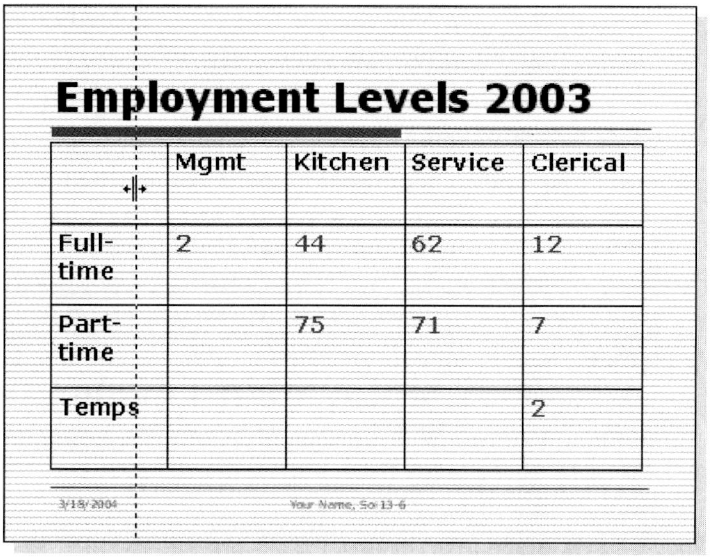

Employment Levels 2003

	Mgmt	Kitchen	Service	Clerical
Full-time	2	44	62	12
Part-time		75	71	7
Temps				2

3/18/2004   Your Name, So 13-6

3. Drag the same column border to the right, making the column wide enough so that the text "Part-time" appears on one line. Now the second column might be too narrow for the word "Kitchen."

4. Use the arrow pointer ⟨↕⟩ to double-click the right border of the "Kitchen" column. Double-clicking a right border makes the column wide enough to accommodate the widest text line in the column. (You'll further adjust the widths of columns later in the lesson.)

5. Move your mouse pointer to the bottom border of the first row.

6. When the pointer changes to ⟨↔⟩, drag the bottom border up, so that the row is approximately half its original height.

7. Drag the bottom border of the second row up, making it a little wider than the first row. Repeat for the third row.

8. Position your pointer on the bottom border of the table, anywhere except near a sizing handle. Make sure you see the arrow pointer ↔ and not the four-pointed arrow ⊕.

9. Drag the bottom row up to make it approximately the same height as the second and third rows.

EXERCISE 13-11 Distribute Columns and Rows Evenly

Use the Distribute Columns Evenly button ⊞ on the Tables and Borders toolbar to easily adjust several columns to be the same width. The Distribute Rows Evenly button ⊞ works in a similar way.

1. Select the "Kitchen," "Service," and "Clerical" columns by dragging across the second, third, and fourth cells in any row (or drag the small, black, down-facing arrow ⬇ just above the top border of the three columns).

2. Click the Distribute Columns Evenly button ⊞ on the Tables and Borders toolbar. The three selected columns are now all the same width.

3. Select the second through fourth cells in the first column.

4. Click the Distribute Rows Evenly button ⊞. Now the second through fourth rows are exactly the same height.

EXERCISE 13-12 Resize a Table

To resize the entire table, drag one of the sizing handles. When you drag, make sure the pointer is one of these shapes ↕ ↔ ⬉ and not the pointer used for changing column width ↔ or row height ↕.

If you hold down (Shift) while dragging a corner sizing handle, the table will resize proportionately. Whenever possible, depending on how large or small you make the table, the relative proportions of row heights and column widths are preserved.

1. On slide 2, click anywhere inside the table. Notice the eight sizing handles around the border. They work just like sizing handles on other PowerPoint objects.

2. Using the diagonal two-pointed arrow ⬉, drag the lower-right corner down and to the right. The table becomes larger, and the relative size of the rows and columns is preserved.

3. Drag the middle sizing handle on the bottom of the table up, making room for two more rows. Refer to Figure 13-11 (on the next page) for the approximate size of your table.

4. Save the presentation as *[your initials]*13-12 in your Lesson 13 folder. Leave it open for the next exercise.

FIGURE 13-11
Resized table

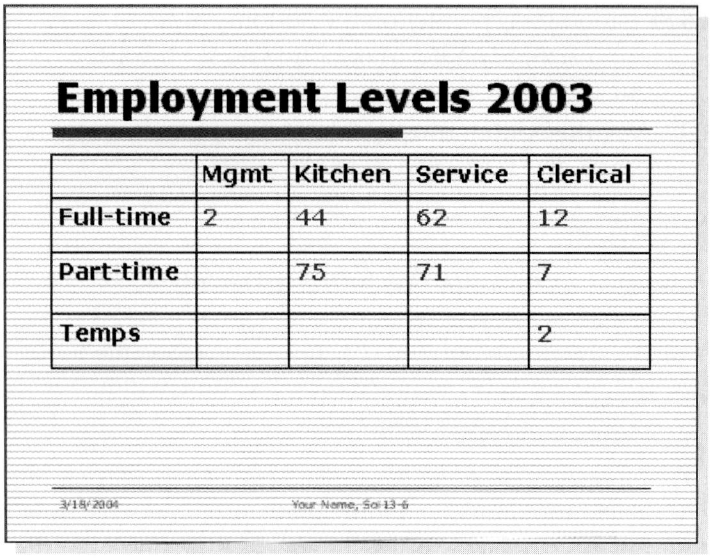

Employment Levels 2003

	Mgmt	Kitchen	Service	Clerical
Full-time	2	44	62	12
Part-time		75	71	7
Temps				2

3/18/2004   Your Name, Soi 13-6

Aligning Text and Numbers

In previous lessons, you aligned text in drawn objects and in text boxes. In a similar way, you can also align text and numbers in a table cell. You can specify that text or numbers appear at the top, middle, or bottom of a cell, and be horizontally left-, center-, or right-aligned.

In addition, you can use cell margin settings to refine even further the position of text and numbers in a cell. A *cell margin* is the space between the text in a cell and its borders.

EXERCISE 13-13 Align Text and Numbers Horizontally

In this exercise, you center the column labels in their cells and right-align the numbers.

1. On slide 2, select the cells in the first row that contain the text "Mgmt," "Kitchen," "Service," and "Clerical."

2. Click the Center button ☰ on the Formatting toolbar (or press Ctrl+E). The text is horizontally centered in each cell. You center text in table cells in the same way as you center text in other PowerPoint objects.

3. Select all the cells that contain numbers and right-align them. (Remember, you can press Ctrl+R to right-align text.)

EXERCISE 13-14 Change the Vertical Position of Text in a Cell

The appearance of a table is often improved by changing the vertical alignment within cells.

1. On slide 2, select the cells in the first row that contain the text "Mgmt," "Kitchen," "Service," and "Clerical."

 2. Click the Align Bottom button ▥ on the Tables and Borders toolbar. The text in the selected cells is now at the bottom edge of the cells.

3. Select all the cells in the second and third rows.

 4. Click the Center Vertically button ▤. The text moves to the middle of the cells.

EXERCISE 13-15 Use Margin Settings to Adjust the Position of Text in a Cell

Sometimes, the horizontal and vertical alignment settings are not able to place text precisely where you want it to be in a cell. You might be tempted to use Spacebar and Enter to adjust the text, but that usually doesn't work well.

You can precisely control where text is placed in a cell by using the cell's margin settings, combined with horizontal and vertical alignment. For example, you can right-align a column of numbers and also have them appear centered in the column.

1. On slide 2, select all the cells that contain numbers (blank cells in the third and fourth row, too).

2. From the Format menu, choose Table. The Format Table dialog box opens.

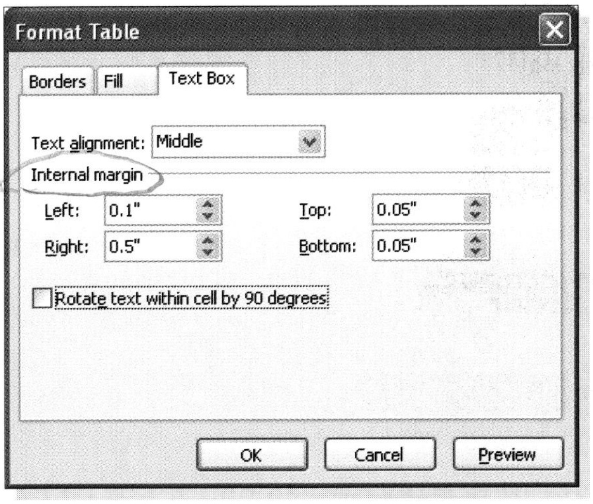

FIGURE 13-12
Using the Format Table dialog box to set cell margins

Format Table

Borders | Fill | Text Box

Text alignment: Middle

Internal margin

Left: 0.1"   Top: 0.05"

Right: 0.5"   Bottom: 0.05"

☐ Rotate text within cell by 90 degrees

OK   Cancel   Preview

3. Click the Text Box tab. Notice that the Text alignment setting is already set to Middle. This is equivalent to clicking the Center Vertically button on the Tables and Borders toolbar.

4. Click the Text alignment list box arrow to see the other settings. Choose Middle again.

5. Under Internal margin, change the Right setting to 0.5", and then click OK. The numbers are still right-aligned, but some space is between the cell border and the numbers.

6. Select all the cells in the first column containing text and change the left margin to 0.2".

FIGURE 13-13
Table with text and
numbers aligned

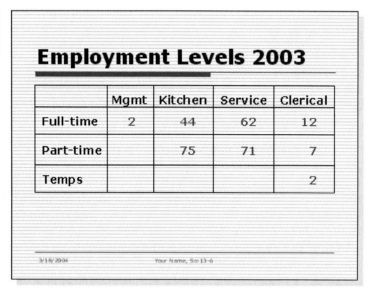

7. Apply the following formatting to the table to make it match the table on slide 2 (and appear as the completed table in Figure 13-13):

- Select the entire table and change the text size to 24 points and make it bold. Make all the numbers medium blue.
- Select the second through the last rows. On the Tables and Borders toolbar, click the Center Vertically button .
- Select the "Kitchen," "Service," and "Clerical" columns, and make them all the same width by clicking the Distribute Columns Evenly button .
- Select the bottom three rows and click the Distribute Rows Evenly button to make them the same height.
- Resize the table, so it fits above the horizontal line at the bottom of the slide. Adjust the table's position, if necessary.

- Select the cells with numbers on the Full-time and Part-time rows, and right-align all the numbers; then give the number cells a 0.5-inch right margin. Repeat for the Temps row.

- Select all the cells in the first column and give them a 0.2-inch left margin.

- Horizontally center the column heading text above the numbers.

8. Update the footer information for this slide. Save the presentation as *[your initials]***13-15** in your Lesson 13 folder. Leave it open for the next exercise.

Applying Fill Colors and Borders

You can dress up a table by adding fill effects to selected cells. You can also add borders to individual cells or the entire table. A convenient way to apply formatting is to use the buttons on the Tables and Borders toolbar.

EXERCISE **13-16** **Add Fill Color to Table Cells**

When you first create a table, the table cells contain no fill, allowing the slide's background to show through. You can apply a fill color or other fill effects, such as a pattern, gradient, or picture effect to one or more cells in your table. Applying fill effects is similar to applying fills to other PowerPoint objects.

1. On slide 2, if the Tables and Borders toolbar is not showing, click the Tables and Borders button 🖳 on the Standard toolbar.

2. If your mouse pointer is a pencil shape, press ⎋Esc to return to the standard mouse pointer.

3. Select all the cells in the top row.

4. Click the arrow for the Fill Color button 🎨 on the Tables and Borders toolbar and then choose medium gray (the fills scheme color).

 TIP: You can also use the Fill Color button 🎨 on the Drawing toolbar to apply fill effects to table cells.

5. Change the font color for the selected row to red.

6. Select the first column in the table, apply the same medium gray fill color, and change the font color to dark red (the accent and hyperlink scheme color).

7. Select all the cells that contain numbers and apply a white fill color.

8. Click outside the table to observe the effect. Now the table has an appearance that distinguishes it from the slide background.

NOTE: Depending on how you first displayed the Tables and Borders toolbar, the toolbar usually disappears when the table is not active and it automatically reappears the next time the table is clicked.

EXERCISE **13-17** **Remove a Fill Effect from a Cell**

You remove the fill effect from a table cell in the same way as for an AutoShape or other object.

1. Select the empty cell in the upper-left corner of the table.

2. Click the list box arrow for the Fill Color button [image] and choose No Fill. The cell now displays the slide's background. For this table, however, the gray color looks better in the corner cell, so click [Undo].

FIGURE 13-14
Fill effects applied
to table cells

Employment Levels 2003

	Mgmt	Kitchen	Service	Clerical
Full-time	2	44	62	12
Part-time		75	71	7
Temps				2

3/18/2004   Your Name, Sol 13-18

3. Leave the presentation open for the next exercise.

EXERCISE **13-18** **Change the Color and Style of Table Borders**

Changing the color and style of table borders is similar to changing the borders of other PowerPoint objects. Table *borders* are the lines forming the edges of cells, columns, rows, and the outline of the table. The Borders button's [image] drop-down list enables you to apply borders to all the cells in a selection, to just an outside border, or to just the inside borders separating one cell from another. Applying table borders is a three-step process:

• First, select the border style, border width, and border color you want.

- Second, select the cells to which you want to apply the border effect.
- Third, click the Borders button ▦ ▾ and choose an option from the drop-down list. (You can float the Borders toolbar.)

TIP: You can also use the Format Table dialog box to change border and fill formatting. Choose T̲able from the F̲ormat menu to open the dialog box. Or, right-click selected table cells and choose Bord̲ers and Fill from the shortcut menu.

1. Select any cell in your table. Open the Border Style list ━━━━ ▾ on the Tables and Borders toolbar.

2. Click the list box arrow for Border Style and choose the dash line. Then click the list box arrow for Border Width 1 pt ▾ and choose 1½ pt.

3. Click the Border Color button ▨ and choose medium blue, the accent scheme color.

4. Click T̲able on the Tables and Borders toolbar and choose S̲elect Table from the menu. The dotted border surrounding the table indicates that the entire table is selected.

FIGURE 13-15
Table menu

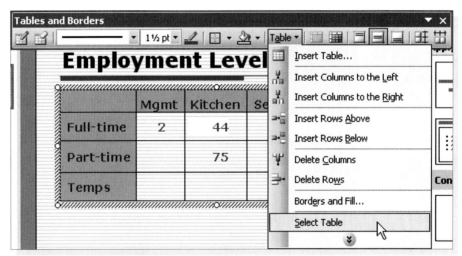

5. Click the list box arrow for the Borders button ▦ ▾; then click the Inside Borders button on the menu. The inside borders of the table are now blue dashed lines.

FIGURE 13-16
Borders menu with
Inside Borders
selected

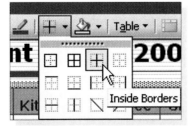

6. With the table still selected, change the options on the Tables and Borders toolbar, so the Border Style is a solid line, the Border Width is 3 pt, and the Border Color is dark red.

7. Click the list box arrow for the Borders button and choose Outside Borders ▦ ▾. The table now has a dark red outside border with dashed blue lines defining each cell.

> ⬤ **TIP:** You can use the pencil tool to change the color and style of a border. Set the border options on the Tables and Borders toolbar. Then, instead of clicking the Borders button ⬛ ▾, click the Draw Table button ▨ and use the pencil to click the borders you want to change.

8. Apply the following formatting to the table to make it match the table on slide 2 and as shown in Figure 13-17:

- Apply a medium gray fill color to the cells in the second row and left column.
- Apply a white fill color to the top row and all the cells with numbers.
- Change the text color to agree with Figure 13-17.
- Format all inside borders as medium blue, 1½-point, dashed lines.
- Format the outside border as a 3-point, dark red, solid line.
- Format the bottom border of the first row with the 2¼-point, red, solid line by using the pencil tool to draw the line that replaces the dashed line.

FIGURE 13-17
Completed table

Estimated Projection				Revised Figures
	Mgmt	Kitchen	Service	Clerical
Full-time	2	52	71	13
Part-time	1	82	87	8
Temps		2	4	6

9. Update the slide's footer for this exercise. Create a handout header and footer: include the date and your name as the header, and the page number and text *[your initials]*13-18 as the footer.

10. Save the presentation as *[your initials]*13-18 in your Lesson 13 folder.

11. View the presentation as a slide show; then preview and print the presentation as handouts, slides per page, grayscale, landscape, scale to fit paper, framed. Keep the presentation open for the next exercise.

Inserting a Microsoft Word Table

PowerPoint offers a wide variety of features that enable you to create interesting and attractive tables. Word tables, however, make some of these features more convenient to use and offer additional features as well. For example, you can sort data in a Word table, and Word enables you to create nested tables.

If you need the advanced table features that Word offers, you can create your table in Word and then copy and paste it onto a PowerPoint slide by using the

Paste Special command on the Edit menu. As is true with Excel charts, you have the option of embedding or linking a Word table on a PowerPoint slide.

EXERCISE 13-19 Insert a Word Table

To preserve all of Word's formatting when you copy a table, make sure you use the Paste Special command on the Edit menu. This feature will link the Word table in PowerPoint. If you use the Paste button 📋 or the Paste command instead, your Word table will be converted into a PowerPoint table, losing any special Word effects that are not supported by PowerPoint.

1. Insert a new slide after slide 4 that uses the Title Only slide layout. Key the title **Kitchen Forecast**.
2. Without closing PowerPoint, start Word and open the file **Brief1**, located on your student data disk.
3. Scroll halfway down the first page until you find the red, white, and blue table with the heading "2004 Estimates."
4. Move your mouse pointer within the table borders. The table move handle 🔘 appears in the upper-left corner of the table.
5. Click the table move handle 🔘 to select the table.
6. Copy the table to the clipboard.
7. Switch to PowerPoint. If slide 5 is not showing, move to slide 5.
8. From the Edit menu, choose Paste Special. The Paste Special dialog box opens.

FIGURE 13-18
Copying a Word table onto a PowerPoint slide

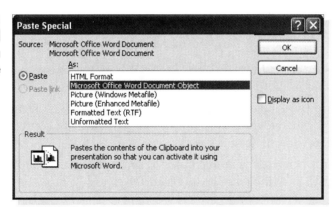

9. In the As list box, choose Microsoft Office Word Document Object. Click OK. The table appears on the slide.

> **NOTE:** To create Word tables from within PowerPoint, open the Insert menu and choose Object. In the Insert Object dialog box, choose Create new; then choose Microsoft Office Word Document from the Object type list. In the Word document window, use Word's table tools to create your table.

10. Make the table approximately 1 inch wider and 1 inch taller. Position it attractively on the slide.

11. Use the Format Object dialog box to recolor the table. Change all the black text to medium blue, change the royal blue lines to medium blue, change the red lines and red text to dark red, and change the light blue fill to medium gray. The cells with numbers were not colored in Word, so they cannot be recolored here.

> **TIP:** When creating a Word table that you are going to link, plan in advance which PowerPoint colors you want to use. You might not be able to use the same colors in Word but, if you make each part of the table a different color, it will be easy to recolor the table to suit your needs after it is on a PowerPoint slide.

EXERCISE 13-20 Make Changes to a Word Table

If you need to make changes to text, numbers, or other formatting in a linked Word table, double-click it to open Word from within PowerPoint. You will have all the Word table tools available to work with.

1. Double-click the table on slide 5. The Word toolbars and menu appear.

2. In the first column, change the text "F/T" to **Full-time** and the text "P/T" to **Part-time**

3. Change the number "46" under "Clean-up" to **48**

4. Press [Ctrl]+[A] to select the entire Word table.

5. Click the Bold button **B** on Word's Formatting toolbar.

6. Select the three cells containing the text "Chefs," "Helpers," and "Clean-up." Change their text color to red by using the Font Color button **A** on Word's Formatting toolbar.

7. Click outside the table border to return to PowerPoint. Adjust the size and position of the table to suit your taste.

8. Create a slide footer for the current slide (slide 5 only) containing today's date and the text *[Your Name], [your initials]*13-20.

9. Create a handout header and footer: include the date and your name as the header, and the page number and text *[your initials]*13-20 as the footer.

FIGURE 13-19
Word table
embedded on a
PowerPoint slide

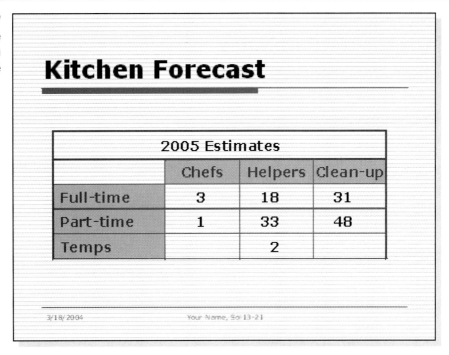

10. Move to slide 1 and save the presentation as *[your initials]***13-20** in your Lesson 13 folder.

11. Print the current slide in full size. If you have a color printer, print it in color.

12. View the presentation as a slide show; then preview and print the presentation as handouts, six slides per page, grayscale, landscape, framed. Close the presentation.

USING ONLINE HELP

This lesson shows you how to insert a PowerPoint table and how to import a Word table. There are other options for inserting a table into PowerPoint.

Use Help to learn more about inserting tables from other programs:

1. In the Ask a Question box, key the search words **Office programs, table** and press Enter.

2. Select the topic **Office programs you can use to create a table**. Read the Help topic.

3. Close Help when you finish.

LESSON 13 Summary

➤ Tables offer a convenient way to quickly organize material on a slide. You can use various menu commands, toolbar buttons, and slide layouts to insert a table, or you can "draw" a table directly on a slide by using the Draw Table button ▣.

➤ Before you can apply special formatting to table cells, you must first select those cells. You can select individual cells, groups of cells, or the entire table.

➤ Use the buttons on the Tables and Borders toolbar to apply fill effects and border effects to individual cells, a group of cells, or the entire table.

➤ Change the overall size of a table by dragging one of its sizing handles with a two-pointed arrow.

➤ Change the width of a column by dragging or double-clicking its border. Change the height of a row by dragging its border.

➤ Rows and columns can be easily inserted or deleted as you develop a table. Select at least one cell in the row or column where you want to insert or delete; then use commands on the Table menu.

➤ While keying text in a table, a quick way to insert a new row at the bottom is to press Tab when you reach the last table cell.

➤ Occasionally, you might want one row or column to have more or fewer cells than the others. You can make this happen by merging a group of cells or splitting an individual cell into two cells.

➤ A diagonal line can be added to a cell to make it appear to be split into two cells. Careful placement of text within the cell completes this illusion.

➤ Applying and removing fill effects is similar to applying fill effects to other PowerPoint objects. Table and cell fills can be gradients, textures, patterns, or pictures.

➤ Before applying a border to cells or the entire table, choose the border style, border width, and border color on the Tables and Borders toolbar. Then select cells and choose an option from the Borders button ▣▾ drop-down list.

➤ Use the text alignment buttons on the Formatting toolbar to control the horizontal position of text in a cell.

➤ Use the Align Top ▤, Center Vertically ▤, and Align Bottom ▤ buttons on the Tables and Borders toolbar to control the vertical position of text within a cell.

➤ To fine-tune the horizontal or vertical position of text, change a cell's margin settings by using the Text Box tab on the Format Table dialog box.

➤ An easy way to insert a Word table is to open the file in Word, select the table, copy it to the clipboard and then use PowerPoint's Paste Special command to insert it on a slide.

➤ Like Excel charts, Word tables can be embedded or linked on a PowerPoint slide. Double-click the table to edit it in Word.

LESSON 13   Command Summary

FEATURE	BUTTON	MENU	KEYBOARD
Insert table		Insert, Table	
Column, select		Table (Tables and Borders toolbar), Select Column	
Row, select		Table (Tables and Borders toolbar), Select Row	
Table, select		Table (Tables and Borders toolbar), Select Table	
Apply fill effect to cells		Table (Tables and Borders toolbar), Borders and Fill, Fill tab	
Apply border effects		Table (Tables and Borders toolbar), Borders and Fill, Borders tab	
Align table text vertically		Table (Tables and Borders toolbar), Borders and Fill, Text Box tab	
Set table cell margins		Table (Tables and Borders toolbar), Borders and Fill, Text Box tab	
Distribute columns evenly			
Distribute rows evenly			
Insert table columns		Table (Tables and Borders toolbar), Insert Columns to the Left, or Insert Columns to the Right	
Insert table rows		Table (Tables and Borders toolbar), Insert Rows Above, or Insert Rows Below	
Delete table columns		Table (Tables and Borders toolbar), Delete Columns	
Draw a table			
Merge table cells		Table (Tables and Borders toolbar), Merge Cells	
Split a table cell		Table (Tables and Borders toolbar), Split Cell	

Concepts Review

TRUE/FALSE QUESTIONS

Each of the following statements is either true or false. Indicate your choice by circling T or F.

T **(F)** 1. You can adjust the width of individual columns in a table, but row heights must all be the same.

(T) F 2. You don't need to be exact when you define the size of a table because it's easy to insert rows and columns later.

(T) F 3. Cell borders can be any color you want.

T **(F)** 4. Borders are available in only one width.

(T) F 5. Text in a table cell can have its vertical position adjusted, independent of other cells.

T **(F)** 6. When you insert a new column, it is always inserted to the left of the currently selected column.

(T) F 7. Cell margins work the same way as text box margins.

T **(F)** 8. If you need to make changes to an embedded Word table, you must delete the table, open the file in Word, make the changes and then copy the edited table back to PowerPoint.

SHORT ANSWER QUESTIONS

Write the correct answer in the space provided.

1. What do you call a box in a table that contains text or numbers?

   CELL

2. Other than dragging down all the cells or using a menu command, how can you select a column in a table?

   BLACK DOWN POINTING ARROW AT TOP OF COLUMN

3. What toolbar contains the Center Vertically button?

   TABLES + BORDERS

4. What menu command selects the entire table?

   TABLE MENU   SHORT CUT

5. What three settings do you specify before using the Borders button ☐▾ to apply a border effect to selected cells?

STYLE   WIDTH   COLOR

6. How do you merge selected cells in a table by using a toolbar?

MERGE   CELLS   BUTTON

7. What is different about splitting a cell diagonally from splitting it horizontally or vertically?

DRAWING   IT   IN

8. What's the quickest way to make a group of selected columns of varying widths all the same width?

DISTRIBUTE   COLUMNS   EVENLY

Answer these questions on a separate page. There are no right or wrong answers. Support your answers with examples from your own experience, if possible.

1. How would you decide whether a table or a chart is a better presentation tool for a particular set of numerical information? Which criteria should govern the use of one form over the other?

2. If you are adding a Word table to a lengthy presentation that includes a variety of slide types, what should you do to ensure that the table slide is visually consistent with the rest of the slides?

Skills Review

EXERCISE 13-21

Create a table, key text, select parts of a table, change column width, and resize the table.

1. Open the file **CookOff** and move to slide 4, which contains the WordArt title "The Winning Fare."

2. Insert a new table by following these steps:

   a. Click the Insert Table button 🔲 on the Standard toolbar.
   b. On the grid that appears, drag to define a table three rows long by two columns wide.

c. If the Tables and Borders toolbar is not showing, click the Tables and Borders button 🔲 on the Standard toolbar.

    d. If the mouse pointer is a pencil, click the Draw Table button 🔲 on the Tables and Borders toolbar to turn off the pencil.

3. Move the table to a new position and change its size by following these steps:

    a. Right-click anywhere inside the table and choose S̲elect Table from the shortcut menu.

    b. Move your mouse pointer over the table's border until you see the four-pointed arrow ⟐.

    c. Using the four-pointed arrow, drag the table to move it to a better position on the slide.

    d. Make the table wider by dragging the right-center sizing handle to the right. Before you drag, make sure the pointer appears as ↔.

4. Change the width of a column by following these steps:

    a. Move your mouse pointer over the border between the two columns until you see the pointer ╫.

    b. Drag the column border to the left, reducing the left column width by about 1 inch.

5. Key text in the table and change the font size by following these steps:

    a. Click the upper-left cell to select it and then key:
      Amy Grand Enter
      Hot Tomato Salsa

    b. Press Tab to move to the next cell and then key:
      Tangy fresh tomato salsa with fresh jalapenos, white corn, lots of garlic, and green and yellow peppers

    c. Select the entire table. Use the Formatting toolbar to change the font size to 20 points.

6. Key the text shown in Figure 13-20 for the remaining cells. Apply bold to each name.

FIGURE 13-20

Juanita McLeod Enter Raspberry Cream Pie	Raspberry yogurt custard in a graham cracker crust that tastes like a million calories
William Steinberg Enter Roasted Chicken and Vegetables	Free-range chicken breasts marinated in garlic, herbs, and lime juice, and roasted with turnips, yellow squash, and red potatoes

7. Resize and reposition the table to create an attractive layout on the slide.

8. Check the grayscale settings and make any necessary changes.

9. Create a slide footer for the current slide (slide 4 only) containing today's date and the text *[Your Name], [your initials]***13-21**.

10. Create a handout header and footer: include the date and your name as the header, and the page number and text *[your initials]***13-21** as the footer.

11. Move to slide 1 and save the presentation as *[your initials]***13-21** in your Lesson 13 folder.

12. Print the current slide in full size. If you have a color printer, print it in color.

13. View the presentation as a slide show; then preview and print the presentation as handouts, six slides per page, grayscale, landscape, framed. Close the presentation.

EXERCISE 13-22

Create a table, apply border and fill options, and change cell alignment and text alignment.

1. Open the file **Operate2**.

2. Insert a new slide after slide 3 that uses the Title Only layout. Key the title **Capital Equipment 2005**

3. Use the Insert Table button ▦ to create a five-row by three-column table.

4. Click the Automatic Layout Options ▨▾ smart tag button at the lower-right corner of the table and choose <u>U</u>ndo Automatic Layout.

5. For the table text, key the information shown in Figure 13-21.

FIGURE 13-21

	Column 1	Column 2	Column 3
Row 1		Leased	Bought
Row 2	Kitchen	9,450	24,350
Row 3	Dining	14,400	18,650
Row 4	Office	10,500	25,500
Row 5	Other	8,252	16,300

6. Align text horizontally by following these steps:

   a. Select the first column by clicking the first cell and dragging down to the last cell.

b. Click the Center button ≣ on the Formatting toolbar (or press Ctrl+E).
  c. Select all the cells in the first row and center that text horizontally.
  d. Select all the cells that contain numbers by dragging diagonally across the cells.

  e. Click the Align Right button ≣ on the Formatting toolbar (or press Ctrl+R) to right-align the numbers.

7. Change cell margin settings by following these steps:

  a. Make sure all the cells that contain numbers are selected.
  b. Right-click the selected cells and then choose Borders and Fill from the shortcut menu. Click the Text Box tab.
  c. In the Internal margin section, key **0.75"** in the Right text box. Click OK.

8. Change the vertical alignment of text and numbers in their cells by following these steps:

  a. Select the entire table by clicking the table's border.
  b. Click the Center Vertically button ▤ on the Tables and Borders toolbar.

9. Change the font size for the entire table to 24 points and make all the text bold.

10. Apply fill effects to table cells by following these steps:

  a. Select all the cells in the first row.

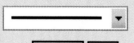

  b. Click the list box arrow on the Fill Color button 🪣 on either the Drawing toolbar or the Tables and Borders toolbar.
  c. Choose Fill Effects and click the Gradient tab.
  d. Set one-color medium blue gradient shading to the darkest setting. Choose the From center shading style and the variant that is darkest at the edges. Click OK.

11. Select the cells in the first column that contain text starting with "Kitchen" through "Other." Apply the same blue gradient fill as in step 10.

12. Select all the cells with numbers and apply a red one-color gradient fill, using the same variant and shading settings as the blue cells.

13. Remove all the table's borders by following these steps:

  a. Select the entire table.
  b. Click the arrow on the Border Style drop-down list ▬▬▬ and choose No Border.
  c. Click the arrow on the Borders button and choose All Borders ⊞.
  d. If the pencil pointer is active, press Esc to restore your standard mouse pointer.

14. Use the table's right-center sizing handle to make the whole table wider. Make the table wide enough so that the numbers appear centered under their column headings.

15. Adjust the table's overall position on the slide to make a pleasing composition.

16. Adjust the table's grayscale settings, so that it will print well on a black-and-white printer.

17. Create a handout header and footer: include the date and your name as the header, and the page number and text *[your initials]*13-22 as the footer.

18. Move to slide 1 and save the presentation as *[your initials]*13-22 in your Lesson 13 folder.

19. Print slide 4 in full size. If you have a color printer, print it in color.

20. View the presentation as a slide show; then preview and print the presentation as handouts, six slides per page, grayscale, landscape, framed. Close the presentation.

EXERCISE 13-23

Draw a table; insert and delete rows and columns; adjust column and row width; apply formatting for text, fill colors, and borders.

1. Open the file **Operate3**.

2. Apply the design template Blends and use the default color scheme. Change the background to a one-color horizontal gradient fill, using white and shading to a medium gray. Choose the variant with the lightest shade in the middle and apply it to all slides.

3. Display slide 5, titled "Reservation Requests."

4. Draw a table on slide 5 by following these steps:

   a. If the Tables and Borders toolbar is not displayed, click the Tables and Borders button 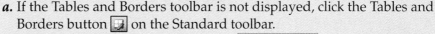 on the Standard toolbar.

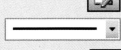

   b. Click the Border Style list box arrow 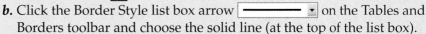 on the Tables and Borders toolbar and choose the solid line (at the top of the list box).

   c. Click the Border Color button 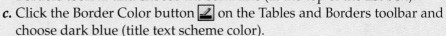 on the Tables and Borders toolbar and choose dark blue (title text scheme color).

   d. Move the Tables and Borders toolbar to the top of the slide to get it out of the way.

   e. If your mouse pointer is not a pencil pointer 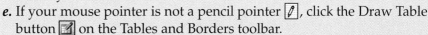, click the Draw Table button on the Tables and Borders toolbar.

   f. Starting on the left side just below the title, drag the pencil pointer diagonally down and across the slide to create a rectangle that fills the available space.

   g. Within the table, draw four vertical lines (to create five columns) and three horizontal lines (to create four rows). They don't need to be the same size.

   h. Press (Esc) to turn off the pencil pointer.

5. For the table's text, key the data in Figure 13-22. It's okay if the text wraps within cells; you will fix the layout in the next few steps.

FIGURE 13-22

	Column 1	Column 2	Column 3	Column 4	Column 5
Row 1		Brunch	Lunch	Dinner	Late Nite
Row 2	Weekday	3	35	75	3
Row 3	Weekends	21	12	100	15
Row 4	Memorial Day	7	5	12	4

6. Reduce the text size to 24 points for the entire table and make it bold. Make all the numbers red and make all the text dark blue.

7. Make all the columns the same width and all the rows the same height by following these steps:

   a. Select the entire table by clicking its border.
   b. Click the Distribute Columns Evenly button ⊞ on the Tables and Borders toolbar.
   c. Click the Distribute Rows Evenly button ⊞ on the Tables and Borders toolbar.

8. If the text "Weekday" or "Weekends" wraps to a second line, make the table a little wider by dragging either the right- or left-center sizing handle. Make sure the pointer appears as ↔.

9. Insert a new row between "Weekends" and "Memorial Day" by following these steps:

   a. Right-click "Memorial Day."
   b. Choose Insert Rows from the shortcut menu.
   c. If the table extends below the bottom of the slide, make it smaller by dragging the bottom-center sizing handle up.

10. Insert a new column to the left of "Brunch" by following these steps:

    a. Click anywhere in the first column.
    b. Click Table on the Tables and Borders toolbar.
    c. Choose Insert Columns to the Right.

11. Delete a column and a row by following these steps:

    a. Select the entire "Late Nite" column (which might extend beyond the right edge of the slide).
    b. Right-click the selection and choose Delete Columns from the shortcut menu.
    c. Select the "Memorial Day" row. Right-click the selection and choose Delete Rows from the shortcut menu.

12. In the second column, key **Breakfast** for the column heading. Key **5** for "Weekday" and **18** for "Weekends." Make the numbers in the "Breakfast" column red. Change the "Weekday" cell to **Weekdays**.

13. Key the following information in the new row:

Holidays[Tab]6[Tab]9[Tab]15[Tab]94

14. Center the table's column headings, right-align the numbers, and use margin settings to make the numbers appear centered under the headings. Center all the text vertically within each cell.

15. Change the table's outside border to a 3-point line (keep it dark blue).

16. Adjust the table's size and position on the slide to make a pleasing composition. You may need to adjust the width of columns so text in the first column does not wordwrap.

17. Adjust the table's grayscale settings so that it will print well on a black-and-white printer.

18. Create a slide footer for the current slide (slide 5 only) containing today's date and the text *[Your Name], [your initials]*13-23.

19. Create a handout header and footer: include the date and your name as the header, and the page number and text *[your initials]*13-23 as the footer.

20. Move to slide 1 and save the presentation as *[your initials]*13-23 in your Lesson 13 folder.

21. Print the current slide in full size. If you have a color printer, print it in color.

22. View the presentation as a slide show; then preview and print the presentation as handouts, six slides per page, grayscale, framed. Close the presentation.

EXERCISE 13-24

Import a Microsoft Word table, edit and format the Word table, format a PowerPoint table, and merge and split cells.

1. Open the file **NewMenu1** and move to slide 4 (which is titled "Menu Analysis").

2. Embed a Microsoft Word table by following these steps:

   a. Without closing PowerPoint, start Word and open the file **NewMenu2**.

   b. Scroll down until the table with the heading "Number of Menu Items" is displayed.

   c. Select the table by moving your mouse pointer onto the table and then click the table move handle ⊞ in the upper-left corner of the table.

   d. Copy the table to the clipboard and then switch to PowerPoint. Move to slide 4, if it is not already active.

   e. In PowerPoint, choose Paste Special from the Edit menu. Choose Microsoft Word Document Object from the As list box and click OK.

3. Format the embedded table by following these steps:

   a. Using the Format Object dialog box, recolor the table by using scheme colors that contrast with the slide's background.

   b. Double-click the table to open Word and then edit the table's numbers to agree with Figure 13-23.

FIGURE 13-23

	Column 1	Column 2	Column 3	Column 4
Row 1		2002	2003	2004
Row 2	Meat	15	14	11
Row 3	Vegetarian	9	10	13

   c. Click outside the table border to return to PowerPoint.
   d. Resize the shaded rectangle behind the table, so that its edges exactly coincide with the table's borders. Use Zoom to be precise.

    TIP: Hold down Alt while dragging the rectangle's edges to fine-tune its size.

   e. Draw a selection rectangle around both the table and the rectangle behind it. Group the two objects and position them attractively on the slide.

4. Check and adjust the grayscale settings for the table as needed.

5. Create a slide footer for the current slide (slide 4 only) containing today's date and the text *[Your Name], [your initials]***13-24**.

6. Save the presentation as *[your initials]***13-24** in your Lesson 13 folder.

7. Print slide 4 in full size. If you have a color printer, print it in color.

8. Merge two cells by following these steps:

   a. Move to slide 5, which contains a table with many rows of text.
   b. Select the two cells in the first row.
   c. Click the Merge Cells button 🔳 on the Tables and Borders toolbar.
   d. Near the top of the center column, merge the two cells that contain the names "Susan Smith" and "Wanda Jacks."
   e. In the same manner, merge the "Jan" and "Feb" cells in the first column, and merge the cell containing "No-Guilt Cherry Cheesecake" with the blank cell below it.

9. Split a cell into two side-by-side cells by following these steps:

   a. Select the cell containing "Susan Smith" and "Wanda Jacks."
   b. Click the Split Cell button 🔳 on the Tables and Borders toolbar.
   c. Move "Wanda Jacks" into the new empty cell.
   d. Remove any extra blank lines from the split cells by clicking on the blank line and pressing Backspace.

10. Split a cell diagonally by following these steps:

a. Make whatever changes are needed, so that the settings on the Tables and Borders toolbar are for a 1-point, solid, gold line (accent and hyperlink scheme color).

b. If your mouse pointer is not a pencil shape, click the Draw Table button on the Tables and Borders toolbar to turn on the pencil tool.

c. Draw a diagonal line in the "Jan Feb" cell from the lower-left corner of the cell to the upper-right corner.

d. In the same way, split the "Mar Apr" cell diagonally.

e. Click the Draw Table button to turn off the pencil.

f. Select the text "Feb" and right-align that line only (press Ctrl+R).

g. Right-align the text "Apr."

11. Apply a Title Only layout to this slide and key the table title for the slide title. Delete the table title row. The table will now fit better below the graphic on the slide master.

12. Adjust the overall size of the table and adjust column widths to create a well-designed slide. Apply solid color fills from the slide color scheme to make the table text easier to read.

13. Create a slide footer for the current slide (slide 5) containing today's date and the text *[Your Name], [your initials]***13-24**.

14. Create a handout header and footer: include the date and your name as the header, and the page number and text *[your initials]***13-24** as the footer.

15. Resave the presentation using the same filename.

16. Print the current slide (slide 5) in full size.

17. View the presentation as a slide show; then preview and print the presentation as handouts, six slides per page, grayscale, framed. Close the presentation.

Lesson Applications

Create a presentation with a table slide, apply border settings, arrange and format text, and change column widths and table size.

1. Open the file **Print1**.
2. Insert three slides after slide 1 and key the text shown in Figure 13-24. Use the Title and Text layout for slides 2 and 3, and use the Title and Content layout for slide 4. On the table, each cell in the first row should contain two lines (press Shift + Enter to start a new line within a cell).

FIGURE 13-24

Slide 2

Print Advertising 2004 ———— Title

- Campaigns use a variety of print media
- Each medium targets a specific market segment
- Every campaign must meet specific sales objectives

Slide 3

Coupon Redemption ———— Title

- Effective measure of return on investment
- Used for promotional purposes in a variety of print media

Slide 4

Coupons Redeemed 2004 ———— Title

	Column 1	Column 2	Column 3	Column 4
Row 1	Newspaper Magazine	Coupons Redeemed	Average Check	Cost of One Ad
Row 2	NY Times	414	$31.50	$6,800
Row 3	NY Magazine	476	$25.00	$2,850
Row 4	NY Runner	1,063	$23.50	$975
Row 5	NY Health	125	$16.25	$650

Table

3. On slide 4, change the table's text color of the first row and the first column to light blue.

4. For the entire table, change all right and left cell margins to 0.2 inches. Using the pointer ⊹, double-click each column border so that each column self-adjusts to fit the widest text in the column.

5. Center the headings for the columns containing numbers.

6. Right-align all numbers; then set the right margins for the cells containing numbers to make the numbers appear centered under their column headings. (Each column will need a different right margin setting.)

7. Vertically center all text and numbers in the table.

8. Remove the cell borders for the entire table. Apply a 3-point purple border to the bottom of row 1 and the right side of column 1.

9. Select the top row of the table and change the line spacing to 0.9 lines. Align the text in the top row with the bottoms of their cells; then reduce the height of the row.

10. Adjust the overall size and position of the table to make an attractive composition on the slide.

11. Review the presentation. Add decorative touches and change bullets or text arrangements on the other slides as you see fit.

Completed table slide

Coupons Redeemed 2004

Newspaper Magazine	Coupons Redeemed	Average Check	Cost of One Ad
NY Times	414	$31.50	$6,800
NY Magazine	476	$25.00	$2,850
NY Runner	1,063	$23.50	$975
NY Health	125	$16.25	$650

Your Name, Sol 13-25   3/18/2004

12. Create a slide footer for the current slide (slide 4) containing today's date and the text *[Your Name], [your initials]*13-25.

13. Create a handout header and footer: include the date and your name as the header, and the page number and text *[your initials]***13-25** as the footer.

14. Save the presentation as *[your initials]***13-25** in your Lesson 13 folder.

15. Print the current slide (slide 4) in full size.

16. View the presentation as a slide show; then preview and print the presentation as handouts, six slides per page, grayscale, landscape, framed. Close the presentation.

EXERCISE 13-26

Edit and format a presentation; insert a table slide; insert rows; change row height, column width, alignment, and cell margins; and create hyperlinks for table text.

1. Open the file **Ads2**. Change the background of the entire presentation to a two-color gradient fill, using medium blue (fills scheme color) and dark blue (background scheme color). Choose the From title shading style with the lightest color in the center.

2. Customize the slide color scheme as follows: change the title text color to a brighter shade of gold, the accent color to a darker shade of red, the accent and hyperlink color to bright turquoise, and the accent and followed hyperlink color to navy blue.

3. On slide 1, change "Student Name" to your name.

4. Insert a table on a new slide after slide 1 and key the text shown in Figure 13-26.

FIGURE 13-26

Advertising Effectiveness	—Slide title		
	Column 1	**Column 2**	**Column 3**
Row 1		New Customers	Total Revenue
Row 2	Newspaper	28%	30%
Row 3	Radio	10%	5%
Row 4	Yellow Pages	6%	12%

Table

5. Apply the following formatting to the table's text:
   - Center the text in the first row.
   - Right-align all the numbers and apply a right indent, so that the numbers appear centered underneath their headings.
   - Apply a 0.25-inch left margin to all the cells in the first column.
   - If necessary, adjust column width of the first row so that "Yellow Pages" is on one line.

6. Insert a row above "Yellow Pages" with the following text:

   Mailers   12%   18%

7. Make the table attractive by adjusting the column widths, row heights, and vertical alignment of cells, as necessary. Position the table in the center of the slide.

8. Fill the cells in the first column with dark blue and the remaining cells with medium blue. Change the column heading text to gold with a black shadow.

9. Remove all the inside borders; then apply a 3-point, solid, red line for the outside border. Add a 3-point, solid, red line to the bottom border of the first row.

10. Create hyperlinks from the text in each of the cells in the first column. Link the text to the appropriate slide. Insert a Return or Home button on the slide master. Format the button as you please and make it link to slide 2, the table slide. (Hint: Select the text; then choose Hyperlink from the Insert menu or press Ctrl+K.)

11. Create a slide footer for the current slide (slide 2) containing today's date and the text *[Your Name], [your initials]*13-26.

12. Create a handout header and footer: include the date and your name as the header, and the page number and text *[your initials]*13-26 as the footer.

13. Check spelling and grayscale settings.

14. Save the presentation as *[your initials]*13-26 in your Lesson 13 folder.

15. Print the current slide (slide 4) in full size.

16. View the presentation as a slide show; then preview and print the presentation as handouts, slides per page, grayscale, landscape, framed. Close the presentation.

Edit and format a presentation including a table slide, add data, change alignment, change table colors, merge cells, and embed a Word table.

1. Open the file **MktSum**.

2. Create your own designs for your title master and slide master using a burgundy and gold color scheme. Use a gradient background blending to the darkest color in the lower corner.

3. Establish your presentation color scheme and modify the scheme, if necessary, when you develop your slides.

4. Use a rectangle with a pattern fill behind the title placeholders and narrow rectangles with a two-color gradient (gold and burgundy) combined with the patterned shape. Use the title slide shown in Figure 13-27 as your example. The design of the slide master is shown in Figure 13-28 with the table design.

5. Change the presentation's font to Tahoma.

FIGURE 13-27
Title slide

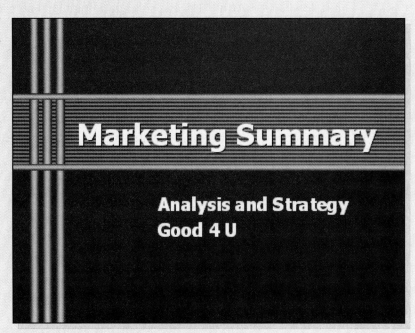

6. Create a table on a new slide after slide 3. Use Figure 13-28 for the slide title, table content, and format.

FIGURE 13-28
Table slide

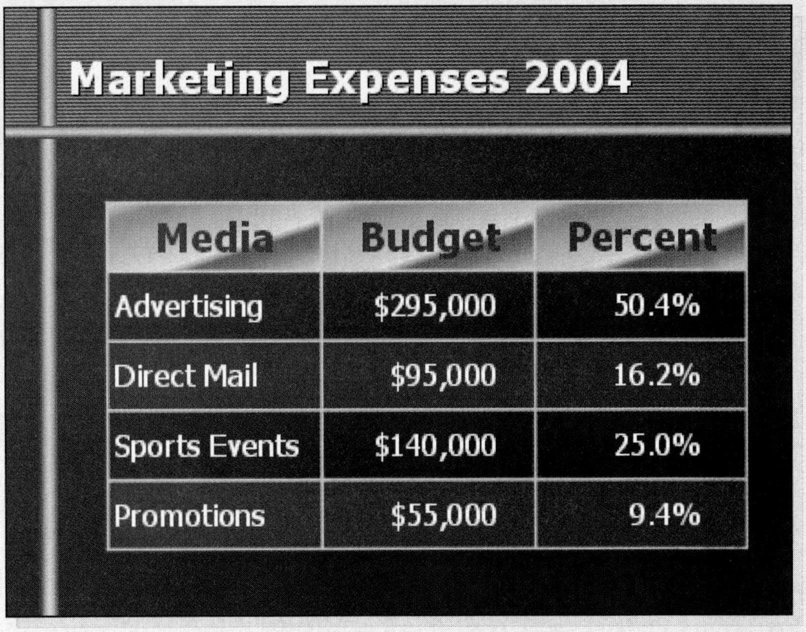

Table slide showing "Marketing Expenses 2004"

Media	Budget	Percent
Advertising	$295,000	50.4%
Direct Mail	$95,000	16.2%
Sports Events	$140,000	25.0%
Promotions	$55,000	9.4%

7. Use appropriate alignment techniques, fill colors, and border treatments. Use a preset gradient color for the heading row fill for a gold appearance.

8. Using the Title Only layout, insert a new slide after slide 4 with the title **Estimated Budget 2005**

9. Open the Word document **AdBudget**. Insert the table in the Word document onto slide 5. (Start Word, open the document, select the table, copy it to the clipboard, and use Paste Special to insert it on the PowerPoint slide.)

10. Using the Recolor command, change the Word table to match the table on slide 4 as much as you can.

TIP: If some of the borders for the inserted table are not showing, try activating the table in Word. Then, while in Word, drag the window's border to make it a little larger. If some of the inside borders are not showing in PowerPoint, increase the line weight on the Word table.

11. Insert a new slide after slide 5 and create a pie chart by using the numbers from the estimated budget for 2005. Use a 3-D pie chart and format it attractively to go with the rest of the presentation. Key **Estimated Budget 2005** as the title. This slide could be used in place of slide 5 to better show the distribution of the budget.

12. Go through the other slides in the presentation and add any decorative touches, changes in layout, animation scheme, etc., that you think would improve the overall look.

13. Create a handout header and footer: include the date and your name as the header, and the page number and text *[your initials]***13-27** as the footer.

14. Check spelling and grayscale settings.

15. Save the presentation as *[your initials]***13-27** in your Lesson 13 folder.

16. View the presentation as a slide show; then preview and print the presentation as handouts, two slides per page, grayscale, framed. Close the presentation.

On Your Own

In these exercises, you work on your own, as you would in a real-life work environment. Use the skills you've learned to accomplish the task—and be creative.

EXERCISE 13-28
Use a packaged food label to create a series of slides describing the food product. Create a title slide with the product's name and manufacturer, and, if possible, a picture of the product logo. Add one or two slides describing in general terms what the product is and why it is a good/bad product. Create a series of slides containing tables that present the information contained in the Nutrition Facts section. Design your own table structures to present the information in a way that you think is easy to understand. In your series of slides, be sure to include all the information contained in the Nutrition Facts section. Format your presentation attractively, picking up colors, fonts, and other style features from the label. Save your presentation as *[your initials]***13-28**. Preview and then print the presentation as handouts.

EXERCISE 13-29
Find a schedule of events from your local newspaper or other source, for example, a movie schedule, TV listing, or a schedule of community or school events. Create a presentation containing a table that lists those events in a way you think is easy to understand. Create a second table listing the three events you think are the most interesting in one column and a description of those events in a second column. The presentation should include a title slide, two table slides, and any other slides you think will enhance your presentation. Use your creativity to make the tables interesting and fun to view. Save the presentation as *[your initials]***13-29**. Preview and then print the presentation as handouts.

EXERCISE 13-30

Create a single-slide presentation with a personal "To Do" list in table format. (If you have a long list, use two or more slides.) Include the following columns: **Priority**, **Task**, **Description**, and **Time Needed**. In the "Priority" column, rate the tasks as **High**, **Medium**, or **Low**. In the "Task" column, use no more than four words, for example, "Walk the dog." In the "Description" column, describe the task by using approximately 15 words or less. In the "Time Needed" column, enter the time in hours. For example, "1/2 hour," "55 hours." Format your table attractively and in keeping with your own personality (making sure it is easy to read). Save the presentation as *[your initials]*13-30. Preview and then print the presentation as a full-size slide(s).

Creating Diagrams for Processes and Relationships

MICROSOFT OFFICE
SPECIALIST
ACTIVITIES
In this lesson:
   PP03S-1-3
   PP03S-1-4
   PP03S-2-2

See Appendix.

OBJECTIVES

After completing this lesson, you will be able to:

1. Create flowchart diagrams.
2. Create an organization chart.
3. Add and rearrange organization chart boxes.
4. Format organization charts.
5. Create other diagrams.

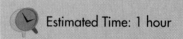 Estimated Time: 1 hour

A *flowchart* is a diagram that is used to show a sequence of events. Flowcharts are usually associated with computer programs, but they can have many other uses.

An *organization chart*—or "org" chart, for short—is a diagram that is typically used by businesses or work groups to show who reports to whom, and who is responsible for what function or task. Org charts can also be useful for describing other types of relationships, such as a family tree.

When neither a flowchart nor an organization chart is right for the information you want to convey, PowerPoint offers a variety of other diagram layouts to help you illustrate a variety of relationships in pictorial format.

Creating Flowchart Diagrams

PowerPoint provides special AutoShapes designed for traditional flowcharts, but you can use any PowerPoint object, including clip art and text placeholders. The shapes are joined to one another with special connector lines.

A *connector line* is a straight, curved, or angled line with special endpoints that can lock onto an object's *connection sites*—blue handles on an object indicating where connector lines can be attached. When you rearrange objects joined with connector lines, the lines stay attached and adjust to the new position of the shapes they connect.

EXERCISE **14-1** **Draw Flowchart AutoShapes**

Along with the Basic Shapes, Block Arrows, and other categories, the AutoShapes menu has a special category containing traditional Flowchart shapes.

1. Open the file **Organize**. Insert a Title Only slide after slide 2 and key the title **New Purchasing Procedure**

2. Choose Flowchart from the AutoShapes menu on the Drawing toolbar. (You might need to expand the menu to see Flowchart.) Float the Flowchart submenu.

3. Choose the second shape in the first row (Flowchart: Alternate Process). In the upper-left corner of the slide, draw a rectangle approximately 1 inch high by 2.5 inches wide.

4. Key **Get purchase pre-approval** in the rectangle.

5. Using the Text Box tab in the Format AutoShape dialog box, turn on the Word wrap text in AutoShape option. (The Resize AutoShape to fit text option should be turned off.) Change the Text anchor point to Middle Centered and change the internal margins to 0.05" all around.

6. Duplicate the AutoShape five times (six boxes total) and arrange the shapes in two columns, approximately as shown in Figure 14-1. Change the text in each AutoShape to match the text in the figure.

 NOTE: Duplicating or copying existing shapes is the fastest way to achieve balance and symmetry in flowcharts.

FIGURE 14-1
Flowchart
AutoShapes
on a slide

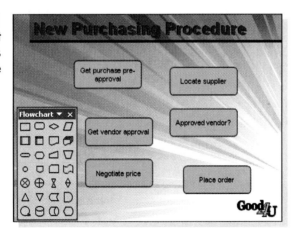

EXERCISE **14-2** Draw Connector Lines

Connector lines come in many shapes, including straight arrow, elbow, and curved. They can be formatted in the same way as ordinary lines; for example, they can be wide dashed lines or thin solid lines.

Connector lines have endpoints that automatically attach to a shape's connection sites. Connector lines have either unlocked connectors or locked connectors. An *unlocked connector* has a green endpoint, indicating that it is not attached to a shape. A *locked connector* has a red endpoint, indicating that it is attached.

1. Choose Connectors from the AutoShapes menu and float the Connectors submenu.

2. Click the Straight Arrow Connector button 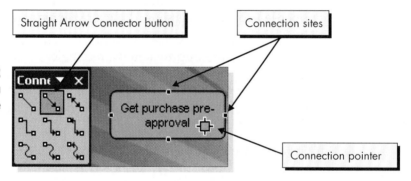 on the floating toolbar and move the pointer over one of the AutoShapes. Notice the blue connection sites that appear. The pointer changes from a cross pointer ⊞ to a connection pointer ⊕.

FIGURE 14-2
Drawing a
connector line

Straight Arrow Connector button

Connection sites

Get purchase pre-approval

Connection pointer

3. Click the connection pointer ⊕ on the connection site that is on the right side of the first AutoShape ("Get purchase pre-approval") and move the pointer to the right. Notice the dashed line that appears.

4. Move the pointer to the second box ("Locate supplier") and click its left connection site to connect the two boxes. Notice that the endpoints of the selected connector are red.

5. Select the first box and change its position slightly. Notice that the two boxes stay connected when you move one.

6. Double-click the Straight Arrow Connector on the floating toolbar. Now you can draw several connector lines without the need to click the button each time.

7. Draw four more connectors, as shown in Figure 14-3 (on the next page). Make sure your arrows are headed in the same direction as shown in the figure.

8. Click the Straight Arrow Connector on the floating toolbar again to deactivate it.

FIGURE 14-3
Connected
flowchart shapes

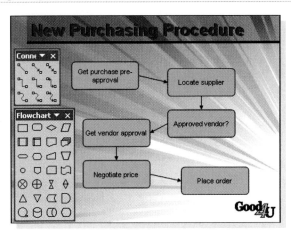

EXERCISE 14-3 Change Flowchart AutoShapes

You can change Flowchart AutoShapes just as you change other AutoShapes. In flowcharts, the diamond shape is traditionally used to signify a decision-making point, where a "Yes" takes one path and a "No" takes another path.

1. Select the "Approved vendor?" box. From the D̲raw menu on the Drawing toolbar, choose C̲hange AutoShape, and then choose F̲lowchart from the submenu. Choose the diamond shape in the first row with the ScreenTip Change Shape to Flowchart: Decision.

2. Drag one of the diamond's side sizing handles to make it slightly wider. Notice that the connection lines adjust and stay connected.

3. Change the last shape in the right column ("Place order") to the first shape in the third row of Flowchart shapes (Terminator). Reduce the height of this AutoShape to approximately 0.75 inches.

4. Below the diamond shape, create a small text box with the text **Yes**. Format it with no border and no fill. Make the text 16-point Arial, center-aligned, and black. Change all its internal margins to 0.00 inches.

 5. Click the Straight Connector button on the floating toolbar to draw a line from the diamond to the top of the "Yes" box.

 6. Click the Elbow Arrow Connector button on the floating toolbar to draw a connector from the bottom of the "Yes" box to the top of the "Negotiate price" box. Notice that the connector automatically bends to make a neat path between the two shapes.

EXERCISE 14-4 Edit Connector Lines

Connector lines are easy to disconnect if you need to make a change. To disconnect a line, select it and drag one of its red endpoints.

1. Move the "Get vendor approval" box to the left, so there is at least 1.5 inches between it and the "Approved vendor?" diamond. Don't be concerned about the overall arrangement of the boxes. You'll fix that later.

2. Copy the "Yes" text box and paste it above the connector that is between "Get vendor approval" and "Approved vendor." Select the word "Yes" and change it to **No**.

3. Select the connector between "Get vendor approval" and "Approved vendor." Drag its right endpoint away from the diamond shape and reconnect it to the left side of the "No" box.

4. Draw a straight connector (without an arrowhead) from the "Approved vendor?" diamond to the right side of the "No" box.

EXERCISE 14-5 Align Flowchart Elements and Apply Finishing Touches

Sometimes it's preferable to have the flowchart connectors point at odd angles but, other times, you'll want them aligned horizontally or vertically.

1. Float the Align or Distribute toolbar (from the Draw menu).
2. Select the three shapes in the right column and the "Yes" box. Using the Align or Distribute toolbar, align their centers relative to one another.
3. Select the three shapes in the left column and align their centers relative to one another. Now all the vertical connectors are straight.
4. Select the two shapes at the top of the slide and align their middles relative to each other. Align the middles of the bottom two shapes.
5. Select the "No" box along with the two middle shapes and align their centers. Now all the connectors are straight and neat.
6. If necessary, select the bottom two shapes and move them down to create more room within the flowchart. You may need to separate the columns of shapes a little more, too, if you don't have enough space.
7. Select the first box ("Get purchase pre-approval") and change it to the Right Arrow on the Block Arrows AutoShape menu. Use the arrow's adjustment and sizing handles to make it large enough to fit the text. Change the arrow fill color to gold (accent and hyperlink scheme color) and its text color to white.

8. Change the fill color of the diamond to red (accent scheme color) and its text color to white. Change the bottom-right shape ("Place order") to green and its text color to white.

9. Apply the Shadow Style 6 object shadow to all the flowchart shapes (but not the connectors or the "Yes" or "No" boxes). Make the shadow color semitransparent black, and nudge it down and to the right to make it more dramatic.

10. Close all the floating toolbars. Select all the shapes of the flowchart and group them. Resize the grouped object to make a pleasing layout.

11. Center the flowchart horizontally, relative to the slide, and adjust its vertical position as needed. Close all the floating toolbars.

12. Adjust the flowchart's grayscale settings.

13. Create a slide footer for this slide only that includes the date and the text *[Your Name], [your initials]*14-5.

FIGURE 14-4
Completed
flowchart

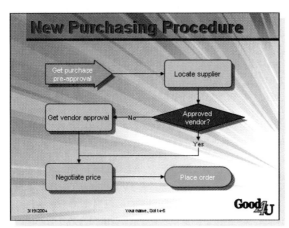

14. Create a folder for Lesson 14. Save the presentation as *[your initials]*14-5 in this new folder.

15. Print the flowchart slide in full size. Leave the presentation open for the next exercise.

Creating an Organization Chart

Organization charts are composed of the same AutoShapes and connector lines that you use in flowcharts. You use the Organization Chart toolbar to insert shapes and modify the layout. You use the Drawing toolbar and the Formatting toolbar to control the colors, fonts, and other style features of the org chart's shapes.

As with tables and Microsoft Graph charts, there are several ways to start an org chart. You can:

- Create a new slide that uses one of the Content layouts; then click the Insert Diagram or Organization Chart button ⟳ in the content placeholder.
- Click the Insert Diagram or Organization Chart button ⟳ on the Drawing toolbar.
- Display the Insert menu and choose Diagram.

Each of these actions opens the Diagram Gallery dialog box, where you can choose Organization Chart or one of the other five diagram types.

EXERCISE 14-6 Start an Org Chart

When you start a new org chart, you begin with a default arrangement of four boxes. Each box is positioned on a *level* in the chart, which indicates its position in the hierarchy of the organization. Level 1 is used for the head of the organization and is usually at the top of an org chart.

Whenever an org chart is active, the Organization Chart toolbar is displayed. It contains commands for inserting additional shapes and for controlling the layout of the org chart, selection commands, and an AutoFormat button.

1. Insert a new slide between slides 2 and 3 that uses the Title and Content layout. Key the title **New Management Structure**

FIGURE 14-5
Selecting a diagram type

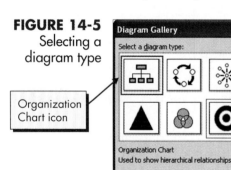

2. Click the Insert Diagram or Organization Chart button ⟳ in the content placeholder. The Diagram Gallery dialog box appears.

3. Select the Organization Chart icon in the upper-left corner and click OK. A "starter" org chart appears within a drawing space. The drawing space is surrounded by black sizing handles and a nonprinting border made up of small diagonal lines.

EXERCISE 14-7 Navigate in an Org Chart and Key Text

Keyboard navigation methods are a convenient way to move from one box to the next in an org chart, especially if you have a large number of boxes to fill. Keying text in an org chart box is just like keying text in a text box.

1. Move your pointer over the top box in the chart. When you see the I-beam, click. The blinking insertion point and the diagonal border tell you the box is activated, so you can enter and edit text.

2. Key **Julie Wolfe &** press (Enter) **Gus Irvinelli** to position the names on two lines. You will later format this text to fit on one line.

3. Press (Enter) to start a new line and key **Co-owners**

4. Press (Esc) to deactivate the box. It has a solid border and gray selection handles, indicating that it is selected but not activated. You can format the border and fill color for the box when you see the gray handles.

 5. Use the Fill Color button 🎨 on the Drawing toolbar to change the box color to gold (accent and hyperlink scheme color). Change the text color to white.

TABLE 14-1   Using the Keyboard to Navigate in an Org Chart

KEY	RESULT
(F2)	Toggles the current box between being selected and activated.
(Esc)	Selects (deactivates) the current box.
(Enter)	Selected box: Selects all the text in the box and activates it. Activated box: Inserts a new line.
(←) or (→)	Selected box: Moves left or right one box on the current level and in the current coworker group. Activated box: Moves one character to the left or right.
(↑) or (↓)	Selected box: Moves up or down one level. Activated box: Moves up or down one line in the box.
(Tab)	Selected box: Moves to the next object on the slide, which might or might not be an org chart box. Activated box: Inserts a tab character at the insertion point.
(Shift)+(Tab)	Selected box: Moves to the previous box or other object on the slide. Activated box: Inserts a tab character at the insertion point.

6. Press (↓) to move to the next-lower level. Press (→) twice, and then press (←). The arrow keys enable you to move to other boxes in the org chart.

7. Press (Shift)+(Tab) to move to the first box in the second level.

NOTE: You can, of course, also move from box to box by clicking, but when you have a large number of boxes to fill, the keyboard navigation tools are more convenient.

8. Press (Enter) to activate the current box; then key the following three lines:
   Administration
   Michael Peters
   Administration Mgr

9. Press (F2) (another way to deactivate a box). All the boxes on the second level become larger to accommodate the text.

10. Press (Tab) to move to the next box, and then press (F2) to activate it. Key the following:
    Sales & Marketing
    Roy Olafsen
    Marketing Mgr

11. Move to the third box and key:
    Operations
    Michele Jenkins
    Head Chef

12. Use (Shift)+click to select all three boxes on the second level. Change their fill color to dark blue (accent and followed hyperlink scheme color) and their text to white.

13. Select the organization chart placeholder and resize it from the bottom to reduce the size of the boxes vertically to make them fit the text with no extra space.

FIGURE 14-6
Org chart with
text and fill colors

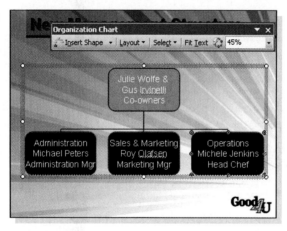

14. Click outside the drawing space to deactivate the org chart.

15. Save the presentation as *[your initials]*14-7 in your Lesson 14 folder. Leave the presentation open for the next exercise.

Adding and Rearranging Organization Chart Boxes

The organization of many companies changes frequently. You might need to promote, demote, or move org chart boxes as the reporting structure changes or becomes more complex.

To expand your org chart, you can insert additional boxes of the following types:

- *Subordinate boxes*—boxes that are connected to a *superior box* (a box on a higher level).
- *Coworker boxes*—boxes that are connected to the same superior box as another box.
- *Assistant boxes*—boxes that are usually placed below a superior box and above subordinate boxes. They have no subordinates.

FIGURE 14-7
Structure of
an org chart

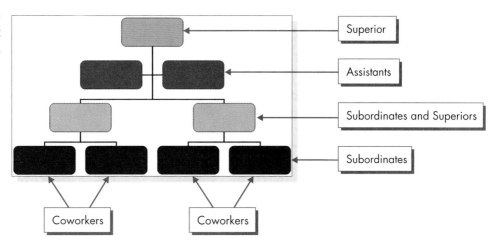

EXERCISE   **14-8**   **Insert Subordinate Boxes**

To add subordinate boxes, first select the box that will be their superior; then click Insert Shape on the Organization Chart toolbar. To insert other types of boxes, click the list box arrow for Insert Shape. For added convenience, you can float the Insert Shape toolbar.

1. If the task pane is displayed, close it to give yourself more room to work. Close the Outline and Slides pane also.

2. Select the first box on the second level, with the name "Michael Peters."

3. Click Insert Shape on the Organization Chart toolbar. A box appears below the selected box.

4. Select the third box in the second level containing the name "Michele Jenkins."

5. Click Insert Shape twice. Two boxes appear under "Michele Jenkins." All the boxes automatically become smaller, so the chart will fit on the slide.

6. Select the box containing the name "Roy Olafsen," and then click Insert Shape three times. Three boxes appear under the selected box. Once again the boxes are resized to fit, and the text is now too small to read. This will be corrected later.

FIGURE 14-8
Org chart
with subordinate
boxes added

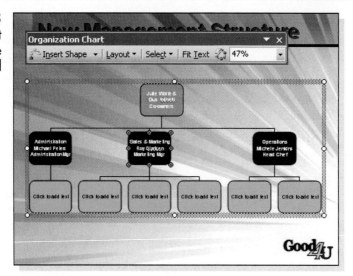

EXERCISE 14-9 Add Assistant and Coworker Boxes

Assistant boxes are used for positions that provide administrative assistance or other support. They are inserted below a selected box, but above the next-lower level.

Coworker boxes are inserted at the same level as the selected box and report to the same superior as the selected box.

1. Select the gold level 1 box.
2. Click the list box arrow for Insert Shape on the Organization Chart toolbar. Choose Assistant from the submenu. A new box is inserted below the gold box, between level 1 and level 2.
3. Reopen the Insert Shape list box on the Organization Chart toolbar and float its submenu. The Insert Shape toolbar makes it easy to insert multiple coworker boxes at one time.
4. Select the first level 3 box, on the far left.
5. Click Coworker on the Insert Shape toolbar three times. There are now nine boxes on the lowest level.

EXERCISE 14-10 Select Boxes and Navigate in a Complex Org Chart

A traditional org chart is a tree structure, branching out to multiple divisions in each lower level. Its structure is similar to the arrangement of folders on a computer storage disk or the diagram of a family tree.

When you use the keyboard to navigate in an org chart, you follow a branch with your arrow keys. In a particular level, you can move left or right within a coworker group, but you cannot jump to a different group. Instead, you must use ⬆️ to go up one or more levels, and then follow another branch back down.

As with other PowerPoint objects, when you want to apply formatting to an object, you must first select it. To select boxes you can:

- Click a box when you see the four-pointed arrow ⊕.
- Use Shift+click or Ctrl+click to select multiple boxes.
- Select a box; then choose Level from the Select menu on the Organization Chart toolbar to select all the boxes on the same level.
- Select a box; then choose Branch from the Select menu on the Organization Chart toolbar to select all the boxes on the same branch below the selected box.
- Draw a selection box around the boxes you want to select.

1. Point to the border of the third box from the left on the lowest level.

2. When you see the four-pointed arrow ⊕, click to select the box. The box should have gray selection handles surrounding it. If you see an insertion point, press Esc.

3. Press ➡️. The right-most box in this coworker group is selected.

4. Press ➡️ again. Nothing happens because the next box to the right is in a different coworker group. You cannot jump from one group to another. Instead, you must travel up one branch, and then down another.

5. Press ⬆️ once. The box's superior is selected.

6. Press ➡️, and then press ⬇️. You selected the box you couldn't jump to in step 4.

7. Press ⬆️ one time to select the dark blue level 2 box.

8. On the Organization Chart toolbar, click the list box arrow for Select and choose Branch from the submenu. Now the dark blue box and all the lower boxes on its branch are selected. Press Esc to turn off the selection.

9. Select any box on level 3. On the Organization Chart toolbar, click the list box arrow for Select and choose Level from the submenu. All the level 3 boxes are selected. Change the level 3 box fill color to green.

10. Press ⬆️ twice to select the gold level 1 box. Click the list box arrow for Select and choose Branch. Now all the boxes are selected, because they all branch from the level 1 box.

11. Use the Font Size list box on the Formatting toolbar to change the text size for all the boxes to 10 points. Some of the text spills over the edges of the boxes, but now the text is easier to read. You'll fix the box sizes later.

12. Using the Shadow Style button 🔲 on the Drawing toolbar, apply an object shadow to the boxes by choosing Shadow Style 6. Change the shadow color to semitransparent black.

13. Click a blank area within the org chart drawing space to deselect all the boxes.

EXERCISE 14-11 Key Text in a Complex Org Chart

Now that the boxes are in place, you can key text in them. Because the text is still small, use Zoom so you can see the text you are keying.

1. Select the assistant box below the level 1 gold box; then zoom to a level that enables you to comfortably see the text, probably between 100 percent and 150 percent.

2. Key **Troy Scott** in the assistant box.

3. In the first three boxes under Michael Peters, key the following employee information on two lines (leave the fourth box blank):

MIS	Billing	HR
Chuck Warden	Sarah Conners	Chris Davis

4. After keying the text in Chris Davis's box, press Esc to deactivate the text box. Press ↑ one time to move to Michael Peters's box, press → to move to Roy Olafsen's box, and press ↓ to move to the first green box under Roy Olafsen.

5. In the three boxes under Roy Olafsen, key the following employee information:

Events	Merchandise	Marketing
Ian Mahoney	Lila Nelson	Evan Johnson

6. In the remaining two boxes under Michele Jenkins, key the following:

Kitchen	Purchasing
Eric Dennis	Jessie Smith

   Notice that the org chart again adjusted the text to a smaller size.

EXERCISE 14-12 Delete Boxes

If you have more boxes than necessary, you can delete them at any time.

1. Scroll to the left, if necessary, to locate the fourth box under Michael Peters (with the text "Click to add text").

2. Select the fourth box. You should see gray selection handles surrounding it. If you see an insertion point instead, press F2 or Esc to deactivate it.

3. Press Delete. The box is removed, and the box next to it is now selected. Use Zoom so you can see the entire slide.

4. Save the presentation as *[your initials]*14-12 in your Lesson 14 folder. Leave the presentation open for the next exercise.

EXERCISE 14-13 **Promote and Demote Boxes**

You move an org chart box and all its selected subordinate boxes by dragging it on top of the box that will be its superior. To promote a box, you move it up a level. To demote a box, you move it down a level. It's similar to promoting and demoting bullets, except that in an org chart, the move is vertical and in bulleted text, the move is horizontal.

It's important to understand that if you want to move a box that has subordinates, you must select all the boxes in the branch and move them as a group. If you don't want the subordinates to move, you must first attach them to a different superior.

1. Select the dark blue box in the center of level 2; then zoom to a level that enables you to read the text and still see several boxes. Use the scroll bars to adjust the view, so that Roy Olafsen's box and his three subordinates are clearly visible.

2. Select Ian Mahoney's box on the left. With the four-pointed arrow ⊕ drag to the right, landing on top of Lila Nelson's box. You will see a dotted outline of the box as you drag.

FIGURE 14-9
Dragging to
demote a box

3. When the dotted line is superimposed on top of Lila Nelson's box, release your mouse button. Now Ian Mahoney reports to Lila Nelson.

4. Edit Lila Nelson's box, changing the first line to **Sales**

5. Edit Ian Mahoney's box, deleting the line containing "Events" and leaving just one line with Ian Mahoney's name.

6. Select Chuck Warden's box (the left-most green box on level 3).

7. Drag Chuck Warden's box on top of the level 1 box. Chuck Warden has now been promoted to level 2.

8. Use the Format Painter button ☑ on the Standard toolbar to make Chuck Warden's box match the other level 2 boxes.

9. Add a third line to Chuck Warden's box with the text **MIS Mgr**

10. Select the center box on level 2—the Roy Olafsen box—and then use the Select menu on the Organization Chart toolbar to select the branch associated with his box.

11. Drag the Roy Olafsen box (and its subordinates) on top of the Michele Jenkins box. Now Roy Olafsen and his subordinates have all been demoted.

12. Drag the Roy Olafsen branch on top of the gold level 1 box. Now the box is restored to level 2, but in a different position—on the right side.

13. Move Jessie Smith's box, so he reports to Michael Peters instead of to Michele Jenkins.

EXERCISE 14-14 Change the Layout of a Branch

Depending on the size of your org chart, you might find it useful to rearrange a group of boxes under a manager. For example, you can arrange the boxes vertically instead of horizontally.

When you want to rearrange coworker boxes, select the superior box (not the branch), click Layout on the Organization Chart toolbar, and choose the layout you want.

1. Add another subordinate box under Michael Peters.

2. Use the Format Painter button 🖌 to apply the formatting of other level 3 boxes to the new box.

3. In the new box, key the following:

   Payroll
   John Larson

4. Select the Michael Peters box, which now has four subordinates (don't select the branch).

5. On the Organization Chart toolbar, click Layout, and then choose Both Hanging. The subordinate boxes are now arranged in two columns below their superior.

FIGURE 14-10
Choosing
a layout for
subordinate boxes

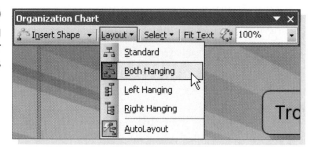

6. With the Michael Peters box still selected, click Layout again and choose Right Hanging. Now the subordinate boxes are arranged in one vertical column, a good arrangement when a large number of boxes are on one level.

7. Select the Roy Olafsen box. Open the Layout menu and choose Left Hanging. Now that the structure of the organization chart is prepared, you will improve its appearance in the next exercises with boxes and text appropriately sized.

8. Change the zoom to Fit; then save the presentation as *[your initials]*14-14 in your Lesson 14 folder. Leave the presentation open for the next exercise.

FIGURE 14-11
New layout
for org chart

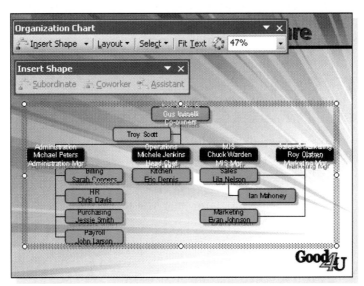

Formatting Organization Charts

You've seen that formatting org chart boxes is similar to formatting other PowerPoint objects. This is also true for formatting the connector lines, which can be any color, width, and line style.

In addition, you can change AutoShapes, change the overall size of an org chart, and move and resize groups of boxes or individual boxes.

EXERCISE 14-15 **Format Org Chart Boxes**

Changing AutoShapes for some boxes can distinguish them from other functions. Usually, you will want to be consistent in how you format certain types of boxes. For example, format all assistant boxes in the same way.

1. Zoom to a setting that enables you to easily read the text; then select the Troy Scott assistant box and use Shift +click to add Ian Mahoney's box (below Lila Nelson) to the selection.

2. From the Draw menu, choose Change AutoShape; then from the Basic Shapes menu, choose Change Shape to Oval.

3. Use the Format Painter button 🖋 to change Ian Mahoney's box to match Troy Scott's box.

4. Select Lila Nelson's box under Roy Olafsen (make sure the gray selection handles are displayed); then right-click the border of the box and choose Select from the shortcut menu and Level from the submenu to select all level 3 boxes.

5. Change the fill color of the level 3 boxes to white.

EXERCISE **14-16** **Format Connecting Lines**

You can select connecting lines by clicking one line at a time, by [Shift]+clicking to select more than one line, or by drawing a selection box around a group of boxes and their lines. You can also choose All Connecting Lines from the Select menu.

1. From the Select menu on the Organization Chart toolbar, choose All Connecting Lines.

2. Using buttons on the Drawing toolbar, change the line color to deep gray (a custom color), and the line style to a solid 3-point line.

3. Zoom to Fit; then save the presentation as *[your initials]***14-16** in your Lesson 14 folder. Leave the presentation open for the next exercise.

EXERCISE **14-17** **Adjust the Overall Size of an Org Chart**

At this point, the org chart is not using the available space on the slide. Once it is made larger, the boxes and text can be scaled to fit the space.

1. In the level 1 box, delete the [Enter] so Gus Irvinelli's name follows Julie Wolfe's name on the same line, even though this adjustment causes the text to extend beyond the box.

2. Drag the top-center sizing handle up, until the level 1 box is positioned just below the slide's title.

3. Drag the bottom-center sizing handle down, until it reaches almost to the bottom of the slide.

4. Hold down [Ctrl] and drag the right-center sizing handle out, until the chart is almost as wide as the slide. Release your mouse button, and then release [Ctrl]. Now the boxes are larger and can accommodate a larger text size.

5. Select all the org chart boxes; then change the text size to 14 points. The level 2 boxes are still not tall enough to accommodate the text. Click a blank area of the chart to deselect the boxes.

6. With the org chart selected, click the Fit Text button on the Organization Chart toolbar. The text adjusts to fit the size of the chart.

EXERCISE 14-18 **Turn Off Automatic Layout to Fine-Tune the Org Chart**

When you first create an org chart, the AutoLayout feature is automatically turned on. This means that as you add boxes and text, PowerPoint automatically inserts those boxes in predetermined positions on the chart, and automatically resizes the text and the overall chart dimensions to fit the slide.

After you have a general org chart structure in place, you can turn off AutoLayout to customize your chart. With AutoLayout turned off, the connectors and shapes that make up an org chart behave exactly like the connector lines and AutoShapes you use to create flowcharts. You can freely insert, reposition, and resize individual boxes anywhere on the chart.

1. From the Layout menu on the Organization Chart toolbar, click AutoLayout at the bottom of the list to turn it off. AutoLayout is a toggle command—it is on by default, so one click turns it off; click it again to turn it on.

2. Select the gold level 1 box. The gray selection handles are now replaced with white sizing handles—the same sizing handles that you see in standard AutoShapes.

3. Change the text size in the level 1 box to 18 points, and adjust the width and height of the box as needed.

4. Select the Troy Scott box; then press ⬆ several times to move this box closer to the level 1 box. Notice that its connector line moves as well.

5. Using any method, select all the dark blue level 2 boxes; then use ⬆ several times to move them closer to the Troy Scott box.

6. Drag down the bottom-center sizing handle on one of the dark blue level 2 boxes (they should all be selected) to increase the height of the boxes. Adjust the height, so that the text fits nicely inside the boxes.

7. Right-click one of the dark blue boxes (they should still all be selected); then choose Format AutoShape from the shortcut menu.

8. In the Format AutoShape dialog box, click the Size tab. Under Scale, change the Width from 100% to 110%, to make each box a little wider. Click OK.

9. Deselect the dark blue boxes; then select just the Chuck Warden box. Use ➡ to adjust its position.

10. Move up slightly the Ian Mahoney oval. Raise up the white rectangles for HR, Purchasing, and Payroll to make that group closer together. Be sure they are evenly spaced.

11. Create a slide footer for this slide only that includes the date and the text *[Your Name], [your initials]*14-18. If necessary, adjust the overall size of the org chart, so that it does not conflict with the footer.

12. Save the presentation as *[your initials]***14-18** in your Lesson 14 folder.

FIGURE 14-12
Completed
org chart slide

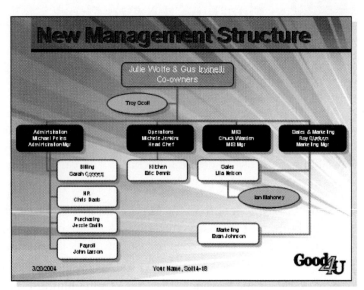

13. Print the org chart slide in full size. Leave the presentation open for the next exercise.

Creating Other Diagrams

Along with flowcharts and org charts, PowerPoint offers five additional types of diagrams to illustrate your thoughts and ideas in a pictorial format.

TABLE 14-2   Additional Diagram Types

DIAGRAM	PURPOSE
Cycle	Illustrates a process that has a continuous cycle
Radial	Illustrates relationships focused on a central element
Pyramid	Illustrates relationships built on a solid foundation
Venn	Illustrates overlapping responsibilities or relationships
Target	Illustrates a process working toward a goal

You start a diagram the same way that you start an org chart: by creating a new slide with a content placeholder, by clicking the Insert Diagram and Organization Chart button 🔄 on the Drawing toolbar, or by displaying the Insert menu and choosing Diagram.

EXERCISE 14-19 Insert a Radial Diagram

A *radial diagram* starts with three circles connected to and surrounding a fourth circle in the center. You can insert as many additional circles as you need to illustrate your message.

1. Insert a new slide after slide 4 that uses the Title and Content layout. Key the title **New Customer Philosophy**

2. Click the Insert Diagram and Organization Chart button 🔄 in the content placeholder and click the Radial icon ❋. Click OK. A "starter" radial diagram and the Diagram toolbar appear with the center circle selected. Notice the drawing space surrounding the diagram. The drawing space works the same way as with an org chart.

3. On the Diagram toolbar, click Insert Shape. A new circle is added to the diagram. It becomes the selected circle.

4. Press ⬅. One of the other outer circles is selected. The outer circles radiate from the center circle, as do the numbers on the face of a clock.

5. Press ⬅ and/or ➡ a few times to select the other outer circles, one at a time.

6. Press ⬆ to select the center circle.

7. With the center circle selected, key **Customer**, and then press Esc or F2 to deactivate the circle.

8. Click the top outer circle (12 o'clock position) and key the information shown under "12 o'clock" in Figure 14-13. Press Enter after the first two words, so the information appears on three lines.

9. Press Esc, and then press ➡ to move to the circle at 3 o'clock.

10. Working in a clockwise direction, key the remaining text shown in Figure 14-13 in the three remaining outer circles.

FIGURE 14-13

12 o'clock	3 o'clock	6 o'clock	9 o'clock
Satisfy	Provide	Provide	Resolve
customer	courteous	excellent	problems
needs	service	quality	promptly

NOTE: If PowerPoint automatically capitalizes the second and third word in each circle, change the letters to lowercase. Automatic capitalization is caused by the way an option is set in the AutoCorrect feature.

EXERCISE 14-20 Format a Diagram

Applying fill effects, line styles, and font attributes to a diagram is similar to formatting an org chart. You select the parts you want to change and use the Formatting toolbar, the Drawing toolbar, and/or the Format AutoShape dialog box to apply the look you want.

As with org charts, commands on the Layout menu of the Diagram toolbar are used to fit the diagram's drawing space to its contents, scale the diagram, and turn on or off the AutoLayout feature.

1. Select the diagram and change the font size to 18 points.

2. From the Layout menu on the Diagram toolbar, choose Fit Diagram to Contents. The drawing space is resized to fit the diagram.

3. Open the Layout menu again and choose Resize Diagram. Black cropping handles appear on the drawing space border.

4. Using Ctrl to resize the diagram from the center, drag sizing handles to make the diagram wider and higher, so the text fits inside the circles without crowding.

5. Apply a different fill color to each outside circle, choosing the gold, green, dark blue, and red scheme colors.

6. Using Shift+click, select the four outer circles. Change the font color to white.

7. Select just the center circle and change its AutoShape to a 16-point star.

8. Using Shift+click, select the four lines that connect the outer circles with the star. Apply Arrow Style 6, so that arrows point to the star, and change the line width of the connecting lines to 3 points.

9. Create a slide footer for this slide only that includes the date and the text *[Your Name], [your initials]*14-20. If necessary, adjust the size of the diagram, so it does not overlap the footer text. (See Figure 14-14 on the next page.)

10. Save the presentation as *[your initials]*14-20 in your Lesson 14 folder.

11. Print the radial diagram slide in full size. Leave the presentation open for the next exercise.

FIGURE 14-14
Completed
radial diagram

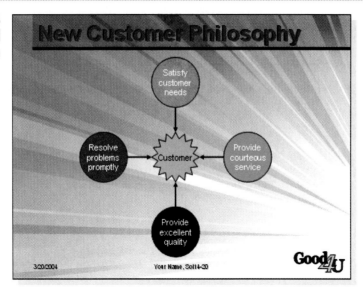

EXERCISE 14-21 Insert a Cycle Diagram

After creating one type of diagram, you will find that creating other types follows a similar process.

1. Insert a new slide after slide 5 that uses the Title and Content layout. Key the title **New Development Cycle**

2. Click the Insert Diagram and Organization Chart button ⊞ in the content placeholder and click the Cycle icon ◯. Click OK. A diagram with three curved shapes and three text placeholders appears.

3. Click Insert Shape on the Diagram toolbar. A fourth shape and a fourth text placeholder are inserted.

4. Experiment with the arrow keys to find out how to navigate from one placeholder to another.

5. Starting with the text box at 2 o'clock and working in a clockwise direction, key the text in Figure 14-15.

FIGURE 14-15

2 o'clock	4 o'clock	8 o'clock	10 o'clock
Survey	Analyze	Develop	Introduce
customer	survey	product	new
needs	results	plan	products

NOTE: If PowerPoint automatically capitalized words, undo the capitalization.

6. Change the font size for all the diagram text to 18 points.

7. Using commands from the Layout menu, make the drawing space fit the diagram. Then scale the diagram, making it proportionately larger all around.

8. Select the four text placeholders and apply red; select the four arrows and apply dark blue.

9. Create a slide footer for this slide only containing today's date and the text *[Your Name], [your initials]***14-21**. If necessary, adjust the size or position of the diagram, so it does not overlap the footer text.

FIGURE 14-16
Completed
cycle diagram

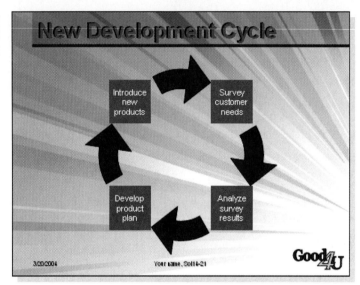

10. Create a handout header and footer: include the date and your name as the header, and the page number and text *[your initials]***14-21** as the footer.

11. Move to slide 1 and save the presentation as *[your initials]***14-21** in your Lesson 14 folder.

12. Print the cycle diagram slide in full size. Preview, and then print the entire presentation as handouts, six slides per page, grayscale, framed. Close the presentation.

USING ONLINE HELP

When you draw a complex diagram by using AutoShapes and connector lines, you might want to simplify the drawing by changing the path the connector lines make.

Use Help to learn more about moving and rerouting connector lines:

1. Click the Microsoft Office PowerPoint Help button 🔘 on the Standard toolbar to open the PowerPoint Help task pane.

2. In the Search for text box, key **connector lines** and click Start Searching arrow.

3. Select the topic Move or reroute a connector.

4. Expand and read all the topics in the help window.

FIGURE 14-17
Help on
moving or
rerouting a
connector

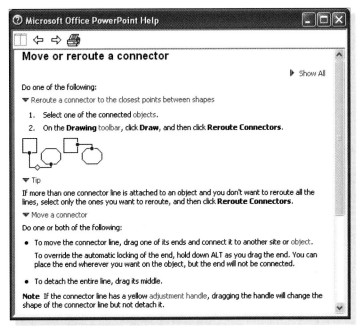

5. Select other topics that interest you.

6. Close Help when you are finished.

LESSON Summary

➤ Flowcharts, organization charts, and other types of nonnumerical diagrams are used to illustrate a variety of relationships in pictorial format.

➤ Flowcharts show a sequence of events or steps in a process. They are made up of flowchart AutoShapes and other AutoShapes that are connected to each other with connector lines.

➤ Connector lines can be straight, curved, or angled lines and can be formatted in any line style. They have special endpoints that lock onto connection sites on AutoShapes.

➤ When a connector endpoint is locked onto an AutoShape, it is red. When it is not attached, it is green. To disconnect a connector, select the connector line; then drag one of its red connectors.

➤ Use the Align and Distribute commands to arrange a flowchart in a symmetrical layout.

➤ Organization charts are used to describe a hierarchical structure, showing who reports to whom, and who is responsible for what function or task. They are made up of the same AutoShapes and connector lines as flowcharts.

➤ The Organization Chart toolbar has commands to insert shapes and modify the layout. The position of shapes is determined by a predefined layout, but you can turn off the AutoLayout feature to arrange and resize shapes to suit your needs.

➤ When AutoLayout is turned off, org chart connectors and shapes can be freely inserted, deleted, repositioned, resized, and reformatted in the same way as flowchart shapes.

➤ A traditional org chart is a tree structure, branching out to multiple divisions in each lower level. When you use the keyboard to navigate in an org chart, you follow a branch with your arrow keys.

➤ You move an org chart box and all its selected subordinate boxes by dragging it on top of the box that will be its superior. To promote a box, you move it up a level. To demote a box, you move it down a level.

➤ When a large number of org chart boxes are on a single level, you can rearrange the boxes in one of three vertical layouts.

➤ In addition to numerical charts, flowcharts, and org charts, PowerPoint offers five additional types of diagrams to illustrate your thoughts and ideas in a pictorial format.

➤ You start a diagram in the same way as you start an org chart. You insert and delete shapes, key text, apply formatting, and size it in the same way.

LESSON 14   Command Summary

FEATURE	BUTTON	MENU	KEYBOARD
Insert flowchart AutoShape		AutoShapes, Flowchart	
Insert connector line		AutoShapes, Connectors	
Insert organization chart or diagram		Insert, Diagram	

continues

LESSON 14 Command Summary *continued*

FEATURE	BUTTON	MENU	KEYBOARD
Insert subordinate box (org chart)		Insert Shape (Organization Chart toolbar)	
Insert coworker box (org chart)		Insert Shape (Organization Chart toolbar), Coworker	
Insert assistant box (org chart)		Insert Shape (Organization Chart toolbar), Assistant	
Select branch (org chart)		Select (Organization Chart toolbar), Branch	
Select level (org chart)		Select (Organization Chart toolbar), Level	
Select all connecting lines (org chart)		Select (Organization Chart toolbar), All Connecting Lines	
Select all assistants (org chart)		Select (Organization Chart toolbar), All Assistants	
Both hanging branch layout		Layout (Organization Chart toolbar), Both Hanging	
Left hanging branch layout		Layout (Organization Chart toolbar), Left Hanging	
Right hanging branch layout		Layout (Organization Chart toolbar), Right Hanging	
Adjust drawing space to fit content		Layout (Organization Chart toolbar), AutoLayout	
Scale text to fit layout		Fit text (Organization Chart toolbar)	
Adjust drawing space to fit diagram		Layout (Diagram toolbar), Fit Diagram to Contents	
Resize a diagram		Layout (Diagram toolbar), Resize Diagram	

Concepts Review

TRUE/FALSE QUESTIONS

Each of the following statements is either true or false. Indicate your choice by circling T or F.

T F **1.** You must turn on AutoLayout if you want to change the size of an individual shape in a diagram.

T F **2.** All the shapes in a diagram must be the same color.

T F **3.** You can use any shapes you want in a flowchart.

T F **4.** An organization chart is one of six types of diagrams available in the Diagram Gallery dialog box.

T F **5.** If you add too many boxes to an org chart, you can always delete the extra boxes.

T F **6.** You can change the color of the boxes in an org chart.

T F **7.** Assistant boxes are usually placed above the box to which they report.

T F **8.** Connection sites are always available for use when you point to an AutoShape.

SHORT ANSWER QUESTIONS

Write the correct answer in the space provided.

1. Under what conditions are connection sites visible on an AutoShape?

_____

2. How do you add more shapes to a diagram?

_____

3. Which shape is often used in a flowchart to show a decision point?

_____

4. How do you access the Connectors submenu?

_____

5. If a selected box in an org chart or diagram has gray selection handles, what command must you use to change the selection handles to white sizing handles?

_____

6. If you have six subordinates reporting to one superior, how do you change the six boxes so they are stacked vertically in two columns?

_____

7. What command sequence can you use to select all the organization chart boxes on a single level?

_____

8. What type of diagram is used to illustrate a continuous cycle relationship?

_____

CRITICAL THINKING

Answer these questions on a separate page. There are no right or wrong answers. Support your answers with examples from your own experience, if possible.

1. Think of a task you had to explain or a job you had to describe to someone and try drawing it in a flowchart format.

2. Org charts are by nature rather detail-oriented. Based on what you learned about designing presentations, how can you ensure that an org chart follows the rule of simplicity?

Skills Review

EXERCISE 14-22

Create and format a flowchart.

1. Open the file **EmpProc1**. Insert a new slide after slide 3 that uses the Title Only layout. Key the title **Procedures**

2. Draw flowchart AutoShapes by following these steps:
   a. Click AutoShapes on the Drawing toolbar, choose Flowchart, and float the submenu.
   b. Choose Flowchart: Process (the rectangle) and draw the shape near the left edge of the slide.

c. Key **Listen to grievance** in the AutoShape. Format the text as 18-point Arial, bold, with a text shadow, and left-aligned.

d. Set the following properties for the AutoShape:

- Turn on word wrapping.
- Set all internal margins to 0.00".
- Set the anchor point to Middle Centered.
- Change the fill color to dark pink.
- Remove the border.
- Apply Shadow Style 6 and make it black (remove semitransparent shadow setting).

3. Draw a Flowchart: Decision shape (the diamond) to the right of the first shape. Key **Employee talked to manager?** Use the Format Painter tool to apply the same text box and object formatting as the first box. Then change the fill color to bright green, the text color to black, and remove the text shadow. Adjust the diamond's size to fit the text.

4. Change the shape of the pink rectangle to a right block arrow and adjust its size and shape to fit the text.

5. Draw a connector line between the two shapes by following these steps:

a. From the AutoShapes menu, choose Connectors and float the Connectors submenu.

b. Click the Straight Arrow Connector and move the pointer on top of the pink AutoShape to display the blue connector sites.

c. Click the connector site at the tip of the arrow.

d. Move the pointer to the green diamond and click the connector site on the left side of the diamond.

e. To change the connector color, select the connector, click the list box arrow for the Line Color button [icon], and choose gray (background scheme color). Increase the line thickness of the connector to 4½ points.

6. Add the remaining three AutoShapes shown in Figure 14-18 (on the next page), coloring and formatting them as shown. Key the text shown inside each AutoShape. Don't worry about aligning the shapes yet.

7. Insert connectors between the shapes as shown in the figure.

 TIP: Use Format Painter to format the connector lines.

8. Insert a text box between the diamond and square with the text **Yes**. Format the text as 16-point Arial, bold, white. Make sure the text box has no fill and no border. Adjust the text box, so it sits just above the connector.

9. Create a similar text box with the text **No**. Position it beside the arrow as shown in the figure.

10. Adjust the grayscale settings for the individual flowchart objects, as needed.

FIGURE 14-18
Completed
flowchart

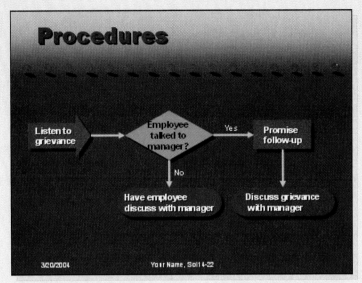

11. Align flowchart AutoShapes by following these steps:
    a. Select the arrow, diamond, "Yes" box, and square in the first row of shapes.
    b. Using the Align and Distribute commands, align their middles relative to one another (not to the slide).
    c. Align the middles of the two purple shapes on the second row.
    d. Select the green diamond, the "No" text box, and the purple shape below it. Align their centers relative to one another, and then group them.
    e. Align the centers of the pink rectangle and the purple shape below it, and group them.
    f. Select the arrow, the diamond group, and the rectangle group. Distribute them horizontally, relative to one another.
    g. Adjust the position of the "Yes" and "No" boxes as needed.

12. Group all the shapes and text boxes in the flowchart, and then center the group horizontally, relative to the slide. Adjust the vertical position of the group, if necessary.

13. Create a slide footer for slide 4 containing today's date and the text *[Your Name], [your initials]***14-22**.

14. Create a handout header and footer: include the date and your name as the header, and the page number and text *[your initials]***14-22** as the footer.

15. Move to slide 1 and save the presentation as *[your initials]***14-22** in your Lesson 14 folder.

16. Print the flowchart slide in full size. Preview, and then print the entire presentation as handouts, four slides per page, landscape, grayscale, framed. Close the presentation.

EXERCISE 14-23

Create a simple org chart, delete boxes, and format boxes.

1. Open the file **Kitchen1**. Insert a new slide after slide 3 that uses the Title and Content layout. Key the title **Operations**

2. Start an organization chart by following these steps:

   a. Click the Insert Diagram or Organization Chart button in the content placeholder.

   b. In the Diagram Gallery dialog box, click the Organization Chart icon. Click OK.

   c. Make sure the top box on the chart that appears is surrounded by gray sizing handles (if not, click the top box), and then key:
      Michele Jenkins
      Head Chef & Operations Mgr

   d. Press (Esc) to deactivate the box; then press (↓) to move to the first box on the second level.

   e. In the first box on the second level, key:
      Eric Dennis
      Asst Chef & Kitchen Mgr

   f. Press (Esc), press (→) to move to the next box, and then key:
      Claudia Pell
      Maitre d' & Service Mgr

3. Delete a box by following these steps:

   a. Press (Esc) to deactivate the second box on the second level.

   b. Press (→) to select the third box on the second level (or click it). Make sure you see the gray selection handles.

   c. Press (Delete).

4. Insert subordinate boxes by following these steps:

   a. Select Eric Dennis's box.

   b. On the Organization Chart toolbar, click Insert Shape twice.

   c. Key the following information in the two boxes:

First box	Second box
G. Robinson	S. Stefano
Sr. Cook	Sr. Cook, Weekends

   d. Using the previous steps a, b, and c, insert two boxes below Claudia Pell and key the following information:

First box	Second box
T. Domina	T. Conway
Banquets	Facilities & Maint

5. Change the formatting of an org chart box by following these steps:

   a. Select the top box.

b. Using the Fill Color button on the Drawing toolbar, choose dark beige (accent scheme color).

    c. Within the box, select just the text "Michele Jenkins," increase its size by two increments, and make it bold.

6. Change the formatting of all the boxes on one level by following these steps:

    a. Click the box for G. Robinson, the first box on the lowest level.

    b. On the Organization Chart toolbar, click Sele<u>c</u>t and choose <u>L</u>evel.

    c. With all the lowest-level boxes selected, change the fill color to light beige (background scheme color).

    d. On the lowest level, make the employee names (but not their titles) bold.

7. For the two second-level boxes (Eric Dennis and Claudia Pell), change the fill color to medium beige (shadows scheme color). Increase the font size for just the employee names on this level by one increment and make them bold.

8. Apply formatting to the entire org chart by following these steps:

    a. Select the top box (Michele Jenkins).

    b. From the Organization Chart toolbar, click Sele<u>c</u>t and choose <u>B</u>ranch to select all the org chart boxes.

    c. Using the Shadow Style button on the Drawing toolbar, apply Shadow Style 1.

9. Turn off AutoFormat, and then adjust the width of the level 1 and level 2 boxes to make them large enough to contain the text.

10. Adjust the grayscale settings for the org chart as needed.

11. Create a slide footer for this slide only containing today's date and the text *[Your Name], [your initials]***14-23**.

12. Create a handout header and footer: include the date and your name as the header, and the page number and text *[your initials]***14-23** as the footer.

13. Move to slide 1 and save the presentation as *[your initials]***14-23** in your Lesson 14 folder.

14. Print the org chart slide in full size. Preview, and then print the entire presentation as handouts, four slides per page, landscape, grayscale, framed. Close the presentation.

EXERCISE 14-24

Add, promote, demote, and rearrange boxes in an existing org chart. Work with the AutoLayout feature.

1. Open the file **Kitchen2**. Move to slide 3 and click the org chart to activate it.

2. Add three subordinate boxes to the G. Robinson level 2 box and key the information shown in Figure 14-19.

FIGURE 14-19

First box	Second box	Third box
Pastry	Cooks	Banquets
G. Gordon	L. Tilson	T. Domina
J. Lemmer	S. Mason	
	J. Fulman	

3. Promote the level 3 Banquets box to level 2 by following these steps:

   a. Select the Banquets box.
   b. Drag the Banquets box up to the top-most box for Eric Dennis.
   c. When you see a dotted box on top of the Eric Dennis box, release the mouse button.

4. Change the organizational style of the boxes under G. Robinson by following these steps:

   a. Select the box for G. Robinson.
   b. On the Organization Chart toolbar, click Layout and choose Right Hanging.
   c. Apply the Left Hanging style to the two boxes under T. Conway.

5. Scale the org chart by following these steps:

   a. Using the sizing handles on the org chart border, make the chart as large as possible to fill the available space.
   b. On the Organization Chart toolbar, click Fit Text.

6. Apply the following formatting to the org chart:

   ● Increase the font size to 14 points (so you can read the text—you'll change the font size again later).

   ● Change the before-paragraph spacing to 0 lines. (From the Format menu, choose Line Spacing.)

   ● Change the fill color for all the boxes except the top box to light blue (background scheme color).

   ● Make the first line of each box bold.

7. Change the position of boxes relative to their coworkers by following these steps:

   a. Select the box for T. Conway and her subordinates (Select, Branch).
   b. Drag the T. Conway box on top of the box for Eric Dennis (at the top of the chart). The T. Conway branch is moved to the right side of level 2.
   c. Drag the G. Robinson branch to the Eric Dennis box to position it to the right of the T. Conway branch.
   d. Drag the S. Stefano box to the Eric Dennis box to position it on the far right side of level 2.

8. Change the font size for the first two levels to 18 points and the third level to 16 points.

9. Adjust the size and position of boxes by following these steps:

    a. On the Organization Chart toolbar, click Layout and choose AutoLayout (to turn it off).

    b. For those boxes that are too small, drag their bottom-center sizing handles to increase their size.

    c. For level 3 boxes, drag the bottom-center sizing handles up to make them slightly smaller.

    d. Adjust the spacing between the boxes, so they all fit together evenly.

10. Adjust the grayscale settings as needed.

11. Create a slide footer for this slide only containing today's date and the text *[Your Name], [your initials]***14-24**. Adjust the position of the slide elements if they conflict with the footer.

12. Create a handout header and footer: include the date and your name as the header, and the page number and text *[your initials]***14-24** as the footer.

13. Move to slide 1 and save the presentation as *[your initials]***14-24** in your Lesson 14 folder.

14. Print the org chart slide in full size. Preview, and then print the entire presentation as handouts, three slides per page, grayscale, framed. Close the presentation.

EXERCISE 14-25

Create and format diagrams.

1. Open the file **Health2**.

2. Insert a new slide after slide 1 that uses the Title and Content layout. Key the title **Heart Smart Living**

3. Create a cycle diagram by following these steps:

    a. Click the Insert Diagram or Organization Chart button ⟳ in the content placeholder.

    b. In the Diagram Gallery dialog box, click the Cycle Diagram icon ⟳. Click OK.

    c. On the Diagram toolbar, click Insert Shape to add a fourth shape to the diagram.

4. Insert text on the diagram by following these steps:

    a. Switch to Grayscale view and zoom to 100 percent so you can see the text boxes clearly.

    b. Press ➡ several times until the gray selection handles are surrounding the text box at 2 o'clock.

    c. Key the text **Get enough** Enter **sleep**

    d. Press Esc. Press → to move to the text box at 4 o'clock and key **Eat right when** Enter **you're out**

    e. Move to the text box at 8 o'clock and key **Eat right** Enter **at home**

    f. In the text box at 10 o'clock, key **Exercise** Enter **regularly**

    g. Close Grayscale view.

5. Format the four curved arrow shapes by following these steps:

    a. Click one of the green arrow shapes.

    b. Using the Line Color button 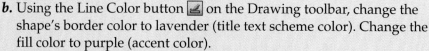 on the Drawing toolbar, change the shape's border color to lavender (title text scheme color). Change the fill color to purple (accent color).

    c. Using the Line Style button ≣, change the border's weight to 4½ pt.

    d. Use the Format Painter button 🖌 to apply the same border and fill color to the other three curved shapes.

6. Format the four text boxes by following these steps:

    a. Click one of the text boxes and make the text bold.

    b. Change the fill color to blue (accent and followed hyperlink color).

    c. With the shape selected, change the AutoShape to an oval. A circle will appear that you will change in the next step.

    d. Use the Format Painter button to apply the color and font changes to the other four text boxes. You will need to select them individually to change their shapes.

7. Change the text boxes by following these steps:

    a. On the Diagram toolbar, click Layout, and then choose AutoLayout to turn off the AutoLayout feature.

    b. Use Shift+click to select the four text boxes and change the font size to 20 points.

    c. Select the two text boxes on the right side of the diagram and use the center right resizing handle to stretch the circle into an oval large enough to hold the text.

    d. Select the two text boxes on the left side of the diagram and use the center left resizing handle to stretch the circle into an oval large enough to hold the text.

    e. Adjust your Zoom, so you can see the entire diagram.

    f. If necessary, adjust the position of the left and right arrows, so they are positioned evenly between the ovals. You may need to move the ovals up or down to allow a little more space.

8. Insert a new slide after slide 4 that uses the Title and Content layout. Key the title **Do What's Good 4 U**

9. Using the content placeholder, insert a radial diagram.

10. Change the radial diagram's size and position by following these steps:

    a. On the Diagram toolbar, click Layout and choose Fit Diagram to Contents.

     b. Click Layout again and choose Expand Diagram.

     c. While holding down Ctrl, drag a corner sizing handle until the diagram is large enough to slightly overlap the slide's title.

     d. Press ⬇ several times until the diagram appears centered vertically in the available space below the title.

11. Key the text shown in Figure 14-20 in the diagram's circles.

FIGURE 14-20

12 o'clock	4 o'clock	8 o'clock	Center
Eat	Play	Walk	Join
With Us	With Us	With Us	Our
			Team

12. Format one of the circles to have a one-color center gradient blue (accent and followed hyperlink) fill with the lightest color in the center and a 4½-point lavender border. Make the text bold.

13. Use Format Painter to apply these settings to the other circles.

14. Adjust grayscale settings for all slides as needed.

15. Create a slide footer for all slides except slide 1 containing today's date and the text *[Your Name], [your initials]*14-25. Adjust the position of the footer elements on the master slide by deleting the number placeholder and moving the Footer Area placeholder to the right side of the slide even with the right edge of the body placeholder. Change to right alignment.

16. Create a handout header and footer: include the date and your name as the header, and the page number and text *[your initials]*14-25 as the footer.

17. Move to slide 1 and save the presentation as *[your initials]*14-25 in your Lesson 14 folder.

18. Print slides 2 and 5 in full size. Preview, and then print the entire presentation as handouts, six slides per page, grayscale, landscape, framed. Close the presentation.

Lesson Applications

Create a flowchart and a diagram.

1. Open the file **NewYear3**. Insert a new slide 2 that uses the Blank layout. Copy the WordArt on slide 1 and paste it on slide 2. Edit the text for **New Year's Eve Reservations** on two lines and resize the WordArt to fit, as shown in Figure 14-21.

2. In the upper-left corner, below the title, draw a Pentagon AutoShape (Block Arrows category, the third item in the fifth row). Make it about 0.75 inches high and 2 inches wide. In the pentagon shape, key **Call friends**

3. Make the text 24-point Arial, bold, white, with a text shadow. Adjust the size of the AutoShape to fit the text. Make its text anchor point Middle Centered and turn on word wrap. Apply a blue fill and a black border.

4. To the right of the pentagon, insert a clip-art image of a telephone (use the search word **phones**). Size the phone to approximately 1 inch square.

5. Draw a Curved Arrow Connector from the point of the pentagon to the left side of the phone. With the connector selected, change the line thickness to 4 1/2 pt and change the line style to Round Dot.

6. Using Figure 14-21 as a guide, duplicate the AutoShape four times, edit the text as shown and change each AutoShape. Apply a purple color to the star shape so it stands out more. Add the smiley face and make it bright yellow with a black line.

FIGURE 14-21
Completed
flowchart

7. Copy the telephone and position it as shown in the figure. Add the connectors, formatting them like the first connector you drew (use Format Painter).

8. Create the "Yes" and "No" text boxes with no fill and no border. Format the text as 18-point Arial, bold, white. Position the text boxes as shown in the figure.

9. Save the presentation as *[your initials]*14-26 in your Lesson 14 folder. Keep it open for the next step.

10. Insert a new slide after slide 2 that uses the Title and Content layout. Copy the WordArt from slide 2 and paste it on slide 3. Edit the WordArt for **New Year's Eve Menu**

11. Create a radial diagram on the new slide and insert six additional shapes (for a total of nine plus one in the center).

12. Adjust the drawing space border to fit the diagram; then expand the diagram proportionately to fill the available space below the title. Leave some room at the bottom of the slide for a footer.

13. Key the text **Great Food** in the center circle; then key the text in Figure 14-22 in the outer circles, starting with the 12 o'clock circle and entering text in each circle moving clockwise.

FIGURE 14-22

Poached Enter Salmon

Texan Enter Tofu

Fresh Enter Fruit

Pecan Enter Pie

Peanut Enter Soup

Veggies Enter & Dip

Sautéed Enter Greens

Corn Enter Relish

Spring Enter Rolls

14. Change the text size for each circle to 20 points. Apply a 6-point solid light purple border and dark purple fill color to each circle.

15. Change the border color individually for each circle, using a variety of bright colors.

16. Apply a 4½-point round dot-line style to the connector lines.

17. Change the center circle AutoShape to a 16-point star. Change the fill color to bright yellow and add a 6-point dark purple border. Change the text to dark purple, too, and make it 24 points.

18. Turn off AutoLayout and make the center star slightly larger.

FIGURE 14-23
Completed diagram

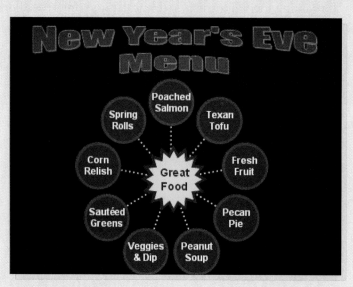

19. Adjust the grayscale settings in the presentation, as needed.

20. Create a handout header and footer: include the date and your name as the header, and the page number and text *[your initials]***14-26** as the footer.

21. Move to slide 1 and save the presentation as *[your initials]***14-26** in your Lesson 14 folder.

22. Preview, and then print the entire presentation as handouts, three slides per page, grayscale, landscape, framed. Close the presentation.

EXERCISE 14-27

Create an organization chart, rearrange boxes, and apply formatting.

1. Open the file **MISdept**. Insert a new slide after slide 2 that uses the Title and Content layout. Key the title **MIS Department Organization**

2. Create an org chart by using the information shown in Figure 14-24 (on the next page). Use whatever boxes, lines, arrangement style, fonts, and colors you think would look good and present the information clearly. Be sure to include all the information shown in the figure.

3. Adjust the grayscale settings in the presentation, as needed.

4. Change the font to 14 points.

5. Turn off AutoLayout and adjust the size of the boxes and adjust their positioning for even spacing.

6. Create a slide footer for slide 3 containing today's date and the text *[Your Name]*, *[your initials]***14-27**.

FIGURE 14-24 Org chart text

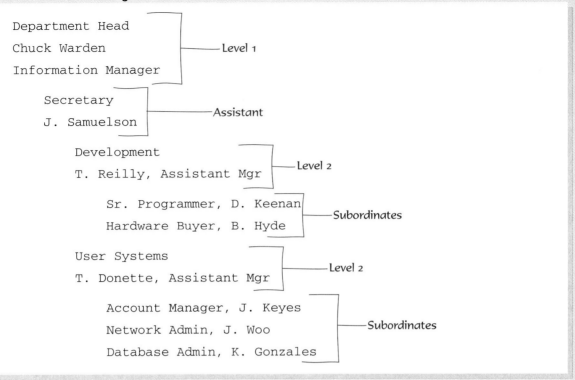

7. Create a handout header and footer: include the date and your name as the header, and the page number and text *[your initials]*14-27 as the footer.

8. Move to slide 1 and save the presentation as *[your initials]*14-27 in your Lesson 14 folder.

9. Print slide 3 in full size. Preview, and then print the entire presentation as handouts, three slides per page, grayscale, framed. Close the presentation.

EXERCISE 14-28 ➕ *Challenge Yourself*

Format organization chart boxes and lines, and change the arrangement, size, and style of the org chart elements.

1. Open the file **Retail2** and move to slide 4.

2. Change the arrangement of all the level 3 boxes to Right Hanging.

3. Size the org chart so that it fills the slide.

4. Remove the fill color from all boxes; then apply the second 4½-point double-line border (with the heaviest line at the top) to the level 1 and level 2 boxes. After applying the line style, change its weight to 8 points and its color to medium gray (shadows scheme color).

5. Change the font for the entire org chart to Arial Black at 18 points.

6. For the level 1 text, change the size to 24 points and the color to blue (fills scheme color).

7. For the level 2 text, change the size to 20 points and the text color to magenta (accent and hyperlink scheme color). Change the fill color to white.

8. For all the level 3 boxes, remove the box border lines and left-align the text.

9. Turn off AutoLayout.

10. Select the first level 3 item in each group and use the ⬆ several times to move the text closer to the level 2 boxes.

11. Repeat this procedure to raise up each of the remaining level 3 items, so they are evenly spaced below the level 2 boxes.

12. Increase the size of the level 1 box, so it holds all the text. Add a white fill.

13. Make other size and position adjustments to individual items or the whole chart to make a pleasing composition.

14. Adjust the grayscale settings in the presentation as needed.

15. Create a slide footer for slide 3 containing today's date and the text *[Your Name]*, *[your initials]***14-28**.

16. Create a handout header and footer: include the date and your name as the header, and the page number and text *[your initials]***14-28** as the footer.

17. Move to slide 1 and save the presentation as *[your initials]***14-28** in your Lesson 14 folder.

18. Print slide 3 in full size. Preview, and then print the entire presentation as handouts, four slides per page, grayscale, landscape, framed. Close the presentation.

On Your Own

In these exercises, you work on your own, as you would in a real-life work environment. Use the skills you've learned to accomplish the task—and be creative.

EXERCISE 14-29

Think of a process with which you are familiar and create a flowchart indicating the steps in the process. For example, baking a cake, preparing for a camping trip, or paying a bill. Keep the process fairly simple—no more than ten steps—and format it so that it is easy to understand and attractive to view. Add a title slide and one or two additional slides giving additional information about the process. Save the presentation as *[your initials]***14-29**. Preview, and then print the presentation as handouts.

EXERCISE 14-30

Create an organization chart of your family tree, starting with one set of great-grandparents and including all the cousins that come from that branch. If you don't want to create your own family tree, choose a famous person, a pedigreed pet, or an imaginary figure. Include a title slide for your presentation and one or two slides describing something of interest about one or more of the people (or pets) on your chart. Use your own creativity to format the presentation and the chart attractively. Save the presentation as *[your initials]*14-30. Preview, and then print the presentation as handouts.

EXERCISE 14-31

Create a diagram to describe a relationship between several functions or departments at your school, work, or other organization. For example, a drama club might have a director, stagehands, costume designer, actors and actresses, musicians, and a playwright. Choose any of the diagram types in the Design Gallery dialog box, except the organization chart. Add a title slide and one or two other slides describing some aspect of the relationship. Save the presentation as *[your initials]*14-31. Preview, and then print the presentation as a full-size slide(s).

Unit 5 Applications

Add a table, a chart, and a flowchart to a presentation.

1. Open the file **HdCount**. Apply the Echo design template and use the default color scheme. Move the "Good 4 U" logo between the title and subtitle.

2. Insert a new slide after slide 3 that uses the Title and Content layout and key the title **Current Breakdown**. Create a table by using the data shown in Figure U5-1.

FIGURE U5-1
Completed table

	Kitchen		Service	
	F/T	P/T	F/T	P/T
Weekdays	13	8	19	9
Weekends	7	13	9	16

3. Merge two cells for "Kitchen" and two cells for "Service."

4. Adjust the column widths so that the text fits attractively, and align the text to match the figure. The overall table dimensions should be approximately 6.25 inches wide by 3.25 inches tall.

5. Apply 3-point dark green borders (text and lines scheme color) to the table's outside border and under the headings as shown in the figure. Apply a pale green fill (fills scheme color) to the entire table with 50% transparency.

6. Adjust text margin spacing so the numbers are positioned below the headings. Position the table attractively on the slide.

7. Insert a new slide after slide 4 that uses the Title and Content layout and key the title **Past, Current, Projected**. Create a column chart by using the data shown in Figure U5-2.

FIGURE U5-2

		Column A	Column B	Column C	Column D
		2002	2003	2004	2005
Row 1	Full-time	41	40	48	38
Row 2	Part-time	30	35	46	61

8. Apply a one-color gradient fill to each column, using colors from the template's color scheme. Move the legend to the bottom, make it slightly wider, center it, and delete its border.

9. Draw an AutoShape at the top of the chart with the text **Projecting 61 P/T, 38 F/T**. Draw an arrow from the text to the top of the 2005 columns. Format the AutoShape and the arrow as you like.

10. Insert a new slide after slide 5. Use the Title Only layout and key the title **Plan for Increasing P/T Headcount**

11. On the new slide 6, create a flowchart showing the five steps in Figure U5-3; place the text for each step in a different AutoShape. Arrange the shapes in clockwise order and draw arrow connector lines from the first shape to the second, from the second to the third, and so on.

FIGURE U5-3

```
Step 1  Advertise P/T positions

Step 2  T. Scott to schedule interviews

Step 3  M. Peters to interview and hire applicants

Step 4  J. Farla to train

Step 5  L. Klein to assign schedules
```

12. Format the shapes, text, and connector lines as you like.

13. Apply one transition to the slides and then apply custom animation on slides 4–6.

14. Check the grayscale settings for all slides.

15. View the presentation as a slide show.

16. Create a slide footer for all slides, except the title slide, containing today's date and the text *[Your Name], [your initials]***u5-1**.

17. Create a handout header and footer: include the date and your name as the header, and the page number and text *[your initials]***u5-1** as the footer.

18. Move to slide 1 and save the presentation as *[your initials]***u5-1** in a new folder for Unit 5 Applications.

19. Print slides 4, 5, and 6 in full size. Preview and then print the entire presentation as handouts, six slides per page, grayscale, landscape, framed. Close the presentation.

UNIT APPLICATION 5-2

Create a presentation with a table, edit and format the table, modify master slides, and create and format a chart.

1. Start a new presentation that uses the Cascade design template and the color scheme with a white background and teak and gray colors (the last sample).

2. On the slide master and title master, move the triangular-shaped graphic made up of vertical lines to the left slightly. Below it insert the picture file

Logo1 as the "Good 4 Ü" logo. Reduce the size of the logo to fit appropriately. Add a thin rectangle in dark blue that spans the slide (.2" × 10") and position it at the top of the vertical lines. Make the one on the slide master to be more narrow (.2"). Make the title text bold on both masters. Change the presentation's fonts to Verdana.

3. Create six slides by using the text in Figure U5-4. Slide 1 should have the **Title Slide** layout; slides 2, 3, and 4 should have the **Title and Text** layout; and slides 5 and 6 should have the **Title and Content** layout.

FIGURE U5-4

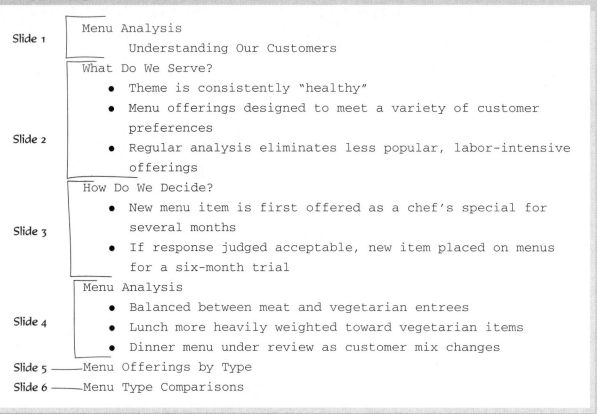

Slide 1

Menu Analysis
Understanding Our Customers

Slide 2

What Do We Serve?
- Theme is consistently "healthy"
- Menu offerings designed to meet a variety of customer preferences
- Regular analysis eliminates less popular, labor-intensive offerings

Slide 3

How Do We Decide?
- New menu item is first offered as a chef's special for several months
- If response judged acceptable, new item placed on menus for a six-month trial

Slide 4

Menu Analysis
- Balanced between meat and vegetarian entrees
- Lunch more heavily weighted toward vegetarian items
- Dinner menu under review as customer mix changes

Slide 5 — Menu Offerings by Type

Slide 6 — Menu Type Comparisons

4. On slide 5, create a table by using the information shown in Figure U5-5.

FIGURE U5-5

	Column 1	Column 2	Column 3	Column 4	Column 5
Row 1		Entrees			
Row 2		Meat	Vegetarian	Appetizers	Desserts
Row 3	Lunch	7	14	6	7
Row 4	Dinner	11	9	8	8

5. Adjust the column widths so that there is no text wrapping. Make the second, third, fourth, and fifth columns all the same size; then adjust the table's position on the slide.

6. Merge the cell containing the text "Entrees" with the cell to its right.

7. Merge the two cells in the first row above "Appetizers" and "Desserts." Then key **Other Items** in the merged cell.

8. Decrease the text size for all the table text to 20 points.

9. Adjust the height of the first two rows to be just high enough to fit the text. Make the other rows approximately 1 inch high.

10. Adjust text alignment and cell alignment to position text and numbers appropriately within the cells. Make sure that numbers are right-aligned and centered under their headings.

11. Remove all the table's borders; then apply deep blue/green 2¼-point borders (text and titles scheme color) to the border of the table.

12. Apply a 50% transparent bright blue fill (accent and hyperlink scheme color) to the cells containing numbers and make the numbers bold.

13. Add a text box under the table with the text **High appeal among female customers** formatted as 20-point Verdana italic. Draw a dark blue/green line with an arrow from the text box to the vegetarian lunches cell.

14. On slide 6, use the data from the table on slide 5 to create a 3-D pie chart showing the percentages of each type of menu offering. (Add lunch and dinner numbers together for each category.) Color the pie slices to harmonize with the presentation.

15. Add data labels to the pie slices, showing percent only. Move the data labels onto each slice, and change their font size to 20 points and recolor if necessary.

16. Move the legend to the bottom of the chart and remove its border. Make the legend slightly wider.

17. Adjust the grayscale settings as needed.

18. View the presentation as a slide show.

19. Create a slide footer for slides 5 and 6 containing today's date and the text *[Your Name]*, *[your initials]***u5-2**.

20. Create a handout header and footer: include the date and your name as the header, and the page number and text *[your initials]***u5-2** as the footer.

21. Move to slide 1 and save the presentation as *[your initials]***u5-2** in your Unit 5 Applications folder.

22. Print slides 5 and 6 in full size. Preview and then print the entire presentation as handouts, six slides per page, grayscale, landscape, framed. Close the presentation.

Create a presentation with two org charts and a diagram.

1. Start a new presentation that uses the Globe design template and the default color scheme. Create three slides and key the text shown in Figure U5-6. Use the Title Slide layout for the first slide, the Title, Text, and Content layout for the second slide, and the Title and Text layout for the third slide.

FIGURE U5-6

Slide 1	Good 4 U Senior Management Current and Future Organization
Slide 2	Why Change What Works? • Current structure designed for a single-restaurant company • Management must be positioned for a national, multi-restaurant organization
Slide 3	Future Structure • Reorganization planned for 2005 • Designed to capitalize on the individual talents of co-owners • Company will be split into two functional areas

2. On slide 2, insert a radial diagram in the content placeholder.

3. Insert three more shapes on the radial diagram, making a total of six shapes in the outer circle plus a center shape.

4. Make the diagram as large as possible without interfering with the other text on the slide.

5. Key **Good** Enter **4 U** in the center shape. For the other shapes, key the text shown in Figure U5-7, starting with "New York" in the 12 o'clock position and moving clockwise.

FIGURE U5-7

```
New Enter York
Miami
Los Enter Angeles
San Enter Francisco
Tucson
More Enter soon
```

6. Change the diagram's text to 18 points, bold. Format the shapes so that they have a dark blue (shadow color) fill color and a 3-point white border. Adjust

the size and position of the diagram to accommodate its text and to work well with the other elements on the slide.

7. Insert a new slide after slide 2 that uses the Title and Content layout. Give it the title **Current Organization**

8. On slide 3, create an org chart for the Good 4 U restaurant by using Figure U5-8. Arrange the chart boxes in an attractive and functional way.

FIGURE U5-8

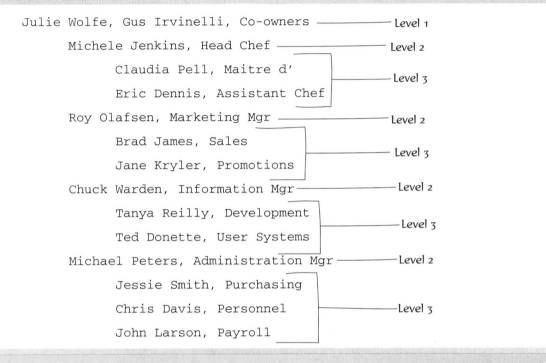

9. Increase the size of the chart, making it as large as possible.

10. Apply dark blue fill color to the boxes. Increase the size of all the text as much as possible (try for 14 points); then make "Gus Irvinelli" and "Julie Wolf" 16 points.

11. Make a copy of slide 3 (the org chart) and paste it as a new slide after slide 4. Change the title of the new slide to **Future Organization**

12. On the org chart, insert two new level 2 boxes. Key **Julie Wolfe** Enter **Co-owner** in the first new box and **Gus Irvinelli** Enter **Co-owner** in the second new box.

13. Make Chuck Warden's and Roy Olafsen's departments report to Gus Irvinelli's level 2 box. Make Michele Jenkins's and Michael Peters's departments report to Julie Wolfe's level 2 box.

14. Format the two new boxes to match the other org chart boxes. Delete the text from the level 1 box; then change its color to white. Insert the picture file **Logo1** sized appropriately.

15. Adjust the size of the boxes so the chart will fit on the slide with even spacing.

16. Review all slides, adjusting the size and position of elements where needed, and adjust grayscale settings.

17. Apply an animation scheme of your choice to all slides in the presentation.

18. View the presentation as a slide show.

19. Create a slide footer for slides 2, 3, and 5 containing today's date and the text *[Your Name]*, *[your initials]*u5-3.

20. Create a handout header and footer: include the date and your name as the header, and the page number and text *[your initials]*u5-3 as the footer.

21. Move to slide 1 and save the presentation as *[your initials]*u5-3 in your Unit 5 Applications folder.

22. Print slides 2, 3, and 5 in full size. Preview and then print the entire presentation as handouts, six slides per page, grayscale, landscape, framed. Close the presentation.

UNIT APPLICATION 5-4 ● *Using the Internet*

Write and design a presentation that uses numerical charts, tables, org charts, and diagrams.

Use the Internet to research a topic of current interest that would lend itself to a presentation including numerical charts, tables, diagrams and/or organization charts. You decide what your topic will be. Here are a few to give you ideas, but you are not limited to these topics:

- The impact of increased security for air travel
- Enrollment information at your local college or university
- How global warming is affecting weather patterns
- How the financial health of Hollywood is affected by the overall economy
- The problems caused by overuse of antibiotics
- The growth of computer use in the general population

Illustrate the information you gathered by using a variety of charts, tables, and diagrams. Be sure to include at least five slides and format them in an attractive way. Prepare a slide listing the resources you used. When the presentation is complete, check spelling and review all the slides in Grayscale view, making any grayscale adjustments that are needed.

In the slide footer, include the text **Prepared by** followed by your name. Include the slide number, but not the date, on all slides. In the handout footer, include the completed filename *[your initials]*u5-4. In the handout header, key **Presented to** and then identify to whom you would be giving this presentation. Include in the handout the date you would be delivering the presentation.

Save the presentation as *[your initials]*u5-4 in your Unit 5 Applications folder. Practice delivering the presentation. Preview and then print the presentation handouts as an appropriate number of slides per page, grayscale, framed. Close the presentation.

Making Presentations Available to Others

Distributing and Presenting Your Work

OBJECTIVES

After completing this lesson, you will be able to:

1. Use PowerPoint with projection equipment.
2. Use Package for CD to prepare presentations for delivery on other computers.
3. Prepare presentations in other formats.
4. Collaborate with others by sending presentations for review and merging reviewer's comments and changes.
5. Publish presentations to the Web.
6. Schedule and deliver broadcast presentations on the Web.

 Estimated Time: 1¼ hours

In this lesson you learn how to use PowerPoint's online tools to navigate through a slide show and to make impromptu notes or record audience feedback while you are presenting. You also learn how to package a presentation so that it can be displayed on other computers, how to publish your work to the Internet or an *intranet* (an Internet-like system that exists only within a company or organization), how to convert your work to 35 mm slides, and how to print overhead transparencies.

You also learn how to collaborate with others, incorporating changes made by reviewers into your presentation, and how to present your work on the Web by using PowerPoint's Broadcast feature.

Presenting with Projection Equipment

When you are presenting with PowerPoint and projection equipment, be sure your equipment is set up well in advance of your presentation and test the equipment and your slide show. Be sure your equipment is arranged in an effective manner so that your computer monitor is visible to you while you are talking. It is better to glance at the monitor than to look at the projected image on a large screen while you are talking. For safety, arrange any necessary cables or electrical cords so that they will not cause you to trip.

The following exercises will introduce you to several of PowerPoint's features that can be very helpful during your delivery of a presentation.

EXERCISE | **15-1** | **Use Onscreen Navigation Tools**

During a slide show, you can navigate from slide to slide or to a specific slide by using a shortcut menu.

1. Open the file **Summertime**. From the Slide Show menu, choose Set Up Show.

2. In the Set Up Show dialog box, change the Show options to Show without animation. For the Advance slides option, choose Manually. Click OK. This turns off any slide animations and timings that might have been set.

> **TIP:** If you're going to be presenting at a live meeting, slide timings are usually not appropriate because you'll want to be flexible with the amount of time spent on individual slides to encourage discussion. Slide timings are most appropriate for self-running presentations.

3. Run the presentation as a slide show, starting with slide 1. Imagine that you are presenting this at a meeting and that the group is commenting and making decisions as you move from slide to slide. You will move back and forth between the slides as your discussion progresses.

4. With slide 1 displayed, right-click anywhere on the screen to display the shortcut menu. The shortcut menu provides a variety of options related to the slide show. Notice that you can click Next or Previous to move forward or backward in the slide show.

FIGURE 15-1
Slide Show menu

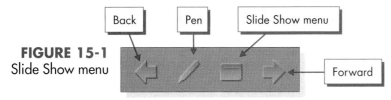

5. Point to <u>G</u>o to slide on the shortcut menu. Notice that slides are listed in order with their titles displayed. Click "3 The Main Course" to go to slide 3.

6. Click the left mouse button repeatedly to advance through slide 2 ("Appetizer Specials") and slide 4 ("Desserts") to display each slide.

7. Another way to move between your slides is with the menu options that are displayed on the lower left of the slide during a slide show.

8. Click the Slide Show menu button ; then point to Go to Slide on the menu. Click slide 2.

> **TIP:** Another way to quickly navigate to slides out of sequence in your slide show is to simply key the number of the slide and press Enter.

EXERCISE 15-2 Record Notes

At any time during a slide show, you can quickly add notes about decisions you make or items you need to follow up on. These notes are recorded as Speaker Notes that you can save and later print as notes pages, or you could copy the text and paste it into Word if necessary.

1. On slide 1, right-click to display the shortcut menu; then choose S<u>c</u>reen and then Spea<u>k</u>er Notes. Key this note and insert the actual date that is one week from the current date.

    Roy Olafsen will take care of convention center details, including room reservations for all attendees. Due date—one week.

FIGURE 15-2
Speaker Notes

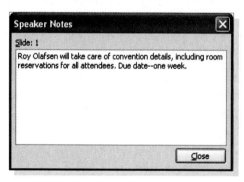

2. Click the Close button.

3. Move to the next slide ("Appetizer Specials") and open Speaker Notes again. Key this note and enter the due date based on the current date.

    Michele Jenkins and her staff will take care of all food preparation issues, including ordering food and arranging for kitchen equipment. Due date: two weeks.

4. Click the Close button.

5. Move to the next slide ("The Main Course") and add the following information as Speaker Notes:

    One menu change is required. The Chicken and Potato Salad did not get good test reviews. Replace it with Black Bean Chicken Salad.

    Michele Jenkins will test. Due date—three weeks
    Question—Do we have enough refrigerator space?

6. Click the Close button.

7. Examine your slides in Normal view and you will notice that the comments you entered while in Slide Show view appear in the Notes pane.

EXERCISE 15-3 **Use Annotation Pens**

During a slide show you can use your mouse pointer to direct your audience's attention to something on your slide. Be careful when using the mouse that you don't move too quickly or display nervous mannerisms by making the mouse move too much.

The *annotation pens* are useful to "draw" on your slides during a slide show with your choice of three different tools. For example, you can use the Ballpoint Pen or the Felt Tip Pen to draw a circle around an important number or underline a word. You can use the Highlighter to draw a wider mark to make something stand out on the slide.

1. With slide 3 displayed, right-click the screen; choose P̲ointer Options and then B̲allpoint Pen from the shortcut menu. The pointer changes to a pen shape.

FIGURE 15-3
Using the pen
during a slide show

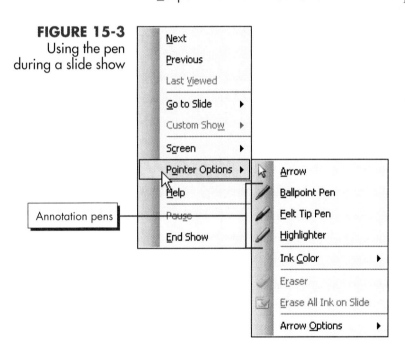

2. Using the Ballpoint Pen pointer, draw an oval around the "Tex-Mex Tofu" at the top left of the list. The pen's blue color is not very noticeable.

3. Right-click the screen, choose P̲ointer Options and then E̲raser from the shortcut menu. Your pointer changes to an eraser, so click on the blue oval to erase it. You can also press E on your keyboard to erase annotations.

4. Right-click the screen, choose P<u>o</u>inter Options and then choose Ink <u>C</u>olor. Choose <u>R</u>ed for the pen color. The pointer changes to a pen shape again.

5. Draw a circle around the "Tex-Mex Tofu" and notice how much better the red shows up.

6. Right-click the screen; choose P<u>o</u>inter Options and then <u>F</u>elt Tip Pen. Draw an oval around "Grilled Swordfish." Notice that the mark made with this pen is thicker.

7. Right-click the screen, choose P<u>o</u>inter Options and then <u>H</u>ighlighter. Check the pen color to select yellow. Draw a mark through "Chicken and Potato Salad."

8. Move to the blank slide 5 and practice with these tools a little more. During a meeting it might be very helpful to draw a quick diagram or to make a sketch about something.

TIP: You don't have to draw precisely when using the annotation pen. Pen marks disappear when you advance the slide, but you will be given the option at the end of the slide show to retain the marks. Then you can use drawing tools to modify them or delete the ones you don't want to keep.

FIGURE 15-4
Annotation pen
samples

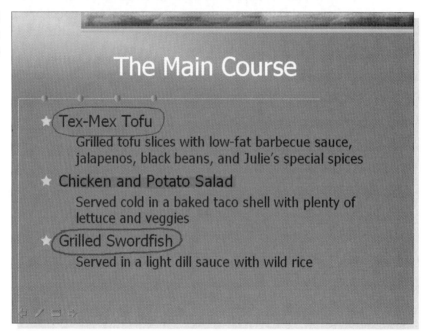

9. Open the shortcut menu again, choose P<u>o</u>inter Options, and then choose <u>A</u>rrow from the submenu to restore the arrow pointer. (Or press the keyboard shortcut Ctrl+A.)

10. Advance through the last slide. When you reach the end of the presentation, click once more to exit the presentation. A message box will automatically appear.

FIGURE 15-5
Message box about
ink annotations

11. Now look at the slides where you used annotation pens. You will see your drawings that can be recolored or resized with line tools. Even though you might have drawn a rectangle shape, you cannot apply fill colors.

EXERCISE 15-4 Blank Slides

During a slide show you may want to blank your computer screen without closing your slide show. You might want to digress from your original topic, or simply have a discussion without an image being projected.

1. With slide 2 displayed in Slide Show view, press the B key to blank the screen to black; press the B key again to return to this slide in your slide show.

2. With slide 2 displayed in Slide Show view, press the W key to blank the screen to white; press the W key again to return to this slide in your slide show.

3. This technique does not require any advance setup and can be used effectively to manage when your slides are displayed.

EXERCISE 15-5 Hide and Unhide Slides

You may decide to include a few extra slides in your presentation in case someone in the audience has a question about these concepts or the slides might be about content you may not have time to cover. You can include these slides as part of your presentation, but hide them so that they will be displayed only if you choose to show them.

1. Click the Slide Sorter button and select slide 3 with the title "Hidden Slide."

2. With slide 3 selected, click the Hide Slide button. (See Figure 15-6 on the next page.)

3. Now the slide will not be displayed during a sequential slide show. Still in Slide Sorter view, select slide 1 and click the slide show button ▦ and then advance through the slides. Slide 3 is not displayed.

4. Still in Slide Show view, from any slide in your presentations press 3 plus Enter. The hidden slide is then displayed.

5. Create a handout header and footer: include the date and your name as the header, and the page number and text *[your initials]*15-5 as the footer.

6. Move to slide 1 and save the presentation as *[your initials]*15-5 in a new folder for Lesson 15. Leave the presentation open for the next exercise.

FIGURE 15-6
Hiding a slide

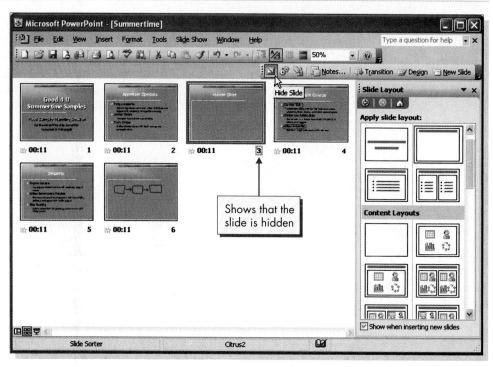

Shows that the slide is hidden

Preparing Presentations for Delivery on Other Computers

The presentations used in this course are small files that fit conveniently on a floppy disk. When you work in a business setting, your presentations might be much more complex and the file too large for a single floppy disk. PowerPoint has a feature called Package for CD that conveniently solves this challenge for you by saving your presentation file and any linked files to a CD or to a folder that you designate to contain the files. This is especially helpful when you need to present with a computer that is not the one used to develop your presentation. You can include a viewer program that makes it possible to display the slide show without PowerPoint.

When your presentation is delivered on a different computer, there is a good possibility that the fonts you chose will not be available. Fortunately, you can *embed*, or save, the fonts used in your presentation so that they will be available wherever your presentation is used.

NOTE: Some third-party TrueType fonts have license restrictions and cannot be embedded. If that is the case, a message will appear to inform you that the font cannot be embedded. All TrueType fonts supplied with Microsoft software can be embedded.

EXERCISE **15-6** **Save Embedded Fonts in a Presentation**

You can embed almost any TrueType font included with the Windows or PowerPoint installation. A *TrueType font* is one that can be sized to any size and that prints exactly the same as it appears on your screen.

FIGURE 15-7
Font types

1. With the presentation *[your initials]*15-5 open, select some text on any slide and then click to open the Font drop-down list on the Formatting toolbar. Notice that the font used in this presentation, Tahoma, is a TrueType font. Most of the fonts available on your computer are likely to be TrueType fonts, indicated by the logo to the left of the fonts.

 NOTE: Fonts that have the printer symbol are available only on the currently selected printer for your computer.

2. Press (Esc) to close the drop-down list. From the File menu, choose Save As.

3. In the Save As dialog box, open the Tools drop-down menu and choose Save Options. The Save Options dialog box opens, displaying many options for saving a file.

FIGURE 15-8
Embedding fonts in the presentation file

4. Locate the section labeled Font options for current document only at the bottom of the dialog box. Check the option Embed TrueType fonts and then select the option Embed all characters (best for editing by others). Click OK to close the Save Options dialog box.

5. Save the presentation as *[your initials]*15-6 in your Lesson 15 folder. The presentation is now saved with the embedded TrueType font Tahoma (the only font used in this presentation).

TIP: If you are concerned about file size and disk space, don't embed TrueType fonts unless necessary. Embedded fonts increase the size of your presentation files.

EXERCISE **15-7** **Save a Presentation by Using Package for CD**

Before using the Package for CD option, decide how you want to store your presentation. You can save it to a CD or you can save it to an empty folder on your hard drive. If you save it to a hard drive folder, you can later copy the contents of the folder to a Zip drive or a CD-R disc, eliminating the need for multiple floppy disks for large presentations.

In this exercise you will save a small presentation to a floppy disk or to a different location that your instructor specifies. Make sure you have a blank formatted disk on hand before beginning.

1. With the file *[your initials]*15-6 open, remove any annotations that you inserted in previous exercises. Select all slides in the Outline and Slide view and then open the Animation Schemes task pane. Choose No Animations to remove the effects that have been applied using the Animation Schemes feature for the placeholders on the title master and the slide master.

2. On slide 1, insert a music file. Choose the Insert menu, Movies and Sounds, Sound from Clip Organizer; then search for WMPAUD6, which is a brief music clip. Click the sound thumbnail to insert it and set it to play automatically as the slide show starts. Right-click the sound icon, choose Edit Sound Object, and choose Hide sound icon during slide show.

3. Save the presentation with these changes as *[your initials]*15-7.

 TIP: If this file doesn't show up when you search for it, you can insert the file from your student data files.

4. Insert a blank formatted disk in your floppy disk drive.

FIGURE 15-9
Package for CD
dialog box

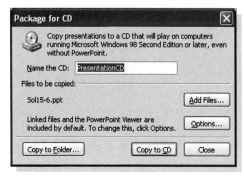

5. Choose Package for CD from the File menu. The Package for CD dialog box appears.

6. Give the CD a name that will identify its content; in the Name the CD box key **Summertime**

 TIP: If you want to package a presentation that's not currently open, choose Add Files and select one or more files on your computer or network.

7. Click the Options button; then on the Options window check both Linked files and Embedded TrueType fonts. As you learned in the previous exercise, embedding fonts will save the fonts you used with your presentation.

Saving linked files will copy the necessary files and maintain all the links to sound or movie files you may have used.

FIGURE 15-10
Options dialog box

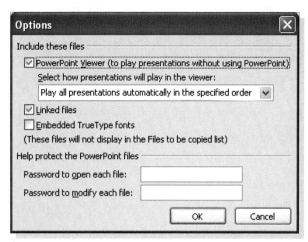

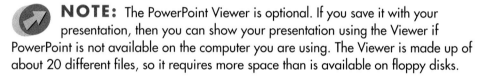

8. Remove the check for PowerPoint Viewer. Click OK.

NOTE: The PowerPoint Viewer is optional. If you save it with your presentation, then you can show your presentation using the Viewer if PowerPoint is not available on the computer you are using. The Viewer is made up of about 20 different files, so it requires more space than is available on floppy disks.

9. Click the Copy to Folder button and then from the Copy to Folder dialog box confirm that the folder name appears as you entered it earlier.

10. Click the Browse button and locate the destination where your Package for CD files should be saved. Choose A:\ drive or whatever drive is appropriate. Click OK.

11. Click Close. The Package for CD process is complete and your presentation file plus linked files are saved in the location you specified.

12. Close the presentation without saving it, and then remove your floppy disk and label it appropriately.

EXERCISE 15-8 Using a Package for CD File

With PowerPoint loaded, using a Package for CD file is easy because it loads just like any other PowerPoint file. The difference is that the presentation file and any linked files have been saved to the folder that you specified.

1. Insert the floppy disk containing the presentation into the A:\ drive. (If you saved it to a different type of medium, insert that medium in the appropriate drive instead.)

FIGURE 15-11
Opening a
presentation saved
with the Package
for CD option

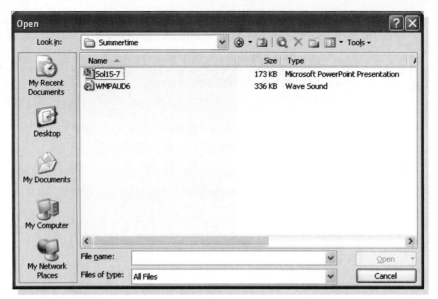

2. Navigate to the Summertime folder under your Lesson 15 folder and open it. At the bottom of the Open dialog box, change the Files of type to All Files. Now you will see your presentation file name and the music file that was automatically saved with it in this folder.

3. Double-click the presentation file to load it and test to be sure the music file plays appropriately.

NOTE: If you had saved PowerPoint Viewer with your files, then you can load your presentation using Windows Explorer and PowerPoint is not required. Using Windows Explorer or My Computer, navigate to where your folder is saved and open it. Double-click the play file to begin your slide show without PowerPoint.

4. Remove the floppy disk from the A:\ drive.

Preparing Presentations for Delivery in Other Formats

Throughout this book, you have viewed presentations on your computer screen and printed them on paper. You can also print presentations on transparency film for use with an overhead projector. Or, you can send your presentation file (by disk, modem, or the Internet) to a *service bureau* where your presentation can be reproduced as 35 mm slide transparencies or full-color overhead transparencies.

You have used the Page Setup dialog box to change slide orientation from landscape to portrait. In the same dialog box, you can resize presentation slides for overhead transparencies, letter paper, 35 mm slides, or custom paper sizes.

 NOTE: Remember, any animation effects that your presentation contains will be lost when presenting as 35 mm slides or overhead transparencies.

TABLE 15-1   Choosing a Presentation Delivery Method

METHOD	MAXIMUM AUDIENCE	ADVANTAGE
Computer monitor	4–20, depending on monitor size	Allows last-minute changes and use of animation
Computer with a large-screen projector	200	Same as preceding
Slide projector	200	Quality color with high color saturation
Overhead projector	200	Simple, and transparencies are inexpensive to create
Presentation broadcast	Any size	Can be sent via the Internet or an intranet to any number of viewers

EXERCISE   15-9   Prepare a Presentation in 35 mm Format

When you want to deliver a presentation in a format other than an on-screen show, you need to change the slide size by using the Page Setup dialog box. For example, 35 mm slides have a different height-to-width ratio (called the aspect ratio) than on-screen slides or overhead transparencies.

1. Start PowerPoint and open the file *[your initials]***15-7**. Delete the music clip from slide 1.

2. From the <u>F</u>ile menu, choose Page Set<u>u</u>p to open the Page Setup dialog box. Notice that the slides have already been formatted for On-screen Show—they are 10 inches wide by 7.5 inches high and have a landscape orientation.

3. Click the <u>S</u>lides sized for drop-down arrow to display the available choices. Notice that there are several sizes from which to choose.

4. Choose 35mm Slides. Notice that the width has changed to 11.25 inches, but the height remains the same as for On-screen Show. (See Figure 15-12 on the next page.)

5. Click OK to close the dialog box. Notice that the 35 mm format is slightly wider than the on-screen format.

FIGURE 15-12
Page Setup
dialog box

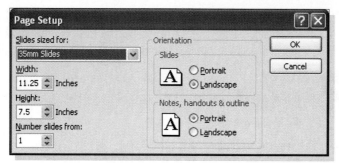

6. Scroll through all the slides and observe any changes in proportions to individual objects. In this case, the body placeholders have simply become wider.

TIP: It is best to choose the output format of a presentation (on-screen, overhead, 35 mm slides, and so on) and the orientation (landscape or portrait) before creating the presentation. However, you might have to change the output format after the presentation is complete. In that case, review each slide because a change in the aspect ratio will change objects, too. You may need to change object proportions, positions, and font sizes.

7. Create a handout header and footer: include the date and your name as the header, and the page number and text *[your initials]***15-9** as the footer.

8. Move to slide 1 and save the presentation as *[your initials]***15-9** in your Lesson 15 folder. Your presentation is now ready to be translated into 35 mm slides for use with a slide projector. You can send the presentation file as an e-mail attachment to a service bureau, or use the Package for CD feature to copy the presentation to a floppy disk, Zip drive, or CD-R and then mail or hand-deliver it to a service bureau for 35 mm slide production.

9. Preview and then print the presentation as handouts, 6 slides per page, grayscale, framed. Notice that the slide miniatures on this printout are slightly shorter and wider than slides formatted for an on-screen presentation.

EXERCISE **15-10** **Prepare a Presentation for Use as Overhead Transparencies**

You can use your printer to print overhead transparencies simply by inserting transparency film in your printer's paper tray. Or, you can copy paper printouts onto transparency film by using a copy machine. Several types of transparency film are available, specially formulated for laser printers, ink-jet printers, and copy machines. Make sure you use the correct film for your printer or copier. You can obtain professional-quality color overhead transparencies by sending your presentation file to a service bureau, just as you would for 35 mm slides.

NOTE: In some rare instances, portrait orientation may work better than landscape. If you are starting a new presentation and know you will need portrait orientation, it is best to change the page setup to portrait before creating any slides. Otherwise, many slide objects will require resizing after changing orientation.

1. With the file *[your initials]***15-9** still open, use the Page Setup dialog box to change the <u>S</u>lides sized for setting to Overhead. This changes the width to 10 inches, keeping the height at 7.5 inches (the same as for an on-screen show), which works well for most overhead projectors.

2. Insert a slide footer for slide 1 only, containing today's date and the text *[Your Name], [your initials]***15-10**.

3. Change the handout footer to reflect the filename *[your initials]***15-10**.

4. Save the presentation as *[your initials]***15-10** in your Lesson 15 folder.

5. Print slide 1, framed, on transparency film if it is available.

TIP: It is important to understand the capabilities of your printer and the type of output it generates. If you are using a small inkjet printer, then you might want to conserve ink and print as fast as possible. Large areas of dark or intense colors will take a long time to print and use a lot of ink. You could choose light background colors and use dark or intense colors for accent colors. For color laser printing, you do not have these limitations.

6. Print the entire presentation as handouts, 6 slides per page, grayscale, framed. Compare this printout to the printout from the previous exercise. Notice the difference in the slide proportions.

7. Close the presentation.

Collaborating with Workgroups

Before delivering a presentation, you might want others to review it and perhaps contribute to it. PowerPoint has some convenient features to make this an easy task. You can send your presentation via e-mail to reviewers or request that they open a copy of your presentation from a shared network folder. Each reviewer can make any changes they want and then send their copy back to you.

When all the reviews are completed, you merge the copies into your original presentation. The merged presentation allows you to accept or reject any changes that reviewers made.

EXERCISE **15-11** **Set Up a Review Cycle**

You have several choices in how to set up a review cycle. You can:

● Send your presentation for review via e-mail by using the Sen<u>d</u> To command on the <u>F</u>ile menu. Using this method, you can send the presentation to all reviewers at the same time or you can use a routing slip to send it to one reviewer, who then sends it on to the next reviewer after making comments and changes.

- Make a uniquely named copy of the presentation for each reviewer, and make the copies available on a shared folder. Each reviewer opens their copy and makes changes to it. When finished, the reviewers notify the author that they have completed their assignment.

- Make copies of the presentation on floppy disks or other removable media and deliver the disks to the reviewers. When the task is completed, the reviewers return the disks to the author.

After all the reviews have been completed, the author merges the reviewed files with the original by using the Compare and Merge Presentations command on the Tools menu.

NOTE: If you have linked files—for example, your presentation is linked to an Excel chart—you must either embed the linked object or include its file in the same directory as the presentation before sending it for review.

1. If your instructor tells you that you will not be using workgroups and e-mail, skip this step, complete only steps 3 and 4 in this exercise and step 4 in Exercise 15-12.

2. Follow your instructor's directions to divide your class into workgroups with three students each. One student should be designated as the author and the other two as reviewers. A presentation will be routed via e-mail for reviewing to members in the group.

3. At your workgroup author's computer, have the student designated as author open the file **MktTrng** from their student disk.

4. Save the presentation as *[your initials]*Orig

5. Choose Send To from the File menu and then choose Mail Recipient (for Review) from the submenu. An e-mail form appears.

6. In the To box, key the e-mail addresses of the two reviewers in your group, separated by a semicolon. (Or, click the Address Book button to the left of the To box and choose the e-mail addresses from the Select Names dialog box.)

7. In the message area, add the following to the existing message:

   Feel free to add any comments or changes that you feel will enhance the presentation.

8. Click the Send button in the upper-left corner of the e-mail window. The e-mail is sent to your outbox.

NOTE: Depending on how your e-mail system is set up, you might need to make a connection to your Internet Service Provider (ISP) and then open Outlook and send any mail that is in your outbox.

FIGURE 15-13
Sending an e-mail
with an attachment
to be reviewed

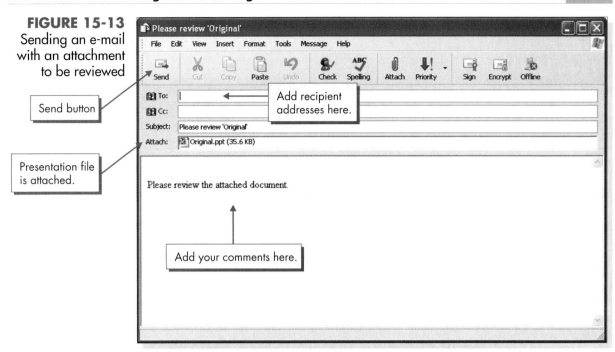

Send button

Presentation file
is attached.

9. Check your e-mail outbox to be sure the e-mails were sent. Close the presentation and close PowerPoint.

EXERCISE 15-12 **Make Changes to a Presentation Submitted for Review**

When the reviewers receive the e-mail, they open the attachment, make any changes, and then send the reviewed presentation back to the author. When you open a presentation that was sent to you for review, the Reviewing toolbar automatically appears.

 NOTE: If the Reviewing toolbar is not displayed, right-click any toolbar and choose Reviewing from the shortcut menu. (See Table 15-2 on the next page.)

1. Log off the author and log on the first reviewer. Retrieve the first reviewer's e-mail. A message from the author along with the attached presentation should appear.

2. Open the e-mail message and double-click the attachment icon.

3. In the Opening Mail Attachment dialog box, choose Open and click OK. If you are asked whether you want to merge changes with the original document, answer No. The presentation opens with the Reviewing toolbar displayed.

TABLE 15-2 Reviewing Toolbar

BUTTON		PURPOSE
	Show/Hide Markup	Shows or hides changes and comment markers
Reviewers...	Reviewers	Displays which reviewer's changes you want to see
	Previous Item	Moves to the previous change marker or change mark
	Next Item	Moves to the next change marker or change mark
	Apply	Applies all suggested changes for the current slide or for the entire presentation
	Unapply	Removes all applied changes for the current slide or for the entire presentation
	Insert Comment	Creates a comment for the current slide
	Edit Comment	Edits a comment's text
	Delete Comment	Deletes the selected comment or deletes all markers on the current slide
	Revisions Pane	Displays or hides the Revisions Pane on the right side of the screen

4. Working as the first reviewer, make the following changes to the presentation: (If you were unable to work with e-mail, use the file *[your initials]*Orig and continue with this step.)

- Slide 1: Replace the text "Good 4 U" with the picture **Logo1** from your student disk. Move the words Employee Training down and logo above those words. Resize the logo to make it slightly smaller.

- Slide 4: Add a fourth bulleted line with the text **Our reputation**

EXERCISE **15-13** **Insert and Edit Comments in a Presentation You Are Reviewing**

In addition to making changes to a presentation you are reviewing, you can also add comments to slides. Comments are similar to the comments you add when working with a word processing program. They are represented on the slide by a *comment marker,* a small colored rectangle in the upper-left corner of a slide. It contains the reviewer's initials. You can read the comment by double-clicking the comment marker, but they will not print on the slides or be seen during a slide show.

Comments can be printed as a separate page when you print one or more slides in the presentation.

1. Return to slide 1. On the Reviewing toolbar, click the Insert Comment button . A colored box appears in which you can key a comment.

FIGURE 15-14
Inserting a comment

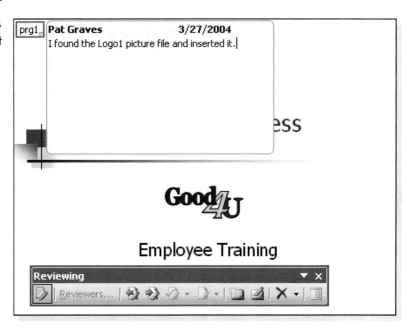

> **NOTE:** If the Reviewing toolbar is not displayed, right-click any toolbar and choose Reviewing from the shortcut menu.

2. Key the following in the comment box:

I found the Logo1 picture file and inserted it.

3. Click outside the comment box to close it. Notice the comment marker (the small colored box in the upper-left corner) with the reviewer's initials and the number "1," indicating the first comment inserted by this reviewer.

4. To edit the comment you keyed, double-click the comment marker and then key the following text at the end of the existing comment:

I hope you like the colors I used.

5. Move to slide 3 ("Marketing Is About People") and insert the following comment:

This slide would be more effective if a picture of happy people was inserted.

6. Click the Save button on the Standard toolbar. If you are working with an e-mail attachment, your changes will be saved in a temporary Internet folder just in case you need to access the file again.

7. If you are not working with an e-mail attachment, skip the rest of this exercise and go on to Exercise 15-14.

   Otherwise, click Reply with Changes on the Reviewing toolbar to send the reviewed presentation back to the author. A reply e-mail is generated automatically.

> **NOTE:** If the e-mail window does not appear, click its button on the Windows taskbar or press [Alt]+[Tab] to find it.

8. At the top of the e-mail message box, key **I have completed my review of the presentation**

9. Click Send; then connect to the Internet, open Outlook, and send the mail that is in your outbox.

10. Close the presentation and close PowerPoint. Log off the first reviewer and log on the second reviewer.

11. As the second reviewer, retrieve the appropriate e-mail from the author and open the attached presentation.

12. Make the following changes to the presentation:
    - Slide 1: Replace the title with WordArt that uses the same text.
    - Slide 3: Change "clients" to **guests** and change "others" to **our staff**
    - Slide 5: Add a fourth bulleted line with the text **Cheerful attitude**

13. Insert the following comments:

    Slide 1: **This would be better if "Good 4 U" was replaced with the logo, but I don't have it.**

    Slide 2: **Each of these bullets could be expanded into a separate slide.**

14. Click the Reply with Changes button on the Reviewing toolbar; then switch to the e-mail message that is automatically generated.

15. Key a short message at the top of the message box and then send the e-mail. Be sure to switch to Outlook (or other e-mail program) and send all the mail in your outbox.

16. Resave the presentation, close it, and close PowerPoint.

17. Log off the second reviewer.

EXERCISE **15-14** **Merge Documents from Multiple Reviewers**

When all the reviews are complete, the author can merge the reviewers' changes into the original document. After merging, the author can look at each change a reviewer made and then decide whether to keep or remove the change.

Instead of using the files you created in the previous exercises, you will start this exercise with a fresh set of files that already contains reviewers' changes and comments.

1. Open the file **Mkt-Orig** and save it as *[your initials]*15-14.
2. From the Tools menu, choose Compare and Merge Presentations. The Choose Files to Merge with Current Presentation dialog box opens.
3. Navigate to your student data disk and select the file **Mkt-Rev1**. With the file selected, hold down Ctrl and select **Mkt-Rev2**. Both files should be selected.
4. Click Merge. The Revisions task pane and the Reviewing toolbar are displayed. Markers on slides indicate changes and comments made by reviewers.

EXERCISE **15-15** **Review, Accept, and Reject Changes from Multiple Reviewers**

When reviewed files are combined with the original, the reviewers' changes are indicated on the slides by change markers. A *change marker* is a small colored marker positioned in the area where a reviewer made a change. Each reviewer's changes are indicated by a different color.

In the Revisions pane on the right, the List tab displays a list of each comment and change for the current slide. The Gallery tab shows the current slide with the changes that each reviewer made.

1. Click the List tab in the Revisions pane; then click the first item listed under Slide changes. The comment associated with this item is displayed on the slide.
2. Click the third item on the list "Title 1: Marketing Our Business." A checkbox with a description of the change appears near the slide's title. In this case, the reviewer deleted the title. (See Figure 15-15 on the next page.)
3. Click the checkbox to accept the change. The title is removed from the slide. The check mark on the change marker indicates that the change was accepted.

4. On the Reviewing toolbar, click the list box arrow for the Apply button ⬚; then choose Apply All Changes to the Current Slide. Both reviewers' changes appear on the slide.
5. Move to slide 2 and click the comment marker in the upper-left corner. Read the comment and then press Delete to delete it.

FIGURE 15-15
Accepting a change

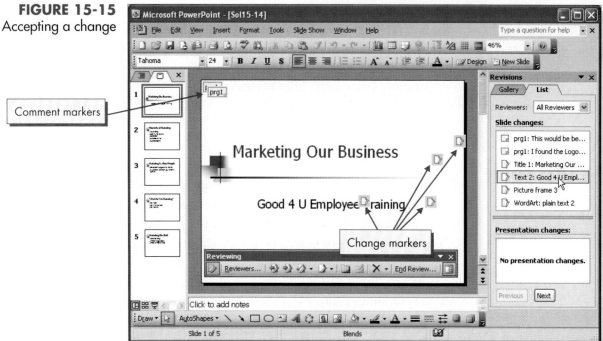

FIGURE 15-16
Multiple changes
listed for one
change marker

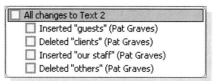

6. Move to slide 3 and click the change marker on the slide. A list of four changes appears. This change marker applies to all changes made in the body text placeholder.

7. Check the first two changes in the list. The word "clients" changes to "guests."

8. Move to slide 4. A different color change marker indicates that the other reviewer made a change to this slide. Click the change marker and then check the box labeled All changes to Text 2. A new bullet line is inserted at the bottom of the slide.

9. Move to slide 1. Click the list box arrow for the Unapply button on the Reviewing toolbar and choose Unapply All Changes to the Presentation. The presentation reverts to its original state.

10. Click the list box arrow for the Apply button on the Reviewing toolbar and choose Apply All Changes to the Presentation. Now all the changes that both reviewers made are applied to the presentation.

11. Scroll through the presentation and notice that all the change markers have a check mark, indicating that they have all been applied.

12. Move to slide 3 and click the change marker next to the body text placeholder. Uncheck the last two items in the list, so that "our staff" changes back to "others."

13. Scroll through all the slides and note the changes that were applied.

14. Click the End Review button on the Reviewing toolbar. Read the question in the question box and then click Yes.

15. Scroll through all the slides. Notice that all the changes you selected have been applied and the change markers have been removed, but the comments remain.

EXERCISE 15-16 **Print Presentation Comments**

The comment markers that appear on the presentation do not appear on a slide show or on printed slides or handouts. If you want to print the comments, check the Include comment pages checkbox at the bottom of the Print dialog box. The comments will print on a separate page (or pages) at the end of whatever else you are printing (slides, handouts, outline, etc).

1. Create a handout header and footer: include the date and your name as the header, and the page number and text *[your initials]*15-16 as the footer.

2. Move to slide 1 and save the presentation as *[your initials]*15-16 in your Lesson 15 folder.

3. From the File menu, choose Print to open the Print dialog box.

4. Set up the dialog box so that all slides will print as handouts, 6 slides per page, grayscale, scale to fit paper, framed.

5. At the bottom of the dialog box, check the Print comments and ink markup checkbox.

6. Click Preview. In the Preview window, move to the second page and change the zoom to 100%. The comments appear, identified by the slide on which they were placed and by the initials of the reviewer.

7. Click Print and then click OK. Close the Preview window and close the presentation.

Publishing Presentations to the Web

For several exercises in this course you have been asked to save presentations as Web pages (in HTML format). Now you will explore more of the options available when you *publish* a presentation to the Web. Publishing a presentation means saving a copy in an HTML format that can be made available on a Web server or a shared folder.

The following are some of the options you can set when you publish a presentation to the Web:

● The title for the Web page. This title appears in the browser's title bar. If you do not specify a title, the title on slide 1 is used.

- What slides you want to publish. You can publish an entire presentation or just a part of it.
- Whether to display the presentation's animations in the browser. (Animations do not always run smoothly in a browser.)
- Whether to display notes pages. They will be displayed in a Notes pane similar to the way they look in Normal view.
- Which browser or browsers to use. If you don't know what browser viewers will use, you can specify multiple browsers. (This creates a larger file.)

Additional Web options are available by clicking Web Options on the Publish as Web Page dialog box.

EXERCISE 15-17 Publish a Presentation as a Web Page

There are two ways you can initiate the process to publish a presentation to the Web:

- From the File menu, choose Save As; then from the Save as type drop-down list, choose Web Page.
- From the File menu, choose Save as Web Page.

1. Open the file **MilSales**.
2. From the File menu, choose Save as Web Page. The Save As dialog box opens. It is very similar to the presentation file Save As dialog box, but it has two additional command buttons: Publish and Change Title.
3. In the Save in box, navigate to your Lesson 15 folder. In the File name box, key *[your initials]***15-17**.

FIGURE 15-17
Saving a presentation as a Web page

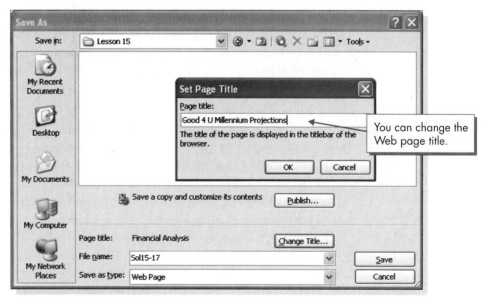

4. Click <u>C</u>hange Title. In the Set Page Title dialog box, key **Good 4 U Millennium Projections** and click OK. This text will appear on the title bar of your browser when you view the Web page.

5. Click <u>P</u>ublish to display the Publish as Web Page dialog box.

6. In the Publish what? section, choose <u>C</u>omplete presentation and deselect the <u>D</u>isplay speaker notes checkbox.

7. In the Browser support section, choose <u>A</u>ll browsers listed above. This option will enable your Web page to be viewed on browsers compatible with either Microsoft Internet Explorer or Netscape Navigator.

8. At the bottom of the dialog box, check <u>O</u>pen published Web page in browser. Checking this box will cause your presentation to automatically display in your browser after it is saved.

FIGURE 15-18
Publish as Web
Page dialog box

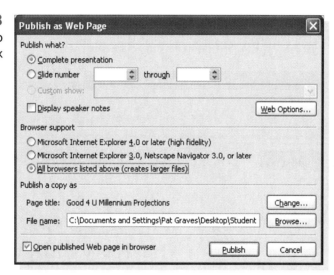

NOTE: This exercise takes you through saving a presentation in HTML format so that it can be viewed on the Web with a suitable browser. To be viewed over the Internet or an intranet, your presentation must be saved in a folder on a file server that is accessible over the Internet. If you have publishing privileges at an Internet or intranet Web site, you can key the site's address (also known as its URL) in the File name text box in the Publish as Web Page dialog box. See your system administrator for more information about available Web sites.

9. Click <u>W</u>eb Options (near the upper-right corner of the dialog box). In the Web Options dialog box, click the General tab. Here you can choose options for how the presentation will appear in a browser window. Make sure the following options are set:

   ● Select <u>A</u>dd slide navigation controls.
   ● In the <u>C</u>olors list box, choose Presentation colors (text color).

- Clear Show slide animation while browsing.
- Select Resize graphics to fit browser window.

10. Click the Files tab. Under File names and locations, make sure Organize supporting files in a folder is checked.

This option collects the many files that publishing a Web page creates in a separate folder. The folder is named *filename*_files, where *filename* is the name you gave to the presentation. For example, if you named the presentation **Finance**, a file with the name **Finance.htm** would be created and a file folder named Finance_files would also be created.

11. Click each of the other tabs in the Web Options dialog box and look at the options available for customizing your Web pages. When you are finished, click OK to close the Web Options dialog box.

12. Click Publish to save the Web page and to close the Publish as Web Page dialog box. After a short period, your browser window appears and displays your presentation as a Web page.

FIGURE 15-19
Presentation displayed in a browser

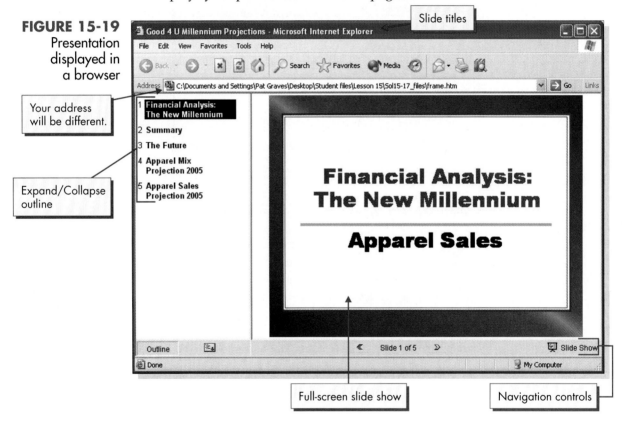

13. Leave the presentation open in the browser window for the next exercise.

EXERCISE 15-18 **Preview a Presentation in a Browser**

As long as your computer has a browser installed on it, you can preview your presentation. You do not have to actually be on-line, because your browser is reading the file from its location on your computer.

1. Notice how the slide titles are displayed at the left. You can click on the titles to display each slide on the larger right area. At the bottom of the Outline pane, you can click the button to expand the outline and bulleted text will be displayed.

2. Browse the presentation by clicking the navigation controls for Next slide and Previous slide.

3. Click the Slide Show button to see the presentation on the full screen. Use the [Spacebar] or left-click to advance forward. Once you have advanced the slides during the full screen slide show, you can use the [Backspace] key to go back one slide at a time. Your navigation controls are not quite as smooth as when you are using PowerPoint.

4. When you are finished, close the browser window.

5. Close the presentation without saving it. (You already saved it as a Web page.) Close PowerPoint.

6. Using My Computer or Windows Explorer, navigate to your Lesson 15 folder. Notice the file *[your initials]***15-17** and the folder *[your initials]***15-17_files**. Both the file and the folder (containing supporting files) are needed to display a Web page.

FIGURE 15-20
My Computer window displaying an HTML file and its folder of supporting files

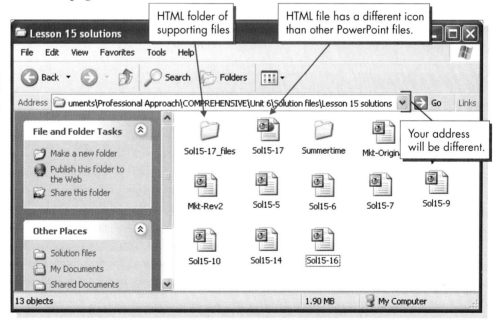

7. Close the My Computer or Windows Explorer window.

 TIP: Even before you save your presentation as a Web page, you can preview the way it will appear in a browser by selecting File, Web Page Preview.

Broadcasting a Presentation on the Web

The Presentation Broadcasting feature enables a speaker to broadcast a presentation over a network in *real time*. When broadcasting in real time, a viewer sees what the presenter is doing at the actual time that it is happening. Along with the presentation's slides, the speaker can broadcast live video and audio, all at the same time.

To broadcast a presentation live, you need to use a third-party partner for PowerPoint online broadcasting and set up an account with them. For that reason, this lesson will save a broadcast to a folder on your hard drive instead of broadcasting live. Viewers can then replay the broadcast at a later time if they have access to the folder where it is saved.

EXERCISE **15-19** **Schedule a Presentation Broadcast**

In this and the following exercises, you have the opportunity to record a narrative along with your presentation as you broadcast it. If your computer is equipped with a microphone, you can read the speaker's notes that accompany the presentation. If you do not have a microphone, you can run the slide show without sound.

Scheduling a broadcast requires that you have read/write access to a shared folder. If you do not, then you can instead record and save a broadcast for later viewing.

1. Open the file MilSales again and save it as a presentation with the filename *[your initials]***15-19**.

2. Print the notes pages for all the slides. You will read the script on the notes pages later while broadcasting the slide show.

3. Ask your instructor if you have read/write access to a shared folder. If you do, then do the following:

From the Sli̲de Show menu, choose O̲nline Broadcast, S̲chedule a Live Broadcast. The Schedule Presentation Broadcast dialog box appears. Skip step 4.

4. If you do not have read/write access to a shared folder, do the following instead of step 3:

From the Sli̲de Show menu, choose O̲nline Broadcast, R̲ecord and Save a Broadcast. The Record Presentation Broadcast dialog box appears.

5. Key the following information in the dialog box:
   - Title: **Good 4 U Apparel Sales**
   - Description: **Discussion of current promotional apparel sales and forecast for future apparel sales**
   - Speaker: *[Your Name]*
   - Copyright: *[Your Name]*
   - Keywords: **Good 4 U; Apparel Sales**
   - E-mail: *[your e-mail address]*

6. Click Settings to open the Broadcast Settings dialog box, and make sure the Presenter tab is displayed.

7. If you have a microphone hooked up to your computer, choose Audio only from the Audio/Video options section. Otherwise, choose None.

FIGURE 15-21
Choosing broadcast setting options

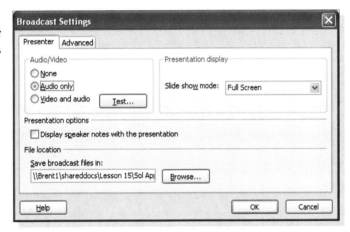

NOTE: It is important that you choose None for the Audio/Video option if you do not have a microphone set up for your computer. If you don't, the process will fail because the program will search for the microphone and will not be able to find it.

8. Under File location, click Browse. The Choose Directory dialog box opens.

9. Navigate to your Lesson 15 folder (or other folder if your instructor directs you to do so).

10. Click the Create New Folder button ☐ on the dialog box toolbar. In the New Folder dialog box, key *[your initials]***Apparel Broadcast** for the folder name. Click OK; then click Select to select the directory and close the Choose Directory dialog box.

11. Click OK to close the Broadcast Settings dialog box.

12. If you are recording a broadcast instead of scheduling a broadcast, skip the rest of this exercise and go on to Exercise 15-20.

Otherwise, in the Schedule Presentation Broadcast dialog box, click Schedule. If the Choose Profile dialog box appears, click OK unless your instructor directs otherwise. A meeting invitation e-mail form appears.

13. In the To box, key an e-mail address for one of your classmates (or to yourself). Clear the Reminder checkbox in the lower-left corner of the form. (Leave the other information on the form unchanged.)

FIGURE 15-22
Meeting invitation
e-mail form

Key addresses of people receiving this presentation broadcast.

Remove reminder.

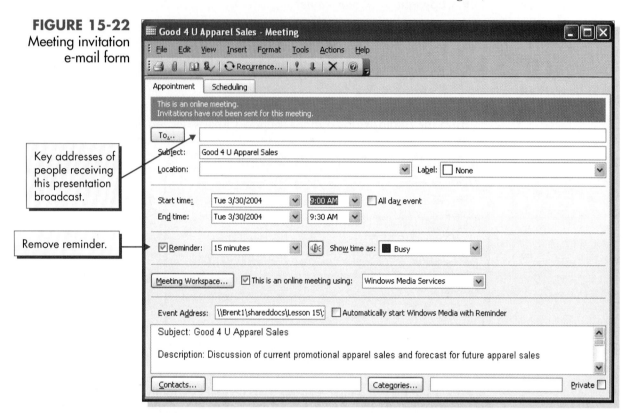

NOTE: If this were a live broadcast, you would set the time and date for sometime in the future and you might also set the Reminder option. For the purpose of this class, you want the time to be as close to the present time as possible. You were instructed to turn off the Reminder option because its pop-up window might appear at an inconvenient time during this exercise.

14. Click Send. A message box should appear, telling you that your broadcast has been successfully scheduled. Click OK.

NOTE: The program Outlook is used to schedule the broadcast. If you do not have a Send button, then close the dialog box and you will be asked if you want to send the message.

EXERCISE 15-20 **Publish a Presentation for Broadcasting on the Web**

If this were a live online broadcast, you would start the following procedure approximately one-half hour before the scheduled broadcast. When you start the procedure, the lobby page appears in your browser with a count-down timer that tells you how much time is left before the broadcast is scheduled to start.

Because this exercise is not using an online broadcasting partner, you will begin the broadcast immediately (or record it if you did not schedule an online broadcast in the previous exercise). No one will be able to view your broadcast while you are presenting it, but it will be recorded and saved to your broadcast folder, where it can be viewed at a later time by anyone who has access to the folder.

1. If you are recording a broadcast instead of scheduling an online broadcast, click Record in the Record Presentation Broadcast dialog box and then skip to step 5.

    Otherwise, choose Online Broadcast from the Slide Show menu and then choose Start Live Broadcast Now.

2. If the Choose Profile dialog box appears, click OK unless your instructor directs otherwise. If a caution box appears, informing you that a program is trying to access e-mail addresses, click Yes.

3. In the Live Presentation Broadcast dialog box, select the event with the title "Good 4 U Apparel Sales."

4. Check the Record this live presentation check box; then click Broadcast. If an information box tells you the time for the broadcast has already passed, click Yes to continue. The Broadcast Presentation dialog box appears, informing you that it is preparing the presentation.

5. If you have a microphone, the Microphone Check dialog box appears. Read the sample text out loud and into your microphone to automatically adjust the microphone's volume. When you are finished, click OK. The Broadcast Presentation dialog box reappears. (See Figure 15-23 on the next page.)

6. Locate the notes pages that you printed earlier and arrange them in slide order, if necessary. When they are ready to read from, click Start.

 NOTE: Read the speaker's notes appropriate for each slide even if you do not have a microphone. This will help you time the slides appropriately.

7. The presentation's first slide appears. Click your left mouse button to make the subtitle appear; then read the notes for the first slide.

8. Advance to the next slide. Use your mouse to make each bullet point appear, one at a time. As each bullet appears, read the appropriate text from the notes page. Continue until the slide show is completed.

9. After the broadcast recording is completed, an information box congratulates you on a successful completion. The location where the

FIGURE 15-23
Performing a
microphone check

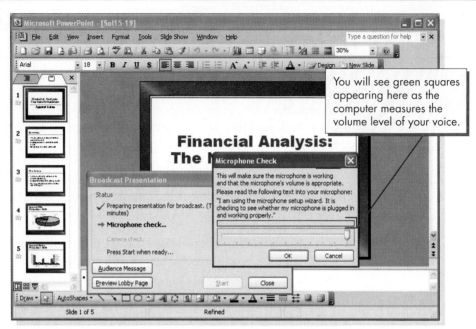

broadcast is saved is shown in this information box. Make a note of the broadcast location so that you can reference it later.

10. Click the Replay Broadcast button to review your recording. After a short period, your browser opens, displaying the *lobby page* for your broadcast. The lobby page displays information about the broadcast and also contains controls similar to a VCR.

FIGURE 15-24
Lobby page for a
presentation
broadcast

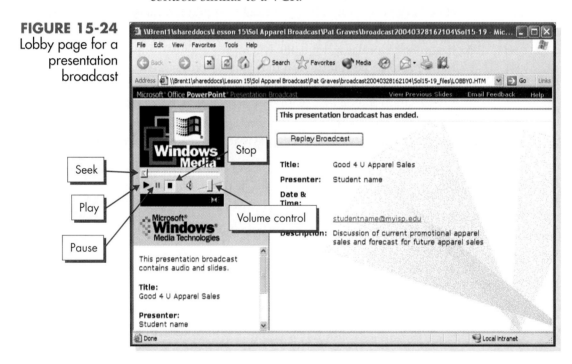

11. Click the Play button on the left panel of the lobby page. When the presentation is finished, close your browser. Close PowerPoint.

EXERCISE 15-21 Access a Presentation Saved as a Web Page

In this lesson you published two presentations to the Web. For the first one (*[your initials]*15-17), you saved an existing presentation as a Web page. For the second one (*[your initials]*15-19), you recorded a slide show broadcast with narration. These procedures both save some files in an HTML format.

The following are some of the ways to access a published presentation:

- Open your browser and key the location of the presentation in the address box.
- Open an e-mail or other document sent to you that contains a hyperlink to the presentation's location and then click the hyperlink.
- Using My Computer or Windows Explorer, navigate to the location of the published presentation, look for its HTML file, and double-click it.

 NOTE: Internet Explorer 4.0 or later is required in order to view a broadcast.

1. Using Windows Explorer or My Computer, navigate to your Lesson 15 folder (or other location where you saved your broadcast).

2. Locate the *[your initials]***Apparel Broadcast** folder and double-click to open it.

If you recorded a broadcast without first scheduling it, skip step 3. Your broadcast is contained in this folder.

If you scheduled a broadcast, a folder labeled with your computer's name or your user ID is contained within this folder. Open the folder. It contains a folder named **Broadcast***[number]*.

3. Open the **Broadcast***[number]* folder.

FIGURE 15-25
Finding the
broadcast file on
your computer

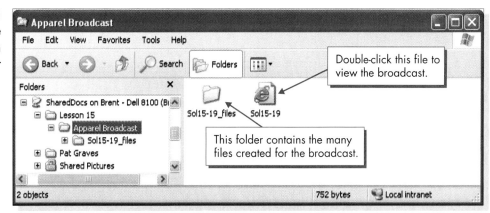

4. Double-click the HTML file *[your initials]***15-21**. Your browser opens to the lobby page of the presentation broadcast that you earlier recorded.

5. Click the Replay button ⌈ Replay Broadcast ⌋ in the left panel to replay the broadcast. When you are finished, close your browser.

USING ONLINE HELP

Publishing a presentation for the Web can be a complex process. When you need more information about the many Web options, Help is available.

Use Help to learn more about publishing a presentation to the Web:

1. Choose Microsoft PowerPoint Office Help from the Help menu to access the PowerPoint Help task pane.

2. In the Search for text box, key **publish** and then click the Start searching button.

3. In the list of topics, select the topic About publishing a presentation to the Web.

4. Read the topic; then select other topics of interest in the search pane.

5. Close the Help window when you are finished.

LESSON Summary

➤ Use the annotation pens during a slide show to call attention to something on a slide, draw an impromptu diagram, or record audience feedback.

➤ During a slide show, you can blank the screen to black by pressing Ⓑ; press Ⓑ again to return to the slide show. To blank to a white screen, press Ⓦ.

➤ Slides can be hidden so that they will not be displayed during a slide show. To go to those slides, key the slide number and press [Enter].

➤ When preparing presentations that will be displayed on other computers, you should embed the fonts you used. That way, you know that your presentation will be displayed with the fonts you used to create it.

➤ The Package for CD saves a presentation with all of its linked files on a CD or other removable medium for use on another computer. When using Package for CD, you have the option of embedding fonts and also of including the PowerPoint Viewer.

➤ The PowerPoint Viewer enables your presentation to be run on a computer that does not have PowerPoint installed. The Viewer is a program containing several files too large for a 3.5" disk, so you will need a large-capacity media storage format to use this feature.

➤ The page size and orientation of presentation slides can be changed to fit your needs. Use the Page Setup dialog box to choose orientation, standard sizes such as 35 mm slide or overhead, or to create a custom size.

➤ Presentations prepared for 35 mm format or for overhead format can be sent to a service bureau via e-mail or disk to be created as 35 mm color slides, color transparencies, or color prints. Overheads (also called overhead transparencies) can also be created by using transparency film in a standard printer.

➤ Presentations can be sent to coworkers or others to be reviewed by e-mail, disk, or a shared folder. Reviewers can make changes and add comments to their copy of the presentation without affecting the original.

➤ Besides making changes to a presentation, reviewers can add comments by clicking the Insert Comment button 🔲 on the Reviewing toolbar. A comment can be read by pointing to a comment marker.

➤ To merge reviewers' copies of a presentation with the original, open the original and choose Tools, Compare and Merge Presentations. The resulting presentation will contain change markers indicating where reviewers made changes.

➤ To see changes made by reviewers, click a change marker. To apply the change, check the box next to the description of the change. To unapply the change, clear the box. Apply all changes to a slide or to the presentation by using the Apply button 🔲 list arrow on the Reviewing toolbar.

➤ Reviewers' comments can be printed by checking the Include comment pages option at the bottom of the Print dialog box.

➤ Publishing a presentation to the Web means saving a presentation as an HTML file in a shared folder or on a Web server. You publish it by choosing Web Page in the Save as type drop-down list in the Save As dialog box. It is only viewable over the Internet if the folder in which it is saved is accessible over the Internet.

➤ If you have an account with a third-party partner for PowerPoint online broadcasting, a broadcast of your presentation can be scheduled and delivered to a large audience via the Internet. The broadcast can include live audio and/or video.

➤ Even if you do not schedule a broadcast, you can record one for later viewing by anyone who has access to the folder where the recorded broadcast is stored.

➤ To access a presentation that was saved as a Web page or one that is a saved broadcast, open your browser and key the address in the Address box. Alternatively, use My Computer or Windows Explorer to navigate to the location where it is saved; then double-click its file icon.

LESSON 15 Command Summary

FEATURE	BUTTON	MENU	KEYBOARD
Package for CD		File, Package for CD	
Merge reviewed documents		Tools, Compare and Merge Presentations	
Publish a presentation to the Web		File, Save as Web Page	
Schedule a presentation broadcast		Slide Show, Online Broadcast, Schedule a Live Broadcast	
Publish a broadcast to the Web		Slide Show, Online Broadcast, Start Live Broadcast Now	
Record and save a broadcast for later viewing		Slide Show, Online Broadcast, Record and Save a Broadcast	

Concepts Review

TRUE/FALSE QUESTIONS

Each of the following statements is either true or false. Indicate your choice by circling T or F.

T F   **1.** Notes can be recorded during a slide show.

T F   **2.** The Felt Tip Pen tool makes a wider mark on a slide than the Highlighter when you use it to annotate a slide.

T F   **3.** Files can be sent over the Internet to a service bureau for printing as 35 mm slides or overhead transparencies.

T F   **4.** Comments from multiple reviewers should be merged one-by-one into a presentation.

T F   **5.** To print reviewers' comments, choose Comments from the Print what drop-down list in the Print dialog box.

T F   **6.** When working on a presentation that will be saved as a Web page, you can preview the presentation in a browser.

T F   **7.** A presentation that you broadcast cannot be saved for later viewing.

T F   **8.** Audio can be included with an online broadcast.

SHORT ANSWER QUESTIONS

Write the correct answer in the space provided.

1. How do you embed a font in a presentation?

_____

_____

2. What file format is used for a Web presentation?

_____

3. Why is it important to use the Package for CD feature when you will be presenting using a computer different from the one you used to develop your presentation?

_____

_____

4. How can you send a presentation to another individual for review?

_____

_____

5. What must you do to your presentation after changing its orientation from landscape to portrait?

_____

6. How do you unapply a reviewer's change by using a change marker?

_____

_____

7. For a presentation saved as a Web page, where does the presentation title appear?

_____

8. How can you view a broadcast that has been saved to a shared folder?

_____

_____

CRITICAL THINKING

Answer these questions on a separate page. There are no right or wrong answers. Support your answers with examples from your own experience, if possible.

1. Think about when and where you might use the various presentation methods you learned about in this course. For example, which methods would be best for small groups, and which would be best for large ones? How might you prepare for a presentation if you were traveling on business?

2. Discuss ways that recording Speaker Notes during a presentation would be useful for you in a meeting or when planning a social event.

Skills Review

EXERCISE 15-22

Record meeting notes and convert them to a Word document.

1. Open the file **ResReqs2** and start a slide show on slide 1.

2. Record meeting minutes and action items by following these steps:

    a. Right-click anywhere on the slide and choose S<u>c</u>reen and then Spea<u>k</u>er Notes from the shortcut menu.

    b. On the Speaker Notes window key **Roy Olafsen, Marketing Manager, opened the meeting at 2:00 p.m. on** *[today's date].*

    c. Click <u>C</u>lose.

    d. Advance to slide 2 ("Reservations Policy"). Create a speaker note and key the following information:

    - Action item: **Research reservation policy studies on the Web.**
    - Assigned to: **Evan Johnson**
    - Due date: *[three weeks from today's date]*

    e. Click <u>C</u>lose.

3. Advance to slide 3 ("Reservations: Advantages"). Create a speaker note and key the following action item: **Create a chart detailing seating capacity and turnaround time for each restaurant.** Assign the action item to **Lila Nelson** with a due date four weeks from today.

4. Advance to slide 4 ("Reservations: Disadvantages") and create the following meeting minutes entry: **A heated discussion took place concerning the advantages and disadvantages of a reservations policy. Everyone agreed to put the reservations policy on hold for six months pending further feasibility studies.**

5. End the slide show and then review the notes pane for each slide to make sure the notes are complete.

6. Create a handout header and footer containing today's date and the text *[Your Name], [your initials]***15-22a** in your Lesson 15 folder.

7. Print the meeting minutes and action items by following these steps:

    a. Choose <u>F</u>ile, Sen<u>d</u> To and choose Microsoft Office <u>W</u>ord and a dialog box will appear.

    b. For the Page layout in Microsoft Office Word option, click Notes <u>n</u>ext to slides.

    c. For the Add slides to Microsoft Office Word document option, select <u>P</u>aste.

    d. Click OK.

    e. A Word document will be created with slide images and your speaker notes arranged in a three-column table.

    f. Above the table, key these items on three lines at the left of the page: **Operations Meeting, Today's Date, Presented by** *[Your Name].* Make Operations Meeting text 20 points, bold, and the other two lines of text 16 points.

    g. Make the table row height less by dragging the bottom border up in each row so that all four table rows fit on one page without crowding the slide images.

    h. Save the Word document as *[your initials]***15-22b** in your Lesson 15 folder.

8. Print the Word document and close Word.

EXERCISE 15-23

Embed fonts using the Package for CD option.

1. Open the file **EventRev**.

2. Save a presentation for viewing on another computer by following these steps:

    a. Insert a blank formatted disk in your A:\ drive (or insert other storage media in the appropriate drive).

    b. From the File menu, choose Package for CD.

    c. In the Package for CD window, for Name the CD: key **SE Revenue NY** Click the Options button.

    d. In the Options window, deselect the first option: PowerPoint Viewer. Select Linked files and Embedded TrueType fonts. Click OK.

    e. In the Package for CD window, click the Copy to Folder button. Browse to choose the appropriate drive and folder where your packed files will be stored (in this case the A:\ drive) and select that location. Click OK.

    f. When the Package for CD process is complete, your presentation file will be saved in the folder you named in step c.

3. Remove the floppy disk from the drive and label it appropriately.

4. Test the presentation to be sure it loads correctly from the floppy disk.

    a. Open Windows Explorer or My Computer and navigate to the A:\ drive (or other location where your Package for CD files are stored).

    b. Locate the **SE Revenue NY** folder and open it. Double-click the **EventRev** presentation and view the slide show.

5. Close the show when you finish viewing it.

6. Make a copy of the **SE Revenue NY** folder and paste it in your Lesson 15 folder. Remember to remove your floppy disk when you finish.

EXRCISE 15-24

Review a presentation, insert comments, merge reviewed presentations, and accept and reject changes.

1. Open the file **Menu3**. Save it as *[your initials]*15-24-Orig in your Lesson 15 folder.

2. Save the file again as *[your initials]*15-24-Rev1 and save it once again as *[your initials]*15-24-Rev2. Close all PowerPoint files.

3. Imagine that you are reviewer 1 and that you received the presentation to review. Open the file *[your initials]*15-24-Rev1. Make the following changes to the presentation:

    a. Choose Options from the Tools menu and click the General tab. In the User information section, key the name **Reviewer 1** and the initials **R1**. Click OK.

This will ensure that the changes you make will be associated with your name.

> **b.** On slide 1, insert the picture file **Logo1** and make it slightly smaller. Create an AutoShape star with a two-color center gradient fill (gold on the outside and white in the middle) and position it behind the logo. Group these two objects together and position the group attractively below the subtitle.
>
> **c.** On slide 3, delete the Chicken and Potato Salad entrée. Insert your own idea of a healthy entrée in its place.

4. Insert a comment on slide 3 by following these instructions:

> **a.** Move to slide 3 and display the Reviewing toolbar.
>
> **b.** Click anywhere in the new entrée you inserted; then click the Insert Comment button 🔲 on the Reviewing toolbar.
>
> **c.** In the colored comment box, key **I removed the Chicken and Potato Salad entree because it got poor reviews from the taste testers.**
>
> **d.** Click outside the comment box to close it.

5. Resave the file and close it.

6. Imagine that you are reviewer 2 and that you received the presentation to review. Open the file *[your initials]*15-24-Rev2. Make the following changes to the presentation:

> **a.** Following step 3a above, open the Options dialog box and click the General tab. Change the user name to **Reviewer 2** and the initials to **R2**.
>
> **b.** Replace the Times New Roman font with Comic Sans MS.
>
> **c.** On slide 1 insert a comment explaining why you changed the font. For example, "We need a more relaxed font for this summertime theme."
>
> **d.** Move to slide 3 and insert a comment stating that you do not like the Chicken and Potato Salad entrée.
>
> **e.** On slide 4, change "Rice Pudding" to **Julie's Cherry Jubilee Pudding**
>
> **f.** Insert a comment explaining why you changed the name of the Rice Pudding dessert. For example: "It needs a jazzier name."

7. Resave the file and close it.

8. Open the file *[your initials]*15-24-Orig. Following step 3a above, change the user name and initials to your name.

9. Merge reviewers' changes into the original presentation by following these steps:

> **a.** From the Tools menu, choose Compare and Merge Presentations.
>
> **b.** In the dialog box, navigate to your Lesson 15 folder and select *[your initials]*15-24-Rev1. Hold down Ctrl and select *[your initials]*15-24-Rev2 (both files should be selected at the same time). Click Merge.
>
> **c.** When the caution box appears, ignore it and click Continue.

10. Read reviewer comments as you go through the slides. Apply and unapply changes made by reviewers by following these steps:

      a. On slide 1, click the comment marker and read about the requested font change.

      b. On slide 1, click the colored change marker below the subtitle. Check the box to the right of the change marker to apply the change.

      c. On slide 3, click the comment marker and read it.

      d. On slide 3, click the change marker to the right of the body text placeholder. Check the box for All changes to Text 2, changing "Chicken and Potato Salad" to the entrée you inserted in its place.

      e. On slide 4, click the comment marker and read it.

      f. On slide 4, click the change marker and then check the box for All changes to Text 2. Clear the All changes to Text 2 check box, unapplying the change.

      g. Click End Review on the Reviewing toolbar to make the changes final and remove the change markers. Click Yes in the question box that appears.

11. Since the second reviewer recommended a font change, replace the Times New Roman font with Comic Sans MS.

12. Create a handout header and footer: include the date and your name as the header, and the page number and text *[your initials]***15-24-Fin** as the footer.

13. Save the presentation as *[your initials]***15-24-Fin** in your Lesson 15 folder.

14. Print comments pages by following these steps:

      a. Open the Print dialog box.

      b. Set up the print options so that all slides will print as handouts, 4 slides per page, grayscale, framed.

      c. At the bottom of the Print dialog box, check the Print comments and ink markup box.

      d. Click Preview. In the Preview window, move to the second page and then zoom to 100%. The comments appear, identified by the slide on which they appear and by the initials of the reviewer.

      e. Click Print and then click OK. Close the Preview window and close the presentation.

EXERCISE 15-25

Broadcast a presentation to the Web and view it in a browser.

1. Open the file **BevNmbrs**. Print the notes pages to use as a script for narration while preparing the broadcast.

2. Set up a recorded online broadcast by following these steps:

      a. From the Slide Show menu, choose Online Broadcast, Record and Save a Broadcast.

      b. Key the following information in the Record Presentation Broadcast dialog box:

        ● Title: **Good 4 U Beverage Sales**

        ● Description: **A presentation to the marketing department**

- Speaker: *[Your Name]*
- Copyright: *[Your Name]*
- Keywords: **Beverage sales; Good 4 U; Marketing**
- E-mail: *[your e-mail address]*

   c. Click Settings and display the Presenter tab.

   d. If you have a microphone attached, select Audio only; otherwise, select None.

   e. Under File location, click Browse and navigate to your Lesson 15 folder (or a shared folder following your instructor's directions).

   f. Click the Create New Folder button 🖾 and give the folder the name *[Your Initials]***BevSales**

   g. Click Select to close the Choose Directory dialog box, and then click OK to close the Broadcast Settings dialog box.

3. Record an online broadcast by following these steps:

   a. In the Record Presentation Broadcast dialog box (which should be open from the previous step), click Record.

   b. If the Microphone Check dialog box appears, turn on your microphone. Follow the directions and read the sample text. When you are finished, click OK.

   c. In the next dialog box, wait until the Start button is activated and then click Start.

   d. Read the script you previously printed on notes pages into your microphone as you advance through the slides. When you are finished, end the slide show.

   e. When the information box appears, write down the location where your broadcast is saved and then click Continue.

4. Play your broadcast by following these steps:

   a. Using My Computer or Windows Explorer, navigate to the location where your broadcast is stored. (See Step 3e above.)

   b. Locate the HTML file **BevNmbrs** and double-click it.

   c. In the browser window that opens, click Replay Broadcast.

5. When the broadcast is complete, close your browser and close the PowerPoint presentation.

Lesson Applications

Create and print meeting notes.

1. Open the file **MktStrat**.

2. Start a slide show and record as speaker notes the following meeting minutes:

   Slide 1. The Marketing Strategy Meeting was called to order on Monday, January 10, 2005 at 1:15 p.m.

   Slide 2. It was generally agreed that there are too many areas targeted in the current marketing strategy and that items will be prioritized to create a stronger focus.

3. Add the following action items:

   Slide 3.
   Assigned to Jane Kryler, due 1/25/2005
   Create a strategy for targeting potential customers' health-conscious interests.

   Assigned to Eric Dennis, due 2/7/2005
   Develop a questionnaire to determine customers' food preferences and develop a plan for doing a survey.

   Slide 5.
   Assigned to Michael Peters, due 3/14/2005
   Investigate the high costs associated with the Miami operation and develop a cost-containment plan for Miami.

4. Add a slide footer with the date and the text *[Your Name],* *[your initials]*15-26a for the Action Items slide only.

5. Save the presentation as *[your initials]*15-26a in your Lesson 15 folder.

6. Check spelling in the presentation.

7. Send the presentation with notes to Word. Arrange the notes beside the slide image. Format the document in Word as follows to fit on one page:
   a. Reduce the text size to 12 points.
   b. Remove the column with slide numbers.
   c. Stretch the edges of the table so the text word-wraps on the fewest possible lines.
   d. Change each slide image to 1.5" height (lock aspect ratio).
   e. Adjust row height to conserve space.
   f. Key **Marketing Strategy Meeting Minutes, Your Name** on the first line of the Word document above the table. Add a blank line after this title text. Adjust the page top and bottom margins if necessary.

8. Save the presentation with recorded minutes in your Lesson 15 folder in Word Document format as *[your initials]*15-26b. Print the document and close Word.

9. Close the presentation.

Change a presentation to 35 mm slide format and use Pack and Go.

1. Open the file **LunchMnu**.
2. Format the presentation for output as 35 mm slides.
3. Review each slide individually, and make adjustments to font size, placeholder size, spacing, and decimal tab position so that all text is uniform in size and aligned correctly.
4. On the handouts, include the date and your name as the header and include the page number and filename *[your initials]*15-27 as the footer.
5. Save the presentation as *[your initials]*15-27 in your Lesson 15 folder.
6. Print as handouts, 4 slides per page, grayscale, landscape, framed.
7. Use the Package for CD to save the presentation on a floppy disk. Be sure to embed the fonts used in the presentation.
8. Test the presentation to be sure that it loads correctly from the floppy disk.

Review a presentation and incorporate reviewers' changes.

1. Open the presentation **JulyFun2**. Save the file as *[your initials]***July-Orig**
2. Save two more copies of the file with the following names: *[your initials]***July-Rev1** and *[your initials]***July-Rev2**
3. Close all PowerPoint files. Open *[your initials]***July-Rev1**. In the Options dialog box, change the user name to **Reviewer 1** and the initials to **R1**
4. Working as reviewer 1, make the following changes:
   - Correct all the spelling errors in the presentation.
   - Change the star bullet color from red to white for all slides.
   - Change the registration time on slide 2 to 6:30 a.m.
   - Insert at least two comments on any slides.
5. Resave the presentation and close it.
6. Open *[your initials]***July-Rev2**. In the Options dialog box, change the user name to **Reviewer 2** and the initials to **R2**
7. Working as reviewer 2, make the following changes:
   - On slide 1, move the title down a little and fix the spelling error.
   - On slide 3, remove the comma and the words "and no seeds to spoil the fun"
   - On slide 4, add the following second-level bullet under "Elbow and knee pads": **Registration number**
   - On slide 4, change the slide title from uppercase to title case.
   - Insert at least two comments.

8. Resave the presentation and close it.

9. Open *[your initials]***July-Orig**. In the Options dialog box, change the user name to *[Your Name]* and the initials to *[your initials]*. Merge the two reviewed documents with it.

10. Accept the following changes that the reviewers made:
    - Slide 1: Spelling changes, new position for title
    - Slide 2: Spelling changes
    - Slide 3: Spelling changes
    - Slide 4: Spelling changes

11. Reject the following changes that the reviewers made:
    - Slide 2: The time change in the first bullet
    - Slide 4: The "Registration number" bullet
    - Slide master: The bullet color change

12. End the review. Read the reviewer comments.

13. Create a handout header and footer: include the current date and your name as header, and the text *[your initials]***15-28** as footer.

14. Save the file as *[your initials]***15-28**. Print it as handouts, grayscale, framed, 6 slides per page, and include the comment pages.

EXERCISE 15-29 *Challenge Yourself*

Save a presentation as a Web page.

1. Open the file **InfoPak**.

2. Add an animation scheme of your choice and insert a MIDI sequence sound file that will play throughout the slide show. Adjust the sound volume to a low level so that it does not conflict with the audio you'll record in step 8.

3. Create speaker's notes for each slide that would be suitable for a broadcast presentation.

4. Check the Grayscale view for all slides and adjust the settings where needed.

5. On the handouts, include the date and your name as the header, and include the page number and filename *[your initials]***15-29** as the footer.

6. Save the presentation as *[your initials]***15-29** in your Lesson 15 folder.

7. Print the notes pages for each slide.

8. Record a broadcast in a new folder under your Lesson 15 folder named *[your initials]***Franchise**. If you have a microphone, record audio for the presentation by using the notes pages as a script. The following information should appear on the lobby page:
    - Title: **Franchise Information Package**
    - Description: **A presentation for new franchisees**

- Speaker: *[Your Name]*
- Copyright: *[Your Name]*
- Keywords: **Franchise information; Good 4 U;**
- E-mail: *[your e-mail address]*

9. View the broadcast in your browser. When you are finished, close the browser and close PowerPoint.

On Your Own

In these exercises you work on your own, as you would in a real-life work environment. Use the skills you've learned to accomplish the task—and be creative.

EXERCISE 15-30
Create a presentation describing how you plan to apply your new PowerPoint skills in the real world. Create at least six slides, including tables, charts, and/or diagrams. Create an attractive and lively presentation. Write a script that you could use if presenting your presentation to an audience, and use the script to create suitable notes pages. Print out the notes pages and read them while you record a presentation broadcast for online viewing. Save your presentation as *[your initials]*15-30. Preview it and then print as handouts.

EXERCISE 15-31
Imagine you are conducting a planning meeting for a fun event such as a class picnic, family reunion, or scout troop camping trip. Create a presentation that lists and organizes tasks that need to be completed to have a successful event. Make the slides interesting and fun to view. Run the presentation as a slide show, and use Speaker Notes to record minutes and action items. Save the presentation as *[your initials]*15-31a. Preview it and then print as handouts. Send the minutes and action items to a Word document. Adjust the format as needed. Save the Word document as *[your initials]*15-31b and print it.

EXERCISE 15-32
Think of a disliked task or chore that you are expected to do or are required to do on a regular basis, either at work, at home, or at school. Create a presentation that builds a case for why you should not be required to do the task. Save the presentation as *[your initials]*15-32a. Make a copy of the presentation with the name *[your initials]*15-32b and have a classmate review it, inserting comments and revisions. When the file is returned to you, merge it with your original file. Accept and reject the suggested changes as you see fit; then save the presentation again as *[your initials]*15-32c. Preview and then print the presentation as handouts, and include the reviewer's comments.

Unit 6 Applications

Write and design a presentation that will be presented as a prerecorded broadcast for viewing via an intranet or shared folder.

Use the Internet to research the most prevalent types of manufacturing industries in the state where you live or go to school.

Create a presentation with at least six slides describing these industries, including historical information and what the future holds for them. Include at least one graph, chart, or diagram and at least one table.

Add visual interest to your presentation by choosing an appropriate design template and color scheme. Customize the template as you see fit and add graphic elements to enhance it.

Compose a script for your presentation and use the script to create suitable notes pages for each slide.

In the slide footer, include the text **Prepared by** followed by your name. Include the slide number on all slides but not the date. In the handout footer, include the completed filename *[your initials]*u6-1. In the handout header, key **Presented to** and then identify to whom you would be giving this presentation. Include in the handout the date you would be delivering the presentation and the page number (so that notes pages will be numbered).

Preview and then print your presentation as handouts; then print the notes pages for each slide. You will read these pages as you create your prerecorded broadcast.

Record and save a broadcast of your presentation in a subfolder under a new folder for Unit 6. Name the subfolder *[your initials]*u6-Broadcast (or use a shared folder provided by your instructor). Be sure to change the settings appropriately, depending on whether you have a microphone available.

As you record your broadcast, read the notes pages that you printed earlier. If you have a microphone, make sure that the microphone is turned on before starting and read your notes into the microphone.

When you are finished recording, write down the broadcast address and then view your broadcast in a browser.

If possible, create an e-mail message that includes a hyperlink to your broadcast and send it to two of your classmates who have access to the folder where your broadcast is stored.

Appendix

APPENDIX

Microsoft Office Comprehensive Certification

TABLE A-1

Microsoft Office Comprehensive Activities Related to Lessons

CODE	ACTIVITY	LESSON
PP03S-1	**Creating Content**	
PP03S-1-1	Create new presentations from templates	2, 3, 9
PP03S-1-2	Insert and edit text-based content	1, 2, 3, 4, 5
PP03S-1-3	Insert tables, charts, and diagrams	10, 12, 13, 14
PP03S-1-4	Insert pictures, shapes, and graphics	6, 7, 12, 14
PP03S-1-5	Insert objects	11, 12, 13
PP03S-2	**Formatting Content**	
PP03S-2-1	Format text-based content	5, 9, 10, 13
PP03S-2-2	Format pictures, shapes, and graphics	6, 7, 8, 14
PP03S-2-3	Format slides	3, 9, 10
PP03S-2-4	Apply animation schemes	11, 12
PP03S-2-5	Apply slide transitions	2
PP03S-2-6	Customize slide templates	9
PP03S-2-7	Work with masters	2, 5, 9, 10
PP03S-3	**Collaborating**	
PP03S-3-1	Track, accept, and reject changes in a presentation	15
PP03S-3-2	Add, edit, and delete comments in a presentation	15
PP03S-3-3	Compare and merge presentations	15
PP03S-4	**Managing and Delivering Presentations**	
PP03S-4-1	Organize a presentation	1, 2, 3, 4, 10, 11
PP03S-4-2	Set up slide shows for delivery	11, 15
PP03S-4-3	Rehearse timing	11
PP03S-4-4	Deliver presentations	1, 15
PP03S-4-5	Prepare presentations for remote delivery	15
PP03S-4-6	Save and publish presentations	1, 4, 15
PP03S-4-7	Print slides, outlines, handouts, and speaker notes	1, 3, 4, 7
PP03S-4-8	Export a presentation to another Microsoft Office program	4

Glossary

35mm slide An output format that creates individual, 35 millimeter slides from each slide in a presentation. These slides are usually prepared by a service bureau and then arranged in a slide carousel tray to project with a 35mm projector. Excellent color is possible, but room illumination usually must be reduced. (15)

3-D effect The illusion of depth. (8)

Action button Button you draw on a slide that has a link associated with it. Although you generally use special shapes for action buttons, any AutoShape or other object that you place on a slide can be set up to act as an action button. Action buttons serve the same purpose as hyperlinks. (11)

Activate Selects a placeholder by clicking it. An activated text placeholder can accept text that you key or it can be moved or resized. (1)

Adjustment handle Yellow diamond–shaped handle found on many AutoShapes used to change a prominent feature of a shape. For example, you can change the size of an arrowhead relative to the body of the arrow, or you can change the tilt of a triangle. (6)

Alignment In text placeholders, the left, center, right, or justify attribute for text positioning. Also refers to how elements are positioned on a slide in relation to other elements. (4)

Animation Creates special visual or sound effects for an object. (11)

Animation scheme Preset visual effects that control how text appears on the screen during a slide show. For example, the title might fly into place in a spiral fashion, and the body text might fly up from the bottom one bullet point at a time. (11)

Animation tag Small, numbered gray box that appears on a slide next to an object to which an animation effect has been applied. The number in the box indicates the order in which the animation will occur and correlates with the item numbers in the custom animation list. (11)

Annotation pen Pointer that you can use to "draw" on the screen during a slide show presentation. Annotation pen marks can be in any color and can be saved with the presentation as drawn objects. (15)

Arrow style Shape of an arrowhead on the end of a line. Arrowheads come in several varieties, including dots and diamonds. They can be placed on either end of a drawn line or on both ends. (7)

Assistant box Box in an organization chart that is usually placed below a superior box and above subordinate boxes. Usually, an assistant box has no subordinates. (14)

AutoContent Wizard A feature that assists you in starting new presentations by providing content suggestions. (2)

AutoCorrect Feature that automatically corrects common spelling errors and typos as you key text. It can be turned on or off, and you can customize it to find errors so it will find errors that you frequently make. (2)

AutoFit Feature that automatically adjusts the size of text when needed so that it fits in its text placeholder. (5)

AutoShape One of a group of predefined shapes that are easy to draw. Available shapes include rectangles, circles, and other basic shapes, arrows, flowchart symbols, stars, banners, callouts, lines, and connectors. (6)

Axis Line that borders one side of the chart plot area. A value axis displays a range of numbers, and a category axis displays category names. (12)

Background The area behind all slide elements that can be filled with solid, patterned, or textured colors. It can also include a picture or other graphics that help to create a theme for your presentation. (9)

Backward Used to adjust object stacking order and move a selected object behind another object. (8)

Bar chart A chart that compares one data element with another data element using horizontal bars. (12)

Bitmap Picture made up of tiny colored dots. The more you enlarge a bitmap, the more blurred it becomes. You can crop bitmaps and easily change the contrast and brightness. Other changes can be made only by using a paint-type graphics program. Examples of bitmaps are pictures created in a paint program, photographs and other images that come from a scanner, and images that come from a digital camera. (6)

Blank presentation One way to start a new presentation with no design elements displayed. (3)

Blank slides During a slideshow, the display screen can blank to black by pressing B or it can blank to white by pressing W. Pressing the same key will redisplay the current slide. (15)

Body text Text in the body of a slide or other document. On a PowerPoint slide, body text is usually placed in a body text placeholder and can be displayed as bulleted text. (1)

Border and Borders The line around AutoShapes and other objects. In a table, line around the table or around cells within a table. (13)

Branch An organization chart box with all of its subordinate boxes. (14)

Broadcast A feature that enables you to transmit a presentation over the Web so viewers can watch it at a designated time. (15)

Browser A software program, such as Microsoft Internet Explorer or Netscape Navigator, that interprets HTML files and formats them into Web pages for viewing on an intranet or on the Internet. (4)

Bullet A small dot, square, or other symbol placed to the left of each item in a list or series of paragraphs to add emphasis and readability. Bullets are often used in presentations and outlines. (1)

Case Text capitalization treatment: UPPERCASE (all capital letters), lowercase (all small letters), Sentence case (first letter only capitalized), Title Case (first letter of all words capitalized). (5)

Cell Rectangle formed by the intersection of a row and a column in a table or a spreadsheet. In a datasheet, a cell is the rectangle formed by the intersection of a row and a column in which you enter one of the data items used to create a chart. (12)

Cell margin Space between the text in a cell and its borders. (13)

Cell pointer Mouse pointer in the shape of a white cross used to select cells in a Microsoft Graph datasheet. (12)

Change marker Small colored marker positioned in the area on a slide where a reviewer made a change. Each reviewer's changes are indicated by a different color change marker. (15)

Chart Diagram that displays numbers in pictorial format, such as slices of a pie shape, or rows of columns of varying height. Charts are sometimes called graphs. (12)

Chart animation Applied through custom animation to animate the chart as a whole or to animate the chart by series. (12)

Chart placeholder Box with the dotted line that appears on slides using the Chart, Text & Chart, and Chart & Text layouts. Double-clicking a chart placeholder opens Microsoft Graph automatically. (12)

Clip art Ready-to-use graphic images that you can insert in a presentation. (6)

Clipboard Temporary storage place for cut and copied items. (3)

Collapse In the Outline pane, to hide the body text so that only the slide titles are displayed. (4)

Collate To print all the pages of one copy before starting to print the first page of the next copy. When pages are not collated, all the copies of page 1 are printed first, then all the copies of page 2, and so on. (1)

Color scheme A set of eight colors used in a slide design template. These colors appear in the background, text and lines, shadows, title text, fills, accents, and text hyperlinks. (3) (9)

Column chart A chart that compares one data element with another data element using vertical bars. (12)

Comment marker Small rectangle appearing in the upper-left corner of a slide that indicates the presence of a reviewer comment. You read a comment by pointing to the comment marker. (15)

Compress picture An optimization feature for reducing file sizes that can be applied to one or all pictures in a presentation. It enables you to reduce a picture's resolution or to discard cropped areas of a picture. (6)

Connection sites Blue handles that appear on an AutoShape, clip art, or text box object when the connector tool is active or when a connector is selected. Connection sites indicate places where a connector can be attached to an object. (14)

Connector line Straight, curved, or angled line with special endpoints that can lock on to connection sites on an AutoShape or other PowerPoint object. (14)

Constrain To control moving or drawing an object in precise increments or proportions. When you constrain a rectangle as you draw it, it becomes a square; a constrained oval becomes a circle. (6)

Content layout Slide layout that includes placeholders for pictures, charts, clip art, and diagrams. (3)

Content placeholder Placeholder designed to hold tables, clip art, pictures, media clips, charts, or diagrams. (5)

Contiguous slides Slides that follow one after another. For example, slides numbered 2, 3, and 4 are contiguous. See "Noncontiguous slides." (2)

Copy Duplicates a selected object or text from a presentation and stores it on the clipboard without removing the selection from its original place. (3)

Coworker box Box in an org chart that is connected to the same superior box as another box. (14)

Crop Trims the vertical or horizontal edges of a picture. (6)

Cropping handles Four heavy black dashes on the sides and the corners of a picture selected for cropping. When you drag one of these handles with the cropping tool, an edge of the picture is cut away (trimmed). (6)

Crosshair pointer The shape of your mouse pointer when drawing objects. (6)

Custom animation Visual effects that you create to control how text, pictures, movies, and other objects move on a slide during a slide show. May include sound. (11)

Custom animation list List on the Custom Animation task pane of all the animation effects applied to objects on the current slide. Items are listed in the order that they will occur during a slide show. (11)

Custom color Colors that you mix on the Custom tab of the Colors dialog box. You can create an infinite variety of custom colors. (7)

Custom show Presentation within a presentation. It displays only specially selected slides instead of all the slides in a show. (11)

Cut Removes a selected object or text from a presentation and stores it on the clipboard. (3)

Cycle diagram Diagram used to illustrate a process that is a continuous cycle. (14)

Dash style Pattern of dashes and dots that make up a line. Styles include solid line, square dot, dash, and combinations of dashes and dots. Dash styles can be applied to object borders, lines, and arrows. (7)

Data series Group of data that relate to a common object or category such as product, geographic area, or year. Often, more than one data series are displayed on a single chart. (12)

Datasheet Table that is part of Microsoft Graph in which you enter numbers and labels used to create a chart. When you start a new chart, the datasheet appears automatically, containing sample data that you can delete or overwrite. (12)

Demote Moves selected text to the next-lower outline or heading level by increasing the indent level. (1)

Design template Custom design that you apply to a presentation to give it a uniform color scheme and a particular "look" through predesigned background graphics and font treatments. (3)

Destination When working with clipboard objects, the presentation, or other document in which the objects are pasted. (3)

Distribute Evenly spaces selected objects, either in relation to one another or across the length or width of a slide. Objects can be distributed either horizontally or vertically. (8)

Docked toolbar Toolbar that is attached to one of the edges of the program window. (1)

Drag Selecting then holding an object by pointing to it or selecting it, then holding down the left mouse button while moving the mouse to a different location. (1)

Duplicate Makes a second copy of a selected object on the same slide. (8)

Embed Saves with the presentation or document file so that the information is always available. For example, embedding fonts in a file ensures that those fonts will be available if the file is loaded on a different computer. (15)

Embedded object An object, such as an Excel chart or a Word table, that is placed in and becomes part of a PowerPoint slide. An embedded object is saved as part of the file in which it is placed. When you make

changes to an embedded object, it does not affect the original file (the source) from which it came. (12)

Emphasis effect Animation effect that you apply to draw attention to an object that is already showing on a slide. (11)

Entrance effect Animation effect that you apply to text or an object to control how it first appears on a slide. (11)

Eraser Used to erase table cell borders. (13)

Exit effect Animation effect that you apply to control how an object leaves (or disappears from) a slide. (11)

Expand In the Outline pane, displays all the text contained in placeholders for each slide. (4)

Explode a pie slice Moves a pie slice out from other slices in a pie chart to add emphasis. (12)

Export Saves a file in a format that can be read by a different application from the one in which it was created. For example, saving a PowerPoint presentation outline in a format that can be used by a word processing program. (4)

Filename Unique name given to a PowerPoint presentation file, a Word document file, or files created by other applications. (1)

Fill color Color of an object. Objects can be filled with a solid color, a pattern, a gradient, a texture, a picture, or have no fill at all. (7)

Find command Locates specified text in a presentation. (2)

First-line indent Paragraph indent style in which the first line is indented to the right of the paragraph. (10)

Flip Reverses an object either horizontally or vertically, creating a mirror image of the original object. (8)

Floating text Text contained in a text box (as differentiated from a text placeholder). Floating text can be formatted by using the tools on the Formatting toolbar, can be easily placed anywhere on a slide, and can be rotated. (6)

Floating toolbar Toolbar that is not attached to the edge of the program window. It can be moved freely by dragging its title bar. (1)

Flowchart Diagram used to show a sequence of events using shapes that have specific meanings. (14)

Font Set of text characters with a specific design—for example, Arial or Times New Roman. (5)

Footer Text that appears at the bottom of each slide, notes page, or handouts page. (2)

Format Painter Button on the Standard toolbar used to copy formatting from one object to another. (7)

Forward Adjusts object stacking order and moves a selected object in front of another object. (8)

Four-pointed arrow Moves placeholders and other objects without resizing them. Can also select text in a bulleted list by clicking the bullet. (2)

Go to Slide A command available using the right-click menu during a slide show to display a particular slide. (15)

Gradient fill Object fill effect in which one color blends or fades into another color. (7)

Grayscale Rendering of slides in shades of gray for printing on a black-and-white printer. (2)

Grid A set of intersecting lines used to align objects that you can show or hide. For the grid you can choose from a range of preset measurements and can use a snap-to option to align on the grid. (10)

Gridline The background lines on a chart that aid interpretation of data quantities. (12)

Group Combines selected objects so that they behave as one object. (8)

Guides Horizontal and vertical lines used to align objects. Guides do not display in a slide show or when printed. (10)

Handout Printout that contains 1, 2, 3, 4, 6, or 9 PowerPoint slides on a page. (1)

Handout master Used to control how objects are positioned on each printed handout page. Often includes header or footer text, date, and page numbers; graphic elements such as a company logo can also be included. (10)

Hanging indent Paragraph indent style where the first line is even with the left of a placeholder while all other lines are indented to the first tab position. This style is most often used with bullets or numbered paragraphs so the bullet or number that begins each paragraph is more noticeable. (10)

Header Text that appears at the top of each slide, notes page, or handouts page. (2)

Hide and unhide slides Slides can remain in a presentation file but be hidden when you run the presentation. This feature can be controlled from the Slide Show menu or in Slide Sorter view. (15)

HTML Acronym for Hypertext Markup Language. See "Hypertext Markup Language." (4)

Hyperlink Text or graphic object you click to move to another slide, another application, or a location on the Internet. Text hyperlinks are displayed with an underline. (4)

Hypertext Markup Language File format used to make a file readable when using a browser on the Internet or on an intranet. (4)

I-beam Mouse pointer that has the shape of an uppercase "I." The I-beam pointer is used to select text or mark the location where you can insert text. (1)

Import Uses a file in an application that was created with a different application. For example, opening an outline from Word in PowerPoint. (4)

Indent markers Two small triangles and a rectangle that appear on the ruler when a text box is selected. The lower triangle controls the left indent setting of the text box; the top triangle controls the first-line indent setting. The rectangle moves both triangles at the same time. (10)

Insertion point Vertical flashing bar indicating the position where text that you key will be inserted. Clicking an I-beam mouse pointer is one way to place an insertion point. (1)

Intranet Internet-like system that exists only within a company or organization. (15)

Landscape Page orientation in which the page is wider than it is tall—as is usually the case in a painting of a landscape. The opposite of portrait. (1)(10)

Legend Box showing the colors and patterns assigned to the data series or categories in a chart. (12)

Less contrast In the Picture toolbar, this button reduces the intensity of the colors in a picture. (6)

Level In organization charts, the position in the hierarchy of the organization being diagrammed. (14)

Line chart A chart that plots trends or shows changes over a period of time. (12)

Line color The color of a line. Lines can be filled with a solid or patterned color. (7)

Line spacing The spacing between lines of text in a paragraph. (10)

Line style Options include single, double, and triple lines of varying line weights. Also used for object borders. (7)

Line weight Thickness of a line measured in points. (7)

Linked object Object, such as an Excel chart or a Word table, that is displayed within a document (the destination) created by a different program. A linked object is merely a pointer to an external file (the source) that contains the data. Only the pointer is saved with the document in which it is placed. When you make changes to a linked object, you are making changes to the actual file that was used to create the object. (12)

Lobby page First page you see when you want to play a presentation broadcast. It displays information about the broadcast and also contains play controls similar to a VCR. (15)

Locked connector Endpoint of a connector line when it is colored red, indicating that it is attached to an AutoShape. (14)

Margin Space between the edge of an object and the text or other material inside the object. For example, a PowerPoint slide typically has a ½-inch margin at the top, bottom, and each side where no text or other objects appear. Text boxes and text placeholders also have margins. (10)

Master slide Slide that stores a design template's arrangement for slides, including the size and position of placeholders, text formatting, and graphic elements. There are two types of master slides: the slide master and the title master. (5)

Menu bar Displays the names of menus you use to perform various tasks. You can open menus by using the mouse or the keyboard. (1)

Merge cells To combine two or more table cells into one larger cell. (13)

Merge comments The process of combining multiple reviewer comments into one presentation. (15)

More contrast In the Picture toolbar, this button increases the intensity of the colors in a picture. (6)

Motion path Path that an object follows as part of an animation effect. You can choose a pre-defined motion path or create a custom path with drawing tools. Motion paths can be resized, rotated, and moved. (11)

Movie In PowerPoint, any motion file such as an animated clip art file or a video file. Movies can be inserted on slides in the same way as clip art. These are also called movie clips and they play during a slide show. (11)

Noncontiguous slides Slides that do not follow one after another. For example, slides numbered 1, 4, 5, and 7 are noncontiguous. See "Contiguous slides." (2)

Normal indent Paragraph indent style in which all the lines in the body of a paragraph are indented the same amount, creating an even left edge. (10)

Normal view This view provides one place for viewing the different parts of your presentation and displays the Outline and Slides pane, Slide pane, and Notes pane. (1)

Notes master Controls how objects are positioned on each printed notes page. Often includes header or footer text, date, and page numbers; graphic elements such as a company logo can also be included. (10)

Notes page Printout containing a slide image at the top of the page and speaker's notes that were entered in the Notes pane underneath. Notes pages are often used by speakers as cue cards during a presentation. (3)

Notes pane Area where you can add presentation notes for either the presenter or the audience. The Notes pane is located below the Slide pane. (1)

Optimize Reducing a presentation's file size by compressing pictures. (8)

Organization chart Diagram used to show the relationships and reporting structure of the people in an organization in a hierarchical format. (14)

Outline and Slides pane Area that can display either an outline of the presentation's text or thumbnails of the presentation's slides. You choose either Outline or Slides by clicking the appropriate tab. (1)

Overhead transparencies An output format that creates individual transparency sheets for projecting with an overhead projector when computer projection is not available. Transparencies can be prepared with an ink jet printer, a laser printer, or a photocopier. (15)

Package for CD Saves a presentation and all the files that link to it for display on a different computer. A viewer can be included so the presentation will display without PowerPoint being loaded. (15)

Paste Inserts an item stored on the clipboard at the current location. (3)

Pencil pointer Used to draw and recolor table borders and cells. (13)

Pie chart A chart that shows the proportions of individual components compared to the whole. (12)

Placeholder Box that can contain title text, body text, pictures, or other objects. Most slide layouts contain placeholders. A placeholder's formatting, size, and position is set on a master slide and can be customized. (1)

Plot area The area of a chart that displays the shapes such as bars or pie slices that represent the data. (12)

Point Unit of measure for the height of the tallest character in a font set. There are 72 points to an inch. (5)

Portrait A vertical orientation for slides or printed pages where the slide or page is taller than it is wide. The opposite of landscape. (1)

Print preview Feature that enables you to see what your printed pages will look like before you actually print them. You can view preview pages in black-and-white, grayscale, or color. (1)

Promote Moves selected text to the next-higher outline or heading level by decreasing the indent. (1)

Proofreaders' marks Special notation used to mark up a printed draft with changes to be made before final printing. Some proofreaders' marks might be confusing if you are unfamiliar with them. For example, a hand-written "=" indicates that a hyphen is to be inserted. (1)

Proportion Relationship between the height and width of an object. When an object is resized, its proportions will be preserved if both the height and width of the object change at the same rate or percentage. An object that is out of proportion is either too tall and skinny, or too short and wide. (6)

Publish To save a copy of a file in HTML format so it can be made available on a Web server or a shared folder. (15)

Pyramid diagram Diagram that illustrates relationships based on a foundation. (14)

Radial diagram Diagram that illustrates relationships focused on or directed to a central element. (14)

Real time Actual time during which events take place. For example, if viewers see your presentation at the same time that you are broadcasting it, they are viewing it in real time over a network. (15)

Recolor picture On the Picture toolbar, a button that enables you to change all the solid colors that make up a clipart image. (6)

Record Notes A command available using the right-click menu during a slide show to record information. The notes are saved as speaker notes and will appear in the Notes pane when the presentation has ended. (15)

Redo Reapplies the previous action such as an editing change. (3)

Regroup Recombines objects that were at one time part of the same group. (8)

Rehearse timings A PowerPoint feature that enables you to record the amount of time you spend on each slide as you practice your presentation. It could also be used to control the speed of advancing slides when audio is recorded to support a self-running presentation. (11)

Replace command Locates specified text in a presentation and replaces it with different text that you specify. (2)

Replace fonts Feature that changes an existing font in a presentation to a different font. (5)

Reset picture On the Picture toolbar, a button that enables you to return a picture to its original state after its colors have been changed. (6)

Reviewer comments Comments inserted during a review of a presentation. Comments from multiple reviewers working collaboratively can be combined and then accepted or rejected to incorporate necessary changes. (15)

Rich text format Standard file type that converts document formatting into instructions that Microsoft programs and many other programs can read and interpret. (4)

Rotation handle Green handle that appears above a selected object. You change the rotation of an object by dragging the rotation handle. You can constrain the rotation to 15-degree increments by holding down (Shift) while rotating the object. (5)

RTF Acronym for rich text format. See "Rich text format." (4)

Sample text Text provided by the AutoContent Wizard that suggests content for your presentation. You change the sample text to suit the needs of your presentation. (2)

Scale Specifies the range of values on a chart's value axis and the interval between values. (12)

ScreenTip Box that identifies the name of an on-screen object when you point to the object. (1)

Scroll bars Used with the mouse to move a slide view or outline text right or left, and up or down. You can also use the vertical scroll bar to move from slide to slide. (1)

Selection rectangle Dotted box that you draw by dragging the mouse pointer to select objects on a slide. All objects contained inside the rectangle are selected. (8)

Service bureau Business that translates computer files into high-quality output in various media, such as slide transparencies, high-resolution full-color prints, and large-format prints. (15)

Shadow effect The illusion that light is shining on an object because a shadow appears behind it. (8)

Sizing handles Small circles on the border of a selected object. Handles are used to change the size and shape of the placeholder or object. (5)

Slide layout Arrangement of text and/or object placeholders that can be applied to a new or existing slide. (3)

Slide master Master slide that includes placeholders for the title and body. Used to control colors, fonts, and background graphics for all slides created with any layout except the Title Slide layout. (5)

Slide pane Area where you create, edit, and display presentation slides. (1)

Slide show The view that displays slides sequentially in full-screen size. Slides can advance manually or automatically with slide timings using a variety of transition effects. Slide shows can display movies and animated elements. (1)

Slide Sorter view Displays several thumbnails of slides making it easy to reorder, add, delete, or duplicate slides and set transition effects. (1)

Slide transition Visual effect that you can apply to enhance the way the screen changes during a slide show as you move from one slide to another. For example, the current

slide could fade to a black screen before the next slide appears. (2)

Snap to Grid Feature that causes objects to align on the grid that may or not be visible when working on a slide. (10)

Sound clips A short sound file. These files can be inserted on a slide or associated with a custom animation sequence. (11)

Source When working with clipboard objects, the presentation or other document from which the objects were cut or copied. (3)

Speaker's notes Notes that can be entered for each slide in a presentation. Speaker's notes can be printed as Notes pages and then used to assist the speaker during a presentation, or they can add supplemental information to include with presentations published on the Web. (3)

Spelling checker Feature that corrects spelling by comparing words to an internal dictionary file. (2)

Split cells Divides a table cell into two smaller cells. (13)

Standard color Premixed color that you choose by clicking a sample on the Standard tab of the Colors dialog box. (7)

Status bar Displays information about the presentation you're working on. It is located at the bottom of the PowerPoint window. (1)

Style checker Feature that checks your presentation for consistency in punctuation and capitalization, as well as the number of fonts and text sizes used. (2)

Subordinate box Box in an organization chart that is connected to a superior box (a box on a higher level). (14)

Summary slide Slide that contains the titles of slides in a presentation. It can be used as an agenda, a wrap-up, or table-of-contents slide with hyperlinks to other slides, custom shows, other presentations, or files created by other programs. (11)

Superior box Box in an organization chart that has subordinate boxes connected to it. (14)

Tables Organized arrangement of information in rows and columns. (13)

Tabs Used to align and indent text on a slide. Tab stops appear on the horizontal ruler. (10)

Target diagram Diagram that illustrates a process that works toward a goal. (14)

Task pane Area that appears at appropriate times on the right side of the PowerPoint window, displaying a list of commands that are relevant to the task on which you are currently working. (1)

Text anchor point Point in a text box or AutoShape where text is attached. For example, you can anchor text to the top of an AutoShape, the middle of an AutoShape, or the bottom of an AutoShape. (10)

Text attributes Styles and effects applied to text. For example, bold, italic, underline, shadow. (5)

Text box A container for text that you can position anywhere on a slide. (5)

Text layout Slide layout that includes only text placeholders. (3)

Thesaurus Finds words with similar meanings. (2)

Thumbnail Miniature version of a graphic image. In PowerPoint, a miniature version of a slide is often referred to as a "thumbnail." (1)

Tick marks Small measurement marks, similar to the marks on a ruler, that cross a chart value or category axis. (12)

Title bar Colored bar (usually blue) at the top of most windows that contains identifying information. In the case of the PowerPoint main window, the title bar contains the name of the presentation. (1)

Title master Master slide that includes text placeholders for the title and subtitle of a Title Slide layout. Used to control colors, fonts, and background graphics for slides created with the Title Slide layout only. (5)

Title text Text that usually appears at the top of a PowerPoint slide. Title text is usually placed in a title text placeholder. (1)

Toggle button Toolbar button that turns a feature on or off by clicking it. (5)

Toolbar Row of buttons that give instant access to a wide range of commands. Each button is represented by an icon and accessed by using the mouse. PowerPoint opens with the Standard and Formatting toolbars

displayed in abbreviated form on one line at the top of the screen and the Drawing toolbar at the bottom of the screen. (1)

Transition, Slide See "Slide transition." (2)

Transparency Allows the color behind an object to show through. (7)

TrueType font Fonts that can be sized to any height and that print exactly as they appear on your screen. Most of the fonts that are automatically installed with Microsoft Office are TrueType fonts. TrueType fonts can be embedded in PowerPoint presentation files and in other Microsoft Office document files. (15)

Undo Reverses the last action such as an editing change. (3)

Ungroup To separate a group of objects into its components. When an object is ungrouped, each of its elements behaves as an individual object. (8)

Unlocked connector Endpoint of a connector line when it is colored green, indicating that it is not attached to an AutoShape. (14)

Vector drawing Picture made up of an arrangement of line segments and shapes that can be scaled to any

size or aspect ratio without blurring. Vector drawings can be modified in PowerPoint by recoloring and by adding, removing, and rearranging individual elements. An AutoShape is an example of a simple vector drawing. (6)

Venn diagram Diagram consisting of overlapping circles that illustrates relationships with overlapping responsibilities. (14)

View buttons Three buttons located on the lower-left corner of the PowerPoint window. You use these buttons to switch between Normal view (the default), Slide Sorter view, and Slide Show view. (1)

Wizard Online guide that leads you through the steps to complete a task. (2)

WordArt Text objects you create with special shape and color effects. (6)

Zoom box Changes the magnification of the Slide pane, Outline and Slides pane, or Slide Show view, whichever one is active. Zoom changes the size at which you view objects, but not their actual size. (1)

Index

I-4

INTERNATIONAL CONTACT INFORMATION

AUSTRALIA
McGraw-Hill Book Company
Australia Pty. Ltd.
TEL +61-2-9900-1800
FAX +61-2-9878-8881
http://www.mcgraw-hill.com.au
books-it_sydney@mcgraw-hill.com

CANADA
McGraw-Hill Ryerson Ltd.
TEL +905-430-5000
FAX +905-430-5020
http://www.mcgraw-hill.ca

**GREECE, MIDDLE EAST, & AFRICA
(Excluding South Africa)**
McGraw-Hill Hellas
TEL +30-210-6560-990
TEL +30-210-6560-993
TEL +30-210-6560-994
FAX +30-210-6545-525

MEXICO (Also serving Latin America)
McGraw-Hill Interamericana Editores
S.A. de C.V.
TEL +525-1500-5108
FAX +525-117-1589
http://www.mcgraw-hill.com.mx
carlos_ruiz@mcgraw-hill.com

SINGAPORE (Serving Asia)
McGraw-Hill Book Company
TEL +65-6863-1580
FAX +65-6862-3354
http://www.mcgraw-hill.com.sg
mghasia@mcgraw-hill.com

SOUTH AFRICA
McGraw-Hill South Africa
TEL +27-11-622-7512
FAX +27-11-622-9045
robyn_swanepoel@mcgraw-hill.com

SPAIN
McGraw-Hill/
Interamericana de España, S.A.U.
TEL +34-91-180-3000
FAX +34-91-372-8513
http://www.mcgraw-hill.es
professional@mcgraw-hill.es

**UNITED KINGDOM, NORTHERN,
EASTERN, & CENTRAL EUROPE**
McGraw-Hill Education Europe
TEL +44-1-628-502500
FAX +44-1-628-770224
http://www.mcgraw-hill.co.uk
emea_queries@mcgraw-hill.com

ALL OTHER INQUIRIES Contact:
McGraw-Hill Technology Education
TEL +1-630-789-4000
FAX +1-630-789-5226
http://www.mhteched.com
omg_international@mcgraw-hill.com